MW01626220

CRYSTAL PALACE

A COMPLETE RECORD 1905-1989

CRYSTAL PALACE

A COMPLETE RECORD 1905-1989

Mike Purkiss with Rev Nigel Sands

Breedon Books Sport

First published in Great Britain by
The Breedon Books Publishing Company Limited
44 Friar Gate, Derby DE1 1DA
1989
Second impression 1990

ISBN 0 907969 54 2

Printed by Butler and Tanner Limited, Frome.
Jacket designed by Graham Hales and printed by Arkle Print, Northampton.

CONTENTS

Acknowledgements

Many people helped in the preparation of this book and special thanks are due to the staff of the Croydon and Lee Green Reference Libraries and to Steve Clark and Dave Barber, of the Football League and Football Assocation respectively, both of whom were Palace supporters in their less impartial days. Mike Davage checked and gave advice on transfer dates and players' dates and places of birth, and Rob Morton kindly lent some of the early photographs. Not least, my wife Margaret was extremely supportive, seeing me locked at my desk day and night, and Tracey gave enormous assistance with typing the manuscript. The invaluable contribution of The Rev Nigel Sands is given in fuller detail elsewhere and I am immensely grateful for his help.

Mike Purkiss

Photographic Acknowledgements

Photographs were supplied by Action Images, Colorsport, Illustrated London News Picture Library and Rob Morton.

Foreword

WHEN Crystal Palace won promotion back to the First Division of the Football League in 1989, it capped the first phase of a revival at Selhurst Park which supporters hope will continue with Palace established as one of the leading clubs in the country. Certainly, there are few better places to be on a Saturday afternoon than Selhurst when the Eagles are in full flight.

This book tells not only the story of that recent revival, but also recounts the history of Crystal Palace FC since the club's formation. Certainly, Palace have earned their place in football history as the first champions of the Third Division and founder members of the Fourth. As a Third Division team they reached an FA Cup semi-final and now they begin another spell in Division One.

Inevitably, the choice of subjects for the section on biographies of Palace 'stars' and for the 'Match to Remember' features has been a personal one and does not pretend to be the definitive list of every Palace 'great' and of every golden memory. How could it, for different supporters see different aspects of their club and each will have his own favourite players and moments. These features provide, however, a fairly representative look at the club down the years.

In compiling the statistics for the book, I used first-hand accounts of matches taken from contemporary newspapers, although these have not always been reliable and where there is doubt, I have accepted the club's official records as supplied by The Rev Nigel Sands MA. Mr Sands became involved in the book when my own work was considerably advanced but that is not to minimize his help. Without him, many points would have gone unanswered and mistakes gone uncorrected. It may also be worth mentioning at this point that team line-ups for the pre-Football League days have been omitted on the grounds that newspaper coverage of the day left a great deal to be desired and there would have been too many gaps and too many areas of doubt.

Given the sheer volume of information contained in this book, it will be surprising if someone, somewhere, does not come up with a different answer on some point or other. Nevertheless, the author, co-author and publishers believe it to be the most accurate and comprehensive work yet attempted on the history of Crystal Palace Football Club.

Virgin
Fly Virgin

The Crystal Palace Story

IT WAS Queen Victoria's Consort, Prince Albert, whose idea for a building made of glass for the Great Exhibition gave birth to the Crystal Palace. In 1851, Queen Victoria opened the Crystal Palace in Hyde Park and three years later it was moved to Sydenham Hill, a grass and woodland area. It became a site for leisure and holiday events and attracted tourists and local visitors, until the building was almost completely destroyed by fire in 1936. Only two towers survived the blaze and they were demolished during World War Two.

Back in 1861, however, the Crystal Palace thrived and that year the staff formed a football team. Ten years later, that original Crystal Palace club became one of the 15 founder entrants to the FA Cup competition.

The early rounds saw many teething troubles and poor organization, which in some way helped the Crystal Palace club. Their first game was against Hitchin and ended in a goalless draw. Under the rules, no replay was required and both teams progressed to the next round. Palace were drawn at home to Maidenhead and won 3-0. The third-round draw gave Palace an away game against The Wanderers. This, too, was drawn (alas, no record of the score survives), but when other clubs withdrew, Crystal Palace and The Wanderers found themselves propelled straight into the semi-final. At the Kennington Oval, Palace lost 3-0 to Royal Engineers.

The following season, Oxford University, who went on to reach that year's Final, knocked Palace out in the first round. In 1874, Swifts beat Palace 1-0 in the first round and in 1875, Palace lost 2-1 at Cambridge University after a drawn game. In 1876, which was the original Crystal Palace's last year in the FA Cup, the 105th Army Regiment lost a first-round replay 3-0 before The Wanderers reversed that scoreline in the next round.

During this short early period, the Palace club saw four of their players capped for England against Scotland. Charles John Chenery appeared in the first-ever international, playing in the forward line in Glasgow on 30 November 1872. Chenery, who also played soccer for The Wanderers and first-class cricket for Surrey, won two more caps in 1873 when he scored, and in 1874. Alex Morten was in goal in 1873, as was A.H.Savage in 1876. Charles Eastlake Smith also played in the 1876 game. Morten had appeared in the unofficial international of 1870, only on that occasion he represented the Scots.

The deeds of the Crystal Palace club after their FA Cup days are lost in the mists of time and they were eventually disbanded. Yet the name became synonymous with the Cup, for the Crystal Palace ground became the venue for the FA Cup Final from 1895.

In 1904, the idea of a new Crystal Palace club was mooted but the Football Association objected to a team representing the company who owned the Cup Final venue. In 1905, however, a new company was formed. They constructed a football club called Crystal Palace and hired the Crystal Palace ground for its matches. That is where the story of the present-day Crystal Palace Football Club begins.

In 1905, the Palace board, under the chairmanship of Sydney Bourne, applied — along with Chelsea and Clapton Orient — to join the Football League. Chelsea and Orient were accepted but the League rejected Palace, who then had difficulty in obtaining entrance to the Southern League, starting in the Second Division.

The Palace board appointed a north-country man, former Middlesbrough manager John Robson, as their new manager and he soon signed up 16 players from the north, plus a couple of local players. A former Aston Villa player and assistant

◀ *Palace's Mark Bright (left) and Gary O'Reilly celebrate David Madden's penalty against Blackburn Rovers in the Second Division promotion play-off at the end of 1988-9.*

secretary at Villa Park, Edmund Goodman, who had lost a leg through injury, became Palace's secretary. Goodman was to have a profound effect on Palace's early development, not least because he also introduced the new club to Villa's colours. Palace, of course, still play in claret and blue.

Crystal Palace's first game was a United Counties match at New Brompton on the day before the Southern League season started. Palace won 3-0 and the same side lined up the next day against Southampton Reserves. All seemed well when Dick Roberts scored in the fourth minute — and even better when Palace led 3-0. However, tiredness crept in and the Saints fought back to win 4-3. Yet from then to the end of the season, Palace were unbeaten in the League, finishing champions and moving up into the Southern League's First Division.

Palace's first season could hardly have been more impressive, although it must be remembered that they considered themselves good enough for the Football League and were actually playing in the Southern League's Second Division. During that initial term they enjoyed a run of 17 consecutive League wins, including a 9-1 victory over Grays Athletic.

In the FA Cup, Palace won 7-1 against Chelsea, who fielded several reserves, before being beaten by Blackpool after two drawn games. In a friendly at Beckenham, incidentally, Palace won 17-2, still their biggest win in any game. At the end of the 1905-06 season, Palace sold skipper Ted Birnie to Chelsea. The former Newcastle United player was the first footballer to be transferred out of the club.

Palace's first year in the First Division of the Southern League was disappointing, but they showed excellent form in the Cup. After beating Rotherham County in the qualifying round at Stamford Bridge — a Rugby Union international was held at the Crystal Palace the same day — Palace were drawn to play the previous year's Cup Finalists, Newcastle United, at St James' Park. The football world was shocked when a goal from Astley, the former Middlesbrough player, gave Palace a 1-0 win.

Newcastle went on to win the Championship and Palace went through as far as the Cup quarter-final where it took a replay before Everton won. The Goodison club went on to win the Cup that year and their England international, Jack Sharp, said afterwards: "The Palace never once slackened . . .I shall always have a profound respect for the team."

That excellent Cup run could not save John Robson's job. Palace finished next to bottom of the Southern League, six points ahead of Northampton Town, and Robson took over Croydon Common, a Southern League club who played at The Nest, the ground that was to become Palace's home after World War One.

Edmund Goodman was given the joint position of secretary-manager. His first transaction was transferring Charles Wallace, Palace's speedy winger, to Aston Villa.

In Goodman's first season as manager there was a dramatic improvement in Palace's League fortunes. They finished in fourth place behind champions QPR, Plymouth and Millwall. In the FA Cup they won at Coventry and Plymouth before going down 1-0 at Grimsby before a record crowd of 8,828.

In March 1908, Bill Davies became the first player to appear in a full international whilst on the club's books, when he turned out for Wales against Scotland at Dens Park, Dundee.

In 1908-09, Palace exceeded their previous season's Cup form with a giantkilling feat over Wolves, the holders. The Londoners held Wolves to a 2-2 draw at Molineux, thanks to goals from Jimmy Beauchop, and won the replay 4-2. In the next round, however, First Division Burnley won a replay 9-0 at Turf Moor. In the League, Palace slipped down to 16th place.

In 1909-10, Palace improved considerably on their Southern League position, finishing seventh. Against the champions, Brighton, they scored a 2-1 win at the

Crystal Palace in 1907 with the United Counties League trophy. Back row (left to right): Balding, Hall, Walker, Edwards, Collier, Lawrence. Second row: Birch (trainer), Brearley, Woodger, Ryan, Wilson, Higgins, Roberts, Baker, E.Goodman (secretary). Seated: Owens, Forster, G.Smith, Innerd, Needham, A.Smith. On ground: Swann, Davies.

Goldstone Ground and drew 0-0 at the Crystal Palace on the last day of the season. At The Nest, Norwich, in October, Palace played before Norwich City's record attendance of 12,078, but most of the crowd for this Monday afternoon game had been to see King Edward VII, who was visiting the city that day, although he did not stay to watch the game. In March 1910, Josh Johnson and Joe Bulcock were chosen to represent the Southern League.

Still Palace progressed and in 1910-11 they edged further up the table to finish fourth, six points behind champions Swindon Town. The start of 1911 saw the good and bad sides of football. In January, 35,000 people packed the Palace to see Everton win a first-round FA Cup tie, 4-0. In February, at Plymouth, three players were sent off — Hanger and Williams for Palace and Butler for Plymouth. All were later suspended.

The following November, forward Charlie Woodhouse, who had proved a useful goalscorer for Palace, died after a short illness and was buried in Elmers End Cemetery. His place in the side was taken by Ted Smith, from Hull City, who scored a hat-trick on his debut at West Ham on 30 December and followed up with another hat-trick in the next game, at home to Bristol Rovers. All this helped Palace to finish 1911-12 in seventh place.

In the Cup, Palace defeated Brentford after a replay and the next First Division visitors were Sunderland. The Wearsiders drew the second-round tie 0-0 before winning the Roker replay with the only goal of the game.

'Ginger' Williams added to Palace's list of capped players when he turned out for Wales against Scotland in March 1912. In the close season, Palace trainer Arthur Birch looked after the FA amateur party in Stockholm.

Highlight of the 1912-13 season was an 8-0 hammering of Southampton. The

Saints had been one of the high-flyers in the Southern League but in recent seasons they had fallen on hard times. On a foggy November day at the Crystal Palace, they went down to their heaviest-ever defeat in a competitive match, with Hewitt (4) and Williams (3) doing most of the damage. Palace, though, were still some way short of championship-winning material. Plymouth Argyle won the title and Palace finished fifth, above Millwall on goal-average.

After FA Cup wins over Glossop and Bury, Palace travelled to Villa Park to meet up with their old player, Charlie Wallace. The game attracted a crowd of over 44,000, who saw Villa win easily. At the end Wallace returned to his old ground where a record crowd for English football — 120,081 — saw Villa beat Sunderland in the Cup Final. Palace had their own moment of glory when they beat West Ham 1-0 in the London Challenge Cup Final.

Around this time, Palace had the services of one of the game's leading figures, albeit in the twilight of his career. The Reverend Kenneth Hunt had won two full England caps, plus 20 at amateur level as well as an Olympic soccer gold medal in 1908 and an FA Cup-winners' medal with Wolves the same year. An Oxford Blue and a member of the Corinthians, Hunt joined Palace from Clapton Orient and played a few games at wing-half. After the war he ended his career with Oxford City.

The 1913-14 season saw Palace enjoy their best Southern League campaign when they fought a close battle with Swindon for the title. On the last day of the season both sides were level on points and both had away games. Swindon drew at Cardiff, but Palace also dropped a point at Gillingham. Thus Swindon took the honours on goal-average.

On 16 March 1914, Horace Colclough became Palace's first English international when he played at left-back against Wales at Cardiff. Colclough's form meant that there was no place for Joe Bulcock, who was transferred to Swansea. Ginger Williams also moved, to Millwall, and Palace's hold on the London Challenge Cup continued when they beat Tottenham 2-1 in the Final at Highbury. Palace also beat Spurs 2-1 in the London Professional Footballers' Charity Fund match at White Hart Lane.

The 1914-15 season started with Britain at war with Germany. Several Palace players joined the Army, although some were still available to play regularly. Shortly into the New Year, the club received a shock when the Admiralty took over the Crystal Palace ground and banned all sports from being played there. Talks of ground-sharing with Millwall came to nothing, and Palace moved to Herne Hill, a ground used by the amateurs, West Norwood, and where the 1911 FA Amateur Cup Final had been staged.

Palace's first game there was the rearranged match against Southampton on 3 March, which the visitors won 2-1. A few weeks earlier, when Palace drew at Birmingham in the first round of the FA Cup, they elected to stage the replay at St Andrew's for financial reasons because home support had dwindled in the early months of the war.

The 1915 FA Cup Final was transferred to Old Trafford and for the next four seasons the Cup and the Football League were suspended in favour of regionalized competitions. Palace played in the London Combination and fielded many local players, amateurs and soldiers stationed in London.

The transient nature of wartime football meant that there were some strange results. In March 1916, for instance, Palace beat Reading 10-1 with Sid Sanders scoring six; in April 1918, West Ham hammered Palace 11-0 with Sid Puddefoot netting seven. A few weeks earlier, Palace had lost 8-0 to Spurs in a match played at Highbury. The war claimed the lives of Harry Hanger and former Palace players Joe Bulcock and 'Ginger' Williams.

Palace in 1920-21, their first season in the Football League. Back row (left to right): Bates, McCracken, Bennett, Alderson, Walkerall, Kennedy. Middle row: Swift (assistant trainer), Greener, Feebury, Cracknell, Swift, Rhodes, Little, W.Jones (trainer). Front row: Storey, Conner, Whitworth, Smith, Menlove, Milligan, Wood. Insets (top right): Bateman, (bottom left): J.T.Jones, (bottom right): Hand.

The last wartime season saw Palace move home yet again, this time to a small ground called The Nest, opposite Selhurst Railway Station. It had been used by Croydon Common, a Southern League club which folded during the war, and on 14 September 1918, Palace played their first competitive game there as hosts, defeating Queen's Park Rangers 4-2.

On 30 August 1919, normal football was resumed and Palace drew 2-2 with Northampton Town at The Nest. Players who returned to the side were Rhodes, Feebury, Hughes, Bateman and Smith. Together with those who had been introduced during wartime soccer, they formed the nucleus of a good side and finished the season in third place, two points behind champions Portsmouth, who won the title on goal-average from Watford. In the FA Cup, Palace returned to Newcastle, scene of an earlier Cup triumph, but this time they lost 2-0.

The Football League, who before the war were against a Third Division, now agreed to a new section and in 1920-21, Crystal Palace kicked off as members of the League. The Third Division was made up of Southern League clubs with the exception of Cardiff City, who were elected to the Second Division. Grimsby Town, who finished bottom of Division Two in 1919-20, dropped down into the Third.

The challenge of League football held no fear for Palace — the opposition was almost exclusively the same as the previous season — and although they started with a defeat at Merthyr and a draw at home to Plymouth Argyle, the Londoners then strung together a run of six consecutive wins which put them at the top of the table. Over Easter they drew with their nearest rivals, Southampton, home and away, and the last 16 games saw Palace undefeated. They were the first champions of Division Three, five points clear of the Saints and with 70 goals scored. Only fourth-placed Swindon had netted more.

Action from the 1921-2 season. Top: Mercer, the Hull City goalkeeper, tips the ball over the bar with Palace's Menlove on the ground. Hull won this game at Palace 2-0 in the London club's first season in Division Two. Bottom: A raid on the Palace goal during an FA Cup tie against Millwall. Little clears for the home side.

Palace's chief marksman in that first League season was Jack Conner, who scored 28 to make him the leading scorer in the division. Conner did not miss a game and goalkeeper Jack Alderson and full-backs Jack Little and Ernie Rhodes were also ever-present.

Football hooligans made headlines, even in the early 1920s, and after Palace lost to Southend in November 1920, the crowd caused trouble and The Nest was closed for one game with the home match against Exeter being played at Southampton.

In the FA Cup, Palace scored a magnificent home victory over that season's First Division runners-up, Manchester City. The effect was rather spoilt, though, when Third Division North Hull City won 2-0 at The Nest in the next round. At least it left Palace free to concentrate on promotion. Two Palace players, Jones (Wales) and McCracken (Ireland), gained international caps towards the end of the season.

On 27 August 1921, Nottingham Forest were the first visitors to The Nest for a Second Division game. Palace won 4-1, then embarked on a poor run which saw them lose their next three games. Thereafter, steady progress saw Palace end the season in 14th position. Forest, incidentally, went on to win the championship.

In the FA Cup, Crystal Palace produced another giantkilling feat, this time a 6-0 hammering of First Division Everton at Goodison Park. True, the Merseysiders were struggling in the League and narrowly avoided relegation that season, but the 41,000 crowd could hardly believe their eyes as Palace goalkeeper Alderson had so little to do that he spent part of the match eating oranges.

Palace went out in the next round, beaten in a replay at Millwall, and soon afterwards Alderson was injured and 'keeper George Irwin, later to become manager of Palace, came in for his debut. At home to Bury in late March, another player made his first appearance when Albert Harry scored twice in the first of more than 400 Football League appearances for Palace. An indication of how Palace's scoring edge had been blunted in Division Two was the fact that Conner was leading scorer again, but this time with only eight goals.

The 1922-3 season proved fairly uneventful — Palace finished 16th in the table and went out of the Cup in the first round at QPR — but in the close season Jack Alderson earned an England cap when he played against France in Paris.

The following season was another struggle in the League — Palace finished 15th — but the Cup again held the interest. After dispatching First Division Spurs in the first round, Palace met another Division One side in the shape of Notts County. After three goalless games, Palace won another Villa Park replay, 2-1. The fourth game took place on a Monday afternoon and on the following Saturday, Palace faced Swindon Town in the third round. On the fringe of the Third Division South promotion race, Swindon produced their own Cup upset, beating Palace 2-1.

The end of the 1923-4 season saw Crystal Palace say goodbye to The Nest. Plans for a new ground had been underway since 1919, when the club first looked at a piece of wasteland at Selhurst, between Park Road, Whitehorse Lane and Holmesdale Road, owned by the London, Brighton & South Coast Railway Company. In January 1922, Palace paid £2,570 for the freehold and work began on erecting London's newest football stadium.

Palace's last game at The Nest was a 3-1 win over Barnsley on 3 May 1924 and another South Yorkshire club, Sheffield Wednesday, were the first visitors to Selhurst Park, on 30 August 1924. Some 25,000 people turned up but the Owls spoiled the celebrations by winning 1-0 with a goal from debutant Billy Marsden, who had joined them from Sunderland that summer.

The next three months, though, produced some fine results for Palace and after beating Wolves on 13 December they moved into fifth place with real hopes of

First Division football. Incredibly, Palace ended the season, not looking forward to football in the top flight, but staring relegation in the face.

After beating Wolves, Palace managed only three more victories that season. They lost their last three games, two of them at home, and allowed Stoke City to survive along with Oldham Athletic, who won at Selhurst in the final match of the season. It was a game which proved to be Palace's last in the Second Division for nearly 40 years.

The new 1925-6 campaign began with five defeats and, although Palace improved with three straight wins, another string of defeats followed and in November, secretary-manager Edmund Goodman reverted to his administrative duties, while Scotsman Alec Maley came down from Hibernian to take charge of playing affairs. Maley's first game was a 5-5 draw at home to Plymouth.

The new manager introduced fresh faces but it was one of Goodman's last signings, Percy Cherrett, who hit the headlines, scoring 26 goals in 35 games. In the end it was enough to lift Palace to 13th place in the Third Division South.

In the FA Cup, at Northampton, Palace were 3-0 down before a late burst earned them a replay. Victory at Selhurst brought Chelsea down for the fourth round and a record crowd of 41,000 (receipts £2,554) saw Cherrett and Hawkins put Palace into the next round.

Again, Palace were involved in a remarkable Cup battle. At Maine Road, against relegation-haunted Manchester City, the Londoners trailed 7-0 at half-time. In the second half, Palace pulled back to 8-4, only for City to add three more. For the first time, Palace had been involved in a first-class match which produced double figures. A crowd of 51,630, paying £3,358, witnessed the 15-goal extravaganza.

The Football Association were pleased with the new ground and awarded Palace an international match on 1 March 1926, when Wales beat England 3-1 before 23,000 spectators. Swansea Town's Fowler scored twice for the Welsh and W.Davies of Cardiff City hit the other. Billy Walker of Aston Villa netted England's lone effort.

Palace began the 1926-7 season in style, despite going a goal behind to Queen's Park Rangers inside 30 seconds of the opening of the campaign at Selhurst Park. The home side recovered to win 2-1. They ended the season with a 6-1 home defeat at the hands of Millwall. In between there were some big wins — seven goals against Norwich and Bristol Rovers, six against Newport and five against Swindon — and some equally big defeats — seven goals scored by Plymouth and six conceded against Swindon. This was a season when defences were still coming to terms with the new offside law introduced in 1925. Overall, Palace played well enough to finish in sixth place.

A defeat at Norwich heralded the start of 1927-8 and although matters improved with two home wins, by the middle of October, Palace had gone another six games without a victory. On 12 October, Alex Maley was deposed and on 21 November, Fred Mavin, formerly manager of Exeter City, was appointed.

By now, Palace had slipped still further, but Mavin's influence was such that the team pulled up the table and by the end of the season had finished fifth — far better placed than anyone dared have hoped. A run of six straight wins in late March and early April helped considerably.

During the 1928 close season, Mavin returned to Exeter to sign left-back Stan Charlton. He was appointed skipper and penalty-taker and missed only one game in 1928-9 as Palace missed promotion to Division Two on goal-average. Champions Charlton Athletic edged clear, helped by a 2-0 win at Selhurst early in the season, although Palace gained revenge with victory at The Valley in early March.

During the season, Palace achieved a run of 17 games without defeat. The sequence ended on 29 March, before a record crowd of 33,100, who saw Queen's Park Rangers win 4-1 at Selhurst.

In October, Palace travelled to Northampton, where Walter Betteridge made his debut at the age of 40, having been signed from Peterborough in the summer as a player-coach. His only game for Palace ended in an 8-1 defeat.

In the FA Cup, Palace met Southern League Kettering Town in the first round. Kettering waived home advantage and travelled to London, where they lost 2-0. Before the season was over, Palace signed three Kettering players and took on two more in the close season. One was centre-forward Peter Simpson, who was to score many fine goals for the Selhurst club.

A Havelock hat-trick helped defeat Luton 7-0 in the Cup and after two games against Millwall, Palace met the 'team of the 1920s' — Huddersfield Town. Huddersfield had won the League Championship three times and had been runners-up twice. The previous season they were beaten FA Cup Finalists and, although their fine team was breaking up, they still managed to beat Palace 5-2.

Peter Simpson was not selected for the start of the 1929-30 season and it was the fifth game, at home to Norwich, when he made his debut. He made up for lost time, however, with a hat-trick in a 3-2 win over the Canaries (although some reports claim that one was an own-goal). Simpson went on to score a total of 37 goals during the season — including one in the Cup at Leeds, when Palace were thrashed 8-1 — as the side finished in ninth place.

The 1930-31 season started with some high scoring and it was Simpson who got most of the goals. Fred Mavin, whose wife was suffering ill health, left Palace on 18 October, although he later returned to the game with Gillingham. He was replaced by Northampton Town manager Jack Tresadern, the former West Ham player. There was a bleak note when Sydney Bourne, chairman of Crystal Palace since the club's inception, died at the age of 77.

Meanwhile the goals continued to rain in — there was a 7-2 win over Exeter when Peter Simpson scored six — and at the end of the season, Palace had totalled 107. Simpson claimed 46 of them — still the club's record for a season — plus another eight in FA Cup matches.

He made the best possible use of non-League opposition, hammering in three goals against Taunton Town and four against Newark, and after three games against Reading, Palace met Everton, now taking the Second Division by storm. The

Palace goalkeeper Imrie gathers the ball as an Everton forward topples over in the Cup game at Selhurst in January 1931.

Merseysiders went to Selhurst seeking to avenge their 1922 Cup defeat by Palace. This time there were no upsets. Dixie Dean scored four and Everton won 6-0.

That season Everton reached the semi-final of the Cup as well as lifting the Second Division title and scoring 121 League goals. Palace, meanwhile, finished second to Notts County in the Third Division South.

The 1930s saw Palace suffer considerable embarrassment at the hands of non-League clubs in the FA Cup. The first was in December 1931, when Bath City won 2-1 in the second round. In the League, Palace finished fourth that season, six points behind champions Fulham and were unbeaten at Selhurst. It was their away form that let them down and they lost 11 games on their travels. Perhaps Palace's fortunes can best be summed up by two results. They beat Torquay United 7-0 on the first day of the season and lost 6-1 at Bristol Rovers in their third game. Coventry beat them 8-0 at Highfield Road and, of course, there was that Cup humiliation at Bath City's Twerton Park.

In July 1932, the Palace players reported back for training and were soon to be shocked when goalkeeper Billy Callender committed suicide. Callender, suffering from depression after the death of his fiancée, hanged himself at the ground. He was only 26.

The sad event cast gloom over Selhurst Park, but Palace started the season well, winning their first four games. Thereafter, however, their form was indifferent and they slipped to fifth place by the end of the season. On 8 October 1932, Watford became the first club to win at Selhurst for 32 matches. Against Brentford, the eventual champions, Palace lost 2-0 at Griffin Park and won 2-1 at Selhurst.

In March, Crystal Palace signed a youngster named Ronnie Rooke, a Guildford-born lad who played with Guildford City and Woking and had trials with Stoke City before joining Palace. Rooke scored consistently for the Reserves but could not establish a regular first-team place. Eventually he went to Fulham, where his career took off, and starred with Arsenal after the war.

In May 1933, secretary Edmund Goodman retired after 28 years service with Crystal Palace. He went to run a grocery shop in Anerley where he lived.

In 1933-4, Palace struggled in the League and finished 12th with Peter Simpson, their leading marksman, sidelined through injury after scoring 20 goals in 25 games. Palace manager Jack Tresadern returned to his former club, Northampton Town, to sign Albert Dawes as cover for Simpson. Dawes responded with 16 goals in 22 games. For some reason, Rooke, later to prove such a successful goalscorer at Craven Cottage, was still out of favour.

In the FA Cup, Palace eliminated Norwich City, the eventual Third Division champions, and after wins over Stockport County and Aldershot, they drew probably the greatest reward of all, a fourth-round tie against Arsenal at Highbury. Just as Huddersfield had been the team of the 1920s, so Arsenal were proving the team of the 30s. In 1933-4 they were in the middle of a hat-trick of League Championships and Palace were no match for them. Before an attendance of 56,177, the biggest crowd ever to watch Palace, the Gunners won 7-0 with goals from Dunne (2), Bastin (2), Beasley (2) and Birkett.

In 1934-5, another FA Cup trip to the West Country ended in humiliation as Yeovil & Petters beat Palace 3-0. Earlier in the season, Dawes scored five goals against Cardiff City and took over as the club's leading marksman, although Simpson was now back to his old form. At the end of a season in which Palace finished fifth, Dawes had netted 19 goals and Simpson 14. Bob Bigg was third-highest scorer with 16.

The following season, when Dawes topped the Third Division South scoring list with 38 goals from 41 League games, he played in an England trial and was later named 12th man against Scotland at Wembley.

Read, Crystal Palace's goalkeeper, punches clear from Clapton Orient's Ted Crawford during a Third Division South game at Lea Bridge in February 1936.

Peter Simpson left Selhurst in the 1935 close season, moving to West Ham after scoring more than 150 League goals for Palace. A benefit match between Palace and the famous amateur club, Corinthians, was held for Simpson at Selhurst Park. Simpson's goalscoring talents were held in check by Bernard Joy, who had just signed for Arsenal and who was the last amateur to play in a full international for England. Alas, poor weather restricted the attendance to around 1,000 and Simpson's financial gain was not as great as it might have been.

Palace began 1935-6 with a new manager. Jack Tresadern had taken over at Spurs in the summer and his place was taken by former Liverpool and England player, Tommy Bromilow.

Behind the scenes, the Palace club lost two chairmen within the first month of the season. Louis Bellatti died and then his successor, R.S.Flew, also passed away. Carey Burnett became the new chairman.

Palace finished the season in sixth position and in the FA Cup, Margate were the latest non-Leaguers to knock out the Selhurst side. In the 1936 close season, Tom Bromilow resigned after a stormy board meeting and director R.S.Moyes took over team affairs. It was Moyes who sold Rooke to Fulham and then let Dawes move to Luton, where he helped the Hatters win promotion at the end of the season.

In December, Moyes resigned, taking up scouting duties instead, and the following month, Bromilow resumed his duties. One of Moyes' signings from his brief reign was the former Sheffield Wednesday and Aston Villa player, Jackie Palethorpe, who had been on Palace's books as an amateur some years before. Palethorpe marked his League debut with two goals as Palace beat Newport County 6-1 and by the end of the season he had scored eight goals in 29 appearances.

As Albert Dawes helped Luton to promotion, Palace finished in 14th place. The following season it was the turn of London neighbours Millwall to achieve Second Division football, while Palace were still out of contention in seventh place.

In the Cup, after a scare against non-League Kettering, Palace beat Accrington Stanley and then drew Bromilow's old club, Liverpool, in the third round. The Merseysiders were then a mid-table First Division club and after a goalless draw at Selhurst, they won the replay in extra-time. Waldron netted for Palace and Shafto for Liverpool in normal time. Then an own-goal by Palace left-half Collins and one from Fagan, five minutes from the end of the extra period, settled the issue in Liverpool's favour. A few weeks later the Football Association ordered Liverpool to publicly retract a comment in their programme which alleged that in the game at Selhurst Park, Palace players had handed out some rough treatment and that it was 'remarkable that Liverpool players had escaped serious injury'.

In the 1938 close season Dawes returned from Luton and finished leading scorer with 12 goals in 29 League games. Palace finished the last season before the war as runners-up to Newport County, missing promotion to Division Two by three points. The vital game between the two challengers took place on 11 February, when Newport visited Selhurst. The Welsh club were eight points clear of Palace but had played two games more. A crowd of over 29,000 saw Palace lead until the dying moments when Chesters, their goalkeeper, was bowled over in a goalmouth scramble and could only watch as the ball trickled agonizingly over the line.

In the 1939 close season, Leicester City tempted Tommy Bromilow to Filbert Street as their new manager and Palace trainer George Irwin, their former goalkeeper, took over. Irwin had little chance to show his paces. After only three League games, war was declared and the Football League closed down for the duration. Most of the players remained but, after signing up for the services or police, their futures were uncertain.

The war years were good footballing times for Crystal Palace. Most of the regular

Crystal Palace in 1938-9. Back row (left to right): Birtley, Horton, Blackman, A.Dawes, Collins, F.Dawes, Owens, Hudgell, Jordan, Robson. Middle row: Gregory, Lievesley, Daniels, Walker, Chesters, Tierney, Shanks, Brooks, Uren, Lewis. Front row: Greener (assistant trainer), G.Stansbury, Dr T.E.M.Wardill (medical officer), C.H.Temple (vice-chairman), E.T.Truett (chairman), R.H.E.Blaxill (director), F.E.Burrell (secretary), T.Bromilow (manager), Irwin (trainer). On ground: Davis, Waldron, Smith, Bryson, Gillespie, Bigg, McLean.

players turned out and in the second half of 1939-40 Palace won the League South Division 'D' championship, one of their most memorable results being a 10-0 win at home to Brighton. In 1940-41 they lifted the South Regional League and reached the London War Cup semi-final. And in 1945-6, as football prepared for normality the following season, Palace were first in the Third Division South (South). Even the ground missed the bombing and Millwall had a spell at Selhurst when The Den was damaged.

As in World War One, the system of guest players was widespread and Palace benefited by having the services of several established footballers from other clubs. Two of Palace's wartime players, Dick Graham and Fred Kurz, were to give the club fine service when peacetime football resumed.

In December 1939, it was announced that the FA had suspended three Palace directors, plus R.S.Moyes (the man who took over as manager when Tommy Bromilow resigned) for 12 months. Another director was banned for six months, two players were fined and the Palace secretary was cautioned. The reason was that money, allegedly spent on directors' expenses, had been used for illegal payments to players. The custom was fairly commonplace in the days of the maximum wage and perhaps Palace were just unlucky to be caught. During the war, Derby County were another club found guilty of such offences and their manager, George Jobey, was suspended *sine die*.

The FA Cup got underway again in 1945-6, when Palace drew on aggregate with Queen's Park Rangers in a two-legged first round and then went out by the only goal of an extra-time replay at Craven Cottage. The Football League, however, did not resume until 1946-7, with the same programme of fixtures as that planned for the aborted 1939-40 season.

Palace lost their opening match, at Mansfield, and there was worse to follow. The following Wednesday evening, at a windswept Elm Park, Palace were 3-0 down to Reading and, although they fought back to 3-2 before half-time, Reading dominated the second half and took their score to ten. It was Palace's biggest-ever defeat in the Football League and goalkeeper Graham was dropped for the next game. He returned to play for several seasons and took Palace to promotion as manager.

In the FA Cup, Palace travelled to Newcastle and were hammered 6-2 with Len Shackleton scoring twice for the Magpies. Several League club scouts were at St James' Park and it was the signal for the Palace side to be broken up. Sunderland equalled the record fee for a full-back when they paid £10,000 for Arthur Hudgell. He began his career as a wing-half but was switched to right-back as one of nine changes in the aftermath of the defeat by Reading. Brentford snapped up Girling and Naylor for a combined fee of £6,500. The latter player turned out as Bark earlier that season, before changing his name by deed poll.

There were few highlights for Palace in that first post-war season, apart perhaps from the 6-1 thrashing of Torquay United on Christmas Day, when Naylor and Girling each scored twice. The following day, Palace lost 2-1 at Plainmoor and managed only five more wins to the end of the season, a run-in which left them in 18th place, albeit nine points above the re-election zone.

Inevitably, perhaps, that kind of return meant that Palace would start 1947-8 with a new manager. He was Jack Butler, the former Arsenal player who had built up quite a reputation as a coach on the Continent. Palace trainer, Bob John, had played alongside Butler in the Gunners' team which lost the 1927 FA Cup Final to Cardiff City.

Butler was well-liked by the players but after two seasons of struggle, the last of which saw Palace finish bottom of the Third Division South, he resigned. In his first campaign, he saw Palace finish in 13th place and win only once away from home — a remarkable 5-0 victory at Watford.

Two of the mainstays of the side were Graham and Kurz, both wartime signings. Graham (the goalkeeper who lost his place after Reading hammered ten past him) was an ever-present. Kurz was leading scorer with 18 goals from 33 League appearances. Towards the end of the season Marcel Gaillard, a Belgian, made a few appearances for Palace at outside-left.

In the FA Cup there was something of a fairy-tale when Tonbridge-born Roy Farrington scored on his first-team debut, in the 2-1 first-round win over Port Vale. It was not the start of a famous career, however, for Farrington made only two more appearances before drifting out of League football.

Palace then beat Bristol City 1-0 at Ashton Gate. Emergency regulations decreed that extra-time should be played in the first game to avoid midweek replays and the resultant absenteeism from factories, and Bert Robson settled the issue for Palace in the first period of extra-time. In the third round, former Bolton and England forward Ray Westwood helped Chester, of the Third Division North, win 1-0 at Selhurst.

The 1948-9 season got off to a miserable start when Reading won 5-1 at Elm Park. There was a similar defeat at Notts County and when the Midlanders visited Selhurst in February, Palace went down 5-1 yet again. Tommy Lawton, who was winning his last England cap when Palace lost at Meadow Lane, headed a magnificent goal and the game attracted Selhurst's best crowd of the season — 30,925.

Palace endured some barren spells. They lost 5-0 at Newport on Christmas Day and that heralded the start of a five-match run in which they failed to score. Palace ended the season at the foot of the table but were comfortably re-elected.

Butler left and his replacement was Ronnie Rooke, the prolific goalscorer who Palace let slip through their fingers before the war. Rooke's playing career was coming to an end, but he still managed to score 21 League goals that season as Palace climbed up the table to finish a satisfactory seventh. Rooke joined the new fashion of player-manager. He also entered the record books as probably the first manager ever to be sent off, when he took an early bath at Millwall.

There was a school of thought that, despite the fact that he was still scoring goals, Rooke would achieve more by concentrating solely on management. After the first three games of the 1950-51 season, however, there was cause to reconsider. Palace lost all those games and scored only once in the process. Rooke returned to the side, scored a penalty in a 2-1 win over Torquay, and ended the season as the club's leading League scorer with five goals, despite leaving Selhurst in November.

Rooke's departure had its root cause in a meeting held in January 1950, at which seven new directors were elected to the Palace board. David Harris, John Dunster, Victor Ercolani, Guy Robson, Ralph Shrager, Arthur Wait and Colonel J.Trevor were the new men. Harris was elected chairman and Wait became vice-chairman. Three directors — G.J.Ellis, L.A.Ward and E.A.Webber — resigned and another, R.E.Edwards, announced his decision to stand down at the annual meeting.

The new men made £20,000 available to strengthen the team and Rooke paid £7,000 to Bradford for inside-forward Les Stevens. He also bought Morris Jones, another inside-forward, from Swindon (£4,000), Charlie Rundle from Spurs (£4,000) and George Smith, a short, stocky wing-half from Southampton (£2,500). In November 1949, incidentally, Palace had sold wing-half Jack Lewis to Bournemouth for £7,500.

Alas, Rooke's signings did not succeed. Stevens, a former Spurs player, made 20 appearances before dropping out of League football. Jones managed 17 games before being transferred to Watford. Smith played in only seven matches and eventually emigrated to Australia.

Rooke's biggest outlay, though, was the club record fee of £10,000 he spent to

Crystal Palace in 1949-50. Back row (left to right): Chilvers, George, Crowe, Blackshaw, Goodyear, Gaillard, Delaney, Harding, Edwards, Bostock, Thomas, Hancox. Middle row: Blackman (assistant trainer), Ross, Broughton, Chase, Murphy, Watson, Bumstead, Graham, Briggs, Saward, Kurz, Buckley, Mulheron, Greener (trainer). Front row: F.Dawes, R.Rooke (manager), F.T.Edwards (secretary), G.Robson (director), Col J.Trevor (director), A.J.Wait (vice-chairman), D.Harris (chairman), J.R.Dunster (director), V.Ercolani (director), R.Shrager (director), C.Slade, Betty Beamish. On ground: Kelly, Surtess, Hanlon.

take former England Amateur international Bill Whittaker to Selhurst Park. Whittaker, who was a late choice for Charlton Athletic's winning 1947 FA Cup Final team, joined Palace from Huddersfield Town in June 1950. Although he made 35 appearances in 1950-51, they were to be his sum total for the club.

Chairman David Harris had been away on a cruise, although he had been kept in touch with developments. Nevertheless, when Harris returned he was apparently surprised by the amount of money that had been spent — and dismayed by the club's position in the table.

Palace's first 18 League games had produced only four wins and the last six games had all been lost. On 29 November they were knocked out of the FA Cup, 4-1 at home to Millwall, and the board recorded its decision: 'Mr R.L.Rooke be placed on indefinite leave of absence, or alternately, the board were prepared to accept his resignation on terms agreeable to all parties'.

In Rooke's place, the Palace board decided to appoint not one manager, but two. Fred Dawes, a former player and Rooke's assistant, and chief scout Charlie Slade took over but their task was a desperately difficult one. Yet, in the very next game, Palace broke their losing sequence when 22-year-old centre-forward Trevor Herbert marked his debut with the only goal of the home game against Walsall. Yet again, however, there was to be no fairy-tale. Herbert, who began his career on Leyton Orient's books, made only seven more League appearances before drifting out of senior football.

Neither did the game herald the start of a Palace revival. At the end of the season they were firmly entrenched at the foot of the Third Division South. Nottingham Forest, that season's champions, hammered in six goals at Selhurst. Norwich City, the eventual runners-up, won 5-0 there and one of their stars was Republic of Ireland winger John Gavin, who was to sign for Palace eight years later.

The Palace board now off-loaded the players which had cost them so much money. Stevens, Rundle, Smith and Whittaker were all given free transfers and Jones was allowed to go to Watford for £1,000. The only outgoing transfer which brought a profit was that of inside-forward Noel Kelly, who went to Nottingham Forest for £7,000. Kelly, who joined Palace from Arsenal in March 1950 and who made 42 League appearances for them, went on to win a Republic of Ireland cap with Forest.

On 11 October 1951, the Palace board dispensed with the services of Fred Dawes, whilst Charlie Slade reverted to the post of chief scout. Into their place came Laurie Scott, the former England full-back whose career at Arsenal had wound down after a succession of injuries.

Palace had begun the season well enough, with a 2-1 home win over Exeter, but in the next game they went down 5-0 at Plymouth, where Worcestershire cricketer George Dews scored twice. After winning 2-1 at Colchester, Palace then lost their next five League games, a dismal run eventually relieved by a 4-0 win at Leyton Orient when Cam Burgess, making only his second appearance, scored a hat-trick.

By the end of the season, Burgess, a £3,000 signing from Chester, was Palace's leading scorer with 21 goals in 22 appearances, and the club had improved slightly

Cup embarrassment against non-League opposition in the 1950s. Top: Finchley's Milne scores from a free-kick against Palace. Bottom: Palace goalkeeper Macdonald is beaten by a shot from Bishop Auckland's Major, who went on to net a hat-trick.

to finish 19th. After Scott's appointment as player-manager, Palace continued their inconsistent ways and Burgess was the one steady influence, although he missed several matches through injury. When he did play he was seemingly always 'on-song' and he scored in six consecutive games in November and December. Alas, Palace won only two of them.

In 1952-3, Palace received the first of several FA Cup shocks at the hands of non-League opposition. After beating Reading in a replay, they lost 3-1 at Finchley. Even then, Palace had been given a second chance. The game was originally scheduled for 6 December and was abandoned because of fog after 61 minutes with the Athenian League side leading 3-1. Four days later, they repeated the scoreline on a bone-hard pitch.

The following season, Palace were beaten 1-0 at Great Yarmouth Town in the first round and in 1954-5, Bishop Auckland won 4-2 at Selhurst Park in the second round.

By then, Palace had yet another new manager. Scott had steered them to 13th place in the Third Division South in 1952-3, but in 1953-4 they were back down to 22nd, albeit ten points from the re-election zone.

The summer of 1953 saw frenzied transfer activity at Selhurst Park. In July, Cam Burgess was sold to York City for less than £1,000. Inside-forward John Rainford went to Cardiff in May, for £3,000 plus wing-half Don Moss. In June, inside-forward Fred Evans was exchanged for Rochdale forward Bert Foulds. And another exchange deal in June involved forward Ray Hancox going to Southend, with wing-half Ray Woods moving in the opposite direction.

Players arriving at Selhurst that summer also included Chelsea inside-forward Ernie Randall, who was signed in June for £1,300 down and the £1,000 balance due four months later. A less expensive signing was Brighton wing-half Cecil Willard, veteran of 190 League games for the Goldstone club. He arrived at Selhurst in July for £150 and later became Palace's trainer.

The year also saw other changes at Selhurst Park. The club's first floodlights were installed and in November, chairman David Harris resigned and his place was taken by Arthur Wait. A few days later, Colonel Trevor also resigned and with Guy Robson having earlier emigrated to Mexico, this left only four of the seven directors who had pumped money into the club upon their election in 1950.

In October 1954, with Crystal Palace again at the wrong end of the table and still smarting from a 7-1 defeat at Watford, Scott was relieved of his duties. Palace's first choice as his successor was Harry Storer, the former Birmingham City and Coventry City manager. Storer had left Highfield Road in December 1953, but he declined Palace's offer and it was July 1955 before he went back into management with one of his former clubs, Derby County.

Storer was a manager with an 'iron-man' reputation, but the man who Palace next approached could hardly have been more different. Cyril Spiers, the former Aston Villa and Tottenham goalkeeper and lately manager of Norwich City and Cardiff City, was a quiet, studious character. Initially he was manager-secretary at Selhurst before handing over the administrative duties to Margaret Montague.

Spiers, like most of his predecessors, did not find life easy as manager of Crystal Palace and at the end of the season the club had missed having to apply for re-election by four points. And, of course, there was the latest Cup disaster, this time at the hands of Bishop Auckland.

At the end of the season the board dispensed with the services of chief scout Charlie Slade. It was later claimed that in 1954, Slade had been one of the parties involved in rejecting a young centre-forward from Kidderminster called Gerry Hitchens. That Hitchens signed for Cardiff in January 1955 and later starred for Aston Villa and England probably had nothing to do with Slade's departure.

Rouse and Edwards of Palace beat off a challenge from Torquay United's Collins in the final match of the 1956-7 season.

No matter how poor results became, it seemed that Palace fans would still support their team and that was a comforting thought when the club had to apply for re-election at the end of 1955-6. Surely the League would not turn its back on a club with such 'gate potential'. Sure enough, Palace were voted back in after a plea from chairman Victor Ercolani, who pointed out that over the past five years, despite the team's poor showing, attendances at Selhurst had averaged 12,000.

The average age of the side was now the lowest in the club's history and in 1956-7 they lifted Palace to 20th place, ensuring that another cap-in-hand approach would be avoided. Mike Deakin was one of the few successes, scoring 16 League goals, but there were some useful looking youngsters on view, none more so than Johnny Byrne. A Surrey lad, Byrne signed professional forms on his 17th birthday in May 1956, made his League debut early the following season and went on to become one of the greatest names in Crystal Palace's history.

Television cameras arrived at Selhurst Park in November 1956, no doubt hoping to record another FA Cup upset when Palace entertained Walthamstow Avenue in the first round. Goals from Murray and Cooper ensured that there would be no shock this time, but Palace eventually went out to Millwall in round three.

Crystal Palace needed to finish in the top half of the table in 1957-8, if they were to avoid being placed in the new Fourth Division that was to take effect the following season. They failed by four points, finishing 14th when 12th place would have taken them into the new Third Division.

George Cooper, who signed from West Midlands non-League club Brierley Hill, headed the scorers with 17 League goals and Tony Collins, who was nearing the end of a career that would eventually encompass eight League clubs, hit a hat-trick at home to Walsall. Full-back Terry Long was the only ever-present and went on to break the club's overall appearance record previously held by Albert Harry.

One bonus was the signing of Johnny McNichol, who was Ted Drake's first signing for Chelsea. McNichol had made his name as a goalscoring inside-forward with the Blues and before them, Brighton. He did not score many goals for Palace but over the next five years gave yeoman service as a hard-working versatile defender and an inspirational club captain.

Before Palace took their place in Division Four, they had yet another new manager. Cyril Spiers paid the price of failure and left in June 1958. His place was taken by George Smith, the former Charlton, Brentford and Queen's Park Rangers centre-half. Smith had served Ipswich as player-assistant manager and then coached in the Channel Islands and with Sheffield United before managing Eastbourne and Sutton United.

Smith was something of an abrasive character and told the Palace board that if he did not win promotion for them within two seasons, then he would resign. In April 1960 he kept his word.

Palace won their first game in Division Four, hammering Crewe Alexandra 6-2 with Deakin and Byrne each grabbing a hat-trick, but overall it was a moderate season and the club finished in seventh place. Deakin (23 goals) and Byrne (17) headed the scorers, but goalkeeper Vic Rouse made national headlines when he became the first player from Division Four to win a full international cap. Rouse replaced the injured Jack Kelsey against Northern Ireland in Belfast on 22 April 1959.

In 1958-9, Palace reached the Southern Floodlit Cup Final and lost 2-1 to Arsenal in front of a 32,000 crowd who paid new record receipts for Selhurst Park.

In August 1959, Palace took two points from their first three games, but there were some big wins to follow. Towards the middle of September they beat Hartlepools United 5-2 and at the end of the month hammered Watford 8-1. On 10 October, Roy Summersby scored four goals as Palace put nine past Barrow.

Alas, all this did not signal the start of a promotion-winning season. There were also some heavy defeats — a 7-1 thrashing at Notts County and a 4-0 reverse at Rochdale — and by the middle of April, Palace were third behind Millwall and Watford. They took only five points from their last five games to finish eighth. Smith remembered his promise and resigned.

Arthur Rowe, manager of Spurs' famous 'Push and Run' side of the 1950s and

Palace in 1958-9. Back row (left to right): Colfar, Roche, Pyke, Rouse, Evans, Sexton, Noakes. Front row: Byrne, Summersby, McNichol, Choules, Deakin, Long, Gavin.

now Palace's assistant manager, stepped up to take over from Smith. He could hardly have had a better start to his first full season in charge as Palace beat Accrington Stanley 9-2 with Byrne and Alan Woan the chief goalscorers.

There followed a 3-2 win over Darlington and a 5-1 success at Doncaster. Palace then won 1-0 at Darlington and the scene was set for a serious promotion challenge. There were a few shocks, none greater than the 4-1 defeat at the hands of Peterborough United, who had just been elected to Division Four in place of Gateshead.

An attendance of 36,478 — then a Fourth Division record — saw The Posh win 2-0 at Selhurst. In the return at London Road, Peterborough won 4-1 before a crowd of more than 21,000 and justice was done when they lifted the Fourth Division title, two points ahead of Palace who were promoted as runners-up.

Peterborough scored a record 134 League goals that season, but Palace were no slouches and hit 110. Leading the scorers was Johnny Byrne with 30, whilst Summersby had 25 to his name. Byrne also gained international honours, playing for England Under-23s. At the end of the season he went on the full England tour to Portugal, Italy and Austria, but did not play.

Palace's home attendances set a new high and the Fourth Division record was broken again when 37,774 saw Millwall win 2-0 at Selhurst at the end of March. Palace averaged over 19,000, easily the best in the Third and Fourth Divisions and a figure bettered by only a handful of Second Division clubs.

Crystal Palace's interest in Cup football was minimal in this promotion season. Darlington won Palace's first-ever League Cup game, 2-0, and Watford knocked them out of the FA Cup in a second-round replay.

Palace took their place in the Third Division and their games attracted managers and scouts from many League clubs. Johnny Byrne was their main target and after he became only the third Third Division player to win a full England cap — against Northern Ireland at Wembley in November 1961 — the pressure on him intensified.

No Third Division club could hope to keep a newly-capped England player and in March, West Ham manager Ron Greenwood paid a British record fee of £65,000 for Byrne, with Ronnie Brett returning in part-exchange for £2,500. Brett had scored 12 goals in 36 League appearances before joining the Hammers in June 1959. In August 1962, a few months after rejoining Palace, Brett was killed in a road accident.

Despite leaving for West Ham in March, Byrne was Palace's second highest scorer (behind Andy Smillie) with 14 goals when the 1961-2 season ended. The club finished 15th in the table and were knocked out of the FA Cup third round in a seven-goal thriller before more than 39,000 spectators at Villa Park.

During the season, Palace signed three players, all of whom were to give the club stalwart service. Two of them were goalkeepers. John Jackson, who signed in March 1962, began a career which saw him make 346 League appearances for Palace, and Bill Glazier, who joined in October 1961, went on to play in 106 League games. The third player was Alan Stephenson, who signed for the club in February 1962 and made the first of 170 League appearances.

Far more experienced were two players signed by Rowe in May 1961. They were West Brom's former England centre-forward, Ronnie Allen, and former Manchester City full-back, Roy Little, who came from Brighton.

Perhaps the outstanding memory of the season was the visit of European Cup giants, Real Madrid. They visited Selhurst for the official switching-on of Palace's new floodlights and on a wet night, some 25,000 fans braved soaking conditions to see Palace lose 4-3.

How different the mood after a few weeks of the 1962-3 season. A poor start saw Palace still looking for their first win after seven games. In the summer they had signed Millwall's Peter Burridge for £10,000, in an attempt to make good the loss of Byrne's goals. Burridge did reasonably well, scoring 14 goals in a season severely disrupted by bad weather, but Byrne was almost impossible to replace.

That elusive first victory came at home to Queen's Park Rangers, but Palace were still struggling desperately and in November, Arthur Rowe resigned through ill health. His replacement was the club's former goalkeeper, Dick Graham, who had been Rowe's assistant since January 1961. The enormity of his task was soon thrust home when Palace crashed out of the FA Cup, 7-2 at Mansfield.

Graham soon went into the transfer market in a bid to save Palace from relegation. In November he bought Bournemouth's centre-forward, Gilbert Dowsett, and the following month former Arsenal centre-forward, Cliff Holton, joined Palace from Northampton Town. Dowsett finished second-highest scorer with 12 goals and Holton was fourth in the list, behind Allen (11 goals), with nine.

It was the combined efforts of these goalscorers which saw Palace edge away from the bottom of the table. There was even a 6-0 win, albeit over soon-to-be-relegated Bradford, and by the end of the season there was convincing evidence that Palace had turned the corner.

Hopes were severely checked by a 5-1 defeat at Coventry on the opening day of the 1963-4 season, a campaign which saw Rowe back at Selhurst in the role of general manager. The defeat by Jimmy Hill's Coventry was a set-back, but Palace overcame it and at the season's end they were promoted as runners-up to the Highfield Road club.

Crystal Palace had only themselves to blame for not finishing top. After a 12-match undefeated run they failed to win any of their last seven games and the championship was decided on goal-average. Palace, of course, could look back to that opening-day defeat by the eventual champions but, even then, they could have wrapped up the title in front of their own supporters on the last day of the season. Nearly 28,000 fans packed into Selhurst, hoping to acclaim the new champions, but a hat-trick from Oldham Athletic's Bob Ledger spoilt the celebrations.

Holton and Burridge were Palace's main scorers, finishing with 20 goals each. Bill Glazier and Bert Howe were ever-present, Brian Wood missed only one game, Burridge two and Holton three. Indeed, Palace used only 20 players in their League programme that season.

The spectre of FA Cup giantkillers still haunted Palace in 1963-4. After hitting eight goals past Harwich & Parkeston, they might have thought that the ghost was laid. Then Yeovil Town, famous giantkillers of old, beat Palace 3-1 on their notorious sloping Huish ground. The time-honoured cliché was, of course, that it left Palace free to concentrate on the League.

Dick Graham never appeared to be worried about what other people thought of him or his methods. Although his ways were not always appreciated by the fans, he had taken Crystal Palace into the Second Division.

In October 1964, he made the unpopular decision to allow Bill Glazier to go to Coventry. The £35,000 fee was then a record for a British goalkeeper but the size of the incoming fee meant little to the fans, who would rather have seen Glazier between the posts. Graham immediately bought West Brom's Welsh international 'keeper, Tony Millington, but by the end of the season he had given way to John Jackson.

Palace made a dreadful start to their first season in Division Two for 40 years. Derby County won 3-2 at Selhurst on the opening day and Palace then lost at Swindon and Swansea. With no points from their first three games, Palace then won five on the trot and that set the pattern for a topsy-turvy season in which they finished a satisfactory seventh.

One man who made a rapid impact for Palace was Keith Smith, the former West Brom forward who was transferred from Peterborough in November 1964. Smith netted six seconds after the start of Palace's game at Derby the following month. He was the first substitute to be used by Palace in a Football League game, when he replaced Ian Lawson against Leyton Orient on 28 August 1965.

In December 1964, Palace signed the former West Brom inside-forward, David Burnside, from Southampton. Burnside, who had gained national fame for his ball-juggling exhibitions on television, scored one of the goals by which Palace beat Nottingham Forest in the fifth round of the FA Cup in February 1965. The game was watched by a record Selhurst crowd of 41,667, a figure pushed up to 45,384 when Leeds beat Palace in the quarter-final.

In May 1965, Cliff Holton was transferred to Watford. Right up to the end of his Palace days, Holton was making major contributions and he finished leading scorer with 11 goals from 35 League appearances. Other outgoing transfers were Kellard (to Ipswich) and Burridge (to Charlton Athletic).

In July, Derek Kevan, the former West Brom and England centre-forward, was signed from Manchester City for £20,000. Eight months later, Kevan was allowed to go to Peterborough and by then, Palace were looking for a new manager.

Dick Graham had come under increasing criticism from supporters and in January 1966, with Palace having won nine of their first 25 League games, he was asked to leave. There had been a series of niggling upsets behind the scenes and the time was right for change. Graham had done a good job at Selhurst Park, taking Palace out of the Third Division, but fresh ideas were needed.

As Graham's replacement, the Palace board earmarked Bert Head, the former Swindon Town boss who was now in charge at Bury. The Gigg Lane club were reluctant to release Head from his contract and Arthur Rowe took over as caretaker manager until April, when Palace finally got their man.

The efforts of Graham, Rowe and then Head saw Palace finish 11th in that disjointed 1965-6 season. In the close season, Head signed Bobby Woodruff from Wolves. Woodruff had played under Head at Swindon and he soon showed his old scoring flair with 18 goals in his first season at Selhurst. They helped Palace to a respectable seventh place in 1966-7 and although the club slipped down to 11th the following season — Woodruff was again top scorer with another 18 goals — there were great days just around the corner.

The side which took Crystal Palace into Division One for the first time in the club's history was built by Head over the preceding months. John Jackson, Terry Long, Steve Kember and David Payne were already on the books when Head took over. He added Bobby Woodruff and then made further important introductions.

Centre-half John McCormick was signed from Aberdeen (along with Tommy White) in May 1966 and later that year Cliff Jackson, an inside-forward who had played under Head at Swindon, came from Plymouth Argyle. In November 1967, Head signed Queen's Park Rangers' veteran winger, Mark Lazarus. In 1968, defender Mel Blyth (from Scunthorpe), left-back John Loughlan (Morton), defender Tony Taylor (Morton), outside-left Colin Taylor (Walsall) and Roger Hoy (Spurs) all joined Palace. Hoy had the unenviable job of understudying Mike England at White Hart Lane.

These were the men who took Palace into Division One. The season began with a 4-0 away win at Cardiff and ended with a 2-1 victory at Blackburn. In between there were some exciting times in a League programme which was the latest to suffer from severe weather conditions.

In the early stages, Palace went up and down the top ten. After a month's interruption because of the ice and snow, Palace began again and with 16 games remaining they were in ninth place, ten points behind the leaders, Derby County, who were surging forward under Brian Clough.

The rest seemed to have done the Selhurst club a power of good, for they did not lose another League game that season. A Woodruff goal gave them victory at Derby and then Kember's goal earned a win at Birmingham. Palace went on swallowing up the backlog of fixtures and on 8 April they stood in second place, two points ahead of Middlesbrough.

The last home game of the season was against Fulham and a crowd of 36,126 saw the Cottagers go 2-0 ahead before goals from Colin Jackson, Lazarus and Kember gave Palace victory. The scenes at Selhurst Park were unrivalled in the club's history and in complete contrast to Palace's last game of the season when less than 5,000 saw them win at Ewood Park. They finished runners-up to Derby, who had roared into Division One with a remarkable run of nine straight wins. Palace were the last side to defeat the champions and finished seven points behind them and six in front of third-placed Charlton Athletic.

John Sewell captained Palace to promotion and John Jackson, Steve Kember and John McCormick were ever-present. Colin Jackson was top scorer with 14 goals.

In the summer, the Arthur Wait Stand went up along the Whitehorse Lane side of Selhurst Park at a cost of £150,000.

Palace's first game in Division One could hardly have provided them with more attractive opposition and a record crowd of 48,610 saw Manchester United held to a 2-2 draw. Just after Christmas, the record was broken again when 49,498 saw the visit of Chelsea. Alas, Chelsea were in a rampant mood and won 5-1.

Palace began the next season with several new players. Alan Birchenall and Bobby Tambling were transferred from Chelsea, Gerry Humphreys from Everton and Peter Wall from Liverpool. Gerry Queen had come from Kilmarnock in the 1969 close season and only he made his mark on Palace's first season in the top flight, appearing in 37 games and scoring nine goals to finish top scorer. With that sort of return enabling Queen to head the list, Palace were obviously short of fire-power and

Crystal Palace staff in 1968-9. Back row (left to right): Lazarus, Long, Woodruff, Blyth, Presland, Bert Head (manager), J.Jackson, McCormick, Snowden, Payne, Hoy. Front: Loughlan, T.Taylor, Tomkins, C.Taylor, Sewell, Kember, C.Jackson, Dawkins, Oliver.

they struggled all along before finishing in 20th place, one point ahead of relegated Sunderland and Sheffield Wednesday.

The 1970-71 season saw Crystal Palace finish 18th in Division One, losing 6-0 at Southampton in their last game. One of the better results was the 2-0 win at Highbury in the fourth round of the Football League Cup. Arsenal lifted the FA Cup and League double that season and Palace's victory was the Gunners' only defeat at Highbury.

In 1971-2, after all the success of recent years, Palace supporters had to endure the old familiar fight against relegation, albeit this time from the First Division. Once again the lack of goals was a major problem and Bobby Tambling's eight in League games made him the club's leading scorer for the season in which Palace finished 20th. Bobby Kellard, who rejoined the club in September after spells at Ipswich, Portsmouth, Bristol City and Leicester, made a massive contribution to the drive for safety.

In November 1972, Head signed Don Rogers from his old club, Swindon Town and Rogers scored a magnificent goal when Palace hammered Manchester United 5-0 in front of the TV cameras. A victory of that proportion over the Old Trafford

Don Rogers outstrips Manchester United's Martin Buchan.

club is always something to savour, but United were in deep trouble and Palace, too, were struggling desperately at the wrong end of the table.

In the spring of 1973, Ray Bloye took over the club from Arthur Wait. Relegation loomed and in March, Palace appointed Malcolm Allison as manager with Head moving over to become general manager. Head, in fact, was soon to leave Selhurst.

Allison immediately blooded a youngster from Scotland, Jim Cannon, who thus began a 16-year career in the Palace team. Cannon had a remarkable debut, being booked against Chelsea and then scoring a goal to help Palace towards their only win in 32 attempts against London sides in the First Division. That rare success could not help Palace and at the end of the season they went down with West Brom.

Twelve months later, Palace were down again. They did not manage their first League win until November and slid into Division Three alongside Swindon and Preston. This was the first season that three clubs were automatically relegated and Palace finished 20th.

Allison was a good coach, but not everybody's idea of the ideal manager. Several of the older players were replaced by youngsters and the biggest surprise was the sale of John Jackson. After 346 League appearances for Palace, the veteran goalkeeper was transferred to Orient in October 1973, after a disagreement with Allison. He joined several former Palace players at Brisbane Road. His place in the Palace goal was taken by Paul Hammond, a former apprentice who had started the season in goal before Jackson made his last five appearances.

◀ *John Burridge punches clear from Liverpool's David Johnson in the goalless draw at Selhurst in 1979-80.*

In September 1974, Palace sold Mel Blyth to Southampton for £60,000. Later that month, Allison pulled off one of his best deals for Palace, transferring Rogers to Queen's Park Rangers in exchange for Ian Evans and Terry Venables. After a few games, Venables took over much of the coaching. Another Allison signing was Peter Taylor, who signed from Southend in October 1973 and who was to follow in Johnny Byrne's footsteps as a Third Division player who was capped for England.

For many years, Crystal Palace were known as the Glaziers. Now the club adopted a new nickname and became officially known as the Eagles. It did not help their fortunes, but at least results began to improve and an excellent scouting system was turning up some talented youngsters. The first to make the top was Kenny Sansom, who captained Palace to victory in the FA Youth Cup Final.

Palace were fast becoming one of the best footballing sides in the Third Division. In 1974-5 they finished in fifth place, with Peter Taylor and Dave Swindlehurst, a former Palace apprentice, finishing joint leading scorers with 14 goals each. Former Arsenal, Brighton and Charlton player Tony Burns was now the regular goalkeeper and Sansom made his first appearance in the League side.

Fifth place again in 1975-6 was overshadowed by Palace reaching the FA Cup semi-final for the first time in the club's history. The season started well and Palace went to the top of the table before the Cup programme began. After coming through the first two rounds, they started a run of away wins, at Scarborough, Leeds, Chelsea and Sunderland, to earn a place in the last four.

In April 1976, Palace met Southampton at Stamford Bridge in a bid to become the first Third Division side to reach a Wembley FA Cup Final. Alas, the team froze on the day and with Taylor soon injured, Palace never enjoyed any of the breaks. It was never an inspiring game. Gilchrist scored Saints' first goal in the 74th minute. Then Channon was fouled and Peach scored from the penalty spot. Former Palace player Mel Blyth eventually collected a winners' medal when Southampton beat Manchester United at Wembley.

With outstanding League games due to the Cup run, Palace lost their top position. Of the seven games remaining after the semi-final, Palace won only one and hopes of a return to Division Two evaporated.

With those hopes went Malcolm Allison and in the summer of 1976, Terry Venables was promoted. His first season at the helm could hardly have been more successful as Palace at last regained their Second Division place. It was a tight finish and Palace earned promotion by winning their last four games. The last game of the season saw them beat promotion rivals, Wrexham, 4-2 with two late goals at the Racecourse Ground.

This left Wrexham needing to win their last game for promotion. The Welsh club lost to Mansfield, who were promoted as champions, and Palace followed them into Division Two in third place behind Brighton.

Palace also lifted the FA Youth Cup in 1977 and retained the trophy the following year, when defender Terry Fenwick again scored the winning goal. The Youth side now formed the basis of the first team and there were international honours for some of Palace's talented squad. Kenny Sansom was elevated to full England status in May 1979.

After finishing ninth in their first season back in Division Two — Swindlehurst was leading scorer with 12 goals, followed by Rachid Harkouk and Nick Chatterton with nine each — Palace embarked on what was to prove one of the most interesting periods in the history of the club.

Although they did not score many goals in 1978-9, Palace did not concede many either. Goalkeeper John Burridge was an ever-present, keeping 21 clean sheets and conceding only 24 goals in the League.

Palace were always in the promotion frame and the last Saturday of the season saw the top five sides all playing away from home. Only West Ham lost. Brighton went top with Stoke, and Sunderland were right behind them. Palace were left to fit in a previously postponed home game against Burnley. A draw would be enough for promotion, but victory would give Palace their first championship since 1921.

On a pleasant sunny evening, the eve of the FA Cup Final, it seemed as though the whole of South London had turned out and the gates at Selhurst Park were were locked an hour before kick-off. Thousands missed a match of high tension, the record crowd of 51,482 seeing late goals by Walsh and Swindlehurst give Palace their win. The cost of the side that clinched the Second Division title was the £105,000 paid for Burridge and Kember.

Venables was given money to produce a side of true First Division material and the record signings of Gerry Francis (£450,000 from Queen's Park Rangers) and Mike Flanagan (£650,000 from Charlton) saw Palace reach top after beating Ipswich 4-1 in September. That sort of form was not maintained and the 'Team of the Eighties', as the Press labelled them, finished in 13th position.

The 1980 close season was one of frenzied transfer activity. Kenny Sansom was sold to Arsenal in August. Clive Allen (who had joined Arsenal from Queen's Park Rangers two months earlier) and goalkeeper Paul Barron moved to Selhurst Park. The deal was confusing but estimates valued Sansom at £1.25 million.

The previous April, Palace had sold striker Dave Swindlehurst to Derby County for £400,000 — the Rams' record signing at that time — and Burridge was in dispute with the manager over personal terms. The goalkeeper moved to Queen's Park Rangers in December.

The troubles off the field transferred to the pitch and after ten games Palace were bottom with only one win — over Middlesbrough with a hat-trick from Allen.

Venables was reported to be in disagreement with the board, but it was still a shock when he resigned in October 1980 and joined Queen's Park Rangers. Several players, plus his back-room staff, were to join him later. The directors gave coach Ernie Walley the job of acting manager, then promoted him to full manager, only to replace him with Malcolm Allison, who returned to Selhurst in December.

Results did not improve, too much money had been spent and relegation was a distinct possibility. The club was in deep trouble and Ron Noades, former chairman of Wimbledon, bought the controlling interest. In January, Noades installed Dario Gradi, his manager at Wimbledon, as Palace's new boss.

It was too late to stop the rot and at the end of 1980-81, Crystal Palace found themselves back in the Second Division. Noades' main worry was the large wage bill, so many of the players were sold. With many new faces settling in, there was no chance of an immediate return to the First Division.

By November, Gradi had left and Steve Kember appointed manager. A fine FA Cup run to the quarter-finals helped relieve the gloom but it was the League that mattered and in the close season, with Palace finishing in 15th place, Kember was axed.

When Palace were promoted as Second Division champions in 1979, Brighton had gone up with them. The Seagulls' manager then was the former Fulham, Spurs and England wing-half, Alan Mullery, who later took charge at Charlton. It was to Mullery that Palace turned in 1982, as replacement for Kember.

For all the good work he had achieved at Brighton, Mullery could not work a miracle for Crystal Palace. Attendances were poor and the team managed only

Palace at the start of 1983-4. Back row (left to right): K.Shellito (coach), A.Mullery (manager), Brooks, Mabbutt, Nebbeling, McCulloch, Phillips, Wood, Lacey, Wilkins, Gilbert, Strong, H.Cribbs (Reserves' coach), R.Woolnough (physiotherapist). Middle row: Giles, Murphy, Hilaire, Cannon, Locke, Cummins, Hughton, Evans. Front row: Martin, Jay, Lindsay, Haistead, Di Palma, Dodman, Carter.

five away wins during his reign. There was precious little money available to buy new players and in his two seasons in charge, Palace finished 15th and 18th.

Midway through 1982-3, goalkeeper Paul Barron was sold to West Brom and his place was taken by David Fry, a former apprentice at Selhurst. Ever-present that season was Vince Hilaire, another player who began his career as an apprentice with Palace. Hilaire helped the Eagles win the Second Division title in 1979 and gained England Youth and Under-23 caps.

In 1983-4, Hilaire missed only two games to again demonstrate his consistency, but Palace were woefully short of goals and Tony Evans, signed from Birmingham City, finished leading scorer with seven. Big George Wood, the former Everton, Arsenal and Scotland goalkeeper, did not miss a game but Palace still fell far short of being realistic promotion hopes.

Chairman Ron Noades returned to his former club, Wimbledon, to bring Dave Bassett to Palace. A former Wimbledon player, Bassett had replaced Dario Gradi as manager when Gradi took over team affairs at Selhurst. The Wimbledon manager was not sure whether he wanted to leave the home-spun atmosphere of Plough Lane and 48 hours later Bassett announced that he wanted to stay at his present club.

There was much speculation about who Palace would appoint to succeed Mullery. The new manager was Steve Coppell, chairman of the PFA and a player who had carved out a fine career with Manchester United and England before injury caused his premature retirement.

Coppell's first season in charge saw Palace finish 15th, an improvement of only

◀ *Mark Bright (Palace) and Graeme Forbes (Walsall) in an aerial challenge during the Simod Cup tie between the clubs at Selhurst in 1988-9.*

three places on the previous season. But the board adopted a sensible approach. Coppell was gaining valuable experience in his new job and Palace's patience has since been totally justified.

In September 1985, Charlton Athletic, who had left their famous old ground at The Valley, played their first 'home' League game at Selhurst Park. For Palace, results were now showing a rapid improvement and at the end of the season they finished in fifth place.

Coppell was quick to find talent in local semi-professional football and he made several signings. The most successful proved to be Andy Gray, from Dulwich, and Ian Wright from Greenwich Borough. Gray finished 1985-6 as Palace's leading scorer with ten League goals, whilst Wright was to make his mark in subsequent seasons.

For 1986-7, the Football League introduced play-off matches to decide certain promotion and relegation issues. Palace just missed out, finishing in sixth place. Wright's eight goals made him joint-highest scorer this time, alongside a player with whom he was forging a remarkable attacking partnership. Mark Bright originally came to Palace on loan from Leicester City before signing for £75,000 in January 1987. The Bright-Wright strike-force was to push Palace towards the First Division.

In 1986-7, Palace hammered Birmingham City 6-0 at Selhurst. The following season they equalled their record away win when they triumphed by the same scoreline at St Andrew's. Now Bright and Wright were really on song. Bright's 24 goals in 1987-8 made him the leading scorer in the top two divisions, with Wright contributing 20 goals.

The season saw Palace again narrowly miss out on the promotion play-offs. Once more they finished sixth, just two points away from the last play-off position, despite winning three of their last four games. Neil Redfearn, the former Bolton, Lincoln and Doncaster midfielder, was ever-present and Geoff Thomas, another midfielder who joined Palace from Crewe, missed only one League game. One link with the past was broken when Jim Cannon, who was given a richly-deserved second testimonial, left Selhurst Park on a free transfer after 571 Football League games for Crystal Palace. To replace Cannon, manager Steve Coppell signed Jeff Hopkins, a tribunal setting the fee at £240,000, which made him Coppell's most expensive signing.

Palace's first scheduled game of the 1988-9 season, against Swindon Town, was postponed because of work being carried out at the County Ground. When Palace finally got underway they faced five clubs either newly promoted or relegated. After six games the prospects of making a serious promotion challenge looked remote, for the Selhurst club had scored only four goals and were still looking for their first League victory. It came with a 4-1 home win over Plymouth on 1 October.

Away from home Palace conceded five goals at Blackburn (losing a nine-goal thriller at Ewood Park on 8 October) and five at West Brom (on 26 November when they managed three in reply). To compound the problems, several first teamers suffered injuries, the worst being to skipper Geoff Thomas, who was crocked in the 4-0 home win over Walsall on 2 January and ruled out for the remainder of the season.

Steve Coppell increased his record transfer signing when he paid £250,000 for Hull City's Alex Dyer in November. Dyer was set to replace Redfearn, who was sold to Watford for £150,000, but he was soon injured and his place taken by Eddie McGoldrick, a £200,00 signing from Northampton Town in January.

The key to Palace's eventual success, though, lay in the return to form of their fine striking partnership of Mark Bright and Ian Wright. By the end of the season the Bright-Wright duo had bagged 44 League goals between them and signed new contracts in the face of media speculation that they would be transferred.

Palace's Cup form was poor in that they went out of the FA Cup and the Littlewoods Cup early on. In the Simod Cup, however, it took Brian Clough's high-flying young Nottingham Forest side to deny Palace their first appearance in a Wembley Cup Final.

That run in the Simod competition seemed to lift the spirits and after Palace had lost at home to Bournemouth on 4 March and a final mid-table position had looked the most likely, the Selhurst club embarked on a run of ten games which brought eight victories and a draw. That sequence elevated Palace into challengers for a place in the end-of-season play-offs and contained a remarkable game against Brighton on Easter Monday. At Selhurst that day, referee Kelvin Morton found himself a place in the record books by awarding five penalties. Palace took four of them, missed three and went on to win 2-1.

The final Saturday of the League season arrived with Palace in with a chance of achieving promotion to Division One outright. They faced already-relegated Birmingham City at Selhurst, whilst Manchester City, who had faltered in their promotion run-in, had to go to Bradford City. If Manchester lost at Valley Parade and Palace beat Birmingham 5-0, then Palace would go up.

It seemed a very tall order and yet Palace got away to a flying start through Wright. Then a pitch invasion by Birmingham followers held up play for 30 minutes and news came through that Bradford City were winning. Although Palace got three more after the restart — Wright completing his hat-trick — hopes were dashed when Manchester City equalized to take runners-up position behind Chelsea. Nevertheless, that still left Palace in the play-offs.

In the two-legged semi-final, Swindon Town were removed to leave Blackburn Rovers between Crystal Palace and the First Division. At Ewood Park, Rovers won 3-1 but McGoldrick's goal for Palace was a vital strike because away goals would count double in the event of a tie on aggregate after extra-time in the second leg.

An all-ticket 30,000 crowd packed Selhurst Park on the first Saturday of June and they were treated to a fine game. Wright made the aggregate score 3-2. In the second half a Madden penalty left it all-square and Palace were technically through, thanks to McGoldrick's effort at Ewood Park, providing that the Londoners could successfully negotiate extra-time.

They did better than that. In the 117th minute, Wright put the issue beyond doubt to leave Palace clear winners. Again the match had been interrupted by a pitch invasion, but this time it was the good old-fashioned sort — sheer jubilation at the prospect of First Division soccer at Selhurst again. Palace had won promotion to the top flight in 1969 and 1979. Now, at the end of another decade, they were back again.

Ian Wright (Palace) and David Mail (Blackburn) in action as Palace pile on the pressure during the 1989 promotion play-off game at Selhurst.

Fly Virgin

Crystal Palace Grounds

The Crystal Palace ground pictured at the end of the last century with the fine glass and iron building in the background.

The Crystal Palace (1905-15)

CRYSTAL Palace Football Club was named after its first home, the site in Upper Sydenham, South London, which rehoused the magnificent glass and metal building built by Joseph Paxton and which was originally in Hyde Park.

The football arena at the Crystal Palace was a large sporting venue which staged FA Cup Finals from 1895 to 1914 and many soccer internationals. When a rugby international was played there in December 1906, Palace were forced to switch their home FA Cup qualifying match against Rotherham to Stamford Bridge.

In 1913 a crowd of 120,081 saw Aston Villa (with former Palace player Charlie Wallace returning to the home of his old club) beat Sunderland in the FA Cup Final.

Palace's first game there was the 4-3 defeat by Southampton Reserves on 2 September 1905. The last was in February 1915, when the Admiralty took over the ground. After World War One, the famous amateur club, Corinthians, played there. A new stadium was eventually built and the Crystal Palace ground is now used for major athletics meetings.

England beat Scotland at the Crystal Palace in 1905 to take the Home International Championship.

Herne Hill (1915-1918)

THE Herne Hill ground lies between the Crystal Palace and Millwall and was used by the amateur club, West Norwood. It staged the 1911 FA Amateur Cup Final, when Bromley beat Bishop Auckland 1-0. Palace's first game there was the rearranged Southern League fixture against Southampton on 3 March 1915, when the Saints won 2-0. The ground is now used for athletics.

The Nest (1918-1924)

THIS is a small ground opposite Selhurst Railway Station and was previously used by Croydon Common FC, a Southern League club which folded during World War One. Queen's Park Rangers were Palace's first visitors at The Nest on 14 September 1918, when Palace won 4-2. Palace played their early Football League games here and after their departure it was rented by Tramway FC. It is no longer used as a football ground.

Football at The Nest in September 1922 when Manchester United were the visitors and won 3-2. Note the electrical railway line running along the side of the ground and the train rattling past.

Selhurst Park (1924 to date)

ONLY five minutes walk from The Nest, the site which was to house Palace's present home of Selhurst Park was purchased for £2,570 freehold in January 1922 from the London, Brighton & South Coast Railway Company.

The site covered 15 acres of land, which was then used primarily as a brickfield and two chimney stacks stood on what is now the Selhurst pitch. One major advantage was that it was within walking distance of three suburban railway stations, Thornton Heath, Selhurst and Norwood Junction, and was banked on two sides, ideal for terracing.

The crowds flock to Selhurst Park for the official opening by the Lord Mayor of London on 30 August 1924.

Archibald Leitch, a famous name in the design of football grounds, drew up plans for the new stadium which was officially opened on 30 August 1924, with the only stand unfinished due to industrial action. Palace played the first match at Selhurst that day, against Sheffield Wednesday. They completed an unwelcome hat-trick of having lost each opening game at a new venue. Indeed, Palace were relegated from Division Two at the end of their first season at Selhurst, although in March 1926, the ground was selected to stage the England-Wales international.

For many years Selhurst Park comprised one stand and open banking around the rest of the ground. Floodlights were installed in September 1953 and were officially 'switched-on' for the visit of Chelsea in a friendly game. In 1962, this rather antiquated lighting system was replaced with an £18,000 set mounted on four pylons at each corner of the ground. Some 25,000 fans saw the great Real Madrid play the first official game under the new lights.

However, it was not until promotion to Division One in 1969 that any major changes were made to Selhurst Park, when the Arthur Wait Stand was completed. In 1983, a Sainsburys supermarket was built on the car-park at the Whitehorse Lane End in a £2 million deal. This resulted in the capacity on the terracing at that end of the ground being reduced.

The attendance record was finally set — and will now surely never be beaten in these days of greatly reduced capacities — at the final game of the 1978-9 season, when 51,801 spectators saw Palace beat Burnley 2-0 to win promotion as Second Division champions. In 1960-61, the attendance record for any Fourth Division match was broken twice at Selhurst, the ultimate figure being 37,774 for the visit of Millwall in March.

The Publishers acknowledge that some of the above information also appears in *The Football Grounds of England & Wales* by Simon Inglis (Collins Willow, 1983).

Action at Selhurst Park in December 1978. Vince Hilaire scores for Palace against Orient.

PALACE MANAGERS

John Robson
1905-1907

WHEN Middlesbrough were elected to the Second Division of the Football League, John Robson was the man they appointed as manager, on an annual salary of £156. In 1902, it was Robson who steered 'Boro into the First Division and three years later, Palace saw him as the man to take charge of their newly-formed team. Within a season he had taken the club into the First Division of the Southern League as champions.

Robson's career at Palace was relatively brief and in April he took charge of another Southern League club, Croydon Common. Robson was manager of Brighton when they won the Southern League championship in 1910. On 28 December 1914, he became manager of Manchester United and remained there until ill health forced his retirement in October 1921. He remained as assistant to new manager John Chapman and his seven years at the helm make him the longest-serving United manager after Sir Matt Busby.

Edmund Goodman
1907-1925

EDMUND Goodman was born in Birmingham on 8 October 1873 and was a reserve player with Aston Villa when he broke his leg and the injury proved so severe that the limb had to be amputated. Goodman was appointed secretary to Palace in 1905 and became their manager in April 1907.

Under his leadership Palace narrowly missed the Southern League championship in 1914, when they finished behind Swindon Town on goal-average, but he was still manager in 1921 when they became the first champions of the new Third Division.

In 1925, after several poor seasons, Palace found themselves back in what was now the Third Division South. Results did not improve and in October that year Goodman reverted to his original job as club secretary. He retired in May 1933 to run a grocery shop in Anerley, South London.

Alex Maley
1925-1927

ALEX Maley was one of several footballing brothers, Tom of Manchester City and Willie of Celtic being the most famous. Alex Maley managed Clyde, Clydebank from 1919 to 1921 and Hibernian from 1921 to 1925. He was appointed Crystal Palace manager in November that year and introduced a few Scottish players to the club. He saw Palace finish 13th and sixth in the Third Division South before returning to Clydebank in October 1927. Later he became a director of Hibernian.

Fred Mavin
1927-1930

FRED Mavin was born in Newcastle in 1885. He played for Newcastle United Reserves, without making a first-team appearance, before signing for New Brompton in 1905. In the close season of 1909, Mavin joined Fulham and in December 1913 returned north to play for Bradford. After World War One he ended his playing career at Reading.

Mavin became manager at Exeter City in 1923, arriving at Selhurst Park in October 1927. He was manager when Palace missed promotion on goal-average behind Charlton in 1928-9. Ill health caused his early retirement, although he made a comeback with Gillingham, from January 1932 until May 1937. He died in Bradford in May 1957.

John Tresadern
1930-1935

'JACK' Tresadern was born in Leytonstone on 26 September 1893 and played for Barking Town before signing for West Ham United in January 1913. He played in the first Wembley FA Cup Final and won two England caps before joining Burnley in October 1924. After a season at Turf Moor, Tresadern took up his first managerial job at Northampton in May 1925, spending the first two seasons as player-manager before a broken leg ended his playing career.

In July 1930 he took charge of Palace and in his first season saw the club again narrowly miss promotion from the Third Division South, this time as runners-up to Notts County. In July 1935, Tottenham Hotspur appointed him as their manager, but his three years at White Hart Lane were not a success and he was far from happy there. In April 1938, his contract at Spurs almost expired, he made a last-minute application for the vacant job of Plymouth Argyle manager.

Tresadern, who rose to the rank of army captain during World War Two, remained as Plymouth manager until a few weeks into the 1947-8 season, when he was effectively sacked. He managed non-League Chelmsford City, Hastings United and Tonbridge. Jack Tresadern died on 26 December 1959, aged 67.

Tom Bromilow
1935-1936 and 1937-1939

TOM Bromilow was a Liverpudlian, born on 7 October 1894. He played for West Dingle Presbyterian Club, asked Liverpool for a trial and signed for them in 1919. He played for the Reds for 11 seasons, winning five England caps and two League Championship medals.

After retiring he coached in Holland before Burnley appointed him manager in October 1932. Bromilow went to Palace in July 1935 but a disagreement with the directors saw him resign the following year. However, he returned on 1 January 1937 and became Palace's third consecutive manager to miss promotion by one place, when the club finished behind Newport County in 1939.

In July 1939, in the wake of that disappointment, Bromilow left to manage Leicester City. He stayed at Filbert Street until May 1942 and saw Leicester win the Midland Cup in 1941 and the War League South in 1942. He returned to the game in 1948, as manager of Newport, but stayed only a short time before becoming a scout for Leicester. Bromilow died on a train at Nuneaton on 4 March 1959, aged 64.

R.S. Moyes
1936

CRYSTAL Palace director Mr R.S.Moyes took over the reins when Tom Bromilow left but his stay was only a short one. He resigned over transfer dealings involving Blore and Palethorpe and became chief scout. In December 1939, Moyes was banned by the FA for 12 months after they discovered that illegal payments had been made to the above-mentioned players.

George Irwin
1939-1947

GEORGE Irwin became the first former Crystal Palace player to manage the club. He was born in Birmingham and joined West Bromwich Albion as a goalkeeper but did not appear in their first team. Irwin arrived at The Nest in 1921, as reserve to Alderson, and then spent three seasons with Reading. He had a spell coaching with Southend United and then went to Sheffield Wednesday as assistant manager, then coach.

Irwin was on the Hillsborough staff when the Owls won the 1935 FA Cup Final. He returned to Palace in 1937, as coach, and was appointed manager in July 1939 until May 1947. Thus the greater part of his days as Palace boss were spent steering the club through the problems of wartime football. He scouted for Palace for a time before being appointed Darlington manager in the close season of 1950. Irwin remained at Feethams for two seasons.

Jack Butler
1947-1949

JACK Butler was born in Colombo, Ceylon, on 14 August 1894 but moved to England at an early age and was playing for West London Schools when Fulham signed him in 1913. He made no League appearances for the Cottagers before going to non-League Dartford and it was Arsenal who gave him his chance after signing him as a centre-forward in 1914.

After wartime service in the Royal Field Artillery, Butler switched to the half-back line, made his League debut in 1919 and went on to become Herbert Chapman's first 'stopper' centre-half. He was in the Gunners' losing FA Cup Final side of 1927. In June 1930, after 267 League games for Arsenal, Butler moved to Torquay United, for £1,000. He made 56 League appearances for them before retiring in 1932. He went to coach in Belgium, including working with the Belgian national team.

During World War Two he was trainer at Leicester City and coached in Copenhagen before becoming manager of Torquay in 1946. Butler, who was capped once by England, joined Crystal Palace in May 1947 and after Palace finished 13th in his first season in charge, they had to seek re-election after his second full term. It was no surprise then, when he left in April 1949. In June 1953 he became manager of Colchester United and also coached in Denmark and again in Belgium. He died in south-east London in January 1961, aged 66.

Ronnie Rooke
1949-1950

RONNIE Rooke was born at Guildford on 7 December 1911 and was a great goalscorer at schoolboy and youth level. He went to Stoke City for a trial but could not settle and eventually signed for Crystal Palace in March 1933. Although he scored regularly for the Reserves, the goals dried up when he appeared in the first team and Palace let him go to Fulham in November 1936.

At Craven Cottage his career blossomed. He netted a hat-trick on his League debut and once scored six goals in an FA Cup match against Bury. He was leading scorer in each of his 11 seasons at Fulham — seven were wartime seasons, when he won one England cap — before a surprise transfer to Arsenal in December 1946. Although he was 33, Rooke prospered in Division One, helping Arsenal avoid relegation and then winning a League Championship medal in 1947-8, when his 33 goals made him the First Division's leading scorer.

In 1949, after 93 goals in 67 appearances for Arsenal, he returned to Crystal Palace as player-manager and was probably the first manager to be sent off, when he received his marching orders at Millwall. The directors made £20,000 available to buy new players, but Rooke enjoyed little success and resigned in November 1950. He was still joint top-scorer at the end of the season. He managed Bedford Town for a while and then worked at Heathrow Airport. Rooke died in July 1985, aged 73.

Fred Dawes
1950-1951

FRED Dawes was born in Frimley Green, Surrey, on 2 May 1911 and, with his brother Albert, was signed by Northampton Town in 1929, as a left-back. He followed Albert to Selhurst Park in February 1936, served Palace during the war and played until injury forced his retirement in October 1949.

Dawes became assistant manager to Rooke and was then asked to join Charlie Slade as a joint manager. After some disappointing results, he was sacked. The FA reinstated him as an amateur and he turned out for Beckenham. He later opened a grocery shop and Crystal Palace kept in touch with this most loyal servant of the club until his death in August 1989.

Charlie Slade
1950-1951

CHARLIE Slade was born in Bristol on 28 January 1891. He started with Stourbridge before moving to Aston Villa in 1913 but, after only three League appearances for Villa, he was transferred to Huddersfield Town. Slade moved to Middlesbrough late in 1922, then joined Darlington, helping them to promotion in his first season. Two years later, after they were relegated, he left Feethams and coached at Rotherham United and Aldershot before scouting for Palace. He shared the manager's job with Fred Dawes and was responsible for the signing of Cam Burgess, who was scoring regularly for Chester in the Third Division North. Burgess repaid Slade's faith with a hatful of goals. Slade eventually reverted to chief scout. He left Palace in June 1955.

Laurie Scott
1951-1954

LAURIE Scott was born in Sheffield on 23 April 1917 and signed professional forms for Bradford City in 1934, as a 17-year-old outside-right. He made 39 League appearances before Arsenal signed him on 12 February 1937 and, by this time a full-back, he was restricted to mostly reserve football due to the brilliance of Male and Hapgood. After the war he established himself and won a League Championship medal in 1948, an FA Cup-winners' medal in 1950 and 17 England caps.

In October 1951, after two cartilage operations, he was appointed player-manager of Crystal Palace. Scott did little to suggest that he was the man to steer Palace out of a crisis. They endured some poor League seasons, culminating in having to seek re-election in 1954, and there were embarrassing FA Cup defeats at the hands of non-League clubs, Finchley and Great Yarmouth. In October 1954, with Palace again low in the Third Division South table, Scott left Selhurst Park. He later coached Hitchin Town and worked on the sales side of a hardware firm. He now lives in Sheffield.

Cyril Spiers
1954-1958

CYRIL Spiers was born in Witton, Birmingham, on 4 April 1902. He started his career as a goalkeeper with Halesowen Town during World War One and afterwards went to Aston Villa. He made his League debut in a 4-3 defeat by Manchester United on Christmas Day 1920. Spiers totalled 104 League appearances for Villa before Tottenham signed him in December 1927.

He was ever-present in 1929-30 and 1930-31 but injury forced him to miss the 1932-3 season. Spiers returned to the Midlands as player-coach with Wolves and made eight appearances. In April 1939, Spiers took the manager's job at Cardiff and in June 1946 he joined Norwich City. He returned to Cardiff in December 1947 and, with the help of local products and young players, he steered the Ninian Park club into Division One.

In October 1954, Crystal Palace persuaded him to become their manager, in succession to Laurie Scott. In his first full season, Palace had to seek re-election to the Third Division South and when Spiers left in 1958, the club had failed to win a place in the new Third Division. His legacy, though, was the signing of Johnny Byrne, who went on to become arguably Palace's greatest-ever player and shared in brighter days at Selhurst Park. Spiers managed Exeter City for a while before being replaced by Jack Edwards, who had captained Palace when Spiers was manager there. Spiers died on 21 May 1967.

George Smith
1958-1960

GEORGE Smith was born in Bromley on 23 April 1915 and played centre-half for Charlton Athletic before World War Two. Smith signed for Brentford during the war and went to Queen's Park Rangers in June 1947. He moved to Ipswich in April 1949, as a player-assistant manager, and resigned in January 1950. As an FA coach, he had spells in the Channel Islands and with Sheffield United. He was manager of Eastbourne and Sutton United before accepting the manager's job at Crystal Palace.

Smith stated that if promotion was not achieved within two years, then he would resign. Palace did not make the Third Division in that time and Smith, true to his word, left Selhurst Park on 12 April 1960, returning to Sheffield United as a coach. Portsmouth appointed him manager in March 1961 and he remained there until 1970, during which time Pompey were in Division Three. Smith, who won an England wartime cap against Wales in 1945, should not be confused with G.C.Smith who played for Southampton and Crystal Palace. George Smith died in November 1983, aged 68.

Arthur Rowe
1960-1962 and 1966

ARTHUR Rowe was born near White Hart Lane on 1 September 1906. He joined Tottenham's nursery side, Northfleet, as an amateur in 1923 and became a professional with Spurs in 1929, making his League debut in 1931. A 'footballing' centre-half, Rowe helped Spurs win promotion to Division One in 1932-3, when he missed only one League game and was capped for England against France. Spurs were relegated in 1935 and four years later, injury ended Rowe's playing career after 201 League and Cup appearances for Tottenham.

He coached in Hungary before war was declared and he returned to Britain to join the Army as a physical training instructor. Rowe became secretary-manager of Chelmsford City in 1945 and built a team which made Chelmsford one of the country's leading non-League clubs. In May 1949, he took over as manager of Spurs, following Joe Hulme's dismissal and, after signing England full-back Alf Ramsey from Southampton, developed the famous 'Push and Run' side which took Spurs from Division Two to the League Championship in successive seasons. In July 1955, ill health which had threatened his career for some time, saw him resign.

In November 1958, Arthur Rowe returned to soccer as assistant manager at Crystal Palace. He was appointed manager in April 1960, after George Smith resigned, and guided Palace to promotion from Division Four in 1960-61, after they started the season with a 9-2 win over Accrington. A poor start to the 1962-3 season saw Rowe again suffer ill health and eventually he resigned in December 1962.

Rowe later scouted for Palace and acted as caretaker manager for four months in 1966. In February 1971 he was manager of the Hall of Fame in London and, in January 1972, assisted Orient as adviser. He lives at Norbury.

Dick Graham
1962-1966

DICK Graham, born in Corby on 6 May 1922, was a wartime goalkeeper with Northampton Town and Leicester City before joining Crystal Palace in 1945. He was in goal at Reading when Palace lost 10-2 in September 1946, but remained first-choice until injury forced his early retirement in 1950.

Graham left football for a short time before West Brom appointed him as their trainer. He returned to Palace as assistant manager to Arthur Rowe in 1960 and took over when Rowe was forced to quit in 1962. A break for the bad winter that year saw Palace resume with fresh spirit and they carried this into the next season, winning promotion to Division Two in 1963-4, when they finished runners-up behind Coventry City on goal-average.

Graham, however, became somewhat unpopular with supporters, who disagreed with his selection policy. The unrest spread to the dressing-room and Palace cancelled his contract, despite his successful managerial record at Selhurst Park.

Graham later managed Orient and Walsall, but his biggest triumph was as Colchester United's manager when they beat Don Revie's Leeds United in the FA Cup. Later, Graham acted as an adviser to Charlton Athletic and non-League Wimbledon.

Bert Head
1966-1973

BERT Head was born in Midsomer Norton on 8 June 1916 and was a centre-half with the local side before signing for Torquay United in 1937. He remained at Plainmoor until February 1952, when he joined Bury, for whom he made 22 League appearances. He then became coach and assistant manager at Gigg Lane.

In October 1956, Swindon Town offered him their manager's job and his signing of young players, who helped Swindon gain promotion in 1963, made him a target for several clubs. Head returned to Bury in the close season of 1965, to the disappointment of Palace, who later bought out his contract.

It was money well spent and Head's 'bargain' team, which cost only £80,000 in transfer fees, won promotion to Division One in 1969, for the first time in Palace's history. After four seasons of struggle and the threat of relegation, however, Head was eventually given the title of 'club manager' and released from looking after team affairs. That did not work out and in 1973 he became manager of Bath City, a club near his home.

Malcolm Allison
1973-1976 and 1980-1981

MALCOLM Allison was born in Dartford, Kent, on 5 September 1927. He started at Bexleyheath and then went to Charlton. West Ham signed him in February 1951 and he made over 250 League and Cup appearances as a classy centre-half before tuberculosis and the loss of a lung ended his playing career.

Allison tried a comeback with Romford before taking the Bath City manager's job and then moved to Plymouth Argyle in May 1964. He went to Manchester City as coach under Joe Mercer and their partnership brought back the glory days to Maine Road before Mercer left in June 1972. Allison became manager but was soon on his way to Selhurst Park, claiming that he could no longer motivate the City players.

In March 1973, Palace paid £10,000 for Allison's services, but the club suffered relegation two years in succession before the signing of his friend, Terry Venables, as player-coach saw fortunes improve and they guided Palace to an FA Cup semi-final. Allison resigned in 1976 and two years later was back at Plymouth.

In July 1979 he returned to Manchester City and then went back to Palace in December 1980, for 55 days before switching to Middlesbrough in October 1982. Allison, who has also held several foreign club appointments, proved an excellent coach and is also one of the most colourful characters in football with his cigars-and-champagne image and his fedora hat.

Terry Venables
1976-1980

TERRY Venables was born in Dagenham on 6 January 1943. His football career began at Chelsea as an amateur and he became the first player to gain England caps at all levels.

With Chelsea he won an FA Youth Cup-winners' medal in 1960-61 and a League Cup-winners' trophy in 1964-5. After being transferred to Spurs in May 1966, he gained an FA Cup-winners' medal and then moved to Queen's Park Rangers in June 1969 before joining Palace in September 1974. Ian Evans came with him and Don Rogers went in the other direction.

Venables made only 14 appearances before being appointed coach under Malcolm Allison. His work on the youth side impressed and he took over as manager in June 1976. Venables soon proved that he could succeed and Palace won promotion from the Third Division in 1976-7. Two seasons later, a record Selhurst Park attendance saw them clinch the Second Division championship and he saw his young side top the First Division table in October 1979 before they dropped to a mid-table position.

After Palace made a poor start to the following season, Venables moved to Queen's Park Rangers in October 1980 and guided them to a Wembley Cup Final, followed by promotion to Division One. He helped Barcelona win the Spanish Championship before returning to London and Spurs in December 1987. He is the co-author of the TV series *Hazell.*

Ernie Walley
1980

ERNIE Walley was born at Caernarfon on 19 April 1933 and started his career with Spurs juniors before signing as a professional in May 1951. He made his League debut against Manchester United on 31 August 1955 but made only five League appearances before he moved to Middlesbrough in May 1958, for £12,000.

After adding another eight appearances to his total, Walley was transferred to Crystal Palace but failed to make a first-team appearance before moving to Gravesend and then Stevenage. He spent eight years as a coach at Arsenal and then served Palace for 13 years in the same capacity before taking over as caretaker manager for two months after Venables left.

In October 1980, Walley reverted to coach under Allison and later Dario Gradi. Eventually, he went to Chelsea as assistant to John Hollins but in March 1988, as Chelsea slithered towards relegation from Division One, Hollins and Walley lost their jobs.

Dario Gradi
1981

DARIO Gradi was born in Italy in 1943 and is one of the few managers never to have played in League football. His amateur career began with Sutton United and he made a Wembley appearance in the 1969 FA Amateur Cup Final and won an England Amateur cap.

Gradi worked as a coach at Chelsea, Derby County and Wimbledon and the latter club appointed him their manager in 1978. He saw Wimbledon promoted to Division Three in only their second season of League football but the following season they were relegated and then bounced back again.

In January 1981, Gradi joined his former Wimbledon chairman, Ron Noades, at Crystal Palace but could not save the team from relegation to Division Two and in November the following season he joined Orient as youth-team coach. In May 1983, Gradi became manager of Crewe Alexandra and in 1988-9 transformed the erstwhile strugglers into a Fourth Division promotion outfit. He also sold Geoff Thomas, John Pemberton and Brian Parkin to Palace.

Steve Kember
1981-1982

STEVE Kember, who was born in Croydon on 8 December 1948, signed professional forms for Palace in December 1965. Kember, who won England Under-23 honours, helped Palace to promotion from Division Two in 1969 before moving to Chelsea in September that year, for a record fee of £170,000. He went to Leicester in July 1975 and returned to Palace in October 1978, again helping them into Division One.

Kember coached Palace's juniors before being the so-called players' choice as manager in November 1981. Palace finished 15th that season and in June 1982 he was dismissed. He is now manager of Whyteleafe.

Alan Mullery MBE
1982-1984

ALAN Mullery was born in Notting Hill on 23 November 1941 and turned professional with Fulham in December 1958, helping the Cottagers into Division One in his first season. An aggressive wing-half, he moved to Spurs in March 1964 for £72,500 and enjoyed some great years at White Hart Lane. He made 372 appearances, was capped 35 times for England (he was the first England player to be sent off in a full international) and won FA Cup, League Cup and UEFA Cup-winners' medals.

In 1972, Mullery returned to Fulham on loan and helped them avoid relegation before signing permanently for £65,000. He was appointed skipper, led Fulham to an FA Cup Final and was awarded the MBE and voted Footballer of the Year in his second career at Craven Cottage.

Mullery retired in 1976 and although everyone thought he was favourite for the vacant job as Fulham manager, he was not appointed and became Brighton's manager instead. Mullery took Brighton into the First Division in 1979, although they lost out to Palace for the championship.

In July 1981 he moved to Charlton Athletic, where he stayed for a year before joining Palace in June 1982. Mullery was not a success at Selhurst Park and in two seasons Palace finished in the bottom half of the Second Division. He was sacked in May 1984 and became Queen's Park Rangers' manager before rejoining Brighton. Mullery eventually lost his job at the Goldstone Ground and took over local club, Ringmer.

Steve Coppell
1984-

STEVE Coppell was born in Liverpool on 9 July 1955 and obtained a degree at Liverpool University before making his League debut for Tranmere Rovers in 1974. In March 1975, Tommy Docherty paid a bargain £40,000 to take Coppell to Manchester United and at Old Trafford his career blossomed as he showed great flair on the wing.

Coppell played in three FA Cup Finals for United, in 1976, 1977 and 1979, gaining a winners' medal in the middle year. He also played in the 1983 Milk Cup Final but missed United's FA Cup win over Brighton that season, through injury. In October that year Coppell, who won 42 full England caps and was PFA chairman, was forced to retire at the early age of 28.

On 3 June 1984, after Wimbledon's Dave Bassett had spent only 48 hours as manager at Palace before returning to Plough Lane, Coppell became the youngest manager in the Football League. He went on to steer Palace clear of the relegation zone and turned them into a promotion-seeking outfit.

In 1988-9 they finally made the play-offs, finishing third in the table, a position which would, until recently, have given Palace automatic First Division football. Justice was done when Coppell's side beat fifth-placed Blackburn Rovers in a two-legged play-off final and there is no doubt that Steve Coppell has become the most popular Crystal Palace manager in recent years.

Palace Stars A-Z

JACK ALDERSON

Goalkeeper Jack Alderson was born in Crook, County Durham, on 28 November 1891 and began his career with Shildon before moving to Middlesbrough in the close season of 1912. Alderson remained an amateur at Ayresome Park and did not make a first-team appearance. In January 1913, he was transferred to Newcastle United for £50 and turned professional, finally making his League debut on 25 January 1913, in the Magpies' 3-1 home win over Woolwich Arsenal. Despite his early baptism for Newcastle, however, it turned out to be his only appearance. He was posted to Woolwich during World War One and signed for Palace in January 1919, for £50. He made his debut on 25 January 1919, against Brentford in the London War League, when Palace lost 6-1. Alderson did not miss a game until February 1922 and was ever-present in Palace's championship-winning side in the initial Third Division season, when he was in his 30th year. After winning an England cap against France in 1923, Alderson was involved in a pay dispute at Palace and played for non-League Pontypridd for a season before Sheffield United signed him in May 1925. He made 122 League appearances for the Blades before joining Exeter City in May 1929. After another 36 League appearances, he was forced to retire through injury. Alderson had a spell on Torquay's staff from November 1930 to March 1931, when he returned to Crook. He died on 17 February 1972.

	S LEAGUE		*F LEAGUE*		*FA CUP*		*TOTAL*	
	App	*Gls*	*App*	*Gls*	*App*	*Gls*	*App*	*Gls*
1919-20	42	0	-	-	1	0	43	0
1920-21	-	-	42	0	2	0	44	0
1921-22	-	-	27	0	3	0	30	0
1922-23	-	-	40	0	1	0	41	0
1923-24	-	-	41	0	6	0	47	0
	42	0	150	0	13	0	205	0

ROY BAILEY

Goalkeeper Roy Bailey first made a name for himself at Selhurst Park when he saved three penalties in a match for Palace Reserves. He was waiting to begin his National Service when Palace called him up for his League debut in March 1950, against Torquay United, when first-choice Dick Graham and reserve Charlie Bumpstead were both injured. Palace went down 3-1 and Bumpstead replaced Bailey for the next game, but the young goalkeeper eventually went on to greater things. Born at Epsom on 26 May 1932, he progressed from the junior ranks to sign professional forms in June 1949. After returning from military service he established himself at Palace and with Jack Edwards had a benefit in 1954. In March 1956, Alf Ramsey signed Bailey for Ipswich Town and he helped the Suffolk club from the Third Division South to the First Division title. After 315 League appearances for Ipswich, Bailey was given a free transfer and went to coach in South Africa. His son, Gary, kept goal for Manchester United and won full England honours.

	LEAGUE		*FA CUP*		*TOTAL*	
	App	*Gls*	*App*	*Gls*	*App*	*Gls*
1949-50	1	0	0	0	1	0
1950-51	2	0	0	0	2	0
1951-52	0	0	0	0	0	0
1952-53	14	0	0	0	14	0
1953-54	45	0	1	0	46	0
1954-55	37	0	0	0	37	0
1955-56	19	0	0	0	19	0
	118	0	1	0	119	0

BEN BATEMAN

A schoolteacher by profession, outside-right Ben Bateman was an England Amateur international during Crystal Palace's Southern League days before World War One. Born in Chelsea on 20 November 1892, Bateman played for the Middlesex amateur club, Sutton Court, before signing for Palace in the close season of 1913. He was one of the players who made the transition to the Football League after the war and he was a regular in the side which won the first Third Division championship in 1920-21, although he did not manage to score a goal. He eventually opened his Football League account in the second match of the following season, netting in a 3-1 defeat at Barnsley. After a season of Second Division football, his place came under threat from Albert Harry and in August 1924, Bateman moved to non-League Dartford.

	S LEAGUE		*F LEAGUE*		*FA CUP*		*TOTAL*	
	App	*Gls*	*App*	*Gls*	*App*	*Gls*	*App*	*Gls*
1913-14	29	2	-	-	2	0	31	2
1914-15	9	0	-	-	0	0	9	0
1919-20	36	2	-	-	1	0	37	2
1920-21	-	-	32	0	2	1	34	1
1921-22	-	-	37	2	3	0	40	2
1922-23	-	-	19	2	0	0	19	2
1923-24	-	-	10	2	0	0	10	2
	74	4	98	6	8	1	180	11

JIMMY BAUCHOP

Jimmy Bauchop was described as the 'catch of the season' when he joined Crystal Palace from Norwich City in March 1908, for he had built up a reputation as a player who was always likely to snatch victory with a late goal. Bauchop was born in Sauchie in May 1886. A classy inside-forward, he began his career with Alloa Athletic before moving to Celtic. Derby County tried to sign him from the Parkhead club but were outbid by Norwich. At Palace, Bauchop proved a regular marksman. In his one full season there he scored 16 League goals, including a hat-trick against Portsmouth, and netted both Palace's goals when they held FA Cup holders Wolves at Molineux. Derby finally got their man in May 1909 and he helped them to the Second Division title in 1911-12. After 135 League games (72 goals) for the Rams, Bauchop moved to Spurs in May 1913. He helped Bradford into Division One in 1914 and after the war he played for Doncaster Rovers and Lincoln City. Bauchop died in Bradford in June 1948.

	S LEAGUE		*FA CUP*		*TOTAL*	
	App	*Gls*	*App*	*Gls*	*App*	*Gls*
1907-08	7	6	0	0	7	6
1908-09	35	16	4	3	39	19
	42	22	4	3	46	25

PETER BERRY

Born in Aldershot on 20 September 1933, Peter Berry is the brother of John Berry, the Manchester United and England international winger whose career ended after he was severely injured in the Munich air disaster. Peter, who began his League career on the right wing but later played at centre-forward and inside-forward, signed professional forms for Crystal Palace in August 1951. After completing his National Service he made his League debut in a 4-0 defeat at the hands of Bristol City at Ashton Gate in January 1954. He scored his first goal for the club in a 4-1 defeat at Coventry the following season and played well for Palace during the difficult years of the 1950s. Alf Ramsey signed him, together with Palace's Jim Belcher, for Ipswich Town in May 1958, but an injury in September 1959 put him out of the game and he eventually retired in June 1961, after making 38 League appearances and scoring six goals for the Suffolk club.

	LEAGUE		*FA CUP*		*TOTAL*	
	App	*Gls*	*App*	*Gls*	*App*	*Gls*
1951-52	0	0	0	0	0	0
1952-53	0	0	0	0	0	0
1953-54	7	0	0	0	7	0
1954-55	26	5	2	0	28	5
1955-56	41	5	2	0	43	5
1956-57	37	8	4	0	41	8
1957-58	40	9	2	0	42	9
	151	27	10	0	161	27

MEL BLYTH

Born in Norwich on 28 July 1944, Mel Blyth was at Norwich as an amateur in 1964 before going to Great Yarmouth Town. Scunthorpe United gave him a second chance in League football in November 1967 and he made 27 League appearances (three goals) for the Iron before Bert Head signed him for Palace, for £9,000 in the close season of 1968. At the end of his first season at Selhurst Park, Blyth had helped Palace gain First Division football for the first time in their history. He was a regular at the centre of the defence for six years but, after seeing Palace suffer relegation two years running, he was transferred to Southampton in September 1974 for £60,000. He was the Saints' Player of the Year in 1975 and the following year won an FA Cup-winners' medal — he was in the side which beat Palace in that year's semi-final at Stamford Bridge. After 105 League games for Southampton, Blyth returned to Selhurst Park on loan in November 1977 before ending his career with Millwall, for whom he made 75 League appearances.

	LEAGUE		*FA CUP*		*FL CUP*		*TOTAL*	
	App	*Gls*	*App*	*Gls*	*App*	*Gls*	*App*	*Gls*
1968-69	31/1	3	1	0	4	0	36/1	3
1969-70	31/2	2	3/1	1	3	0	37/3	3
1970-71	38	0	2	0	5	2	45	2
1971-72	41	2	2	0	3	0	46	2
1972-73	39	0	4	0	1	0	44	0
1973-74	29	1	0	0	3	0	32	1
1974-75	4	1	0	0	0	0	4	1
1977-78	6	0	0	0	0	0	6	0
	219/3	9	12/1	1	19	2	250/4	12

It was striker Mark Bright's goals, as much as anything, which gave Crystal Palace promotion from Division Two in 1989. Bright was born in Stoke-on-Trent on 6 June 1962 and began his career in non-League football with Leek Town. In August 1982, his local Football League club, Port Vale, signed him and after making slow progress, he finally established himself in 1983-4, with nine goals in 26 League games. In July 1984, Leicester City paid £33,000 for Bright's signature but in 16 League games in his first season at Filbert Street, he failed to score. Six goals in 24 games in 1985-6 gave rise to the hope that he had at last made the transition from Third to First Division football. Soon after the start of the 1986-7 season, however, he was injured and managed only two League games before joining Crystal Palace on loan in November 1986. His fitness now established, Bright signed permanently in January 1987, for £75,000, and finished the season as joint leading scorer. The following term saw his partnership with Wright develop and Bright won the Golden Shoe Award for topping the Second Division scorers' list with 24 League goals.

	LEAGUE		*FA CUP*		*FL CUP*		*TOTAL*	
	App	*Gls*	*App*	*Gls*	*App*	*Gls*	*App*	*Gls*
1986-87	28	8	2	0	0	0	30	8
1987-88	38	24	0/1	0	2	1	40/1	25
1988-89	46	20	1	0	3	1	50	21
	112	52	3/1	0	5	2	120/1	54

MARK BRIGHT

ALBERT BURGESS

Inside-forward 'Cam' Burgess — his full name was Albert Campbell Burgess — was discovered by Bolton Wanderers, playing local amateur football at Bromborough. Burgess, who was born at Birkenhead on 21 September 1919, made his debut for Bolton in 1939-40, at Burnley in the North-West Division of the War Regional League. After the war he made five appearances in the Trotters' First Division side, scoring three goals, before moving into the Third Division North with Chester in October 1948. At Sealand Road, Burgess became a regular scorer, netting 64 goals in 111 League games. Palace chief scout Charlie Slade, then acting as co-manager with Fred Dawes, purchased this small, nippy forward in September 1951, for £3,000. Although Burgess failed to score on his debut, at home to Bristol Rovers, in his second appearance he netted a second-half hat-trick against Leyton Orient at Brisbane Road. Thereafter, Burgess was in prolific form and was Palace's most effective goalscorer since Dawes and Simpson. He scored 21 goals in 22 League games in his first season; in his second campaign he registered three hat-tricks in four games. In July 1953, Burgess left Palace for 'personal reasons' and moved to York City for £850. It was money well spent and Burgess scored 14 goals in 33 games in his one season at Bootham Crescent. In the close season of 1954 he went into non-League football with Runcorn, a club near his birthplace.

	LEAGUE		*FA CUP*		*TOTAL*	
	App	*Gls*	*App*	*Gls*	*App*	*Gls*
1951-52	22	21	0	0	22	21
1952-53	25	19	3	0	28	19
	47	40	3	0	50	40

JOHN BURRIDGE

Over the last decade John Burridge has proved to be one of the game's goalkeeping 'characters'. Universally known as 'Budgie', even his pre-match warm-up routine has provided entertainment. Burridge, born at Workington on 3 December 1951, began his career as an apprentice with Workington before being loaned to Blackpool in April 1971. The following month he signed for the Seasiders for £10,000, the first of several moves which took him to ten clubs in 18 years. He went to Aston Villa in September 1975, for £100,000, and won a League Cup medal with them. A loan spell at Southend ended when Palace signed Burridge in March 1978 for £65,000. He made his League debut in a goalless draw against Brighton at Selhurst Park on 18 March. The following season he conceded only 24 goals as Palace won the Second Division title, but after a pay dispute he followed Terry Venables to QPR in December 1980, for £200,000. Burridge joined Wolves in September 1982, for £75,000 after a month's loan, and was ever-present as they won promotion to Division One. Wolves were relegated and Burridge joined Derby County on loan in September 1984, but refused a permanent move and signed for Sheffield United for £10,000. In August 1987 he was off again, this time to Southampton for £30,000. He has now made around 600 League appearances.

	LEAGUE		*FA CUP*		*FL CUP*		*TOTAL*	
	App	*Gls*	*App*	*Gls*	*App*	*Gls*	*App*	*Gls*
1977-78	10	0	0	0	0	0	10	0
1978-79	42	0	4	0	4	0	50	0
1979-80	36	0	3	0	3	0	42	0
1980-81	0	0	-	-	0	0	0	0
	88	0	7	0	7	0	102	0

JOHN BYRNE

Johnny Byrne, a goalscoring forward whose silky skills delighted London fans for well over a decade, would be a strong contender for the title of Crystal Palace's greatest-ever player. Born in West Horsley, Surrey, on 13 May 1939, Byrne was recommended by Vince Blore, the club's pre-war goalkeeper. Byrne joined Palace in May 1956, just as they were seeking re-election to Division Three South, and made his League debut in October 1956. His early years at Selhurst saw Palace continue to struggle but gradually their fortunes improved and in 1960-61 his 30 goals helped achieve promotion from Division Four. The first Fourth Division player to be capped for England Under-23s, Byrne won one full cap with Palace, against Northern Ireland in November 1961. Despite coming in for close attention from defenders, he missed few games and it was no surprise when West Ham's Ron Greenwood paid an English record fee of £65,000 to sign him in March 1962. Byrne became a great star for West Ham. Dangerous in front of goal, he needed little space to work himself into a scoring position. He began an extended run in the England team and won an FA Cup-winners' medal in 1964, when he was voted 'Hammer of the Year'. He missed the 1965 European Cup-winners' Cup Final after injuring a knee in the England-Scotland match a few weeks earlier, but played in the 1966 League Cup Final before rejoining Palace in February 1967, for £45,000, after scoring 107 goals in 205 League and Cup games for the Hammers. Palace were now in Division Two but Byrne was past his best and in March 1968, Fulham paid £25,000 for him. He saw them drop from First to Third Division in consecutive seasons and played a few games in the half-back line. In June 1969 he signed for Durban City (South Africa). Byrne later managed Hellenic (Cape Town) and settled in South Africa.

JOHN BYRNE

	LEAGUE		*FA CUP*		*FL CUP*		*TOTAL*	
	App	*Gls*	*App*	*Gls*	*App*	*Gls*	*App*	*Gls*
1956-57	14	1	0	0	-	-	14	1
1957-58	28	7	1	0	-	-	29	7
1958-59	45	17	5	3	-	-	50	20
1959-60	42	16	4	3	-	-	46	19
1960-61	42	30	3	1	0	0	45	31
1961-62	32	14	3	3	1	0	36	17
1966-67	14	1	0	0	0	0	14	1
1967-68	22	4	2	1	1	0	25	5
	239	90	18	11	2	0	259	101

BILLY CALLENDER

Born in Prudhoe on 5 January 1903, goalkeeper Billy Callender was another player to join Crystal Palace from local football in the North-East, during the years after World War One. He made his debut on 22 March 1924, in a 1-0 win against South Shields at The Nest after replacing the injured Jack Alderson. It proved to be his only game of the season and he was also restricted to only one appearance the following season, when he came in for the last game — a 1-0 home defeat by Oldham Athletic in a vital relegation battle that saw Oldham survive and Palace go down. Callender finally won a regular place in the second half of the 1925-6 season, although he had the uncomfortable experience of conceding 11 goals in an FA Cup match against Manchester City at Maine Road in February 1926. In 1926-7 he was an ever-present for Palace and played for the Football League against the Army at Millwall in October that season. In 1932, Billy Callender met a tragic end, taking his own life at the ground after a training session. He had apparently been depressed following the death of his fiancée.

	LEAGUE		*FA CUP*		*TOTAL*	
	App	*Gls*	*App*	*Gls*	*App*	*Gls*
1923-24	1	0	0	0	1	0
1924-25	1	0	0	0	1	0
1925-26	21	0	3	0	24	0
1926-27	42	0	2	0	44	0
1927-28	19	0	2	0	21	0
1928-29	41	0	7	0	48	0
1929-30	25	0	1	0	26	0
1930-31	24	0	5	0	29	0
1931-32	28	0	2	0	30	0
	202	0	22	0	224	0

JIM CANNON

Born in Glasgow on 2 October 1953, defender Jim Cannon had a trial with Manchester City before returning home. A Palace scout recommended that Bert Head should sign him, however, and Cannon joined the Selhurst Park staff as an apprentice in October 1970. He won Scottish Youth international honours before Malcolm Allison gave him a first-team chance against Chelsea on 31 March 1973. Cannon had an eventful debut. He was booked and scored one of Palace's goals in their only League victory over a London First Division side that season. Palace dropped straight through into Division Three and as they tried to win back their place, Cannon's presence in the centre of defence was a considerable boost to their chances. He was ever-present when promotion was finally achieved in 1976-7 and in 1985 he broke Terry Long's club record for the number of League appearances. Cannon had a testimonial against Spurs in March 1988 and continued to give Palace magnificent service until he was given a free transfer in the 1988 close season. Cannon, who was Palace's Player of the Year in 1978, 1985 and 1987, joined Croydon before moving to Dartford in November 1988, where he teamed up with another former Palace star, Peter Taylor, who was player-manager there.

	LEAGUE		*FA CUP*		*FL CUP*		*TOTAL*	
	App	*Gls*	*App*	*Gls*	*App*	*Gls*	*App*	*Gls*
1972-73	3	1	0	0	0	0	3	1
1973-74	13/1	1	0	0	1	0	14/1	1
1974-75	34/2	3	2	0	0/1	0	36/3	3
1975-76	40	2	8	0	2	0	50	2
1976-77	46	2	6	0	3	0	55	2
1977-78	39	2	1	0	4	1	44	3
1978-79	41	2	4	0	4	0	49	2
1979-80	42	4	3	0	3	0	48	4
1980-81	33	1	1	0	4	0	38	1
1981-82	42	1	5	1	4	2	51	4
1982-83	41	1	4	0	5	0	50	1
1983-84	30	2	2	0	2	0	34	2
1984-85	40	2	2	0	2	0	44	2
1985-86	42	1	1	0	4	0	47	1
1986-87	42	1	2	0	4	0	48	1
1987-88	40	4	1	0	1	0	42	4
	568/3	30	42	1	43/1	3	653/4	34

Born in Orpington, Kent, on 29 January 1932, centre-half Len Choules was an amateur with Sutton United before turning professional with Crystal Palace in May 1951. He made his League debut in a 1-1 draw against Ipswich Town on 22 April 1953 and although his early days with Palace came at a low ebb in the club's fortunes, he remained to help them win promotion to Division Three in 1961. Choules was an ever-present for Palace in 1956-7 and his one representative honour came in 1954 when he was selected to play for an FA XI against Oxford University. Choules enjoyed two testimonials at Selhurst Park before being given a free transfer in 1962, when he decided to retire from the game.

	LEAGUE		*FA CUP*		*FL CUP*		*TOTAL*	
	App	*Gls*	*App*	*Gls*	*App*	*Gls*	*App*	*Gls*
1952-53	4	0	0	0	-	-	4	0
1953-54	27	1	1	0	-	-	28	1
1954-55	26	0	2	1	-	-	28	1
1955-56	28	1	2	0	-	-	30	1
1956-57	46	0	4	0	-	-	50	0
1957-58	39	0	3	0	-	-	42	0
1958-59	44	0	5	0	-	-	49	0
1959-60	20	1	3	0	-	-	23	1
1960-61	12	0	0	0	0	0	12	0
1961-62	13	0	0	0	1	0	14	0
	259	3	20	1	1	0	280	4

LEN CHOULES

GEORGE CLARKE

Born in Bolsover, Derbyshire, in 1901, outside-left 'Nobby' Clarke, as he was known to teammates and supporters, worked as a miner at Welbeck Colliery when Mansfield Town, then a non-League club, signed him. Aston Villa paid £500 for his signature in August 1922, but Clarke made only one appearance for Villa, in a 4-1 defeat at West Brom on 28 February 1925, before Palace manager Edmund Goodman, a former Villa reserve player, returned to his old club for Clarke in May 1925. Goodman remained in office for only another six months but Clarke remained at Selhurst Park and missed only one game in his first season. Indeed, wingers Clarke and Harry (on the right flank) were a familiar feature of Palace teams for several seasons. They were the regular wingers in the sides which finished Third Division South runners-up in 1928-9 and 1930-31, before Clarke was transferred to Queen's Park Rangers in the 1933 close season. He remained at Loftus Road for only one season and ended his career at Folkestone. He died on 11 February 1977, aged 76.

	LEAGUE		*FA CUP*		*TOTAL*	
	App	*Gls*	*App*	*Gls*	*App*	*Gls*
1925-26	41	9	4	1	45	10
1926-27	42	13	2	0	44	13
1927-28	40	22	3	0	43	22
1928-29	31	7	7	1	38	8
1929-30	32	4	0	0	32	4
1930-31	39	20	7	4	45	24
1931-32	38	19	2	1	40	20
1932-33	11	4	1	0	12	4
	274	98	25	7	299	105

HORACE COLCLOUGH

Born in Meir, Staffordshire, in about 1890, Horace Colclough appeared at right-back for Crewe Alexandra before signing for Crystal Palace in the close season of 1912. At Palace, he was converted to the left-back position and took over from Joe Bulcock. On 16 March 1914, Colclough made history when he became the first player to appear in a full international match for England whilst on Crystal Palace's books. He stepped in as replacement for Jesse Pennington against Wales at Cardiff and did well in a 2-0 win. Colclough also represented the Southern League XI and appeared in 82 Southern League matches for Palace before World War One. He was injured during the war and retired from the game.

	S LEAGUE		*FA CUP*		*TOTAL*	
	App	*Gls*	*App*	*Gls*	*App*	*Gls*
1912-13	11	0	1	0	12	0
1913-14	34	0	2	0	36	0
1914-15	38	0	2	0	40	0
	83	0	5	0	88	0

TOM CRILLY

Tom Crilly was born at Stockton-on-Tees on 20 July 1895 and joined Hartlepools United from Stockton in 1919. He was ever-present for two seasons of North-Eastern League football and missed only one game when Hartlepools were elected to the Third Division North in 1921-2. In August 1922, Crilly and Harry Thoms followed manager Cecil Potter to Derby County. Crilly established himself immediately at Derby and in his first five seasons at the Baseball Ground he missed only 24 games, forming a magnificent full-back partnership with Albert Chandler. He helped Derby into the First Division and made over 200 League and FA Cup appearances before being transferred to Palace, again with Thoms, in May 1928. He went to Selhurst on a free transfer and for some of his time there formed another good full-back partnership, this time with Charlton. Crilly was in the side which finished Third Division South runners-up in 1928-9 and 1930-31. In June 1933 he went to Northampton Town and skippered the Cobblers before being appointed player-manager of Scunthorpe United in May 1935. He left the Old Show Ground in April 1937 and became a publican in Derby, looking after the Rams' juniors sides during the war. Crilly died at Derby on 18 January 1960.

	LEAGUE		*FA CUP*		*TOTAL*	
	App	*Gls*	*App*	*Gls*	*App*	*Gls*
1928-29	18	0	2	0	20	0
1929-30	20	0	0	0	20	0
1930-31	36	1	6	0	42	1
1931-32	19	0	2	0	21	0
1932-33	23	0	0	0	23	0
	116	1	10	0	126	1

WILLIAM DAVIES

Born in Rhayader in 1884, winger Billy Davies signed for Stoke in 1904 and joined Crystal Palace in October 1907, when he took over from outside-right Charlie Wallace, who had been transferred to Aston Villa. Davies enjoyed a brief, but successful, career in Palace's Southern League side and in March 1908 he became the club's first current international when he was selected to play for Wales against Scotland at Dundee. West Brom signed him in August 1908 but, after making 52 League appearances and scoring four goals for the Throstles, he returned to Palace in August 1910 and was capped again in 1914, when he played against England at Cardiff. Whilst with West Brom he had been capped twice, against England and Scotland. Davies continued to play for Palace until the outbreak of World War One ended his career.

	S LEAGUE		*FA CUP*		*TOTAL*	
	App	*Gls*	*App*	*Gls*	*App*	*Gls*
1907-08	32	3	3	1	35	4
1910-11	31	3	1	0	32	3
1911-12	31	6	4	0	35	6
1912-13	34	2	3	1	37	3
1913-14	33	5	2	0	35	5
1914-15	33	2	1	0	34	2
	194	21	14	2	208	23

ALBERT DAWES

Born in Frimley Green on 23 April 1907, Bert Dawes was the eldest of two brothers. He started his career with Northampton Town and was a firm favourite with the Cobblers' fans, so it was a shock when he was allowed to join Crystal Palace in December 1933, as cover for the injured Simpson. The 1935-6 season was Dawes' best and he was the Football League's second-highest goalscorer with 38 goals that term. He was also 12th man for England on one occasion. Luton Town, who were seeking promotion, signed him in December 1936 for a large fee. Dawes helped the Hatters achieve the championship but, after 44 appearances for them, he returned to Selhurst Park in February 1938. His form declined and Dawes joined his local club, Aldershot, in the close season of 1939. Yet again he returned to Palace, making many appearances during the war years. Dawes, who played cricket for Northamptonshire, died at Goring-by-Sea, Sussex, on 23 June 1973.

	LEAGUE		*FA CUP*		*TOTAL*	
	App	*Gls*	*App*	*Gls*	*App*	*Gls*
1933-34	22	16	0	0	22	16
1934-35	31	19	1	0	32	19
1935-36	41	38	2	1	43	39
1936-37	11	2	2	0	13	2
1937-38	15	4	0	0	15	4
1938-39	29	12	2	0	31	12
	149	91	7	1	156	92

MIKE DEAKIN

Centre-forward Mike Deakin was born in Birmingham on 25 October 1933 and was on Wolves' books as an amateur in 1951. He was playing in the Birmingham League with Bromsgrove when he became Cyril Spiers' first signing for Crystal Palace in November 1954 and made his League debut at Brighton the next day. Deakin was one of the few successes in a struggling side in the mid-1950s — he scored a hat-trick at Southend in October 1955, but Palace still lost — and in the first season of the Fourth Division he weighed-in with 23 goals. In October 1959 he joined Northampton Town, in exchange for Alan Woan, and helped the Cobblers towards promotion from Division Four in 1960-61. After 31 goals in 45 League games for Northampton, Deakin joined Woan at Aldershot in February 1961. He made 17 League appearances for the Shots (five goals) before ending his League career and signing for Nuneaton Borough. His brother, Alan Deakin, an England Under-23 international wing-half, made 231 League appearances for Aston Villa and 50 for Walsall between 1959 and 1971.

	LEAGUE		*FA CUP*		*TOTAL*	
	App	*Gls*	*App*	*Gls*	*App*	*Gls*
1954-55	19	4	0	0	19	4
1955-56	38	8	0	0	38	8
1956-57	37	16	3	0	40	16
1957-58	12	4	1	3	13	7
1958-59	34	23	4	4	38	27
1959-60	3	1	0	0	3	1
	143	56	8	7	151	63

JACK EDWARDS

Born in Risca, Monmouthshire, on 6 July 1929, Jack Edwards was an amateur with Cardiff City and Lovells Athletic and played in the 1948 Army Cup Final, when two players were killed by lightning. Like Len Choules, Edwards played through Palace's worst days and was skipper in many of his appearances. He was given a free transfer to Rochdale in the close season of 1959 and added another 68 games to his total with them. Later he took up a coaching position at Ashford and then became manager at Exeter, replacing Cyril Spiers in February 1963. Exeter gained promotion but Edwards resigned in January 1965. He went to Torquay United, then returned to Exeter before having a spell as assistant manager at Plymouth Argyle. Edwards then had a long spell at Leeds United as a scout.

	LEAGUE		*FA CUP*		*TOTAL*	
	App	*Gls*	*App*	*Gls*	*App*	*Gls*
1949-50	11	0	1	0	12	0
1950-51	9	0	0	0	9	0
1951-52	26	0	1	0	27	0
1952-53	11	0	0	0	11	0
1953-54	12	0	1	0	13	0
1954-55	30	0	2	0	32	0
1955-56	35	0	2	0	37	0
1956-57	45	0	4	0	49	0
1957-58	29	0	2	0	31	0
1958-59	15	0	3	0	18	0
	223	0	16	0	239	0

IAN EVANS

Tall defender Ian Evans, who was born at Egham on 30 January 1952, was an apprentice with Queen's Park Rangers before signing as a full-time professional in January 1970. He was with Rangers when they won promotion to the First Division in 1972-3 and then joined Crystal Palace in an exchange deal which took Don Rogers to Loftus Road in September 1974. Evans was an ever-present member of the Palace team which restored Second Division football to Selhurst Park in 1976-7. He broke into the Welsh side and won all his 13 full caps whilst a Palace player. In the home game against Fulham in October 1978, Evans broke a leg in a challenge with George Best. After regaining fitness he could not win back his place and in December 1979 he signed for Barnsley, for £80,000 after originally being on loan. He helped the Yorkshire club to promotion from Division Three in 1980-81, before having short loan periods at Exeter City and Cambridge United. Evans returned to Palace as coach, then assistant to Steve Coppell. After Palace beat Bradford City, then managed by Terry Yorath who had just left Swansea, Evans became manager at Vetch Field in February 1989.

	LEAGUE		*FA CUP*		*FL CUP*		*TOTAL*	
	App	*Gls*	*App*	*Gls*	*App*	*Gls*	*App*	*Gls*
1974-75	38	3	2	0	0	0	40	3
1975-76	45	7	8	1	3	0	56	8
1976-77	46	3	6	1	3	0	55	4
1977-78	8	1	0	0	4	0	12	1
1978-79	0	0	0	0	0	0	0	0
1979-80	0	0	0	0	0	0	0	0
	137	14	16	2	10	0	163	16

TERRY FENWICK

Terry Fenwick, who was born at Seaham, County Durham, on 17 November 1959, played a major part in Crystal Palace winning the FA Youth Cup two seasons in succession. In 1977, in a two-legged Final against Everton, Fenwick scored the only goal; 12 months later he did the same again, in a one-off Final against Aston Villa at Highbury. He made his League debut in the number-nine shirt, at White Hart Lane in December 1977, and played 20 games in defence when Palace won the Second Division championship in 1978-9. When Sansom left Selhurst Park in 1980, it was Fenwick who took over from him at left-back, but in December that year, with Palace heading towards relegation, Fenwick rejoined Terry Venables, who was by then manager of Queen's Park Rangers. Venables signed Fenwick for £110,000 and the player had the pleasure of scoring QPR's goal in the 1982 FA Cup Final against Tottenham at Wembley, although Spurs went on to win the replay. Twelve months later, Fenwick won a Second Division championship medal and in May 1984 he was awarded his first England cap, coming on as substitute for Alvin Martin at Wrexham. Since then Fenwick has won 20 caps. When Venables took over as manager of Spurs in December 1987, he signed Fenwick again, this time for £550,000.

	LEAGUE		*FA CUP*		*FL CUP*		*TOTAL*	
	App	*Gls*	*App*	*Gls*	*App*	*Gls*	*App*	*Gls*
1976-77	0	0	0	0	0	0	0	0
1977-78	10	0	0	0	0	0	10	0
1978-79	20/4	0	4	1	0/1	0	24/5	1
1979-80	11/4	0	3	1	0	0	14/4	1
1980-81	21	0	0	0	4	0	25	0
	62/8	0	7	2	4/1	0	73/9	2

Hard-tackling defender Billy Gilbert first made his mark at Selhurst Park as a member of Crystal Palace's successful FA Youth Cup team of the late-1970s. He was born at Lewisham on 10 November 1959 and made his League debut for Palace in a 3-1 defeat at Blackpool on 4 October 1977. The following season, Palace won the Second Division title and Gilbert missed only one game — the 2-1 win at Roker Park in March. In May 1984, after making over 250 first-team appearances for Palace, Gilbert was transferred to Portsmouth for £100,000. He was a vital member of the Pompey team which won promotion to the First Division in 1987, when he played alongside Noel Blake in the centre of defence, but 12 months later the Fratton Park club were back in Division Two and Gilbert's career had taken a nosedive. Beset by injuries and illness, his appearances were restricted and in May 1989, at the end of his contract, he was given a free transfer.

	LEAGUE		*FA CUP*		*FL CUP*		*TOTAL*	
	App	*Gls*	*App*	*Gls*	*App*	*Gls*	*App*	*Gls*
1976-77	0	0	0	0	0	0	0	0
1977-78	18	0	1	0	0	0	19	0
1978-79	41	1	4	0	4	0	49	1
1979-80	40	1	3	0	3	0	46	1
1980-81	38/1	0	1	0	4	0	43/1	0
1981-82	31	0	1	0	3	0	35	0
1982-83	34	0	4	0	3	0	41	0
1983-84	33/1	1	3	1	2	0	38/1	2
	235/2	3	17	1	19	0	271/2	4

BILLY GILBERT

BILL GLAZIER

Born in Nottingham on 2 August 1943, Bill Glazier had the most appropriate name for a Palace player, the Glaziers being the club's nickname at the time. He also proved to be one of their best players. Glazier started on Torquay's books as a trialist and went to Selhurst Park in October 1961, making his League debut against Halifax Town on 13 January 1962. He was an ever-present when Palace were promoted to Division Two and Jimmy Hill, then manager of Coventry City, caused a stir when he paid a record fee, for a goalkeeper, of £35,000 for Glazier in October 1964. Glazier broke a leg but returned to the Coventry side in their Second Division championship-winning season of 1966-7. After 346 appearances for the Sky Blues, he was given a free transfer and moved to Brentford in June 1975. He gained three England Under-23 caps and was 12th man for the Football League side. He became a Brighton hotelier.

	LEAGUE		*FA CUP*		*FL CUP*		*TOTAL*	
	App	*Gls*	*App*	*Gls*	*App*	*Gls*	*App*	*Gls*
1961-62	13	0	0	0	0	0	13	0
1962-63	35	0	3	0	0	0	38	0
1963-64	46	0	2	0	1	0	49	0
1964-65	12	0	0	0	1	0	13	0
	106	0	5	0	2	0	113	0

JIMMY HAMILTON

Jimmy Hamilton was born in Hetton-le-Hole, County Durham, and was stationed in London during Army service with the Coldstream Guards when he went to Palace for a trial in 1922. Hamilton, who represented the Army at boxing, was signed by Palace in December that year and made his League debut the following season, against Bradford City on 27 October 1923. Alas, these were difficult times for Palace and the following season Hamilton found himself in the side relegated from Division Two along with Coventry City. A tough-tackling half-back, Hamilton played in the Palace team which narrowly missed promotion in 1928-9 and made ten appearances when Palace again finished runners-up in 1930-31. In the close season of 1931 he returned north-east and joined Hartlepools United. He skippered United, making 49 appearances before joining Gateshead in 1933. He was player-coach at Redheugh Park before being appointed manager of Hartlepools in July 1935, when he replaced Jack Carr. The outbreak of war in September 1939 ended Hamilton's managerial career at the Victoria Ground.

	LEAGUE		*FA CUP*		*TOTAL*	
	App	*Gls*	*App*	*Gls*	*App*	*Gls*
1923-24	9	0	1	0	10	0
1924-25	25	1	2	0	27	1
1925-26	22	1	0	0	22	1
1926-27	16	0	2	0	18	0
1927-28	40	1	3	0	43	1
1928-29	24	1	7	1	31	2
1929-30	34	0	1	0	35	0
1930-31	10	0	0	0	10	0
	180	4	16	1	196	5

ALBERT HARRY

Born in Kingston, Surrey, on 8 March 1897, Bert Harry was spotted by Edmund Goodman, playing in the Surrey Cup Final. Goodman signed the winger in the close season of 1921 and he made his League debut against Bury on 25 March 1922, scoring twice. He was in Palace's Third Division South runners-up sides of 1929 and 1931 and his total of 411 League games was a club record until Terry Long beat it in 1960. In May 1934, Harry left Selhurst Park for Dartford, subsequently joining Shrewsbury Town, who were then in the Midland League. After Shrewsbury he retired from the game and became a publican in Oakmoor, Staffordshire. Bert Harry died in 1966.

	LEAGUE		*FA CUP*		*TOTAL*	
	App	*Gls*	*App*	*Gls*	*App*	*Gls*
1921-22	8	2	0	0	8	2
1922-23	24	2	1	0	25	2
1923-24	33	2	6	0	39	2
1924-25	41	2	2	0	43	2
1925-26	40	4	4	0	44	4
1926-27	15	1	0	0	15	1
1927-28	31	8	0	0	31	8
1928-29	41	8	7	2	48	10
1929-30	40	4	0	0	40	4
1930-31	41	9	6	0	47	9
1931-32	42	5	2	0	44	5
1932-33	39	6	1	0	40	6
1933-34	15	0	1	0	16	0
	410	53	30	2	440	55

Vince Hilaire was born in Forest Gate, East London, on 10 October 1959 and was spotted by a Palace scout, playing for East London Schools. He signed professional forms in October 1976 and made his League debut at Lincoln City on 2 March 1977, coming on as substitute in a 3-2 defeat. This skilful winger added two more substitute appearances before making a full appearance. He became a favourite with the Selhurst Park crowd and won England Youth and Under-23 caps. He helped Palace to the Second Division title in 1979. More a goalmaker than a scorer, he became unsettled at Palace and joined Luton Town in an exchange with Trevor Aylott, plus a £100,000 fee. He moved to Portsmouth and joined Leeds United in July 1988.

	LEAGUE		*FA CUP*		*FL CUP*		*TOTAL*	
	App	*Gls*	*App*	*Gls*	*App*	*Gls*	*App*	*Gls*
1976-77	0/3	0	0	0	0	0	0/3	0
1977-78	26/4	2	0	0	2	0	28/4	2
1978-79	25/6	6	1/1	0	4	0	30/7	6
1979-80	42	5	3	1	3	1	48	7
1980-81	31	4	0	0	2	0	33	4
1981-82	33/3	5	5	2	3	0	41/3	7
1982-83	42	5	4	0	5	1	51	6
1983-84	40	2	3	0	2	2	45	4
	239/16	29	16/1	3	21	4	276/17	36

VINCE HILAIRE

PHILIP HOADLEY

Philip Hoadley was born in Battersea, South London, on 6 January 1952, and started in junior football before making Palace history as their youngest-ever player. On 27 April 1968, aged 16, he came on as substitute at Bolton. Hoadley had one game in the promotion season of 1969-70 and then made his presence felt in the following two seasons before going to Orient, where he joined a number of former Palace men. Hoadley signed for the Os in September 1971, for £30,000. He had a good spell there before moving to Norwich City for £110,000 in August 1978. After three years at Carrow Road, he went to play in Hong Kong football in February 1982 but injury forced his retirement and he returned home to become a publican.

	LEAGUE		*FA CUP*		*FL CUP*		*TOTAL*	
	App	*Gls*	*App*	*Gls*	*App*	*Gls*	*App*	*Gls*
1967-68	0/2	0	0	0	0	0	0/2	0
1968-69	1	0	0	0	0	0	1	0
1969-70	24/5	0	2/2	0	5	1	31/7	1
1970-71	31/1	1	0/2	0	3	0	34/3	1
1971-72	6/3	0	0	0	1	0	7/3	0
	62/11	1	2/4	0	9	1	73/15	2

CLIFF HOLTON

Cliff Holton was playing as a full-back for amateurs Oxford City when he was recommended to Arsenal by former Gunners and Palace player, Alf Haynes. Holton, who was born in Oxford on 29 April 1929, joined Arsenal in November 1947 but it was three years before he made his League debut, his progress restricted by National Service. Arsenal manager Tom Whittaker saw his potential as a centre-forward and, after making his League debut on Boxing Day 1950, Holton scored regularly for the next three seasons. His first FA Cup tie for Arsenal was the 1952 Final. The Gunners lost the Wembley game but Holton collected a League Championship medal the following season. He switched to wing-half in his latter Highbury days and, after 216 League and Cup appearances (88 goals), signed for Watford in October 1958 for £9,000. He scored a club record 42 goals as Watford won promotion from Division Four in 1959-60. He joined Northampton in September 1961, again breaking a club scoring record. In December 1962 he was transferred to Palace for £10,000 and made his debut on Boxing Day, at home to Millwall. The following season, Holton made it a hat-trick of Third Division promotions, missing only three League games as Palace finished runners-up to Coventry. It was something of a shock for Palace fans when Dick Graham sold him back to Watford in May 1965, because Holton had been a regular in the side which finished seventh in Division Two. He played for Charlton and Leyton Orient before a knee injury caused his retirement in November 1969.

	LEAGUE		*FA CUP*		*FL CUP*		*TOTAL*	
	App	*Gls*	*App*	*Gls*	*App*	*Gls*	*App*	*Gls*
1962-63	23	9	0	0	0	0	23	9
1963-64	43	20	2	3	1	0	46	23
1964-65	35	11	4	5	4	1	43	17
	101	40	6	8	5	1	112	49

ARTHUR HUDGELL

Born in Hackney on 28 December 1920, Arthur Hudgell was signed by Crystal Palace from Eton Manor in December 1937, although he did not make his first-team debut until Palace were playing in wartime regional football. He became a first-team regular in the first post-war season of 1946-7 but when Palace played in an FA Cup tie at Newcastle, a Sunderland scout saw him and Hudgell signed for the Wearsiders in January 1947, for £10,000 — which was then a record fee for a full-back. He missed Sunderland's famous FA Cup defeat at Yeovil but went on to make 260 League appearances for the Roker Park side before retiring in May 1956.

	LEAGUE		*FA CUP*		*TOTAL*	
	App	*Gls*	*App*	*Gls*	*App*	*Gls*
1946-47	25	1	1	0	26	1
	25	1	1	0	26	1

John Jackson is arguably the best goalkeeper ever to play for Crystal Palace. Jackson, who was born in Hammersmith on 5 September 1942 and began his football career at St Clement's Dane School, won England Youth honours before he signed for Palace in March 1962. He was the reserve 'keeper until Glazier's transfer and then ousted Welsh international Tony Millington to make the first-team spot his own. Jackson made 222 consecutive League appearances, being an ever-present in Palace's promotion-winning season of 1968-9. He missed only four games in the club's Division One days before seeing Palace relegated in consecutive seasons. After a disagreement with Malcolm Allison he moved to Orient and with the O's he made 210 consecutive League appearances. Millwall signed Jackson in August 1979 and he was ever-present in his first season at The Den. In the close season of 1981, Millwall gave him a free transfer and he had short spells with Ipswich Town, Hereford United and Brighton. Jackson, who now lives in Brighton, played for the Football League against the Scottish League in March 1971.

	LEAGUE		*FA CUP*		*FL CUP*		*TOTAL*	
	App	*Gls*	*App*	*Gls*	*App*	*Gls*	*App*	*Gls*
1964-65	17	0	2	0	2	0	21	0
1965-66	38	0	0	0	1	0	39	0
1966-67	38	0	1	0	1	0	40	0
1967-68	42	0	2	0	1	0	45	0
1968-69	42	0	2	0	4	0	48	0
1969-70	42	0	4	0	5	0	51	0
1970-71	42	0	2	0	6	0	50	0
1971-72	42	0	2	0	3	0	47	0
1972-73	38	0	3	0	1	0	42	0
1973-74	5	0	0	0	0	0	5	0
	346	0	18	0	24	0	388	0

JOHN JACKSON

JOSHUA JOHNSON

Born in Tibshelf, Derbyshire, Josh Johnson was a lay preacher who started his football career with Ripley Athletic. He was signed by Aston Villa but did not appear in the first team before joining Plymouth Argyle, for whom he made six Southern League appearances. Johnson joined Palace in November 1907, going on to make 274 Southern League appearances up to the beginning of World War One. In the close season of 1919 he returned to the Midlands and signed for Nottingham Forest, retiring after two seasons at the City Ground. He represented the Southern League three times whilst with Palace.

	S LEAGUE		*FA CUP*		*TOTAL*	
	App	*Gls*	*App*	*Gls*	*App*	*Gls*
1907-08	23	0	3	0	26	0
1908-09	38	0	4	0	42	0
1909-10	41	0	0	0	41	0
1910-11	36	0	1	0	37	0
1911-12	34	0	4	0	38	0
1912-13	37	0	3	0	40	0
1913-14	35	0	2	0	37	0
1914-15	32	0	2	0	34	0
	276	0	19	0	295	0

Joe Jones was born in Rhosymedre, South Wales, in 1887 and was signed by Stoke from his local club, Treharris, in September 1910. He made several appearances in the Southern League, gained a cap for Wales and had a further season at Stoke after the war before Palace signed him in June 1920. This tall, balding centre-half helped the side to their first major honour as the first champions of the Third Division. He also made further international appearances. In July 1922, Jones moved to Coventry City, where he spent two seasons before ending his League career at Crewe, whom he joined in May 1924. Jones gained 15 Welsh caps altogether, five while with Palace. He died in Stoke on 23 July 1941, aged 53.

	LEAGUE		*FA CUP*		*TOTAL*	
	App	*Gls*	*App*	*Gls*	*App*	*Gls*
1920-21	25	4	2	0	27	4
1921-22	36	2	3	0	39	2
	61	6	5	0	66	6

JOE JONES

BOBBY KELLARD

Bobby Kellard, a small, stocky ball-winning wing-half, served eight League clubs and had two spells with Crystal Palace, helping them to promotion from Division Three in his first season at Selhurst. He was born in Edmonton on 1 March 1943 and signed full-time professional forms for Southend United in May 1960. Kellard won England Youth international caps and after 106 League appearances for Southend he was transferred to Palace in September 1963. Two years and 76 League appearances later, he moved to Ipswich Town (13 appearances) and then his travels took him to Portsmouth (March 1966; 91 appearances), Bristol City (July 1968; 77) and Leicester City (August 1970; 48) before he rejoined Palace in September 1971. Kellard stayed for 15 months before returning to Portsmouth in December 1972, after making another 44 appearances for a Palace team destined to drop out of Division One at the end of that season. After 62 games for Pompey he ended his career with spells at Hereford United and Torquay United, for whom he made three appearances each. Kellard also played in South Africa and in 1976 became manager of Chelmsford City.

	LEAGUE		*FA CUP*		*FL CUP*		*TOTAL*	
	App	*Gls*	*App*	*Gls*	*App*	*Gls*	*App*	*Gls*
1963-64	24	2	1	0	1	0	26	2
1964-65	40	3	4	0	4	0	48	3
1965-66	13	1	0	0	1	0	14	1
1971-72	32	3	2	0	0	0	34	3
1972-73	12/2	1	0	0	1	0	13/2	1
	121/2	10	7	0	7	0	135/2	10

In September 1971, Steve Kember brought Crystal Palace their record incoming transfer fee when Chelsea paid £170,000 for his midfield skills. Born at Croydon on 8 December 1948, Kember was signed as an apprentice for Palace by Dick Graham in July 1965. He turned full-time professional on his 17th birthday and made his League debut at Bristol City on New Year's Day 1966. He won England Youth and Under-23 caps and helped Palace to the First Division in 1969. After more than 200 League appearances he joined Chelsea and played in 130 League games for them (five as sub) before the Stamford Bridge club were relegated in 1975. He stayed in the First Division with Leicester City (115 appearances) before returning to Selhurst Park in October 1978, for £50,000. Kember helped Venables' young side to the Second Division championship and had spells in the North American Soccer League with Vancouver Whitecaps. He served Palace as youth trainer and then manager (see *Palace Managers*).

	LEAGUE		*FA CUP*		*FL CUP*		*TOTAL*	
	App	*Gls*	*App*	*Gls*	*App*	*Gls*	*App*	*Gls*
1965-66	11/2	2	1	0	0	0	12/2	2
1966-67	39	10	1	0	1	0	41	10
1967-68	41	7	2	0	1	0	44	7
1968-69	42	8	2	0	4	0	48	8
1969-70	35	3	0	0	5	0	40	3
1970-71	39	5	2	0	3	0	44	5
1971-72	9	0	0	0	1	0	10	0
1978-79	29	0	4	1	0	0	33	1
1979-80	10/3	1	3	1	1	0	14/3	2
	255/5	36	15	2	16	0	286/5	38

STEVE KEMBER

JACK LEWIS

Wing-half Jack Lewis, whose proper name was John, was born in Walsall on 26 August 1919. He was on West Bromwich Albion's books as a junior before signing for Crystal Palace in the summer of 1938 and made his debut in a goalless draw against Bristol Rovers in April 1939. After the war he was a regular member of Palace's League side for three seasons, playing in a team which struggled at the foot of the Third Division South. His personal form was quite impressive, however, and he was selected for a London XI (along with Dick Graham) to play in Brussels in 1948. In November 1949, Palace transferred him to Bournemouth for £7,500. He moved to Reading in July 1951 and was in the side which missed promotion in 1951-2, finishing runners-up five points behind Plymouth. In April 1952 Lewis scored two goals for Reading in their 3-1 win over Palace at Elm Park. They helped him equal Arthur Grimsdell's record, for a half-back, of 14 goals in a season and before the end of the campaign the former Palace man set a new best of 15. Lewis stayed at Elm Park for another season. Then, after 74 League games (17 goals), he went into non-League soccer with Kettering Town. Later he became a publican.

	LEAGUE		*FA CUP*		*TOTAL*	
	App	*Gls*	*App*	*Gls*	*App*	*Gls*
1938-39	1	0	0	0	1	0
1945-46	-	-	3	0	3	0
1946-47	42	1	1	0	43	1
1947-48	36	2	1	0	37	2
1948-49	31	2	1	0	32	2
1949-50	14	1	0	0	14	1
	124	6	6	0	130	6

Right-back Jack Little did not miss a game when Crystal Palace became the first champions of the Football League in 1920-21. The previous season he had been an ever-present when Palace finished third in the Southern League and he extended it to 87 games before being injured in the third match of 1921-2. Born at Seaton Delaval, he played for Scotswood before joining Barnsley in 1908. In 1911, Little moved to Croydon Common and was left-back in a defence which conceded only 14 goals as Croydon won the Second Division of the Southern League. Common, of course, played at The Nest, a ground which Palace were to use after the war. Little signed for Palace in 1919 and formed a fine partnership with Ernie Rhodes at full-back. He joined Sittingbourne in the 1926 close season and was granted a benefit against Palace.

	S LEAGUE		*F LEAGUE*		*FA CUP*		*TOTAL*	
	App	*Gls*	*App*	*Gls*	*App*	*Gls*	*App*	*Gls*
1919-20	42	0	-	-	1	0	43	0
1920-21	-	-	42	0	2	0	44	0
1921-22	-	-	36	0	3	0	39	0
1922-23	-	-	39	0	1	0	40	0
1923-24	-	-	36	0	6	0	42	0
1924-25	-	-	27	0	2	0	29	0
1925-26	-	-	19	0	4	0	23	0
	42	0	199	0	19	0	260	0

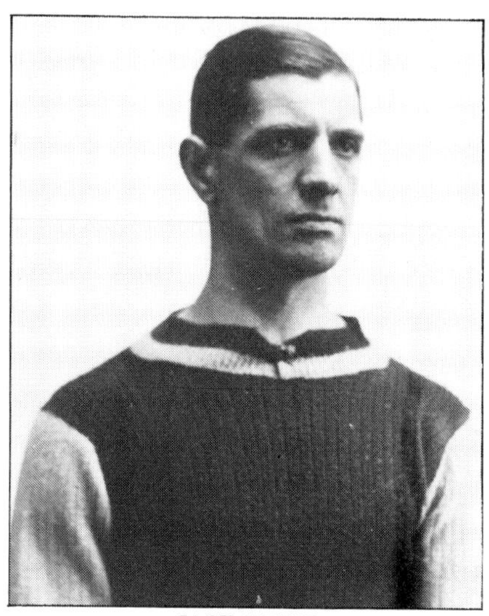

JACK LITTLE

TERRY LONG

Born in Tylers Green, Beaconsfield, on 17 November 1934, Terry Long spent three seasons as an amateur with Arsenal before rejoining his local side, Wycombe Wanderers, from where Palace signed him on 12 May 1955. Long made his League debut against Walsall on 24 September 1955 and his consistent play earned him a run of 214 consecutive League appearances from September 1956 to March 1961. Long's stay at Selhurst Park saw promotion from the Fourth to the First Division but unfortunately Bert Head never gave him a game in the top flight. Long had a benefit against an All Stars XI in October 1966. He totalled 432 League appearances, plus ten as a substitute, beating Bert Harry's club record. Long's record, of course, has since been passed by Jim Cannon. Long became coach under Head but was sacked when Allison took over as manager. He joined George Petchey, first at Orient then at Millwall. In November 1980 he was acting manager at The Den, after Petchey's departure.

	LEAGUE		*FA CUP*		*FL CUP*		*TOTAL*	
	App	*Gls*	*App*	*Gls*	*App*	*Gls*	*App*	*Gls*
1955-56	13	0	0	0	-	-	13	0
1956-57	42	1	4	0	-	-	46	1
1957-58	46	4	3	0	-	-	49	4
1958-59	46	4	5	0	-	-	51	4
1959-60	46	0	4	0	-	-	50	0
1960-61	43	0	3	0	1	0	47	0
1961-62	45	0	3	1	1	0	49	1
1962-63	39	2	2	0	1	0	42	2
1963-64	27	0	0	0	0	0	27	0
1964-65	17	1	2	0	3	0	22	1
1965-66	32	1	1	0	1	0	34	1
1966-67	20/5	1	1	0	0	0	21/5	1
1967-68	14/5	1	2	0	1	0	17/5	1
1968-69	2	0	0	0	0	0	2	0
	432/10	15	30	1	8	0	470/10	16

Red-haired John McCormick, who was affectionately known as 'Big Mac' by Crystal Palace supporters, was born in Glasgow on 18 July 1936. McCormick was a pillar of strength during Palace's first spell in Division One and earned the club's Player of the Year award in 1972. He started his career with St Roch before signing for Third Lanark in 1959. McCormick joined Aberdeen in the close season of 1964 and in May 1966 he was one of Bert Head's first — and best — signings for Palace. When he arrived at Selhurst Park he replaced Alan Stephenson, who signed for West Ham in March 1968. McCormick was an ever-present in the promotion-winning team of 1968-9 and continued to serve Palace in the top flight October 1972. He was then awarded a benefit, which realized £7,000, and allowed to leave on a free transfer. He signed for Wealdstone, who were managed by Eddie Presland, and helped them win the Southern League title.

	LEAGUE		*FA CUP*		*FL CUP*		*TOTAL*	
	App	*Gls*	*App*	*Gls*	*App*	*Gls*	*App*	*Gls*
1966-67	2	0	0	0	1	0	3	0
1967-68	27	1	0	0	1	0	28	1
1968-69	42	3	2	0	4	0	48	3
1969-70	41	1	4	0	5	0	50	1
1970-71	32	0	2	1	6	0	40	1
1971-72	35	1	2	0	3	0	40	1
1972-73	15	0	0	0	1	0	16	0
	194	6	10	1	21	0	225	7

JOHN McCORMICK

HARRY McDONALD

Full-back Harry McDonald came into League football at the comparatively late age of 24. He was born in Salford on 11 September 1926 and was playing for Ashton United when he was recommended to Palace by Charlie Slade. Manager Ronnie Rooke signed McDonald in September 1950 and the following month he made his debut at left-back. It was hardly a happy start, for Palace crashed 5-0 at Bournemouth, and soon Slade, the scout who spotted him, was his joint manager, alongside Fred Dawes. McDonald appeared intermittently that season as Palace finished bottom of the Third Division South and had to apply for re-election. Thereafter, he established himself, albeit in a team that was continually struggling. He scored one goal for Palace, in a 3-1 win against Northampton Town in September 1954. He moved to Kettering Town the following year and then gave Gravesend sterling service, making 324 appearances for them and helping them win the Southern League title.

	LEAGUE		*FA CUP*		*TOTAL*	
	App	*Gls*	*App*	*Gls*	*App*	*Gls*
1950-51	12	0	1	0	13	0
1951-52	40	0	0	0	40	0
1952-53	30	0	3	0	33	0
1953-54	38	0	0	0	38	0
1954-55	20	1	2	0	22	1
	140	1	6	0	146	1

JOHNNY McNICHOL

Inside-forward Johnny McNichol, who was born in Kilmarnock on 20 August 1925, was a youngster with Scottish club, Hurlford Juniors, when Newcastle United signed him during World War Two. McNichol did not manage a first-team game for the Magpies and in August 1948 was transferred to Brighton & Hove Albion. McNichol spent four seasons at the Goldstone Ground, making 158 appearances and scoring 36 goals in the Third Division South. In August 1952, Chelsea paid £15,000 for him and McNichol helped the Londoners to their first League Championship, in 1954-5 under Ted Drake. Altogether McNichol scored 60 goals in 181 appearances for Chelsea. Crystal Palace manager Cyril Spiers needed a general to guide his young side and in March 1958 he signed McNichol. The player made 153 consecutive League appearances and skippered the team in their Fourth Division promotion season of 1960-61. After leaving Palace he was player-manager of Tunbridge Wells Rangers and later worked for both Brighton and Palace in their pools departments.

	LEAGUE		*FA CUP*		*FL CUP*		*TOTAL*	
	App	*Gls*	*App*	*Gls*	*App*	*Gls*	*App*	*Gls*
1957-58	12	7	0	0	0	0	12	7
1958-59	46	4	5	0	0	0	51	4
1959-60	46	3	4	0	0	0	50	3
1960-61	46	1	3	0	1	0	50	1
1961-62	29	0	3	0	0	0	32	0
1962-63	10	0	0	0	0	0	10	0
	189	15	15	0	1	0	205	15

JERRY MURPHY

Jerry Murphy, a left-sided midfield player, did not score many goals for Crystal Palace but he certainly helped make many for his colleagues. Born in Stepney on 23 September 1959, he began at Selhurst Park as an apprentice and was another member of Palace's successful FA Youth Cup side to progress to League soccer. In 1978-9, when Palace won the Second Division title, Murphy was almost an ever-present and he capped his first season in Division One by making three appearances for the Republic of Ireland, qualified by the fact that his father was Irish. He managed relatively few appearances in the 1980-81 relegation season but, thereafter, was a regular. After nine years at Selhurst he was given a free transfer, only to be signed by First Division Chelsea in August 1985. He made 34 League appearances and scored three goals for the Stamford Bridge club before injury caused his contract to be cancelled in March 1988.

	LEAGUE		*FA CUP*		*FL CUP*		*TOTAL*	
	App	*Gls*	*App*	*Gls*	*App*	*Gls*	*App*	*Gls*
1976-77	0/1	0	0	0	0	0	0/1	0
1977-78	4/4	0	0	0	0	0	4/4	0
1978-79	40/1	5	4	0	4	1	48/1	6
1979-80	36/1	3	2/1	0	3	1	41/2	4
1980-81	15/4	2	1	0	4	2	20/4	4
1981-82	24/1	2	5	0	3	1	32/1	3
1982-83	30	2	3	0	3	0	36	2
1983-84	30/2	3	0	0	1	0	31/2	3
1984-85	35/1	3	2	0	4	0	41/1	3
	214/15	20	17/1	0	22	5	253/16	25

Born in Newport on 10 November 1959, Peter Nicholas was a member of Palace's FA Youth Cup-winning sides. He was a hard-tackling half-back, who gained Welsh Schools, Youth, Under-21 and full caps. Nicholas signed professional forms in December 1976 and made his debut at Millwall on the opening day of the 1977-8 season, in a 3-0 victory. He saw Palace promoted to Division One, as champions, in 1979 before joining Kenny Sansom at Arsenal in March 1981, for a fee of £400,000. Nicholas moved back to Palace, originally on loan. He made more Welsh appearances while playing for Palace on loan, but was still registered with the Gunners, a fact which confuses the issue over whether he is Palace's most-capped player. After a row between Palace and the Welsh FA over injury payments, he moved to Luton Town in January 1985. A surprising transfer to Aberdeen saw Nicholas gain more Welsh caps, this time as a Scottish League player. When his child became ill he returned south, to Chelsea, in July 1988, for a fee of £350,000.

	LEAGUE		*FA CUP*		*FL CUP*		*TOTAL*	
	App	*Gls*	*App*	*Gls*	*App*	*Gls*	*App*	*Gls*
1977-78	23	1	1	0	0	0	24	1
1978-79	37	3	4	1	4	0	45	4
1979-80	39	2	1	0	3	0	43	2
1980-81	28	1	1	0	3	0	32	1
1983-84	25	3	3	0	0	0	28	3
1984-85	22	4	1	0	4	1	27	5
	174	14	11	1	14	1	199	16

PETER NICHOLAS

ALF NOAKES

Alf Noakes was born in Stratford, East London, on 14 August 1933 and signed for his local club, West Ham United, in August 1950, aged 17. He never made the first team at Upton Park and went on loan to Sittingbourne before signing for Crystal Palace in June 1955. He made his League debut in the ninth match of the 1955-6 season, wearing the number-11 shirt in a 3-1 defeat at Southampton. After that, Noakes switched from the forward line to wing-half before settling down as Palace's regular left-back. He became a favourite with the crowd at Selhurst Park and, although his early days with the club were spent struggling at the foot of the Third Division South, he missed only six League games when Palace won promotion from Division Four in 1960-61. In July 1962, former Palace manager George Smith signed Noakes for Portsmouth but, after making only 13 League appearances for Pompey, he was given a free transfer.

	LEAGUE		*FA CUP*		*FL CUP*		*TOTAL*	
	App	*Gls*	*App*	*Gls*	*App*	*Gls*	*App*	*Gls*
1955-56	18	1	2	0	-	-	20	1
1956-57	31	1	3	0	-	-	34	1
1957-58	22	0	0	0	-	-	22	0
1958-59	45	6	5	0	-	-	50	6
1959-60	37	5	2	0	-	-	39	5
1960-61	40	1	2	0	0	0	42	1
1961-62	2	0	0	0	0	0	2	0
	195	14	14	0	0	0	209	14

DAVID PAYNE

Dave Payne must qualify as a local-born player, having first seen the light of day at the Mayday Hospital, Thornton Heath, on 25 April 1947. He played for Palace juniors before signing professional forms in October 1964 and made his League debut as a 17-year-old at Preston on 5 December 1964. He proved to be one of Dick Graham's best signings and was a versatile player, although he was used mainly as a defender in the side which took Palace to the First Division for the first time in the club's history. He made one international appearance, coming on as a substitute for England Under-23s. In August 1973, Payne was one of the Palace players who joined George Petchey at Orient. He broke a leg in April 1974, but returned to take his appearances tally for Orient to 88 (plus five as a substitute) before becoming youth-team coach at Millwall, whom he helped win the FA Youth Cup.

	LEAGUE		*FA CUP*		*FL CUP*		*TOTAL*	
	App	*Gls*	*App*	*Gls*	*App*	*Gls*	*App*	*Gls*
1964-65	7	0	0	0	1	0	8	0
1965-66	27/2	0	0	0	0	0	27/2	0
1966-67	40	2	1	0	1	0	42	2
1967-68	39	2	2	0	1	0	42	2
1968-69	30	3	2	0	3	1	35	4
1969-70	27	1	4	0	2	0	33	1
1970-71	31	0	1	0	6	1	38	1
1971-72	41	1	2	0	3	0	46	1
1972-73	39/1	0	4	1	1	0	44/1	1
	281/3	9	16	1	18	2	315/3	12

GEORGE PETCHEY

George Petchey was born in Whitechapel on 24 June 1931 and was yet another East Ender who started his career with West Ham United. Petchey signed for the Hammers in August 1948 and made two League appearances, both at inside-left in the Second Division in 1951-2. In July 1953, he was transferred to Queen's Park Rangers, where he made a name for himself as a tough-tackling wing-half. He became a great favourite at Rangers and made 255 League appearances in six years with the club. Queen's Park Rangers' fans were dismayed when Petchey was transferred to Crystal Palace in May 1960. In his first season he was an ever-present as Palace won promotion to the Third Division. He also helped Palace into the Second Division in 1964, before an eye injury caused his retirement. His last appearance was the FA Cup match at home to Leeds United in March 1965. Petchey became youth-team manager at Palace and was later assistant to Bert Head. Orient gave him his first manager's job in July 1972 and he took over at Millwall in January 1978. In 1986 he was helping run Brighton's junior teams.

	LEAGUE		*FA CUP*		*FL CUP*		*TOTAL*	
	App	*Gls*	*App*	*Gls*	*App*	*Gls*	*App*	*Gls*
1960-61	46	7	3	0	1	0	50	7
1961-62	40	1	3	0	1	0	44	1
1962-63	33	2	0	0	0	0	33	2
1963-64	24	2	0	0	1	0	25	2
1964-65	0	0	1	0	0	0	1	0
	143	12	7	0	3	0	153	12

The rock upon which Palace's successful Third Division championship season of 1920-21 was built consisted of the defence of goalkeeper John Alderson and full-backs Jack Little and Ernie Rhodes. All three were ever-present as Palace lifted the title at the first attempt. The trio were all North-Easterners and Rhodes was born at South Bank. He first played for Grangetown, near Middlesbrough, before joining Sunderland in June 1902. Rhodes made over 100 appearances for the Roker Park side before switching to Brentford in April 1908. Again he ran up a century of appearances before being transferred to Gravesend in the close season of 1913. He stayed there for only a few months before Edmund Goodman signed him for Palace in October. Mainly a reserve up to the war, Rhodes won a permanant place as Palace moved into the Football League. He missed only two games in Palace's first season of Second Division football before age caught up with him. He finished his career at Sheppey United.

	S LEAGUE		*F LEAGUE*		*FA CUP*		*TOTAL*	
	App	*Gls*	*App*	*Gls*	*App*	*Gls*	*App*	*Gls*
1913-14	6	0	-	-	0	0	6	0
1914-15	0	0	-	-	0	0	0	0
1919-20	40	0	-	-	1	0	41	0
1920-21	-	-	42	0	2	0	44	0
1921-22	-	-	40	0	3	0	43	0
1922-23	-	-	7	1	0	0	7	1
	46	0	89	1	6	0	141	1

ERNIE RHODES

DON ROGERS

When Bert Head was manager of Crystal Palace he signed several players from his former club, Swindon Town, but he had to wait seven years before clinching the signature of talented winger Don Rogers. Born at Paulton, near Bath, on 25 October 1945, Rogers signed professional forms for Swindon in October 1962. He was one of the best wingers in the business and could have joined a more glamorous club, yet chose to spend his peak years with Swindon. He saw the Wiltshire side relegated from Division Two, but was rewarded in 1969 when he scored two goals at Wembley as Third Division Swindon beat First Division Arsenal in the Football League Cup Final. He helped Swindon win promotion and also lift the Anglo-Italian Cup before a fee of £150,000 took him to Selhurst Park in November 1972, after he had made exactly 400 League appearances for Swindon. In his first season at Selhurst he scored brilliant televised goals against Everton and Manchester United (Palace beat United 5-0) but at the end of the campaign, Palace were relegated and Rogers' brief taste of First Division football was over. In September 1974, Malcolm Allison transferred Rogers to Queen's Park Rangers, in a deal which saw Ian Evans move in the opposite direction. Rogers made 13 League appearances (plus five as substitute) for Rangers before returning to Swindon. He made another 11 League appearances for them (plus one sub) and opened a sports shop in the town. Rogers won England Youth and Under-23 caps and represented the Football League.

	LEAGUE		*FA CUP*		*FL CUP*		*TOTAL*	
	App	*Gls*	*App*	*Gls*	*App*	*Gls*	*App*	*Gls*
1972-73	26	13	4	2	0	0	30	15
1973-74	41	15	1	0	1	0	43	15
1974-75	2/1	0	0	0	1/1	0	3/2	0
	69/1	28	5	2	2/1	0	76/2	30

Born in Swansea on 16 March 1936, Vic Rouse came from a footballing family, his father and grandfather both having long spells with several clubs. Rouse signed as an amateur for Millwall and turned professional with Palace in August 1956, making his debut at home to Swindon Town on 13 October that year, in a 0-0 draw. He took over from Bailey and improved so much that he was capped by Wales. On 22 April 1959 he became the first player from Division Four to be capped in a full international, when he played against Northern Ireland in Belfast. Rouse was ever-present when Palace were promoted to the Third Division in 1961 but was later replaced by Glazier. In August 1963 he was transferred to Oxford United, but left for Orient who were then managed by Dave Sexton. Orient suffered relegation to the Third Division and after only three games the following season, Rouse left to play in the North American Soccer League. He returned to England and joined the Metropolitan Police, training and managing their soccer team in the Southern League.

	LEAGUE		*FA CUP*		*FL CUP*		*TOTAL*	
	App	*Gls*	*App*	*Gls*	*App*	*Gls*	*App*	*Gls*
1956-57	25	0	1	0	-	-	26	0
1957-58	42	0	2	0	-	-	44	0
1958-59	36	0	4	0	-	-	40	0
1959-60	45	0	4	0	-	-	49	0
1960-61	46	0	3	0	0	0	49	0
1961-62	33	0	3	0	1	0	37	0
1962-63	11	0	0	0	1	0	12	0
	238	0	17	0	2	0	257	0

VIC ROUSE

KENNY SANSOM

Born in Camberwell on 26 September 1958, Kenny Sansom signed for Palace as a junior in December 1975 and was England Youth captain and gained Under-23 full caps while at Selhurst. He played in Palace's FA Youth Cup-winning side and was the club's Player of the Year in 1977 and 1979. He made his League debut in the last game of the 1974-5 season, a 2-0 defeat at Tranmere. Sansom became a regular the following season and helped Palace to promotion from Division Three in 1977 and to the Second Division championship in 1979. His ambition to play for Arsenal was realized when he became the first 'million-pound full-back', although Paul Barron, valued at £400,000, helped reduce the actual fee to £950,000. It was part of a complicated deal which took Clive Allen to Palace. Sansom is now the most-capped England full-back. He skippered Arsenal to consecutive League Cup Finals, collecting a winners' medal in 1987 and a losers' medal the following year. In the summer of 1988, Sansom was in dispute with Arsenal manager George Graham and was dropped. Newcastle United manager Jim Smith signed him for £300,000 in December 1988, only for Sansom to return to London with QPR in June 1989.

	LEAGUE		*FA CUP*		*FL CUP*		*TOTAL*	
	App	*Gls*	*App*	*Gls*	*App*	*Gls*	*App*	*Gls*
1974-75	1	0	0	0	0	0	1	0
1975-76	6	0	0	0	0	0	6	0
1976-77	46	0	6	0	3	0	55	0
1977-78	41	2	1	0	4	0	46	2
1978-79	42	0	4	1	4	0	50	1
1979-80	36	1	0	0	3	0	39	1
	172	3	11	1	14	0	197	4

JOHN SEWELL

John Sewell started with Bexleyheath and signed for Charlton Athletic in January 1955, teaming up with Don Townsend as the regular full-backs at The Valley. Sewell, who was born at Brockley on 7 July 1936, was transferred to Crystal Palace in October 1963 and helped the club win promotion to Division Two. When Stephenson was transferred, Sewell became captain and led the side into the First Division in 1969. He left for Orient in August 1971, on a free transfer, but soon afterwards became actively involved in the North American Soccer League, where he played for and managed several clubs. Sewell, who was booked only once in his playing career, was known as one of football's smartest dressers.

	LEAGUE		*FA CUP*		*FL CUP*		*TOTAL*	
	App	*Gls*	*App*	*Gls*	*App*	*Gls*	*App*	*Gls*
1963-64	18	0	2	1	0	0	20	1
1964-65	22	0	0	0	2	0	24	0
1965-66	28	1	1	0	0	0	29	1
1966-67	26	0	1	0	1	0	28	0
1967-68	31	0	0	0	1	0	32	0
1968-69	35/1	1	2	0	3	0	40/1	1
1969-70	37	2	4	0	3	2	44	4
1970-71	31/2	2	2	0	5	0	38/2	2
	228/3	6	12	1	15	2	255/3	9

PETER SIMPSON

Born in Leith, Edinburgh, on 13 November 1904, Peter Simpson started with local club, St Bernards, before going to Southern League side, Kettering Town. He helped them win the championship two seasons running, in 1928 and 1929. Crystal Palace were drawn against Kettering in the FA Cup and, although Palace won, manager Fred Mavin signed several players from the non-Leaguers, going back for Simpson in the close season of 1929. He made his League debut against Norwich City at home, scoring a hat-trick in a 3-0 victory, although some records state that one was an own-goal. Simpson finished the season with 36 League goals and the following term he improved his total to 46 goals, plus eight in the Cup, when Palace were Third Division South runners-up to Notts County. Simpson gave Palace magnificent service, scoring well over 150 League and Cup goals before injury slowed him down and he was transferred to West Ham United in the 1935 close season, in exchange for Wood. He had short spells at Reading and Aldershot before retiring from football and buying a shop in Croydon. He died in March 1974, aged 69.

	LEAGUE		*FA CUP*		*TOTAL*	
	App	*Gls*	*App*	*Gls*	*App*	*Gls*
1929-30	34	36	1	1	35	37
1930-31	42	46	6	8	48	54
1931-32	31	23	2	1	33	24
1932-33	20	14	1	1	21	15
1933-34	25	20	4	1	29	21
1934-35	28	14	1	0	29	14
	180	153	15	12	195	165

ALAN STEPHENSON

Alan Stephenson was born in Cheshunt on 26 September 1944. A tall, lean centre-half, he came through the junior ranks at Selhurst Park before making his League debut against Bradford on 24 March 1962, when he was 17 years old and after signing full-time professional forms the previous month. It was his only game that season and he made only one appearance the following term before gaining a regular place in the 1963-4 season. Stephenson helped Palace gain promotion in 1964 and captained the team in 1966. He also won England Under-23 honours. Ron Greenwood paid £80,000, a West Ham record fee, to sign him in March 1968 and he made 106 League appearances (plus two as a substitute) before being sold to Portsmouth in May 1972 for a fee of £32,000, after an earlier loan period with Fulham. Bobby Moore, in his biography, claimed that Greenwood had 'ruined' Stephenson and the player certainly failed to live up to his early potential. Stephenson went to South Africa in the close season of 1975 before returning to Orient as coach. He then left football to run a public house.

	LEAGUE		*FA CUP*		*FL CUP*		*TOTAL*	
	App	*Gls*	*App*	*Gls*	*App*	*Gls*	*App*	*Gls*
1961-62	1	0	0	0	0	0	1	0
1962-63	1	1	0	0	0	0	1	1
1963-64	26	2	0	0	1	0	27	2
1964-65	40	4	4	0	4	0	48	4
1965-66	40	4	1	0	1	0	42	4
1966-67	42	1	1	0	1	0	44	1
1967-68	20	1	2	0	0	0	22	1
	170	13	8	0	7	0	185	13

ROY SUMMERSBY

Born in Lambeth on 19 March 1935, Roy Summersby signed professional forms for Millwall in March 1952, after playing for the juniors at The Den. This small inside-forward was mainly a reserve until 1957, when he finally established himself in the first team. In December 1958, however, after making 87 League appearances (14 goals) in six years at Millwall, he was transferred to Crystal Palace. Summersby made his League debut for Palace at Walsall in the first season of the Fourth Division and became a regular, making 123 consecutive League appearances, most of them alongside Johnny Byrne. He played a major part in Palace's promotion to Division Three in 1960-61, when he was ever-present and scored 25 goals to finish second-highest scorer behind Byrne. In May 1963, he joined former Palace manager, George Smith, at Portsmouth but after 12 League appearances for Pompey he moved into non-League soccer with Chelmsford City and then Hillingdon Borough.

	LEAGUE		*FA CUP*		*FL CUP*		*TOTAL*	
	App	*Gls*	*App*	*Gls*	*App*	*Gls*	*App*	*Gls*
1958-59	25	9	0	0	0	0	25	9
1959-60	46	15	4	0	0	0	50	15
1960-61	46	25	3	0	1	0	50	25
1961-62	42	8	3	0	0	0	45	8
1962-63	17	2	3	1	0	0	20	3
	176	59	13	1	1	0	190	60

Goalscoring forward Bobby Tambling was a great servant to Chelsea before being transferred to Crystal Palace in 1970. Born at Storrington, Sussex, on 18 September 1941, he joined Chelsea straight from school in July 1957 and in 302 League appearances (four as substitute) for the Blues he scored 164 goals. Tambling, a former schoolboy international, won three full England caps and 13 at Under-23 level. He scored a goal for Chelsea in the 1964-5 League Cup Final, which they won on aggregate against Leicester City, and also netted their goal when they lost 2-1 to Spurs in the 1967 FA Cup Final. He was a member of the side promoted to Division One in 1962-3. In January 1970, Tambling played three games on loan to Palace before Bert Head signed him in June that year. He went to Selhurst with Alan Birchenall for a joint fee of £140,000. Tambling spent two years as a first-team regular but was in the Reserves by the time Palace suffered relegation in successive seasons. In October 1973, Tambling moved to Cork Hibernians in the League of Ireland. He is a Jehovah's Witness.

	LEAGUE		*FA CUP*		*FL CUP*		*TOTAL*	
	App	*Gls*	*App*	*Gls*	*App*	*Gls*	*App*	*Gls*
1969-70	3	0	0	0	0	0	3	0
1970-71	26	4	0	0	3	2	29	6
1971-72	33	8	1	2	3	1	37	11
1972-73	4/1	0	0	0	0	0	4/1	0
1973-74	1	0	0	0	1	0	2	0
	67/1	12	1	2	7	3	75/1	17

BOBBY TAMBLING

PETER TAYLOR

Peter Taylor was born in Rochford on 3 January 1953 and as a schoolboy he had trials with Spurs and Palace before signing as a junior for his home side, Southend United, in January 1971. He helped Southend gain promotion to Division Three before Malcolm Allison saw this small left-footed winger as his saviour and signed him in October 1973, for £110,000. Taylor was Palace's Player of the Year that season, as Palace were relegated to the Third Division, but his trickery and running stopped the club sliding further and advanced his claim for an England place. He was Player of the Year again in 1976 and was sold to Tottenham Hotspur in September that year, for a record fee of £400,000, which meant that he missed Palace's promotion at the end of the season. With Spurs he suffered relegation, then promotion before going to Orient in November 1980. There followed spells at Oldham Athletic (on loan), Maidstone United, Exeter City, Chelmsford and Dartford, whom he joined as manager in the close season of 1986. He won four England caps while he was a Third Division player with Palace.

	LEAGUE		*FA CUP*		*FL CUP*		*TOTAL*	
	App	*Gls*	*App*	*Gls*	*App*	*Gls*	*App*	*Gls*
1973-74	32	6	1	0	0	0	33	6
1974-75	43	14	2	0	3	1	48	15
1975-76	41	12	8	4	3	0	52	16
1976-77	6	1	0	0	3	1	9	2
	122	33	11	4	9	2	142	39

Tony Taylor, a small but versatile Scottish footballer, began as a forward before making the left-back position his own. Taylor, who was born in Glasgow on 6 September 1946, was transferred to Palace from Morton in October 1968, for £15,000, after spells with Celtic and Kilmarnock. In his first season he saw Palace promoted to Division One as runners-up to Derby and he played regularly in the top flight. Relegation in successive seasons saw Palace back in the Third Division and in August 1974, Taylor moved to Southend United. He made 56 League appearances at Roots Hall and then had brief spells with Swindon Town, Bristol Rovers, Portsmouth and Northampton Town before going to Canada to work as a coach. He remained in that country but still visits Selhurst Park on trips to England.

	LEAGUE		*FA CUP*		*FL CUP*		*TOTAL*	
	App	*Gls*	*App*	*Gls*	*App*	*Gls*	*App*	*Gls*
1968-69	25	2	0/1	0	0	0	25/1	2
1969-70	30/2	1	3	0	3/1	0	36/3	1
1970-71	36/1	2	2	0	6	2	44/1	4
1971-72	41	2	2	0	3	1	46	3
1972-73	40	1	4	0	1	0	45	1
1973-74	20	0	0	0	1	0	21	0
	192/3	8	11/1	0	14/1	3	217/5	11

TONY TAYLOR

GEOFF THOMAS

Geoff Thomas, who was born in Manchester on 5 August 1964, is one of several successful signings from the lower divisions made by Steve Coppell. Thomas joined Palace from Crewe Alexandra in May 1987, for £50,000, and quickly established himself as a Selhurst favourite — in his very first season he was elected the club's Player of the Year. In his second season he was appointed captain in place of Jim Cannon, only for injury to force him out of the side. Thomas began his career with Rochdale in 1981 and made his League debut for the Dale at Hereford United in October 1982. After making 11 League appearances for the Spotland club, he was transferred to Crewe in March 1984, when former Palace manager Dario Gradi signed him for the Cheshire side.

	LEAGUE		*FA CUP*		*FL CUP*		*TOTAL*	
	App	*Gls*	*App*	*Gls*	*App*	*Gls*	*App*	*Gls*
1987-88	41	6	1	0	3	0	45	6
1988-89	22	5	1	0	3	1	26	6
	63	11	2	0	6	1	71	12

BILL TURNER

Born in Tipton, Staffordshire, on 16 November 1901, Bill Turner, an England Schoolboy international, went to Bromsgrove before being signed by Crystal Palace on 4 May 1925. In 11 seasons at Selhurst Park, he played in eight different positions and played in the runners-up sides in seasons 1928-9 and 1930-31. After 284 League appearances he returned to Bromsgrove. Turner, who was nicknamed 'Rubber', had a reputation as a player who gave 100 per cent effort in every game.

	LEAGUE		*FA CUP*		*TOTAL*	
	App	*Gls*	*App*	*Gls*	*App*	*Gls*
1925-26	11	1	0	0	11	1
1926-27	22	5	2	0	24	5
1927-28	31	7	3	0	34	7
1928-29	7	0	0	0	7	0
1929-30	26	5	1	0	27	5
1930-31	21	3	6	0	27	3
1931-32	38	4	2	0	40	4
1932-33	35	4	1	0	36	4
1933-34	38	6	4	1	42	7
1934-35	26	0	0	0	26	0
1935-36	26	1	2	0	28	1
	281	36	21	1	302	37

CHARLIE WALLACE

Charlie Wallace was born in Sunderland on 20 January 1885 and played for local club Southwick before joining Palace in July 1905. He was signed as a reserve for Palace's initial season of 1905-06 but, after establishing himself in the first team, he became a firm favourite with the fans. He helped Palace gain promotion to the Southern League First Division before being snapped up by Aston Villa in the close season of 1907. Once more Wallace became a great favourite with home fans and for the next nine seasons he was a Villa regular, playing in two FA Cup-winning sides (1913 and 1920) and in Villa's League Championship team of 1909-10. He made 314 League appearances for Villa before moving to Oldham Athletic in the close season of 1921. Wallace returned to Villa Park as coach and scout in 1923 and was a club steward until his retirement in 1960. Wallace, who was capped three times by England, worked as a painter and decorator after finishing full-time football. He died on 26 January 1970, soon after his 85th birthday.

	S LEAGUE		*FA CUP*		*TOTAL*	
	App	*Gls*	*App*	*Gls*	*App*	*Gls*
1905-06	19	5	7	0	26	5
1906-07	37	8	7	0	44	8
	56	13	14	0	70	13

Outside-left John Whibley arrived at Crystal Palace from his home-town club, Sittingbourne, in 1911. Before World War One he was a reserve player who managed only 20 games in three seasons. After the war, Whibley established himself and in the first three seasons of Palace's Football League career he maintained a regular place. He won a Third Division championship medal in 1920-21 and kept his spot for two seasons as Palace sought to consolidate their position in Division Two. Towards the end of 1922-3 he lost his place to Hand and in the close season returned to Sittingbourne.

	S LEAGUE		*F LEAGUE*		*FA CUP*		*TOTAL*	
	App	*Gls*	*App*	*Gls*	*App*	*Gls*	*App*	*Gls*
1911-12	0	0	-	-	0	0	0	-
1912-13	3	0	-	-	0	0	3	0
1913-14	9	2	-	-	0	0	9	2
1914-15	8	1	-	-	1	0	9	1
1919-20	35	9	-	-	1	0	36	9
1920-21	-	-	32	5	1	0	33	5
1921-22	-	-	29	5	1	1	30	6
1922-23	-	-	30	5	0	0	30	5
	55	12	91	15	4	1	150	28

JOHN WHIBLEY

GEORGE WHITWORTH

Centre-forward George Whitworth was born in Northampton on 14 July 1896 and started his career at Rushden Windmill FC before going to Northampton Town in 1914. He guested for Palace during World War One and, after scoring regularly on his return to Northampton, it took a large fee to take him to The Nest. He signed in 1922 and made his mark in Palace's first season of Second Division football. Whitworth continued to find the net regularly until Palace were relegated in 1925, when he was transferred to Sheffield Wednesday. There was intense competition for places at Hillsborough — that season the Owls won the Second Division title — and Whitworth did not make the first team. In November 1925 he moved to Hull City and scored 31 goals in 67 League appearances for the Tigers before ending his career with Midland League Peterborough United, whom he joined in the close season of 1928.

	LEAGUE		*FA CUP*		*TOTAL*	
	App	*Gls*	*App*	*Gls*	*App*	*Gls*
1921-22	6	2	0	0	6	2
1922-23	36	17	1	0	37	17
1923-24	38	16	5	1	43	17
1924-25	31	13	1	1	32	14
	111	48	7	2	118	50

Centre-half Brian Wood signed for West Bromwich Albion in January 1958, but did not make a League appearance for the Throstles before Dick Graham signed him for Crystal Palace in May 1961. Born at Hamworthy, Poole, on 8 December 1940, Wood went to Selhurst Park on a free transfer and made his League debut in December 1961, in a 5-0 defeat at Swindon. Despite the result, Wood held his place and in 1963-4 he missed only one game as Palace won promotion to the Second Division. Alas, Wood twice suffered a broken leg — one coming in an FA Cup game at home to Bury in January 1964 — and in December 1966, Dick Graham, who was now at Orient, re-signed his old player. Wood enjoyed a complete recovery and made 58 appearances for Orient, followed by two seasons at Colchester United (71 appearances) and six at Workington (202 appearances, plus two as sub), before retiring in 1975.

	LEAGUE		*FA CUP*		*FL CUP*		*TOTAL*	
	App	*Gls*	*App*	*Gls*	*App*	*Gls*	*App*	*Gls*
1961-62	18	0	1	0	0	0	19	0
1962-63	44	0	1	1	1	0	46	1
1963-64	45	1	2	1	0	0	47	2
1964-65	21	0	1	1	2	0	24	1
1965-66	5	0	0	0	1	0	6	0
1966-67	9/1	0	0	0	0	0	9/1	0
	142/1	1	5	3	4	0	151/1	4

BRIAN WOOD

GEORGE WOOD

George Wood, a tall, blond Scottish international goalkeeper, joined Palace on a free transfer from Arsenal in 1983. He went straight into the first team and did not miss a League game for two seasons. Wood was born in Douglas on 26 September 1952 and began his career with East Stirling. He is one of the few goalkeepers in the game to have scored a goal, when he netted from a goal-kick against Queen of the South. In January 1972, Blackpool paid £7,000 for him as cover for John Burridge and that began a period of remarkable consistency for Wood. He made 117 League appearances for Blackpool and was ever-present in his last season at Bloomfield Road. In August 1977, Everton paid £150,000 for his signature and Wood did not miss a game in his first two seasons at Goodison Park. His form earned him three caps before mistakes crept into his play and he lost his place to Martin Hodge. In August 1980, Everton sold him to Arsenal for £150,000 and Wood made 60 League appearances in three years at Highbury before Alan Mullery signed him for Palace. He played in 119 consecutive League matches before injury halted his run. He was ever-present for another term before being given a free transfer. In January 1988, Cardiff City snapped him up and Wood went on to win a Welsh Cup-winners' medal.

	LEAGUE		*FA CUP*		*FL CUP*		*TOTAL*	
	App	*Gls*	*App*	*Gls*	*App*	*Gls*	*App*	*Gls*
1983-84	42	0	3	0	2	0	47	0
1984-85	42	0	2	0	4	0	48	0
1985-86	39	0	1	0	4	0	44	0
1986-87	42	0	2	0	4	0	48	0
1987-88	27	0	1	0	3	0	31	0
	192	0	9	0	17	0	218	0

BOBBY WOODRUFF

Inside-forward Bobby Woodruff was born at Highworth, Wiltshire, on 9 November 1940 and was a junior at Swindon Town, where he was coached by Bert Head. Woodruff became a member of Town's successful young side which gained promotion to the Second Division in 1962-3. He made 180 League appearances for Swindon before being transferred to First Division Wolves for £40,000 in March 1964. Woodruff became known for his long throw 'specials' and, after 59 appearances for Wolves, he was signed by Head in June 1966, for £35,000. He helped Palace to promotion to the First Division in 1968-9, but played only a few games in the top-flight before joining Cardiff City in November 1969 for £25,000. After five seasons and 141 games for Cardiff, Woodruff moved to Newport County. He appeared in 52 League games for them before finishing his career in Welsh League soccer. His son, Bobby junior, also played for Newport and Swindon.

	LEAGUE		*FA CUP*		*FL CUP*		*TOTAL*	
	App	*Gls*	*App*	*Gls*	*App*	*Gls*	*App*	*Gls*
1966-67	42	18	1	0	1	0	44	18
1967-68	42	18	1	0	1	0	44	18
1968-69	30	11	2	0	3/1	0	35/1	11
1969-70	9/2	1	0	0	4	0	13/2	1
	123/2	48	4	0	9/1	0	136/3	48

IAN WRIGHT

Together with Mark Bright, Ian Wright formed the lethal scoring spearhead which kept Crystal Palace in the promotion hunt in 1989. Wright's goals, coupled with a devastating burst of speed over the first five yards, made him a tremendous asset to a side seeking First Division football. He was born in Woolwich on 3 November 1963 and was signed by Steve Coppell from Greenwich Borough in August 1985. In his first season he made 32 League appearances (half of them as substitute), while learning his trade. He has been a regular ever since and a favourite with the Palace supporters. He has been watched by First Division club scouts and a transfer fee of £1 million has been mentioned. Wright was second-highest scorer for Palace in 1987-8, scoring a hat-trick in the final game against Birmingham. He was then voted Palace's Player of the Year in 1988-9.

	LEAGUE		*FA CUP*		*FL CUP*		*TOTAL*	
	App	*Gls*	*App*	*Gls*	*App*	*Gls*	*App*	*Gls*
1985-86	16/16	9	1	0	1	0	18/16	9
1986-87	37/1	9	1	0	4	1	42/1	10
1987-88	41	20	1	0	3	3	45	23
1988-89	41/1	24	1	0	2	1	44/1	25
	135/18	62	4	0	10	5	149/18	67

Rachid Harkouk (left) of Palace and Manny Andruszewski of Southampton.

Match to Remember 1 2 September 1905

Crystal Palace 3 Southampton Reserves 4

Roberts, Needham, Thompson *Soye 3, Hoskins*

A GOOD crowd turned out to see the first game of South London's newest club when Crystal Palace entertained Southampton Reserves in the Second Division of the Southern League. They paid 6d (3p) to enter the ground and one shilling (5p) to sit in the stand.

Manager John Robson had seen Palace win 3-0 in a United Counties League game at New Brompton the day before and, although the club had 16 players on their books, Robson retained that side to meet the Saints only 24 hours later.

Southampton were one of the leading clubs in the Southern League — their first team was continually challenging for honours — but it was Palace who took an early lead. The home side won the toss and elected to play with the wind in their favour. After only four minutes, Dick Roberts scored with a 'fast, low shot'.

Seven minutes later, Archie Needham beat three defenders before netting a superb goal and there was now no stopping Palace. George Thompson put them 3-0 ahead before Irishman Jimmy Soye pulled a goal back for Southampton before half-time.

After a frantic first 45 minutes, the pace slackened in the second half as the Palace players began to feel the effects of turning out on consecutive days. Dick Harker left the field with an injury and the rapidly-tiring ten-man Palace paid the price.

Soye scored his second goal of the game and then completed his hat-trick to draw Southampton level in a match they appeared to have lost before half-time. There were still ten minutes left on the referee's watch and even then the visitors were not finished. Bert Hoskins, who later managed Wolves, got through a flagging Palace defence and beat Bob Hewitson to score the winner. It turned out to be Palace's only Southern League defeat of the season. They recovered from this initial set-back to take the Second Division title at the very first attempt.

Crystal Palace: Hewitson; Walker, Edwards, Innerd, Birnie, Astley, Thompson, Harker, Watkins, Needham, Roberts.
Southampton Reserves: Burrows; Hartshorne, Weston, Huxton, Hogg, Metcalfe, Cohan, Brown, Soye, Locke, Hoskins.

Attendance: 3,000

Match to Remember 2 18 November 1905

Crystal Palace 7 Chelsea 1

Innerd 2, Watkins 3 (1 pen), Needham, Harker *O'Hara*

AFTER victories over Clapham and the Grenadier Guards, Palace were drawn against Chelsea in the FA Cup. Chelsea were in their first season of existence and had gone straight into the Football League, while Palace had not even been accepted to the top Southern League division. There was no doubt that South London fans relished the prospect of a giantkilling act.

In fact, the challenge facing Crystal Palace was not quite as great as it might first appear, for Chelsea had a Second Division match scheduled for the same day and the team which faced Palace in the Cup included several reserves. Palace, meanwhile, had Edwards on the injured list and his place was taken by Grant.

From the start, the home side attacked and Wilf Innerd soon put them ahead and then added another with what a local reporter described as 'a brilliant shot'. Walter Watkins made it 3-0 and then further extended Palace's lead from the penalty-spot, late in the first half.

The Palace players, now firmly in command of the match, could have been forgiven for thinking that the game was already theirs, but perhaps they thought back to the opening day of the season when Southampton Reserves had fought back from a seemingly hopeless position.

Palace came out for the second half, full of spirit and determination. Archie Needham worked his way through to score their fifth goal, Dick Harker netted the sixth and then Watkins completed his hat-trick for the seventh. With time running out, O'Hara scored a consolation effort for the visitors.

Palace went on to beat Luton in the next round before falling to Blackpool in a second replay at neutral Villa Park, after two 1-1 draws.

Crystal Palace: Hewitson; Walker, Grant, Innerd, Birnie, Astley, Wallace, Harker, Watkins, Needham, Roberts.
Chelsea: Byrne; Harris, Miller, Craigie, Wolff, J.T.Robertson, Tonner, J.A.S.Robertson, O'Hara, Donoghy, Goodwin.

Attendance: 3,500

Several Crystal Palace players also appeared in first-class cricket. Amongst them were L.Fishlock (Surrey and England), G.S.Watson (Kent and Leicestershire) A.G.Dawes (Northants) B.Harrison (Hampshire) and E.Presland (Essex).

Match to Remember 3 12 January 1907

Newcastle United 0 Crystal Palace 1

Astley

THROUGHOUT the history of Crystal Palace there have been some magnificent results in the FA Cup and this first-round tie against Newcastle United, one of the greatest sides of the Edwardian era, must rank as one of Palace's greatest ever feats.

The home side, who were to win the First Division Championship that season and had played in the previous two FA Cup Finals, were regarded as 100 per cent home bankers, particularly since they had not been beaten at St James' Park since 25 November 1905. They fielded many fine players, perhaps the best known of whom was England international, Colin Veitch.

It was no surprise that Palace, who, incidentally, fielded several players with northern connections, were on the defensive from the start. Gradually, though, they began to force their way back into the game with George Woodger and Dick Roberts — who was playing against his old club — prominent in the attack as Palace gained a toe-hold. The visitors even had the ball in the Newcastle net, only for the effort to be disallowed for offside.

Scottish international Jimmy Howie suffered a similar disappointment when he found the back of the Palace net and was ruled offside. Had that 'goal' been allowed, then perhaps the floodgates would have opened. Instead, the result probably turned on that moment. Just before half-time, Astley, who was having a relatively quiet time for Palace, broke away to score.

There was now the very real prospect of a Cup sensation and whatever was said in the Newcastle dressing-room at half-time did nothing to prevent it. Indeed, on three occasions Palace came close to increasing their lead, but each time goalkeeper Jimmy Lawrence saved the First Division leaders.

Palace had plenty of Cup action ahead of them that season. They beat Fulham and Brentford in replays before going down 4-0 at Everton in yet another replay.

Newcastle United: Lawrence; McCombie, McCracken, Gardner, Veitch, McWilliam, Rutherford, Howie, Speedie, Orr, Gosnell.
Crystal Palace: Hewitson; Needham, Edwards, Innerd, Ryan, Forster, Wallace, Harker, Astley, Woodger, Roberts.

Attendance: 28,000

Match to Remember 4 21 January 1909

Crystal Palace 4 Wolverhampton Wanderers 2

Lawrence, Garratt, Bauchop, Needham **(after extra-time)** *Hedley, Radford*

CRYSTAL Palace were gaining quite a reputation for Cup giantkilling and their 2-2 draw at Molineux brought the FA Cup holders, Wolverhampton Wanderers, back to the scene of Wolves' triumph over Newcastle United the previous April.

Palace fans were relishing the prospect of another Cup shock, but their hopes were dented within a minute of the kick-off when Wolves took the lead with a goal by Hedley. Palace came back and the amateur Billy Lawrence equalized in the ninth minute from a John Brearley pass.

Soon after, Jimmy Bauchop, the former Celtic and Norwich City inside-forward who had scored both Palace's goals in the first game at Wolves, got the ball in the net again but this time was ruled offside. When Charlie Ryan limped off just before the break, it seemed as though the fates were conspiring against Palace, but he soon returned and the Londoners were still level at half-time.

Palace had the wind in their favour after the interval, but it was still Wolves who went on the attack. Both sides suffered injuries, with Palace's Ted Collins having a spell on the touch-line. When Collins returned, however, he was soon on hand to lay on a chance which George Garratt put away. The Palace fans threw their hats in the air, for giantkilling dreams looked like coming true.

There were only eight minutes remaining when Hedley got through and created a chance for Radford and the Wolves man levelled the scores again and sent the game into extra-time.

As the extra period ticked away, both teams tired in what was becoming a Cup marathon. Then Palace found new energy as Bauchop restored their lead in the 103rd minute. Just before the final whistle, Archie Needham ran the length of the field to seal the tie with Palace's fourth goal.

Palace had one more moment of glory, a goalless draw with Burnley before the Lancashire club won the replay 9-0 at Turf Moor.

Crystal Palace: Johnson; Collins, Collyer, Innerd, Ryan, Brearley, Garratt, Lawrence, Bauchop, Woodger, Needham.
Wolverhampton Wanderers: Lunn; Jones, Collins, Shelton, Hunt, Bishop, Harrison, Blunt, Hedley, Radford, Pedley.

Attendance: 12,300

Match to Remember 5 28 August 1920

Merthyr Town 2 Crystal Palace 1

Walker, Chesser *Milligan*

FIFTEEN years after their formation as a professional club, Crystal Palace played their very first Football League game, in the newly-formed Third Division which mostly comprised clubs from the Southern League.

The fixture planners did not do Palace any favours for this opening game in the League, for the trip to South Wales took so long that the kick-off had to be rearranged for 5pm.

The Welsh club fielded their strongest team which was captained by Tommy Barber, who had played for Palace the previous season.

Both sides set out to attack but it was Merthyr who took the lead through their other new signing, Walker from Coventry, in the 25th minute. Soon after the restart, however, Palace drew level when John Conner's clever approach work ended with A.G.Milligan marking his debut by netting Crystal Palace's first-ever goal in the Football League.

The Palace forwards were having the best of the chances, but they could not put them away and it was Chesser who restored the Welshmen's lead with a goal that the Palace players claimed was offside.

That unsettled the Palace team but it was not a sign of things to come. Palace ended the season as the first champions of the new Third Division — to be renamed the Third Division South the following season when the Northern section was formed.

Merthyr Town: Lindon; Copeland, Clarke, Brown, Jennings, Crowe, Williams, Barber, Walker, Chesser, Nicholas.
Crystal Palace: Alderson; Little, Rhodes, McCracken, Jones, Feebury, Bateman, Conner, Smith, Milligan, Whibley.

Attendance: 15,000

Albert Feebury, who joined Palace from Coventry City in 1914, was one of the players whose careers spanned the Southern League and the Football League.

Match to Remember 6 27 August 1921

Crystal Palace 4 Nottingham Forest 1

Jones, Conner, Smith, Whibley *Tinsley*

THE summer of 1921 was one of great anticipation for Crystal Palace players, officials and supporters alike as they looked forward to the club's first season in the Second Division. Palace's first game in their new surroundings was against Nottingham Forest, who had finished in 18th position the previous season.

On a fine afternoon, Palace skipper Ted Smith won the toss and chose to defend the Station end. It was not long before Palace opened their account in Division Two, when the balding head of Tom Jones rose above the Forest defence to head his side into the lead. Palace's joy was short-lived, however, for Tinsley soon put Forest back on level terms.

The Palace forwards kept Sam Hardy, the former England goalkeeper, busy and it was John Conner who restored the Londoners' lead before half-time.

In the second half Smith seemed to kick the ball from Hardy's grasp, but the referee allowed the goal and then John Whibley made a fine run to beat the goalkeeper for the fourth goal. Before the end Ernie Rhodes, the Palace left-back, burst the ball when taking a kick.

Forest beat Palace in the return match 2-1 at the City Ground and went on to regain their First Division place as champions. Palace, meanwhile, finished 14th as they consolidated their position as a Football League club.

Crystal Palace: Alderson; Little, Rhodes, McCracken, Jones, Feebury, Bateman, Conner, Smith, Menlove, Whibley.
Nottingham Forest: Hardy; Bulling, Jones, Bolton, F.Parker, Armstrong, Harold, Spavin, R.Parker, Tinsley, Burton.

Attendance: 20,000

John Conner restored Palace's lead before half-time.

Match to Remember 7 7 January 1922

Everton 0 Crystal Palace 6

Whibley, Menlove 2, Conner 2, Wood

ALTHOUGH Everton were not enjoying one of their better seasons — they were 15th in Division One at the time — few people could have imagined that Second Division Crystal Palace would achieve such a remarkable result when the sides were drawn together in the first round of the FA Cup.

Rain had fallen heavily on the Friday before the match and again on the Saturday morning, but the sun was shining brightly as the brass band played prior to the teams emerging from the dressing-rooms.

Everton had been right down in the relegation zone earlier that season, but picked up seven points out of eight over the Christmas period and looked to be on something of a run. Palace, meanwhile, were struggling in their first season in the Second Division. Indeed, the Everton programme editor remarked in his notes: 'The Blues have a fairly easy task'.

A large crowd gave the teams a tremendous reception and reserved a special welcome for Everton goalkeeper Ferns, who had just passed a fitness test. He was soon in action but could do nothing to prevent John Whibley giving Palace an early lead.

In the 24th minute, Bert Menlove added the second goal with a shot in the corner of the net. Everton, who played a close-passing game, never threatened and half-time arrived with Palace still commanding a 2-0 lead.

When the teams came out for the second half, someone in the crowd threw an orange towards Palace goalkeeper Jack Alderson, who obliged by peeling the fruit and taking a few bites as his colleagues pressed home their advantage at the other end of the field.

John Conner scored their third goal with a hooked shot over his shoulder and in the 73rd minute Menlove added a fourth. Wood got the fifth and, with the minutes ticking away, Conner scored the sixth. Once again, Crystal Palace had achieved an historic Cup shock.

Everton: Ferns; MacDonald, Livingstone, Brown, Fleetwood, Peacock, Chedgzoy, Fazackerley, Irvine, Wall, Harrison.
Crystal Palace: Alderson; Little, Rhodes, McCracken, Jones, Feebury, Bateman, Conner, Menlove, Wood, Whibley.

Attendance: 41,000

Oldest and Youngest: Phil Hoadley is Crystal Palace's youngest-ever Football League debutant. Hoadley was 16 when he made his first appearance on 27 April 1968. The oldest player to make his League debut for Palace is Wally Betteridge, who was 41 when he made his bow on 27 October 1928.

Match to Remember 8 30 January 1926

Crystal Palace 2 Chelsea 1

Cherrett, Hawkins *Thain*

THE highlight of Crystal Palace's 1925-6 season was their FA Cup run. Despite being relegated from Division Two at the end of the previous season, Palace were still exempt until the third round of the competition and after beating Northampton in a replay — Palace were 3-0 down after 75 minutes of the first game — they were given a home tie against Chelsea, who were chasing promotion to Division One.

The prospect of a Cup clash between the South London clubs had football fans buzzing and Palace, in particular, relished their visit. Percy Cherrett, who scored two goals in each of the games against Northampton, was playing and Palace fancied their chances of going through to the fifth round.

Selhurst Park had been opened only 18 months earlier and the attendance record for the new ground stood at 25,000, set on Boxing Day 1924 for the visit of Portsmouth. It was obvious that this was now going to be far exceeded and with the terraces almost full the fans still trooped in. Indeed, the 41,000 attendance was to stand as a Selhurst Park record for over 40 years.

Once the game got underway, the spectators were not disappointed. Cherrett soon brought the Palace fans to their toes when his shot hit a goal-post. Then, with half-time approaching, he put Palace ahead with a fierce shot. At the other end, Billy Callender was in good form and at the half-time whistle, Palace supporters gave the players a great ovation.

Early second-half pressure by Chelsea came to nothing before Alf Hawkins added a second goal for the home side. Thain pulled one back for Chelsea but it was too late to save the game. Palace fell to Manchester City at Maine Road in the fifth round.

Crystal Palace: Callender; Little, Cross, McCracken, Coyle, Greener, Harry, Blakemore, Cherrett, Hawkins, Clarke.
Chelsea: McKenna: Smith, Barrett, Priestley, Rodger, Ferguson, Crawford, Thain, Turnbull, Wilding, McNeil.

Attendance: 41,000

At least two well-known figures in the entertainment world were on Crystal Palace's books. John Salthouse, of ITV's The Bill, *was a junior at Selhurst Park between 1968 and 1970 before injury forced his retirement. Commentator Stuart Hall, best-known for BBC TV's* It's A Knockout *played for Palace Reserves in 1953.*

Match to Remember 9 20 February 1926

Manchester City 11 Crystal Palace 4

Austin (pen), Johnson, Roberts 5, Browell 3, Hicks *Cherrett 2, Clarke, McCracken*

OVER 50,000 people turned up to see a Manchester City side that was scoring plenty of goals this season — the first in which the present-day offside law was in use. As defenders came to terms with the new law — the number of players needed between a forward and the goal was reduced from three to two — goals rained in all over the country and this fifth-round FA Cup tie was no exception.

City had the best possible start when they were awarded a penalty after only three minutes. Austin netted the spot-kick and then Johnson, Roberts and Browell (2) made the score 5-0. The visitors suffered even further when Blakemore was injured and had to leave the field. Roberts added two more goals against ten-man Palace before half-time.

Soon after the restart, Percy Cherrett scored from Harry's cross, only for Browell to complete his hat-trick. Cherrett joined in with another goal, then George Clarke added his name to the score-sheet.

When McCracken reduced the arrears, Palace hoped that their earlier comeback at Northampton could be repeated, but time began to run out and Palace heads dropped. As Roberts added the ninth and tenth goals, his personal tally went up to five. Then, with time nearly up, Hicks, the last City forward to score, made it 11.

Manchester City: Goodchild; Cookson, McCloy, Coupland, Cowan, Pringle, Austin, Browell, Roberts, Johnson, Hicks.
Crystal Palace: Callender; Little, Cross, McCracken, Coyle, Greener, Harry, Blakemore, Cherrett, Hawkins, Clarke.

Attendance: 51,630

Alan Devonshire began as a junior with Crystal Palace, for whom his father, Les, had played League soccer in the early 1950s. Palace released Alan, who joined Southall before signing for West Ham United in October 1976. He went on to make over 300 Football League appearances for the Hammers and was capped eight times by England.

Match to Remember 10 — 4 October 1930

Crystal Palace 7 Exeter City 2

Simpson 6, Butler — *Varco, Greener (og)*

AFTER Palace had scored 20 goals in their first eight games of the season, including a 7-1 win over Newport in their previous home game, a good crowd turned up at Selhurst Park hungry for more. Of course, they had to take into account the fact that in their most recent game, Palace had lost 6-2 at Gillingham.

On this occasion, though, it was almost all Palace and for one man in particular, the visit of Exeter for this Third Division South match was a landmark. Peter Simpson went into the record books by scoring six goals in a game, the only time that feat has been achieved by a Palace player.

Yet the star player was outside-right Albert Harry, who provided the passes and crosses for all seven Palace goals. The first came in the ninth minute when Harry crossed for Simpson to head home. The centre-forward completed a first-half hat-trick and Exeter got a goal from Varco, who Palace claimed was offside.

Exeter applied more pressure at the start of the second half and gave Billy Callender plenty to do in the early stages. Then Simpson went on the rampage again and Butler netted Palace's seventh goal. Palace even scored Exeter's second when Greener deflected a Doncaster cross past Callender.

Crystal Palace: Callender; Crilly, Charlton, Rivers, Wilde, Greener, Harry, Havelock, Simpson, Butler, G.Clarke.
Exeter City: Davies; Baugh, Miller, R.Clarke, Ditchburn, Barber, Armfield, Purcell, Varco, Houghton, Doncaster.

Attendance: 12,805

In July 1979, Steve Mackenzie was transferred from Crystal Palace to Manchester City for £250,000, without having made a League appearance for Palace. Mackenzie scored a spectacular goal for City against Spurs in the 1981 FA Cup Final before being sold to West Brom for £650,000 in July that year. Selhurst Park eventually became his home ground after he joined Charlton Athletic in June 1987.

Maurice Edelston scores one of his goals against Palace.

Match to Remember 11 4 September 1946

Reading 10 Crystal Palace 2

Deverall 2, Barney, Edelston 3, McPhee 4 — *Waldron, Reece*

A CROWD of over 8,000 turned up to see Reading meet Crystal Palace on only the second Saturday since the Football League got back to normal after the competition had been suspended in 1939.

Palace had lost their opening game 3-1 at Mansfield and manager George Irwin made three changes for the visit to his former club, giving Felton his debut at right-back. As it turned out, it was Felton's only League game for Palace.

It was a windy evening and within 15 minutes, Reading were 3-0 ahead through Deverall, Barney and Edelston. Before half-time, though, Palace had pulled back to 3-2 with goals from Ernie Waldron and Tom Reece.

The second half was only two minutes old when Edelston scored from the penalty-spot after McPhee had been brought down. McPhee made it 5-2 and Deverall netted Reading's sixth. McPhee completed his hat-trick to take Reading's lead to 8-2 and then Edelston completed his treble with the ninth goal. McPhee's fourth goal took Reading into double-figures and left Palace to contemplate their worst-ever defeat in a Football League game.

Irwin responded to the defeat by introducing five new players for the next game, which Palace won 2-1 at home to Bristol Rovers. They went on to finish 18th in the Third Division South.

Reading: Groves; Glidden, Gulliver, McKenna, Ratcliffe, Young, Chitty, Edelston, McPhee, Barney, Deverall.
Crystal Palace: Graham; Felton, Dawes, J.Lewis, Bassett, Hudgell, Kurz, Reece, Waldron, Burrell, Girling.

Attendance: 8,165

Match to Remember 12 10 October 1959

Crystal Palace 9 Barrow 0

Colfar 2, Gavin, Summersby 4 (1 pen), Byrne 2

ALTHOUGH Palace had beaten Watford 8-1 in late September, the fact that they followed up with four consecutive defeats surely meant that nobody who went to Selhurst Park for this Fourth Division match could have imagined that they were about to witness their club's biggest-ever League victory.

Even when Ray Colfar opened the scoring midway through the first half, there was no immediate hint of what was to come. Then John Gavin netted direct from a corner and Roy Summersby added two more goals in the 42nd and 44th minutes.

The second half was all one-way. Colfar added the fifth goal and Summersby completed his hat-trick for Palace's sixth. Then Cahill handled and Summersby made it 7-0 from the penalty-spot. Byrne had a goal disallowed before adding the eighth in the 82nd minute. In the last seconds, Johnny Byrne made it 9-0. The following Wednesday, Palace won 11-1 in a friendly against a Caribbean XI.

Crystal Palace: Rouse; Long, Noakes, Truett, Evans, McNichol, Gavin, Summersby, Sexton, Byrne, Colfar.
Barrow: Heys; Lindores, Cahill, O'Connor, Robinson, McNab, Kerr, Murdoch, Robertson, Bannan, Kemp.

Attendance: 9,566

Selhurst Park in the the late 1950s, showing the recently installed floodlights.

Johnny McNichol (right) and Francisco Gento exchange pennants before the kick-off.

Match to Remember 13 — 18 April 1962

Crystal Palace 3 Real Madrid 4

Heckman, Smillie, Long — *Di Stefano, Gento, Puskas, Sanchis*

THIS prestige friendly match was something of a coup by Crystal Palace, as it was the first visit to London by the European Cup-holders. Palace guaranteed their visitors £10,000, which resulted in increased admission charges. The fans were happy to pay and nearly 25,000 of them turned up, despite heavy rain.

The match was to mark the switching-on of the new floodlights at Selhurst Park. Real Madrid fielded the same side that had beaten Standard Liège in the European Cup semi-final the previous week, whilst Palace had Johnny Byrne guesting after his record transfer to West Ham the previous month.

After six minutes, Di Stefano headed Real into the lead from a Puskas pass. Gento, the flying left winger, soon added a second, but Palace retaliated with a goal from Heckman after a good move between Byrne and Ronnie Brett. Three minutes later, Puskas beat Rouse with a 25-yard free-kick and Sanchis increased the lead to 4-1 by half-time.

The second half saw Bill Glazier in goal for Palace and he was to remain undefeated, whilst Andy Smillie scored for Palace in the 53rd minute. This was followed by Terry Long's magnificent 30-yard shot which hit the net. Palace could not find the equalizing goal, but the fans still went home happy after a feast of good football.

Crystal Palace: Rouse(Glazier); McNichol, Little, Long, Wood, Petchey, Brett, Summersby, Byrne, Smillie, Heckman(Lewis).
Real Madrid: Araquistain(Vicente); Casao, Miera, Sanchis(Ruiz), Santa-Maria(Marquitos), Pachin, Tejada, Del Sol(Pepillo), Di Stefano, Puskas, Gento.

Attendance: 24,740

Match to Remember 14 19 April 1969

Crystal Palace 3 Fulham 2

Kember, Lazarus, C.Jackson *Dear, Large*

CRYSTAL Palace arrived at this last home game of the season knowing that they still needed one point to be assured of First Division football for the first time in the club's history.

Palace were unbeaten in the League since January — a run of 14 games — whilst Fulham were bottom of the table and already doomed to relegation. The theory was that the Cottagers had nothing left to play for, yet the Palace crowd were shocked after only six minutes when Dear put the visitors ahead.

Palace fought back, but could not penetrate a Fulham rearguard which included Johnny Byrne at left-half. Indeed, in the 35th minute, Large made it 2-0 to Fulham. At half-time Bert Head used all his managerial experience to calm the players' nerves. He apparently succeeded, for Palace settled down and pulled a goal back through Steve Kember.

Kember's goal lifted the team's spirits and on the hour, Mark Lazarus became a Selhurst hero when he equalized. The crowd was now in full voice and Cliff Jackson wrapped the game up with the winning goal four minutes later. For the first time in their 64-year history, Crystal Palace were about to step into the First Division.

Crystal Palace: J.Jackson; Sewell, Loughlan, Payne, McCormick, Hoy, Lazarus, Kember, C.Jackson, A.Taylor, C.Taylor.
Fulham: McClelland; Moreline, Callaghan, Horne, Roberts, Byrne, Jones, Lloyd, Dear, Large, Conway.

Attendance: 36,126

Palace goalkeeper John Jackson, seen here in typically brave action, was one of the heroes as the Selhurst club clinched First Division football for the first time in their history.

Palace at the start of 1969-70. Mel Blyth (back row, second left) and Gerry Queen (front row, extreme left) scored Palace's goals in the club's first-ever game in Division One.

Match to Remember 15 — 9 August 1969

Crystal Palace 2 Manchester United 2

Blyth, Queen — *Charlton, Morgan*

THIS was Crystal Palace's first game in the First Division and they were rewarded with a visit from the best-supported club in the Football League. Manchester United's appearance at Selhurst Park took the attendance to a new record.

A warm, sunny day greeted the sides and it took Palace only 11 minutes to open their account in Division One. The honour went to Mel Blyth, whose header from a corner found the net. In the 24th minute, Bobby Charlton equalized for United but Palace regained the lead five minutes before half-time, Gerry Queen, Palace's new signing from Kilmarnock, marking his debut with a goal.

The second half saw star-studded United put Palace under pressure and it was not long before they levelled the scores again, this time through Willie Morgan, who chalked up his first goal of the season.

Crystal Palace: J.Jackson; Sewell, Loughlan, Hoy, McCormick, Hynd, Lazarus(A.Taylor), Kember, C.Jackson, Queen, Blyth.
Manchester United: Rimmer; Dunne, Burns, Crerand, Foulkes, Sadler, Morgan, Kidd, Charlton, Law, Best.

Attendance: 48,610

Match to Remember 16 — 9 November 1970

Arsenal 0 Crystal Palace 2

Queen, Tambling (pen)

CRYSTAL Palace did not enjoy a particularly memorable season in 1970-71 — they finished 18th in the First Division — but, for many fans, there was one enduring memory. It was this fourth-round Football League Cup replay against an Arsenal team who were on their way to a remarkable double of Football League Championship and FA Cup success.

Palace's earlier League Cup games — a replay win over Rochdale and victory over Lincoln City — had hardly prepared them for this hurdle. Nevertheless, they fought out a goalless draw with Arsenal in front of a 40,451 crowd at Selhurst Park and now braved the white-hot atmosphere of Highbury.

The Gunners were in second place in Division One and Palace were seventh, yet it was Palace who took the lead against the run of play, Gerry Queen beating Bob Wilson with a fine effort.

In the second half, Arsenal did everything but score and eventually Palace drew further away and sealed the game with a Bobby Tambling penalty. In the next round Palace lost 4-2 at Old Trafford but, inevitably, nothing could take away the glory of this win over all-powerful Arsenal. Indeed, it was the Gunners' only defeat of the season.

Arsenal: Wilson; Rice, McNab, Kelly, McLintock, Roberts, Armstrong, Storey, Radford, Kennedy, Graham.
Crystal Palace: Jackson; Sewell(Loughlan), Wall, Payne, McCormick, Hoadley, Taylor, Scott, Queen, Birchenhall, Tambling.

Attendance: 45,026

Tony Taylor gave a good account of himself as Palace enjoyed one of their few golden moments in 1970-71

Match to Remember 17 16 December 1972

Crystal Palace 5 Manchester United 0

Mulligan 2, Rogers 2, Whittle

IN any other era, a 5-0 thrashing of Manchester United would be considered a magnificent performance — and so perhaps was this Palace feat, just before Christmas 1972. Alas, their victory was shaded by the fact that United were bottom of the First Division and Palace were already in desperate relegation trouble.

Palace manager Bert Head made two new signings — Don Rogers from his old club, Swindon, and Alan Whittle from Everton — but United were once again having trouble with George Best, who was missing from their team.

Television cameras were at Selhurst Park to record what proved to be Palace's best performance of the season. It appeared that there was only one team in the game as Palace attacked time and time again.

Paddy Mulligan came forward to score the first goal in the ninth minute and then repeated his effort in the 42nd minute with a shot that left Stepney helpless. The second period showed no change. From the start Rogers added the third goal, followed by one from Whittle. Rogers got his second and the team's fifth.

United's manager, Frank O'Farrell, was sacked on the following Monday morning and at the end of the season, Palace dropped out of Division One. United followed them 12 months later.

Crystal Palace: Jackson; Mulligan, Taylor, Philip, Bell, Blyth, Hughes, Payne, Whittle, Cooke, Rogers.
Manchester United: Stepney; O'Neill, Dunne(Law), Young, Sadler, Buchan, Morgan, MacDougall, Kidd, Davies, Storey-Moore.

Attendance: 38,897

David Payne enjoyed a fine game as Palace hammered Manchester United.

Ian Evans, one of the Palace stars who helped steer the Third Division side into an FA Cup semi-final.

Match to Remember 18 — 6 March 1976

Sunderland 0 Crystal Palace 1

Whittle

AFTER a brilliant start to the season — seven wins and a draw in their first eight League games — Palace began to falter at Christmas, but then embarked on a remarkable FA Cup marathon which saw them reach the semi-final stage, playing away at every stage from the third round.

They had travelled to Scarborough, Leeds, Chelsea and now Roker Park. Sunderland were in third position in the Second Division and unbeaten at home, but Palace feared no one.

A capacity crowd saw an exciting, but goalless, first half in this quarter-final tie. The second half produced one golden moment and it belonged to Alan Whittle. A long clearance by Paul Hammond found Peter Taylor, who beat two defenders to cross for Whittle. The Palace star crashed the ball into the net for only his second goal of the season.

His effort gave Palace a share of soccer history as only the fourth Third Division side to play in an FA Cup semi-final. Southampton ended their Wembley dream at Stamford Bridge.

Sunderland: Montgomery; Malone, Bolton, Towers, Clarke, Moncur, Kerr, Longhorn, Holden, Robson, Finney.
Crystal Palace: Hammond; Wall, Cannon, Holder, Jeffries, Evans, M.Hinshelwood, Chatterton, Whittle, Swindlehurst, Taylor.

Attendance: 50,800

Match to Remember 19 11 May 1979

Crystal Palace 2 Burnley 0

Walsh, Swindlehurst

AFTER a great season, Palace found the last match, a previously postponed game against mid-table Burnley, to be one of the most important games in the history of the club. The issue was quite clear — a win for the championship or a draw for promotion as runners-up.

Prior to this encounter, nobody had ever thought that Palace would see several thousand fans locked out of Selhurst Park and the gates closed an hour before kick-off.

The tension was electric on a warm, sunny evening as the home side attacked from the start. Jerry Murphy and Paul Hinshelwood had shots blocked, while Jim Cannon went close, his effort hitting the woodwork.

The young players, whom manager Terry Venables had groomed into a fine defensive team, now chose to go for the goal that would give them the title and their enterprise was rewarded when Vince Hilaire's fine cross was met by Ian Walsh. Dave Swindlehurst scored a second goal and Palace's delight was complete — the championship of Division Two, their first major honour since 1921.

Crystal Palace: Burridge; Hinshelwood, Sansom, Kember, Cannon, Gilbert, Nicholas, Murphy, Swindlehurst, Walsh, Hilaire.
Burnley: Stevenson; Scott, Brennan, Noble, Thomson, Rodaway, Hall, Ingram, Morley, Kindon, James.

Attendance: 51,482

Vince Hilaire, whose fine cross laid on a goal for Ian Walsh.

Eric Gates beats John Burridge for Ipswich's only goal.

Match to Remember 20 29 September 1979

Crystal Palace 4 Ipswich Town 1

Swindlehurst, Hinshelwood, Francis (pen), Cannon — *McCall*

THIS was a match which marked a special occasion — Palace sitting atop the First Division. It was too early in the season to think about winning the League Championship, but the young Venables side was burdened with the tag of 'The Team of the 1980s'.

Prior to this game, Palace were in second place, behind Nottingham Forest on goal-average. Their opponents were Bobby Robson's entertaining Ipswich side and the near-30,000 crowd saw a superb display of attacking football on a pleasant autumn day.

Palace were rewarded with the first goal in the 17th minute, when Dave Swindlehurst cracked home Vince Hilaire's cross. On the half-hour, a header from Paul Hinshelwood increased their lead. The third goal came when Swindlehurst was brought down and Gerry Francis scored from a twice-taken penalty. With only a minute to the interval, Ipswich pulled a goal back through McCall.

In the second half, Palace created a fourth goal, winning the ball from an Ipswich corner and setting up a beautiful move which ended with Jim Cannon, who had run 80 yards, volleying home.

Crystal Palace: Burridge; Hinshelwood, Sansom, Nicholas, Cannon, Gilbert, Murphy, Francis, Swindlehurst, Flanagan, Hilaire.
Ipswich Town: Cooper; Burley, Mills(Osborne), Thijssen, Osman, Butcher, Wark, Muhren, Mariner, Gates, McCall.

Referee: T.Glasson (Salisbury) *Attendance: 29,885*

Match to Remember 21 3 June 1989

Crystal Palace 3 Blackburn Rovers 0

Wright 2, Madden (pen)

PALACE returned to the First Division after eight years, their final victory coming amid scenes of utter jubilation at Selhurst Park. Trailing 3-1 from the first leg of the play-off final, they needed at least a two-goal margin and a clean sheet if they were to go into the top flight.

In the 16th minute, Palace found the first of those goals, the result of a flowing move from one end of the pitch to the other. It ended with Ian Wright poking home Pardew's low cross. Indeed, the way the ball was played to Wright summed up what Palace must do to win, for earlier high balls pumped up to Wright and Bright had instead been snapped up by Hendry and Mail in Blackburn's defence.

One minute into the second half Palace achieved their two-goal objective. McGoldrick ran straight at a nervous defence and when Mail tripped him, referee George Courtney pointed to the penalty-spot. Up stepped David Madden to overcome the electric atmosphere and send Gennoe the wrong way.

Palace now needed to hold that lead through extra-time and in the 117th minute they went one better. With thousands of Palace supporters now right up to the touch-lines, Eddie McGoldrick got over a cross from the right flank. This time there were no Blackburn heads to deny Wright, whose glancing header ignited the pent-up emotions of a crowd living on a knife's edge. The Palace fans swarmed on to the pitch to celebrate the fact that justice had been done. Palace, who had finished third in the Second Division, had gained their rightful reward over fifth-placed Blackburn.

The Lancashire club had gone to Selhurst to defend but, when they needed to push forward after conceding two vital goals, they gave Palace's rearguard a thorough examination. In the end it was the home side's great organization which complemented Wright's cutting edge to send them up.

Crystal Palace: Suckling; Pemberton, Burke, Madden, Hopkins, O'Reilly, McGoldrick, Pardew, Bright, Wright, Barber.
Blackburn Rovers: Gennoe; Atkins, Sulley, Reid, Hendry, Mail, Gayle(Ainscow), Millar, Miller(Curry), Garner, Sellars.

Referee: G.Courtney (Spennymoor) *Attendance: 30,000*

Opposite: Ian Wright (Palace) and David Mail (Blackburn) tussle for the ball in the play-off second leg.

Palace in the Football League 1920-21 to 1988-89

	P	W	D	L	F	A	Pts	Pos
DIVISION THREE								
1920-21	42	24	11	7	70	34	59	1st
DIVISION TWO								
1921-22	42	13	13	16	45	51	39	14th
1922-23	42	13	11	18	54	62	37	16th
1923-24	42	13	13	16	53	65	39	15th
1924-25	42	12	10	20	38	54	34	21st
DIVISION THREE SOUTH								
1925-26	42	19	3	20	75	79	41	13th
1926-27	42	18	9	15	84	81	45	6th
1927-28	42	18	12	12	79	72	48	5th
1928-29	42	23	8	11	81	67	54	2nd
1929-30	42	17	12	13	81	74	46	9th
1930-31	42	22	7	13	107	71	51	2nd
1931-32	42	20	11	11	74	63	51	4th
1932-33	42	19	8	15	78	64	46	5th
1933-34	42	16	9	17	71	67	41	12th
1934-35	42	19	10	13	86	64	48	5th
1935-36	42	22	5	15	96	74	49	6th
1936-37	42	13	12	17	62	61	38	14th
1937-38	42	18	12	12	67	47	48	7th
1938-39	42	20	12	10	71	52	52	2nd
1939-46			War years					
1946-47	42	13	11	18	49	62	37	18th
1947-48	42	13	13	16	49	49	39	13th
1948-49	42	8	11	23	38	76	27	22nd
1949-50	42	15	14	13	55	54	44	7th
1950-51	46	8	11	27	33	84	27	24th
1951-52	46	15	9	22	61	80	39	19th
1952-53	46	15	13	18	66	82	43	13th
1953-54	46	14	12	20	60	86	40	22nd
1954-55	46	11	16	19	52	80	38	20th
1955-56	46	12	10	24	54	83	34	23rd
1956-57	46	11	18	17	62	75	40	20th
1957-58	46	15	13	18	70	72	43	14th
DIVISION FOUR								
1958-59	46	20	12	14	90	71	52	7th
1959-60	46	19	12	15	84	64	50	8th
1960-61	46	29	6	11	110	69	64	2nd
DIVISION THREE								
1961-62	46	14	14	18	83	80	42	15th
1962-63	46	17	13	16	68	58	47	11th
1963-64	46	23	14	9	73	51	60	2nd
DIVISION TWO								
1964-65	42	16	13	13	55	51	45	7th
1965-66	42	14	13	15	47	52	41	11th
1966-67	42	19	10	13	61	55	48	7th
1967-68	42	14	11	17	56	56	39	11th
1968-69	42	22	12	8	70	47	56	2nd
DIVISION ONE								
1969-70	42	6	5	21	34	68	27	20th
1970-71	42	12	11	19	39	57	35	18th
1971-72	42	8	13	21	39	65	29	20th
1972-73	42	9	12	21	41	58	30	21st
DIVISION TWO								
1973-74	42	11	12	19	43	56	34	20th
DIVISION THREE								
1974-75	46	18	15	13	66	57	51	5th
1975-76	46	18	17	11	61	46	53	5th
1976-77	46	23	13	10	68	40	59	3rd
DIVISION TWO								
1977-78	42	13	15	14	50	47	41	9th
1978-79	42	19	19	4	51	24	47	1st
DIVISION ONE								
1979-80	42	12	16	14	41	50	40	13th
1980-81	42	6	7	29	47	83	19	22nd
DIVISION TWO								
1981-82	42	13	9	20	34	45	48	15th
1982-83	42	12	12	18	43	52	48	15th
1983-84	42	12	11	19	42	52	47	18th
1984-85	42	12	12	18	46	65	48	15th
1985-86	42	19	9	14	57	52	66	5th
1986-87	42	19	5	18	51	53	62	6th
1987-88	44	22	9	13	86	59	75	6th
1988-89	46	23	12	11	71	49	81	3rd

SUMMARY

SNS	P	W	D	L	F	A	Pts
DIVISION ONE							
6	252	53	74	125	241	381	180
DIVISION TWO							
20	846	311	231	304	1053	1047	985
DIVISION THREE							
7	318	137	97	84	489	366	371
DIVISION THREE SOUTH							
26	1124	414	281	429	1761	1819	1109
DIVISION FOUR							
3	138	68	30	40	284	204	166
62	2678	983	713	982	3828	3817	2811

1905-06

Manager: J.R.Robson

1	Sep	2	(h)	Southampton Res	L 3-4	Roberts, Needham, Thompson	3,000
2		16	(a)	Swindon Res	W 2-1	Birnie, Harker	
3		18	(a)	West Ham U Res	D 0-0		
4		23	(h)	Leyton	D 0-0		5,000
5	Oct	14	(h)	Fulham Res	W 5-0	Wallace, Watkins 2, Needham 2	1,500
6		21	(a)	Southern U	W 1-0	Watkins	
7	Nov	4	(h)	Grays U	W 9-1	Birnie, Harker 2, Watkins 2, Needham, Astley, Roberts, Walker	
8		25	(a)	Watford Res	W 3-1	Roberts 2, Ross	
9	Dec	13	(h)	Reading Res	W 3-0	Harker, Watkins, Roberts	3,000
10		23	(h)	Swindon Res	W 3-0	Astley, Ross 2	
11		26	(h)	Portsmouth Res	W 1-0	Needham	2,000
12	Jan	6	(a)	Wycombe W	W 4-1	Thompson, Needham, Wallace 2	
13		20	(h)	St Leonards	W 3-1	Woodger 2, Thompson	3,000
14		27	(a)	Grays U	W 3-0	Walker 2, Needham	
15	Feb	10	(h)	West Ham Res	W 3-1	Woodger 2, Needham	2,000
16		21	(a)	St Leonards	W 3-0	Needham 2, Wallace	
17		28	(h)	Southern U	W 4-0	Needham 2, Woodger, Opp own-goal	
18	Mar	3	(h)	Watford Res	W 4-0	Roberts, Needham 2, Woodger	4,000
19		10	(a)	Southampton Res	W 2-0	Thompson, Needham	
20		24	(a)	Reading Res	W 1-0	Needham	
21	Apr	7	(a)	Leyton	W 2-1	Wallace, Needham	
22		13	(a)	Portsmouth Res	D 1-1	Watkins	7,000
23		14	(h)	Wycombe W	W 4-0	Woodger 2, Moody, Needham	
24		17	(a)	Fulham Res	D 2-2	Needham, Harker	5,000

FINAL LEAGUE POSITION: 1st in Southern League, Division Two.

Appearances
Goals

FA Cup

1Q	Oct	7	(h)	Clapham	W 7-0	Watkins 3 (2 pens), Innerd, Astley, Roberts, Harker	1,500
2Q		26	(a)	Grenadier Gds	W 3-0	Harker, Wallace, Astley	1,200
3Q	Nov	18	(h)	Chelsea	W 7-1	Watkins 3, Innerd 2, Harker, Needham	3,000
4Q	Dec	9	(h)	Luton T	W 1-0	Harker	5,000
1	Jan	15	(a)	Blackpool	D 1-1	Harker	2,500
R		19	(h)	Blackpool	D 1-1	Birnie	4,000
2R		22	(n†)	Blackpool	L 0-1		5,000

†Played at Villa Park, Birmingham.

Appearances
Goals

1906-07

Manager: J.R.Robson

1	Sep	1	(h)	Northampton T	W 3-0	Woodger 2, Harker	7,000
2		8	(a)	Queen's Park R	L 0-1		7,900
3		15	(h)	Fulham	L 0-3		8,000
4		19	(h)	Reading	W 4-1	Harker, Woodger, Roberts, Hodgkinson	
5		22	(a)	Southampton	D 1-1	Edwards (pen)	4,500
6		29	(h)	West Ham U	D 1-1	Wallace	10,000
7	Oct	6	(a)	Tottenham H	L 0-3		18,000
8		13	(h)	Swindon T	W 3-2	Wallace 3	7,000
9		20	(a)	Norwich C	L 2-4	Edwards (pen), Woodger	9,000
10		27	(h)	Luton T	L 0-1		8,000
11	Nov	3	(a)	Bristol R	D 1-1	Wallace	5,000
12		10	(a)	Brentford	L 0-2		6,000
13		17	(h)	Millwall	W 3-0	Roberts, Wallace, Innerd	6,000
14		24	(a)	Leyton	W 4-0	Astley 2, Wallace, Harker	
15	Dec	1	(h)	Portsmouth	W 1-0	Woodger	7,500
16		15	(h)	Plymouth	L 0-2		
17		22	(a)	Brighton & HA	L 1-2	Wallace	5,000
18		26	(a)	Watford	L 0-2		3,000
19		29	(a)	Northampton T	L 1-2	Roberts	3,000
20	Jan	5	(h)	Queen's Park R	W 5-1	Astley 4, Harker	6,000
21		19	(a)	Fulham	L 1-2	Astley	15,000
22		26	(h)	Southampton	D 1-1	Roberts	6,500
23	Feb	9	(h)	Tottenham H	L 0-1		8,000
24		16	(a)	Swindon T	L 1-2	Astley	5,000
25	Mar	2	(a)	Luton T	L 1-2	Astley	8,000
26		16	(h)	Brentford	L 0-3		7,000
27		23	(a)	Millwall	L 0-2		10,000
28		25	(a)	West Ham U	D 1-1	Harker	
29		29	(a)	Reading	D 1-1	Weston	10,000
30		30	(h)	Leyton	W 1-0	Woodger	7,000
31	Apr	1	(h)	Watford	L 1-3	Roberts (pen)	10,000
32		6	(a)	Portsmouth	L 0-6		7,000
33		13	(h)	New Brompton	L 1-3	Edwards (pen)	5,500
34		17	(h)	Bristol R	D 3-3	Astley, Roberts, Woodger	2,000
35		20	(a)	Plymouth A	D 0-0		
36		24	(h)	Norwich C	L 0-1		2,000
37		27	(h)	Brighton & HA	D 2-2	Harker, Edwards (pen)	4,000
38		29	(a)	New Brompton	L 2-4	Harker, Roberts	3,000

FINAL LEAGUE POSITION: 19th in Southern League, Division One.

Appearances

Goals

FA Cup

Q	Dec	8	(h†)	Rotherham C	W 4-0	Roberts 2, Harker, Opp own-goal	
1	Jan	12	(a)	Newcastle U	W 1-0	Astley	28,000
2	Feb	2	(a)	Fulham	D 0-0		28,000
R		6	(h)	Fulham	W 1-0	Woodger	20,000
3		23	(h)	Brentford	D 1-1	Harker	31,123
R		27	(a)	Brentford	W 1-0	Roberts	21,478
4	Mar	9	(h)	Everton	D 1-1	Astley	35,000
R		13	(a)	Everton	L 0-4		34,340

†Played at Stamford Bridge, London.

Appearances

Goals

1907-08

Manager: Edmund Goodman

1	Sep	4	(h)	Northampton T	L 0-2		5,000
2		7	(a)	Southampton	W 3-2	Davies, Woodger, Edwards (pen)	
3		14	(h)	Plymouth A	L 0-4		8,000
4		21	(a)	West Ham U	L 0-1		
5		28	(h)	Queen's Park R	L 2-3	Roberts 2	8,000
6	Oct	5	(a)	Tottenham H	W 2-1	Innerd, Needham	20,000
7		7	(a)	Northampton T	D 1-1	Innerd	
8		12	(h)	Swindon T	W 4-1	Woodger 3, Owens	8,000
9		19	(h)	New Brompton	D 3-3	Owens, Davies, Woodger	8,000
10		26	(a)	Luton T	L 0-4		
11	Nov	2	(h)	Brighton & HA	W 2-1	Owens, Innerd	10,000
12		9	(a)	Portsmouth	W 1-0	Swann	9,000
13		16	(h)	Bradford	D 1-1	Roberts (pen)	11,000
14		23	(a)	Millwall	L 0-1		6,000
15		30	(h)	Brentford	W 2-1	Roberts, Woodger	7,000
16	Dec	7	(a)	Bristol R	L 1-2	Roberts	6,000
17		14	(h)	Leyton	W 3-0	Swann 2, Roberts	5,000
18		21	(a)	Reading	L 1-2	Brearley	3,500
19		25	(a)	Norwich C	W 1-0	Brearley	10,0000
20		28	(h)	Watford	W 3-1	Roberts (pen), Woodger 2	8,000
21	Jan	4	(h)	Southampton	W 1-0	Roberts (pen)	8,000
22		18	(h)	West Ham U	L 1-3	Woodger	8,000
23		25	(a)	Queen's Park R	W 2-1	Smith, Swann	8,000
24	Feb	8	(a)	Swindon T	D 0-0		5,000
25		12	(h)	Tottenham H	L 0-2		8,000
26		15	(a)	New Brompton	D 2-2	Smith, Woodger	2,000
27		29	(a)	Brighton & HA	W 1-0	Owens	4,000
28	Mar	4	(h)	Luton T	W 4-2	Needham, Owen 2, Davies	
29		7	(h)	Portsmouth	D 2-2	Woodger, Ryan	10,000
30		14	(a)	Bradford	W 1-0	Owens	7,000
31		21	(h)	Millwall	W 2-0	Needham, Bauchop	13,000
32		28	(a)	Brentford	D 1-1	Bauchop	9,000
33	Apr	4	(h)	Bristol R	D 1-1	Woodger	10,000
34		8	(a)	Plymouth A	D 1-1	Bauchop	
35		11	(a)	Leyton	D 0-0		5,000
36		18	(h)	Reading	W 2-0	Bauchop, Woodger	12,000
37		20	(h)	Norwich C	W 2-1	Needham, Bauchop	13,000
38		25	(a)	Watford	L 1-4	Bauchop	

FINAL LEAGUE POSITION: 4th in Southern League, Division One.

Appearances
Goals

FA Cup

1	Jan	11	(a)	Coventry C	W 4-2	Woodger 2, Roberts, Davies	9,992
2	Feb	1	(a)	Plymouth A	W 3-2	Swann, Roberts, Smith	17,830
3		22	(a)	Grimsby T	L 0-1		8,828

Appearances
Goals

1908-09

Manager: Edmund Goodman

1	Sep	1	(a)	Coventry C	D 1-1	Bauchop	5,000
2		5	(h)	Leyton	W 5-1	Bauchop 2, Woodger, Swann 2	10,000
3		12	(a)	West Ham U	W 1-0	Woodger	9,900
4		16	(h)	Southampton	L 2-3	Swann, Bauchop	
5		19	(h)	Brighton & HA	W 4-0	McGibbon 3, Bauchop	10,000
6		26	(a)	Plymouth A	D 0-0		8,000
7		30	(h)	Norwich C	W 4-0	Woodger, Haywood, McGibbon, Lawrence	
8	Oct	3	(a)	Brentford	W 3-1	Haywood, Barker, McGibbon	6,000
9		5	(a)	Southampton	D 4-4	McGibbon 3, Lawrence	5,000
10		10	(h)	Luton T	W 2-0	McGibbon, Woodger	10,000
11		15	(a)	Norwich C	L 0-2		5,000
12		17	(a)	Swindon T	L 0-4		6,000
13		21	(h)	Queen's Park R	W 3-0	McGibbon, Lawrence 2	
14		24	(h)	Portsmouth	W 3-2	Bauchop 3	9,500
15		31	(a)	Exeter C	D 1-1	McGibbon	10,000
16	Nov	7	(h)	Northampton T	L 2-3	Swann 2	12,000
17		14	(a)	New Brompton	L 1-2	McGibbon	7,000
18		21	(h)	Millwall	W 2-1	Swann, Bauchop	10,000
19		28	(a)	Southend	L 0-1		4,000
20	Dec	12	(a)	Bristol R	D 2-2	Ryan, Lawrence	6,000
21		19	(h)	Watford	W 3-1	McGibbon 2, Swann	8,000
22		26	(a)	Reading	D 2-2	Woodger 2	11,000
23	Jan	2	(a)	Leyton	L 0-2		4,000
24		9	(h)	West Ham U	D 2-2	Bauchop, Woodger	
25		23	(a)	Brighton & HA	L 0-3		5,000
26		30	(h)	Plymouth	L 0-1		6,000
27	Feb	13	(a)	Luton T	L 1-4	Bauchop	5,000
28		20	(h)	Swindon T	D 1-1	Swann	7,000
29		27	(a)	Portsmouth	D 1-1	Bauchop	5,000
30	Mar	6	(h)	Exeter C	D 0-0		1,500
31		13	(a)	Northampton	L 0-1		7,000
32		17	(h)	Southend U	L 1-3	Brearley	
33		20	(h)	New Brompton	L 1-2	Bauchop	4,500
34		27	(a)	Millwall	L 1-2	Swann	
35		31	(h)	Brentford	W 3-1	Woodger 2, Bauchop	
36	Apr	3	(a)	Queen's Park R	D 1-1	Swann	8,000
37		10	(h)	Coventry C	L 0-1		
38		12	(h)	Reading	D 0-0		5,000
39		17	(h)	Bristol R	W 4-1	Lee 2, Swann, Bauchop	4,000
40		24	(a)	Watford	L 1-5	Bauchop	4,000

FINAL LEAGUE POSITION: 16th in Southern League, Division One. Appearances

Goals

FA Cup

1	Jan	16	(a)	Wolves	D 2-2	Bauchop 2	18,653
R		21	(h)	Wolves	W 4-2	Garratt, Lawrence, Bauchop, Needham	12,300
2	Feb	6	(h)	Burnley	D 0-0		17,076
R		10	(a)	Burnley	L 0-9		14,000

Appearances

Goals

1909-10

Manager: Edmund Goodman

No.	Month	Day	Venue	Opponents	Result	Score	Scorers	Att.
1	Sep	1	(h)	Brentford	W	1-0	Payne	4,500
2		4	(a)	Coventry C	D	1-1	Collyer (pen)	8,000
3		8	(h)	Bristol R	W	3-1	Hanger, Payne, Woodger	
4		11	(h)	Watford	D	1-1	Payne	10,000
5		13	(a)	Brentford	L	0-1		
6		18	(a)	Reading	D	1-1	Williams	4,000
7		25	(h)	Southend U	W	6-0	Williams 5, Payne	10,000
8	Oct	2	(a)	Leyton	W	1-0	Payne	14,000
9		9	(h)	Plymouth A	W	3-0	Payne, Woodger, Hughes	10,000
10		13	(h)	Norwich C	W	4-0	Payne 3, Williams	5,000
11		16	(a)	Southampton	W	3-0	Payne 3	
12		23	(h)	Croydon Com	W	2-0	Williams, Woodger	17,500
13		25	(a)	Norwich C	L	0-1		11,000
14		30	(a)	Millwall	W	2-0	Williams, Payne	
15	Nov	6	(h)	New Brompton	W	6-2	Payne 4, Williams 2	12,000
16		13	(a)	Northampton T	L	0-1		10,000
17		17	(a)	Portsmouth	L	0-2		4,000
18		20	(h)	Queen's Park R	L	0-1		15,000
19		27	(a)	Luton T	W	4-2	Young 2, Williams, Payne	4,000
20	Dec	4	(h)	Swindon T	W	2-0	Payne 2	6,000
21		11	(h)	Exeter C	W	3-0	Williams 2, Hughes	7,000
22		18	(a)	Brighton & HA	W	2-1	Payne, Williams	7,000
23	Jan	1	(a)	Bristol R	D	1-1	Spottiswood	
24		8	(h)	Coventry C	L	1-2	Payne (pen)	
25		22	(a)	Watford	L	0-3		4,000
26		29	(h)	Reading	D	1-1	Woodger	4,000
27	Feb	12	(h)	Leyton	L	1-2	Woodger	
28		19	(a)	Plymouth A	L	0-2		5,000
29		23	(a)	Southend U	L	0-3		
30		26	(h)	Southampton	W	2-0	Woodger 2	
31	Mar	5	(a)	Croydon Com	W	1-0	Young	'Record crowd'
32		9	(h)	Portsmouth	W	4-2	Young 2, Garratt, Woodger	
33		12	(h)	Millwall	W	4-1	Williams 2, Young, Woodger	4,000
34		19	(a)	New Brompton	L	1-3	Young	5,000
35		25	(a)	West Ham U	L	1-3	Williams	15,000
36		26	(h)	Northampton T	W	1-0	Williams	10,000
37		28	(h)	West Ham U	L	2-4	Payne 2	20,000
38	Apr	2	(a)	Queen's Park R	W	2-1	Gibson, Payne	10,000
39		9	(h)	Luton T	L	1-3	Williams	
40		16	(a)	Swindon T	L	1-2	Griffin	
41		23	(a)	Exeter C	L	0-2		
42		30	(h)	Brighton & HA	D	0-0		10,000

FINAL LEAGUE POSITION: 7th in Southern League, Division One. Appearances

Goals

FA Cup

Round	Month	Day	Venue	Opponents	Result	Score	Scorers	Att.
1	Jan	15	(h)	Swindon T	L	1-3	Payne	15,000

Appearances

Goals

1910-11

Manager: Edmund Goodman

1	Sep	3	(a)	Swindon T	D 0-0		
2		10	(h)	Bristol R	W 1-0	Hanger	8,000
3		14	(a)	Exeter C	W 4-3	Payne 3, Davies	
4		17	(h)	Norwich C	L 0-3		6,000
5		24	(a)	Brentford	L 1-2	Payne	
6	Oct	1	(h)	Leyton	W 5-4	Woodhouse, Hughes 2 (2 pens), Lawrence, Davies	
7		5	(h)	Portsmouth	L 0-1		4,000
8		8	(a)	Watford	D 1-1	Hanger	4,000
9		15	(h)	Plymouth A	W 6-1	Garratt, Williams 2, Woodhouse 2, Hewitt	
10		22	(a)	Southampton	W 3-0	Hughes 2, Woodhouse	
11		29	(h)	Southend U	D 0-0		6,000
12	Nov	5	(a)	Coventry C	W 2-0	Williams, Woodhouse	8,000
13		12	(h)	New Brompton	W 3-2	Collins, Hewitt, Woodhouse	8,000
14		19	(a)	Millwall	W 1-0	Williams	18,000
15		26	(h)	Queen's Park R	W 2-1	Garratt, Hewitt	9,000
16	Dec	3	(a)	West Ham U	D 1-1	Woodhouse	8,000
17		10	(h)	Luton T	W 3-1	Spottiswood, Woodhouse, Hughes	
18		17	(a)	Portsmouth	D 0-0		7,000
19		24	(h)	Northampton T	D 0-0		
20		26	(a)	Brighton & HA	L 0-2		
21		27	(h)	Brighton & HA	D 1-1	Hewitt	
22		31	(h)	Swindon T	L 2-5	Woodhouse, Williams	12,000
23	Jan	7	(a)	Bristol R	D 3-3	Hanger, Woodhouse, Hewitt	
24		21	(a)	Norwich C	W 1-0	Hewitt	4,000
25		28	(h)	Brentford	D 1-1	Payne	8,000
26	Feb	4	(a)	Leyton	W 1-0	Woodhouse	5,000
27		11	(h)	Watford	W 1-0	Williams	6,000
28		18	(a)	Plymouth A	L 1-5	Davies	
29		25	(h)	Southampton	D 2-2	Hewitt, Woodhouse	
30	Mar	4	(a)	Southend	D 0-0		
31		11	(h)	Coventry C	W 2-0	Hewitt, Woodhouse	
32		18	(a)	New Brompton	L 0-2		
33		25	(h)	Millwall	W 1-0	Woodhouse	
34	Apr	1	(a)	Queen's Park R	D 0-0		
35		8	(h)	West Ham U	W 4-1	Williams, Woodhouse, Bulcock, Garratt	10,000
36		15	(a)	Luton T	D 1-1	Williams	
37		17	(h)	Exeter C	W 1-0	Woodhouse	
38		18	(a)	Northampton T	L 0-5		4,000

FINAL LEAGUE POSITION: 4th in Southern League, Division One.

Appearances
Goals

FA Cup

1	Jan	14	(h)	Everton	L 0-4		35,000

Appearances
Goals

1911-12

Manager: Edmund Goodman

1	Sep	2	(h)	West Ham U	W 1-0	Williams	14,000
2		9	(a)	Bristol R	D 0-0		10,000
3		16	(h)	Swindon T	D 2-2	Harker, Hewitt	8,000
4		23	(a)	Northampton T	D 1-1	Hewitt	9,000
5		30	(h)	Brighton & HA	D 1-1	Williams	10,000
6	Oct	7	(a)	Stoke	L 1-2	Williams	14,000
7		14	(h)	Coventry C	W 3-0	Woodhouse 2, Hughes (pen)	10,000
8		21	(a)	Leyton	W 3-1	Williams, Woodhouse, Davies	3,000
9		28	(h)	Norwich C	W 6-0	Hewitt 2, Woodhouse 2, Williams 2	8,000
10	Nov	4	(a)	Luton T	W 1-0	Woodhouse (pen)	5,000
11		11	(a)	Southampton	W 4-2	Hewitt, Davies, Williams 2	
12		25	(a)	Reading	L 0-2		4,000
13	Dec	9	(a)	New Brompton	D 1-1	Harker	5,000
14		16	(h)	Exeter C	W 5-0	Williams, Harker, Davies 2, Hewitt	8,000
15		23	(a)	Brentford	L 0-1		5,000
16		25	(a)	Queen's Park R	L 2-3	Williams 2	22,000
17		26	(h)	Queen's Park R	W 3-0	Williams 2, Davies	
18		30	(a)	West Ham U	W 6-1	Smith 3, Harker 3	8,000
19	Jan	6	(h)	Bristol R	W 4-1	Smith 3, Harker	4,000
20		20	(a)	Swindon T	L 1-2	Smith	6,000
21		27	(h)	Northampton T	L 1-2	Smith	10,000
22	Feb	10	(h)	Stoke	L 1-2	Smith	10,000
23		17	(a)	Coventry C	L 2-3	Myers, Smith	5,000
24		24	(h)	Leyton	D 1-1	Smith	
25		28	(h)	Plymouth	L 0-1		
26	Mar	2	(a)	Norwich C	D 1-1	Bourne	6,300
27		9	(h)	Luton T	W 3-1	Smith 2, Williams	
28		16	(h)	Southampton	W 3-1	Smith 2, Bourne	5,000
29		20	(a)	Watford	L 0-2		
30		23	(a)	Plymouth A	L 1-3	Bourne	
31		30	(h)	Reading	D 1-1	Williams	
32	Apr	5	(a)	Millwall	L 1-2	Bourne	
33		6	(h)	Watford	W 2-0	Smith, Hewitt	6,000
34		8	(h)	Millwall	W 3-0	Davies, Hewitt 2	14,000
35		9	(a)	Brighton & HA	L 1-4	Smith	
36		13	(h)	New Brompton	D 1-1	Smith	6,000
37		20	(a)	Exeter C	D 1-1	Hewitt	
38		27	(h)	Brentford	W 2-0	Smith, Garratt	4,000

FINAL LEAGUE POSITION: 7th in Southern League, Division One. Appearances

Goals

FA Cup

1	Jan	13	(a)	Brentford	D 0-0		19,000
R		17	(h)	Brentford	W 4-0	Smith, Hewitt, Hanger, Harker	9,000
2	Feb	3	(h)	Sunderland	D 0-0		20,000
R		7	(a)	Sunderland	L 0-1		34,000

Appearances

Goals

1912-13

Manager: Edmund Goodman

1	Sep	4	(h)	Brentford	W	3-1	Smith, Garratt, Hewitt	2,000
2		7	(a)	Swindon T	L	0-1		7,000
3		14	(h)	Portsmouth	W	2-0	Smith, Davies	9,000
4		18	(a)	Brentford	L	1-2	Bulcock	4,200
5		21	(a)	Exeter C	D	1-1	Smith	4,000
6		28	(h)	West Ham U	D	1-1	Smith	15,000
7	Oct	5	(a)	Brighton & HA	W	2-1	Smith (pen), Hewitt	6,000
8		12	(h)	Coventry C *	W	3-0	Smith, Hewitt, Davies	9,000
9		19	(a)	Watford	D	1-1	Williams	5,000
10		26	(h)	Merthyr T	W	2-1	Hewitt, York	6,000
11	Nov	2	(h)	Stoke	W	1-0	Smith	6,000
12		9	(a)	Plymouth A	D	0-0		10,000
13		16	(h)	Southampton	W	8-0	Williams 3, Hewitt 4, York	8,000
14		23	(a)	Reading	L	0-2		10,000
15		30	(h)	Norwich C	W	1-0	Smith	6,000
16	Dec	7	(a)	Gillingham	W	2-1	Smith, Hanger	9,000
17		14	(h)	Northampton T	D	2-2	Smith 2 (1 pen)	5,500
18		21	(a)	Queen's Park R	L	0-2		9,800
19		25	(a)	Millwall	W	1-0	Hewitt	10,000
20		26	(h)	Millwall	W	2-0	Smith (pen), Williams	14,000
21		28	(h)	Swindon T	W	1-0	Smith	7,000
22	Jan	4	(a)	Portsmouth	L	0-2		12,000
23		18	(h)	Exeter C	L	0-1		8,000
24		25	(a)	West Ham U	D	1-1	Hewitt	14,000
25	Feb	8	(h)	Brighton & HA	D	1-1	Smith	14,000
26		15	(a)	Coventry C	W	2-1	Smith, York	5,000
27	Mar	1	(a)	Merthyr T	D	1-1	Hanger	10,000
28		8	(a)	Stoke	D	0-0		9,000
29		15	(h)	Plymouth A	W	1-0	Smith (pen)	8,000
30		21	(a)	Bristol R	D	2-2	Smith 2	9,000
31		22	(a)	Southampton	L	0-1		8,000
32		24	(h)	Bristol R	W	3-0	York, Williams 2	20,000
33		29	(h)	Reading	W	4-2	Williams, Smith 3	10,000
34	Apr	5	(a)	Norwich C	D	2-2	Smith, Williams	5,000
35		12	(h)	Gillingham	L	0-1		8,000
36		19	(a)	Northampton T	L	1-2	Smith (pen)	6,000
37		23	(h)	Watford	W	2-1	Hewitt, Smith	5,000
38		26	(h)	Queen's Park R †	L	1-2	Smith	6,000

FINAL LEAGUE POSITION: 5th in Southern League, Division One. Appearances

*H.Collyer benefit match. †J.Johnson benefit match. Goals

FA Cup

1	Jan	11	(h)	Glossop	W	2-0	Smith, Williams	8,000
2	Feb	1	(h)	Bury	W	2-0	Smith, Davies	14,000
3		22	(a)	Aston Villa	L	0-5		44,500

Appearances

Goals

1913-14

Manager: Edmund Goodman

1	Sep	4	(a)	Northampton T	D 1-1	Williams	
2		6	(h)	Portsmouth	W 3-1	Hewitt, Smith 2 (1 pen)	
3		13	(a)	Millwall	D 0-0		
4		17	(h)	Northampton T	W 3-0	Smith 2, Williams	
5		20	(h)	Exeter C	D 0-0		
6		27	(a)	Cardiff C	W 2-1	Williams, Bateman	
7	Oct	4	(h)	Swindon T	L 0-1		
8		11	(a)	Bristol R	W 1-0	Smith	
9		18	(h)	Merthyr T	W 3-1	Smith, Williams, Hewitt	
10		25	(a)	West Ham U	W 2-1	Williams, Smith	
11	Nov	1	(h)	Plymouth A	D 2-2	Whibley, Smith	
12		8	(a)	Southampton	D 2-2	Smith 2 (1 pen)	
13		15	(h)	Reading	W 5-1	Davies, Smith 2, Keene, Hewitt	12,000
14		22	(a)	Queen's Park R	L 0-3		10,000
15		29	(a)	Coventry C	L 0-2		
16	Dec	6	(h)	Watford	W 3-0	Bright 2, Smith	6,000
17		20	(h)	Gillingham	W 1-0	Smith	6,000
18		25	(a)	Southend U	D 3-3	Davies, Bright, Hughes	
19		26	(h)	Southend U	D 0-0		15,000
20		27	(a)	Portsmouth	D 1-1	Smith	16,000
21	Jan	3	(h)	Millwall	W 3-0	Smith 2, Hewitt	
22		17	(a)	Exeter C	D 1-1	Davies	
23		24	(h)	Cardiff C	W 4-0	Bright, Smith 2, Davies	
24	Feb	7	(a)	Swindon T	W 2-0	Bright, Bateman	
25		14	(h)	Bristol R	W 5-3	Smith 2, Davies, Bright 2	
26		21	(a)	Merthyr T	W 1-0	Smith (pen)	
27		28	(h)	West Ham U	L 1-2	Smith	12,000
28	Mar	7	(a)	Plymouth	D 0-0		
29		14	(h)	Southampton	D 0-0		
30		21	(a)	Reading	L 1-2	Davies	
31		28	(h)	Queen's Park R	W 2-1	Bright, Smith	
32	Apr	2	(a)	Norwich C	D 0-0		
33		4	(h)	Coventry C	W 3-1	Whibley, Smith, Hughes	
34		10	(a)	Brighton & HA	D 0-0		
35		11	(a)	Watford	D 1-1	Hughes	5,000
36		13	(h)	Brighton & HA	D 0-0		20,000
37		18	(h)	Norwich C	W 3-0	Hughes, Hewitt 2	
38		25	(a)	Gillingham	D 1-1	Smith	8,000

FINAL LEAGUE POSITION: 2nd in Southern League, Division One.

Appearances

Goals

FA Cup

1	Jan	10	(h)	Norwich C	W 2-1	Hewitt, Smith	8,898
2		31	(a)	West Ham U	L 0-2		18,000

Appearances

Goals

1914-15

Manager: Edmund Goodman

1	Sep	5	(a)	Bristol R	D	1-1	Collins	6,500
2		10	(a)	Norwich C	L	1-2	Hewitt	2,000
3		12	(h)	Brighton & HA	L	0-2		
4		19	(a)	Croydon Com	D	1-1	York	8,000
5		26	(h)	Cardiff C	L	0-2		6,000
6	Oct	3	(a)	Reading	L	0-3		5,000
7		10	(h)	Exeter C	D	0-0		4,000
8		17	(a)	Southampton	W	3-2	Smith 2, York (pen)	
9		24	(h)	Luton T	L	2-3	Smith, Whibley	
10		31	(a)	Northampton T	L	1-2	Hewitt	
11	Nov	7	(h)	Portsmouth	W	1-0	Smith	
12		14	(a)	Watford	L	0-1		4,000
13		21	(h)	Swindon T	W	3-1	Smith, Keene 2	6,000
14		28	(a)	Plymouth A	W	4-1	Smith 3 (1 pen), Middleton	
15	Dec	5	(h)	Southend U	D	1-1	Middleton	
16		12	(a)	West Ham U	W	2-1	Smith, Middleton	5,000
17		19	(h)	Queen's Park R	D	2-2	Hewitt, Smith	3,000
18		25	(a)	Millwall	D	0-0		
19		26	(h)	Millwall	L	0-1		
20		28	(h)	Norwich C	W	2-1	Middleton, Hughes	1,000
21	Jan	2	(h)	Bristol R	W	1-0	Smith	3,000
22		30	(a)	Cardiff C	L	0-5		12,000
23	Feb	6	(h)	Reading	W	4-1	Hooper, Smith 2, Feebury	4,000
24		13	(a)	Exeter C	D	1-1	Davies	
25		27	(a)	Luton T	W	2-1	Smith 2	
26	Mar	3	(h)	Southampton	L	1-2	Smith	
27		6	(h*)	Northampton T	D	1-1	Lane	3,000
28		11	(h*)	Croydon Com	L	1-5	Smith (pen)	
29		13	(a)	Portsmouth	L	0-1		6,000
30		20	(h*)	Watford	L	0-1		
31		27	(a)	Swindon T	L	2-5	Hughes, Smith	
32	Apr	2	(a)	Gillingham	L	0-3		
33		3	(h*)	Plymouth A	W	2-1	Middleton, Davies	
34		5	(h*)	Gillingham	W	1-0	Lane	
35		10	(a)	Southend U	W	3-2	Lane, Hewitt, Smith	3,000
36		17	(h*)	West Ham U	W	2-1	Lane 2	4,000
37		24	(a)	Queen's Park R	L	2-3	Hooper, Smith	6,000
38	May	1	(a)	Brighton & HA	L	0-1		2,000

FINAL LEAGUE POSITION: 15th in Southern League, Division One. — Appearances

*Played at Herne Hill. — Goals

FA Cup

1	Jan	9	(a)	Birmingham	D	2-2	Davies, Middleton	18,000
R		16	(a†)	Birmingham	L	0-3		17,000

†Played at St Andrew's, Birmingham. — Appearances

Goals

1915-16

Manager: Edmund Goodman

1	Sep	4	(a)	Croydon C	L 1-2	Lawrence	3,000
2		11	(h)	Arsenal	W 3-1	Whitworth 2, Lawrence	3,500
3		18	(a)	Brentford	L 0-1		2,500
4		25	(h)	West Ham U	W 2-0	Whitworth 2	2,500
5	Oct	2	(a)	Tottenham H	W 4-2	Sanders 2, York, Poulton	1,800
6		9	(h)	Chelsea	L 1-5	Rogers	4,000
7		16	(h)	Queen's Park R	W 1-0	Marsh	
8		23	(a)	Fulham	L 0-5		
9		30	(h)	Clapton O	L 1-2	Dunn (og)	
10	Nov	6	(a)	Watford	L 1-7	Green	
11		13	(h)	Croydon C	W 4-2	Sanders, Fordham, Lockton, Keene	600
12		20	(a)	Arsenal	D 2-2	Lockton, Sanders	
13		27	(h)	Brentford	W 1-0	Hughes	
14	Dec	4	(a)	West Ham U	L 1-3	Fordham	
15		11	(h)	Tottenham H	W 4-2	Lockton 3, Fordham	3,000
16		18	(a)	Chelsea	L 1-6	Sanders	
17		25	(h)	Millwall	L 0-1		
18		27	(a)	Millwall	L 1-4	Lockton	
19	Jan	1	(a)	Queen's Park R	L 1-5	Rogers	
20		8	(h)	Fulham	D 2-2	Keene, Sanders	
21		15	(a)	Clapton O	W 3-2	Sanders 3	
22		22	(h)	Watford	D 1-1	Dobson	

FINAL LEAGUE POSITION: 9th in London Combination (Principal Competition) — Appearances

Goals

Supplementary Competition

23	Jan	29	(a)	Croydon C*	W 2-0	Lockton, Gilboy	
24	Feb	5	(h)	Millwall	L 1-5	Sanders	
25		12	(a)	Chelsea	W 1-0	Keene	
26		19	(h)	Watford	W 1-0	Gilboy	
27	Mar	4	(h)	Reading	W 10-1	Sanders 6, Gilboy 2, Keene, Marsh	
28		11	(a)	Clapton O	W 5-1	Sanders, Lockton 2, Martin, Keene	
29		18	(h)	Chelsea	W 4-2	Lockton 3, Gilboy	
30		25	(a)	Watford	L 0-4		
31	Apr	1	(h)	Brentford	W 6-3	Booth 2, Martin, Keene 3	
32		8	(a)	Reading	D 1-1	Sanders	
33		15	(h)	Clapton O	W 2-1	Redward (og), Sanders	
34		21	(a)	Tottenham H	L 1-3	Hughes	
35		22	(h)	Tottenham H	W 4-0	Keene 2, Gilboy, Marsh	10,000
36		29	(a)	Millwall	D 2-2	Noon, Cracknell	
37	May	6	(a)	Brentford	L 3-6	Shields, Keene, Lawrence	

FINAL LEAGUE POSITION: 6th in London Combination (Supplementary Competition) — Appearances

*Played in aid of War Comforts Fund — Goals

1916-17

Manager: Edmund Goodman

1	Sep	2	(h)	Brentford	W	4-0	Lockton 4
2		9	(a)	Chelsea	L	1-4	Lockton
3		16	(h)	Arsenal	W	1-0	Hughes
4		23	(a)	Luton T	L	1-3	Johnson
5		30	(h)	Reading	W	5-3	Lawrence 2, Gilboy, Shields, Hughes
6	Oct	7	(a)	Millwall	L	2-3	Keene, Fox
7		14	(h)	Watford	L	0-1	
8		21	(a)	Clapton O	D	2-2	Shields 2
9		28	(h)	Fulham	W	1-0	Driver
10	Nov	4	(a)	Queen's Park R	L	0-1	
11		11	(h)	West Ham U	L	1-8	Beech
12		18	(a)	Tottenham H	L	1-3	Shields
13		25	(a)	Brentford	L	1-3	Opp own-goal
14	Dec	2	(h)	Chelsea	D	1-1	Shields
15		9	(a)	Arsenal	W	2-1	Peach, Ekington
16		16	(h)	Luton T		*	
17		23	(a)	Portsmouth	D	2-2	Burton, Kennett
18		25	(h)	Southampton	D	2-2	Shields, Keene
19		26	(a)	Southampton	D	2-2	Gilboy, Keene
20		30	(h)	Millwall	D	1-1	Dunk
21	Jan	6	(a)	Watford	D	2-2	Shields 2
22		13	(h)	Clapton O	W	3-0	Sanders, Hughes, Shields
23		20	(a)	Fulham	L	3-4	Sanders, Hughes, Whalley
24		27	(h)	Queen's Park R	W	4-0	Sanders 2, Beech 2
25	Feb	3	(a)	West Ham U	L	0-1	
26		10	(h)	Tottenham H	L	0-1	
27		17	(h)	Clapton O	W	3-0	Shields, Fenwick, Beech
28		24	(a)	Tottenham H	L	1-4	Ritchie
29	Mar	3	(h)	West Ham U	W	3-1	Beech 2, Keene
30		10	(a)	Queen's Park R	L	2-3	McGlover, Shields
31		17	(h)	Arsenal	W	1-0	Dunk
32		24	(h)	Southampton	W	4-2	Lockton 2, Shields, Keene
33		31	(a)	Clapton O	W	4-1	Lockton 2, Ritchie, Lancaster
34	Apr	6	(a)	Portsmouth	W	2-1	York, Booth
35		7	(h)	Tottenham H	L	0-3	
36		9	(h)	Portsmouth	L	2-3	Hewitt, Carr
37		14	(a)	West Ham U	L	1-2	Lancaster
38		21	(h)	Queen's Park R	W	3-0	Hill, Keene, Shields
39		28	(a)	Arsenal	L	0-4	
40	May	5	(a)	Southampton		*	

FINAL LEAGUE POSITION: 8th in London Combination — Appearances

*Games v Luton Town (h) and Southampton (a) were not played — Goals

1917-18

Manager: Edmund Goodman

1	Sep	1	(h)	Tottenham H	L 2-4	Whitworth, Sanders	2,000
2		8	(a)	Fulham	L 1-7	Hill	
3		15	(h)	Chelsea	L 0-3		
4		22	(a)	Queen's Park R	L 1-4	Keene	
5		29	(h)	Brentford	W 4-0	Keene 2, York, Slade	
6	Oct	6	(a)	Clapton O	W 3-2	Sanders, Colley, Whitworth	
7		13	(h)	Arsenal	W 2-0	Sanders, Lowe	
8		20	(a)	Millwall	W 2-1	Slade, York	
9		27	(a)	Tottenham H	L 0-1		5,000
10	Nov	3	(h)	Fulham	W 2-1	Slade, York	
11		10	(a)	Chelsea	W 1-0	Slade	
12		17	(h)	Queen's Park R	W 4-1	Slade, Hughes, Hill, Keene	
13		24	(a)	Brentford	L 0-3		
14	Dec	1	(h)	Clapton O	W 3-1	Gibbs, Hughes, York	
15		8	(a)	Arsenal	W 2-0	Slade, Smart	
16		15	(h)	Millwall	L 1-5	Martin	
17		22	(h)	Tottenham H	L 2-3	York, Smart	2,000
18		25	(a)	West Ham U	L 1-2	Slade	
19		26	(h)	West Ham U	W 4-0	Gibbs, Smart, Slade, Cracknell	
20		29	(a)	Fulham	D 1-1	Piggott	
21	Jan	5	(h)	Chelsea	D 0-0		
22		12	(a)	Queen's Park R	L 1-2	Cartwright	
23		19	(h)	Brentford	L 3-4	Wiggins, Chester 2	
24		26	(a)	Clapton O	D 0-0		
25	Feb	2	(h)	Arsenal	L 1-4	Slade	
26		9	(h)	West Ham U	D 1-1	Keene	
27		16	(a)	Tottenham H	L 0-8		7,000
28		23	(h)	Fulham	W 5-2	Jameson 2, Hughes, Slade, Cartwright	
29	Mar	2	(a)	Chelsea	L 0-2		
30		9	(h)	Queen's Park R	L 0-2		
31		16	(a)	Brentford	W 2-0	Jameson, York	
32		23	(h)	Clapton O	W 3-1	Gibbs 2, Slade	
33		29	(a)	Millwall	W 3-1	Dunk 2, Jameson	
34		30	(a)	Arsenal	L 0-3		
35	Apr	1	(h)	Millwall	L 0-2		
36		6	(a)	West Ham U	L 0-11		4,000

FINAL LEAGUE POSITION: 7th in London Combination

Appearances
Goals

War Fund Matches

Apr	13	(a)	Queen's Park R	L 1-2	Armstrong	
	20	(h)	Queen's Park R	W 3-1	Lancaster, Whitworth, Pale	
	27	(h)	Clapton O	W 2-0	Dunk, Jameson	
May	4	(a)	Clapton O	W 2-0	Cartwright, Lancaster	

Appearances
Goals

1918-19

Manager: Edmund Goodman

1	Sep	7	(a)	Clapton O	W 2-1	Howarth 2	3,000
2		14	(h)	Queen's Park R	W 4-2	Keene 3, Turner	3,000
3		21	(a)	Millwall	W 2-0	Whitworth 2	
4		28	(h)	Fulham	W 1-0	Beech	5,000
5	Oct	5	(a)	Brentford	W 3-2	Keene, Dunk 2	3,000
6		12	(h)	West Ham U	D 0-0		4,000
7		19	(a)	Tottenham H	L 0-2		10,000
8		26	(h)	Arsenal	W 2-1	Keene, Dunk	5,000
9	Nov	2	(h)	Clapton O	W 6-1	Bird 2, Keene, Beech, Whitworth 2	
10		9	(a)	Queen's Park R	L 2-3	Whitworth, Bates	
11		16	(h)	Millwall	D 2-2	Beech, Castle	4,000
12		23	(a)	Fulham	L 1-5	Beech	
13		30	(h)	Brentford	L 0-4		6,000
14	Dec	7	(a)	West Ham U	L 0-2		
15		14	(h)	Tottenham H	W 6-3	Whitworth 5, Cartwright	2,500
16		21	(a)	Arsenal	D 3-3	Stephenson, Cartwright, Lockton	
17		25	(a)	Chelsea	W 2-0	Stephenson, Whitworth	10,000
18		26	(h)	Chelsea	D 0-0		12,000
19		28	(a)	Clapton O	W 4-0	Lockton, Whitworth 2, Cartwright	
20	Jan	4	(h)	Queen's Park R	L 0-2		
21		11	(a)	Millwall	L 1-2	York	
22		18	(h)	Fulham	L 1-4	Beech	6,000
23		25	(a)	Brentford	L 1-6	Bateman	
24	Feb	1	(h)	West Ham U	W 3-0	Smith 3	
25		8	(a)	Tottenham H	L 2-4	Beech, Whitworth	14,000
26		15	(h)	Chelsea	W 1-0	Humphries	10,000
27		22	(h)	Clapton O	W 4-1	Humphries, Whitworth 2, Smith	
28	Mar	1	(a)	Queen's Park R	L 2-3	Humphries, Draper (og)	
29		8	(h)	Millwall	L 1-4	Humphries	
30		15	(a)	Fulham	D 1-1	Smith	
31		22	(h)	Brentford	L 2-3	Bateman, Kimpton	10,000
32		29	(a)	West Ham U	W 3-1	Smith, Whitworth 2	16,000
33	Apr	5	(h)	Tottenham H	D 2-2	Edmonds, Smith	12,000
34		12	(a)	Chelsea	L 0-3		12,000
35		18	(h†)	Arsenal	L 0-3		
36		21	(a)	Arsenal	L 2-3	Smith 2	

FINAL LEAGUE POSITION: 7th in London Combination

†Played at Millwall.

London Victory Cup

Feb	17	(h)	Brentford	W 1-0	Stephenson	
Apr	19	(n†)	Chelsea	L 0-4		22,000

†Played at Arsenal Stadium, Highbury, London.

1919-20

Manager: Edmund Goodman

No	Month	Date	Venue	Opponents	Result	Score	Scorers	Att
1	Aug	30	(h)	Northampton T	D	2-2	Middleton, Whibley	
2	Sep	3	(a)	Portsmouth	D	0-0		
3		6	(a)	Watford	L	1-4	Whibley	
4		10	(h)	Portsmouth	W	2-1	E.Smith, Middleton	
5		13	(a)	Southend U	D	1-1	Conner	
6		20	(h)	Norwich C	W	3-1	Conner, Whibley, E.Smith	
7		27	(a)	Brentford	D	0-0		
8	Oct	4	(h)	Merthyr T	D	1-1	E.Smith	
9		11	(a)	Plymouth A	D	0-0		
10		15	(h)	Swindon T	L	1-2	Wood	4,000
11		18	(h)	Bristol R	W	5-1	E.Smith 4, Whibley	
12		25	(a)	Reading	D	0-0		
13	Nov	1	(h)	Southampton	W	3-0	Conner 2, E.Smith	
14		8	(a)	Luton T	W	4-1	Bateman, Conner, E.Smith, Barber	
15		15	(h)	Gillingham	W	4-1	Conner, E.Smith 2, Whibley	
16		22	(a)	Swansea T	W	1-0	Conner	
17	Dec	6	(a)	Cardiff C	L	1-2	Hughes (pen)	
18		13	(h)	Queen's Park R	W	1-0	Conner	
19		20	(a)	Swindon T	D	2-2	E.Smith, Whibley	
20		25	(a)	Brighton & HA	W	3-2	E.Smith 2, Whibley	
21		26	(h)	Brighton & HA	W	4-0	Conner, E.Smith, Barber 2	15,000
22		27	(h)	Millwall	W	1-0	Cracknell	17,000
23	Jan	3	(a)	Northampton T	W	1-0	E.Smith	
24		17	(h)	Watford	W	2-1	Barber 2	15,000
25		24	(h)	Southend U	D	0-0		15,000
26		31	(a)	Norwich C	L	0-2		
27	Feb	7	(h)	Brentford	D	1-1	Wood	12,000
28		14	(a)	Merthyr T	W	1-0	Conner	
29		28	(a)	Bristol R	L	0-1		
30	Mar	3	(h)	Plymouth A	W	1-0	Barber	6,000
31		6	(h)	Reading	W	2-1	Conner, E.Smith	10,000
32		13	(a)	Southampton	L	1-5	Conner	
33		17	(h)	Exeter C	W	1-0	Conner	5,000
34		20	(h)	Luton T	W	4-1	Menlove 2, Green, Whibley	
35		27	(a)	Gillingham	W	4-2	Conner, Menlove 3	
36	Apr	2	(a)	Newport C	L	0-1		
37		3	(h)	Swansea T	W	2-1	Conner, Green	
38		5	(h)	Newport C	W	3-0	Bates, Conner 2	15,000
39		10	(a)	Exeter C	L	1-2	E.Smith	
40		17	(h)	Cardiff C	D	1-1	Menlove	
41		24	(a)	Queen's Park R	W	3-2	Bateman, E.Smith, Whibley	
42	May	1	(a)	Millwall	D	1-1	Conner	

FINAL LEAGUE POSITION: 3rd in Southern League, Division One.

Appearances
Goals

FA Cup

No	Month	Date	Venue	Opponents	Result	Score	Scorers	Att
1	Jan	10	(a)	Newcastle U	L	0-2		15,000

Appearances
Goals

1920-21

Manager: Edmund Goodman

No	Month	Date	Venue	Opponent	Result	Score	Scorers	Attendance
1	Aug	28	(a)	Merthyr T	L	1-2	Milligan	15,000
2	Sep	1	(h)	Plymouth A	D	0-0		9,500
3		4	(h)	Merthyr T	W	3-0	Conner 2, Whibley	12,500
4		8	(a)	Plymouth A	W	1-0	Storey	12,000
5		11	(a)	Norwich C	W	1-0	Whibley	11,000
6		18	(h)	Norwich C	W	1-0	Conner	14,000
7		25	(a)	Brentford	W	4-0	Smith 2, Whibley, Menlove	13,000
8	Oct	2	(h)	Brentford	W	4-2	Whibley, Conner, Feebury, Smith	15,000
9		9	(a)	Bristol R	L	1-2	Conner	20,000
10		16	(h)	Bristol R	W	3-0	Smith 2, Conner	16,000
11		23	(a)	Reading	L	0-1		10,000
12		30	(h)	Reading	W	2-0	Smith, Menlove	18,000
13	Nov	3	(h)	Southend U	L	2-3	Conner, Capper (og)	9,000
14		6	(a)	Luton T	D	2-2	Conner, Whibley	10,000
15		13	(h)	Luton T	W	2-1	Conner, Feebury	12,000
16		20	(a)	Exeter C	D	1-1	Conner	
17		27	(h†)	Exeter C	W	2-1	Storey, Smith	12,000
18	Dec	4	(a)	Swansea T	D	0-0		20,000
19		11	(h)	Swansea T	L	0-1		9,000
20		18	(a)	Queen's Park R	L	0-3		
21		25	(a)	Brighton & HA	W	2-0	Conner 2	14,000
22		27	(h)	Brighton & HA	W	3-2	Feebury, Smith 2	22,000
23	Jan	1	(h)	Queen's Park R	D	0-0		15,000
24		15	(a)	Millwall	W	1-0	Conner	
25		22	(h)	Millwall	W	3-2	Wood, Menlove 2	
26	Feb	5	(a)	Grimsby T	L	0-1		
27		9	(h)	Grimsby T	W	2-0	Menlove, Wood	6,000
28		12	(a)	Newport C	W	1-0	Conner	15,000
29		19	(h)	Newport C	W	2-0	Conner 2	16,000
30		26	(a)	Gillingham	W	1-0	Conner	
31	Mar	5	(h)	Gillingham	W	4-1	Jones 2, Conner, Wood (pen)	12,000
32		12	(a)	Swindon T	W	3-1	Jones, Feebury, Conner	12,000
33		19	(h)	Swindon T	W	1-0	Wood	20,000
34		26	(h)	Portsmouth	W	3-0	Bates, Conner, Wood	18,000
35		28	(a)	Southampton	D	1-1	Bates	20,000
36		29	(h)	Southampton	D	1-1	Wood	20,000
37	Apr	2	(a)	Portsmouth	D	0-0		18,353
38		9	(h)	Watford	D	2-2	Conner 2	16,000
39		16	(a)	Watford	D	1-1	Conner	8,000
40		23	(h)	Northampton T	W	5-1	Storey 2, Conner 2, Jones	
41		30	(a)	Northampton T	D	2-2	Conner 2	8,000
42	May	7	(a)	Southend U	W	2-0	Conner 2	

FINAL LEAGUE POSITION: 1st in Division Three — Appearances

†Played at The Dell, Southampton, after The Nest was closed due to crowd trouble. — Goals

FA Cup

No	Month	Date	Venue	Opponent	Result	Score	Scorers	Attendance
1	Jan	8	(h)	Manchester C	W	2-0	Menlove, Bateman	18,500
2		29	(h)	Hull C	L	0-2		

Appearances

Goals

Alderson	Little	Rhodes	McCracken	Jones	Feebury	Bateman	Conner	Smith E	Milligan	Whibley	Bates	Menlove	Storey	Collier	Wood	Swift	Hand	Kennedy	
1	2	3	4	5	6	7	8	9	10	11									1
1	2	3	4	5	6	7	8	9	10	11									2
1	2	3	4		6	7	8	9		11	5	10							3
1	2	3	4		6		8	9		11	5	10	7						4
1	2	3	4		6		8	9		11	5	10	7						5
1	2	3	4		6		8	9		11	5	10	7						6
1	2	3	4		6		8	9		11	5	10	7						7
1	2	3	4		6		8	9		11	5	10	7						8
1	2	3	4		6		8	9		11	5	10	7						9
1	2	3	4		6		8	9		11	5	10	7						10
1	2	3		4	6		8	9		11	5	10	7						11
1	2	3	4		6		8	9		11	5	10	7						12
1	2	3	4		6		8	9		11	5	10	7						13
1	2	3	4			7	9			11	5	10	8	6					14
1	2	3	4		6	7	9			11	5	10	8						15
1	2	3	4		6	7	9			11	5	10	8						16
1	2	3	4		6	7	10	9		11	5		8						17
1	2	3	4		6	7	10	9		11	5		8						18
1	2	3	4		6	7	8	9			5	10	7		11				19
1	2	3		4	6	7	10				5		8		11	9			20
1	2	3		4	6	7	9	10			5		8		11				21
1	2	3		4	6	7	9	10			5		8		11				22
1	2	3		4	6	7	9	10			5		8		11				23
1	2	3		4	6	7	8			11	5	10			9				24
1	2	3		4	6	7	8			11	5	10			9				25
1	2	3		4	6	7	8				5	10			9		11		26
1	2	3		4	6	7	8				5	10			9		11		27
1	2	3			6	7	9			11	5				10		8	4	28
1	2	3		4	6	7	9			11	5		8		10				29
1	2	3		4	6	7	9			11	5		8		10				30
1	2	3		4	6	7	9			11	5		8		10				31
1	2	3		4	6	7	9			11	5		8		10				32
1	2	3		4	6	7	9			11	5		8		10				33
1	2	3		4	6	7	9			11	5		8		10				34
1	2	3		4	6	7	9			11	5		8		10				35
1	2	3		4	6	7	9				5	10	8		11				36
1	2	3		4	6	7	9				5		8		10		11		37
1	2	3		4	6	7	8				5	9			10		11		38
1	2	3		4	6	7	9			11	5		8				10		39
1	2	3		4	6	7	9			11	5		8				10		40
1	2	3		4	6	7	9			11	5		8				10		41
1	2	3		4	6	7	9			11	5		8				10		42
42	42	42	18	25	41	32	42	19	2	32	40	21	33	1	19	1	9	1	
				4	4		29	9	1	5	2	5	4		6				

1 own-goal

Alderson	Little	Rhodes	McCracken	Jones	Feebury	Bateman	Conner	Smith E	Milligan	Whibley	Bates	Menlove	Storey	Collier	Wood	Swift	Hand	Kennedy	
1	2	3		4	6	7	8			11	5	9			10				1
1	2	3		4	6	7	8				5	9			10			11	2
2	2	2		2	2	2	2			1	2	2			2			1	
						1						1							

1921-22

Manager: Edmund Goodman

1	Aug	27	(h)	Nottingham F	W 4-1	Jones, Conner, Smith, Whibley	20,000
2		29	(a)	Barnsley	L 1-3	Bateman	12,000
3	Sep	3	(a)	Nottingham F	L 1-2	Wood	18,000
4		7	(h)	Barnsley	L 0-1		
5		10	(h)	Rotherham C	W 2-0	Menlove, Wood	12,000
6		17	(a)	Rotherham C	D 1-1	Smith	
7		24	(h)	Sheffield W	D 2-2	Conner 2	14,000
8	Oct	1	(a)	Sheffield W	L 0-1		18,000
9		8	(h)	Fulham	W 2-0	Conner, Menlove	20,000
10		15	(a)	Fulham	D 1-1	Conner	32,000
11		22	(h)	Blackpool	W 1-0	Hand	15,000
12		29	(a)	Blackpool	W 3-1	Dreyer, Whibley, Hand	
13	Nov	5	(h)	Clapton O	W 1-0	Hand	18,000
14		12	(a)	Clapton O	D 0-0		19,000
15		19	(a)	Wolves	W 1-0	Feebury (pen)	14,000
16	Dec	3	(a)	Stoke	L 1-5	McGrory (og)	
17		7	(h)	Wolves	D 1-1	Menlove	8,000
18		10	(h)	Stoke	L 0-2		14,000
19		17	(a)	Leeds U	D 0-0		
20		24	(h)	Leeds U	L 1-2	Whibley	10,000
21		26	(h)	Notts C	W 1-0	Conner	
22		27	(a)	Notts C	L 2-3	Conner, Whibley	
23		31	(a)	Hull C	L 0-1		
24	Jan	14	(h)	Hull C	L 0-2		
25		21	(h)	Bristol C	D 1-1	Menlove	
26	Feb	4	(h)	South Shields	L 1-2	Menlove	
27		8	(a)	Bristol C	W 2-1	Menlove 2	
28		11	(a)	South Shields	D 1-1	Waite	
29		18	(h)	Port Vale	D 0-0		
30		25	(a)	Port Vale	L 0-3		
31	Mar	4	(h)	West Ham U	L 1-2	Cartwright	
32		11	(a)	West Ham U	L 0-2		22,000
33		18	(a)	Bury	W 2-1	Whitworth, Bateman	8,000
34		25	(h)	Bury	W 4-1	Wood, Whibley, Harry 2	10,000
35	Apr	1	(a)	Leicester C	L 0-2		12,000
36		8	(h)	Leicester C	W 1-0	McCracken	10,000
37		15	(a)	Derby C	L 0-2		12,000
38		17	(h)	Bradford	D 1-1	Cartwright	10,000
39		18	(a)	Bradford	D 0-0		
40		22	(h)	Derby C	W 3-1	Conner, Jones, Cartwright	7,000
41		29	(a)	Coventry C	D 1-1	Cartwright	
42	May	6	(h)	Coventry C	D 1-1	Whitworth	10,000

FINAL LEAGUE POSITION: 14th in Division Two

Appearances

Goals

FA Cup

1	Jan	7	(a)	Everton	W 6-0	Whibley, Menlove 2, Conner 2, Wood	41,000
2		28	(h)	Millwall	D 0-0		25,000
R	Feb	1	(a)	Millwall	L 0-2		35,000

Appearances

Goals

Alderson	Little	Rhodes	McCracken	Jones	Feebury	Bateman	Conner	Smith	Menlove	Whibley	Dreyer	Cartwright	Hand	Wood	Kennedy	Storey	Wells	Waite	Allen	Nixon	Forward	Irwin	Whitworth	Harry	Greener	
1	2	3	4	5	6	7	8	9	10	11																1
1	2	3	4	5		7	8	9	10		6	11														2
1	2	3	4	5		7		9			6	11	8	10												3
1		3	4	5		7		9			6	11	8	10	2											4
1		3	4	5		7			9		6	11		10	2	8										5
1		3	4	5		7		8	9		6	11		10	2											6
1	2	3	4	5		7	8		9		6	11		10												7
1	2	3	4	5		7	9		10		6	11				8										8
1	2	3	4	5	6	7	9		10	11						8										9
1	2	3	4	5		7	9		10	11	6		8													10
1	2	3		5		7	9		10	11	6		8				4									11
1	2	3	4	5		7	8		9	11	6		10													12
1	2	3	4	5		7	8		9	11	6		10													13
1	2	3	4	5	6	7			9	11	8		10													14
1	2	3	4	5	6	7			9		8	11	10													15
1	2	3	4	5	6		9			11	8		10			7										16
1	2	3		5	6	7			9	11	4		10					8								17
1	2	3	4		5	7			9	11	6		10					8								18
1	2	3	4	5	6	7			9				11	10				8								19
1		3	4	5	6	7		9		11				10				8	2							20
1		3	4	5	6	7	8		9	11				10					2							21
1		3	4		6	7	8		9	11				10					2	5						22
1	2	3	4	5	6	7	8		9	11				10												23
1	2	3	4		6	7	8		9	11	5			10												24
1	2			5		7	8		9	11	6			10			4		3							25
1	2	3	4			7			9		6		11			8				5	10					26
1	2	3	4	5					10	11	6		7			8		9								27
	2	3	4	5		7			10	11	6					8		9				1				28
	2		4	5		7	9		10	11	6					8			3			1				29
	2	3	4	5		7			10	11	6					8		9				1				30
	2	3		5	6	7			9	11	4	10				8						1				31
	2	3	5		6					11	4	10				7		9				1				32
	2	3		5	6	7				11	4			10		8						1	9			33
	2	3	4	5	6	7				11				10		8						1		9		34
	2	3			6	7				11				10		8	4			5		1		9		35
	2	3	4	5	6	7				11						8						1	9	10		36
	2	3	4	5		7				11	6					8						1	9	10		37
	2	3	4	5		7				11	6	10										1	9	8		38
	2	3	4	5						11		10				7						1	9	8	6	39
	2	3	4	5			9				6	10	11			7		8				1				40
	2	3	4	5	6	7						10	11			8						1		9		41
	2	3		5	6	7						10	11				4					1	9	8		42
27	36	40	35	36	21	37	17	6	27	29	29	15	18	15	3	19	4	9	5	3	1	15	6	8	1	
			1	2	1	2	8	2	7	5	1	4	3	3				1					2	2		

1 own-goal

Alderson	Little	Rhodes	McCracken	Jones	Feebury	Bateman	Conner	Smith	Menlove	Whibley	Dreyer	Cartwright	Hand	Wood	
1	2	3	4	5	6	7	8		9	11				10	1
1	2	3	4	5		7	8		9		6	11		10	2
1	2	3	4	5		7	8		9		6	11	10		R
3	3	3	3	3	1	3	3		3	1	2	2	1	2	
							2		2	1				1	

1922-23

Manager: Edmund Goodman

1	Aug	26	(a)	Manchester U	L 1-2	Whitworth	30,000
2		30	(h)	Coventry C	D 0-0		8,000
3	Sep	2	(h)	Manchester U	L 2-3	Waite, Whitworth	12,000
4		7	(a)	Coventry C	L 1-2	Morgan	14,000
5		9	(h)	Fulham	D 0-0		12,000
6		16	(a)	Fulham	L 1-2	Feebury (pen)	26,000
7		23	(h)	Leicester C	L 0-1		10,000
8		30	(a)	Leicester C	L 0-3		16,000
9	Oct	7	(h)	Hull C	D 1-1	Waite	10,000
10		14	(a)	Hull C	D 1-1	Nixon	10,000
11		21	(a)	Bury	L 1-2	Whitworth	10,000
12		28	(h)	Bury	D 1-1	Feebury	12,000
13	Nov	4	(a)	Sheffield W	L 1-3	Rhodes (pen)	17,000
14		6	(a)	Rotherham U	L 1-4	Johnson	7,000
15		11	(h)	Sheffield W	W 2-0	Bateman, Whitworth (pen)	10,000
16		18	(h)	Barnsley	W 2-0	Whitworth, Johnson	12,000
17		25	(a)	Barnsley	W 2-1	Hand, Whibley	11,000
18	Dec	2	(a)	Blackpool	L 0-4		10,000
19		9	(h)	Blackpool	D 1-1	Dreyer	10,000
20		16	(a)	Port Vale	L 0-2		4,000
21		23	(h)	Port Vale	W 2-0	Millard, Douglas	9,000
22		25	(a)	Derby C	L 0-6		17,000
23		26	(h)	Derby C	D 2-2	Morgan 2	10,000
24		30	(a)	Bradford C	D 1-1	Harry	12,000
25	Jan	6	(h)	Bradford C	W 2-0	Whitworth 2	12,000
26		20	(a)	Southampton	W 2-0	Whitworth, Whibley	13,000
27		27	(h)	Southampton	W 1-0	Whibley	9,000
28	Feb	10	(h)	Rotherham U	W 4-0	Millard, Whibley, Morgan, Harry	6,000
29		17	(a)	Clapton O	L 1-3	Whitworth	22,000
30		24	(h)	Clapton O	W 2-0	Whitworth, Morgan	15,000
31	Mar	3	(a)	Stockport C	D 2-2	Whitworth 2	5,000
32		10	(h)	Stockport C	W 3-0	Johnson 2, Whibley	10,000
33		17	(h)	Leeds U	W 1-0	Whitworth	15,000
34		24	(a)	Leeds U	L 1-4	Johnson	8,000
35		30	(h)	Notts C	L 0-1		9,000
36		31	(h)	West Ham U	L 1-5	Blakemore	10,000
37	Apr	2	(a)	Notts C	W 4-0	Morgan, Whitworth, Hand 2	20,000
38		7	(a)	West Ham U	D 1-1	Bateman	25,000
39		14	(h)	South Shields	D 1-1	Blakemore	9,000
40		21	(a)	South Shields	L 0-2		4,000
41		28	(h)	Wolves	W 5-0	Whitworth 3, Blakemore, Morgan	7,000
42	May	5	(a)	Wolves	L 0-1		

FINAL LEAGUE POSITION: 16th in Division Two

Appearances
Goals

FA Cup

1	Jan	13	(a)	Queen's Park R	L 0-1		18,030

Appearances
Goals

Alderson	Little	Rhodes	McCracken	Millard	Feebury	Bateman	Ward	Whitworth	Morgan	Whibley	Waite	Dreyer	Allen	Greener	Forward	Harry	Cross	Cartwright	Nixon	Conner	Hand	Johnson	Blakemore	Douglas	Wells	Irwin	
1	2	3	4	5	6	7	8	9	10	11																	1
1	2	3	4	5	6	7	8	9	10	11																	2
1	2	3	4	5	6	7		9	10	11	8																3
1	2	3	4	5		7		9	10	11	8	6															4
1	2		4		5	7	8	9	10	11			3	6													5
1	2		4		5	7	8	9	10	11			3	6													6
1	2		4		5	7		8		11	9		3	6	10												7
1	2				5			9	10	11	8	4	3	6		7											8
1			4	5	6			9		11	8		3			7	2	10									9
1	2		4					8		11				6		7	3	10	5	9							10
1	2		4		6			8		11				10		7	3		5	9							11
1	2		4		9			8		11	10			6		7	3		5								12
1		3	4			7				11				6	10	9	2		5		8						13
1		3	4			7								6	10	9	2	11	5			8					14
1	3		6			11		9		7				4			2		5		10	8					15
1	2		4			7		9		11				6			3		5		8	10					16
1	2		4			7		9		11		5		6			3				8	10					17
1	2		4			7		9		11		5		6			3				8	10					18
1	2		4					8		11		5		6		9	3				7	10					19
1	2		4						11	8	10	5		6		7	3						9				20
1	2		4	5						11		6				7	3					8	9	10			21
1	2		4					8	11			5		6		7	3						9	10			22
1	2		4						10	11		6				7	3					8	9		5		23
1	2		4	5					10			6				7	3				11	8	9				24
1	2		4	5				9	10			6				7	3				11	8					25
1	2		4	5				9	10	11		6				7	3					8					26
1	2		4	5				9	10	11		6				7	3					8					27
	2		4	5				9	10	11		6				7	3					8				1	28
	2		4	5				9	10	11		6				7	3					8				1	29
1	2		4	5				9	10	11		6				7	3					8					30
1	2		4	5				9	10	11		6				7	3					8					31
1	2		4	5				9	10	11		6				7	3					8					32
1	2		4	5				9	10	11		6				7	3					8					33
1	2	3	4	5		7		9	10					6				11				8					34
1	2		4	5				9	10			6				7	3				11	8					35
1	2		4	5				9	10			6				7	3				11		8				36
1	2		4	5		7		9	10			6					3				11		8				37
1	2		4	5		7		9	10			6					3				11		8				38
1	2		4	5		7		9	10			6					3				11		8				39
1	2		4	5		7		9	10			6					3				11		8				40
1	2		4	5		7		9	10					6			3				11		8				41
1	2			5		7		9	10			6		4			3				11		8				42
40	39	7	40	25	10	20	4	36	29	29	7	26	5	19	3	24	33	4	7	2	16	20	12	2	1	2	
		1		2	2	2		17	7	5	2	1				2			1		3	5	3	1			

Alderson	Little	Rhodes	McCracken	Millard	Feebury	Bateman	Ward	Whitworth	Morgan	Whibley	Waite	Dreyer	Allen	Greener	Forward	Harry	Cross	Cartwright	Nixon	Conner	Hand	Johnson	Blakemore	Douglas	Wells	Irwin	
1	2		4	5				9	10			6				7	3				11	8					1
1	1		1	1				1	1			1				1	1				1	1					

1923-24

Manager: Edmund Goodman

1	Aug	25	(h)	Port Vale	L	1-2	Hoddinott	12,000
2		27	(a)	Leeds U	L	0-3		10,000
3	Sep	1	(a)	Port Vale	W	4-3	Millard, Bateman, Johnson, Whitworth	14,000
4		5	(h)	Leeds U	D	1-1	Whitworth	8,000
5		8	(h)	Fulham	D	1-1	Whitworth (pen)	12,000
6		15	(a)	Fulham	L	0-1		10,000
7		22	(h)	Blackpool	W	3-1	Millard, Whitworth, Blakemore	
8		29	(a)	Blackpool	L	0-2		12,000
9	Oct	6	(h)	Nelson	D	1-1	Blakemore	10,000
10		13	(a)	Nelson	L	2-4	Morgan, Whitworth	
11		20	(h)	Bradford C	W	3-0	Whitworth, Hand, Bateman	12,000
12		27	(a)	Bradford C	W	1-0	Hoddinott	13,000
13	Nov	3	(h)	Hull C	D	0-0		10,000
14		10	(a)	Hull C	D	2-2	Morgan 2	10,000
15		17	(a)	Stoke	D	1-1	Morgan	5,000
16		24	(h)	Stoke	W	5-1	Hoddinott 3, Morgan, Hand	
17	Dec	1	(a)	Derby C	L	0-5		11,237
18		8	(h)	Derby C	L	0-1		8,000
19		15	(h)	Sheffield W	W	3-0	Whitworth 3	10,000
20		22	(a)	Sheffield W	L	0-6		10,000
21		25	(a)	Bristol C	D	0-0		10,000
22		26	(h)	Bristol C	W	1-0	Hoddinott	10,000
23		29	(a)	Coventry C	D	0-0		15,000
24	Jan	5	(h)	Coventry C	W	3-1	Whitworth, Hoddinott, Morgan	15,000
25		19	(h)	Leicester C	W	4-3	Whitworth 2, Hoddinott, Morgan	10,000
26		26	(a)	Leicester C	L	0-1		
27	Feb	9	(a)	Clapton O	L	0-1		
28		16	(h)	Stockport C	D	1-1	Hoddinott	10,000
29	Mar	1	(h)	Oldham A	L	2-3	Hoddinott 2 (1 pen)	8,000
30		8	(a)	Oldham A	L	0-1		9,915
31		10	(a)	Stockport C	D	2-2	Harry 2	
32		15	(a)	South Shields	L	0-2		8,000
33		22	(h)	South Shields	W	1-0	Blakemore	8,000
34		29	(a)	Bury	D	1-1	Hand	15,000
35	Apr	5	(h)	Bury	W	1-0	Whitworth	12,000
36		12	(a)	Manchester U	L	1-5	Hand	8,000
37		18	(h)	Southampton	D	0-0		8,000
38		19	(h)	Manchester U	D	1-1	Whitworth (pen)	6,000
39		21	(a)	Southampton	L	0-1		10,000
40		22	(h)	Clapton O	W	2-1	Blakemore, Whitworth	6,000
41		26	(a)	Barnsley	L	2-5	Harry, Whitworth	4,000
42	May	3	(h)	Barnsley	W	3-1	Hoddinott 2, Blakemore	

FINAL LEAGUE POSITION: 15th in Division Two

Appearances
Goals

FA Cup

1	Jan	12	(h)	Tottenham H	W	2-0	Morgan 2	17,000
2	Feb	2	(h)	Notts C	D	0-0		19,500
R		6	(a)	Notts C	D	0-0		20,600
2R		6	(n†)	Notts C	D	0-0		11,370
3R		18	(n†)	Notts C	W	2-1	Hoddinott, Hand	6,000
3		23	(h)	Swindon T	L	1-2	Whitworth	20,000

†Played at Villa Park, Birmingham.

Appearances
Goals

Alderson	Little	Cross	McCracken	Millard	Feebury	Bateman	Whitworth	Hoddinott	Morgan	Osbourne	Nixon	Harry	Allen	Johnson	McKenna	Blakemore	Greener	Hand	Cracknell	Hamilton	Nicholson	Callender	Forward	
1	2	3	4	5	6	7	8	9	10	11														1
1	2	3	4		6		8	9	10	11	5	7												2
1	2		4	5	6	7	8	9	11				3	10										3
1	2		4	5	6	7	8	9	11					10	3									4
1	2	3	4	5	6	7	8	9	11					10										5
1	2	3	4	5	6	7	8	9	11					10										6
1	2	3	4	5	6	7	8		10			11				9								7
1		3	4	5	6	7	8		10			11			2	9								8
1	2	3	4	5			8		10			7				9	6	11						9
1	2	3	4	5	6		8		10			7				9		11						10
1	2	3	4		6	7	8	9	10									11	5					11
1	2	3	4		6		8	9	10									11	5	7				12
1	2	3	4		6		8	9	10			7						11	5					13
1	2	3	4		6		8	9	10			7						11	5					14
1	2	3	4		6		8	9	10			7						11	5					15
1	2	3	4		6		8	9	10			7						11	5					16
1	2	3	4		6		8	9	10			7						11	5					17
1	2	3	4		6	7	8	9	10									11	5					18
1	2	3	4		6		8	9	10			11							5		7			19
1	2	3	4	8	6			9	10			11							5		7			20
1	2	3					8	9	10			7	4				6	11	5					21
1	2	3					8	9	10			7	4				6	11	5					22
1	2	3					8	9	10			7	4				6	11		5				23
1	2	3	4				8	9	10			7					6	11	5					24
1	2	3	4				8	9	10			7					6	11	5					25
1	2	3	4				8	9	10			7					6	11	5					26
1	2						8	9	10		3	7	4				6	11	5					27
1	2	3	4				8	9	10	11		7	6						5					28
1	2	3	4				8	9				7		10			6	11		5				29
1	2	3	4					9	10	11		8					6	7		5				30
1	2	3	4					9	10	11	6	7						8		5				31
1	2	3	4			7	8	9	10								6	11	5					32
	2	3	4					9	10			7				8	6	11	5			1		33
1	2	3	4				9		10			7				11	6	8		5				34
1	2	3	4				9			11		7				10	6	8		5				35
1	2	3					9		8			7				10	6	11	4	5				36
1		2	4				8	9	10		3	7					6	11	5					37
1		2	4				8	9	10		3	7					6	11	5					38
1	2	3	4				9		10			7				8	6		5				11	39
1		2	4				9				3	7		10		8	6			5			11	40
1		2	4				9		11		3	7		10		8	6		5					41
1		2	4				8	9	11		3	7				10	6		5					42
41	36	39	37	10	19	10	38	32	39	6	8	33	6	7	2	12	21	27	25	9	2	1	2	
				2		2	16	13	7			2		1		5		5						

Alderson	Little	Cross	McCracken	Millard	Feebury	Bateman	Whitworth	Hoddinott	Morgan	Osbourne	Nixon	Harry	Allen	Johnson	McKenna	Blakemore	Greener	Hand	Cracknell	Hamilton	Nicholson	Callender	Forward	
1	2	3	4				8	9	10			7					6	11	5					1
1	2	3	4				8	9	10			7					6	11	5					2
1	2	3	4				8	9	10			7					6	11	5					R
1	2	3	4				8	9	10			7					6	11	5					2R
1	2		4					9	10		3	7		8				11	6	5				3R
1	2		4				8	9	10		3	7					6	11	5					3
6	6	4	6				5	6	6		2	6		1			5	6	6	1				
							1	1	2									1						

1924-25

Manager: Edmund Goodman

1	Aug	30	(h)	Sheffield W	L 0-1		25,000
2	Sep	1	(a)	Coventry C	W 4-1	Hamilton, Whitworth, Blakemore 2	16,000
3		6	(a)	Clapton O	L 0-3		
4		13	(h)	Hull C	W 1-0	Blakemore	15,000
5		20	(h)	Southampton	W 3-1	Whitworth 2, Blakemore	15,000
6		27	(a)	Chelsea	D 2-2	Harry, Whitworth	40,000
7	Oct	1	(h)	Coventry C	D 0-0		8,000
8		4	(h)	Stockport C	W 3-0	Hoddinott, Blakemore 2	
9		6	(a)	Oldham A	W 2-0	Blakemore, Osbourne	7,661
10		11	(a)	Manchester U	L 0-1		27,750
11		18	(h)	Leicester C	L 0-2		20,000
12		25	(a)	Blackpool	W 1-0	Whitworth	
13	Nov	1	(h)	Derby C	W 2-0	Blakemore, Osbourne	10,000
14		8	(a)	South Shields	D 1-1	Whitworth	
15		15	(h)	Bradford C	W 4-1	Whitworth 3 (1 pen), Blakemore	12,000
16		22	(a)	Port Vale	L 0-3		
17		29	(h)	Middlesbrough	D 2-2	Hoddinott, Whitworth	
18	Dec	6	(a)	Barnsley	L 0-3		
19		13	(h)	Wolves	W 2-1	Hoddinott, Hand	12,000
20		20	(a)	Fulham	L 1-3	Whitworth	18,000
21		25	(a)	Portsmouth	D 0-0		18,000
22		26	(h)	Portsmouth	L 1-2	Harry	25,000
23		27	(a)	Sheffield W	W 1-0	Whitworth	
24	Jan	3	(h)	Clapton O	L 0-1		
25		17	(a)	Hull C	L 0-5		
26		24	(a)	Southampton	L 0-2		9,000
27	Feb	7	(a)	Stockport C	L 0-1		
28		14	(h)	Manchester U	W 2-1	Hoddinott 2	11,250
29		28	(h)	Blackpool	L 1-2	Osbourne	
30	Mar	7	(a)	Derby C	L 0-3		15,381
31		12	(a)	Leicester C	L 1-3	Groves	
32		14	(h)	South Shields	D 0-0		
33		21	(a)	Bradford C	D 0-0		15,000
34		28	(h)	Port Vale	D 0-0		
35	Apr	1	(h)	Chelsea	W 1-0	Whitworth	20,0000
36		4	(a)	Middlesbrough	D 0-0		
37		10	(h)	Stoke	L 0-1		15,000
38		11	(h)	Barnsley	L 0-1		
39		13	(a)	Stoke	D 1-1	Blakemore	
40		18	(a)	Wolves	L 1-3	Groves	20,000
41		25	(h)	Fulham	L 1-2	Blakemore	10,000
42	May	2	(h)	Oldham A	L 0-1		17,500

FINAL LEAGUE POSITION: 21st in Division Two

Appearances

Goals

FA Cup

1	Jan	10	(h)	South Shields	W 2-1	Blakemore, Whitworth	22,000
2		31	(a)	Hull C	L 2-3	Hoddinott, Groves	20,085

Appearances

Goals

Harper	Little	Cross	McCracken	Cracknell	Greener	Harry	Whitworth	Hoddinott	Morean	Hand	Hamilton	Blakemore	Groves	Jones	Osbourne	Nixon	Strang	Blake	McKenna	Hedley	Johnson	Middlemiss	Pettit	Callender	
1	2	3	4	5	6	7	8	9	10	11															1
1	2	3	4		6	7	8	9		11	5	10													2
1	2	3	4		6	7	8	9		11	5	10													3
1	2	3	4		6	7	8	9		11	5	10													4
1	2	3	4		6	7	9				5	10	8	11											5
1	2	3	4		6	7	9				5	10	8	11											6
1	2	3	4		6	7	9			11	5	10	8												7
1	2	3		4	6	7	9	8			5	10			11										8
1	2	3		4	6	7	9	8			5	10			11										9
1	2			4	6	7	9	8			5	10			11	3									10
1	2		4	3	6	7	9	8			5	10			11										11
1	2	3		4	6	7	9	8				10			11		5								12
1	2	3		4	6	7	9	8			5	10			11										13
1	2	3		4	6	7	9	8			5	10			11										14
1	2	3	4	5	6	7	9	8				10			11										15
1	2			4	6	7	9	8				10			11		5	3							16
1	2			4	6	7	9	8		10	5				11	3									17
1	2		4	6		7		9		8	5	10			11	3									18
1	2	3			6	7	9	8		10	5				11		4								19
1	2	3			6	7	9	8		10	5				11		4								20
1	2	3		4	6	7	9	8		10					11	5									21
1	2	3		4	6	7	9	8		10	5				11										22
1	2	3		4	6	7	9	8		10	5				11										23
1	2	3		4	6		9	8		10	5				11				7						24
1	2			4	6	7	9	8		11	5	10								3					25
1	2	3	4	5	6	7	9	8		11		10													26
1	2	3	4		6	7	9		11		5		8								10				27
1		3	4		6	7		9	11	10	5		8					2							28
1		3	4		6	7		9			5	10	8		11			2							29
1		3	4		6	7		9				10			11		5	2			8				30
1		3	4		6	7		9				10	8		11		5	2							31
1		3			6	7		10		11	4	9	8				5	2							32
1		3	4		6	7		8		10	5	9			11			2							33
1		3	4		6	7	9	8	11			10					5	2							34
1		3	4	6		7	9	8		11		10					5	2							35
1		3	4		6	7	9	11		8		10					5	2							36
1		3	4		6	7	9			8		10			11		5	2							37
1		3	4		6	7	9		10	8		11					5	2							38
1		3				7			10			9	8	11		5		2				4	6		39
1		3	4		6	7		11	10			9	8			5		2							40
1		3	4			7			10			9	8	11		6	5	2							41
		3	4			7		9				10	8		11	6	5	2						1	42
41	27	36	25	19	37	41	31	34	8	22	25	32	12	4	23	8	14	16	1	1	2	1	1	1	
						2	13	5		1	1	11	2		3										

Harper	Little	Cross	McCracken	Cracknell	Greener	Harry	Whitworth	Hoddinott	Morean	Hand	Hamilton	Blakemore	Groves	Jones	Osbourne	Nixon	Strang	Blake	McKenna	Hedley	Johnson	Middlemiss	Pettit	Callender	
1	2	3		4	6	7	9	8		11	5	10													1
1	2	3	4		6	7		9	11		5	10	8												2
2	2	2	1	1	2	2	1	2	1	1	2	2	1												
							1	1				1	1												

1925-26

Manager: Edmund Goodman until 24 November 1925, then Alec Maley.

1	Aug	27	(h)	Millwall	L 1-2	Blakemore	23,617
2	Sep	2	(a)	Plymouth A	L 2-6	Blakemore 2	12,934
3		5	(a)	Northampton T	L 0-4		9,005
4		12	(h)	Aberdare A	L 0-1		12,471
5		19	(a)	Brighton & HA	L 2-3	Hand 2	11,738
6		23	(h)	Bristol C	W 5-2	Cherrett 2, Blakemore 3	8,078
7		26	(h)	Watford	W 4-0	Hand, Cherrett 3	14,065
8	Oct	3	(h)	Brentford	W 2-0	Cherrett, Clarke	15,724
9		7	(a)	Bristol C	L 0-1		6,144
10		10	(h)	Bristol R	L 0-2		14,272
11		17	(a)	Swindon T	L 1-3	Cherrett	7,564
12		24	(h)	Exeter C	W 3-2	Harry, Blakemore (pen), Clarke	11,332
13		31	(a)	Luton T	L 2-3	Turner, Blakemore (pen)	7,980
14	Nov	7	(h)	Queen's Park R	W 1-0	Cherrett	11,829
15		14	(a)	Charlton A	D 1-1	Harry	11,465
16		21	(h)	Gillingham	L 0-2		11,879
17		28	(h)	Plymouth A	D 5-5	Hoddinott 2, Cherrett, Hawkins 2	12,300
18	Dec	19	(h)	Bournemouth	W 3-1	Harry, Cherrett, Clarke	10,682
19		25	(a)	Norwich C	L 3-4	Cherrett, Blakemore 2 (1 pen)	8,166
20		26	(h)	Norwich C	W 2-0	Cherrett, Clarke	20,208
21		28	(a)	Reading	L 1-2	Cherrett	12,452
22	Jan	2	(a)	Millwall	L 0-1		18,126
23		16	(h)	Northampton T	W 1-0	Blakemore	7,113
24		25	(a)	Merthyr T	L 0-4		2,755
25	Feb	6	(a)	Watford	L 0-3		6,693
26		10	(h)	Newport C	W 4-2	Blakemore (pen), Cherrett 2, Hawkins	4,228
27		13	(a)	Brentford	L 2-3	Coyle, Hawkins	10,140
28		27	(h)	Swindon T	W 1-0	Coyle (pen)	11,534
29	Mar	6	(a)	Exeter C	W 1-0	Cherrett	5,996
30		10	(h)	Brighton & HA	W 2-1	Cherrett, Clarke	5,871
31		13	(h)	Luton T	W 3-0	Greener, Cherrett 2	12,306
32		20	(a)	Queen's Park R	W 3-1	Blakemore, Harry, Clarke	8,389
33		24	(a)	Bristol R	L 1-3	Cherrett	2,417
34		27	(h)	Charlton A	W 4-1	Cherrett, Hawkins 2, Clarke	11,179
35	Apr	2	(h)	Southend U	W 3-0	Hamilton, Blakemore, Cherrett	17,260
36		3	(a)	Gillingham	D 1-1	Clarke	7,371
37		5	(a)	Southend U	L 1-5	Cherrett	10,908
38		10	(h)	Merthyr T	W 3-0	Cherrett, Blakemore 2	11,411
39		17	(a)	Newport C	W 3-2	Blakemore 3	4,477
40		19	(a)	Aberdare A	L 0-2		2,839
41		24	(h)	Reading	W 3-0	Cherrett 2, Clarke	20,758
42	May	1	(a)	Bournemouth	L 1-6	Hawkins	6,051

FINAL LEAGUE POSITION: 13th in Division Three South

Appearances

Goals

FA Cup

3	Jan	9	(a)	Northampton T	D 3-3	Cherrett 2, Blakemore	14,467
R		13	(h)	Northampton T	W 2-1	Cherrett 2	15,000
4		30	(h)	Chelsea	W 2-1	Cherrett, Hawkins	‡41,000
5	Feb	20	(a)	Manchester C	L 4-11	Cherrett 2, Clarke, McCracken	51,630

‡Record attendance

Appearances

Goals

Harper	Blake	Cross	McCracken	Strang	Greener	Harry	Turner	Blakemore	Keenan	Clarke	Callender	Nixon	Little	Cracknell	Smith L	Pettit	Hamilton	Groves	Hand	Cherrett	Hawkins	Hoddinott	Hampton	Coyle	Hunt	Moore	Osbourne	Hedley	
1	2	3	4	5	6	7	8	9	10	11																			1
	2	3		5	4	7	8	9	10	11	1	6																	2
1		3				7	8	9	10	11			2	4	5	6													3
1	2	3			6	7		9	10	11				4			5	8											4
1	2	3		5	6	7		10		11							4		8	9									5
1	2	3		5	6	7		10		11							4		8	9									6
1	2	3		5	6	7		10		11							4		8	9									7
1	2	3		5	6	7		10		11							4		8	9									8
1	2	3	4	5	6	7		10		11									8	9									9
1	2	3	4	5	6	7		10		11									8	9									10
1	2	3		5	6			10		11							4	8	7	9									11
1	2	3	4	5	6	7		10		11									8	9									12
1	2	3	4		6	7	8	10		11							5			9									13
1	2	3	4		6	7	8	10		11							5			9									14
1	2	3			6	7	8	10		11				5			4			9									15
1	2	3	4		6	7	8	5		11										9	10								16
1	2	3	4		6	7		5		11										9	10	8							17
		3	4		6	7		10		11			2							9		8	1	5					18
		3	4		6	7		10		11			2							9		8	1	5					19
		3	4		6	7		10		11			2							9		8	1	5					20
		3			6	7		10		11			2							9		8		5	1	4			21
		3	4		6	7		10		11			2							9		8		5	1				22
		3	4		6	7		8			1		2								10	9		5			11		23
		3	4		6	7		10		11	1		2							9		8		5					24
		3	4		6	7				11	1		2							9	10	8		5					25
		3	4		6	7		8		11	1		2							9	10			5					26
			4		6	7		8		11	1	3	2							9	10			5					27
		3	4		6	7	8			11	1		2							9	10			5					28
		3			6	7		8		11	1		2				4			9	10			5					29
		3			6	7		8		11	1		2				4			9	10			5					30
		3			6	7		8		11	1		2				4			9	10			5					31
		3			6	7		8		11	1		2				4			9	10			5					32
		3			6	7		8		11	1		2				4			9	10			5					33
		3			6	7		8		11	1		2				4			9	10			5					34
		3			6	7		8		11	1		2				4			9	10			5					35
		3			6	7	8			11	1		2				4			9	10			5					36
		3	4		6	7	8			11	1						5			9		10		2					37
		2			6	7	8	10		11	1						4			9				5				3	38
		2			6	7		8		11	1						4				10	9		5				3	39
		2			6	7		8		11	1						4				10	9		5				3	40
	2	3			6	7		8		11	1						4			9	10			5					41
	2	3	4		6			8		11	1						5			9	10	7							42
16	18	41	20	10	41	40	11	38	4	41	21	2	20	3	1	1	23	2	8	35	19	13	3	24	2	1	1	3	
					1	4	1	19		9							1		3	26	7	2		2					

Harper	Blake	Cross	McCracken	Strang	Greener	Harry	Turner	Blakemore	Keenan	Clarke	Callender	Nixon	Little	Cracknell	Smith L	Pettit	Hamilton	Groves	Hand	Cherrett	Hawkins	Hoddinott	Hampton	Coyle	Hunt	Moore	Osbourne	Hedley	
		3	4		6	7		10		11			2							9		8		5	1				3
		3	4		6	7		10		11	1		2							9		8		5					R
		3	4		6	7		8		11	1		2							9	10			5					4
		3	4		6	7		8		11	1		2							9	10			5					5
		4	4		4	4		4		4	3		4							4	2	2		4	1				
			1					1		1										7	1								

1926-27

Manager: Alec Maley

1	Aug	28	(h)	Queen's Park R	W 2-1	Blakemore, Cherrett	18,261
2	Sep	1	(a)	Brighton & HA	D 1-1	Hilley	7,209
3		4	(a)	Charlton A	W 2-1	Clarke 2	13,499
4		8	(h)	Watford	L 0-1		12,350
5		11	(h)	Bristol C	W 4-2	Blakemore 3, Clarke	16,902
6		15	(a)	Watford	W 2-1	Cherrett 2	7,000
7		18	(a)	Bournemouth	D 1-1	Cherrett	7,504
8		25	(h)	Plymouth A	D 1-1	Blakemore	20,497
9	Oct	2	(a)	Newport C	L 1-2	Flood	6,985
10		9	(h)	Aberdare A	D 0-0		13,003
11		16	(h)	Brentford	W 4-3	Flood, Cherrett, Blakemore, Clarke	14,860
12		23	(a)	Northampton T	D 1-1	Blakemore	5,676
13		30	(h)	Norwich C	W 7-1	Flood, Turner, Cherrett 4, Clarke	12,184
14	Nov	6	(a)	Luton T	L 0-1		7,343
15		13	(h)	Southend U	W 5-3	Cherrett 2, Clarke 3	4,101
16	Dec	4	(a)	Swindon T	L 1-6	Cherrett	6,190
17		18	(a)	Millwall	L 0-1		15,445
18		25	(a)	Coventry C	L 1-3	Cherrett	12,507
19		27	(h)	Coventry C	L 1-2	Blakemore	18,220
20	Jan	1	(h)	Brighton & HA	W 2-0	Blakemore, Clarke	14,346
21		15	(a)	Queen's Park R	W 2-0	Grant, Cherrett	11,506
22		22	(h)	Charlton A	W 2-1	Cherrett, Smith (og)	7,606
23		29	(a)	Bristol C	L 4-5	Turner, Cherrett 2, Grant	11,938
24	Feb	5	(h)	Bournemouth	D 2-2	Grant, Cherrett	11,474
25		9	(h)	Exeter C	W 1-0	Cherrett	4,454
26		12	(a)	Plymouth A	L 1-7	Hawkins	11,781
27		19	(h)	Newport C	W 6-2	Orr, Grant, Cherrett 2, Blakemore 2	10,328
28		26	(a)	Aberdare A	W 3-2	Greener, Smith, Harry	745
29	Mar	5	(a)	Brentford	L 0-3		8,205
30		12	(h)	Northampton T	W 3-0	Greener, Hilley, Grant	11,460
31		16	(h)	Bristol R	W 7-4	Turner 2, Cherrett 2, Blakemore, Clarke 2	5,327
32		19	(a)	Norwich C	W 1-0	Orr	7,087
33		26	(h)	Luton T	D 1-1	Cherrett	9,264
34	Apr	2	(a)	Southend U	L 1-3	Cherrett	6,270
35		9	(h)	Merthyr T	D 1-1	Cherrett	5,968
36		15	(a)	Gillingham	L 1-2	Blakemore	7,584
37		16	(a)	Exeter C	L 1-3	Turner	6,182
38		18	(h)	Gillingham	D 2-2	Cherrett, Blakemore	10,386
39		23	(h)	Swindon T	W 5-0	Cherrett 2, Blakemore 2, Clarke	10,670
40		30	(a)	Bristol R	L 1-4	Clarke	5,905
41	May	2	(a)	Merthyr T	W 2-1	Cherrett 2	1,435
42		7	(h)	Millwall	L 1-6	Cherrett	12,896

FINAL LEAGUE POSITION: 6th in Division Three South

Appearances
Goals

FA Cup

1	Nov	27	(h)	Norwich C	D 0-0		15,000
R	Dec	2	(a)	Norwich C	L 0-1		9,821

Appearances
Goals

Callender	Cross	Orr	Hamilton	Coyle	Greener	Harry	Blakemore	Cherrett	Hilley	Clarke	Smith L	Flood	Hopkin	Gallagher	Turner	Tonner S	Grant	Nixon	Hawkins	Morgan	Barnes V	
1	2	3	4	5	6	7	8	9	10	11												1
1	2	3	4	5	6	7	8	9	10	11												2
1	2	3	4	5	6	7	8	9	10	11												3
1	2	3	4	5	6	7	8	9	10	11												4
1	2	3	4		6		10	9		11	5	7	8									5
1	2	3	4		6		10	9		11	5	7	8									6
1	2	3	4		6		10	9		11	5	7	8									7
1	2	3	4		6	7	10	9		11	5	8										8
1	2	3	4		6	7	10	9		11	5	8										9
1	2	3			6	7		9	10	11	5	8		4								10
1	2	3			6		10	9		11	5	7		4	8							11
1	2	3			6		10	9		11	5	7		4	8							12
1	2	3			6		10	9		11	5	7		4	8							13
1	2	3			6		10	9		11	5	7		4	8							14
1		3	5				10	9	6	11		7		4	8	2						15
1	3						10	9	6	11	5	7		4	8	2						16
1	2					7	9		6	11	5		3	4	8		10					17
1	2					7	10	9	6	11	5		3	4	8							18
1						7	10	9	6	11	5		2	4	8			3				19
1		3				7	10	9	6	11	5		2	4			8					20
1	2	3			4	7	10	9	6	11	5						8					21
1	2	3			4		10	9	6	11	5	7					8					22
1	2	3						9	6	11	5	7		4	8		10					23
1	2	3	4				10	9	6	11	5	7					8					24
1	2	3	4				10	9	6	11	5	7					8					25
1	2	3				7	8	9	6	11	5			4					10			26
1	2	3			4	7	10	9	6	11	5						8					27
1	2	3			4	7	10	9	6	11	5						8					28
1	2	3		5	4		10	9	6	11					8		7					29
1	2	3			4		10	9	6	11	5				8		7					30
1	2	3			4		10	9	6	11	5				8		7					31
1	3	9			6				10	11	5		2	4	8		7					32
1	2	3					10	9	6	11	5			4	8		7					33
1	2	3					10	9	6	11	5	7		4			8					34
1	2	3					10	9	6	11	5			4	8					7		35
1	2	3	5				10	9	6	11		7		4			8					36
1	2	3	5				10	9	6	11		7		4	8							37
1	2	3			5		10	9	6	11		7		4	8							38
1	2	3			5		10	9	6	11				4	7		8					39
1		3			5		10	9	6	7			2	4	8						11	40
1	2	3	5		6		10	9	8	11				4	7							41
1	2	3	5		6		8	9	10	11				4	7							42
42	38	38	16	5	27	15	39	40	33	42	29	20	9	24	22	2	17	1	1	1	1	
		2			2	1	16	32	2	13	1	3			5		5		1			

1 own-goal

Callender	Cross	Orr	Hamilton	Coyle	Greener	Harry	Blakemore	Cherrett	Hilley	Clarke	Smith L	Flood	Hopkin	Gallagher	Turner	Tonner S	Grant	Nixon	Hawkins	Morgan	Barnes V	
1	2	3	5				10	9	6	11		7		4	8							1
1	3		5				10	9	6	11		7		4	8	2						R
2	2	1	2				2	2	2	2		2		2	2	1						

1927-28

Manager: Alec Maley until 12 October 1927, then Fred Mavin from 21 November 1927.

1	Aug	27	(a)	Norwich C	L 1-4	Hallam	13,140
2		29	(h)	Exeter C	W 2-0	Hallam, Clarke	11,329
3	Sep	3	(h)	Northampton T	W 1-0	Hilley	13,771
4		7	(a)	Exeter C	D 2-2	Williamson, Hilley	5,906
5		10	(a)	Southend U	L 1-6	Clarke	6,808
6		17	(h)	Brighton & HA	D 1-1	Hamilton	13,557
7		24	(a)	Bournemouth	D 2-2	Flood, Turner	5,933
8	Oct	1	(h)	Brentford	L 0-2		11,552
9		8	(a)	Luton T	L 1-6	Clarke (pen)	8,844
10		15	(h)	Millwall	L 0-4		18,930
11		22	(h)	Queen's Park R	D 1-1	Clarke	7,115
12		29	(a)	Watford	L 1-2	Turner	7,346
13	Nov	5	(h)	Charlton A	W 5-0	Turner, Havelock 2, Clarke 2	16,694
14		12	(a)	Swindon T	D 3-3	Flood, Hopkins, Turner	7,608
15		19	(h)	Newport C	W 2-0	Clarke 2	8,863
16	Dec	3	(h)	Gillingham	D 2-2	Harry, Hopkins	4,299
17		17	(h)	Merthyr T	W 2-0	Harry, Barnes	6,809
18		24	(a)	Plymouth A	L 1-5	Harry	11,515
19		27	(a)	Torquay U	W 2-0	Hopkins, Brown	3,353
20		31	(h)	Norwich C	W 2-1	Clarke, Hopkins	7,446
21	Jan	7	(a)	Northampton T	D 1-1	Greener	9,860
22		14	(a)	Walsall	D 1-1	Hopkins (pen)	4,279
23		21	(h)	Southend U	W 4-1	Tonner 2, Brown, Clarke	10,606
24		28	(a)	Brighton & HA	L 2-4	Hopkins, Clarke	4,494
25	Feb	4	(h)	Bournemouth	W 6-1	Clarke 3, Hopkins, Tonner 2	10,862
26		11	(a)	Brentford	L 1-2	Turner	7,580
27		13	(a)	Coventry C	D 2-2	Hopkins, Tonner	2,059
28		18	(h)	Luton T	W 3-2	Tonner 2, Salt	13,370
29		25	(a)	Millwall	D 1-1	Clarke	27,736
30	Mar	3	(a)	Queen's Park R	L 0-2		16,468
31		10	(h)	Watford	W 2-1	Hopkins, Tonner	9,851
32		14	(h)	Torquay U	W 3-2	Hopkins, Clarke, Turner	4,842
33		17	(a)	Charlton A	W 4-0	Hopkins 2, Clarke, Harry	11,083
34		24	(h)	Swindon T	W 1-0	Harry	8,373
35	Apr	6	(h)	Bristol R	W 3-2	Clarke 2, Mulcahy	16,126
36		7	(h)	Walsall	W 5-1	Hopkins, Clarke 2, Harry, Mulcahy	12,530
37		9	(a)	Bristol R	D 1-1	Harry	6,275
38		14	(a)	Gillingham	L 1-3	Mulcahy	3,623
39		21	(h)	Coventry C	W 1-0	Mulcahy	5,908
40		26	(a)	Newport C	W 3-0	Clarke, Hopkins, Harry	2,554
41		28	(a)	Merthyr T	D 2-2	Mulcahy, Turner	2,169
42	May	5	(h)	Plymouth A	L 0-2		12,218

FINAL LEAGUE POSITION: 5th in Division Three South

Appearances

Goals

FA Cup

1	Nov	26	(a)	Dartford	W 3-1	Hopkins 2, Smith	6,227
2	Dec	10	(a)	Swindon T	D 0-0		16,360
R		14	(h)	Swindon T	L 1-2	Hopkins	8,500

Appearances

Goals

Callender	Orr	Cross	Gallagher	Hamilton	Hilley	Flood	Williamson	Tonner J	Hallam	Clarke	Greener	Turner	Kelly	Hopkins	Grant	Holmes	Smith	Hunt	Harry	Barnes	James	Havelock	Brown	Ivey	Salt	Mulcahy	
1	2	3	4	5	6	7	8	9	10	11																	1
1	2	3	4	5	6	7	8	9	10	11																	2
1	2	3	4	5	10	7	9			11	6	8															3
	2	3	4	5	6	7	9	10		11		8	1														4
		3	4	5	6	7		10		11		8	1	2	9												5
	2		4	5	6	7		10		11		8	1		9	3											6
	2		4	5	6	7	9	10		11		8	1			3											7
	2		4	5	6	7		10		11		8	1		9	3											8
	2			5		7	9	10		11	6	8	1			3	4										9
	2			5				9		11	6	8				3	4	1	7	10							10
1	2		4	5	6			10		11		8				3			7		9						11
1	2		4	5	6					11		8			10	3			7		9						12
1	2			4		7				11	6	8		10		3	5					9					13
		2	4			8				11	6	10	1	9		3	5		7								14
		2		4		7				11	6	8	1	10		3	5					9					15
		2		4		8				11	6	10	1	9		3	5		7								16
		2		4							6	8	1	9		3	5		7	11			10				17
		2		4				8			6		1	9		3	5		7	11			10				18
		2		4				8		11	6		1	9		3			7				10	5			19
		2		4				8		11	6		1	9		3	5		7				10				20
		2		4				8		11	6		1	9		3	5		7				10				21
		2		4				8		11	6		1	9		3	5		7				10				22
	3	2		4				8		11	6		1	9					7				10		5		23
	3	2		4				8		11	6		1	9					7				10		5		24
	3	2		4				10		11	6	8	1	9					7						5		25
	3	2		4				10		11	6	8	1	9					7						5		26
	3	2		4		8		10		11	6		1	9					7						5		27
1	3	2		4				10		11	6			9					7						5	8	28
1	3	2		4				10		11	6	8		9					7						5		29
1	3	2						10		11	6	8		9			4		7						5		30
1	3	2		4				10		11	6	8		9					7						5		31
1	3	2		4						11	6	8		9					7						5	10	32
1	3	2		4						11	6	8		9					7						5	10	33
1	3	2		4						11	6	8		9					7						5	10	34
1	3	2		4						11	6	8		9					7						5	10	35
1	3	2		4						11	6	8		9					7						5	10	36
	3	2		4						11	6	8	1	9					7						5	10	37
	3	2		4						11	6	8	1	9					7						5	10	38
1	3	2		4						11	6	8		9					7						5	10	39
1	3	2		4						11	6	8		9					7						5	10	40
1	3	2		4						11	6	8		9					7						5	10	41
1	3	2		4						11	6	8		9					7						5	10	42
19	32	34	11	40	10	14	6	24	2	40	33	31	22	31	4	17	12	1	31	3	2	2	8	1	20	12	
				1	2	2	1	8	2	22	1	7		14					8	1		2	2		1	5	

Callender	Orr	Cross	Gallagher	Hamilton	Hilley	Flood	Williamson	Tonner J	Hallam	Clarke	Greener	Turner	Kelly	Hopkins	Grant	Holmes	Smith	Hunt	Harry	Barnes	James	Havelock	Brown	Ivey	Salt	Mulcahy	
		2		4		7				11	6	8	1	10		3	5					9					1
1		2		4		8				11	6	10		9		3	5			7							2
1		2		4		8				11	6	10		9		3	5			7							R
2		3		3		3				3	3	3	1	3		3	3			2		1					
														3			1										

1928-29

Manager: Fred Mavin

1	Aug	25	(h)	Watford	W 3-0	Harry, Gill, Davis	19,466
2	Sep	1	(a)	Walsall	L 1-3	Walsh	7,243
3		5	(h)	Fulham	W 2-1	Moyle, Griffiths	15,005
4		8	(h)	Newport C	D 1-1	Davis	14,796
5		10	(a)	Fulham	D 2-2	Griffiths 2	11,239
6		15	(a)	Norwich C	W 1-0	Harry	9,892
7		22	(a)	Swindon T	L 2-3	Charlton (pen), Gill	7,999
8		29	(h)	Torquay U	W 2-0	Havelock 2	14,091
9	Oct	6	(a)	Gillingham	W 1-0	Harry	5,923
10		13	(h)	Plymouth A	L 1-4	Gill	17,980
11		20	(h)	Charlton A	L 0-2		12,551
12		27	(a)	Northampton T	L 1-8	James	7,299
13	Nov	3	(h)	Coventry C	L 0-3		12,470
14		10	(a)	Luton T	L 3-5	Havelock 3	9,606
15		17	(h)	Brentford	W 1-0	Harry	11,323
16	Dec	1	(h)	Merthyr T	W 2-0	Butler 2	9,100
17		15	(h)	Exeter C	W 1-0	Griffiths	6,041
18		22	(a)	Brighton & HA	W 5-1	Havelock 2, Butler 3	3,899
19		25	(a)	Bristol R	D 1-1	Griffiths	12,106
20		26	(h)	Bristol R	W 5-2	Harry, Havelock, Butler 2, Clarke	9,083
21		29	(a)	Watford	D 3-3	Havelock 2, Clarke	9,693
22	Jan	5	(h)	Walsall	D 1-1	O'Brien (og)	9,057
23		19	(a)	Newport C	W 3-1	Havelock, Griffiths, Clarke	3,399
24	Feb	2	(h)	Swindon T	W 6-1	Charlton (pen), Thoms, Havelock, Griffiths 2, Clarke	10,364
25		9	(a)	Torquay U	W 2-1	Havelock, Clarke	4,178
26		23	(a)	Plymouth A	D 1-1	Hamilton	9,213
27	Mar	2	(a)	Charlton A	W 3-1	Griffiths, Butler, Clarke	2,644
28		6	(h)	Norwich C	W 2-1	Havelock 2	9,171
29		9	(h)	Northampton T	W 1-0	Butler	25,072
30		16	(a)	Coventry C	W 3-1	Charlton (pen), Clarke, Griffiths	12,289
31		23	(h)	Luton T	W 3-0	Harry, Havelock 2	22,981
32		29	(h)	Queen's Park R	L 1-4	Havelock	33,160
33		30	(a)	Brentford	W 4-2	Harry, Griffiths 2, Butler	13,314
34	Apr	1	(a)	Queen's Park R	D 1-1	Griffiths	19,341
35		6	(h)	Bournemouth	L 1-3	Griffiths	20,792
36		10	(a)	Southend U	L 0-3		3,084
37		13	(a)	Merthyr T	D 2-2	Harry, Griffiths	2,750
38		20	(h)	Southend U	W 3-2	Havelock, Charlesworth, Dunsire	16,327
39		24	(a)	Bournemouth	L 0-2		5,005
40		27	(a)	Exeter C	W 2-1	Charlesworth, Griffiths	5,743
41	May	1	(h)	Gillingham	W 3-0	Havelock, Griffiths 2	15,679
42		4	(h)	Brighton & HA	W 1-0	Charlton (pen)	22,146

FINAL LEAGUE POSITION: 2nd in Division Three South — Appearances / Goals

FA Cup

1	Nov	24	(h)	Kettering T	W 2-0	Butler, Clarke	13,000
2	Dec	8	(h)	Bristol R	W 3-1	Harry, Charlton, Havelock	13,500
3	Jan	12	(a)	Luton T	D 0-0		14,200
R		16	(h)	Luton T	W 7-0	Havelock 3, Wilde, Griffiths, Butler, Hamilton	17,000
4		26	(a)	Millwall	D 0-0		40,460
R		30	(h)	Millwall	W 5-3	Butler 3, Griffiths, Harry	26,405
5	Feb	16	(a)	Huddersfield T	L 2-5	Griffiths, Charlton (pen)	19,000

Appearances
Goals

Callender	Crilly	Charlton	Moyle	Thoms	Greener	Harry	Gill	Walsh	Davis	Clarke	Salt	Griffiths	Fletcher	Turner	Mulcahy	Havelock	Wetherby	Smith	James	Butler	Hamilton	Wilde	Imrie	Charlesworth	Dunsire	Betteridge	Conaty	
1	2	3	4	5	6	7	8	9	10	11																		1
1	2	3	4		6	7	8	9	10	11								5										2
1	2	3	4		6	7	8		10	11	5	9																3
1	2	3	4		6	7	8		10		5	9	11															4
1	2	3				7	8			11	5	9		10	4												6	5
1	2	3				7	8	9			5		11	10	4												6	6
1	2	3				7	8			11	5			10	4	9											6	7
1		3			6	7	8		10	11	5				4	9	2											8
1	2	3			6	7	8				5		11	10	4	9												9
1	2	3			6	7	8				5		11	10	4	9												10
1		3	4	5		7		9			6		11	8	10		2											11
1		3		5		7				11	6				4	8			9	10						2		12
1	2	3			6	7				11	5		10	8					9		4							13
1		3		5	6	7		9		11						8		2		10	4							14
1	2	3		5	6	7		9		11						8		4		10								15
1	2	3			6	7		9		11						8				10	4	5						16
1	2	3			6	7						9	11			8				10	4	5						17
1		3			6	7				11		9				8	2			10	4	5						18
1		3			6	7				11		9				8	2			10	4	5						19
1		3			6	7				11		9				8	2			10	4	5						20
1		3			6	7				11		9				8	2			10	4	5						21
1		3			6	7				11		9				8	2			10	4	5						22
1		3			6	7				11		9				8	2			10	4	5						23
1		3		5		7				11	6	9				8	2			10	4							24
1		3				7				11	6	9				8	2			10	4	5						25
1		3			6	7		9		11						8	2			10	4	5						26
1		3			6	7				11		9				8	2			10	4	5						27
1		3			6	7				11		9				8	2			10	4	5						28
1	3				6	7				11		9				8	2			10	4	5						29
1		3			6	7				11		9				8	2			10	4	5						30
1		3			6	7				11		9				8	2			10	4	5						31
1		3			6	7				11		9				8	2			10	4	5						32
1		3				7					6	9				8	2			10	4	5		11				33
1		3				7					6	9				8	2			10	4	5		11				34
1		3				7					6	9				8	2			10	4	5		11				35
1		3				7					6	9			2	8					4	5		11	10			36
1		3			6	7						9			2	8					4	5		11	10			37
	2	3			6	7				11	4					8						5	1	9	10			38
1		3			6	7				11	4	10			2	8						5		9				39
1	2	3			6					11	4	9				8				10		5		7				40
1	2	3			6	7				11	4	9				8				10		5						41
1	2	3			6	7				11	4	9				8				10		5						42
41	18	41	5	6	31	41	10	8	5	31	22	27	7	7	11	34	20	3	2	26	24	26	1	8	3	1	3	
		4	1	1		8	3	1	2	7		18				20				10	1			2	1			

1 own-goal

Callender	Crilly	Charlton	Moyle	Thoms	Greener	Harry	Gill	Walsh	Davis	Clarke	Salt	Griffiths	Fletcher	Turner	Mulcahy	Havelock	Wetherby	Smith	James	Butler	Hamilton	Wilde	Imrie	Charlesworth	Dunsire	Betteridge	Conaty	
1	2	3			6	7		9		11						8				10	4	5						1
1	2	3			6	7				11		9				8				10	4	5						2
1		3			6	7				11		9				8	2			10	4	5						3
1		3			6	7				11		9				8	2			10	4	5						R
1		3				7				11	6	9				8	2			10	4	5						4
1		3		5		7				11	6	9				8	2			10	4							R
1		3			6	7				11		9				8	2			10	4	5						5
7	2	7		1	5	7		1		7	2	6				7	5			7	7	6						
		2				2				1		3				4				5	1	1						

1929-30

Manager: Fred Mavin

1	Aug	31	(h)	Queen's Park R	D 1-1	Havelock	20,268
2	Sep	2	(a)	Southend U	L 2-3	Wilde, Griffiths	6,954
3		7	(a)	Fulham	W 2-1	Griffiths, Barrett (og)	23,273
4		9	(h)	Southend U	L 1-2	Havelock	13,279
5		14	(h)	Norwich C	W 3-2	Simpson 3	14,067
6		18	(a)	Bournemouth	L 1-2	Simpson	6,635
7		21	(a)	Swindon T	L 1-3	Simpson	6,606
8		25	(h)	Newport C	W 1-0	Simpson	9,445
9		28	(a)	Gillingham	D 1-1	Simpson	6,818
10	Oct	5	(h)	Northampton T	L 1-3	Turner	17,562
11		12	(a)	Exeter C	L 1-6	Simpson	6,158
12		19	(h)	Brighton & HA	D 2-2	Fishlock, Charlton (pen)	13,882
13		26	(a)	Bristol R	W 3-2	Simpson, Wilde, Havelock	6,498
14	Nov	2	(h)	Brentford	W 2-1	Duthie 2	16,939
15		9	(a)	Clapton O	L 1-2	Simpson	14,114
16		16	(h)	Coventry C	W 4-3	Charlton (pen), Clarke, Havelock, Duthie	2,862
17		23	(a)	Watford	D 1-1	Havelock	5,646
18		30	(h)	Swindon T	W 1-0	Simpson	11,128
19	Dec	7	(a)	Torquay U	D 2-2	Havelock 2	3,400
20		14	(h)	Merthyr T	W 6-1	Wilde, Simpson 3, Havelock 2	10,625
21		21	(a)	Plymouth A	L 1-6	Simpson	15,728
22		25	(a)	Walsall	D 0-0		5,612
23		26	(h)	Walsall	W 5-1	Harry 2, Simpson 2, Butler	19,940
24		28	(a)	Queen's Park R	L 1-4	Butler	12,709
25	Jan	4	(h)	Fulham	W 4-3	Havelock, Simpson 2, Fishlock	17,732
26		18	(a)	Norwich C	D 2-2	Turner, Simpson	10,348
27	Feb	1	(h)	Gillingham	W 5-1	Turner, Simpson 3, Harry	8,783
28		8	(a)	Northampton T	L 0-2		8,480
29		15	(h)	Exeter C	D 1-1	Simpson	11,966
30		22	(a)	Brighton & HA	W 2-1	Simpson 2	11,530
31	Mar	1	(h)	Bristol R	W 3-0	Butler 2, Turner	13,078
32		8	(a)	Brentford	L 0-2		19,555
33		15	(h)	Clapton O	W 3-0	Havelock 2, Harry	14,649
34		22	(a)	Coventry C	L 0-1		10,360
35		29	(h)	Watford	D 1-1	Turner	12,310
36	Apr	5	(a)	Newport C	D 0-0		3,324
37		12	(h)	Torquay U	W 4-2	Charlesworth 3, Clarke	9,555
38		18	(a)	Luton T	D 2-2	Simpson 2	9,135
39		19	(a)	Merthyr T	L 2-5	Simpson 2	842
40		21	(h)	Luton T	W 4-1	Simpson 3, Clarke	15,167
41		26	(h)	Plymouth A	W 3-0	Clarke, Simpson 2	18,649
42	May	3	(h)	Bournemouth	D 1-1	Simpson	18,649

FINAL LEAGUE POSITION: 9th in Division Three South

Appearances

Goals

FA Cup

3	Jan	11	(a)	Leeds U	L 1-8	Simpson	31,418

Appearances

Goals

Callender	Wetherby	Charlton	Hamilton	Wilde	Greener	Harry	Havelock	Griffiths	Butler	Clarke	Turner	Duthie	Simpson	Fishlock	Charlesworth	Rivers	Dunsire	Crilly	Swan	Imrie	Jamieson	Barrie	
1	2	3	4	5	6	7	8	9	10	11													1
1	2	3	4	5	6	7	8	9	10	11													2
1	2	3	4	5	6	7	8	9		11	10												3
1	2	3	4	5	6	7	8	9		11	10												4
1	2	3	4	5		7	8		10	11		6	9										5
1	2	3	4	5		7	8	6		11			9	10									6
1	2	3	4	5		7		10			8	6	9	11									7
1	2	3	4	5		7	8		10			6	9	11									8
1	2	3	4	5		7			10		8	6	9	11									9
1	2	3	4	5		7				10	8	6	9	11									10
1	2	3	4	5					10		8	6	9	11	7								11
1	2	3	4	5		7		10				6	9	11		8							12
1	2	3	4	5		7	8			11		10	9			6							13
1	2	3	4	5		7		10		11		8	9			6							14
1	2	3	4	5		7			10	11		8	9			6							15
1	2	3	4	5		7	8			11		10	9			6							16
1	2	3	4	5		7	8			11		10	9			6							17
1	2	3	4	5		7	8			11		10	9			6							18
1	2	3	4	5		7	8			11			9			6	10						19
1	2	3	4	5		7	8			11			9			6	10						20
1	2	3	4	5	6	7	8		10	11			9										21
1	2		4	5	6	7	8		10				9	11				3					22
1	2		4	5	6	7			10		8		9	11				3					23
1	2		4	5	6	7			10		8		9	11				3					24
1	2	3		5			8		10		7		9	11		6			4				25
		3		5		7				11	8		9			6		2	4	1	10		26
		3		5		7				11	8		9			6		2	4	1	10		27
				5		7				11	8		9			6		3	4	1	10	2	28
		3		5		7				11	8		9			6		2	4	1	10		29
	2			5	6	7			10	11	8		9					3	4	1			30
	2		4	5	6	7		9	10	11	8							3		1			31
	2		4	5	6	7	9		10	11	8							3		1			32
	2		4	5	6	7	9		10	11	8							3		1			33
	2		4	5	6	7			10	11	8		9					3		1			34
	2		4	5	6	7			10		8		9	11				3		1			35
	2		4		6	7			10	11	8		9					3		1		5	36
	2		4		6	7			10	11	8				9			3		1		5	37
	2		4	5	6	7			10	11	8		9					3		1			38
	2		4	5	6	7			10	11	8		9					3		1			39
	2		4		6	7				11	8		9		10			3		1		5	40
	2				6	7				11	8		9		10	4		3		1		5	41
	2				6	7				11	8		9		10	4		3		1		5	42
25	38	25	34	37	21	40	18	9	22	32	26	13	34	12	5	16	2	20	6	17	4	6	
		2		3		4	12	2	4	4	5	3	36	2	3								

1 own-goal

Callender	Wetherby	Charlton	Hamilton	Wilde	Greener	Harry	Havelock	Griffiths	Butler	Clarke	Turner	Duthie	Simpson	Fishlock	Charlesworth	Rivers	Dunsire	Crilly	Swan	Imrie	Jamieson	Barrie	
1	2	3	4	5			8		10		7		9	11		6							3
1	1	1	1	1			1		1		1		1	1		1							
													1										

1930-31

Manager: Fred Mavin until 18 October 1930, then Jack Tresadern.

1	Aug	30	(a)	Southend U	W 4-2	Havelock, Butler 2, Simpson	7,413
2	Sep	3	(a)	Torquay U	L 1-3	Frost	6,163
3		6	(h)	Luton T	W 5-1	Clarke, Frost, Simpson 3	15,237
4		8	(h)	Northampton T	D 0-0		10,040
5		13	(a)	Bristol R	L 1-2	Simpson	5,799
6		17	(a)	Northampton T	D 0-0		11,253
7		20	(h)	Newport C	W 7-1	Simpson 3, Butler, Havelock, Harry, Clarke	12,625
8		27	(a)	Gillingham	L 2-6	Clarke, Simpson	7,123
9	Oct	4	(h)	Exeter C	W 7-2	Simpson 6, Butler	12,805
10		11	(a)	Brighton & HA	D 1-1	Clarke	9,730
11		18	(h)	Fulham	W 5-2	Harry 2, Clarke 2, Simpson	21,110
12		25	(a)	Coventry C	W 5-3	Simpson 3, Havelock, Clarke	11,460
13	Nov	1	(h)	Walsall	W 6-3	Simpson, Rivers, Havelock 2, Clarke, Butler	13,668
14		8	(a)	Queen's Park R	L 0-4		12,040
15		15	(h)	Norwich C	W 2-1	Butler 2	10,415
16		22	(a)	Thames	W 2-0	Simpson 2	3,117
17	Dec	6	(a)	Notts C	D 2-2	Simpson 2	11,935
18		17	(h)	Watford	W 6-1	Simpson 4, Clarke 2	5,127
19		20	(a)	Bournemouth	D 0-0		5,077
20		25	(a)	Brentford	L 2-8	Crilly (pen), Clarke	11,770
21		26	(h)	Brentford	W 5-1	Clarke 2, Simpson, Wilde, Harry	15,853
22		27	(h)	Southend	W 3-1	Butler, Simpson, Clarke	16,466
23	Jan	3	(a)	Luton T	W 2-1	Simpson, Butler	6,051
24		17	(h)	Bristol R	L 0-2		14,849
25		26	(a)	Newport C	L 1-2	Simpson	1,967
26		31	(h)	Gillingham	W 5-0	Simpson 3, Harry, Lane	15,042
27	Feb	10	(a)	Exeter C	L 3-4	Simpson 2, Clarke	5,756
28		14	(h)	Brighton & HA	L 0-1		16,986
29		21	(a)	Fulham	L 0-2		15,433
30		28	(h)	Coventry C	W 1-0	Lane	10,546
31	Mar	7	(a)	Walsall	L 1-2	Simpson	3,384
32		14	(h)	Queen's Park R	W 4-0	Clarke 2, Turner, Harry	14,366
33		21	(a)	Norwich C	L 1-2	Simpson	7,756
34		28	(h)	Thames	W 2-1	Simpson, Butler	12,071
35	Apr	3	(h)	Swindon T	W 3-1	Turner, Simpson 2	12,283
36		4	(a)	Clapton O	L 2-3	Clarke, Butler	7,414
37		6	(a)	Swindon T	D 4-4	Turner, Simpson 3	4,842
38		11	(h)	Notts C	D 1-1	Harry	19,638
39		18	(a)	Watford	W 2-0	Harry, Butler	5,377
40		20	(h)	Clapton O	W 3-1	Lane 2, Butler	6,567
41		25	(h)	Bournemouth	W 1-0	Clarke	7,754
42	May	2	(h)	Torquay U	W 5-0	Simpson, Butler 2, Clarke, Harry	12,172

FINAL LEAGUE POSITION: 2nd in Division Three South

Appearances
Goals

FA Cup

1	Nov	29	(h)	Taunton T	W 6-0	Clarke, Simpson 3, Greener, Butler	13,038
2	Dec	13	(h)	Newark T	W 6-0	Butler, Simpson 4, Clarke	15,300
3	Jan	10	(h)	Reading	D 1-1	Butler	22,800
R		14	(a)	Reading	D 1-1	Clarke	15,873
2R		19	(n†)	Reading	W 2-0	Clarke, Simpson	19,737
4		24	(h)	Everton	L 0-6		38,000

†Played at Stamford Bridge, London.

Appearances
Goals

Imrie	Wetherby	Charlton	Frost	Barrie	Greener	Harry	Havelock	Simpson	Butler	Clarke	Hamilton	Crilly	Watson	Callender	Wilde	Rivers	Lloyd	Legg	Turner	Brennen A	Fishlock	Lane	Charlesworth	Nicholas	Wilcockson	
1	2	3	4	5	6	7	8	9	10	11																1
1	2	3	4	5	6	7	8	9	10	11																2
1	2	3	4	5	6	7	8	9	10	11																3
1	2	3		5	6	7	8	9	10	11	4															4
1	2	3		5	6	7	8	9	10	11	4															5
1		3	4	5	6	7		9	10	11		2	8													6
1		3		5	6	7	8	9	10	11	4	2														7
1		3		5	6	7	8	9	10	11	4	2														8
		3			6	7	8	9	10	11		2		1	5	4										9
		3			6	7		9	10	11		2		1	5	4	8									10
		3			6	7	8	9	10	11		2		1	5	4										11
		3			6	7	8	9	10	11		2		1	5	4										12
	2				6	7	8	9	10	11		3		1	5	4										13
					6	7	8	9	10	11		3		1	5	4		2								14
	2				6	7		9	10	11		3		1	5	4			8							15
				3	6	7	8	9	10	11		2		1	5	4										16
				3	6	7		9	10	11		2		1	5	4			8							17
				3	6	7		9	10	11		2		1	5	4			8							18
				3	6	7		9	10	11		2		1	5	4			8							19
				3	6	7		9	10	11		2		1	5	4				8						20
		3			6	7		9	10	11		2		1	5	4			8							21
		3			6	7		9	10	11		2		1	5	4			8							22
		3			6	7		9	10	11		2		1	5	4			8							23
		3			6	7		9	10			2		1	5	4			8		11					24
1		3				7		9			6	2	8		5	4				10	11					25
1		3			6	7		9	10			2			5	4						8	11			26
1				3	6	7		9	10	11		2			5	4						8				27
1		3			6	7		9	10	11		2			5	4						8				28
1		3			6	7		9	10	11		2			5				4			8				29
1		3		5		7		9	10	11		2			6	4						8				30
1		3		5		7		9	10	11		2				4			6			8				31
1		3			6	7		9		11	4	2			5				10			8				32
1		3			6	7		9		11	4	2			5				10			8				33
		3			6	7		9	10	11	4	2		1	5				8							34
		3			6	7		9	10	11	4	2		1	5				8							35
		3			6	7		9	10	11		2		1		4			8					5		36
		3		2				9	10	11				1		4	6		7			8		5		37
		3			6	7		9	10	11		2		1					4			8		5		38
		3			6	7		9	10	11		2		1					4			8		5		39
		3			6	7		9	10	11		?		1					4			8		5		40
		3			6	7		9	10	11		2		1					4			8		5		41
		3			6	7		9	10	11		2		1					4			8		5		42
17	7	33	4	17	38	41	13	42	39	39	9	36	2	25	26	24	2	1	21	2	2	14	1	7		
			2			9	5	46	14	21		1			1	1			3			4				

Imrie	Wetherby	Charlton	Frost	Barrie	Greener	Harry	Havelock	Simpson	Butler	Clarke	Hamilton	Crilly	Watson	Callender	Wilde	Rivers	Lloyd	Legg	Turner	Brennen A	Fishlock	Lane	Charlesworth	Nicholas	Wilcockson	
				3	6	7		9	10	11		2		1	5	4			8							1
				3	6	7		9	10	11		2		1	5	4			8							2
		3			6	7		9	10	11		2		1	5	4			8							3
		3			6	7		9	10	11		2		1	5	4			8							R
		3			6	7		9	10	11		2		1	5	4			8							2R
1		3				7		9	10	11		2			5	4			8						6	4
1		4		2	5	6		6	6	6		6		5	6	6			6						1	
					1			8	3	4																

1931-32

Manager: Jack Tresadern

1	Aug	29	(h)	Torquay U	W 7-0	Simpson 4, Lane, Butler, Clarke	18,479
2		31	(a)	Clapton O	W 3-1	Simpson 3	7,344
3	Sep	5	(a)	Bristol R	L 1-6	Clarke	12,979
4		9	(a)	Brighton & HA	W 3-0	Simpson, Lane, Turner	11,175
5		12	(h)	Queen's Park R	D 1-1	Clarke	11,000
6		16	(h)	Brighton & HA	W 2-0	Charlesworth, Clarke	12,071
7		19	(a)	Bournemouth	L 1-4	Lane	9,638
8		26	(h)	Coventry C	D 2-2	Clarke 2	16,259
9	Oct	3	(h)	Watford	W 2-1	Lane, Simpson	20,953
10		10	(a)	Mansfield T	D 1-1	Clarke	10,849
11		17	(a)	Gillingham	D 0-0		4,856
12		24	(h)	Luton T	D 1-1	Clarke	15,327
13		31	(a)	Cardiff C	W 3-1	Simpson 2, Butler	6,757
14	Nov	7	(h)	Northampton T	W 4-0	Simpson 3, Harry	16,119
15		14	(a)	Reading	L 0-3		9,114
16		21	(h)	Southend U	W 3-2	Clarke (pen), Butler, Simpson	29,335
17	Dec	5	(h)	Thames	W 2-1	Simpson, Charlton (pen)	14,106
18		19	(h)	Exeter C	W 3-0	Clarke 3	8,905
19		25	(h)	Swindon T	D 0-0		17,713
20		26	(a)	Swindon T	L 2-3	Cropper, Clarke	9,905
21	Jan	2	(a)	Torquay U	L 1-3	Fowler (og)	2,703
22		9	(h)	Mansfield T	W 2-1	Clarke, Charlesworth	10,817
23		16	(h)	Bristol R	W 5-0	Harry, Greener, Clarke, Charlesworth, Wilcockson	10,691
24		18	(a)	Fulham	L 0-4		8,446
25		28	(a)	Queen's Park R	D 2-2	Harry 2	8,369
26		30	(h)	Bournemouth	D 1-1	May	12,493
27	Feb	6	(a)	Coventry C	L 0-8		11,459
28		17	(a)	Watford	W 2-1	Simpson, Murphy	4,854
29		27	(h)	Gillingham	W 1-0	Turner	11,596
30	Mar	5	(a)	Luton T	L 0-3		6,105
31		12	(h)	Cardiff C	W 5-0	Clarke, Turner, Simpson 3	13,206
32		19	(a)	Northampton T	L 0-5		6,685
33		25	(h)	Norwich C	W 3-1	May 2, Simpson	18,974
34		26	(h)	Reading	D 1-1	Murphy	15,987
35		28	(a)	Norwich C	L 2-3	Simpson, Lane	16,412
36	Apr	2	(a)	Southend U	L 0-1		8,745
37		9	(h)	Fulham	W 2-0	Simpson, Clarke	21,326
38		13	(a)	Brentford	D 1-1	Clarke	5,816
39		16	(a)	Thames	W 3-1	May, Harry, Lane	1,348
40		23	(h)	Brentford	W 1-0	Clarke	12,138
41		30	(a)	Exeter C	W 1-0	Turner	5,538
42	May	7	(h)	Clapton O	D 0-0		10,286
	FINAL LEAGUE POSITION: 4th in Division Three South						Appearances
							Goals

FA Cup

1	Nov	28	(a)	Reading	W 1-0	Clarke	14,135
2	Dec	12	(a)	Bath C	L 1-2	Simpson	
							Appearances
							Goals

Callender	Crilly	Charlton	Turner	Nicholas	Greener	Harry	Lane	Simpson	Butler	Clarke	Barrie	Wilde	Dunn	Parry	Rivers	Charlesworth	Manders	Jewitt	Lloyd	Murphy	Fishlock	Cropper	May	Wilcockson	Clifford	
1	2	3	4	5	6	7	8	9	10	11																1
1		3	4		6	7	8	9	10	11	2	5														2
1		3	4	5	6	7	8	9	10	11	2															3
			4		6	7	8	9	10	11	2	5	1	3												4
			8		6	7			10	11	2	5	1	3	4	9										5
			8		6	7			10	11	2	5	1	3	4	9										6
			4		6	7	8		10	11	2	5	1	3		9										7
		3	8		6	7			10	11	2		1	5			9	4								8
	2	3	4		6	7	8	9	10	11			1	5												9
1		3	4		6	7	8	9	10	11		5		2												10
1		3	4		6	7	8	9	10	11		5		2												11
1		3	4		6	7	8	9	10	11		5		2												12
1		3	4	5		7	8	9	10	11				2					6							13
1		3	4	5		7	8	9	10	11				2					6							14
1		3	4	5		7	8	9	10	11				2					6							15
1		3	4			7		9	10	11	2	5							6	8						16
1	2	3	4			7		9	10			5							6	8	11					17
1	2	3	4		6	7			10	11		5								8		9				18
1	2	3	4		6	7		9		11		5								10			8			19
1	2	3	6			7	8		10	11				5	4							9				20
1	2		4		6	7	8		10	11	3			5								9				21
1	2		4		6	7			10	11	3			5		9				8						22
1	2		4		6	7				11	3	5				9							8	10		23
1	2		4		6	7				11	3	5				9							8	10		24
	2	3	4			7		9		11		5	1						6				8	10		25
	2	3	4			7		9	10	11		5	1						6				8			26
	2	3	4		6	7	10	9				5	1								11		8			27
			10		6	7		9		11	3	5	1	2					4	8						28
			10		6	7		9		11	3	5	1	2					4	8						29
			8		6	7		9		11	3	5	1	2					4					10		30
			8		6	7		9		11	3	5	1	2					4				10			31
			8			7		9		11	3	5	1	2	6				4				10			32
1		3	8			7		9				5		2	4						11		10	6		33
1		3	10	5		7								2	4	9				8	11				6	34
1		3		5		7	8	9		11		4		2									10		6	35
1		3		5		7	8	9		11		4		2	6								10			36
1	3			5		7	8	9		11		4		2	6								10			37
1	3		10	5		7	8	9		11		4		2	6											38
1	3			5		7	8	9		11		4		2	6								10			39
1	3		8	5		7		9		11		4		2	6								10			40
1	3		8	5		7		9		11		4		2	6								10			41
1	3		8	5		7		9		11		4		2	6								10			42
28	19	22	38	14	24	42	20	31	21	38	17	31	14	30	13	7	1	1	12	8	4	3	16	5	2	
		1	4		1	5	6	23	3	19						3				2		1	4	1		

1 own-goal

Callender	Crilly	Charlton	Turner	Nicholas	Greener	Harry	Lane	Simpson	Butler	Clarke	Barrie	Wilde	Dunn	Parry	Rivers	Charlesworth	Manders	Jewitt	Lloyd	Murphy	Fishlock	Cropper	May	Wilcockson	Clifford	
1	2	3	4			7		9	10	11		5							6	8						1
1	2	3	4			7		9	10	11		5							6	8						2
2	2	2	2			2		2	2	2		2							2	2						
								1		1																

1932-33

Manager: Jack Tresadern

1	Aug	27	(a)	Bristol R	W 3-2	Simpson 2, Roberts	13,588
2		31	(h)	Brighton & HA	W 5-0	Doncaster, May, Roberts 2, Simpson	13,704
3	Sep	3	(h)	Aldershot	W 3-0	Roberts, May, Doncaster	12,167
4		7	(a)	Brighton & HA	W 2-1	Simpson, Roberts	9,302
5		10	(a)	Queen's Park R	L 1-2	Simpson	15,955
6		17	(h)	Southend U	W 4-1	Manders 2, Doncaster, May	19,419
7		24	(a)	Exeter C	D 1-1	May	8,734
8	Oct	1	(a)	Gillingham	L 0-2		9,827
9		8	(h)	Watford	L 0-3		12,095
10		15	(a)	Cardiff C	D 1-1	Doncaster	7,144
11		22	(h)	Torquay U	W 2-1	Roberts, Rivers	10,031
12		29	(a)	Brentford	L 0-2		17,827
13	Nov	5	(h)	Coventry C	L 1-3	Simpson	12,203
14		12	(a)	Bristol C	D 3-3	Simpson, May 2	7,804
15		19	(h)	Northampton T	W 2-0	Roberts, Harry	6,463
16	Dec	3	(h)	Swindon T	W 4-3	Goddard, Turner, Wilde, Harry	8,936
17		10	(a)	Bournemouth	L 2-3	May, Walters	2,862
18		17	(h)	Newport C	D 0-0		8,644
19		24	(a)	Luton T	D 1-1	Berry	7,042
20		26	(h)	Reading	D 1-1	Manders	10,400
21		27	(a)	Reading	W 3-2	Harry, Roberts, Berry	21,180
22		31	(h)	Bristol R	W 2-0	Manders, Roberts	10,636
23	Jan	7	(a)	Aldershot	L 1-3	Roberts	7,979
24		14	(a)	Clapton O	L 1-4	Manders	3,130
25		21	(h)	Queen's Park R	L 0-1		8,157
26	Feb	1	(a)	Southend U	W 2-1	Berry, Manders	3,008
27		4	(h)	Exeter C	D 2-2	Walters, Roberts	10,361
28		11	(h)	Gillingham	W 5-1	Berry, Harry, Lester (og), Roberts, Manders	8,280
29		18	(a)	Watford	L 0-1		5,425
30		25	(h)	Cardiff C	W 4-1	Simpson 3, Harry	5,805
31	Mar	4	(a)	Torquay U	L 1-2	Walters	3,467
32		11	(h)	Brentford	W 2-1	Roberts, Manders	20,261
33		18	(a)	Coventry C	L 2-6	Goddard, Manders	14,610
34		25	(h)	Bristol C	D 2-2	Clarke, Goddard	9,641
35	Apr	1	(a)	Northampton T	L 0-1		4,799
36		8	(h)	Clapton O	W 2-1	Manders, Goddard	8,394
37		14	(h)	Norwich C	W 4-0	Turner, Goddard, Clarke 2	18,265
38		15	(a)	Swindon T	L 0-1		4,642
39		17	(a)	Norwich C	L 0-3		20,540
40		22	(h)	Bournemouth	W 3-0	Simpson 2, Clarke	7,825
41		29	(a)	Newport C	W 3-1	Turner 2, Walters	5,168
42	May	6	(h)	Luton T	W 3-0	Harry, Simpson 2	6,554

FINAL LEAGUE POSITION: 5th in Division Three South

Appearances

Goals

FA Cup

1	Nov	26	(h)	Brighton & HA	L 1-2	Simpson	14,870

Appearances

Goals

Dunn	McGregor	Parry	Wilde	Nicholas	Rivers	Harry	May	Simpson	Roberts	Doncaster	Crilly	Turner	Manders	Hopkins	Clarke	Clifford	Goddard	Berry	Barrie	Walters	Turnball	Nash	Brown	Smith T	Goodcliffe	
1	2	3	4	5	6	7	8	9	10	11																1
1	2	3	4	5	6	7	8	9	10	11																2
1	2	3	4	5	6	7	8	9	10	11																3
1	2	3	4	5	6	7	8	9	10	11																4
1		3	4	5	6	7	8	9	10	11	2															5
1		3	4	5	6	7	8		10	11		2	9													6
1		3	4	5	6	7	8		10	11		2	9													7
1		3	4	5	6	7	8		10	11		2	9													8
1		3	4	5	6	8		9	10			2		7	11											9
1		3	4		6	7		9	10	11		2	8			5										10
1		3	5		6			9	10	11		2	8	7		4										11
1		3	5		6			9	10	11		2		7		4	8									12
1		3	5		6			9	10	11		2		7		4	8									13
1		3	5		6	7	8	9	10			2				4		11								14
1		3	4		6	7	8	9	10			2						11	5							15
1		3	4	5		7	8	9		11		2				6	10									16
1			4			7	10	9			3	2				6		11	5	8						17
1			4			7	10	9		11	3	2				6			5	8						18
1		2	4		6	7			8		3		9					11	5	10						19
1			4		6	7			8		3	2	9					11	5	10						20
1			4		6	7			8		3	2	9					11	5	10						21
1			4		6	7			8			2	9					11	5	10	3					22
1			4		6	7			8		3	2	9					11	5	10						23
1		3	4	5		7			8			2	9			6	10	11								24
			4		6	7			8	10	3		9					11	5		2	1				25
1					6	7			8		3	2	9					11	5	10			4			26
1					6	7			8		3	2	9					11	5	10			4			27
1						7			8		3	2	9					11	5	10			4	6		28
1					6	7			8		3	2						11	5	10			4		9	29
1						7		9	8		3	2	10					11	5				4	6		30
1						7			10		3	2	9					11	5	8			4	6		31
1		3				7			8			2	9		11		10		5				4	6		32
1		3			4	7			8			2	9		11		10		5					6		33
1		3				7			8		2	4	9		11		10		5					6		34
1		3				7					2	8	9		11		10		5				4	6		35
1		3				7					2	8	9		11		10		5				4	6		36
1		3			6	7					2	8	9		11		10		5				4			37
1		3				7					2	8	9		11		10		5				4	6		38
1		3				7		10			2	8	9		11	6			5				4			39
1		3			6	7		9			2	8			11		10		5				4			40
1		3			6	7		9			2	8			11				5	10			4			41
1		3	6			7		9			2	8						11	5	10			4			42
41	4	29	26	11	28	39	13	20	31	15	23	35	25	4	11	10	12	17	26	14	2	1	15	9	1	
			1		1	6	7	14	13	4		4	10		4		5	4		4						

1 own-goal

Dunn	McGregor	Parry	Wilde	Nicholas	Rivers	Harry	May	Simpson	Roberts	Doncaster	Crilly	Turner	Manders	Hopkins	Clarke	Clifford	Goddard	Berry	Barrie	Walters	Turnball	Nash	Brown	Smith T	Goodcliffe	
1		3	4		6	7	8	9	10			2			11				5							1
1		1	1		1	1	1	1	1			1			1				1							
								1																		

1933-34

Manager: Jack Tresadern

1	Aug	26	(a)	Southend U	W 4-0	Simpson 2, Earle, Norris	10,285
2		31	(a)	Bristol R	W 1-0	Simpson	17,657
3	Sep	2	(h)	Coventry C	W 2-1	Norris, Simpson	17,888
4		6	(h)	Bristol R	L 1-2	Norris	15,843
5		9	(a)	Reading	D 0-0		11,172
6		13	(h)	Luton T	D 2-2	Simpson, Roberts	9,457
7		16	(h)	Watford	W 4-3	Turner, Simpson, Earle 2	14,542
8		23	(a)	Charlton A	L 2-4	Roberts 2	10,532
9		30	(h)	Bournemouth	W 4-1	Norris, Simpson 2, Roberts	13,502
10	Oct	7	(a)	Cardiff C	L 0-4		9,022
11		14	(h)	Exeter C	D 0-0		10,698
12		21	(a)	Bristol C	D 2-2	Turner, Simpson	8,919
13		28	(h)	Clapton O	W 3-2	Manders, Simpson, Haywood	11,693
14	Nov	4	(a)	Swindon T	L 2-3	Turner, Manders	8,908
15		11	(h)	Brighton & HA	W 2-1	Simpson 2	10,562
16		18	(a)	Aldershot	W 4-0	Simpson 4	4,297
17	Dec	2	(a)	Northampton T	L 2-4	Roberts, Simpson	5,034
18		16	(a)	Queen's Park R	L 1-2	Simpson	12,849
19		23	(h)	Newport C	D 1-1	Simpson	10,755
20		25	(h)	Norwich C	L 0-1		22,126
21		26	(a)	Norwich C	L 0-2		16,386
22		30	(h)	Southend U	D 1-1	Edwards	8,383
23	Jan	6	(a)	Coventry C	L 1-5	Simpson	17,065
24		20	(h)	Reading	D 0-0		12,416
25		31	(a)	Watford	L 1-3	Dawes	2,391
26	Feb	3	(h)	Charlton A	W 1-0	Manders	9,324
27		10	(a)	Bournemouth	D 1-1	Dawes	4,852
28		17	(h)	Cardiff C	W 3-2	Rooke, Turner, Dawes	6,290
29		24	(a)	Exeter C	W 2-1	Rooke, Dawes	5,948
30	Mar	3	(h)	Bristol C	L 0-1		10,947
31		10	(a)	Clapton O	L 0-2		11,907
32		17	(h)	Swindon T	D 0-0		8,327
33		24	(a)	Brighton & HA	L 1-4	Turner	5,356
34		30	(h)	Gillingham	W 3-2	Dawes 2, Crompton	12,836
35		31	(h)	Aldershot	W 4-1	Dawes 3, Manders	9,362
36	Apr	2	(a)	Gillingham	W 5-0	Dawes 2, Manders, Crompton, Goddard	9,089
37		7	(a)	Luton T	L 1-2	Turner	6,841
38		14	(h)	Northampton T	L 1-2	Dawes	7,984
39		21	(a)	Torquay U	L 1-2	Goddard	3,052
40		25	(h)	Torquay U	W 4-1	Goddard, Haynes, Dawes, Crompton	3,683
41		28	(h)	Queen's Park R	W 4-1	Dawes 3, Crompton	7,777
42	May	5	(a)	Newport C	L 0-1		3,930

FINAL LEAGUE POSITION: 12th in Division Three South — Appearances / Goals

FA Cup

1	Nov	25	(h)	Norwich C	W 3-0	Roberts, Manders, Turner	22,905
2	Dec	9	(a)	Stockport C	W 2-1	Simpson, Manders	15,000
3	Jan	13	(h)	Aldershot	W 1-0	Manders	23,628
4		27	(a)	Arsenal	L 0-7		56,177

Appearances

Goals

Dunn	Haywood	Parry	Brown	Barrie	Wilde	Turner	Norris	Simpson	Roberts	Earle	Parker	Nicholas	Lowe	Finn	Harry	Thompson	Manders	Clarke W	Smith WS	May	Edwards	Rossiter	Haynes	Dawes A	Rooke	Robertson	Ward	Crompton	Goddard	
1	2	3	4	5	6	7	8	9	10	11																				1
1	2	3	4		6	7	8	9	10		11	5																		2
1	2	3	4		6	7	8	9	10			5	11																	3
1	2	3	4		6	7	8	9				5	11	10																4
1	2	3		5	6	4	8	9		11					7	10														5
1	2	3		5	6	4	8	9	10	11					7															6
1	2	3	4	5	6	7	8	9		11							10													7
1	2	3	4	5	6		8	9	10	11					7															8
1	2	3	4	6			8	9	10	11				5	7															9
1	2	3	4	5			8	9	10	11				6	7															10
1	2	3	4	5			8	9	10		11			6	7															11
1	2	3	4	5	6	7		9	10								8	11												12
1	2	3	4		5	7		10									9	11	6	8										13
1	2	3			5	7		10	8								9	11	6		4									14
1		3	6		5	7		9	10								8	11			4	2								15
1		3			6	7		9	10								8	11			4	2	5							16
1		3				7		9	10								8	11	6		4	2	5							17
1		3			4	7		9	10								8	11	6			2	5							18
1	2	3			5	7		9	8									11	6		4			10						19
1		3			5	7				4		2						11	6	8				10	9					20
1	2				5	7		9		6		3				11	8				4			10						21
1				5	6	7						3					8	11			4	2		10	9					22
	2			5	6	11		9	10			3					8	7			4					1				23
1	2	3			5	10		9		11							8	7			4						6			24
1		3			5	10		9							7			11			4	2		8			6			25
		3			5	4		10						6	7		8					2		9		1		11		26
		3			5	4		9						6	7		8					2		10		1		11		27
		3			5	8								6	7							2	4	10	9	1		11		28
1		3			4	8								6	7							2	5	10	9			11		29
1		3			4	8								6	7							2	5	10	9			11		30
1		3	4		6	8									7		9					2	5	10				11		31
1		3	4		6	8									7		9					2	5	10				11		32
1		3			6	4									7		8					2	5	10	9			11		33
1	2	3			5	7											8		6				4	10				11	9	34
1		3			5	7											8					2	4	10			6	11	9	35
1		3			5	7											8					2	4	10			6	11	9	36
1		3			5	7											8					2	4	10			6	11	9	37
1		3			5	7											8					2	4	10			6	11	9	38
1		3			5	7											8					2	4	10			6	11	9	39
1		3			5	8												7			6	2	4	10				11	9	40
1		3			5	8												7			6	2	4	10				11	9	41
1		3			5	8												7			6	2	4	10				11	9	42
38	19	39	14	11	38	38	11	25	16	10	2	7	2	9	15	2	23	16	7	2	13	22	18	22	6	4	7	17	9	
	1					6	4	20	5	3							5				1		1	16	2			4	3	

Dunn	Haywood	Parry	Brown	Barrie	Wilde	Turner	Norris	Simpson	Roberts	Earle	Parker	Nicholas	Lowe	Finn	Harry	Thompson	Manders	Clarke W	Smith WS	May	Edwards	Rossiter	Haynes	Dawes A	Rooke	Robertson	Ward	Crompton	Goddard	
1		3			5	7		9	10								8	11	6		4	2								1
1		3			4	7		9	10								8	11	6			2	5							2
1	2	3			5	10		9		11							8	7					4				6			3
1		3			5	10	4	9							7		8	11				2					6			4
4	1	4			4	4	1	4	2	1					1		4	4	2		1	3	2				2			
						1		1	1								3													

1934-35

Manager: Jack Tresadern

1	Aug	25	(a)	Aldershot	D 2-2	Bigg, Dawes	6,091
2		30	(a)	Queen's Park R	D 3-3	Carson, Bigg, Dawes	9,415
3	Sep	1	(h)	Cardiff C	W 6-1	Dawes 5, Bigg	17,641
4		5	(h)	Queen's Park R	L 2-3	Simpson 2	15,843
5		8	(a)	Brighton & HA	L 0-3		10,560
6		15	(h)	Luton T	W 2-1	Simpson, Dawes	13,416
7		22	(a)	Southend U	W 4-1	Manders 2, Crompton, Carson	7,032
8		29	(h)	Bristol R	W 2-0	Simpson 2	15,556
9	Oct	6	(a)	Charlton A	D 2-2	Dawes, Simpson	21,157
10		13	(h)	Coventry C	W 3-1	Dawes, Crompton, Carson	20,943
11		20	(a)	Clapton O	L 0-2		12,105
12		27	(h)	Gillingham	W 2-0	Dawes 2	12,942
13	Nov	3	(a)	Bristol C	W 1-0	Bigg	11,289
14		10	(h)	Millwall	D 1-1	Dawes	10,736
15		17	(a)	Bournemouth	D 1-1	Simpson	4,828
16	Dec	1	(a)	Newport C	W 3-2	Manders, Carson 2	4,317
17		15	(a)	Reading	L 1-6	Carson	8,756
18		22	(h)	Northampton T	W 2-0	Collins, Bigg	9,318
19		25	(a)	Torquay U	L 1-7	Dawes	2,893
20		26	(h)	Torquay U	D 2-2	Simpson, Manders	19,025
21		29	(h)	Aldershot	W 3-0	Rooke, Collins, Manders	9,972
22	Jan	5	(a)	Cardiff C	L 0-2		9,648
23		12	(h)	Watford	D 0-0		11,288
24		19	(h)	Brighton & HA	W 3-0	Carson, Manders, Simpson	11,189
25		26	(a)	Exeter C	W 6-0	Manders 2, Carson 3, Bigg	3,718
26		30	(a)	Luton T	D 2-2	Simpson, Bigg	3,410
27	Feb	2	(h)	Southend U	W 1-0	Simpson	13,313
28		9	(a)	Bristol R	L 3-5	Carson, Bigg, Simpson	7,028
29		16	(h)	Charlton A	L 1-2	Simpson	27,110
30		23	(a)	Coventry C	D 1-1	Carson	15,041
31	Mar	1	(h)	Clapton O	W 1-0	Bigg	13,214
32		9	(a)	Gillingham	L 0-2		2,712
33		16	(h)	Bristol C	W 3-1	Rooke 2, Manders	10,357
34		23	(a)	Millwall	L 2-3	Dawes, Rooke	9,630
35		30	(h)	Bournemouth	W 1-0	Dawes	8,029
36	Apr	6	(a)	Watford	L 0-2		6,588
37		13	(h)	Newport C	W 6-0	Bigg 3, Manders 2, Purdon	8,323
38		19	(h)	Swindon T	W 7-0	Dawes 2, Manders 2, Purdon, Bigg 2	13,506
39		20	(h)	Exeter C	L 0-1		9,382
40		22	(a)	Swindon T	D 1-1	Simpson	5,660
41		27	(h)	Reading	W 3-1	Bigg, Collins, Manders	8,969
42	May	4	(a)	Northampton T	L 2-3	Bigg, Dawes	4,629

FINAL LEAGUE POSITION: 5th in Division Three South

Appearances

Goals

FA Cup

1	Nov	28	(a)	Yeovil & Petters	L 0-3		10,000

Appearances

Goals

Dunn	Purdon	Owens	Haynes	Wilde	Smith	Carson	Handley	Simpson	Dawes	Bigg	Heineman	Turner	Collins	Parry	Manders	Crompton	Rossiter	Brown TB	Tizard	Barnes	Reed	Rooke	Waldren	
1	2	3	4	5	6	7	8	9	10	11														1
1	2	3	4	5	6	7	8	9	10	11														2
1	3	2	4	5	6	7	8	9	10	11														3
1	3	2	4	5		7	8	9	10	11	6													4
1	3	2	4	5		7		9		11	6	8	10											5
1		2	4	5		7	8	9	10	11	6			3										6
1		2	4	5		7		9	10		6			3	8	11								7
1		2	4	5		7		9	10		6			3	8	11								8
1		2	4	5		7		9	10		6			3	8	11								9
1		2	4	5		7		9	10		6			3	8	11								10
1		2	4	5		7		9	10		6				8	11	3							11
1		2		5	6	7		9	10	11	4			3	8									12
1		2		5		7		9	10	11	6	4			8			3						13
1		2	4	5		7		9	10	11	6			3	8									14
1		2	4	5		7		9	10	11	6			3	8									15
		2	4	5		7		9	10	11			6		8			3	1					16
		2	4	5		7			10	11			6		9			3	1	8				17
		2	8	5		7			10	11		4	6	3	9				1					18
		2	8	5		7			10	11		4	6		9			3	1					19
1				5	6	7		9	10			4		2	8	11		3						20
1		2		5								7	6	3	8	11					4	9	10	21
1		2		5								7	6	3	8	11					4	9	10	22
1		2		5		7		9	10			4	6	3	8	11								23
1		2		5		7		9	10	11	6	4		3	8									24
1		2		5		7		9	10	11	6	4		3	8									25
1		2		5		7		9		11	6	4	10	3	8									26
1		2		5		7		9	10	11	6	4		3	8									27
1		2		5		7		9		11	6	4	10	3	8									28
1		2		5		7		9		11	6	4	10	3	8									29
1		2		5		7		9		11	6	4	10	3	8									30
1		2		5		7				11	6	4	10	3	8							9		31
1		2		5		7		9		11	6	4	10	3	8									32
1		2		5		7			10	11	6	4		3	8							9		33
1		2		5		7			10	11	6	4		3	8							9		34
1		2		5		7			10	11	6	4		3	8							9		35
1	7	2		5	6				9	11		4	10	3	8									36
1	7	2		5	6			9		11		4	10	3	8									37
1	7	2		5	6				9	11		4	10	3	8									38
1		2		5		7				11	6	4	10	3	8							9		39
1	7	2		5				9	10	11	6	4		3	8									40
1	7	2	5	4	6				9	11		3	10		8									41
1	7	2	5	4	6				9	11		3	10		8									42
38	11	41	20	42	11	34	5	28	31	33	25	26	20	30	36	9	2	4	4	1	2	7	2	
	2					12		14	19	16			3		14	2						4		

Dunn	Purdon	Owens	Haynes	Wilde	Smith	Carson	Handley	Simpson	Dawes	Bigg	Heineman	Turner	Collins	Parry	Manders	Crompton	Rossiter	Brown TB	Tizard	Barnes	Reed	Rooke	Waldren	
1		2	4	5		7		9	10		6			3	8	11								1
1		1	1	1		1		1	1		1			1	1	1								

1935-36

Manager: Tom Bromilow

1	Aug	31	(h)	Cardiff C	W 3-2	Bigg 3	16,694
2	Sep	4	(a)	Southend U	L 1-7	Turner	7,580
3		7	(a)	Gillingham	W 2-0	Dawes 2	8,914
4		11	(h)	Southend U	W 3-0	Carson, Dawes, Manders	11,954
5		14	(h)	Bournemouth	W 2-0	Dawes 2	15,651
6		16	(a)	Northampton T	L 1-3	Goodliffe	6,319
7		21	(a)	Luton T	L 0-6		13,206
8		23	(h)	Northampton T	W 6-1	Dawes 4, Bigg, Carson	5,134
9		28	(h)	Notts C	D 0-0		16,153
10	Oct	5	(a)	Bristol R	W 4-2	Dawes 2, Carson 2	10,568
11		12	(h)	Clapton O	D 2-2	Dawes, Waldron	16,619
12		19	(h)	Aldershot	W 2-1	Dawes, Manders	11,741
13		26	(a)	Torquay U	L 2-3	Dawes, Carson	4,440
14	Nov	2	(h)	Millwall	W 5-0	Birtley, Dawes 3, Blackman	19,239
15		9	(a)	Coventry C	L 1-8	Birtley	20,818
16		16	(h)	Watford	L 1-2	Dawes	9,376
17		23	(a)	Queen's Park R	L 0-3		13,414
18	Dec	7	(a)	Exeter C	L 0-1		3,337
19		18	(h)	Newport C	W 6-0	Bigg 2, Blackman 3, Dawes	2,165
20		25	(a)	Swindon T	W 2-0	Blackman, Bigg	5,450
21		26	(h)	Swindon T	W 5-1	Blackman 3, Smith, Dawes	15,867
22		28	(a)	Cardiff C	D 1-1	Bigg	7,411
23	Jan	4	(h)	Gillingham	D 1-1	Blackman	11,726
24		15	(h)	Brighton & HA	W 4-0	Dawes 3, Blackman	3,030
25		18	(a)	Bournemouth	W 5-2	Dawes 2, Blackman, Birtley, Wood	6,926
26		29	(h)	Luton T	W 5-1	Dawes 2, Birtley 2, Blackman	6,804
27	Feb	1	(a)	Notts C	L 1-3	Dawes	8,385
28		8	(h)	Bristol R	W 5-2	Wood, Dawes 2, Blackman, Bigg	11,050
29		22	(a)	Aldershot	W 3-1	Birtley, Wood, Bigg	3,807
30		26	(a)	Clapton O	L 0-1		5,699
31		29	(h)	Coventry C	W 3-1	Dawes, Blackman 2	14,638
32	Mar	7	(a)	Newport C	W 5-2	Blackman, Birtley, Dawes 3	3,232
33		14	(h)	Torquay U	W 1-0	Wood	15,324
34		21	(a)	Watford	L 2-3	Blackman, Bigg	10,432
35		28	(h)	Queen's Park R	L 0-2		22,389
36	Apr	4	(a)	Brighton & HA	L 1-2	Waldron	5,879
37		10	(h)	Reading	W 2-0	Blackman, Dawes	23,025
38		11	(h)	Exeter C	D 2-2	Blackman, Dawes	10,059
39		13	(a)	Reading	W 1-0	Waldron	18,716
40		18	(a)	Millwall	L 0-4		14,498
41		25	(h)	Bristol C	W 6-1	Bigg, Waldron 2, Edwards, Dawes 2	6,244
42		29	(a)	Bristol C	L 0-2		5,099

FINAL LEAGUE POSITION: 6th in Division Three South

Appearances
Goals

FA Cup

1	Nov	30	(a)	Bristol C	W 1-0	Dawes	13,997
2	Dec	14	(a)	Margate	L 1-3	Blackman	

Appearances
Goals

Read	Smith W	Waterfield	Haynes	Wilde	Smith WS	Turner	Manders	Rooke	Dawes A	Bigg	Comrie	Owens	Parry	Carson	Goddard	Goodcliffe	Waldren	Dunn	Rumbold	Purdon	Thorpe	Birtley	Blackman	Booth	Collins	Levene	Hanson	Wood	Turton	Dawes F	Edwards	No.
1	2	3	4	5	6	7	8	9	10	11																						1
1	3		4	5	6	7	9		10	11	8	2																				2
1			2	5	6	4	9		10	11			3	7	8																	3
1			2	5	6	4	9		10	11			3	7	8																	4
1			2	5	6	4	9		10	11			3	7	8																	5
1			2	5	6	4	8		10	11			3	7		9																6
1			2	5	6	4	8		10	11			3	7			9															7
				5	6	4	8		9	11		2		7			10	1	3													8
			2	5	6	4	8		9	11				7			10	1	3													9
			4	5	6		8		9	11		2		7			10	1	3													10
			4	5	6		8		9	11		2		7			10	1	3													11
				5	6	2	8		9	11			3	7			10	1		4												12
				5	6	4			9	11	8			7			10	1	3		2											13
				5	6	4			10	11		2					8	1			3	7	9									14
				5	6	4		9	10	11		2					8	1			3	7										15
		3			6				10	11		9		7			8	1		5	2	4										16
				5		4			10	11			3	7				1				8	9	2	6							17
				5		4			10				3				8	1				7	9	2		6	11					18
				5		4			10	11			3	7				1				8	9	2		6						19
				5	6	4			10	11			3	7				1				8	9	2								20
				5	8	4			10	11			3	7				1					9	2	6							21
				5	8	4			10	11			3	7				1					9	2	6							22
				5	8	4			10	11			3	7				1					9	2	6							23
				5		4			10	11		2						1				8	9	3	6			7				24
				5		4			10	11		2						1				8	9	3	6			7				25
				5		4			10	11		2						1				8	9	3	6			7				26
				5		4			10	11		2						1				8	9	3	6			7				27
				5					10	11		2						1				8	9	3	6	4		7				28
				5		4			10	11								1				8	9	3	6			7	2			29
1				5		4			10	11												8	9		6			7	2	3		30
1				5					10	11												8	9		6			7	2	3	4	31
1				5					10	11												8	9		6			7	2	3	4	32
1				5					10	11												8	9		6			7	2	3	4	33
1				5				7	10	11												8	9		6				2	3	4	34
1				5				7	10	11												8	9		6				2	3	4	35
1				5						11		2					8			4		7	9		10	6				3		36
1				5					10	11		2					8					7	9		6					3	4	37
1				5					10	11		2					8					7	9		6	4				3		38
				5					10	11		2					8	1				7	9		6					3	4	39
				5					10	11		2					8	1				7	9		6					3	4	40
				5					10	11		2					8	1				7	9		6					3	4	41
				5					10	11		2					8	1				7	9		6					3	4	42
16	2	2	10	41	20	26	12	4	41	41	2	19	13	18	3	1	18	26	5	3	4	26	27	13	23	5	1	10	7	13	10	
					1	1	2		38	12				5		1	5					7	19					4			1	

Read	Smith W	Waterfield	Haynes	Wilde	Smith WS	Turner	Manders	Rooke	Dawes A	Bigg	Comrie	Owens	Parry	Carson	Goddard	Goodcliffe	Waldren	Dunn	Rumbold	Purdon	Thorpe	Birtley	Blackman	Booth	Collins	Levene	Hanson	Wood	Turton	Dawes F	Edwards	No.
				5	6	4			10	11			3				8	1				7	9	2								1
				5		4			10	11			3	7				1				8	9	2		6						2
				2	1	2			2	2			2	1			1	2				2	2	2		1						
									1														1									

1936-37

Manager: R.S.Moyes from July to December 1936, Tom Bromilow from January 1937.

1	Aug	29	(a)	Clapton O	D 1-1	Quayle	12,647
2	Sep	2	(h)	Notts C	L 1-2	Quayle	11,740
3		5	(h)	Walsall	W 3-1	Blackman, Waldron, Bigg	9,936
4		7	(a)	Notts C	W 1-0	Waldron	7,042
5		12	(a)	Luton T	L 2-5	Birtley, Blackman	14,187
6		19	(h)	Cardiff C	D 2-2	Birtley, McMenemy	18,348
7		23	(h)	Queen's Park R	D 0-0		9,467
8		26	(a)	Gillingham	L 0-2		6,441
9	Oct	3	(a)	Exeter C	L 2-3	Birtley, Bigg	6,080
10		10	(h)	Reading	W 3-1	Blackman, McMenemy, Bigg	15,981
11		17	(h)	Newport C	W 6-1	Birtley 2, Dawes, Collins, Palethorpe 2	14,882
12		24	(a)	Southend U	L 1-2	Palethorpe	10,281
13		31	(h)	Watford	W 2-0	Dawes, Birtley	7,707
14	Nov	7	(a)	Brighton & HA	L 0-1		7,768
15		14	(h)	Bournemouth	D 2-2	Waldron 2	14,108
16		21	(a)	Northampton T	L 0-2		14,163
17	Dec	5	(a)	Millwall	L 0-3		19,063
18		19	(a)	Aldershot	D 2-2	Liddle, McMenemy	3,278
19		25	(a)	Bristol C	L 0-1		13,346
20		26	(h)	Clapton O	L 2-3	Coulston, Bigg	15,120
21		28	(h)	Bristol C	W 1-0	Blackman	4,195
22	Jan	2	(a)	Walsall	L 0-1		6,145
23		9	(h)	Luton T	L 0-4		15,211
24		16	(h)	Swindon T	W 2-0	Blackman, Bigg	7,648
25		20	(h)	Bristol R	W 3-0	Bigg, Blackman 2	3,769
26		23	(a)	Cardiff C	D 1-1	Bigg	9,415
27		30	(h)	Gillingham	D 1-1	Bigg	6,506
28	Feb	6	(h)	Exeter C	W 8-0	Birtley (pen), Blackman 2, Watson 2, Bigg 3	10,019
29		13	(a)	Reading	D 1-1	Watson	9,783
30		20	(a)	Newport C	D 1-1	Waldron	8,319
31		27	(h)	Southend U	D 1-1	Palethorpe	8,830
32	Mar	6	(a)	Watford	L 1-3	Waldron	7,671
33		13	(h)	Brighton & HA	W 2-0	Palethorpe 2	16,255
34		20	(a)	Bournemouth	L 1-3	Blackmore	5,047
35		26	(h)	Torquay U	D 0-0		15,370
36		27	(h)	Northampton T	D 2-2	Palethorpe (pen), Waldron	9,523
37		29	(a)	Torquay U	L 0-3		3,861
38	Apr	3	(a)	Bristol R	L 0-1		6,282
39		14	(h)	Millwall	W 1-0	Gillespie	6,781
40		17	(a)	Swindon T	L 0-4		6,306
41		24	(h)	Aldershot	W 3-0	Blackman, Palethorpe, Birtley	6,816
42	May	1	(a)	Queen's Park R	W 3-1	Fielding, Blackman, Gillespie	6,142

FINAL LEAGUE POSITION: 14th in Division Three South

Appearances
Goals

FA Cup

1	Nov	28	(h)	Southend U	D 1-1	Birtley	15,932
R	Dec	2	(a)	Southend U	L 0-2		9,000

Appearances
Goals

Knox	Owens	Dawes F	Telling	Walker	Collins	Birtley	Quayle	Blackman	Watson	Bigg	McMenemy	Coulston	Waldron	Dunn	Levene	Wilde	Dawes A	Rooke	Liddle	Palethorpe	Blore	Robson	Beresford	Stanbury	Reeve	Gillespie	Fielding	Lievesley	
1	2	3	4	5	6	7	8	9	10	11																			1
1	2	3		5	6		8	9		11	4	7	10																2
	2	3		5	6		8	9		11	4	7	10	1															3
	2	3	4	5			8	9		11		7	10	1	6														4
	2	3			6	7	8	9		11	4			1		5	10												5
	2	3		5	6	7		9		11	4		8	1			10												6
1	2	3		5	6			9		11	4	7	8				10												7
	2	3		5	6		8			11	4	7	10	1				9											8
	2	3		5		8		9		11	4		10	1	6				7										9
	2	3		5	6	8		9		11	4			1			10		7										10
	2	3		5	6	8				11	4			1			10		7	9									11
	2	3		5	6	8				11	4			1			10		7	9									12
	2	3		5	6	8				11	4	7					10			9	1								13
	2	3		5	6	8				11	4	7					10			9	1								14
	2	3		5	6	7				11	4		8				10			9	1								15
	2	3		5	6	7				11	4		8	1			10			9									16
	2	3	4	5		8		7	11				10		6					9	1								17
	2	3		5	11						4				6		10		7	9	1	8							18
	2	3		5		8				11	4		10		6				7	9	1								19
	2	3		5		4		9		11	10	7			6						1		8						20
	2	3		5	10	4		9		11		7			6						1	8							21
	2	3		5		8				11	4	7	10		6					9				1					22
	2	3		5		8		9	10	11	4	7			6						1								23
	2	3		5		7		9		11	4				6					10	1		8						24
	2	3		5		8		9		11	4	7			6					10	1								25
	2	3		5	6	8		9	7	11					4					10	1								26
	2	3		5	6	8		9	7	11					4					10	1								27
	2	3		5	6	4		9	7	11			8							10	1								28
	2	3		5	6	4		9	7	11			8							10	1								29
	2	3		5	6			9	7	11			8		4					10	1								30
	2	3		5	6			9	7				8		4					10	1				11				31
	2	3		5	6	4		9	7				11							10	1					8			32
	2	3		5	6			9	7						4					10	1					8	11		33
	2	3		5	6			9							4				7	10	1					8	11		34
	2	3		5	6	4		9	7				8							10	1						11		35
	2	3		5	6	4							10						7	9	1					8	11		36
	2	3		5		7		9			6					4				10	1	8					11		37
	2	3		5				9			6					4			7	10	1		8				11		38
	2	3		5	6						4		10						7	9	1					8	11		39
	2	3		5	6						4		10						7	9	1					8	11		40
	2	3		5	6	4		9											7	10	1					8	11		41
	2	3		5	4			9											7	10	1					8	11	6	42
3	42	42	3	41	31	28	6	29	12	28	25	12	21	10	17	3	11	1	13	29	28	3	3	1	1	8	10	1	
					1	8	2	12	3	11	3	1	7				2		1	8						2	1		

Knox	Owens	Dawes F	Telling	Walker	Collins	Birtley	Quayle	Blackman	Watson	Bigg	McMenemy	Coulston	Waldron	Dunn	Levene	Wilde	Dawes A	Rooke	Liddle	Palethorpe	Blore	Robson	Beresford	Stanbury	Reeve	Gillespie	Fielding	Lievesley	
	2	3		5	6	8				11	4						10		7	9	1								1
	2	3		5	6	8		7		11	4						10			9	1								R
	2	2		2	2	2		1		2	2						2		1	2	2								
						1																							

1937-38

Manager: Tom Bromilow

1	Aug	28	(h)	Aldershot	D 1-1	Walker	17,123
2	Sep	1	(a)	Swindon T	L 0-4		8,776
3		4	(a)	Millwall	D 2-2	Blackman, Gillespie	25,894
4		8	(h)	Swindon T	L 0-1		8,879
5		11	(h)	Reading	W 3-1	Waldron 3	12,677
6		15	(h)	Watford	W 4-1	Collins, Waldron 2, Quayle	6,391
7		18	(a)	Bournemouth	L 0-1		8,520
8		25	(a)	Notts C	W 1-0	Blackman	18,164
9	Oct	2	(h)	Newport C	W 3-0	Blackman 2, Waldron	15,362
10		9	(a)	Bristol C	D 0-0		13,262
11		16	(h)	Brighton & HA	W 3-2	Waldron 2, Blackman	19,121
12		23	(a)	Queen's Park R	L 0-1		12,982
13		30	(h)	Southend U	W 2-1	Waldron, Palethorpe	15,324
14	Nov	6	(a)	Clapton O	W 2-0	Pritchard 2	11,125
15		13	(h)	Torquay U	W 4-1	Palethorpe 2, Waldron, Pritchard	13,718
16		20	(a)	Mansfield T	L 0-2		8,207
17	Dec	18	(a)	Cardiff C	L 2-4	Blackman 2	18,374
18		27	(a)	Exeter C	D 2-2	Waldron, Blackman	12,263
19		28	(h)	Exeter C	D 2-2	Robson, Pritchard	6,450
20	Jan	1	(a)	Aldershot	L 0-1		5,400
21		15	(h)	Millwall	D 0-0		22,355
22		20	(h)	Bristol R	W 3-2	Gregory, Horton, Pritchard	5,492
23		22	(a)	Reading	L 2-3	Waldron, Robson	11,016
24		29	(h)	Bournemouth	L 0-1		10,485
25	Feb	3	(a)	Northampton T	D 1-1	Gillespie	3,672
26		5	(h)	Notts C	W 3-1	Davis, Smith, Waldron	16,244
27		12	(a)	Newport C	D 0-0		7,933
28		19	(h)	Bristol C	D 1-1	Smith	16,129
29		26	(a)	Brighton & HA	L 1-2	Gregory	9,707
30	Mar	5	(h)	Queen's Park R	W 4-0	Blackman 2, Dawes, Pritchard	25,522
31		12	(a)	Southend U	D 2-2	Blackman, Smith	6,300
32		16	(h)	Walsall	W 3-1	Blackman 2, Lievesley	5,242
33		19	(h)	Clapton O	W 1-0	Blackman	15,395
34		26	(a)	Torquay U	D 0-0		3,358
35	Apr	2	(h)	Mansfield T	W 4-0	Collins, Davis, Smith 2	13,105
36		9	(a)	Bristol R	L 0-1		5,316
37		15	(h)	Gillingham	W 3-0	Dawes, Blackman 2	15,390
38		16	(a)	Northampton T	L 0-1		14,057
39		18	(a)	Gillingham	W 4-2	Davis 2, Dawes 2	6,602
40		23	(a)	Walsall	D 1-1	Horton	3,975
41		30	(h)	Cardiff C	W 1-0	Smith	9,018
42	May	7	(a)	Watford	W 2-1	Horton, Waldron	13,713

FINAL LEAGUE POSITION: 7th in Division Three South

Appearances
Goals

FA Cup

1	Nov	27	(h)	Kettering T	D 2-2	Gillespie, Davis	9,778
R	Dec	2	(a)	Kettering T	W 4-0	Pritchard 2, Blackman, Waldron	7,514
2		11	(a)	Accrington S	W 1-0	Owens	5,400
3	Jan	8	(h)	Liverpool	D 0-0		33,000
R		12	(a)	Liverpool	L 1-3*	Waldron	35,918

*After extra-time

Appearances
Goals

Blore	Owens	Dawes FW	Daniels	Walker	Lievesley	Davis	Fielding	Jordan	Palethorpe	Pritchard	Birtley	Waldren	Chesters	Booth	Collins	Gillespie	Blackman	Turton	Quayle	Horton	Robson	Gregory F	Shanks	Smith T	Dawes AG	
1	2	3	4	5	6	7	8	9	10	11																1
1	2	3		5	6	7	8	9		11	4	10														2
	2			5	6		11		10	7			1	3	4	8	9									3
	2			5	6		11		10	7			1	3	4	8	9									4
		3		5	6					7	8	10	1		4			2	9	11						5
		3		5	6					7	8	10	1		4			2	9	11						6
	2	3		5	4					7	8	10	1		6				9	11						7
	2	3		5	4					7		10	1		6	8	9			11						8
	2	3		5	4					7		10	1		6	8	9			11						9
	2	3		5	4					7		10	1		6	8	9			11						10
	2	3		5	4					7		8	1		6		9			11	10					11
	2	3		5	4					7		10	1		6		9		8	11						12
	2	3		5	4		11		9	7		10	1		6						8					13
	2	3		5	4		11		9	7	6	10	1								8					14
	2	3		5	4	7			9	11	6	10	1								8					15
		3		5	4	7	8		9	11	6		1					2			10					16
		3		5	4	7				11		10	1		6	8	9					2				17
				5	4					7		10	1	3	6		9			11	8	2				18
				5	4					7		10	1	3	6		9			11	8	2				19
				5	4	8				7	10		1		6		9	2		11		3				20
					4				9	7		10	1	3	6	8				11		2	5			21
					4					7		10	1	3	6		9			11	8	2	5			22
				5	4					7		10	1	3	6		9			11	8	2				23
				5	4	7			9	11		10	1	3	6						8	2				24
				5	4	7				11		10	1	3	6	8		2				9				25
				5	4	7				11		10	1	3	6		9					2		8		26
				5	4	7				11		10	1	3	6		9					2		8		27
	2			5	4	7				11			1		6		9					3		8	10	28
1	2			5	4		11			7					6		9					3		8	10	29
1	2			5	4		11			7					6		9					3		8	10	30
1	2			5	4	7	11								6		9					3		8	10	31
	2			5	4	7	11						1		6		9					3		8	10	32
	2			5	4	7	11						1		6		9					3		8	10	33
	2			5	4								1		6		9			11	7	3		8	10	34
	2			5	4	7							1		6		9			11		3		8	10	35
	2			5	4	7							1		6		9			11		3		8	10	36
	2			5	4								1		6		9			11	7	3		8	10	37
	2			5	4								1		6		9			11	7	3		8	10	38
	2			5	4	7							1		6		9			11		3		8	10	39
	2			5	4	7			9				1		6					11		3		8	10	40
	2			5	4						6		1				9			11	10	3		8	7	41
	2			5	4							10	1		6		9			11		3		8	7	42
5	27	15	1	40	42	18	12	2	10	30	9	23	37	12	36	8	29	5	4	23	14	26	2	17	15	
				1	1	4			3	6		14			2	2	16		1	3	2	2		6	4	

Blore	Owens	Dawes FW	Daniels	Walker	Lievesley	Davis	Fielding	Jordan	Palethorpe	Pritchard	Birtley	Waldren	Chesters	Booth	Collins	Gillespie	Blackman	Turton	Quayle	Horton	Robson	Gregory F	Shanks	Smith T	Dawes AG	
	2	3		5	4	7			9	11		10	1		6	8										1
	2	3		5	4	7				11		10	1		6	8	9									R
	2	3		5	4	7				11		10	1		6	8	9									2
				5	4				9	7		10	1	3	6	8		2		11						3
				5	4				9	7		10	1	3	6	8		2		11						R
	3	3		5	5	3			3	5		5	5	2	5	5	2	2		2						
	1					1				2		2				1	1									

1938-39

Manager: Tom Bromilow

1	Aug	27	(a)	Bournemouth	D	1-1	Blackman	9,075
2		31	(a)	Notts C	W	1-0	Lievesley	10,434
3	Sep	3	(h)	Watford	W	2-0	Blackman 2	18,910
4		7	(h)	Northampton T	W	2-0	Horton, A.Dawes	14,570
5		10	(a)	Port Vale	L	0-2		10,478
6		17	(h)	Swindon T	D	1-1	Horton	20,100
7		24	(a)	Torquay U	W	2-1	Gregory 2	3,988
8	Oct	1	(h)	Clapton O	W	4-2	Gregory 3, Horton	19,182
9		8	(a)	Newport C	L	0-2		10,631
10		15	(a)	Walsall	D	1-1	A.Dawes	7,726
11		22	(h)	Brighton & HA	W	1-0	Horton	18,999
12		29	(a)	Queen's Park R	W	2-1	Smith, A.Dawes	17,440
13	Nov	5	(h)	Southend U	W	4-3	Smith, Lievesley, Blackman, Steele	17,685
14		12	(a)	Exeter C	D	4-4	Steele, A.Dawes 2, F.Dawes 1	5,523
15		19	(h)	Cardiff C	W	2-0	A.Dawes 2	17,898
16	Dec	3	(h)	Reading	D	0-0		15,565
17		17	(h)	Mansfield T	W	6-2	A.Dawes, Robson 3, Gregory, Smith	10,224
18		24	(h)	Bournemouth	W	3-0	Robson, Bigg 2	4,403
19		26	(h)	Aldershot	W	3-0	Steele, Robson, A.Dawes	5,417
20		27	(a)	Aldershot	L	1-2	A.Dawes	7,003
21		31	(a)	Watford	L	1-4	Robson	9,853
22	Jan	14	(h)	Port Vale	W	1-0	Wilson	13,773
23		18	(a)	Ipswich T	L	1-2	A.Dawes	5,352
24		21	(a)	Swindon T	D	2-2	Smith, Robson	11,825
25		28	(h)	Torquay U	L	1-3	Blackman	14,342
26	Feb	4	(a)	Clapton O	L	0-4		8,890
27		11	(h)	Newport C	D	1-1	Wilson	29,155
28		18	(h)	Walsall	W	4-0	Steele 2, Gregory, A.Dawes	13,906
29		25	(a)	Brighton & HA	D	0-0		7,146
30	Mar	4	(h)	Queen's Park R	L	0-1		13,328
31		11	(a)	Southend U	L	1-3	Steele	6,244
32		18	(h)	Exeter C	W	3-2	Wilson 2, Waldron	9,152
33		25	(a)	Cardiff C	W	1-0	Smith	11,910
34	Apr	1	(h)	Ipswich T	W	3-0	Robson, Wilson, Smith	13,764
35		7	(h)	Bristol C	W	3-2	Robson, Smith, Waldron	21,913
36		8	(a)	Reading	L	1-3	Collins	10,131
37		10	(a)	Bristol C	D	1-1	F.Dawes	11,055
38		15	(h)	Bristol R	D	0-0		11,714
39		17	(a)	Bristol R	W	2-1	Smith, Robson	4,610
40		22	(a)	Mansfield T	D	0-0		3,016
41		29	(h)	Notts C	W	5-1	Wilson, Robson, Steele 2, Waldron	6,841
42	May	6	(a)	Northampton T	D	0-0		4,056

FINAL LEAGUE POSITION: 2nd in Division Three South

Appearances
Goals

FA Cup

1	Nov	26	(h)	Queen's Park R	D	1-1	Blackman	33,276
R		28	(a)	Queen's Park R	L	0-3		16,000

Appearances
Goals

Jubilee Game

Aug	20	(h)	Brighton & HA	W	5-0	Horton 3, Dawes 2†	8,298

†Some reports credit Horton 2, A.Dawes 3

Appearances
Goals

Chesters	Owens	Dawes FW	Lievesley	Walker	Collins	Davis	Smith	Blackman	Dawes AG	Horton	Gregory	Waldron	Steele	Birtley	Gillespie	Bigg	Robson	Reece	Wilson	Daniels	Shanks	Tootill	Jordan	Lewis	
1	2	3	4	5	6	7	8	9	10	11															1
1	2	3	4	5	6	7	8	9	10	11															2
1	2	3	4	5	6	7	8	9	10	11															3
1	2	3	4	5	6	7	8	9	10	11															4
1	2	3	4	5	6	7	8	9	10	11															5
1	2	3	4	5	6	7	8	9	10	11															6
1	2	3	4	5	6		8		7	11	9	10													7
1	2	3	4	5	6	7	8		10	11	9														8
1	2	3	4	5	6	7	8			11	9	10													9
1	2	3	4	5	6		8		10	11	9		7												10
1	2	3		5	6		8		10	11	9		7	4											11
1	2	3	4	5	6		8	9	10	11			7												12
1	2	3	4	5	6		8	9	10	11			7												13
1	2	3	4	5	6			9	10	11			7		8										14
1	2	3	4	5	6			9	10				7		8	11									15
1		3	4	5	6		8	9	10		2		7			11									16
1		3	4	5	6		8		9		2		7			11	10								17
1		3	4	5	6		8		9		2		7			11	10								18
1		3	4	5	6		8		9		2		7			11	10								19
1		3	4	5	6		8		9		2		7			11	10								20
1	2	3	4	5			8		9				7			11	10	6							21
1	2	3	4		6		8		9				7				10		11	5					22
1	2	3			6		8		9				7	4			10		11	5					23
1	2	3	4		6		7	9	8								10		11	5					24
1	2	3	4		6		7	9	8								10		11	5					25
1	2	3	4		6		8				9	10					7		11	5					26
1	2	3	4		6		8		10		9		7						11		5				27
1	2	3	4		6		8		10		9		7						11		5				28
1	2	3	4		6		8		10		9		7						11		5				29
1	2	3	4		6		8		10		9		7						11		5				30
1	2	3			6		8	9					7		10				11	4	5				31
1	2	3	4				8		9			10	7					6	11		5				32
	2	3	4				8			11		10	7				9	6			5	1			33
1	2	3			6		8					10	7				9	4	11		5				34
1	2	3	6				8					10	7				9	4	11		5				35
1	2	3			6		8					10	7				9	4	11		5				36
1	2	3	4		6		8						7		10		9		11		5				37
1	2	3					8					10	7				9		11		5		4	6	38
1	2	3					8						7		10		9	6	11		5		4		39
1	2	3					8					10	7				9	6	11		5		4		40
1		3					8				2	10	7				9	6	11		5		4		41
1		3					8				2	10	7				9	6	11		5		4		42
41	35	42	32	21	33	8	40	14	29	15	17	12	30	2	5	7	20	10	20	6	16	1	5	1	
		2	2		1		8	5	12	4	7	3	8			2	11		6						

Chesters	Owens	Dawes FW	Lievesley	Walker	Collins	Davis	Smith	Blackman	Dawes AG	Horton	Gregory	Waldron	Steele	Birtley	Gillespie	Bigg	Robson	Reece	Wilson	Daniels	Shanks	Tootill	Jordan	Lewis	
1	2	3	4	5	6		8	9	10				7			11									1
1	2	3	4	5	6		8	9	10	11			7												R
2	2	2	2	2	2		2	2	2	1			2			1									
								1																	

Chesters	Owens	Dawes FW	Lievesley	Walker	Collins	Davis	Smith	Blackman	Dawes AG	Horton	Gregory	Waldron	Steele	Birtley	Gillespie	Bigg	Robson	Reece	Wilson	Daniels	Shanks	Tootill	Jordan	Lewis
1	2	3	4	5	6	7	8		10	11													9	
1	1	1	1	1	1	1	1		1	1													1	
									2	3														

1939-40

Manager: George Irwin

1	Aug	26	(a)	Mansfield T	W 5-4	Steele, Robson, Waldron 3	7,658
2		30	(a)	Reading	L 0-5		9,277
3	Sep	2	(h)	Bristol R	W 3-0	Waldron 2, Smith	7,033

FINAL LEAGUE POSITION: 7th in Division Three South — Appearances, Goals

League South 'A' Division

4	Oct	21	(a)	West Ham U	W 6-2	Bark, Blackman 3, Robson, Gregory (pen)	6,700
5		28	(h)	Watford	D 3-3	Bark, Wilson, Blackman	3,000
6	Nov	4	(a)	Arsenal	L 0-5		7,306
7		11	(h)	Charlton A	L 3-4	Gregory, Bark 2	6,725
8		18	(a)	Clapton O	L 3-5	Blackman 2, Robson	3,000
9		25	(h)	Southend U	W 4-2	Gregory 3 (2 pens), Blackman	3,724
10	Dec	2	(h)	Norwich C	W 1-0	Smith	5,400
11		9	(a)	Tottenham H	W 3-1	Smith 3	4,265
12		16	(h)	Millwall	W 4-1	Smith, Robson 2, E.Smith (og)	5,600
13		25	(a)	Watford	L 1-5	Blackman	3,000
14		26	(h)	Arsenal	L 0-3		10,400
15		30	(a)	Charlton A	L 4-5	Wilson, Robson, Blackman, Gregory (pen)	1,910
16	Jan	6	(h)	Clapton O	D 1-1	Smith	3,600
17		13	(a)	Southend U	L 1-3	Smith	2,000
18		17	(h)	West Ham U	L 0-3		896
19	Feb	28	(h)	Tottenham H	D 1-1	Smith	1,700
20	Apr	13	(a)	Norwich C	L 2-5	Robson, Gregory (pen)	4,000
21	May	25	(a)	Millwall	L 2-7	Gregory (pen), Blackman	4,332

FINAL LEAGUE POSITION: 7th in League South 'A' Division — Appearances, Goals

League South 'D' Division

22	Feb	10	(a)	Brighton & HA	W 3-1	Smith, Robson, Bark	1,739
23		17	(h)	Reading	W 4-1	Gregory, Smith, Robson, Bark	1,139
24		24	(a)	Queen's Park R	W 5-2	Gillespie 2, Smith 2, Wilson	6,500
25	Mar	2	(h)	Norwich C	W 2-0	Gillespie, Robson	4,600
26		9	(a)	Watford	L 2-5	A.Dawes, Bark	4,611
27		16	(h)	Aldershot	L 3-4	Gregory 2, Robson	4,948
28		22	(a)	Clapton O	W 1-0	Wilson	5,000
29		23	(h)	Southend U	W 5-2	Robson 4, Bark	6,742
30		25	(h)	Clapton O	W 7-1	Wilson 2, Bark 2, Robson, Smith, Gregory	7,892
31		30	(a)	Bournemouth	W 3-2	Robson 2, Blackman	5,000
32	Apr	6	(h)	Brighton & HA	W 10-0	Bark 3, Robson 3, Gregory, Blackman, Smith, Wilson	7,529
33	May	8	(a)	Reading	W 4-2	Robson 2, A.Dawes, Wilson	
34		13	(a)	Queen's Park R	D 2-2	Smith, Robson	3,954
35		18	(h)	Bournemouth	W 6-0	A.Dawes 3, Smith 2, Blackman	3,442
36		29	(h)	Watford	W 2-1	A.Dawes, Wilson	3,335
37	Jun	1	(a)	Aldershot	L 2-3	Owens, A.Dawes	1,300
38		5	(a)	Southend U	L 0-3		500
39		8	(a)	Norwich C	W 3-1	Robson 2, A.Dawes	1,000

FINAL LEAGUE POSITION: 1st in League South 'D' Division — Appearances, Goals

Football League War Cup

1	Apr	20	(h)	Tottenham H	W 4-1	Wilson 2, Robson, Bark	15,423
		27	(a)	Tottenham H	L 1-2	Robson	12,376
2	May	4	(a)	Arsenal	L 1-3	Robson	15,021
		11	(h)	Arsenal	L 0-2		21,406

Appearances
Goals

Jubilee Fund

	Aug	19	(a)	Brighton & HA	D 3-3	Robson, Waldron 2	4,500

Appearances
Goals

Chesters	Owens	Dawes F	Lievesley	Shanks	Collins	Steele	Smith	Robson	Waldron	Wilson	Reece	Tootill	James	Gregory F	Millbank	Hudgell	Bark	Blackman	Gillespie	Gregory M	Bigg	Dawes A	Lewis J	Milligan	Joy B	Taylor H	
1	2	3	4	5	6	7	8	9	10	11																	1
1	2	3	4	5		7	8	9	10	11	6																2
	2	3	4	5		7	8	9	10	11	6	1															3
2	3	3	3	3	1	3	3	3	3	3	2	1															
						1	1	1	5																		

Chesters	Owens	Dawes F	Lievesley	Shanks	Collins	Steele	Smith	Robson	Waldron	Wilson	Reece	Tootill	James	Gregory F	Millbank	Hudgell	Bark	Blackman	Gillespie	Gregory M	Bigg	Dawes A	Lewis J	Milligan	Joy B	Taylor H	
		3			4		8	7		11		1		2	5	6	10	9									4
		3			4		8	7		11		1		2	5	6	10	9									5
		3			4		8	7				1	11	2	5	6	10	9									6
	2				4		8	7		11		1		3	5	6	10	9									7
	2				4			8		11		1		3	5	6	10	9	7								8
	4				6			8		11		1		2	5	3	10	9	7								9
	4				6		8			11		1		2	5	3	10	9	7								10
	4				6		8	9		11		1		2	5	3	10		7								11
	4				6		8	9		11		1		2	5	3	10		7								12
1	4	3		5	6		8						11	2			10	9	7								13
	4				6		8	9		11		1		2	5	3	10		7								14
		3			4		8	10		11		1		2	5	6		9	7								15
		3			4		8	9		11		1		2	5	6	10		7								16
		3			4		8	9		11		1		2	5	6	10		7								17
					6		8	9		7		1	11	2	5	3	10			4							18
1	4				6		10	9		7				2	5	3		8			11						19
	4				6		8	9		11		1		2	5	3	10	7									20
	4				6		8	9				1		2	5	3		7	11			10					21
2	11	7		1	18		16	16		15		16	3	18	17	17	15	12	11	1	1	1					
							8	6		2				8			4	10									

1 own-goal

Chesters	Owens	Dawes F	Lievesley	Shanks	Collins	Steele	Smith	Robson	Waldron	Wilson	Reece	Tootill	James	Gregory F	Millbank	Hudgell	Bark	Blackman	Gillespie	Gregory M	Bigg	Dawes A	Lewis J	Milligan	Joy B	Taylor H	
1	4				6		8	9		11				2	5	3	10		7								22
	4				6		8	9		11		1		2	5	3	10		7								23
1	4				6		8	9		11				2	5	3	10		7								24
1	4				6		8	9		11				2	5	3	10		7								25
								9		11		1		2	5	3	10		7			8	4	6			26
	4				6		8	9		11		1		2	5	3	10	7									27
	4				6		8	9		11		1		2	5	3		7				10					28
	4						8	9		11		1		2	5	3	10	7				6					29
	4				6		8	9		11		1		2	5	3	10	7									30
	4				6		8	9		11		1		2		3	10	7					5				31
	4				6		8	9		11		1		2	5	3	10	7									32
	4				6		8	9		11		1		2	5	3			7			10					33
	4				6		8	9				1		2	5	3		7	11			10					34
	4				6		8	9		11		1		2	5	3		7				10					35
	4				6		8	9		11		1		2		3		7				10			5		36
	7				6		8					1		2		3		9	11	4		10				5	37
	2	3			6		8	7				1				5		9	11	4		10					38
	2	3			11		8	9				1				6		7		4		10				5	39
3	17	2			16		17	17		14		15		16	13	18	10	12	9	3		10	2	1	1	2	
	1						9	19		7				5			9	3	3			8					

Chesters	Owens	Dawes F	Lievesley	Shanks	Collins	Steele	Smith	Robson	Waldron	Wilson	Reece	Tootill	James	Gregory F	Millbank	Hudgell	Bark	Blackman	Gillespie	Gregory M	Bigg	Dawes A	Lewis J	Milligan	Joy B	Taylor H	
	4				6		8	9		11		1		2	5	3	10	7									40
	4				6		8	9		11		1		2	5	3	10	7									41
	4				6		8	9		11		1		2	5	3	10	7									42
	4				6		8	9		11		1		2	5	3		7				10					43
	4				4		4	4		4		4		4	4	4	3	4				1					44
								3		2							1										

Chesters	Owens	Dawes F	Lievesley	Shanks	Collins	Steele	Smith	Robson	Waldron	Wilson	Reece	Tootill	James	Gregory F	Millbank	Hudgell	Bark	Blackman	Gillespie	Gregory M	Bigg	Dawes A	Lewis J	Milligan	Joy B	Taylor H
1	2	3	4	5	6		8	9	10	7			11													
1	1	1	1	1	1		1	1	1	1			1													
								1	2																	

1940-41

Manager: George Irwin

1	Aug	31	(h)	Chelsea	W 6-3	Robson, A.Dawes, Blackman, M.Gregory, A.Wilson 2	1,157
2	Sep	7	(h)	Brighton & HA	W 5-2	Robson, Blackman, A.Dawes, A.Wilson 2	1,508
3		14	(a)	Millwall	L 0-1*		600
4		21	(h)	Norwich C	W 7-1	A.Dawes 2, Blackman 3, Robson 2	1,040
5		28	(h)	Millwall	W 2-1	A.Dawes 2	1,600
6	Oct	5	(a)	Norwich C	L 1-3	Waite	1,200
7		12	(a)	Watford	W 2-1	Robson 2	1,000
8		19	(h)	Clapton O	W 6-2	Blackman, A.Dawes 2, Robson 3	1,500
9		26	(a)	Southampton	W 4-1	A.Dawes 3, Waite	1,000
10	Nov	2	(a)	Bournemouth	L 2-3	Blackman, A.Dawes	2,000
11		16	(a)	Clapton O	W 4-2	A.Wilson, Robson 2, Blackman	200
12		23	(h)	Southend U	L 1-2	Blackman	1,097
13		30	(a)	Arsenal	D 2-2	F.Gregory, Robson	761
14	Dec	7	(h)	Bournemouth	W 6-0	A.Dawes 4, Gillespie, Robson	1,121
15		14	(a)	Chelsea	W 2-1	Blackman, A.Dawes	940
16		21	(h)	Arsenal	D 3-3	Robson, Bark, Gillespie	4,400
17		25	(h)	Charlton A	L 0-2		4,015
18		28	(a)	Brighton & HA	W 5-1	Robson 2, Gillespie, A.Dawes 2	1,000
19	Mar	8	(h)	Millwall	W 5-3	Hudgell 2, Blackman, Robson, M.Gregory	5,000
20		15	(a)	Brentford	W 3-2	Bark, Smith 2	4,000
21		22	(h)	Brentford	W 5-0	Hudgell (pen), Bark, Robson 2, A.Wilson	2,638
22		29	(h)	Fulham	D 1-1	Robson	3,000
23	May	10	(a)	Tottenham H	D 1-1	Robson	3,000
24		17	(h)	Southend U	W 7-0	Gillespie 2, Collins, Blackman, Smith, Robson 2	2,519
25		24	(a)	Aldershot	W 3-0	Hudgell 2 (2 pens), A.Wilson	2,000
26	Jun	2	(h)	Reading	L 1-3	A.Dawes	5,500
27		7	(a)	Millwall	L 2-3	Smith, Robson	2,000

FINAL LEAGUE POSITION: 1st in South Regional League (decided on goal average) — Appearances

*Abandoned after 30 minutes but counted towards final table. — Goals

London War Cup

28	Jan	4	(a)	Brentford	D 2-2	A.Dawes 2	1,000
29		11	(h)	Brentford	D 2-2	A.Dawes, Robson	2,841
30		25	(h)	Fulham	W 5-2	A.Dawes 3, Robson, Smith	2,000
31	Feb	1	(a)	Aldershot	D 3-3	Smith, Blackman, Robson	2,000
32		8	(h)	Chelsea	D 3-3	Blackman, Robson, A.Dawes	3,703
33	Mar	1	(a)	Fulham	W 4-1	Robson 4	2,500
34	Apr	5	(a)	Chelsea	W 3-1	A.Wilson 2, Robson	2,491
35		12	(h)	Queen's Park R	L 1-2	Blackman	4,353
36		14	(h)	Aldershot	W 1-0	Robson	
37		19	(a)	Queen's Park R	L 1-2	Robson	2,300
SF	May	31	(a)	Reading	L 1-4	Blackman	7,000

Appearances
Goals

Football League War Cup

1	Feb	15	(h)	Queen's Park R	L 0-1		3,700
		22	(a)	Queen's Park R	L 2-3	Robson, Smith	3,500

Appearances
Goals

Tootill	Hudgell	Dawes FW	Gregory M	Millbank	Collins	Blackman	Dawes A	Robson	Bark	Wilson A	Taylor	Gillespie	Wate E	Halliday	Eastman D	Ridley T	Gregory F	Smith T	Revill	Lievesley	Wilson R	Jackson J	
1	2	3	4	5	6	7	8	9	10	11													1
1	2	3	4		6	7	10	9		11	5	8											2
1	2	3	4		6	7	10	9		11	5		8										3
1	2	3	4	5	6	7	10	9				11	8										4
1	2	3	4	5	6	7	10	9				11	8										5
1	2		4		11	7		9			5	10	8	6	3								6
1	2	3	4	5	6	7	10	9				11	8										7
1	2	3	4	5	6	7	10	9				11	8										8
1	2	3	4	5	6	7	10	9				11	8										9
1	2	3	4		6	7	10	9			5		8			11							10
1	2	3	4	5	6	8	10	9		7						11							11
1	2	3	4		6	7	10	9			5	11	8										12
1	6	3	4	5			10	9		11			8				2	7					13
1	2	3	4		6	7	10	9			5	11						8					14
1		3	4	5	6	7	10	9		11					2			8					15
1		3	4	5	6		7	9	10			11					2	8					16
1		3	2		6	4	7	9	10	11	5							8					17
1		3	2	5	6	4	10	9				11	7					8					18
1	2	3	4	5	6	10		9		11								8	7				19
1	2	3	4	5	6	7		9	10			11						8					20
1	2	3	4	5	6	7		9	10	11								8					21
1	2	3	4	5	6			9	10			11						8	7				22
1		3	5		4	10		9				11		6				8		2	7		23
1		3	2	5	4	10		9		11		7		6				8					24
1	3		4	5	6	10		9		11		7						8		2			25
1	6	3	4	5	10	7	8	9				11								2			26
1	2	3	5		6	4		9	10	11		7						8					27
27	21	25	27	18	26	24	18	27	7	12	7	18	11	3	2	2	2	14	2	3	1		
	5		2		1	12	20	24	3	7		5	2				1	4					

Tootill	Hudgell	Dawes FW	Gregory M	Millbank	Collins	Blackman	Dawes A	Robson	Bark	Wilson A	Taylor	Gillespie	Wate E	Halliday	Eastman D	Ridley T	Gregory F	Smith T	Revill	Lievesley	Wilson R	Jackson J	
1		3	2	5	6	4	10	9				7				11		8					28
1		3	2	5	6	4	10	9		11			7					8					29
1	2	3	5		4	7	10	9				11		6				8					30
1	2	3	5		4	7	10	9				11		6				8					31
1	2	3	4	5	6	7	10	9		11								8					32
	2	3	4	5	6	10		9		11								8			7	1	33
1	2	3	4	5	6	10		9		11								8	7				34
1	2	3	4	5	6	10		9		11		7						8					35
1	2	3	4	5	6	10		9				7	8						7				36
1	2	3	5		6	10		9		11		7						8		4			37
1	2	3	4	5	6	7		9	10	11								8					38
10	9	11	11	8	11	11	5	11	1	7		6	2	2		1		10	2	1	1	1	
						4	7	11		2								2					

Tootill	Hudgell	Dawes FW	Gregory M	Millbank	Collins	Blackman	Dawes A	Robson	Bark	Wilson A	Taylor	Gillespie	Wate E	Halliday	Eastman D	Ridley T	Gregory F	Smith T	Revill	Lievesley	Wilson R	Jackson J	
1	2	3	4	5	6	7		9		11		10						8					1
1	2	3	4	5	6	10		9		11		7						8					
2	2	2	2	2	2	2		2		2		2						2					
								1										1					

1941-42

Manager: George Irwin

1	Aug	30	(h)	Millwall	W 2-0	Robson, Gillespie	4,764
2	Sep	6	(a)	Arsenal	L 2-7	Hawks, Robson	6,207
3		13	(h)	Queen's Park R	W 2-1	Robson, A.Dawes	4,500
4		20	(a)	Reading	L 2-6	Robson, Blackman	4,000
5		27	(a)	Brighton & HA	D 2-2	Hudgell (pen), Robson	4,000
6	Oct	4	(a)	Brentford	W 2-1	Blackman, Smith	4,700
7		11	(h)	Clapton O	W 2-0	Wilson, A.Dawes	3,400
8		18	(h)	Fulham	W 3-1	Bark, Robson 2	5,000
9		25	(a)	Tottenham H	D 1-1	Robson	4,807
10	Nov	1	(h)	Portsmouth	W 3-1	Collins, Robson 2	5,493
11		8	(a)	Chelsea	L 0-1		3,000
12		15	(h)	Charlton A	W 4-0	Gillespie 2, Robson 2	5,300
13		22	(a)	West Ham U	W 5-0	Bark 2, Blackman, Gillespie, Robson	5,000
14		29	(h)	Watford	W 6-1	Gillespie, Blackman, A.Dawes, Wilson, Bark 2	4,800
15	Dec	6	(a)	Aldershot	W 2-1	Collins, Robson	2,000
16		13	(a)	Millwall	L 0-1		5,100
17		25	(a)	Queen's Park R	W 3-1	Smith 3	
18		27	(h)	Reading	D 1-1	Robson	6,550
19	Jan	3	(h)	Brighton & HA	W 10-1	Robson 4, Gillespie 2, A.Dawes 2, Smith 2	4,771
20		10	(h)	Brentford	W 2-0	A.Dawes (pen), Bark	6,000
21		17	(a)	Clapton O	L 0-4		2,000
22		31	(h)	Tottenham H	D 2-2	A.Dawes (pen), Henley	5,300
23	Feb	7	(a)	Portsmouth	L 1-3	Wilson	4,515
24		14	(h)	Chelsea	W 3-2	Robson, M.Gregory, A.Dawes	5,583
25		21	(a)	Charlton A	L 1-3	Bark	2,760
26		28	(h)	West Ham U	D 1-1	Robson	7,790
27	Mar	7	(a)	Watford	L 1-2	Bark	500
28		14	(h)	Aldershot	L 1-2	Bark	5,700
29	May	9	(h)	Arsenal	D 3-3	A.Dawes 2, Geldard	10,024
30		23	(a)	Fulham	L 3-4	J.F.Smith, Collins, G.Lewis	3,000
				FINAL LEAGUE POSITION: 6th in London League			Appearances
							Goals

London War Cup

31	Mar	21	(a)	Chelsea	D 3-3	Bark, Robson, A.Dawes	4,412
32		28	(h)	Portsmouth	L 0-2		7,329
33	Apr	4	(h)	Chelsea	L 0-3		5,900
34		6	(a)	Portsmouth	L 1-2	A.Dawes	11,671
35		11	(a)	Fulham	L 1-4	Hiles (og)	6,000
36		18	(h)	Fulham	L 3-4	McPhee 2, A.Dawes (pen)	3,378
				Crystal Palace finished 4th in the London War Cup Qualifying Group 4 and thus did not qualify for the semi-finals.			Appearances
							Goals

Tootill	Hudgell	Dawes FW	Gregory M	Millbanks	Collins	Gillespie	Smith T	Robson	Bark	Wilson	Blackman	Hawkes	Dawes AG	Fuller	Raynor	Lester	Morris	Young	Reece	Sibley	Gregory FC	Chivers	Scaife	Muttitt	Bartram	Henley	Boulton	Hooper	Oakes John	Geldard	Duncan	Catlin	Lewis J	Hitchin	Lewis G	Tweedy	Hobbins	Forder	
1	2	3	4	5	6	7	8	9	10	11																												1
1	2	3	5		6	7	8	9		11	4	10																										2
1	2	3	4	5	6			9	10	11	7		8																									3
1	2	3	4		6	7		9		11	10	8		5																								4
1	2	3	4	5	6	8		9	10	11					7																							5
1	2	3	4	5	6	7	8		10	11	9																											6
1	2	3	4	5	6	7			10	11	9		8																									7
1	2	3	4	5	6	7	8	9	10	11																												8
1		3	4	5	6	10	8	9		11	7					2																						9
1	2	3	4	5	6		8	9	10	11			7																									10
1	2	3	4	5	6		8	9	10	11	7																											11
1	2	3	4		6	7	8	9		11			10				5																					12
1	2	3	4		6	8		9	10	11	7						5																					13
1	3				6	8		9	10	11	7		4				5				2																	14
1	3				6	10	8	9		11	7						5	2	4																			15
1	2	3			6	8		9		11	10						5		4	7																		16
1	2	3		5	6	11	7	9			8		10				4																					17
1	2			5	6	10	8	9		11	7		3				4																					18
1	3				6	10	8	9		11	7		2				5					4																19
1	3		4		6		8	9	10	11			7				5						2															20
1	2	3			6	7	8	9		11			10				5							4														21
	2	3	4		6	11	8	9					7				5								1	10												22
1	2	3			6	7	8	9		11			10				5									4												23
1	2	3	4		6			9	10	11	7		8				5																					24
	2	3	4		6	7	8	9	10	11							5										1											25
1	2	3	4		6		8	9	10	11			7				5								1													26
1	2	3			6		8	9	10		7		11				5									4												27
	2	3	4		6	7	8	9	10				11				5																					28
	2	3	4		6			9		11			10														1	5	7	8								29
1	2				6	8		9		11																					3	4	5	10				30
26	29	24	20	11	30	22	20	28	16	26	16	2	17	1	1	1	17	1	2	1	1	1	1	1	2	3	1	1	1	1	1	1	1	1	1				
	1		1		3	7	6	21	9	3	4	1	10												1				1					1				

Tootill	Hudgell	Dawes FW	Gregory M	Millbanks	Collins	Gillespie	Smith T	Robson	Bark	Wilson	Blackman	Hawkes	Dawes AG	Fuller	Raynor	Lester	Morris	Young	Reece	Sibley	Gregory FC	Chivers	Scaife	Muttitt	Bartram	Henley	Boulton	Hooper	Oakes John	Geldard	Duncan	Catlin	Lewis J	Hitchin	Lewis G	Tweedy	Hobbins	Forder	
	2	3			6	7	8	9	10	11			4				5																		1			31
	2	3	4		6		8	9	10	11			7				5																			1		32
	2	3			6	7		9					10				5																			1		33
1	2	3	4		6	11		8			7		10				5																				9	34
1	2	3	4		6	11					7		10				5						8													9	35
1	2	3	4		6				10	7			8				5																					36
3	6	6	4		6	4	2	4	3	3	2		6				6						1											1	2	2	
								1	1				3																									

1 own-goal

J.F.Smith played number 7 in Match 30 and scored once; Weale played number 11 in Match 33; Mather played number 4 in Match 33; Mulligan played number 8 in Match 33; McPhee played number 9 in Match 36 and scored twice; Halford played number 11 in Match 36.

1942-43

Manager: George Irwin

1	Aug	29	(a)	Tottenham H	W 3-1	Wilson, Robson 2	5,623
2	Sep	5	(h)	Clapton O	W 5-3	M.Gregory, Smith, Robson 2, Gillespie	4,431
3		12	(a)	West Ham U	D 2-2	Wilson, Lowes	7,000
4		19	(h)	Queen's Park R	L 0-1		5,600
5		26	(a)	Brighton & HA	W 8-1	A.Dawes 2, Smith, Wilson, Bark 2, Robson, Ford (og)	1,350
6	Oct	3	(a)	Charlton A	D 4-4	Bark, A.Dawes (pen), Robson 2	4,396
7		10	(h)	Fulham	L 2-4	Dawes 2 (1 pen)	4,608
8		17	(a)	Portsmouth	L 1-2	Bark	6,374
9		24	(a)	Chelsea	L 1-4	Robson	7,824
10		31	(h)	Arsenal	L 1-7	Bark	12,900
11	Nov	7	(a)	Watford	L 3-5	A.Dawes, Ware, Wilson	1,970
12		14	(a)	Aldershot	L 2-3	Bastin, Smith	4,000
13		21	(h)	Southampton	W 2-1	Bark, Robson	3,368
14		28	(h)	Tottenham H	D 0-0		4,893
15	Dec	5	(a)	Clapton O	W 2-1	A.Dawes, Bastin	2,800
16		12	(h)	West Ham U	D 0-0		5,127
17		19	(a)	Queen's Park R	L 0-3		3,900
18		25	(a)	Millwall	L 1-2	Gillespie	4,000
19		26	(h)	Millwall	D 2-2	Bark, A.Dawes	6,350
20	Jan	2	(h)	Brighton & HA	L 1-4	Lowes	2,667
21		9	(h)	Charlton A	L 0-2		2,850
22		16	(a)	Fulham	W 2-1	Wright, Smith	3,824
23		23	(h)	Portsmouth	L 1-2	Wright	4,365
24		30	(h)	Chelsea	L 0-2		4,172
25	Feb	6	(a)	Arsenal	L 0-9		7,926
26		13	(h)	Watford	L 0-2		2,750
27		20	(h)	Aldershot	W 5-2	A.Dawes 2, Ward 2, Potts	2,500
28		27	(a)	Southampton	L 1-5	Blackman	8,000

FINAL LEAGUE POSITION: 15th in Football League — South

Appearances
Goals

Football League Cup — South

29	Mar	6	(a)	Luton T	D 0-0		3,000
30		13	(h)	Portsmouth	L 0-1		4,763
31		20	(a)	Charlton A	L 0-1		3,836
32		27	(h)	Luton T	W 4-0	Wilson, Smith 3	3,000
33	Apr	3	(a)	Portsmouth	D 3-3	Smith 3	9,137
34		10	(h)	Charlton A	L 0-4		6,394

Crystal Palace played in Group 4 of the Qualifying Competition but did not qualify for the semi-finals

Appearances
Goals

Hudgell	Dawes FW	Gregory M	Lewis J	Morris	Dawes AG	Smith TJ	Robson	Bark	Wilson	Batey	Lewis G	Poland	Reece	Gillespie	Brown	Bassett	Young	Ware	Ford	Blackman	Harding	Lowes AR	Millbank	Joslin	Scaife	Bastin	Tootill	Johnson	Henley	Wright	Waller	Bratley	Ward	Allen	Briscoe	Finch	Smith C	Spencer	
2	3	4	5	6	7	8	9	10	11																														1
3		4	5		2	8	9		11	6	10			7																									2
2	3	4		5		8	9		11			1	6	7																									3
3			5		2	8	9	10	11			1	4	7																									4
6	3				8	7	9	10	11			1	4		2	5																							5
	3				8	7	9	10	11			1	6		4		2	5																					6
	3			6	4	8	9			5				10					1																				7
	3		6		2	7	9	10	11		8				5				1	4																			8
	3				11		9	10					6					5	1	7	2	8																	9
	3				4	7	9	10	11		8	1	6				2						5																10
					6	7		10	11									9	1		2		5																11
				5		7	9	10	11				6							4	2			1	3	8													12
		3		4		8	9	10	11				6			5				7	2						1												13
	3			6	4	7	9	10	11						5						2					8	1												14
	3				2	8	9		11				6	7						4						10	1												15
	3				2	7	9							11		5				4							1	6	8										16
	3				4	8	9		11					7			2			6						10	1												17
	3				4	8	9		11			1		7		5				6	2																		18
	3				2	7	9	10				1	6	11		5						4				8													19
						7	10					1		11		5	2			4		9			3			6											20
	3				8				11		10			7		5				4		9					1	6											21
	3				2	10	7					1		11		5				6		8								9	4								22
	3				2	10	7		11											6		8					1			9	5		4						23
						10			11					8		5				4				1						9	6	2					7		24
	3	2				10	8		11							5				4				1				6		9							7		25
		4			8	10								11		5											1			9	6	2	7						26
	3				9				7							5				6													10			11		4	27
2	3				10	8														6			5				1										7	4	28
6	20	6	4	6	22	25	22	12	20	2	4	9	10	14	4	12	4	3	4	16	6	6	3	3	2	5	9	4	1	5	4	2	4			1	3	2	
		1			10	4	9	7	4					2				1		1		2				2				2			2						

1 own-goal

Hudgell	Dawes FW	Gregory M	Lewis J	Morris	Dawes AG	Smith TJ	Robson	Bark	Wilson	Batey	Lewis G	Poland	Reece	Gillespie	Brown	Bassett	Young	Ware	Ford	Blackman	Harding	Lowes AR	Millbank	Joslin	Scaife	Bastin	Tootill	Johnson	Henley	Wright	Waller	Bratley	Ward	Allen	Briscoe	Finch	Smith C	Spencer	
3			4		10		9		11					7						6											2							5	29
	3		4		9				11		10			7		5				2																		6	30
	3		4		2	8			11											9									6						7	10		5	31
	3		5		10	8			7							5	2			9							1									11		4	32
	3		5		2	8			11		10									9							1							5	7			4	33
					4	8	10		7								2			9							1		6					5		11			34
1	4		5		6	4	2		6		2			2		2	2			6							3		2		1			2	2	3		5	
						6			1																														

Hobbins played number 1 in Match 1; M.Turner played number 1 in Match 2; Driver played number 10 in Match 3 & number 8 in Match 30; Collins played number 6 in Match 4; F.C.Gregory played number 2 in Match 7; Hawkes played number 7 in Match 7; Mennie played number 11 in Match 7; Lowe played number 4 in Match 9; Fletcher played number 3 in Match 11; Fenton played number 4 in Match 11; J.Smith played number 8 in Match 11; Barnes played number 5 in Match 15; Milton played number 10 in Match 16; Farmer played number 5 in Match 17; Perritt played number 10 in Match 18; C.E.Williams played number 8 in Match 20; Buckley played number 3 in Match 24; Delaney played number 3 in Match 26; Williams played number 1 in Matches 27, 29 & 30; Winter played number 2 in Match 27; Potts played number 8 in Match 27 and scored once; Davie played number 9 in Match 28; Girling played number 11 in Match 28; C.J.Walker played number 8 in Match 29; Walker played number 1 in Match 31; Kirk played number 3 in Match 34.

1943-44

Manager: George Irwin

1	Aug	28	(a)	Tottenham H	D 1-1	Wilson	8,139
2	Sep	4	(h)	Clapton O	W 5-2	Smith 2, Bryant 2, A.Dawes	4,653
3		11	(a)	Luton T	W 2-1	Redfern, Wilson	4,000
4		18	(h)	Reading	L 1-5	Wilson	7,500
5		25	(h)	Brentford	D 1-1	Wilson	5,131
6	Oct	2	(h)	West Ham U	L 1-6	Spencer	7,040
7		9	(a)	Fulham	W 5-4	A.Dawes 2, Wilson, Ward, Somerfield	8,000
8		16	(h)	Portsmouth	L 2-3	A.Dawes 2	7,065
9		23	(a)	Chelsea	L 1-2	A.Dawes	8,373
10		30	(h)	Arsenal	D 1-1	Briscoe	14,000
11	Nov	6	(a)	Watford	W 4-2	Wilson, Ferrier 2, Biggs	3,783
12		13	(h)	Aldershot	W 4-1	Robson 2, Ferrier 2	5,121
13		20	(a)	Southampton	D 2-2	Smith, Robson	7,000
14		27	(h)	Tottenham H	W 3-0	Ferrier, Wilson 2	6,138
15	Dec	4	(a)	Clapton O	W 6-1	Robson, Cuthbertson, Girling, Smith 2, Ferrier	1,200
16		11	(h)	Luton T	W 5-0	Ferrier 2, A.Dawes 2, Girling	2,767
17		18	(a)	Millwall	L 1-5	Girling	2,055
18		25	(a)	Brighton & HA	W 3-1	Ferrier 2, Smith	6,800
19		27	(h)	Brighton & HA	W 6-2	Ferrier 3, Smith, Robson, Allen	3,500
20	Jan	1	(a)	Reading	W 3-0	G.Lewis, Wilson, Ferrier	5,000
21		8	(h)	Watford	W 1-0	Ferrier	5,000
22		22	(a)	West Ham U	L 0-3		9,500
23		29	(h)	Fulham	W 6-2	Ferrier 2, A.Dawes, Smith, Wilson, Robinson	7,000
24	Feb	5	(a)	Portsmouth	L 0-1		8,309
25		12	(h)	Chelsea	W 1-0	Allen	10,692
26	Apr	8	(a)	Arsenal	L 2-5	Smith, Robson	11,563
27		10	(a)	Brentford	L 0-2		7,500
28		22	(h)	Millwall	W 2-0	Robson, A.Dawes	5,270
29		29	(a)	Aldershot	W 6-0	Wilson, Robson, Ferrier 2, A.Dawes, Smith	5,000
30	May	6	(h)	Southampton	D 0-0		5,000

FINAL LEAGUE POSITION: 5th in Football League — South

Appearances
Goals

Football League Cup — South

31	Feb	19	(a)	Brentford	W 4-3	Girling, Ferrier 2, J.Lewis	4,110
32		26	(h)	Brighton & HA	L 2-3	Wilson 2	6,000
33	Mar	4	(h)	Charlton A	W 5-1	Smith, Wilson, A.Dawes 2, Robson	6,000
34		11	(h)	Brentford	L 1-2	Wilson	8,659
35		18	(a)	Brighton & HA	W 4-2	A.Dawes 2, Robson, Spencer	3,500
36		25	(a)	Charlton A	D 0-0		19,722

Crystal Palace finished 2nd in Group 'A' of the Qualifying Competition and did not qualify for the semi-finals

Appearances
Goals

Williams	McCrae	Dawes FW	Dawes A	Spencer	Russell	Redfern	Smith T	Bryant	Gallagher	Wilson A	Wilson CF	Blackman	Young	Flavell	Bassett	Humphries	Robson	Lewis G	Mountford	Tootill	Tennant	Millbank	Brophy	Ward	Page	Cabrelli	Ferrier	Girling	Cuthburtson	Allen K	Robinson J	Pond	Robinson P	Nunns	Lewis J	Tunney	Bray	Embleton	
1	2	3	4	5	6	7	8	9	10	11																													1
1	2	3	6	4		7	8	9	10	11	5																												2
1		3		5		8		9		11		6																											3
1		3	6	8			8	9		11		4	2	7																									4
1		3	2	4			8			11				7	5	6	9	10																					5
1			3	4			8		10	11				7	5	6	9		2																				6
		3	10			7				11									2	1	4	5	6	8															7
		3	10	5		7				11							9		2		4			8															8
		3	10				8			7									2	1			4		5	6	9	11											9
		3	8	4						11							10		2	1					5	6	9												10
		3	8	5						11							7		2	1						6	9												11
		3	10	4			8			11							7		2	1					5	6	9												12
			10	5			8			11			3				7		2	1	4						9												13
				5			8			11			2				4	10		1						6	9												14
			3	4			8									5	7		2	1						6	9	11	10										15
		3	10	4			8					6				5	7		2	1							9	11											16
			3	4			8			10							7		2	1		5				6	9	11											17
			3	4			8			10						5	7		2	1						6	9	11											18
			3	4			8					10				5	7		2	1						6	9			11									19
			6	4			8			11			3			5	7	10	2	1							9												20
			10				8					4	3			5	7		2	1						6	9	11											21
			11	5			8						3				7		2	1						6	9		10										22
			4	5			10			11			3				7		2	1						6	9						4						23
			3	4			8			11					5		7		2	1						6	9	10											24
							8						3		5		7	10	2	1						6	9			11		4							25
			5				8			11		6					7		2	1							10				4			9		3			26
			10				8			11		6					7		2	1											4			9	5	3			27
			6	5			8			11			3				7	10	2	1							9										4		28
			10	5			8			11		6	3				7		2	1							9									4			29
			9				8			11		6	3				7	10	2	1															5	4			30
6	2	12	27	23	1	5	25	4	3	24	1	9	11	3	4	8	24	6	24	23	3	2	2	2	3	14	20	7	2	2	2	1	1	2	2	4	1		
			11	1		1	10	2		11							8	1						1			19	3	1	2			1						

Williams	McCrae	Dawes FW	Dawes A	Spencer	Russell	Redfern	Smith T	Bryant	Gallagher	Wilson A	Wilson CF	Blackman	Young	Flavell	Bassett	Humphries	Robson	Lewis G	Mountford	Tootill	Tennant	Millbank	Brophy	Ward	Page	Cabrelli	Ferrier	Girling	Cuthburtson	Allen K	Robinson J	Pond	Robinson P	Nunns	Lewis J	Tunney	Bray	Embleton	
				5			8						3				7	10	2	1						6	9	11							5				31
				4			8			11			3		5		7	10	2	1						6	9												32
			9				8			11			3		5		7	10	2	1						6							4						33
			6	5			8			11			3				7	10	2	1							9						4						34
			4	5						11			3				7	10	2	1						6	9											8	35
			10	5			8			11			3				7		2	1						6	9						4						36
			4	5			5			5			6		2		6	5	6	6						5	5	1					3		1			1	
			4	1			1			4							2										2	1							1				

Lambert played number 2 in Match 3; Grogan played number 4 in Match 3; Franko played number 7 in Match 7; Gilbert played number 10 in Match 3; A.R.J.Brown played number 10 in Match 4; Somerfield played number 9 in Match 7 and scored once; J.Brown played number 1 in Match 8; Henley played number 6 in Match 8; Briscoe played number 7 in Match 10 and scored once; Murfitt played number 4 in Match 11; Biggs played number 10 in Match 11 and scored once; Malpass played number 6 in Match 13; L.Compton played number 3 in Match 14; Thompson played number 7 in Match 14; Collins played number 4 in Match 22.

1944-45

Manager: George Irwin

1	Aug	26	(h)	Queen's Park R	W 7-4	Driver, Kurz 3, Wilson 2, Somerfield	7,000
2	Sep	2	(a)	Watford	W 4-2	Kurz, Driver 2, R.Williams (og)	7,500
3		9	(h)	Brighton & HA	W 5-2	Blackman 3, Wilson, Robson	6,000
4		16	(a)	Chelsea	L 2-8	A.Dawes, Robson	20,000
5		23	(a)	Fulham	L 2-6	Wilson, Spencer	8,000
6		30	(h)	Luton T	D 1-1	Robson	7,000
7	Oct	7	(h)	Tottenham H	L 1-3	A.Dawes	10,000
8		14	(a)	Reading	L 1-4	Kurz	6,000
9		21	(a)	Aldershot	W 4-0	Somerfield 4	4,000
10		28	(h)	Arsenal	W 4-3	Mountford, Somerfield, Parlane, Kurz	14,369
11	Nov	4	(a)	Millwall	W 2-1	Somerfield, Conner	6,000
12		11	(h)	Clapton O	W 6-1	Kurz 3, Wilson, Mountford, Somerfield	4,950
13		18	(a)	Brentford	W 2-1	Wilson, Stock	11,100
14		25	(h)	West Ham U	W 3-0	Jones, Somerfield, Kurz	11,600
15	Dec	2	(a)	Queen's Park R	D 0-0		8,661
16		9	(h)	Watford	L 2-3	Somerfield, Wilson	5,897
17		16	(a)	Brighton & HA	W 3-0	Somerfield 2, Cheetham	3,500
18		23	(h)	Portsmouth	W 1-0	A.Dawes	7,160
19		26	(a)	Portsmouth	L 1-9	Blackman	13,063
20		30	(h)	Chelsea	D 3-3	Somerfield, F.Dawes, Kurz	10,106
21	Jan	6	(h)	Fulham	L 0-2		6,000
22		20	(a)	Tottenham H	L 1-3	Adams (og)	11,015
23		27	(h)	Reading	W 4-1	Jones 2, Somerfield, Kurz	2,000
24	Mar	17	(h)	Aldershot	W 3-1	A.Dawes 2, Wilson	4,419
25		24	(a)	Arsenal	L 0-1		9,619
26		31	(h)	Millwall	W 2-1	G.Lewis, Wilson	9,272
27	Apr	2	(a)	Luton T	D 3-3	Blackman, A.Dawes, Betts	
28		14	(a)	Clapton O	D 1-1	Stevens	2,500
29		21	(h)	Brentford	W 6-1	Kurz 2, Ferrier 3, Betts	6,492
30		28	(a)	West Ham U	L 0-5		6,257

FINAL LEAGUE POSITION: 6th in Football League — South

Appearances
Goals

Football League Cup — South

31	Feb	3	(a)	Southampton	L 1-4	Cheetham	10,000
32		10	(h)	Charlton A	L 0-2		7,000
33		17	(h)	Chelsea	D 1-1	Cheetham	12,000
34		24	(h)	Southampton	D 3-3	Robson, Kurz, Stevens	9,000
35	Mar	3	(a)	Charlton A	L 0-1		10,000
36		10	(a)	Chelsea	L 0-2		20,690

Crystal Palace finished 5th in Group 4 of the Qualifying Competition and did not qualify for the semi-finals

Appearances
Goals

Tootill	Mountford	Dawes F	Dawes A	Millbank	Phillips	Driver	Somerfield	Kurz	Lowes	Wilson	Lievesley	Reece	Robson	Blackman	Lewis G	Ferrier	Spencer	Briscoe	Townsend	Hudgell	Parlane	McFarlane	Harding	Moore	Jones	Challis	Cheetham	Lewis J	Betts	Gillespie	Stephens	Stevens	Bradshaw	Ferrier R	McCormick	Clarkson	Barrett	Tickeridge	
1	2	3	4	5	6	7	8	9	10	11																													1
1	2	3		5	6	7	8	9	10	11	4																												2
1	2	3	8							11	5	6	7	9	10																								3
1	2	3	10				8					6	7	9	11																								4
	2			5	6		8		10	11			9			3	4	7																					5
1	2	3	6							11	4		10					7	5																				6
1	2		8				9			11	4		10	6			5	7		3																			7
1	2		7					9	10	11			6				5			3	8																		8
	2						10			11			7	9		3	5			6	8	1		4															9
1	2						10	9		11						3	5	7		6	8			4															10
	3		8				10											7	5	6		1	2	4															11
	2				6		10	9		11			7			3			5	4		1			8														12
	2		7		6					11					10	3	5			4		1			8														13
	2				6		10	9								3	5			4	8	1			11	7													14
	2				6		10	9		11						3	5			4		1			8	7													15
					6		10	9		11						3	5			4		1	2		8	7													16
	2				6		10	7						11		3	5			4		1			8		9												17
	2		4				8			11						3	5			6					7		9												18
			2							11				6			5			3					4	7													19
1	2	7			6		8	9		11					10	3	5			4																			20
	2		7				8	9		11				4		3	5			6		1																	21
	2				6		10	9		11						3				4	8	1			7			5											22
	2				4		10	7		11						3	5			6		1			8		9												23
	2		9							7					8		5			6		1						4	11		3								24
	2		9		6			7		11					10	3	5			4		1																	25
1	2		4				10	9		11			7		8	3	5			6																			26
1	2		10											9			5			6									11		3								27
1		11	4					9								3				6			2									8	7						28
1			4					8							10	3	5			6			2						11	7				9					29
1			9					8							10	3	5						2					4	11						6	7			30
14	25	7	18	3	13	2	19	18	4	22	4	2	9	8	9	19	21	5	3	23	5	13	5	3	10	4	3	3	4	1	2	1	1	1	1	1			
	2	1	6			3	14	14		9			3	5	1		1				1				3		1		2			1		3					

2 own-goals

Tootill	Mountford	Dawes F	Dawes A	Millbank	Phillips	Driver	Somerfield	Kurz	Lowes	Wilson	Lievesley	Reece	Robson	Blackman	Lewis G	Ferrier	Spencer	Briscoe	Townsend	Hudgell	Parlane	McFarlane	Harding	Moore	Jones	Challis	Cheetham	Lewis J	Betts	Gillespie	Stephens	Stevens	Bradshaw	Ferrier R	McCormick	Clarkson	Barrett	Tickeridge	
	2									11			7	6	10					3		1			7		9	4											31
	2	7			6		10			11						3											9	4		8							5		32
	2		8									4		7						6		1					9					10						3	33
	2							9		11			7							6		1			7			5			3	10							34
	2						10	9								3				6								4				8							35
	2						10			11			7			3				6		1			7		9	4											36
	6	1	1		1		3	2		4		1	3	2	1	3				5		4			3		4	5		1	1	3					1	1	
								1					1														2					1							

Burke played number 4 in Match 3; Stewart played number 5 in Match 4; Cruikshank played number 1 in Match 5; Redfern played number 8 in Match 6; Foreman played number 9 in Match 6; Wales played number 4 in Match 8; Conner played number 9 in Match 11 and scored once; Buchanan played number 11 in Match 11; Stock played number 9 in Match 13 and scored once; Brown played number 1 in Matches 18 & 19; Morrad played number 10 in Matches 18 & 21; Storen played number 8 in Match 19; Ramplin played number 10 in Match 19; Jackman played number 10 in Match 24; Hurrell played number 8 in Match 25; Young played number 2 in Match 27; Scarr played number 7 in Match 27; Stanley played number 8 in Match 27; Blair played number 5 in Match 28; Horn played number 10 in Match 28; Gregory played number 1 in Match 33; Paton played number 11 in Match 34; Muir played number 4 in Match 35; Taylor played number 1 in Match 36; Ward played number 7 in Match 36; Burley played number 11 in Match 36; Spence played number 4 in Matches 32, 34, 36 & 37.

1945-46

Manager: George Irwin

1	Aug	25	(h)	Aldershot	D 0-0		7,000
2	Sep	1	(a)	Aldershot	W 5-2	Kurz, Wilson, Surtees, A.Dawes 2	5,000
3		5	(h)	Reading	D 2-2	Kurz 2	7,000
4		8	(a)	Bristol C	W 2-1	F.Dawes, Wilson	12,000
5		12	(h)	Cardiff C	W 3-0	Addinall 2, A.Dawes	5,000
6		15	(h)	Bristol C	L 0-1		11,000
7		19	(a)	Reading	W 4-3	Addinall 2, Fagan, Wilson	5,052
8		22	(a)	Brighton & HA	L 3-7	Kurz, Stevens 2	10,000
9		29	(h)	Brighton & HA	W 5-1	Bark 2, Kurz, Robson, Ferrier	12,000
10	Oct	6	(a)	Exeter C	W 1-0	Blackman	11,000
11		13	(h)	Exeter C	W 2-1	Kurz, Blackman	15,000
12	Nov	3	(a)	Swindon T	W 3-1	Kurz 2, Robson	12,000
13		10	(h)	Swindon T	W 10-1	Blackman 3, Kurz 3, Robson 2, Stamp, Wilson	10,000
14	Dec	1	(a)	Bristol R	D 1-1	Kurz	12,897
15		15	(a)	Torquay U	W 2-1	Kurz, Blackman	3,000
16		19	(h)	Bristol R	W 1-0	Kurz	4,000
17		22	(h)	Torquay U	W 5-0	Kurz 2, Stamp, G.Lewis 2	8,000
18		25	(h)	Bournemouth	W 4-1	Kurz 3, Stamp	10,000
19		26	(a)	Bournemouth	L 1-2	Kurz (pen)	10,000
20		29	(a)	Cardiff C	L 1-6	Kurz	25,000
FINAL LEAGUE POSITION: 1st in Division Three South (South Region)							Appearances
							Goals

League Cup Qualifying Competition

21	Jan	12	(a)	Brighton & HA	D 2-2	Smith, G.Lewis	16,000
22		19	(h)	Brighton & HA	W 6-1	Kurz 2, G.Lewis 2, Reece 2	10,000
23	Feb	2	(h)	Aldershot	W 6-0	Lievesley 3, Reece 2, G.Lewis	8,000
24		9	(h)	Reading	D 3-3	Lievesley, Kurz, Reece	10,000
25		16	(a)	Reading	W 2-0	G.Lewis, Reece	11,000
26		23	(h)	Bournemouth	W 2-1	Smith, Kurz	10,000
27	Mar	2	(a)	Bournemouth	L 0-4		8,000
28		9	(h)	Norwich C	L 2-3	Lievesley, Kurz	12,000
29		16	(a)	Norwich C	L 1-6	Kurz	10,982
30		23	(h)	Exeter C	W 3-0	Hudgell, Kurz 2	12,000
31		30	(a)	Exeter C	W 3-2	Kurz 2, Reece	8,500
32	Apr	3	(a)	Aldershot	W 3-0	Kurz, Bark, Reece	1,500
33		6	(h)	Bristol C	L 1-2	Kurz	15,000
34		13	(a)	Bristol C	D 2-2	J.Lewis, Waldron	16,264
35		20	(h)	Cardiff C	D 1-1	Girling	17,500
36		22	(a)	Cardiff C	L 0-3		29,000
FINAL LEAGUE POSITION: 4th in League Cup Qualifying Competition							Appearances
							Goals

FA Cup

1	Jan	5	(a)	Queen's Park R	D 0-0		20,080
		9	(h)	Queen's Park R	D 0-0*		16,200
R		16	(n†)	Queen's Park R	L 0-1		24,600
				†Played at Craven Cottage, Fulham. *After extra-time.			Appearances
							Goals

Ford	Dawes FW	Hudgell	Reece	Hindle	Lewis J	Wilson	Jackman	Kurz	Male	Allen	Matthewson	Dawes AG	Surtees	Fagan	Stevens	Harding	Humphries	Blackman	Addinal	Bark	Forder	Gregory F	Millbanks	Robson	Lewis G	Stamps	Graham	Morris	Collins	Bassett	Lievesley	Chivers	Smith	Eastman	Gillespie	Girling	Burrell	Waldron	
1	2	3	4	5	6	7	8	9	10	11																													1
1	2	3	4		6	11		9	10		5	7	8																										2
	3	6	4			11		9			5	7		8	10																								3
1	11	3	4		6	7			10			8				2	5	9																					4
	3	6	4		10	11						7		8		2	5		9																				5
1	2	3	4		6	11			8			7					5			10																			6
1	3		4			11		7				6		8					9		2		5																7
1	3	6	4			11		8	10			2			9								5		7														8
1	3	6			4	11		8									5			10		2		7															9
1	3	6			4	11		8									5	9				2		7	10														10
1	3	6			4	11		8									5	9				2		7	10														11
1	3	6			4	11		8								2	5	9						7	10														12
1	3	6			4	11		8									5	9				2		7		10													13
	3	6			4	11		9									5					2		8	10		1						7						14
	3	6			4	11		9									5	7				2			10		1						8						15
	3	6			4	11		9									5	7				2				10	1						8						16
	3				6			9									5	4				2			11	10	1	7					8						17
	3	6			4			9									5	7				2		8		10	1									11			18
	3	6			4			9									5	7				2		8	11	10	1												19
	2	3			4	11		9									5								10		1	7	6				8						20
11	20	18	8	1	17	17	1	17	5	1	2	7	1	3	2	3	15	10	2	2	1	10	2	8	9	5	7	2	1				5			1			
	1					4		20				3	1	1	2			6	4	2				5	2	3													

Ford	Dawes FW	Hudgell	Reece	Hindle	Lewis J	Wilson	Jackman	Kurz	Male	Allen	Matthewson	Dawes AG	Surtees	Fagan	Stevens	Harding	Humphries	Blackman	Addinal	Bark	Forder	Gregory F	Millbanks	Robson	Lewis G	Stamps	Graham	Morris	Collins	Bassett	Lievesley	Chivers	Smith	Eastman	Gillespie	Girling	Burrell	Waldron	
	3	6			4			9														2		8	11		1		7	5			10						21
	3	6	10		4			8														2			11		1	7		5	9								22
	3	6	10		4			8														2			11		1			5	9		7						23
	3	6	10		4	11		8														2					1			5	9		7						24
	3	6	10		4			8														2			11		1			5	9		7						25
	3	6	10		4	11		8														2					1			5	9		7						26
	3	2	8		6			9																	11		1			5		4	7				10		27
	3	6	10		4			8														2			11		1			5	9		7						28
	3	6	8		4	11		7												10		2	5				1				9								29
	3	6	4		5	11		9												10		2					1						7				8		30
	3	6	10		4	7		9										11				2					1			5			8						31
		6	8		4	7		9												10	3	2					1			5						11			32
		6	8		4	7		9				3								10		2					1			5						11			33
			6		4															10							1			5	3		7	2		11		8	34
		3	6		4	7												9		8							1			5				2		11	10		35
		6			4	7																					1			5	3			2		11	10	9	36
	11	15	14		16	9		13				1						2		6	1	12	1	1	6		16	1	1	14	9	1	10	3		5	4	2	
		1	8		1			12												1					5						5		2			1		1	

Ford	Dawes FW	Hudgell	Reece	Hindle	Lewis J	Wilson	Jackman	Kurz	Male	Allen	Matthewson	Dawes AG	Surtees	Fagan	Stevens	Harding	Humphries	Blackman	Addinal	Bark	Forder	Gregory F	Millbanks	Robson	Lewis G	Stamps	Graham	Morris	Collins	Bassett	Lievesley	Chivers	Smith	Eastman	Gillespie	Girling	Burrell	Waldron	
	3	6	8		4	11		9														2			10		1			5					7				1
	3	6			4	11		9										7				2			10		1			5			8						2
	3	6			4	11		9														2		8	11		1			5			10						R
	3	3	1		3	3		3										1				3		1	3		3			3			2		1				

Hughes played number 1 in Match 3; Winter played number 2 in Match 3; McFarlane played number 1 in Match 4; Corbett played number 9 in Match 5; Woodward played number 10 in Match 7; Ferrier played number 9 in Match 9 and scored once; Stewart played number 9 in Match 34; Healey played number 8 in Match 36.

1946-47

Manager: George Irwin

1	Aug	31	(a)	Mansfield T	L 1-3	Girling	9,508
2	Sep	4	(a)	Reading	L 2-10	Reece, Waldron	8,241
3		7	(h)	Bristol R	W 2-1	Kurz, Corbett	18,141
4		11	(h)	Brighton & HA	W 1-0	Robson	11,983
5		14	(a)	Southend U	L 0-2		9,288
6		18	(h)	Reading	W 2-1	Burrell 2	9,617
7		21	(h)	Queen's Park R	D 0-0		27,517
8		26	(a)	Norwich C	W 3-2	Naylor 2, Burrell	12,264
9		28	(a)	Leyton O	W 1-0	Naylor	11,802
10	Oct	5	(h)	Ipswich T	D 1-1	Hudgell (pen)	20,873
11		12	(a)	Watford	L 0-1		9,904
12		19	(a)	Exeter C	L 1-2	Girling	9,928
13		26	(h)	Port Vale	L 1-2	J.Lewis	14,492
14	Nov	2	(a)	Bristol C	L 0-3		26,418
15		9	(h)	Swindon T	W 4-1	Reece, Kurz 2, Naylor	15,741
16		16	(a)	Bournemouth	L 0-4		13,383
17		23	(h)	Cardiff C	L 1-2	Naylor	25,296
18	Dec	7	(h)	Notts C	W 2-1	Kurz, Girling	12,461
19		21	(h)	Aldershot	D 0-0		6,696
20		25	(h)	Torquay U	W 6-1	Naylor 2, Girling 2, Russell, Head (og)	11,786
21		26	(a)	Torquay U	L 1-2	G.Lewis	7,584
22		28	(h)	Mansfield T	D 1-1	Naylor	15,347
23	Jan	4	(a)	Bristol R	L 1-2	Robson	13,341
24		18	(h)	Southend U	L 0-3		18,968
25		25	(a)	Queen's Park R	W 2-1	Mycock, Girling	13,022
26	Feb	1	(h)	Leyton O	W 2-0	Naylor, Russell	8,326
27		8	(a)	Ipswich T	D 1-1	Robson	9,168
28		15	(h)	Watford	W 2-0	Mycock, Robson	10,779
29		22	(h)	Exeter C	W 1-0	Mycock	7,097
30	Mar	15	(a)	Swindon T	L 0-1		13,711
31		22	(h)	Bournemouth	L 0-1		11,825
32		29	(a)	Cardiff C	D 0-0		24,214
33	Apr	4	(h)	Walsall	D 1-1	Jones	2,906
34		5	(h)	Norwich C	L 0-1		13,315
35		7	(a)	Walsall	D 3-3	Reece, Russell, Robson	13,315
36		12	(a)	Notts C	D 0-0		14,890
37		19	(h)	Northampton T	D 2-2	Millbank, Russell	10,920
38		26	(a)	Aldershot	W 2-0	Reece, Kurz	4,125
39	May	3	(a)	Brighton & HA	L 0-1		6,957
40		6	(a)	Northampton T	L 0-1		5,690
41		23	(h)	Bristol C	D 0-0		11,634
42		25	(a)	Port Vale	L 2-4	Russell, Robson	10,414

FINAL LEAGUE POSITION: 18th in Division Three South

Appearances
Goals

FA Cup

3	Jan	11	(a)	Newcastle U	L 2-6	Naylor 2	43,183

Appearances
Goals

Graham	Eastman	Dawes	Lewis J	Bassett	Hudgell	Coates	Lewis G	Kurz	Burrell	Girling	Felton	Waldron	Reece	Lucas	Webb	Mycock	Corbett	Robson	Bark/Naylor	Guthrie	Russell	Millbank	Harding	Howells	Jones	Hann	Deakin	
1	2	3	4	5	6	7	8	9	10	11																		1
1		3	4	5	6			7	10	11	2	9	8															2
		2	5		3	7		9		11			6	1	4	8	10											3
		2	5		3	7		9		11			6	1	4	8		10										4
		2	5		3	7		9		11			6	1	4	8		10										5
1		3	4	5	2		7	9	10	11			6						8									6
1		3	4	5	2		7	9	10	11			6						8									7
1		3	4	5	2			9	10	11		7	6						8									8
1		3	4	5	2			9	10	11		7	6						8									9
1		3	4	5	2		7		10	11			6					9	8									10
1		3	4	5	2		8	7	10	11			6					9										11
1		3	4	5	2			9	10	11		8	6					7										12
1		3	4	5	2		8	9	10	11			6					7										13
1		3	4	5	2		10	9		11			8					7		6								14
1		3	4	5	2		7	9		11			8						10	6								15
1		3	4	5	2		7	9		11			8						10	6								16
1		3	4	5	2		7	9		11								8	10	6								17
1		3	4	5	6		7	9		11									10	2	8							18
1		3	4	5	2		7	9		11			6						10		8							19
1		3	4	5	2		7	9		11			6						10		8							20
1		3	4	5	2		7	9		11			6						10		8							21
1		3	4	5	2		7	9		11			6					8	10									22
1		3	4	5	6			9		11								7	10		8	2						23
		3	4	5	2		7	8		11			6	1				9	10									24
1		3	4	5	2		7			11			6			8		9	10									25
1		3	4	5						11			6			7		9	10		8		2					26
1		3	4	5			11						6			7		9	10		8		2					27
1		3	4	5			11		10				6			7		9			8		2					28
1		3	4	5			11	10					6			7		9			8		2					29
1		3	4	5			10						6			7		9			8		2	11				30
1		3	4	5				10	11				6			7		9			8		2					31
1		3	4					10	11				6			7		9			8	5	2					32
1		3	4					10	11				6					9			8	5	2		7			33
1		3	4					10	11				6			7		9			8	5	2					34
1		3	4				11	9					6			7		10			8	5	2					35
1		3	4				11	10					9			7					8	5	2			6		36
1		3	4				11	10					6			7		9			8	5	2					37
1		3	4				11	10					6			7		9			8	5					2	38
1		3	4				11	10					6			7		9			8	5					2	39
1		3	4				11	7					6			10		9			8	5					2	40
1		3	4				10	8					6			7		9				5	2	11				41
1		3	4					10					6			7		9			8	5	2	11				42
38	1	42	42	28	25	4	28	36	15	26	1	4	38	4	3	20	1	28	18	5	21	12	14	3	1	1	3	
			1		1		1	5	3	6		1	4			3	1	6	9		5	1			1			

1 own-goal

Graham	Eastman	Dawes	Lewis J	Bassett	Hudgell	Coates	Lewis G	Kurz	Burrell	Girling	Felton	Waldron	Reece	Lucas	Webb	Mycock	Corbett	Robson	Bark/Naylor	Guthrie	Russell	Millbank	Harding	Howells	Jones	Hann	Deakin	
1		3	4	5	2		7	8		11			6					9	10									3
1		1	1	1	1		1	1		1			1					1	1									
																			2									

1947-48

Manager: Jack Butler

1	Aug	23	(a)	Leyton O	D 1-1	Kurz	18,243
2		27	(h)	Aldershot	W 1-0	Russell	11,205
3		30	(h)	Torquay U	W 2-1	Mycock, Burrell	14,490
4	Sep	3	(a)	Aldershot	L 0-2		5,209
5		6	(a)	Swindon T	D 0-0		17,619
6		8	(a)	Bristol R	D 1-1	Kurz	12,430
7		13	(h)	Port Vale	W 2-0	Reece, Mycock	15,063
8		17	(h)	Bristol R	D 0-0		12,172
9		20	(a)	Queen's Park R	L 0-1		25,199
10		27	(h)	Watford	L 1-2	Robson	16,764
11	Oct	4	(a)	Brighton & HA	D 1-1	Robson	10,240
12		11	(a)	Exeter C	L 0-2		7,992
13		18	(h)	Newport C	W 2-1	Kurz, Robson	16,353
14		25	(a)	Southend U	L 1-2	Kurz	10,560
15	Nov	1	(h)	Notts C	D 1-1	Howe (og)	16,019
16		8	(a)	Swansea T	L 0-2		19,584
17		15	(h)	Bournemouth	W 2-0	Kurz 2	14,244
18		22	(a)	Ipswich T	L 0-3		12,387
19	Dec	6	(a)	Walsall	D 1-1	Somerfield	10,669
20		20	(h)	Leyton O	W 2-0	G.Lewis, Clough	9,994
21		25	(h)	Northampton T	W 1-0	Mycock	15,095
22		27	(a)	Northampton T	L 1-3	Mycock	9,631
23	Jan	3	(a)	Torquay U	D 3-3	Clough, Somerfield, Howells	6,016
24		17	(h)	Swindon T	D 1-1	Clough	11,881
25		24	(h)	Walsall	L 2-3	Clough, Somerfield	11,705
26		31	(a)	Port Vale	L 1-4	Kurz	13,419
27	Feb	14	(a)	Watford	W 5-0	Clough 2, Gaillard, G.Lewis, Kurz	14,767
28		28	(h)	Exeter C	L 1-2	Kurz	15,627
29	Mar	6	(a)	Newport C	L 1-3	Burrell	8,732
30		13	(h)	Southend U	D 0-0		14,458
31		15	(h)	Queen's Park R	L 0-1		22,086
32		20	(a)	Notts C	L 0-1		30,558
33		26	(a)	Norwich C	L 1-3	Mycock	24,802
34		27	(h)	Swansea T	W 4-0	Kurz 3, Clough	16,036
35		29	(h)	Norwich C	W 2-0	Kurz 2	20,724
36	Apr	3	(a)	Bournemouth	D 0-0		16,597
37		5	(h)	Bristol C	W 4-0	Kurz 2, G.Lewis, Clough	13,405
38		10	(h)	Ipswich T	W 2-1	J.Lewis, Kurz	18,151
39		12	(h)	Brighton & HA	D 0-0		16,463
40		17	(a)	Bristol C	L 0-2		12,560
41		20	(a)	Reading	D 0-0		8,582
42		24	(h)	Reading	W 2-1	Mycock, Kurz	11,735

FINAL LEAGUE POSITION: 13th in Division Three South

Appearances
Goals

FA Cup

1	Nov	29	(h)	Port Vale	W 2-1	Farrington, Clough	16,000
2	Dec	13	(a)	Bristol C	W 1-0*	Robson	22,327
3	Jan	10	(h)	Chester	L 0-1		22,000

*After extra-time

Appearances
Goals

Graham	Harding	Dawes F	Lewis J	Bassett	Reece	Robson	Mycock	Kurz	Russell	Lewis G	Burrell	Millbank	Stubbs	Clough	Deakin	Somerfield	Howells	Buckley	Gaillard	Farrington	
1	2	3	4	5	6	7	8	9	10	11											1
1	2	3	4	5	6	7	8	9	10	11											2
1	2	3	4	5	6		7	9	8	11	10										3
1	2	3	4	5	6		7	9	8	11	10										4
1	2	3	4	5	10	9	7	8		11		6									5
1	2	3	4	5	10	9	7	8		11		6									6
1	2	3	4	5	10	9	7	8		11		6									7
1	2	3	5		6	9	8		10	11			4	7							8
1	2		4	5	10	9	8			11		6		7	3						9
1	2		4	5	6	9	8		10	11		3		7							10
1	2		4	5	6	9	8		10	11				7	3						11
1	2		4	5	6	9	8		10	11				7	3						12
1	2	3		5	6	9		8	10	7		4		11							13
1	2	3		5	6	9	10	8		7		4		11							14
1	2	3	4		6			9	8	11		5		7		10					15
1	2	3	4		6		7	9			8	5				10	11				16
1	2	3	4		6		7	9		8		5		11		10					17
1	2	3			6		7	9	8			5	4	11		10					18
1	2	3	4			9	7	10				5				8	11	6			19
1	2	3			6	9	7	10		8		5		11				4			20
1	2	3			6	9	7	10		8		5		11				4			21
1	2	3			6	9	7			8		5		11		10		4			22
1	2	3	4		6	10				8		5		7		9	11				23
1	2	3	4		6	10	7			8		5		11		9					24
1	2	3	4		6		7	10		8		5		11		9					25
1		3	4	2	6	10	7	9				5		11				8			26
1	2	3	4				8	9		10		5		7				6	11		27
1	2	3	4				8	9		10		5		7				6	11		28
1	2	3	4				8	9	10		11	5		7				6			29
1	2	3	4				8	9		10		5		7				6	11		30
1	2	3	4				8	9		10		5		7				6	11		31
1	2	3	4		10	8	7	9				5		11				6			32
1	2	3	4		10		7	9	8			5		11				6			33
1	2	3	4	5			7	9	8	10				11				6			34
1	2	3	4	5			7	9	8	10				11				6			35
1	2	3	4	5			7		8	10				11		9		6			36
1	2	3	4	5			7	9	8	10				11				6			37
1	2	3	4	5			7	9	8	10				11				6			38
1	2	3	4	5			7	9	8					11				6		10	39
1	2	3	4	5	10		7	9	8					11				6			40
1	2	3	4	5			7	9	8					11				6		10	41
1	2	3	4	5			7	9	8	10				11				6			42
42	41	38	36	23	28	20	39	33	22	32	4	26	2	33	3	10	3	21	4	2	
			1		1	3	6	18	1	3	2			8		3	1		1		

1 own-goal

Graham	Harding	Dawes F	Lewis J	Bassett	Reece	Robson	Mycock	Kurz	Russell	Lewis G	Burrell	Millbank	Stubbs	Clough	Deakin	Somerfield	Howells	Buckley	Gaillard	Farrington	
1	2	3			6		7	9				5		11		10		4		8	1
1	2	3			6	9	7	10		8		5		11				4			2
1	2	3	4		6	10	7			8		5		11		9					3
3	3	3	1		3	2	3	2		2		3		3		2		2		1	
							1							1						1	

1948-49

Manager: Jack Butler

1	Aug	21	(a)	Reading	L 1-5	Kurz	17,712
2		25	(h)	Swansea T	D 1-1	Broughton	13,464
3		28	(h)	Millwall	D 1-1	Davidson	30,556
4	Sep	2	(a)	Swansea T	L 0-3		14,277
5		4	(h)	Watford	W 3-1	Broughton, Clough, Beresford	16,003
6		8	(h)	Bristol R	W 1-0	Kurz	10,827
7		11	(a)	Bournemouth	L 0-2		17,517
8		13	(a)	Bristol R	L 0-1		14,509
9		18	(h)	Ipswich T	D 1-1	Chase	18,982
10		25	(a)	Notts C	L 1-5	Kurz	24,061
11	Oct	2	(h)	Walsall	L 1-3	Kurz	16,300
12		9	(a)	Aldershot	L 0-3		8,109
13		16	(h)	Brighton & HA	L 0-2		15,170
14		23	(a)	Bristol C	L 0-2		14,913
15		30	(h)	Swindon T	D 1-1	Broughton	12,290
16	Nov	6	(a)	Norwich C	L 0-3		23,890
17		13	(h)	Exeter C	D 1-1	Thomas	13,350
18		20	(a)	Southend U	W 1-0	Clough	10,357
19	Dec	4	(a)	Leyton O	D 1-1	Kurz	12,336
20		25	(a)	Newport C	L 0-5		15,115
21		27	(h)	Newport C	L 0-1		10,951
22	Jan	1	(a)	Millwall	L 0-1		19,484
23		8	(h)	Reading	L 0-1		10,842
24		15	(a)	Watford	L 0-2		7,410
25		22	(h)	Bournemouth	W 2-1	Thomas, Broughton	13,862
26		29	(h)	Northampton T	D 2-2	Kurz, Lewis	13,972
27	Feb	5	(a)	Ipswich T	L 2-3	Thomas 2	10,226
28		12	(h)	Port Vale	D 1-1	Kurz	12,409
29		19	(h)	Notts C	L 1-5	Thomas	30,925
30		26	(a)	Walsall	L 1-3	Davidson	10,913
31	Mar	5	(h)	Aldershot	W 2-1	Clough 2	9,856
32		12	(a)	Brighton & HA	D 1-1	Thomas	15,413
33		19	(h)	Bristol C	W 4-0	Lewis, Chilvers, McCormick, Roberts (og)	11,840
34		26	(a)	Swindon T	L 0-1		11,678
35	Apr	2	(h)	Norwich C	D 1-1	Kurz	16,501
36		9	(a)	Exeter C	L 1-3	Kurz	7,625
37		16	(h)	Southend U	W 2-1	Gaillard 2	14,168
38		18	(h)	Torquay U	L 0-1		12,140
39		19	(a)	Torquay U	L 0-2		7,552
40		23	(a)	Northampton T	L 2-3	Kurz, McCormick	7,717
41		30	(h)	Leyton O	W 2-1	Kurz 2	7,869
42	May	7	(a)	Port Vale	D 0-0		7,821

FINAL LEAGUE POSITION: 22nd in Division Three South

Appearances
Goals

FA Cup

1	Nov	27	(h)	Bristol C	L 0-1*	16,700

*After extra-time

Appearances
Goals

Graham	Harding	Dawes	Lewis	Bassett	Buckley	Broughton	Beresford	Kurz	Freeman	Clough	George	Davidson	Chase	Mullen	Stubbs	Farrington	Briggs	Chilvers	Taylor	Sille	Howells	Thomas J	Mulheron	Bumstead	Wyatt	Ross	McCormick	Gaillard	Murphy	Bostock	Saward	Rainford	
1	2	3	4	5	6	7	8	9	10	11																							1
1	2	3	4	5	6	7	8	9	10	11																							2
1	2		4	5	6	7		9		11	3	10	8																				3
1	2		4	5	6	7		9		11	3		8	10																			4
1	2		4	5	6	7	10	9		11	3		8																				5
1	2		4	5	6	7		9		11	3	10	8																				6
1	2		4	5	6	7	10	9		11	3		8																				7
1			4	5	6	7		9		11	3		8		2	10																	8
1	2		4		6	7	10	9		11	3		8				5																9
1	2		4		6	7		9		11	3	10	8				5																10
1	2			5	6			9		7	3		8					4	10	11													11
1	2				6	7		9			3	10	8				5	4		11													12
1	2	3	4		6	7		10		11			8				5				9												13
1	2	3	4	5	6		8	9		7		10								11													14
1	2	3	5		6	11		8		7		10		4								9											15
1	2	3	5		6	11				7		10		4							9		8										16
1	2	3		5	6	7				11		10		4								9	8										17
1	2	3		5	6	7	8			11				4							9		10										18
1	2	3	4		6	7		8		11			5								9		10										19
1	2	3	4		6	7		9					5	11								10	8										20
	2	3	4		6	7		9						11			5					10	8	1									21
	2	3	5		6	7		9				10		11									8	1		4							22
	2	3	5		6	7		9		11				10				4					8	1									23
	2		4	5	6	7		9		11				10									8	1	3								24
	2	3	4	5	6	7		10		11												9	8	1									25
	2	3	4	5	6	7		10		11				8								9		1									26
	2			5	6	7		10		11			8					4				9		1	3								27
	2	3		5		7		10		11			4									9		1		6	8						28
	2	3	4			7		9		11			5									10		1		6	8						29
		3		5						7	2	11	4					6				9	10	1			8						30
		3		5		11		9		7	2		4					6				10		1			8						31
		3	4					9		7	2		5					6				10		1			8	11					32
			4					9		7	2		5					6				10		1	3		8	11					33
			4			10				7	2		5					6				9		1	3		8	11					34
			4			10		9		7	2		5					6						1	3		8	11					35
			4			10		9		7	2		5					6						1	3		8	11					36
1	2		4			10		9		7			5					6							3		8	11					37
1	2		4			10		9		7			5					6									8	11	3				38
1						10		9					5					6								2	8	11	3	7	4		39
1						10		9			2		5					6									8	11	3	7	4		40
1			4			8		9			2						5	6				10						11	3	7			41
1						10		9			2						5	6					4					11	3	7		8	42
26	30	20	31	19	27	37	7	37	2	34	20	10	27	11	1	1	7	17	1	3	4	15	12	16	7	4	13	11	5	4	2	1	
			2			4	1	12		4		2	1					1				6					2	2					

1 own-goal

Graham	Harding	Dawes	Lewis	Bassett	Buckley	Broughton	Beresford	Kurz	Freeman	Clough	George	Davidson	Chase	Mullen	Stubbs	Farrington	Briggs	Chilvers	Taylor	Sille	Howells	Thomas J	Mulheron	Bumstead	Wyatt	Ross	McCormick	Gaillard	Murphy	Bostock	Saward	Rainford	
1	2	3	4		6	7				11			5	8							9		10										1
1	1	1	1		1	1				1			1	1							1		1										

1949-50

Manager: Ronnie Rooke

No	Month	Day	Venue	Opponents	Result	Score	Scorers	Attendance
1	Aug	20	(a)	Exeter C	L	1-2	Hanlon	12,180
2		24	(h)	Leyton O	D	1-1	Rooke	17,764
3		27	(h)	Ipswich T	W	2-0	Rooke 2	19,173
4	Sep	1	(a)	Leyton O	D	2-2	Rooke, Blackshaw	14,868
5		3	(a)	Port Vale	L	0-2		13,788
6		7	(h)	Walsall	W	2-0	Hanlon, Thomas	12,264
7		10	(h)	Notts C	L	1-2	Lewis	26,847
8		17	(a)	Southend U	D	0-0		13,797
9		24	(h)	Bristol R	W	1-0	Rooke	15,466
10	Oct	1	(a)	Bournemouth	L	0-2		16,738
11		8	(a)	Millwall	W	3-2	Rooke, Mulheron, McMillen (og)	30,043
12		15	(h)	Swindon T	D	2-2	Thomas 2	15,954
13		22	(a)	Torquay U	L	0-1		7,018
14		29	(h)	Aldershot	W	2-1	Hanlon, Rooke	13,299
15	Nov	5	(a)	Nottingham F	L	0-2		18,471
16		12	(h)	Northampton T	L	0-4		12,486
17		19	(a)	Norwich C	L	0-2		23,558
18	Dec	3	(a)	Bristol C	L	0-2		15,304
19		13	(h)	Exeter C	W	5-3	Kurz 2, Mulheron, Blackshaw, Howells	7,416
20		24	(a)	Ipswich T	D	4-4	Watson, Rooke 2, Howells	9,460
21		26	(h)	Watford	W	2-0	Rooke, Blackshaw	15,065
22		27	(a)	Watford	D	0-0		16,985
23		31	(h)	Port Vale	L	0-1		12,609
24	Jan	7	(a)	Brighton & HA	D	0-0		13,289
25		14	(a)	Notts C	W	1-0	Kurz	31,381
26		21	(h)	Southend U	W	2-1	Kurz, Howells	13,509
27		28	(h)	Newport C	W	1-0	Kurz	9,875
28	Feb	4	(a)	Bristol R	D	0-0		17,259
29		11	(h)	Brighton & HA	W	6-0	Rooke 3, Kurz, Chase, Howells	13,973
30		18	(h)	Bournemouth	W	1-0	Rooke	22,322
31		25	(h)	Millwall	W	1-0	Blackshaw	30,432
32	Mar	4	(a)	Swindon T	L	2-4	Kurz 2	15,217
33		11	(h)	Torquay U	L	1-3	Rooke (pen)	20,533
34		18	(a)	Aldershot	D	0-0		8,034
35		25	(h)	Nottingham F	D	1-1	Rooke (pen)	17,480
36	Apr	1	(a)	Northampton T	D	2-2	Rooke 2	10,277
37		7	(h)	Reading	D	1-1	Rooke	22,644
38		8	(h)	Norwich C	W	2-0	Rooke, Thomas	18,067
39		10	(a)	Reading	W	2-1	Blackshaw, Kelly	12,730
40		15	(a)	Newport C	D	2-2	Kurz, Rooke	11,459
41		22	(h)	Bristol C	D	1-1	Kurz	17,263
42	May	6	(a)	Walsall	L	1-3	Hanlon	5,379

FINAL LEAGUE POSITION: 7th in Division Three South

Appearances
Goals

FA Cup

No	Month	Day	Venue	Opponents	Result	Score	Scorers	Attendance
1	Nov	26	(a)	Newport C	L	0-3		13,000

Appearances
Goals

Graham	George	Dawes	Lewis	Watson	Chilvers	Hanlon	Kurz	Rocke	Mulheron	Gaillard	Blackshaw	Chase	Broughton	Thomas J	Surtees	Ross	Clelland	Edwards	Sherwood	Howells	Delaney	Murphy	Harding	Bailey	Kelly	Bumstead	Penn	Buckley	
1	2	3	4	5	6	7	8	9	10	11																			1
1	2	3	4	5	6		8	9	10	11	7																		2
1	2	3	4		6	11	10	9	8		7	5																	3
1	2	3	4	5	6	11	8	9			7	10																	4
1	2	3	4	5	6	11					8	10	7	9															5
1	2	3	4	5	6	11		8		10				9	7														6
1	2	3	4	5	6	11		8						9	7	10													7
1	2	3	4	5	6	11	8	9		10					7														8
1	2	3	4	5	6	11	8	9		10							7												9
1	2	3	4	5	6	11		9	8					10			7												10
1	2		4	5	6	11		9	8				7	10				3											11
1	2		4	5	6	11		9	8				7	10				3											12
1	2			5	6	11		9	8				7	10				3	4										13
1	2		4	5		11		9	8				7	10		6		3											14
1	2		4	5		11			8				7	10		6		3		9									15
1	2			5	6	11			8				7	10				3	4	9									16
1	2			5	6	11		9	8			4	7	10				3											17
1				5				9	8		7	4		10		6		3		11	2								18
1				5			10	9	8		7	4				6				11	2	3							19
1				5			10	9	8		7	4				6				11	2	3							20
1				5			10	9	8		7	4				6		2		11		3							21
1				5			10	9	8		7	4				6		2		11		3							22
1				5			10	9	8		7	4				6		2		11		3							23
1				5			10	9	8		7	4				6				11		3	2						24
1				5			10	9			7	4		8		6				11		3	2						25
1				5			10	9			7	4		8		6				11		3	2						26
1				5			9	10	8		7					6				11		3	2					4	27
1				5			9	10	8		7	4				6				11		3	2						28
1				5			9	10	8		7	4				6				11		3	2						29
1				5			9	10	8		7	4				6				11		3	2						30
1				5			9	10	8		7	4			11	6						3	2						31
1				5			9	10	8		7	4			11	6						3	2						32
				5		11	9	10			7	4				6						3	2	1	8				33
				5			9	10		11	7	4				6						3	2		8	1			34
				5				9	8		7	4				6						3	2		10	1	11		35
				5		11		10	7			4		9								3	2		8	1		6	36
1				5		11		10			7	4		9								3	2		8			6	37
1				5		11		10			7	4		9								3	2		8			6	38
1				5		11		10			9	4	7									3	2		8			6	39
1				5		11	9	10			7	4										3	2		8			6	40
1	3			5		11	9	10			7	4											2		8			6	41
1	3			5		11	9	10			7	4											2		8			6	42
38	19	10	14	41	15	24	25	39	26	6	28	28	9	17	5	21	2	11	2	15	3	22	19	1	10	3	1	8	
			1	1		4	10	21	2		5	1		4						4					1				

1 own-goal

Graham	George	Dawes	Lewis	Watson	Chilvers	Hanlon	Kurz	Rocke	Mulheron	Gaillard	Blackshaw	Chase	Broughton	Thomas J	Surtees	Ross	Clelland	Edwards	Sherwood	Howells	Delaney	Murphy	Harding	Bailey	Kelly	Bumstead	Penn	Buckley	
1	2			5	6	11		9	8			4	7	10				3											1
1	1			1	1	1		1	1			1	1	1				1											

1950-51

Manager: Ronnie Rooke until 29 November 1950, then Fred Dawes/Charlie Slade.

1	Aug	19	(h)	Aldershot	L 0-2		24,968
2		23	(a)	Torquay U	L 1-4	Stevens	11,776
3		26	(a)	Swindon T	L 0-2		13,699
4		30	(h)	Torquay U	W 2-1	Whittaker, Rooke (pen)	11,212
5	Sep	2	(h)	Colchester U	L 1-3	Thomas	22,544
6		6	(a)	Bristol C	L 0-2		13,422
7		9	(a)	Bristol R	D 1-1	Hanlon	16,804
8		13	(h)	Bristol C	W 1-0	Stevens	12,937
9		16	(a)	Millwall	L 0-1		29,874
10		23	(h)	Brighton & HA	L 0-2		17,800
11		30	(a)	Newport C	W 4-2	Rooke 2, Kelly, Jones	10,114
12	Oct	7	(h)	Gillingham	W 4-3	Jones 2, Rooke 2 (1 pen)	18,896
13		14	(a)	Bournemouth	L 0-5		14,187
14		21	(h)	Exeter C	L 0-1		16,133
15		28	(a)	Southend U	L 2-5	Stevens, Thomas	10,387
16	Nov	4	(h)	Reading	L 0-3		12,479
17		11	(a)	Plymouth A	L 0-4		18,414
18		18	(h)	Ipswich T	L 1-3	Kelly	12,146
19	Dec	2	(h)	Walsall	W 1-0	Herbert	12,083
20		9	(a)	Watford	L 0-1		7,987
21		23	(h)	Swindon T	W 2-0	Kelly 2	7,267
22		25	(h)	Northampton T	D 0-0		11,001
23		26	(a)	Northampton T	L 0-2		12,607
24		30	(a)	Colchester U	L 0-1		8,587
25	Jan	6	(a)	Nottingham F	L 0-1		12,923
26		13	(h)	Bristol R	W 1-0	Kurz	10,632
27		20	(h)	Millwall	D 1-1	Kurz	22,392
28		27	(h)	Nottingham F	L 1-6	Kurz	17,179
29	Feb	3	(a)	Brighton & HA	L 0-1		6,790
30		10	(a)	Leyton O	L 0-2		11,763
31		17	(h)	Newport C	D 1-1	Rundle	9,990
32		24	(a)	Gillingham	D 0-0		11,478
33	Mar	3	(h)	Bournemouth	L 0-1		13,323
34		10	(a)	Exeter C	W 2-1	Broughton, Herbert	6,534
35		17	(h)	Southend U	L 0-2		12,898
36		24	(a)	Reading	D 1-1	Saward	16,720
37		26	(h)	Port Vale	L 0-2		11,320
38		31	(h)	Plymouth A	L 0-1		10,411
39	Apr	7	(a)	Ipswich T	D 1-1	Thomas	11,032
40		14	(h)	Leyton O	D 1-1	Evans (pen)	10,390
41		18	(h)	Norwich C	L 0-5		14,782
42		21	(a)	Walsall	D 0-0		7,838
43		26	(a)	Port Vale	D 2-2	Marsden 2	7,069
44		28	(h)	Watford	D 1-1	Marsden	5,258
45	May	2	(a)	Aldershot	L 0-3		4,279
46		5	(a)	Norwich C	L 1-3	Thomas	15,693

FINAL LEAGUE POSITION: 24th in Division Three South — Appearances / Goals

FA Cup

1	Nov	29	(h)	Millwall ‡	L 1-4	Kelly	14,817

‡After an abandoned match (34 minutes) on 25 November. — Appearances / Goals

Graham	Harding	Murphy	Smith	Watson	Whittaker	Stevens	Kelly	Rundle	Jones	Hanlon	Blackshaw	Kurz	Thomas J	George	Rooke	Bumstead	Ross	Briggs	McDonald	Chilvers	Buckley	Broughton	Herbert	Saward	Cushlow	Marsden	Bailey	Hughes	Evans	Edwards	Hancox	Rainford	
1	2	3	4	5	6	7	8	9	10	11																							1
1	2	3	4	5	6	8			10	11	7	9																					2
1	2	3	4	5	6	8			10	11	7		9																				3
1	2		4	5	6	7	8			11		9		3	10																		4
1	2		4	5	6	7	8			11			9	3	10																		5
	2		4	5	6		10		8	11	7		9	3		1																	6
	2		4	5	6		10		8	11	7		9	3		1																	7
	2				6	7	10		8	11			9	3		1	4	5															8
		2			6	7	10		8	11			9	3		1	4	5															9
		2		9	6	11	10		8			7		3		1	4	5															10
		2			6	11	10		8			7		3	9	1	4	5															11
		2			6	11	10		8			7		3	9	1	4	5															12
1					6	11	10		8			7		2	9		4	5	3														13
1		4			6	11	10		8			7		2	9				3	5													14
1		4				11			9	10		7	8	2					3	5	6												15
1	2	4			5	11	7	9	8	10				3							6												16
1	2			4	5	7	8	9		11			10	3							6												17
1	2			4	5	11	8	9	10										3		6	7											18
	2			5			8	10		11				3		1				6	4	7	9										19
	2			5			8	10		11				3		1				6	4	7	9										20
	2			5			8	10		11				3		1				6	4	7	9										21
	2			5			8	10		11				3		1				6	4	7	9										22
	2			5			8	10		11		9		3		1				6	4	7											23
	2			5			8	10		11			9	3		1				6		7		4									24
	2			5			8		10	11			9	3		1				6		7		4									25
	2			5	4		8	10		11		9		3		1				6		7											26
	2			5	4		8		10	11		9		3		1				6		7											27
	2			5	4		8	10		11		9		3		1				6		7											28
	2				4	7		10		11		9				1			3	6					5	8							29
	2				4	11	8	10				7				1			3	6					5	9							30
	2				4	7	8	10		11									3	6					5	9	1						31
	2				4	7	8	10		11									3	6					5	9	1						32
	2				4		8	10		11		7							3	6			9		5			1					33
	2				4			10		11									3	6		7	9	8	5			1					34
	2				4			10		11				3						6			9	8	5			1	7				35
	2				4			8		11									3	6			9	10	5			1	7				36
	2				4		7			11		8								6				10	5			1	9	3			37
	2				4		8			11										6		7		10	5			1	9	3			38
	2				4		8	10		11			9							6		7			5			1		3			39
	2				4			10		11			9							6		7			5			1	8	3			40
	2				4					11			9							6		7			5	10		1	8	3			41
	2				8					11						1	4			6	9	7			5	10				3			42
					4					11				2		1	8			6		10			5	9				3	7		43
										11				2		1	8			6	4	10			5	9				3	7		44
										11				2		1				6	4	10			5	9			7	3		8	45
	2									11		9	10			1			3	6	4	8			5				7	3			46
11	36	10	7	20	35	20	32	22	17	39	4	17	14	28	6	24	9	6	12	30	13	21	8	7	18	9	2	9	8	9	2	1	
					1	3	4	1	3	1		3	4		5							1	2	1		3			1				

Graham	Harding	Murphy	Smith	Watson	Whittaker	Stevens	Kelly	Rundle	Jones	Hanlon	Blackshaw	Kurz	Thomas J	George	Rooke	Bumstead	Ross	Briggs	McDonald	Chilvers	Buckley	Broughton	Herbert	Saward	Cushlow	Marsden	Bailey	Hughes	Evans	Edwards	Hancox	Rainford	
	2			5	4	11	8	9	10							1			3		6	7											1
	1			1	1	1	1	1	1							1			1		1	1											
							1																										

1951-52

Manager: Fred Dawes/Charlie Slade until 11 October, then Laurie Scott.

1	Aug	18	(h)	Exeter C	W 2-1	Marsden, Hanlon	15,464
2		22	(a)	Plymouth A	L 0-5		15,252
3		25	(a)	Colchester U	W 2-1	Price, Devonshire	10,135
4		29	(h)	Plymouth A	L 0-1		14,167
5	Sep	1	(a)	Millwall	L 1-3	McGeachie (pen)	22,436
6		3	(a)	Bristol R	L 0-4		14,467
7		8	(h)	Swindon T	L 0-1		14,264
8		12	(h)	Bristol R	L 0-1		10,289
9		15	(a)	Leyton O	W 4-0	Burgess 3, Evans	12,461
10		22	(h)	Walsall	W 2-1	Burgess, Rundle	16,901
11		29	(a)	Shrewsbury T	L 1-2	Burgess	12,493
12	Oct	6	(h)	Gillingham	L 0-2		20,380
13		13	(a)	Torquay U	W 5-1	Burgess 2, Evans 2, Devonshire	7,085
14		20	(h)	Ipswich T	W 3-1	Burgess 2, Price	21,220
15		27	(a)	Bristol C	L 0-2		18,857
16	Nov	3	(h)	Port Vale	W 3-1	Broughton, Evans 2	16,401
17		10	(a)	Northampton T	L 2-5	Burgess 2	14,845
18		17	(h)	Reading	L 1-2	Burgess	14,679
19	Dec	1	(h)	Southend U	W 1-0	Burgess	16,037
20		8	(a)	Bournemouth	W 2-1	Burgess 2	7,153
21		22	(h)	Colchester U	D 2-2	Burgess 2	11,618
22		25	(h)	Brighton & HA	L 1-2	Burgess	15,439
23		26	(a)	Brighton & HA	L 3-4	Marsden, Price, Evans	24,228
24		29	(h)	Millwall	D 1-1	Marsden	20,834
25	Jan	5	(a)	Swindon T	W 2-0	Price, Evans	10,663
26		12	(h)	Aldershot	L 0-2		12,981
27		19	(h)	Leyton O	W 2-1	Marsden, Price	14,266
28		26	(a)	Walsall	L 0-3		4,666
29	Feb	2	(a)	Norwich C	L 0-1		18,277
30		9	(h)	Shrewsbury T	D 1-1	Burgess	13,514
31		16	(a)	Gillingham	D 4-4	Thomas, Burgess, Evans, McGeachie (pen)	11,991
32		23	(h)	Norwich C	W 2-0	Thomas, Burgess	19,491
33	Mar	1	(h)	Torquay U	D 1-1	Bennett	15,178
34		8	(a)	Ipswich T	D 1-1	McGeachie	10,352
35		15	(h)	Bristol C	W 2-1	Bennett, Thomas	13,285
36		22	(a)	Port Vale	L 0-2		11,686
37		26	(a)	Exeter C	W 1-0	Evans	4,242
38	Apr	5	(a)	Reading	L 1-3	Bennett	11,561
39		11	(a)	Watford	L 0-2		10,273
40		12	(h)	Newport C	D 1-1	McGeachie (pen)	14,933
41		14	(h)	Watford	W 2-0	McGeachie (pen), Evans	12,143
42		19	(a)	Southend U	L 0-4		7,728
43		24	(a)	Newport C	L 0-1		6,942
44		26	(h)	Bournemouth	D 2-2	Hancox 2	10,765
45		30	(a)	Aldershot	L 0-3		5,617
46	May	3	(h)	Northampton T	D 3-3	Marsden 2, Rainford	7,214
						FINAL LEAGUE POSITION: 19th in Division Three South	Appearances
							Goals

FA Cup

1	Nov	24	(h)	Gillingham	L 0-1		21,868
							Appearances
							Goals

Bumstead	Harding	McDonald	Price	Cushlow	McGeachie	Devonshire	Broughton	Marsden	Rainford	Hanlon	Hughes	Briggs	Hancox	Rundle	Evans	Thomas J	Edwards	Burgess	Anderson	Scott	Chilvers	Bennett R	Nelson	George	
1	2	3	4	5	6	7	8	9	10	11															1
1	2	3	4	5	6	7	8	9	10	11															2
	2	3	4		6	7	8	9		11	1	5	10												3
1	2	3	4		6	7	8	9		11		5		10											4
1	2	3	4		6	7	8	9		11		5		10											5
1	2	3	4		6	11	8	9				5			7	10									6
1		3	4		6	7	8			11		5		10	9		2								7
1		3	4		6	11	7	8				5			9		2	10							8
1		3	4		6	11	7					5		8	9		2	10							9
1		3	4		6	11	7					5		8	9		2	10							10
1		3	4		6		7			11		5		8	9		2	10							11
		3	4		6	7	11				1	5		8	9		2	10							12
		3	4		6	11	7					5		8	9		2	10	1						13
		3	4		6	11	7		8			5			9			10	1	2					14
		3	6		4	11	7		8			5			9			10	1	2					15
		3	6		4	11	7		8			5			9			10	1	2					16
		3	6		4	11	7		8			5			9			10	1	2					17
		3	6		4		7		8	11		5			9			10	1	2					18
		3			4	7			8	11		5			9			10	1	2	6				19
		3			4	7			8	11		5			9			10	1	2	6				20
		3			4	7			8	11		5			9			10	1	2	6				21
		3			4	7			8	11		5			9			10	1	2	6				22
			10		4			9	8	11		5			7		3		1	2	6				23
			10		4			9	8	11		5			7		3		1		6			2	24
			10		4			9	8	11		5			7		3		1		6			2	25
			10		4			9	8	11		5			7		3		1		6			2	26
			10		4			9	8	11		5			7		3		1	2	6				27
			10		4			9	8	11		5			7		3		1	2	6				28
		3	10		4			9	8			5			7				1	2	6	11			29
		3			4			9	8			5			7			10	1	2	6	11			30
		3			4				8			5			7	9		10	1	2	6	11			31
		3			4				8			5			7	9	2	10	1		6	11			32
		3			4				8		1	5			7	9	2	10			6	11			33
		3			4				8		1	5		10	7	9	2				6	11			34
		3			4				8		1	5		10	7	9	2				6	11			35
		3			4				8		1	5		10	7	9	2				6	11			36
		3			4		7		8	11	1	5		10	9		2				6				37
		3		5	4		7		8		1			10	9		2				6	11			38
		3		5	4		7		8		1			10	9		2				6	11			39
		3		5	4				8					10	9		2		1	7	6	11			40
		3		5	4				8						9		2	10	1	7		11	6		41
		3		5	4		10							8	9		2		1	7		11	6		42
		3		5	4		7		8					10	9				1	2		11	6		43
		3		5	4			9	8	11			10		7				1	2			6		44
		3		5	4			9	8	11			10		7		2		1				6		45
		3			4		7	9	8			5	10				2		1			11	6		46
10	6	40	24	10	46	20	24	18	34	21	9	36	4	16	40	7	26	22	27	20	22	15	6	3	
			5		5	2	1	6	1	1			2	1	10	3		21				3			

Bumstead	Harding	McDonald	Price	Cushlow	McGeachie	Devonshire	Broughton	Marsden	Rainford	Hanlon	Hughes	Briggs	Hancox	Rundle	Evans	Thomas J	Edwards	Burgess	Anderson	Scott	Chilvers	Bennett R	Nelson	George	
1			10		4		7			11		5		8	9		3			2	6				1
1			1		1		1			1		1		1	1		1			1	1				

1952-53

Manager: Laurie Scott

1	Aug	23	(a)	Brighton & HA	L 1-4	Marsden	23,905
2		26	(h)	Gillingham	D 0-0		15,754
3		30	(h)	Newport C	W 2-1	Simpson, Bennett	14,642
4	Sep	3	(a)	Gillingham	L 0-1		13,023
5		6	(a)	Millwall	D 0-0		25,932
6		10	(h)	Reading	L 0-3		11,546
7		13	(a)	Bristol C	L 0-5		17,163
8		17	(a)	Reading	L 1-4	Devonshire	9,988
9		20	(h)	Torquay U	D 2-2	Devonshire, Marsden	12,557
10		24	(h)	Norwich C	D 1-1	Thomas	7,544
11		27	(a)	Northampton T	L 1-5	Bennett	12,805
12	Oct	1	(a)	Ipswich T	L 0-2		5,763
13		4	(h)	Leyton O	D 2-2	Fell, Grimshaw	17,040
14		11	(h)	Walsall	W 4-1	Burgess 3, Fell	13,685
15		18	(a)	Shrewsbury T	D 1-1	Fell	8,221
16		25	(h)	Queen's Park R	W 4-2	Burgess 3, Rainford	19,181
17	Nov	1	(a)	Swindon T	W 6-3	Burgess 3, Rainford 3	9,106
18		8	(h)	Aldershot	W 3-0	Burgess, Thomas 2	17,979
19		29	(a)	Coventry C	L 2-4	Burgess 2	11,628
20	Dec	13	(a)	Bristol R	L 0-2		20,042
21		20	(h)	Brighton & HA	W 2-1	Simpson 2	10,081
22		26	(a)	Watford	L 0-2		12,422
23	Jan	3	(a)	Newport C	L 2-3	Burgess, George (pen)	8,062
24		10	(h)	Bournemouth	W 1-0	Rainford	12,394
25		17	(h)	Millwall	L 0-1		24,830
26		24	(h)	Bristol C	L 1-3	George (pen)	12,296
27		31	(a)	Bournemouth	L 2-4	Thomas, Burgess	7,724
28	Feb	7	(a)	Torquay U	D 1-1	Hancox	6,077
29		14	(h)	Northampton T	W 4-3	Burgess 3, Thomas	6,409
30		21	(a)	Leyton O	D 0-0		12,240
31		28	(a)	Walsall	W 4-2	Burgess 2, Devonshire, Thomas	5,931
32	Mar	7	(h)	Shrewsbury T	L 1-2	Thomas	13,300
33		14	(a)	Queen's Park R	D 1-1	Rainford	12,972
34		19	(a)	Colchester U	L 0-3		3,382
35		21	(h)	Swindon T	W 3-0	Simpson 3	10,462
36		28	(a)	Aldershot	W 1-0	Thomas	5,673
37	Apr	3	(a)	Southend U	D 2-2	Simpson 2	10,341
38		4	(h)	Colchester U	W 3-1	Thomas, Rainford, Briggs	12,373
39		6	(h)	Southend U	D 0-0		12,845
40		11	(a)	Norwich C	L 1-5	Simpson	16,270
41		15	(h)	Exeter C	W 2-0	Simpson 2	4,916
42		18	(h)	Coventry C	D 2-2	Grimshaw, Downs	13,192
43		22	(h)	Ipswich T	D 1-1	Devonshire	10,135
44		25	(a)	Exeter C	L 0-2		7,357
45		29	(h)	Watford	W 1-0	Grimshaw	6,675
46	May	1	(h)	Bristol R	W 1-0	Thomas	5,712

FINAL LEAGUE POSITION: 13th in Division Three South

Appearances
Goals

FA Cup

1	Nov	22	(h)	Reading	D 1-1	Rainford	24,340
R		26	(a)	Reading	W 3-1	Fell 2, Rainford	8,167
2	Dec	10	(a)	Finchley ‡	L 1-3	Thomas	4,500

‡Following an abandoned game (61 minutes, fog) on 6 December with Finchley leading 3-1.

Appearances
Goals

Match	Anderson	Scott	Edwards	Price	Briggs	Chilvers	Broughton	Rainford	Marsden	Simpson	Bennett R	MacDonald D	McDonald H	Burgess	Evans	Nelson	Hancox	Devonshire	Andrews	Thomas R	Hanlon	George	Grimshaw	Fell	Higgins	Bailey	Harding	Downs	Choules	Besagni	Braithwaite
1	1	2	3	4	5	6	7	8	9	10	11																				
2		2		4	5	6	7	8		9	11	1	3	10																	
3		2		4	5	6		8		9	11	1	3	10	7																
4		2			5	6			9		11	1	3	10	7	4	8														
5		2			5	6		8	9		11	1	3	10	7	4															
6		2			5	6	9	8			11	1	3	10		4		7													
7	1	2			5		9						3	10		4		7	6	8	11										
8	1		2		5		9						3			4	8	7	6	10	11										
9	1		2	4	5	6		8	9		11		3					7		10											
10	1		2	4	5	6		8	9		11		3					7		10											
11	1		3	4	5	6		8	9		11							7		10		2									
12			3	4	5	6		8	9		11	1						7		10		2									
13			3	4	5	6						1		10				11		9		2	8	7							
14				4	5	6						1	3	10				11		9		2	8	7							
15				4	5	6						1	3	10				11		9		2	8	7							
16					5	6		8				1	3	10				11		9		2	4	7							
17					5	6		8				1	3	10				11		9		2	4	7							
18					5	6		8				1	3	10				11		9		2	4	7							
19					5	6		8				1	3	10				11		9		2	4	7							
20		2				6		8		9		1	3					11		10			4	7							5
21					5	6				9		1	3	10				11		8		2	4	7							
22						6		10		9		1	3					11		8		2	4	7							5
23					5	6		8		9		1	3	10				11				2	4	7							
24					5	6		8		9		1	3	10		4		11				2		7							
25						6				9		1	3	10				11		8		2	4	7							5
26					5	6					11	1	3		9		8	10				2	4	7							
27						6					11	1	3	10			8			9		2	4	7	5						
28	1					6							3	10			8	11		9		2	4	7	5						
29	1					6							3	10			8	11		9		2	4	7	5						
30	1					6							3	10			8	11		9		2	4	7	5						
31	1												3	10			8	11	6	9		2	4	7	5						
32	1												3	10			8	11	6	9		2	4	7	5						
33								8					3	10				11	6	9		2	4	7	5	1					
34								8						10				11	6	9		3	4	7	5	1	2				
35					5					9							8		6	10		3	4	7		1	2	11			
36					5					9							8		6	10		3	4	7		1	2	11			
37					5					9							8		6	10		3	4	7		1	2	11			
38					5			9					3				8		6	10		2	4	7		1		11			
39			3		5			8		9									6	10			4	7		1	2	11			
40			3		5			8		9								11	6	10		2	4			1		7			
41			3		5			8		9									6	10		2	4	7		1		11			
42			3		5			8		9								11	6	10		2	4			1		7			
43					5			8		9								11	6	10		2	4			1		7	3		
44								8		9								11	6	10		2	4		5	1		7	3		
45					5			8										11	6	10		2	4			1		7	3	9	
46					5			4									8		6	10		2		7		1		11	3	9	
	11	8	11	10	34	28	5	28	7	18	12	21	30	25	4	6	14	33	18	37	2	34	32	29	9	14	5	12	4	2	3
					1			7	2	11	2			19			1	4		10		2	3	3				1			

Round	Anderson	Scott	Edwards	Price	Briggs	Chilvers	Broughton	Rainford	Marsden	Simpson	Bennett R	MacDonald D	McDonald H	Burgess	Evans	Nelson	Hancox	Devonshire	Andrews	Thomas R	Hanlon	George	Grimshaw	Fell	Higgins	Bailey	Harding	Downs	Choules	Besagni	Braithwaite
1					5	6		8				1	3	10				11		9		2	4	7							
R					5	6		8				1	3	10				11		9		2	4	7							
2		2			5	6		8				1	3	10				11		9			4	7							
		1			3	3		3				3	3	3				3		3		2	3	3							
								2												1				2							

1953-54

Manager: Laurie Scott

1	Aug	20	(h)	Northampton T	D 2-2	Thomas, Foulds	13,935
2		22	(h)	Southampton	W 4-3	Thomas 2, Randall, Foulds	17,790
3		24	(a)	Shrewsbury T	D 1-1	Thomas	11,845
4		29	(a)	Colchester U	L 1-4	Andrews	6,811
5	Sep	2	(h)	Shrewsbury T	W 3-2	Randall 2, Thomas	11,877
6		5	(a)	Millwall	D 2-2	Fell, Thomas	21,997
7		7	(a)	Newport C	W 3-1	Foulds, Devonshire, Randall	6,913
8		12	(h)	Bristol C	L 1-2	Randall	18,723
9		16	(h)	Newport C	W 3-0	Randall 2, Thomas	8,730
10		19	(a)	Aldershot	W 2-1	Randall, Fell	8,308
11		21	(a)	Queen's Park R	D 1-1	Willard	7,485
12		26	(h)	Swindon T	W 3-2	Fell, Randall, Briggs	18,766
13		30	(h)	Queen's Park R	L 0-3		9,409
14	Oct	3	(a)	Walsall	L 0-1		11,020
15		10	(h)	Bournemouth	W 3-1	Thomas 2, Downs	15,756
16		17	(a)	Coventry C	D 0-0		13,554
17		24	(h)	Gillingham	L 1-2	Choules	18,856
18		31	(a)	Northampton T	L 0-6		12,450
19	Nov	7	(h)	Torquay U	W 4-1	Foulds, Thomas 2, Andrews	10,195
20		14	(a)	Watford	L 1-4	Andrews	14,547
21		28	(a)	Southend U	W 2-1	Randall, Thomas	7,748
22	Dec	5	(h)	Reading	W 1-0	Hanlon	12,085
23		19	(a)	Southampton	L 1-3	Willard	12,221
24		25	(h)	Norwich C	W 1-0	Thomas (pen)	11,742
25		26	(a)	Norwich C	L 1-2	Bennett	21,293
26	Jan	2	(h)	Colchester U	L 0-1		7,154
27		9	(a)	Exeter C	L 0-7		7,382
28		16	(h)	Millwall	L 2-3	Bennett, Willard	16,320
29		23	(a)	Bristol C	L 0-4		17,552
30		30	(h)	Exeter C	D 0-0		5,595
31	Feb	4	(h)	Aldershot	D 0-0		8,375
32		13	(a)	Swindon T	D 1-1	Thomas	8,907
33		20	(h)	Walsall	W 1-0	Tilston	10,370
34		27	(a)	Bournemouth	L 0-2		8,740
35	Mar	6	(h)	Coventry C	W 3-1	Thomas 2, Tilston	10,519
36		13	(a)	Brighton & HA	L 0-3		19,312
37		20	(h)	Southend U	W 4-2	Tilston 2, Thomas 2	9,371
38		27	(a)	Torquay U	L 0-1		5,662
39	Apr	3	(h)	Watford	D 1-1	Simpson	9,553
40		8	(a)	Leyton O	L 0-2		5,346
41		10	(a)	Reading	L 1-4	Devonshire	7,467
42		16	(a)	Ipswich T	L 0-2		18,290
43		17	(h)	Leyton O	D 2-2	Morton, Thomas	12,516
44		19	(h)	Ipswich T	D 1-1	Simpson	15,660
45		24	(a)	Gillingham	L 2-3	Morton, Thomas	8,729
46		28	(h)	Brighton & HA	D 1-1	Morton	12,515

FINAL LEAGUE POSITION: 22nd in Division Three South

Appearances
Goals

FA Cup

1	Nov	21	(a)	Great Yarmouth	L 0-1		8,000

Appearances
Goals

Bailey	George	McDonald H	Willard	Briggs	Andrews	Fell	Thomas R	Randell	Foulds	Downs	Devonshire	Higgins	Hanlon	Bennett K	Woods	Moss	Choules	Simpson	Edwards	Chilvers	Berry	Tilston	Potter	Morton	
1	2	3	4	5	6	7	8	9	10	11															1
1	2	3	4	5	6	7	8	9	10	11															2
1	2	3	4	5	6		8	9	10	7	11														3
1	2	3	4		6	7	8	9	10	11		5													4
1	2	3	4		6	7	8	9	10	11		5													5
1	2	3	4	5	6	7	8	9	10		11														6
1	2	3	4	5	6	7	8	9	10		11														7
1	2	3	4	5	6	7	8	9	10		11														8
1	2	3	4	5	6	7	8	9	10		11														9
1	2	3	4	5	6	7	8	9	10				11												10
1	2	3	4	5	6	7	8	9	10				11												11
1	2	3		5	6	7	8	9	10				11		4										12
1	2	3		5	6	7	8	9					11	10	4										13
1	2	3	4	5	6	7	8	9					11	10											14
1		3	4	5		7	8	9		11				10		6	2								15
1		3	4	5		7	8		10	11						6	2	9							16
1	2	3	4	5		7	8		10	11						6	9								17
1	2	3	4	5		7	8		10	11						6	9								18
1			4	5	8	7	9		10		11						2		3	6					19
1			4	5	9	7	8		10		11						2		3	6					20
1		3	4	5			10	9		7			11	8			2			6					21
1		3	4	5			8	9		7			11	10			2			6					22
1		3	4	5		7	10	9					11	8			2			6					23
1			4	5		7	10	9					11	8			2	6	3						24
1			4	5	9	7	10						11	8			2		3	6					25
1			4	5	9	7	8						11			10	2	6	3						26
1			4	5	9	7	10						11	8			2	6	3						27
1	2	3	8	5		7	9						11	10		4		6							28
1		3	8	5	9						10		11			4		6	2		7				29
1		3	4	5		7	9				10		11	8			2	6							30
1		3	4	5		7	9						11	8			2	6				10			31
1		3	4	5		7	9						11	8			2	6				10			32
1		3	9	5			8						11		4		2	6			7	10			33
1		3	9	5			8						11		4		2	6			7	10			34
1		3	9	5		7	8						11		4		2	6				10			35
1		3	9	5		7	8						11		4		2	6				10			36
1		3	9	5			8						11		4		2	6			7	10			37
1		3		5			8				10		11		4		2	6			7	9			38
1		3		5			8						11	10	4		2	6			7	9			39
		3		5			8						11	10	4		2	6			7	9	1		40
1	2	3			9	7	8				10		11		4		5	6							41
1		3		5	6	7	8				10		11		4				2					9	42
1		3		5	6	7	8				11				4				2			10		9	43
1		3		5	6	7	8						11		4			10	2					9	44
1				5	6	7	8						11	10	4		2		3					9	45
1				5	6	7	8						11	10	4		2		3					9	46
45	18	38	35	43	26	36	45	19	17	11	13	2	30	17	16	7	27	19	12	6	7	11	1	5	
			3	1	3	3	20	10	4	1	2		1	2			1	2				4		3	

1			4	5	6	7	8	9	10		11						2		3						1
1			1	1	1	1	1	1	1		1						1		1						

1954-55

Manager: Laurie Scott until October 1954, then Cyril Spiers.

1	Aug	21	(a)	Exeter C	L 0-2		12,465
2		26	(a)	Northampton T	D 1-1	Grieve	11,735
3		28	(h)	Colchester U	D 0-0		14,348
4	Sep	1	(h)	Northampton T	W 3-1	McDonald, Thomas, Addinall	11,626
5		4	(a)	Norwich C	L 0-2		14,542
6		7	(a)	Watford	L 1-7	Devonshire	11,861
7		11	(h)	Southend U	D 2-2	Willard 2	11,526
8		15	(h)	Watford	D 1-1	Addinall	9,549
9		18	(a)	Aldershot	L 0-3		7,002
10		22	(a)	Bournemouth	L 1-4	Andrews (pen)	10,486
11		25	(h)	Swindon T	D 0-0		11,540
12		29	(h)	Bournemouth	W 2-1	Grieve, Belcher	6,165
13	Oct	2	(a)	Leyton O	L 1-2	Devonshire	16,422
14		9	(h)	Reading	D 1-1	Belcher	14,305
15		16	(a)	Shrewsbury T	D 1-1	Andrews	7,322
16		23	(h)	Walsall	W 3-1	Hearn, Belcher, Russon (og)	11,416
17		30	(a)	Millwall	L 2-5	Hanlon, Briggs (pen)	19,427
18	Nov	6	(h)	Torquay U	D 1-1	Devonshire	11,673
19		13	(a)	Brighton & HA	L 0-1		16,440
20		27	(a)	Coventry C	L 1-4	Berry	14,839
21	Dec	4	(h)	Southampton	L 1-2	Briggs (pen)	9,875
22		18	(h)	Exeter C	D 1-1	Devonshire	7,010
23		25	(h)	Newport C	W 2-1	Deakin 2	8,934
24		27	(a)	Newport C	W 1-0	Rutter	13,025
25	Jan	1	(a)	Colchester U	L 0-2		5,806
26		8	(h)	Gillingham	L 0-2		8,379
27		22	(a)	Southend U	L 2-3	Andrews 2 (1 pen)	5,100
28		29	(a)	Gillingham	L 1-2	Belcher	11,338
29	Feb	5	(h)	Aldershot	W 3-2	Grieve, Belcher 2	8,076
30		12	(a)	Swindon T	D 0-0		4,959
31		19	(h)	Leyton O	D 1-1	Randall	12,789
32		26	(a)	Reading	L 0-5		5,389
33	Mar	5	(h)	Shrewsbury T	D 2-2	Deakin, Tilston	7,348
34		12	(a)	Walsall	W 4-1	Berry, Belcher 2, Cooper	10,773
35		19	(h)	Millwall	D 1-1	Andrews (pen)	13,708
36		26	(a)	Torquay U	D 2-2	Belcher, Berry	4,373
37	Apr	2	(h)	Brighton & HA	W 1-0	Berry	11,869
38		8	(h)	Queen's Park R	W 2-1	Deakin, Belcher	17,238
39		9	(a)	Brentford	L 0-3		12,013
40		11	(a)	Queen's Park R	L 0-1		8,974
41		16	(h)	Coventry C	W 1-0	Cooper	9,464
42		19	(a)	Bristol C	L 0-3		27,657
43		23	(a)	Southampton	D 2-2	Andrews, Belcher	8,788
44		27	(h)	Brentford	D 1-1	Berry	8,170
45		30	(h)	Bristol C	L 1-2	Tilston	14,425
46	May	4	(h)	Norwich C	W 2-0	Andrews (pen), Belcher	7,379

FINAL LEAGUE POSITION: 20th in Division Three South

Appearances
Goals

FA Cup

1	Nov	20	(a)	Swindon T	W 2-0	Hanlon, Randall	11,359
2	Dec	11	(h)	Bishop Auckland	L 2-4	Choules, Thomas	20,155

Appearances
Goals

Bailey	Choules	McDonald H	Woods	Briggs	Simpson	Grieve	Thomas	Addinall	Tilston	Devonshire	Moss	Belcher	Andrews	Edwards	Saunders	Willard	Hearn	Hanlon	Gunning	Berry	Greenwood A	Greenwood R	MacDonald D	Deakin	Randall	Taylor	Rutter	Cooper	McDonald G	Hynon	Felton	
1	2	3	4	5	6	7	8	9	10	11																						1
1	2	3	6	5		7	8	9	10	11	4																					2
1	2	3		5		7	8	9	10	11		4	6																			3
1	2	3		5		7	8	9	10	11	4		6																			4
1		3		5		7	8	9	10	11	4		6	2																		5
1		3		5		7	8	9	10	11			6	2	4																	6
1	2			5		7		9					6	3	4	8	10	11														7
1	2	3		5		7		9					6		4	8	10	11														8
1	2	3		5		7		9					6		4	8	10		11													9
1	2	3				7		9				8	6		5	4	10		11													10
1	2	3		5		7	8	9		10			6			4		11														11
1	2	3		5		11	9			10		8	6			4				7												12
1	2	3		5		11	9			10		8	6			4				7												13
1	2	3		5		11	9			10		8	6			4				7												14
1	2	3		5			9			10		8	6			4		11		7												15
1	2	3		5						10		9	6			4	8	11		7												16
1		3		5				9				8	6			4	10	11		7	2											17
	6			5			8		9	10		4						11		7	2	3	1									18
	2			5					10			4	6				8	11		7		3	1	9								19
	8	6		5			10					4		2				11		7		3	1	9								20
		6		5			10		8			4		2				11		7		3	1		9							21
1	8	3		5					9	11		4	6	2										10		7						22
1	8								9	11		4	6	2	5							3		10		7						23
1									9	11		4	6	2	5					7		3		10			8					24
1									9	11		4	6	2	5					7		3		10			8					25
1						7						4	6	2	5		10		11			3		9			8					26
1						7			10		4	8	6	2	5				11			3		9								27
1						7			10		4	8	6	2	5				11			3		9								28
1						7			10		4	8	6	2	5				11			3		9								29
1						7			10		4	8	6	2	5				11			3		9								30
1						7			10		4	8	6	2	5				11			3			9							31
1						7			10		4	8	6	2	5				11			3			9							32
1									10		4	8	6	2	5				11	7		3		9								33
1		3							9		4	8	6	2	5				11	7								10				34
1									9		4	8	6	2	5				11	7		3						10				35
1									9		4	8	6	2	5				11	7		3						10				36
1											4	8	6	2	5				11	7		3		9				10				37
1											4	8	6	2	5				11	7		3		9				10				38
1											4	8	6	2	5				11	7		3		9				10				39
1	4											8	6	2	5				11	7		3		9				10				40
	9								10		4	8	6	2	5					7			1					11	3			41
						7			10			4	6	2	5				11	8		3	1							9		42
	4								10			8	6	2	5				11	7		3	1								9	43
	4								10			8	6	2	5				11	7		3	1	9								44
	4								10			8	6	2	5				11	7		3	1	9								45
1	4								10			8	6	2	5				11	7		3		9								46
37	25	20	2	21	1	22	14	12	29	17	17	38	41	30	29	11	8	10	23	26	2	26	9	19	3	2	3	8	1	1	1	
		1		2		3	1	2	2	4		12	7			2	1	1		5				4	1		1	2				

1 own-goal

Bailey	Choules	McDonald H	Woods	Briggs	Simpson	Grieve	Thomas	Addinall	Tilston	Devonshire	Moss	Belcher	Andrews	Edwards	Saunders	Willard	Hearn	Hanlon	Gunning	Berry	Greenwood A	Greenwood R	MacDonald D	Deakin	Randall	Taylor	Rutter	Cooper	McDonald G	Hynon	Felton	
	8	6		5			10					4		2				11		7		3	1		9							1
	8	6		5			10		9			4		2				11		7		3	1									2
	2	2		2			2		1			2		2				2		2		2	2		1							
	1						1											1							1							

1955-56

Manager: Cyril Spiers

1	Aug	20	(h)	Northampton T	L 2-3	Deakin, Tilston	13,841
2		24	(a)	Torquay U	D 1-1	Tilston	9,267
3		27	(a)	Aldershot	D 1-1	Belcher	7,203
4		31	(h)	Torquay U	W 3-0	Tilston, Berry, Moss (pen)	11,245
5	Sep	3	(a)	Millwall	D 1-1	Belcher	16,497
6		5	(a)	Queen's Park R	W 3-0	Tilston, Brett 2	9,083
7		10	(h)	Brighton & HA	L 1-2	Tilston	20,284
8		14	(h)	Queen's Park R	D 1-1	Belcher	10,543
9		17	(a)	Southampton	L 1-3	Andrews	11,530
10		22	(a)	Newport C	W 1-0	Andrews	6,601
11		24	(h)	Shrewsbury T	L 0-1		13,899
12		28	(h)	Walsall	W 2-0	Murray 2	7,298
13	Oct	1	(a)	Ipswich T	D 3-3	Berry, Belcher, Deakin	15,332
14		8	(h)	Watford	L 1-2	Belcher	13,993
15		15	(a)	Brentford	L 0-3		13,636
16		22	(h)	Coventry C	W 3-0	Cooper 3	7,734
17		29	(a)	Southend U	L 3-4	Deakin 3	12,107
18	Nov	5	(h)	Exeter C	L 0-1		12,631
19		12	(a)	Leyton O	L 0-8		13,547
20		26	(a)	Norwich C	L 1-3	Moss	14,556
21	Dec	3	(h)	Bournemouth	L 1-3	Murray	9,047
22		17	(a)	Northampton T	D 1-1	Gunning	9,302
23		24	(h)	Aldershot	W 1-0	Gunning	6,526
24		26	(a)	Swindon T	D 0-0		9,082
25		27	(h)	Swindon T	L 0-2		10,710
26		31	(h)	Millwall	D 2-2	Deakin, Tilston	12,248
27	Jan	7	(h)	Colchester U	D 1-1	Tilston	6,488
28		14	(a)	Brighton & HA	L 0-5		13,602
29		21	(h)	Southampton	L 0-2		8,848
30		28	(a)	Gillingham	D 1-1	Pierce	4,281
31	Feb	11	(h)	Ipswich T	W 1-0	Deakin	5,739
32		18	(a)	Watford	W 2-0	Pierce, Bateman (og)	4,865
33		25	(h)	Brentford	L 0-2		10,054
34	Mar	3	(a)	Coventry C	W 3-1	Gunning, Pierce, Kirk (og)	17,082
35		10	(h)	Southend U	L 1-2	Williamson (og)	13,093
36		17	(a)	Exeter C	L 1-6	Deakin	6,826
37		24	(h)	Leyton O	L 1-2	Gunning (pen)	19,165
38		30	(h)	Reading	L 2-3	Moyse, Choules	13,463
39		31	(a)	Colchester U	W 4-2	Murray 2, Noakes, Berry	7,397
40	Apr	2	(a)	Reading	L 0-1		9,886
41		7	(h)	Norwich C	W 2-0	Berry, Cooper	9,446
42		14	(a)	Bournemouth	L 0-1		5,981
43		21	(h)	Gillingham	L 1-3	Berry	10,495
44		26	(a)	Walsall	L 0-4		6,277
45		28	(h)	Newport C	W 1-0	Belcher	7,635
46		30	(a)	Shrewsbury T	L 0-2		9,663

FINAL LEAGUE POSITION: 23rd in Division Three South

Appearances
Goals

FA Cup

1	Nov	19	(h)	Southampton	D 0-0		16,864
R		23	(a)	Southampton	L 0-2		11,883

Appearances
Goals

Bailey	Edwards	Greenwood	Moss	Saunders	Andrews	Berry	Belcher	Deakin	Tilston	Gunning	Brett	Choules	Noakes	Cooper	Murray	Long	Sanders	Morgan	Potter	Pierce	Felton	Moyes	Fry	Harrison	
1	2	3	4	5	6	7	8	9	10	11															1
1	2	3	4	5	6	7	8	9	10	11															2
1	2	3	4	5	6	7	8	9	10	11															3
1	2	3	4	5	6	7	8	9	10	11															4
1	2	3	4	5	6	7	8	9	10		11														5
1	2	3	4		6	7	8	9	10		11	5													6
1	2	3	4		6	7	8	9	10		11	5													7
1	2	3	4	5	6	7	8	9	10		11														8
1	2	3	4	5	6	7	8	9	10				11												9
1	2	3	4		6	7	8	11	9			5		10											10
1	2	3	4		6	7	8	11	9			5		10											11
1	2	3	6			7	8	9		11		5			10	4									12
1	2	3	6			7	8	9		11		5			10	4									13
1	2	3	6			7	8	9		11		5			10	4									14
1	3		6	5		11	8				7	2	4	9	10										15
1			4	5		11	8	9			7	2	3	10			6								16
1			4	5		11	8	9			7	2	3	10			6								17
1			4	5		11	8	9			7	2	3	10			6								18
1			4	5		11	8	9				2	3	10			6	7							19
	2		4	5					9		7	3	10	11	8		6		1						20
	2		4	5		11	8	9			7	3			10		6		1						21
		3	4	5	6	7		9		11		2		8					1	10					22
		3	4	5	6	7		9	8	11		2							1	10					23
		3	4	5	6	7		9	8	11			2						1	10					24
		3	4	5	6	7		9		11	8		2						1	10					25
		3	4	5	6	7		9	8	11			2						1	10					26
		3	4	5	6			9	8	11	7	2							1	10					27
		3	4		6			9	10	11	7	2			8				1		5				28
	2	3	4	5	6	7		9		11				8					1	10					29
	2	3	4	5		7		9		11			6	8					1	10					30
	2	3		5		7	4	9		11				8		6			1	10					31
	2	3		5		7	4	9		11				8		6			1	10					32
	2	3		5		7	4	9		11				8		6			1	10					33
	2	3		5		7	4			11				8		6			1	10		9			34
	2	3		5		7	4	9		11				8		6			1	10					35
	2	3		5		7	4	9		11				8		6			1	10					36
	2	3					4	7		11		5		8		6			1	10		9			37
	2	3					4	7		11		5		8		6			1	10		9			38
	2	3				9	4			11		5	6	10	8								1	7	39
	2	3				9	4	7		11		5	6	10	8								1		40
	2	3				9	4			11		5	6	10	8								1	7	41
	2	3				9	4			11		5	6	10	8								1	7	42
	2	3				9	4	7		11		5	6	10	8								1		43
	2	3	6			9	4	7	10			5			8					11			1		44
	2			5		9	4			11		3	7		8	6			1	10					45
	2			5		9	4			11		3	7		8	6			1	10					46
19	35	37	31	30	19	41	36	38	18	31	13	28	18	24	15	13	6	1	21	19	1	3	6	3	
			2		2	5	6	8	7	4	2	1	1	4	5					3		1			

3 own-goals

Bailey	Edwards	Greenwood	Moss	Saunders	Andrews	Berry	Belcher	Deakin	Tilston	Gunning	Brett	Choules	Noakes	Cooper	Murray	Long	Sanders	Morgan	Potter	Pierce	Felton	Moyes	Fry	Harrison	
	3		4	5		7	8			11	9	2	6	10					1						1
	3		4	5		7	8			11	9	2	6	10					1						R
	2		2	2		2	2			2	2	2	2	2					2						

1956-57

Manager: Cyril Spiers

1	Aug	18	(a)	Norwich C	L 0-1		16,057
2		22	(h)	Colchester U	L 2-4	Whitear, Murray	9,980
3		25	(h)	Coventry C	D 1-1	Proudler (pen)	9,657
4		27	(a)	Colchester U	D 3-3	Harrison, Deakin, Berry	6,979
5	Sep	1	(a)	Southampton	L 0-3		14,118
6		5	(h)	Reading	D 1-1	Long	10,575
7		8	(h)	Exeter C	D 0-0		11,801
8		12	(a)	Reading	W 2-1	Deakin 2	11,209
9		15	(h)	Millwall	D 2-2	Harrison, Deakin	16,112
10		19	(h)	Newport C	W 2-1	Berry, Cooper	14,132
11		22	(a)	Southend U	D 1-1	Cooper	10,504
12		27	(a)	Newport C	D 2-2	Cooper, Thomas (og)	8,108
13		29	(h)	Northampton T	D 1-1	Berry	13,904
14	Oct	6	(a)	Gillingham	L 1-4	Cooper	8,567
15		13	(h)	Swindon T	D 0-0		13,459
16		20	(a)	Brentford	D 1-1	Pierce	11,345
17		27	(h)	Aldershot	W 2-1	Deakin 2	11,846
18	Nov	3	(a)	Watford	W 4-1	Murray 2, Belcher, Pierce	8,785
19		10	(h)	Shrewsbury T	L 0-1		13,700
20		24	(h)	Ipswich T	L 1-3	Harrison	10,431
21	Dec	1	(a)	Bournemouth	D 2-2	Berry, Hughes (og)	9,584
22		15	(h)	Norwich C	W 4-1	Berry, Noakes, Pierce, Englefield (og)	8,371
23		25	(h)	Queen's Park R	W 2-1	Belcher, Pierce	9,988
24		26	(a)	Queen's Park R	L 2-4	Berry, Pierce	5,307
25		29	(h)	Southampton	L 1-2	Belcher	15,769
26	Jan	12	(a)	Exeter C	L 1-2	Harrison	5,015
27		19	(a)	Millwall	L 0-3		16,192
28		26	(h)	Plymouth A	W 2-1	Berry 2	10,656
29	Feb	2	(h)	Southend U	W 2-0	Deakin, Pierce	9,545
30		9	(a)	Northampton T	L 0-1		8,651
31		16	(h)	Gillingham	L 1-2	Belcher (pen)	11,410
32		23	(a)	Swindon T	L 1-3	Pierce	6,499
33	Mar	2	(h)	Brentford	L 0-2		11,679
34		9	(a)	Torquay U	L 0-3		5,110
35		11	(a)	Plymouth A	W 1-0	Deakin	13,374
36		16	(h)	Watford	D 0-0		8,830
37		23	(a)	Shrewsbury T	D 1-1	Murray	6,674
38		30	(h)	Walsall	W 3-0	Murray 2, Deakin	9,338
39	Apr	1	(a)	Coventry C	D 3-3	Deakin 2, Byrne	5,626
40		6	(a)	Ipswich T	L 2-4	Murray, Deakin	12,559
41		13	(h)	Bournemouth	D 1-1	Pierce	8,571
42		19	(h)	Brighton & HA	D 2-2	Pierce, Deakin	15,514
43		20	(a)	Aldershot	L 1-2	Deakin	4,685
44		22	(a)	Brighton & HA	D 1-1	Deakin	11,382
45		27	(a)	Walsall	W 2-1	Deakin, Murray	9,748
46	May	1	(h)	Torquay U	D 1-1	Pierce	22,627

FINAL LEAGUE POSITION: 20th in Division Three South

Appearances

Goals

FA Cup

1	Nov	17	(h)	Walthamstow Ave	W 2-0	Murray, Cooper	17,760
2	Dec	8	(a)	Brentford	D 1-1	Pierce	16,750
R		12	(h)	Brentford	W 3-2*	Pierce 3	23,137
3	Jan	5	(a)	Millwall	L 0-2		26,790

*After extra-time

Appearances

Goals

Potter	Choules	Greenwood	Belcher	Proudler	Long	Harrison	Whitear	Berry	Murray	Deakin	Edwards	Moss	Morris	Gunning	Cotton	Noakes	Pierce	Cooper	Rouse	McDonald G	Byrne	Moyse	Sanders	No.
1	2	3	4	5	6	7	8	9	10	11														1
1	2		4	5		7	8	9	10		3	6	11											2
1	5	3	4	6		7	10	8		9	2			11										3
1	5	3	4	6		7		8		9	2			11	10									4
1	5	3	4	6		7		8		9	2			11	10									5
1	5		4		6	7		8			2			11	10	3	9							6
1	5		4		6	7		8			2			11	10	3	9							7
1	5		4		6	7		8		9	2		11			3	10							8
1	5		4		6	7		8		9	2		11			3	10							9
1	5		4		6	7		8		9	2		11			3		10						10
1	5		4		6	7		8		9	2		11			3		10						11
1	5		4		6	7		8		9	2		11			3		10						12
1	5	3	4		6	7		8		9	2		11					10						13
1	5	3	4	9	6	7		8			2		11					10						14
	5		4		6	11		7			2						8	10	1	3	9			15
	5				4			7		9	2						8	10	1	3		11	6	16
	5		8		4	11		7		9	2					3		10	1				6	17
	5		4		8	11		7	9		2						10		1	3			6	18
	5		4		8	11		7	9		2						10		1	3			6	19
	5				4	11		7	8	9	2							10	1	3			6	20
1	5		8		4	7		9	10	11	2									3			6	21
1	5		8		4	7		9		11	2					6	10			3				22
1	5		8		4	7		9		11	2					6	10			3				23
1	5		8		4	7		9		11	2					6	10			3				24
1	5		8		4	7		9		11	2					6	10			3				25
1	5		8		4	7		9		11	2					6	10			3				26
1	5		4		6	11		7			2					3	10	8			9			27
	5		4		6	7		8		9	2			11			10		1	3				28
	5		4		6	7		8		9	2			11		3	10		1					29
	5		4		6	7		8		9	2			11		3	10		1					30
	5		4		6	7		8	11	9	2					3	10		1					31
	5		4		6	7	11	8		9	2					3	10		1					32
	5		4		6	11	8	7		9	2					3	10		1					33
	5	3			4	7		9	8		2			11				10	1				6	34
	5	3			4	7			8	9	2					10			1		11		6	35
	5	3			4	7			8	9	2					10			1		11		6	36
	5			6	4	7			8	9	2					3	10		1		11			37
	5			6	4	7			8	9	2					3	10		1		11			38
	5			6	4	7			8	9	2					3	10		1		11			39
	5			6	4	7			8	9	2					3	10		1		11			40
	5			6	4	7			8	9	2					3	10		1		11			41
	5			6	4	7			8	9	2					3	10		1		11			42
	5			6	4	7			8	9	2					3	10		1		11			43
	5			6	4			7	8	9	2					3	10		1		11			44
	5			6	4			7	8	9	2					3	10		1		11			45
	5			6	4			7	8	9	2					3	10		1		11			46
21	46	9	31	16	42	42	5	37	20	37	45	1	8	9	4	31	30	11	25	12	14	1	9	
			4	1	1	4	1	8	8	16						1	10	4			1			

3 own-goals

Potter	Choules	Greenwood	Belcher	Proudler	Long	Harrison	Whitear	Berry	Murray	Deakin	Edwards	Moss	Morris	Gunning	Cotton	Noakes	Pierce	Cooper	Rouse	McDonald G	Byrne	Moyse	Sanders	No.
	5		8		4	11		7	9		2							10	1	3			6	1
1	5		8		4	7		9		11	2					6	10			3				2
1	5		8		4	7		9		11	2					6	10			3				R
1	5		8		4	7		9		11	2					6	10			3				3
3	4		4		4	4		4	1	3	4					3	3	1	1	4			1	
									1								4	1						

1957-58

Manager: Cyril Spiers

1	Aug	24	(a)	Norwich C	L 2-3	Deakin, Byrne	21,571
2		28	(h)	Millwall	L 0-1		22,680
3		31	(h)	Bournemouth	W 3-0	Byrne, Cooper 2	13,752
4	Sep	2	(a)	Millwall	L 0-3		20,159
5		7	(a)	Walsall	L 1-2	Cooper	11,768
6		11	(h)	Gillingham	W 3-0	Byrne, Cooper, Harrison	7,343
7		14	(h)	Coventry C	W 2-0	Cooper, Berry	11,543
8		18	(a)	Gillingham	L 0-3		6,324
9		21	(a)	Shrewsbury T	D 0-0		7,607
10		25	(a)	Torquay U	D 1-1	Deakin	4,665
11		28	(h)	Reading	D 2-2	Berry, Cooper	12,577
12	Oct	2	(h)	Torquay U	D 1-1	Cooper	6,498
13		5	(a)	Northampton T	W 2-1	Cooper 2	7,594
14		12	(h)	Swindon T	W 4-1	Cooper 2, Byrne, Berry	14,953
15		19	(a)	Aldershot	L 1-4	Proudler (pen)	6,214
16		26	(h)	Plymouth A	W 3-0	Deakin, Pierce, Cooper	14,532
17	Nov	2	(a)	Port Vale	L 0-4		13,602
18		9	(h)	Newport C	D 2-2	Cooper (pen), Deakin	11,082
19		23	(h)	Brighton & HA	L 2-4	Cooper, Harrison	15,757
20		30	(a)	Southend U	D 1-1	Long	10,706
21	Dec	14	(a)	Exeter C	W 1-0	Harrison	5,493
22		21	(h)	Norwich C	L 0-3		11,478
23		25	(a)	Brentford	W 3-0	Harrison, Berry 2	12,394
24		26	(h)	Brentford	W 2-1	Harrison, Pierce	16,797
25		28	(a)	Bournemouth	L 1-3	Byrne	13,073
26	Jan	11	(h)	Walsall	W 4-1	Collins 3, Pierce	10,587
27		18	(a)	Coventry C	D 2-2	Pierce, Harrison	8,211
28		25	(a)	Southampton	L 1-2	Cooper	13,046
29	Feb	1	(h)	Shrewsbury T	W 3-0	Long, Berry, Pierce	11,739
30		8	(a)	Reading	D 2-2	Cooper, Collins	11,062
31		15	(h)	Northampton T	L 1-3	Long	16,245
32		22	(a)	Swindon T	D 0-0		10,316
33	Mar	1	(h)	Aldershot	D 1-1	Cooper	12,569
34		8	(a)	Plymouth A	L 0-1		18,719
35		15	(h)	Port Vale	W 1-0	McNichol	13,577
36		22	(a)	Brighton & HA	L 2-3	Harrison, Pierce	19,611
37		25	(a)	Watford	L 1-2	McNichol	4,304
38		29	(h)	Exeter C	W 2-0	McNichol, Collins	10,601
39	Apr	4	(h)	Colchester U	D 1-1	Byrne	17,787
40		5	(a)	Newport C	D 0-0		4,118
41		7	(a)	Colchester U	D 1-1	Berry	9,528
42		12	(h)	Southend U	W 2-0	Pierce, McNichol	12,843
43		16	(h)	Queen's Park R	L 2-3	Brett, Long	18,712
44		19	(a)	Queen's Park R	L 2-4	Brett, Byrne	11,868
45		23	(h)	Watford	W 4-2	McNichol 2, Berry 2	10,139
46		26	(h)	Southampton	L 1-4	McNichol	10,480

FINAL LEAGUE POSITION: 14th in Division Three South — Appearances / Goals

FA Cup

1	Nov	16	(a)	Margate	W 3-2	Deakin 3	‡ 8,200
2	Dec	7	(h)	Southampton	W 1-0	Berry	14,794
3	Jan	4	(h)	Ipswich T	L 0-1		21,940

‡Ground attendance record — Appearances / Goals

Rouse	Edwards	Noakes	Long	Choules	Proudler	Berry	Belcher	Deakin	Pierce	Byrne	Truett	Cooper	Farrell	Harrison	Brown	Greenwood	Murray	Muxworthy	Sanders	Potter	Hopgood	Collins	Redmond	Brett	McNichol	
1	2	3	4	5	6	7	8	9	10	11																1
1	2	3	4	5	6	7	8	9	10	11																2
1	2	3	4	5	6	7		9		11	8	10														3
1	2	3	4	5	6	7				11	8	10	9													4
1	2	3	4	5	6	7		9		8		10		11												5
1	2	3	4	5		7	8			9		10		11	6											6
1	2	3	4	5		7	8			9		10		11	6											7
1	2	3	4	5		7	8			9		10		11	6											8
1	2		4			7	6		10		5		9			3	8	11								9
1	2		4			7	8	9			5					3	10	11	6							10
1	2		4			7	6	9		10	5	8		11		3										11
1	2		4		5	7	6	9		10		8		11		3										12
1	2		4		5		6	9	10	7		8		11		3										13
1	2		4		5	7			10	9	6	8		11		3										14
1	2		4		5	7			10	9		8		11		3			6							15
1	2		4	5			6	9	10	7		8		11		3										16
	2		4	5			6	9	10	7		8		11		3				1						17
	2		4	5			6	9	10	7		8		11		3					1					18
	2		4	5			6	9	10			8		7		3					1	11				19
1	2		4	5			8					10	9	7		3			6			11				20
1	2		4	5		9	8					10		7		3			6			11				21
1	2	3	4	5		9	8					10		7					6			11				22
1	2		4	5		9	8		10	11				7		3			6							23
1	2		4	5		9	8		10	11				7		3			6							24
1			2	5		9	8		10	11	4			7		3			6							25
1			4	5		8			10				9	7		3			6			11	2			26
1			4	5		8			10			9		7		3			6			11	2			27
1	2		4	5		8			10			9		7		3			6			11				28
1	2		4	5		8			10			9		7		3			6			11				29
1	2		4	5		8			10			9		7		3			6			11				30
1	2		4	5		8			10			9		7		3			6			11				31
1		2	4	5		8			10			9		7		3			6			11				32
1		2	4	5		8			10			9		7		3			6			11				33
1		2	4	5		9			10					7		3			6			11		8		34
1		2	4	5		9			10					7		3			6			11			8	35
1		2	4	5		9			10					7		3			6			11			8	36
1		2	4	5		9			10					7		3			6			11			8	37
1	2		4	5		8				9						3			6			11		7	10	38
1		2	4	5		8				9						3			6			11		7	10	39
1		2	4	5		8				9						3			6			11		7	10	40
1		2	4	5		9	8			11						3			6					7	10	41
1		2	4	5		9			10	11						3			6					7	8	42
1		2	4	5		9			10	11						3			6					7	8	43
1		2	4	5		9			10	11						3			6					7	8	44
1		2	4	5		9	8			11				7		3			6						10	45
		2	4	5		9	8			11				7		3			6		1				10	46
42	29	23	46	39	9	40	23	12	28	28	7	25	4	33	3	37	2	2	29	1	3	19	2	8	12	
			4		1	9		4	7	7		17		7								5		2	7	

Rouse	Edwards	Noakes	Long	Choules	Proudler	Berry	Belcher	Deakin	Pierce	Byrne	Truett	Cooper	Farrell	Harrison	Brown	Greenwood	Murray	Muxworthy	Sanders	Potter	Hopgood	Collins	Redmond	Brett	McNichol	
	2		6	5			4	9	10		11	8		7		3					1					1
1	2		8	5		9	4		10					7		3			6			11				2
1			4	5		9			10	11		8		7		3			6				2			3
2	2		3	3		2	2	1	3	1	1	2		3		3			2		1	1	1			
						1		3																		

1958-59

Manager: George Smith

1	Aug	23	(h)	Crewe A	W 6-2	Deakin 3, Byrne 3	13,551
2		27	(h)	Chester	D 3-3	Byrne 2, Deakin	18,170
3		30	(a)	Northampton T	L 0-3		11,288
4	Sep	3	(a)	Chester	L 2-3	Deakin 2	7,993
5		6	(h)	Workington T	D 1-1	Byrne	13,352
6		9	(a)	Watford	D 2-2	Deakin 2	10,327
7		13	(a)	York C	D 1-1	Collins	8,368
8		17	(h)	Watford	W 3-0	Collins, Truett, Harrison	16,034
9		20	(h)	Bradford	W 2-0	Deakin, Collins	14,134
10		22	(a)	Hartlepools U	L 1-4	Deakin	8,368
11		27	(a)	Port Vale	W 3-2	Long, Truett 2	13,952
12	Oct	1	(h)	Hartlepools U	L 1-2	Deakin	16,596
13		4	(a)	Millwall	L 1-2	Deakin	20,446
14		8	(h)	Southport	W 1-0	Collins	13,780
15		11	(h)	Gateshead	W 3-1	Brett 2, Pierce	13,643
16		18	(a)	Oldham A	L 0-3		6,884
17		25	(h)	Barrow	D 2-2	Pierce (pen), Long	14,046
18	Nov	1	(a)	Carlisle U	D 3-3	Pierce, Deakin, Noakes	7,384
19		8	(h)	Gillingham	W 4-1	Collins 2, Brett 2	13,640
20		22	(h)	Coventry C	D 1-1	McNichol	12,319
21		29	(a)	Shrewsbury T	L 1-2	Byrne	4,135
22	Dec	13	(a)	Walsall	W 2-0	Summersby, Byrne	5,361
23		20	(a)	Crewe A	L 1-4	Summersby	4,586
24		26	(a)	Aldershot	W 2-1	Deakin 2	6,080
25		27	(h)	Aldershot	W 4-1	Byrne 2, Collins, Priestley	19,344
26	Jan	1	(a)	Southport	W 2-0	Byrne, Summersby	2,280
27		3	(h)	Northampton T	D 1-1	Priestley	17,462
28		24	(h)	Darlington	W 4-1	Byrne, Long, Noakes, Summersby	12,909
29		31	(h)	York C	D 0-0		16,175
30	Feb	7	(a)	Bradford	L 0-5		6,276
31		14	(h)	Port Vale	D 1-1	McNichol	13,305
32		21	(h)	Millwall	W 4-0	Noakes (pen), Deakin, Byrne, Collins	18,365
33		28	(a)	Gateshead	W 3-1	Long, Deakin, Summersby	3,614
34	Mar	7	(h)	Oldham A	W 4-0	Deakin 2, Collins, Noakes	13,735
35		14	(a)	Barrow	L 0-1		2,862
36		16	(a)	Workington T	W 4-0	Deakin 2, Summersby 2	4,096
37		21	(h)	Carlisle U	L 0-2		15,319
38		27	(h)	Torquay U	W 3-1	Noakes 2, Byrne	18,971
39		28	(a)	Gillingham	D 1-1	Byrne	8,714
40		30	(a)	Torquay U	W 2-0	Byrne, Brett	5,318
41	Apr	4	(h)	Exeter C	D 1-1	McNichol	20,977
42		11	(a)	Coventry C	L 0-2		12,503
43		15	(a)	Exeter C	L 1-3	Brett	8,556
44		18	(h)	Shrewsbury T	W 4-3	Deakin, McNichol, Byrne, Brett	9,027
45		25	(a)	Darlington	W 4-1	Brett, Deakin, Colfar, Summersby	2,643
46		29	(h)	Walsall	L 1-3	Summersby	8,848

FINAL LEAGUE POSITION: 7th in Division Four

Appearances
Goals

FA Cup

1	Nov	15	(a)	Ashford	W 1-0	Collins	6,500
2	Dec	6	(h)	Shrewsbury T	D 2-2	Deakin 2	16,207
R		11	(a)	Shrewsbury T	D 2-2*	Byrne 2	6,000
2R		15	(n†)	Shrewsbury T	W 4-1	Collins, Byrne, Deakin 2	8,062
3	Jan	10	(a)	Sheffield U	L 0-2		22,179

†Played at the Molineux Grounds, Wolverhampton. *After extra-time.

Appearances
Goals

Rouse	Edwards	Noakes	Truett	Choules	Long	Harrison	McNichol	Deakin	Byrne	Collins	Greenwood	Hopgood	Skingley	Brett	Farrell	Peirce	Nastri	Proudler	Cooper	Priestley	Summersby	Colfar	Howe	Barnett	Evans	Sanders	
1	2	3	4	5	6	7	8	9	10	11																	1
1	2		4	5	6	7	8	9	10	11	3																2
1	2	3	4	5	6	7	8	9	10	11																	3
1	2	3	4	5	6	7	8	9	10	11																	4
1	2	3	4	5	6	7	8	9	10	11																	5
1	2	3	4	5	6	7	8	9	10	11																	6
1	2	3	4	5	6	7	8	9	10	11																	7
1	2	3	4	5	6	7	8	9	10	11																	8
1	2	3	4	5	6	7	8	9	10	11																	9
1	2	3	4	5	6	7	8	9	10	11																	10
		3	4	5	6	7	8	9	10	11		1	2														11
		3	4	5	6	7	8	9	10	11		1	2														12
		3	4	5	6	7	8	9	10	11		1	2														13
		3	4	5	6	7	8	9	10	11		1	2														14
		3		5	6		4		8	11		1	2	7	9	10											15
		3		5	6		4		8	11		1	2	9		10	7										16
		3		5	6		4		8	11		1	2	9		10	7										17
		3		5	6		4	9	8	11		1	2	7		10											18
		3			6		4	9	8	11		1	2	7		10		5									19
		3		5	6		4		8	11		1	2			9			10	7							20
1		3		5	6		4		8	11			2	9		10				7							21
1		3		5	6		4	9	10	11	2									7	8						22
1	2	3		5	6		4	9	10	11										7	8						23
1	2	3		5	6		4	9	10	11										7	8						24
1	2	3		5	6		4	9	10	11										7	8						25
1	2	3		5	6		4	9	10	11										7	8						26
1	2	3		5	6		4	9	10	11										7	8						27
1		2		5	6		4		10					9						7	8	11				3	28
1		3		5	6		4		10					9						7	8	11	2				29
1		3		5	6		4							9		10				7	8	11	2				30
1		3			6		4	9	10	11										7	8		2			5	31
1		3		5	6		4	9	10	11										7	8		2				32
1		3		5	6		4	9	10	11										7	8		2				33
1		3		5	6		4	9	10	11										7	8		2				34
1		3		5	6		4	9	10	11										7	8		2				35
1		3		5	6		4	9	10	11										7	8		2				36
1		3		5	6		4	9	10	11										7	8		2				37
1		3		5	6		4	9	10	11										7	8		2				38
1		3		5	6		4	9	10	11										7	8		2				39
1		3		5	6		4		10					7							8	11	2	9			40
1		3		5	6		4		10					7							8	11	2	9			41
1		3		5	6		4		10											7	8	11	2	9			42
1		3		2	6		4	9	10					7							8	11			5		43
1		3		2	6		4	9	10					7							8	11			5		44
1		3		2	6		4	9	10					7							8	11			5		45
1		3		2	6		4		10					7							8	11		9	5		46
36	15	45	14	44	46	14	46	34	45	36	2	10	11	15	1	8	2	1	1	21	25	10	14	4	4	2	
		6	3		4	1	4	23	17	9				8		3				2	9	1					

Rouse	Edwards	Noakes	Truett	Choules	Long	Harrison	McNichol	Deakin	Byrne	Collins	Greenwood	Hopgood	Skingley	Brett	Farrell	Peirce	Nastri	Proudler	Cooper	Priestley	Summersby	Colfar	Howe	Barnett	Evans	Sanders	
		3		5	6	7	4		8	11		1	2	9		10											1
1	2	3		5	6		4	9	10	11				7						8							2
1	2	3		5	6		4	9	10	11				7						8							R
1	2	3		5	6		4	9	10	11				7						8							2R
1		2		5	6		4	9	8	11						10				7						3	3
4	3	5		5	5	1	5	4	5	5		1	1	4		2				4						1	
								4	3	2																	

1959-60

Manager: George Smith

1	Aug	22	(a)	Carlisle U	D 2-2	Deakin, Noakes (pen)	7,011
2		24	(a)	Oldham A	L 0-1		5,224
3		29	(h)	Notts C	D 1-1	Byrne	16,466
4	Sep	3	(h)	Oldham A	W 3-2	Summersby, Gavin, Roche	16,405
5		5	(a)	Walsall	L 0-3		11,593
6		7	(a)	Stockport C	W 1-0	Noakes	11,882
7		12	(h)	Hartlepools U	W 5-2	Byrne 2, Sexton, Noakes 2	14,722
8		16	(h)	Stockport C	W 3-1	Gavin, Sexton, Bryne	18,534
9		19	(a)	Crewe A	D 1-1	Roche	7,786
10		23	(h)	Watford	W 8-1	Byrne 2, Colfar 2, Roche 2, Gavin, Noakes	21,938
11		26	(h)	Chester	L 3-4	Colfar, Byrne, Summersby	18,312
12		29	(a)	Watford	L 2-4	Summersby, Sexton	14,881
13	Oct	3	(a)	Southport	L 1-3	Byrne	4,210
14		7	(a)	Bradford	L 1-3	Summersby	3,220
15		10	(h)	Barrow	W 9-0	Summersby 4, Byrne 2, Colfar 2, Gavin	9,566
16		17	(a)	Aldershot	L 0-1		6,751
17		24	(h)	Darlington	W 2-0	Sexton, Summersby	14,936
18		28	(h)	Millwall	L 1-2	Easton	28,929
19		31	(a)	Gateshead	W 2-0	Rees, Byrne	3,901
20	Nov	7	(h)	Rochdale	W 4-0	Woan, Byrne, Sexton, Summersby	14,906
21		21	(h)	Doncaster R	W 4-0	Sexton 2, Roche, Woan	15,263
22		28	(a)	Northampton T	W 2-0	Byrne, Roche	8,121
23	Dec	12	(a)	Millwall	L 0-1		17,147
24		19	(h)	Carlisle U	W 2-1	Summersby (pen), Roche	9,045
25		28	(h)	Gillingham	D 3-3	McNichol, Summersby, Byrne	18,248
26	Jan	2	(a)	Notts C	L 1-7	Woan	15,804
27		16	(h)	Walsall	L 1-2	Woan	14,925
28		23	(a)	Hartlepools U	W 1-0	Woan	3,981
29		30	(h)	Torquay U	D 1-1	Woan	15,764
30	Feb	6	(h)	Crewe A	W 4-0	Woan, Roche, Sexton 2	13,567
31		13	(a)	Chester	W 1-0	Sexton	5,132
32		20	(h)	Southport	D 2-2	Sexton, Byrne	13,612
33		25	(a)	Workington T	D 1-1	Woan	3,687
34		27	(a)	Barrow	W 1-0	Roche	5,949
35	Mar	5	(h)	Aldershot	D 1-1	McNichol	16,575
36		12	(a)	Darlington	D 1-1	McNichol	4,834
37		19	(h)	Gateshead	D 2-2	Summersby (pen), Byrne	13,868
38		26	(a)	Rochdale	L 0-4		2,562
39	Apr	2	(h)	Workington T	L 0-1		12,214
40		9	(a)	Doncaster R	W 2-1	Summersby, Roche	6,105
41		15	(h)	Exeter C	W 1-0	Roche	15,831
42		16	(h)	Northampton T	L 0-1		15,943
43		18	(a)	Exeter C	D 2-2	Gavin 2	6,591
44		23	(a)	Torquay U	L 1-2	Gavin	7,293
45		27	(h)	Bradford	W 1-0	Summersby	9,920
46	May	4	(a)	Gillingham	D 0-0		5,077

FINAL LEAGUE POSITION: 8th in Division Four

Appearances

Goals

FA Cup

1	Nov	14	(h)	Chelmsford C	W 5-1	Byrne 3, Woan, Sexton	17,249
2	Dec	5	(a)	Margate	D 0-0		8,203
R		9	(h)	Margate	W 3-0	Roche 2, Woan	28,753
3	Jan	9	(a)	Scunthorpe U	L 0-1		12,561

Appearances

Goals

Rouse	Long	Noakes	McNichol	Choules	Summersby	Gavin	Sexton	Deakin	Byrne	Colfar	Roche	Howe	Evans	Truett	Barnett	Priestley	Rees	Easton	Woan	Pyke	Hopgood	Lunnis	
1	2	3	4	5	6	7	8	9	10	11													1
1	2	3	4	5	6	7	8	9	10	11													2
1	2	3	4	5	6	7	8	9	10	11													3
1	2	3	4	5	6	7	8		10	11	9												4
1	2	3	4	5	6	7	8		10	11	9												5
1	2	3	4	5	6	7	8		10	11	9												6
1	2	3	4	5	6	7	8		10	11	9												7
1	2	3	4	5	6	7	8		10	11	9												8
1	2		4	5	6	7	8		10	11	9	3											9
1	2	3	4	5	6	7	8		10	11	9												10
1	2	3	4	5	6	7	8		10	11	9												11
1	2		4		6	7	8		10	11	9	3	5										12
1	2	3	6		8	7	9		10	11			5	4									13
1	2	3	6		8	7	9		10	11			5	4									14
1	2	3	6		8	7	9		10	11			5	4									15
1	2	3	6		8	7			10	11			5	4	9								16
1	2	3	6	5	4		8		10		9					7	11						17
1	2	3	6	5	4		8				9					7	11	10					18
1	2	3	6	5	4		9		10		7						11		8				19
1	2	3	6	5	4		9		10		7						11		8				20
1	2	3	6	5	4		9		10		7						11		8				21
1	2	3	6		4		8		10	11	7		5					9					22
1	2		6	5	4	7			10	11	9	3							8				23
1	2		6		4				10	11	7	3	5		9				8				24
1	2		6	5	4				10	11	7	3			9				8				25
1	2		6	5	4				10	11	9	3				7			8				26
1	2		6	5	4				10		9	3				7	11		8				27
1	2	3	6		4		9		10		7		5				11		8				28
1	2	3	6		4		9		10		7		5				11		8				29
1	2	3	6		4		9				7		5	8			11		10				30
1	2	3	6		4		9		10		7		5				11		8				31
1	2	3	6		4		9		10	11	7		5						8				32
1	2	3	6		4	7	9		10				5				11		8				33
1	2		3		4	7			10		9		5	6			11		8				34
1	2		3		4	7			10		9		5	6			11		8				35
1	2		6		4	7			10		9	3	5				11		8				36
1	2	3	6		4	7			10	11	9		5						8				37
1	2	3	6		4	7			10	11	8		5						9				38
1	2	3	6		4				11		7		5	8				10	9				39
1	2	3	6		4				11		7		5	8		10			9				40
1	2	3	6		4				11		7		5	8		10			9				41
1	2	3	6		4				11				5	8		10	7		9				42
1	2	3	6		8	7			10		9		5				11			4			43
1	2	3	6		8	7			10		9		5				11			4			44
	4	3	6		8	7				11	9		5						10		1	2	45
1	4	3	6		8	7				11			5					9	10			2	46
45	46	36	46	20	46	27	27	3	42	26	36	8	26	11	3	7	17	4	25	2	1	2	
		5	3		15	7	11	1	16	5	11						1	1	8				

Rouse	Long	Noakes	McNichol	Choules	Summersby	Gavin	Sexton	Deakin	Byrne	Colfar	Roche	Howe	Evans	Truett	Barnett	Priestley	Rees	Easton	Woan	Pyke	Hopgood	Lunnis	
1	2	3	6	5	4		9		10		7						11		8				1
1	2	3	6	5	4				10	11	9					7		8					2
1	2		6	5	4				10	11	9	3				7			8				R
1	2		6	5	4				10	11	9	3				7			8				3
4	4	2	4	4	4		1		4	3	4	2				3	1	1	3				
							1		3		2								2				

1960-61

Manager: Arthur Rowe

1	Aug	20	(h)	Accrington S	W 9-2	Byrne 3, Woan 3, Heckman 2	15,653
2		24	(h)	Darlington	W 3-2	Woan, Byrne, Summersby	21,784
3		27	(a)	Doncaster R	W 5-1	Woan 2, Byrne 2, Gavin	6,511
4		31	(a)	Darlington	W 1-0	Byrne	5,607
5	Sep	3	(h)	Hartlepools U	D 2-2	McNichol, Woan	19,099
6		7	(h)	Peterborough U	L 0-2		† 36,478
7		10	(a)	Wrexham	W 2-1	Byrne, Gavin	10,609
8		12	(a)	Peterborough U	L 1-4	Heckman	21,171
9		17	(h)	Carlisle U	D 1-1	Summersby	15,867
10		20	(a)	Southport	D 3-3	Gavin, Byrne, Lunnis	5,434
11		24	(a)	Rochdale	D 2-2	Petchey, Summersby	4,819
12		28	(h)	Southport	W 5-0	Byrne 4, Noakes	15,969
13	Oct	1	(h)	Mansfield T	W 4-1	Summersby 3, Woan	15,018
14		3	(a)	Stockport C	L 2-5	Woan 2	10,729
15		8	(h)	Barrow	W 4-2	Woan, Uphill 2, Petchey	13,845
16		15	(a)	Gillingham	W 2-1	Summersby 2	10,999
17		22	(h)	Bradford	W 4-1	Heckman, Byrne, Gavin, Petchey	14,946
18		29	(a)	Northampton T	W 2-1	Uphill, Byrne	13,943
19	Nov	12	(a)	Oldham A	L 3-4	Heckman 2, Byrne	18,435
20		19	(h)	Workington T	W 4-2	Summersby 2, Heckman, Uphill	17,006
21	Dec	3	(h)	Crewe A	D 0-0		11,161
22		10	(a)	York C	W 2-0	Petchey, Heckman	6,538
23		17	(a)	Accrington S	W 3-2	Byrne, Summersby, Heckman	3,385
24		26	(a)	Exeter C	W 3-2	Gavin, Byrne, Summersby	7,551
25		27	(h)	Exeter C	D 0-0		28,551
26		31	(h)	Doncaster R	W 5-1	Uphill 2, Byrne, Summersby, Gavin	17,911
27	Jan	7	(a)	Chester	L 0-3		4,243
28		14	(a)	Hartlepools U	W 4-2	Heckman, Summersby, Byrne, Woan	4,430
29		21	(h)	Wrexham	W 3-2	Woan, Byrne 2	15,353
30		28	(h)	Chester	W 5-1	Byrne 3, Summersby 2	14,150
31	Feb	4	(a)	Carlisle U	L 0-2		4,464
32		11	(h)	Rochdale	W 4-1	Gavin 2, Heckman, Bushby (og)	17,655
33		18	(a)	Mansfield T	W 2-1	Summersby, Petchey	5,874
34		25	(a)	Barrow	W 3-0	Byrne, Heckman, Summersby	3,724
35	Mar	4	(h)	Gillingham	W 2-0	Byrne, Summersby	22,559
36		11	(a)	Bradford	L 1-3	Petchey	17,017
37		18	(h)	Northampton T	L 2-3	Summersby, Heckman	20,688
38		25	(a)	Aldershot	L 1-2	Petchey	11,389
39		31	(h)	Millwall	L 0-2		† 37,774
40	Apr	1	(h)	Oldham A	W 2-1	Byrne 2	13,964
41		3	(a)	Millwall	W 2-0	Heckman, Barnett	15,748
42		8	(a)	Workington T	L 0-1		3,776
43		19	(h)	Aldershot	W 2-1	Barnett, Summersby	19,983
44		22	(a)	Crewe A	W 2-1	Summersby, Jones (og)	6,163
45		26	(h)	Stockport C	W 2-1	Summersby 2	15,822
46		27	(h)	York C	W 1-0	Summersby	17,885

FINAL LEAGUE POSITION: 2nd in Division Four

†Fourth Division attendance record (broken twice)

Appearances

Goals

FA Cup

1	Nov	5	(h)	Hitchin	W 6-2	Uphill 2, Byrne, Gavin 2, Heckman	21,118
2		26	(h)	Watford	D 0-0		33,699
R		29	(a)	Watford	L 0-1		28,500

Appearances

Goals

League Cup

1	Oct	12	(a)	Darlington	L 0-2		9,940

Appearances

Goals

Rouse	Long	Noakes	Petchey	Evans	McNichol	Gavin	Woan	Byrne	Summersby	Heckman	Kerrins	Lunnis	Jones	Easton	Colfar	Choules	Uphill	Truett	Barnett	Lewis	Swannell	
1	2	3	4	5	6	7	8	9	10	11												1
1	2	3	4	5	6	7	8	9	10		11											2
1	5	3	4		6	7	8	9	10	11		2										3
1	5	3	4		6	7	8	9	10	11		2										4
1	5	3	4		6	7	8	9	10	11			2									5
1	5	3	4		6	7	8	9	10	11		2										6
1	5	3	4		6	7		9	10	11		2		8								7
1	5	3	4		6	7		9	10	11		2		8								8
1	5	3	4		6	7		9	10	11		2		8								9
1	5	3	4		6	7		9	8	11		2			10							10
1	5		4		6	7		9	8	11		2	3		10							11
1	4	2	6		3	7	10	9	8	11						5						12
1	4	2	6		3	7	10	9	8	11						5						13
1	4		6		3	7	10	9	8	11		2				5						14
1	4		6	5	3	7	10		8	11		2					9					15
1	4	3	6	5	2	7	10		8	11							9					16
1	4	3	6	5	2	7		10	8	11							9					17
1	4		6	5	2	7		10	8	11			3				9					18
1	4		6	5	2	7		10	8	11			3				9					19
1	4	3	6	5	2	7		10	8	11							9					20
1	4	3	6	5	2	7		10	8	11							9					21
1	4	3	6	5	2	7		10	8	11							9					22
1	4	3	6	5	2	7		10	8	11							9					23
1	4	3	6	5	2	7		10	8	11							9					24
1	4	3	6	5	2	7		10	8	11							9					25
1	4	3	6	5	2	7		10	8	11							9					26
1	4	3	6	5	2	7	10	9	8	11												27
1	4	3	6	5	2	7	10	9	8	11												28
1	4	3	6	5	2	7	10	9	8	11												29
1	4	3	6	5	2	7	10	9	8	11												30
1	4	3	6	5	2	7	10	9	8	11												31
1	4	3	6	5	2	7		8	10	11							9					32
1	4	3	6	5	2	7		10	8	11							9					33
1	4	3	6	5	2	7		10	8	11							9					34
1	4	3	6	5	2	7		10	8	11							9					35
1		3	6	5	2	7		10	8		11						9	4				36
1	4	3	6	5	2	7		10	8	11							9					37
1	4	3	6		2	7		10	8	11						5	9					38
1	4	3	6		2	7		9	8						11	5		10				39
1	4		6		2			10	8			3			11	5	9		7			40
1	4	3	6		2			10	8	11						5	9		7			41
1	4	3	6		2				8	10					11	5	9		7			42
1	4	3	6		2			10	8	11						5	9		7			43
1		3	6		2				8	10	11					5	9	4	7			44
1	4	3	6		2			9	8	10	11					5			7			45
1		3	6		2			9	8	10	11					5			7	4		46
46	43	40	46	25	46	39	16	42	46	42	5	11	4	3	5	12	24	3	7	1		
		1	7		1	8	13	30	25	14		1					6		2			

2 own-goals

Rouse	Long	Noakes	Petchey	Evans	McNichol	Gavin	Woan	Byrne	Summersby	Heckman	Kerrins	Lunnis	Jones	Easton	Colfar	Choules	Uphill	Truett	Barnett	Lewis	Swannell	
1	4		6	5	2	7		10	8	11			3				9					1
1	4	3	6	5	2	7		10	8	11							9					2
1	4	3	6	5	2		7	10	8	11							9					R
3	3	2	3	3	3	2	1	3	3	3			1				3					
						1		1		1							3					

Rouse	Long	Noakes	Petchey	Evans	McNichol	Gavin	Woan	Byrne	Summersby	Heckman	Kerrins	Lunnis	Jones	Easton	Colfar	Choules	Uphill	Truett	Barnett	Lewis	Swannell	
	4		6	5	3		10		8	7	11	2							9		1	1
	1		1	1	1		1		1	1	1	1							1		1	

1961-62

Manager: Arthur Rowe

1	Aug	19	(a)	Torquay U	W 2-1	Summersby, Byrne	10,319
2		23	(h)	Notts C	W 4-1	Werge, Summersby, Smillie 2	28,567
3		26	(h)	Swindon T	W 3-1	Allen 2 (2 pens), Byrne	24,184
4		31	(a)	Notts C	D 0-0		11,633
5	Sep	2	(a)	Halifax T	D 1-1	Allen	9,583
6		6	(h)	Northampton T	L 1-4	Little	25,535
7		9	(h)	Queen's Park R	D 2-2	Smillie, Allen	27,179
8		16	(a)	Barnsley	W 3-0	Uphill, Allen, Byrne	6,699
9		20	(h)	Lincoln C	L 1-3	Smillie	19,601
10		23	(h)	Portsmouth	L 1-2	Heckman	24,586
11		27	(a)	Lincoln C	L 2-3	Byrne, Smillie	8,793
12		30	(h)	Southend U	D 2-2	Byrne, Lewis	15,388
13	Oct	3	(a)	Watford	L 2-3	Smillie, Heckman	14,228
14		7	(a)	Shrewsbury T	W 5-1	Byrne 2, Allen 2, Uphill	7,909
15		11	(h)	Watford	D 1-1	Lewis	23,390
16		14	(h)	Peterborough U	W 5-2	Allen 2, Byrne 2, Uphill	28,886
17		17	(a)	Northampton T	D 1-1	Heckman	13,827
18		20	(a)	Reading	L 1-2	Heckman	14,432
19		28	(h)	Newport C	W 2-0	Summersby, Smillie	17,885
20	Nov	11	(h)	Grimsby T	W 4-1	Smillie 3, Heckman	13,661
21		17	(a)	Coventry C	W 2-0	Allen, Uphill	13,757
22	Dec	2	(a)	Port Vale	W 1-0	Smillie	9,761
23		9	(h)	Bristol C	L 2-3	Allen, Uphill	17,365
24		16	(h)	Torquay U	W 7-2	Uphill 2, Heckman 2, Byrne, Smillie, Lancaster (og)	13,884
25		23	(a)	Swindon T	L 0-5		7,707
26		26	(a)	Hull C	W 4-2	Petchey, Byrne, Heckman, Opp own-goal	7,559
27	Jan	13	(h)	Halifax T	W 4-3	Uphill, Heckman, Byrne, Opp own-goal	17,696
28		20	(a)	Queen's Park R	L 0-1		18,003
29		27	(h)	Brentford	D 2-2	Lewis, Uphill	19,323
30	Feb	3	(h)	Barnsley	L 1-3	Summersby	14,095
31		10	(a)	Portsmouth	L 1-2	Byrne	22,541
32		17	(a)	Southend U	D 2-2	Heckman, Allen	8,733
33		24	(h)	Shrewsbury T	W 2-1	Smillie, Allen	12,493
34	Mar	3	(a)	Peterborough U	L 1-4	Byrne	12,095
35		7	(a)	Bradford	L 0-2		3,606
36		10	(h)	Reading	L 3-4	Summersby 2, Truett	12,507
37		17	(a)	Newport C	L 1-2	Truett	2,276
38		21	(h)	Hull C	L 1-2	Summersby	7,041
39		24	(h)	Bradford	D 0-0		8,527
40		30	(a)	Grimsby T	D 0-0		12,535
41	Apr	7	(h)	Coventry C	D 2-2	Smillie, Brett	8,438
42		13	(a)	Brentford	L 2-4	Summersby, Uphill	9,926
43		20	(a)	Bournemouth	L 0-1		13,499
44		21	(h)	Port Vale	D 0-0		10,519
45		23	(h)	Bournemouth	D 0-0		11,319
46		28	(a)	Bristol C	D 2-2	Smillie 2	7,199
FINAL LEAGUE POSITION: 15th in Division Three							Appearances
							Goals

FA Cup

1	Nov	4	(h)	Portsmouth	W 3-0	Byrne, Heckman 2	30,464
2		25	(a)	Bridgewater	W 3-0	Smillie, Heckman 2	6,045
3	Jan	6	(a)	Aston Villa	L 3-4	Byrne 2, Uphill	39,011
							Appearances
							Goals

League Cup

1	Sep	13	(a)	Queen's Park R	L 2-5	Smillie 2	10,561
							Appearances
							Goals

Rouse	McNichol	Little	Long	Choules	Petchey	Werge	Summersby	Byrne	Smillie	Allen	Noakes	Lunnis	Uphill	Heckman	Lewis	Evans	Cartwright	Wood	Glazier	Easton	Truett	Brett	Stone	Stephenson	
1	2	3	4	5	6	7	8	9	10	11															1
1	2	3	4	5	6	7	8	9	10	11															2
1	2	3	4	5	6	7	8	9	10	11															3
1		3	4	5	6	7	8	9	10	11	3														4
1		3	4	5	6	7	8	9	10	11		2													5
1		3	4	5	6	7	8	9	10	11	2														6
1		3	4	5	6			8	10	7		2	9	11											7
1		3	4	5	6			8	10	7		2	9	11											8
1		3	4	5	6		8		10	7		2	9	11											9
1		3	4	5	6			8	7			2	9	11	10										10
1		3	4	5	6			8	10			2	9	11	7										11
1		3	4	5	6		8	9	10			2		11	7										12
1		3	4	5	6		8	9	10			2		11	7										13
1		3	2		6		4	8		9			10	11	7	5									14
1		3	2		6		4	8		9			10	11	7	5									15
1		3	2		6		4	8		10			9	11	7	5									16
1		3	2		6		4	8		10			9	11	7	5									17
1		3	2		6		4	8		10			9	11	7	5									18
1	3		2		6		4	8	10				9	11	7	5									19
1	3		2		6		4	8	10	7			9	11		5									20
1	3		2		6		4	8	10	7			9	11		5									21
1	3		2		6		4		10	7			9	11		5	8								22
1	3		2		6		4	8	10	7			9	11		5									23
1	3		2		6		4	8	10	7			9	11		5									24
1	3		2		6		4	8	10	7				11			9	5							25
1	3		2		6		4	8	10	7			9	11				5							26
	3		2		6		4	8		7			9	11	10			5	1						27
	3		2		6		4	8		7			9	11	10			5	1						28
	3		2		6		4	8		7			9	11	10			5	1						29
	3		2		6	11	4	8					9		7		10	5	1						30
		3	2		6	7	4	9	10						8			5	1	11					31
		3	2		6	7	4	8	10	9				11				5	1						32
	3		2		6	7	4	8	10	9				11		5			1						33
	3		2		6	7	8	9	10					11	4	5			1						34
	3		4		6	7	8		10			2		11		5			1		9				35
	3		4		6		8		10			2		11		5			1		7	9			36
	3		4				8			9		2		11				5	1		7	10	6		37
1	2	3	4				6		10	8				11			7	5				9			38
1	2	3	4				8		10				9				7	6				11		5	39
1	2	3	4				8		10				9	11		5		6				7			40
1	2	3	4			6	8		10				9	11				5				7			41
1	2	3	4			6	8		10				9	11				5				7			42
	2	3	4		6		8		10				9	11				5	1			7			43
	2	3	4		6	7	8		10				9		11			5	1						44
1	2	3			6	7	4		10					11	8		9	5							45
1	2	3	4		6	7	8		10					11			9	5							46
33	29	29	45	13	40	17	42	32	36	28	2	11	27	36	18	16	7	18	13	1	3	8	1	1	
		1			1	1	8	14	16	13			10	10	3						2	1			

3 own-goals

Rouse	McNichol	Little	Long	Choules	Petchey	Werge	Summersby	Byrne	Smillie	Allen	Noakes	Lunnis	Uphill	Heckman	Lewis	Evans	Cartwright	Wood	Glazier	Easton	Truett	Brett	Stone	Stephenson	
1	3		2		6	7	4	8	10				9	11		5									1
1	3		2		6		4	8	10	7			9	11		5									2
1	3		2		6		4	8		7			9	11			10	5							3
3	3		3		3	1	3	3	2	2			3	3		2	1	1							
			1					3	1				1	3											

Rouse	McNichol	Little	Long	Choules	Petchey	Werge	Summersby	Byrne	Smillie	Allen	Noakes	Lunnis	Uphill	Heckman	Lewis	Evans	Cartwright	Wood	Glazier	Easton	Truett	Brett	Stone	Stephenson	
1		3	4	5	6			8	10	7		2	9	11											1
1		1	1	1	1			1	1	1		1	1	1											
									2																

1962-63

Manager: Arthur Rowe until November 1962, then Dick Graham.

1	Aug	18	(h)	Halifax T	D 0-0		17,598
2		22	(a)	Shrewsbury T	L 1-3	Cartwright	6,827
3		25	(a)	Bristol R	L 0-2		10,889
4		29	(h)	Shrewsbury T	D 2-2	Burridge, Allen	15,755
5	Sep	1	(h)	Brighton & HA	D 2-2	Petchey, Stephenson	18,464
6		3	(a)	Queen's Park R	L 1-4	Smillie	16,353
7		8	(a)	Carlisle U	D 2-2	Summersby, Uphill	6,591
8		12	(h)	Queen's Park R	W 1-0	Summersby	21,958
9		15	(h)	Swindon T	D 0-0		16,326
10		20	(a)	Hull C	D 0-0		9,718
11		22	(a)	Peterborough U	D 0-0		12,856
12		29	(h)	Barnsley	L 1-2	Allen	14,062
13	Oct	2	(a)	Northampton T	L 1-3	Lewis	14,204
14		6	(h)	Southend U	L 2-3	Smillie 2	13,186
15		10	(h)	Northampton T	L 1-2	Smillie	13,319
16		13	(a)	Colchester U	W 2-1	Smillie 2	6,282
17		20	(h)	Notts C	D 1-1	Smillie	13,700
18		27	(a)	Bournemouth	L 0-3		10,455
19	Nov	10	(a)	Bradford	L 1-2	Allen	5,811
20		17	(h)	Watford	L 0-1		10,716
21	Dec	1	(h)	Reading	W 2-1	Allen, Heckman	12,391
22		8	(a)	Port Vale	L 1-4	Allen	6,537
23		15	(a)	Halifax T	D 2-2	Burridge, Long	20,055
24		26	(h)	Millwall	W 3-0	Burridge, Allen (pen), Dowsett	20,414
25	Jan	12	(a)	Brighton & HA	W 2-1	Burridge, Holton	12,333
26	Feb	2	(a)	Swindon T	L 0-1		9,895
27	Mar	9	(a)	Notts C	W 2-0	Dowsett 2	5,536
28		16	(h)	Bournemouth	W 1-0	Allen	16,191
29		20	(h)	Bristol R	W 2-1	Holton 2	15,451
30		23	(a)	Coventry C	L 0-1		17,860
31		27	(h)	Colchester U	L 0-1		11,898
32		30	(h)	Bradford	W 6-0	Burridge 2, Petchey, Allen, Holton, Dowsett	9,146
33	Apr	1	(a)	Millwall	D 1-1	Dowsett	21,996
34		6	(a)	Watford	W 4-1	Holton 3, Dowsett	8,471
35		12	(a)	Wrexham	W 4-3	Dowsett 2, Allen, Werge	10,820
36		13	(h)	Bristol C	W 3-2	Burridge, Holton, Dowsett	14,645
37		15	(h)	Wrexham	W 5-0	Burridge 3, Long, Metcalfe (og)	17,332
38		19	(a)	Reading	W 1-0	Holton	9,839
39		24	(h)	Peterborough U	L 0-2		21,777
40		27	(h)	Port Vale	W 2-1	Dowsett, Burridge	13,183
41	May	1	(h)	Hull C	D 1-1	Dowsett	11,210
42		7	(a)	Bristol C	D 1-1	Burridge	8,732
43		15	(h)	Coventry C	D 0-0		12,672
44		18	(h)	Carlisle U	W 3-0	Burridge, Long, Allen	10,242
45		20	(a)	Southend U	L 0-1		7,962
46		22	(a)	Barnsley	W 4-0	Burridge, Allen, Dowsett, Forster	3,807

FINAL LEAGUE POSITION: 11th in Division Three

Appearances
Goals

FA Cup

1	Nov	3	(h)	Hereford U	W 2-0	Wood, Werge	15,317
2		24	(h)	Mansfield T	D 2-2	Burridge, Allen (pen)	13,414
R		26	(a)	Mansfield T	L 2-7	Phillips (og), Summersby	17,118

Appearances
Goals

League Cup

2	Sep	26	(a)	Leeds U	L 1-2	Long	7,274

Appearances
Goals

Glazier	McNichol	Townsend	Long	Wood	Summersby	Lewis	Cartwright	Burridge	Smillie	Imlach	Petchey	Allen	Stephenson	Evans	Werge	Dodge	Heckman	Uphill	Rouse	Howe	Little	Lunnis	Newman	Dowsett	Holton	Forster	Fuller	
1	2	3	4	5	6	7	8	9	10	11																		1
1	2	3	4	5	6	7	8	9	10								11											2
1	2	3	4	5	6	7	8	9	10	11																		3
1	2	3	4	5		7		10	8	11	6	9																4
1	2	3	4			7		10	8	11	6	9	5															5
1		3	2		7				8	11	6	9		5	7	4												6
1		3	2	5	8				10	11	6	7				4		9										7
		3	2	4	7			10		11	6	7		5				9	1									8
		3	2	4	7			10		11	6	9		5				8	1									9
		3	2	4	7			10		11	6	9		5				8	1									10
	3		2	4	8	7		10						5	6		11	9	1									11
		3	2	4		7		10				8		5	6		11	9	1									12
			2	4	8	7		9	10					5	6			8	1		3							13
	7	3	4	5	8				10						6		11		1	2		9						14
	11	3	4	5					10		6				8			9	1	2			7					15
	4			5				11	10		6				8			9	1	2	3		7					16
	4			5	8			11	10		6							9	1	2	3		7					17
				5	8		9	11	10						6	4			1	2	3		7					18
1				6	4				10			11		5	8			9		2	3		7					19
1				6	4				10			11		5	8			9		2	3		7					20
1			4	5	8				10		6	7					11			2	3			9				21
1			4	5	8				10		6	7					11			2	3			9				22
1		3	4	5		7		8			6	10			11					2				9				23
1		3	4	5				8			6	7			11					2				9	10			24
1		3	4	5				8			6	7			11					2				9	10			25
1		3	4	5				8			6	7			11					2				9	10			26
1		3	4	5				8			6	7			11					2				9	10			27
1		3	4	5		8					6	7			11					2				9	10			28
1		3		5				8			4	11			7					2	6			9	10			29
1		3		5		11		8			6	7			4					2				9	10			30
1		3	4	5				8			6	7			11					2				9	10			31
1		3	4	5				8			6	7			11					2				9	10			32
1		3	4	5				8			6	7			11					2				9	10			33
1		3	4	5				8			6	7			11					2				9	10			34
1		3	4	5				8			6	7			11					2				9	10			35
1		3	4	5				8			6	7			11					2				9	10			36
1		3	4	5				8			6	7			11					2				9	10			37
1		3	4	5				8			6	7			11					2				9	10			38
1		3	4	5				8			6	7			11					2				9	10			39
1		3	4	5				8			6	7			11					2				9	10			40
1		3	4	5		6		8				7			11					2				9	10			41
1		4	5	3		7		10				11			8					2				9	6			42
1		4	5	5				10			8	11			7					2				9	6			43
1		4	5	5				10			8	11			7					2				9	6			44
1		4	5	5				10			8	11								2				9	6	7		45
1		6	2	5				10				7								4				9	8	11	3	46
35	10	37	39	44	17	13	4	37	17	9	33	36	1	9	32	3	6	12	11	33	9	1	6	26	23	2	1	
			3		2	1	1	14	7		2	11	1		1		1	1						12	9	1		

1 own-goal

Glazier	McNichol	Townsend	Long	Wood	Summersby	Lewis	Cartwright	Burridge	Smillie	Imlach	Petchey	Allen	Stephenson	Evans	Werge	Dodge	Heckman	Uphill	Rouse	Howe	Little	Lunnis	Newman	Dowsett	Holton	Forster	Fuller	
1				6	4				10			11		5	8			9		2	3		7					1
1			4		6			8	10			11		5	7			9		2	3							2
1			4		8			9	10			11		5	6			7		2	3							R
3			2	1	3			2	3			3		3	3			3		3	3		1					
				1	1			1				1			1													

1 own-goal

Glazier	McNichol	Townsend	Long	Wood	Summersby	Lewis	Cartwright	Burridge	Smillie	Imlach	Petchey	Allen	Stephenson	Evans	Werge	Dodge	Heckman	Uphill	Rouse	Howe	Little	Lunnis	Newman	Dowsett	Holton	Forster	Fuller	
			4	5		7		10				8			6		11	9	1	2	3							2
			1	1		1		1				1			1		1	1	1	1	1							
			1																									

1963-64

Manager: Dick Graham

No	Month	Day	Venue	Opponent	Res	Score	Scorers	Att
1	Aug	24	(a)	Coventry C	L	1-5	Burridge	26,037
2		28	(a)	Reading	D	0-0		10,118
3		31	(h)	Mansfield T	W	3-1	Burridge, Petchey, Werge	14,180
4	Sep	7	(a)	Brentford	L	1-2	Wood	15,883
5		11	(h)	Reading	W	4-1	Spiers (og), Dowsett, Burridge, Werge	12,059
6		14	(h)	Shrewsbury T	W	3-0	Dowsett 2, Allen	14,469
7		18	(a)	Luton T	W	4-0	Allen 2, Holton, Dowsett	6,152
8		21	(a)	Bristol C	D	1-1	Burridge	9,782
9		28	(h)	Port Vale	W	2-0	Dowsett, Holton	15,044
10	Oct	2	(h)	Luton T	D	1-1	Dowsett	16,304
11		5	(a)	Notts C	D	1-1	Burridge	7,207
12		9	(h)	Watford	W	2-0	Burridge 2	16,913
13		12	(h)	Millwall	W	2-1	Holton 2	25,056
14		15	(a)	Watford	L	1-3	Allen (pen)	9,595
15		19	(a)	Oldham A	L	1-3	Burridge	17,458
16		23	(a)	Crewe A	W	2-0	Allen, Holton	5,883
17		26	(h)	Bristol R	W	1-0	Burridge	18,389
18		30	(h)	Crewe A	W	1-0	Burridge	15,178
19	Nov	2	(a)	Queen's Park R	W	4-3	Holton 2, Burridge 2	9,826
20		9	(h)	Wrexham	W	2-1	Holton 2	16,601
21		23	(h)	Hull C	D	2-2	Allen (pen), Whitehouse	16,929
22		30	(a)	Barnsley	L	0-2		5,539
23	Dec	14	(h)	Coventry C	D	1-1	Stephenson	18,942
24		21	(a)	Mansfield T	D	1-1	Petchey	5,526
25		26	(a)	Southend U	L	1-2	Burridge	8,392
26		28	(h)	Southend U	W	3-0	Holton, Stephenson, Imlach	16,168
27	Jan	4	(a)	Bournemouth	L	3-4	Burridge 2, Holton	8,491
28		11	(h)	Brentford	W	1-0	Burridge	16,630
29		18	(a)	Shrewsbury T	D	1-1	Werge	4,303
30		25	(h)	Peterborough U	W	1-0	Holton	15,308
31	Feb	1	(h)	Bristol C	W	1-0	Kellard	16,539
32		8	(a)	Port Vale	W	2-1	Holton 2	8,204
33		15	(h)	Notts C	W	2-0	Holton, Burridge	15,867
34		22	(a)	Millwall	W	1-0	Burridge	20,264
35		29	(h)	Colchester U	D	0-0		15,421
36	Mar	7	(a)	Bristol R	W	3-1	Burridge 2, Kellard	10,598
37		14	(h)	Queen's Park R	W	1-0	Allen	15,370
38		18	(h)	Walsall	W	1-0	Whitehouse	12,784
39		28	(h)	Bournemouth	W	2-1	Holton, Whitehouse	22,175
40		30	(a)	Walsall	D	2-2	Holton, Whitehouse	5,356
41	Apr	4	(a)	Hull C	D	1-1	Holton (pen)	6,602
42		11	(h)	Barnsley	L	1-2	Whitehouse	21,205
43		15	(a)	Colchester U	D	1-1	Imlach (pen)	5,633
44		18	(a)	Peterborough U	D	1-1	Whitehouse	11,837
45		22	(a)	Wrexham	D	2-2	Whitehouse, Holton (pen)	3,492
46		25	(h)	Oldham A	L	1-3	Holton (pen)	27,967

FINAL LEAGUE POSITION: 2nd in Division Three

Appearances
Goals

FA Cup

Rd	Month	Day	Venue	Opponent	Res	Score	Scorers	Att
1	Nov	16	(h)	Harwich & Parkeston	W	8-2	Burridge, Holton 3, Allen 2, Sewell, Howe	15,759
2	Dec	7	(a)	Yeovil T	L	1-3	Wood	10,925

Appearances
Goals

League Cup

Rd	Month	Day	Venue	Opponent	Res	Score	Scorers	Att
2	Sep	25	(a)	Bristol R	L	0-2		4,859

Appearances
Goals

Glazier	Howe	Townsend	Long	Wood	Petchey	Allen	Holton	Dowsett	Burridge	Werge	Kellard	Fuller	Stephenson	Birch	Sewell	Lucas	Whitehouse	Imlach	Brooks	Forster	
1	2	3	4	5	6	7	8	9	10	11											1
1	2	3	4	5	6	7	8	9	10	11											2
1	2	3	4	5	6	7	8	9	10	11											3
1	2	3	4	5	6	7	9		10	11	8										4
1	2	3	4	5	6	7	8	9	10	11											5
1	2	3	4	5	6	7	8	9	10	11											6
1	2	3	4	5	6	7	8	9	10	11											7
1	2	3	4	5	6	7	8	9	10	11											8
1	2	3	4	5	6	7	8	9	10	11											9
1	2	3	4	5	6		8	9	10	11	7										10
1	2	3	4	5	6	7	8	9	10	11											11
1	2	3	4	5	6	7	8	9	10	11											12
1	2	3	4	5	6	7	8	9	10	11											13
1	2	3	4	5	6	7	8	9	10	11											14
1	2	3	4	5	6	7	8	9	10	11											15
1	2	3		5		7	8	9	10			4	6	11							16
1	4	3		5		7	8	9	10					11	2	6					17
1	4	3		5		7	8	9	10					11	2	6					18
1	4	3				7	9		10	11	8		5		2	6					19
1	4	3		5		7	9		10	11	8				2	6					20
1	4	3		5		7	9		10		11				2	6	8				21
1	4	3		5		7	9		10		11				2	6	8				22
1	4			5	6	7			10		11		3	9	2		8				23
1	4			5	6	7	9		10		11		3		2		8				24
1	4			5	6	7	9		10		11		3		2		8				25
1	4			5	3		9				11		6	8	2	10		7			26
1	4			5	3		9		10		11		6		2	8		7			27
1	4	3		5			9		10	7			6		2	8		11			28
1	4	3		5			9		10	7			6		2	8		11			29
1	4	3		5		7	9		10				6		2	8		11			30
1	4	3		5			9		10		8		6		2			11	7		31
1	4	3		5			9		10		8		6		2			11	7		32
1	4	3		5			9		10				6		2		8	11	7		33
1	4	3		5			9		10				6		2		8	11	7		34
1	4	3	2	5			9		10				6				8	11	7		35
1	4	3	2	5		7	9		10		11		6				8				36
1	4	3	2	5		7	9		10		11		6				8				37
1	4	3	2	5			9	7	10		1		6				8				38
1	4	3	2	5			9		10		7		6				8	11			39
1	4	3	2	5			9		10		7		6				8	11			40
1	4	3	2	5			9		10		11		6				8		7		41
1	4	3	2	5			9		10		11		6				8		7		42
1	4		2	5	3				10		7		6			8	9	11			43
1	4		2	5	3				10		7		6			8	9	11			44
1	4		2	5	3		9	10		7	11		6				8				45
1	4		2	5	3		9		10	7	11		6				8				46
46	46	37	27	45	24	27	43	19	44	21	24	1	26	5	18	13	19	14	7		
				1	2	7	20	6	20	3	2		2				7	2			

1 own-goal

Glazier	Howe	Townsend	Long	Wood	Petchey	Allen	Holton	Dowsett	Burridge	Werge	Kellard	Fuller	Stephenson	Birch	Sewell	Lucas	Whitehouse	Imlach	Brooks	Forster	
1	4	3		5		11	9		10	7	8				2	6					1
1	4	3		5		11	9		10	7					2	6	8				2
2	2	2		2		2	2		2	2	1				2	2	1				
	1			1		2	3		1						1						

Glazier	Howe	Townsend	Long	Wood	Petchey	Allen	Holton	Dowsett	Burridge	Werge	Kellard	Fuller	Stephenson	Birch	Sewell	Lucas	Whitehouse	Imlach	Brooks	Forster	
1	6	3			4		8			10	11	2	5	9						7	2
1	1	1			1		1			1	1	1	1	1						1	

1964-65

Manager: Dick Graham

No	Month	Day	Venue	Opponent	Result	Scorers	Attendance
1	Aug	22	(h)	Derby C	L 2-3	Holton, Burridge	22,935
2		25	(a)	Swindon T	L 0-2		17,446
3		29	(a)	Swansea T	L 1-2	Whitehouse	13,000
4	Sep	2	(h)	Swindon T	W 3-1	Holton, Dowsett 2	18,517
5		5	(h)	Rotherham U	W 2-1	Burridge 2	18,200
6		12	(a)	Norwich C	W 2-1	Holton 2 (1 pen)	20,893
7		15	(a)	Charlton A	W 2-1	Kellard, Dowsett	31,498
8		19	(h)	Plymouth A	W 2-1	Holton, Dowsett	21,074
9		26	(h)	Bury	L 0-2		19,299
10		30	(h)	Charlton A	W 3-1	Allen 3	29,878
11	Oct	3	(a)	Leyton O	W 1-0	Burridge	17,711
12		7	(h)	Ipswich T	D 1-1	Werge	22,690
13		10	(a)	Bolton W	L 0-3		13,484
14		17	(h)	Middlesbrough	W 3-1	Whitehouse 2, Kellard	18,055
15		24	(a)	Newcastle U	L 0-2		28,750
16		31	(h)	Northampton T	L 1-2	Holton	21,331
17	Nov	7	(a)	Southampton	W 1-0	Burridge	20,161
18		14	(h)	Huddersfield T	W 3-0	Smith 2, Kellard	14,084
19		21	(a)	Coventry C	D 0-0		24,145
20		28	(h)	Cardiff C	D 0-0		18,188
21	Dec	5	(a)	Preston NE	L 0-1		11,390
22		12	(a)	Derby C	D 3-3	Burridge 2, Smith	11,828
23		19	(h)	Swansea T	D 3-3	Holton 2, Long	13,585
24		26	(h)	Portsmouth	W 4-2	Burnside 2, Smith, Stephenson	18,758
25		28	(a)	Portsmouth	D 1-1	Holsgrove	15,450
26	Jan	2	(a)	Rotherham U	L 0-1		9,385
27		16	(h)	Norwich C	W 2-0	Holton, Burnside	17,103
28		23	(a)	Plymouth A	D 1-1	Smith	15,582
29	Feb	6	(a)	Bury	L 1-3	Smith	5,580
30		13	(h)	Leyton O	W 1-0	Woods	17,776
31		27	(a)	Middlesbrough	D 0-0		12,071
32	Mar	13	(a)	Northampton T	D 1-1	Cutler	17,350
33		17	(h)	Preston NE	W 1-0	Holton	14,976
34		20	(h)	Southampton	L 0-2		12,737
35		27	(a)	Huddersfield T	L 0-2		10,255
36	Apr	3	(h)	Coventry C	D 2-2	Holsgrove, Woods	15,900
37		7	(h)	Bolton W	W 2-0	Smith, Stephenson	14,022
38		10	(a)	Cardiff C	D 0-0		10,000
39		16	(a)	Manchester C	W 2-0	Smith 2	15,885
40		17	(h)	Newcastle U	D 1-1	Stephenson	21,756
41		19	(h)	Manchester C	D 1-1	Stephenson	12,175
42		24	(a)	Ipswich T	L 2-3	Holton, Burnside	14,642

FINAL LEAGUE POSITION: 7th in Division Two

Appearances
Goals

FA Cup

Round	Month	Day	Venue	Opponent	Result	Scorers	Attendance
3	Jan	9	(h)	Bury	W 5-1	Burnside, Wood, Holton 3	18,672
4		30	(a)	Southampton	W 2-1	Holton, Smith	26,398
5	Feb	20	(h)	Nottingham F	W 3-1	Burnside, Burridge, Holton	‡41,667
6	Mar	10	(h)	Leeds U	L 0-3		‡45,384

‡Ground attendance record

Appearances
Goals

League Cup

Round	Month	Day	Venue	Opponent	Result	Scorers	Attendance
2	Sep	23	(a)	Tranmere R	W 2-0	Holton, Burridge	11,098
3	Oct	26	(h)	Southampton	W 2-0	Burridge 2	11,538
4	Nov	4	(a)	Leicester C	D 0-0		11,141
R		11	(h)	Leicester C	L 1-2	Burridge	15,808

Appearances
Goals

Glazier	Long	Howe	Wood	Stephenson	Holsgrove	Holton	Whitehouse	Kellard	Burridge	Allen	Jackson	Townsend	Werge	Birch	Lucas	Imlach	Sewell	Dowsett	Millington	Smith	Woods	Payne	Burnside	Horobin	Cutler	Fuller	Petchey	
1	2	3	4	5	6	7	8	9	10	11																		1
		2		5	4			10		7	1	3	6	8	9	11												2
1	4	3		5		7	8	9	10				11		6		2											3
1		3	5	6		9	4	10	8							11	2	7										4
1		3	5	6		9	4	10	8							11	2	7										5
1		3	5	6		9	4	8	10							11	2	7										6
1		3	5	6		9	4	10	8							11	2	7										7
1		3		5		9	4	10	8						6	11	2	7										8
1		3		6		9	4	8	10			5				11	2	7										9
1		3	5	6		9	4	10	8	7			11				2											10
1		3	5	6		9	4	10	8	7			11				2											11
1		3	5	6		9	4	8	10	7			11				2											12
1		3	5	6	9		4	8	10				11			7	2											13
	4	3	5	6		9	10	8		11			7				2		1									14
	4	3	5	6		9	10	8		11			7				2		1									15
		6		5		9	4	10	8			3	7				2	11	1									16
	2	3	5			8	4	11	10							7	6		1	9								17
	2	3	5	6		9	4	11	10							7			1	8								18
	2	3	6	5		9	4	11					10			7			1	8								19
	2	3	5	4			6	11	10		1					7				8	9							20
	2	3	5	4			6	11			1							7		8	10	9						21
	2	4	5			9	6	11	7								3		1	10	8							22
	6		3	5		9	4	11	8								2		1	10	7							23
		3	5	4	6	9	7	11			1						2			10			8					24
		3	5	4	6	9	10	11		7							2		1				8					25
		3	5	4		9	6	11		7							2		1	10			8					26
	2	3		5	6	9	7	11	4										1	10			8					27
		3		5	6	9	4	11			1						2			10	7		8					28
	2	4		5	6	9	3	11											1	10			8	7				29
		2		5	6		3	11			1									10	9	4	8	7				30
		2		5	4	9		11			1		3							7	6		10	8				31
	2			5	4		7	11	8		1									10	3		6		9			32
	2			4	6	5	3	9			1									8	10		7		11			33
	3	4		5	6	8	7	10			1									9	2		11					34
		2		5	6								11				4		1	10	7	3	8		9			35
	4	2		6	11	5	9				1							8			7			10		3		36
		3		5	4	9	2	11	6		1									10	7		8					37
		3		5	4	9	2	11	6		1									10	7		8					38
		3		5		9	2	11	6		1									10	7	4	8					39
		3		5		9	2	11	6		1									10	7	4	8					40
		3		5		9	2	11	6		1									10	7	4	8					41
		3		5	7	9	2	11	6		1									10		4	8					42
12	17	39	21	40	18	35	39	40	26	9	17	3	12	1	3	12	22	9	13	24	17	7	18	4	3	1		
	1			4	2	11	3	3	7	3			1					4		9	2		4		1			

Glazier	Long	Howe	Wood	Stephenson	Holsgrove	Holton	Whitehouse	Kellard	Burridge	Allen	Jackson	Townsend	Werge	Birch	Lucas	Imlach	Sewell	Dowsett	Millington	Smith	Woods	Payne	Burnside	Horobin	Cutler	Fuller	Petchey	
	2	3	5	4	6	9	7	11											1	10			8					3
		2		5	6	9	3	11	4		1									10			8	7				4
	3	2		5	4	9	7	11	6		1												10	8				5
		2		5	6	9	3	11											1	10			8	7			4	6
	2	4	1	4	4	4	4	4	2		2								2	3			4	3			1	
			1			5			1											1			2					

Glazier	Long	Howe	Wood	Stephenson	Holsgrove	Holton	Whitehouse	Kellard	Burridge	Allen	Jackson	Townsend	Werge	Birch	Lucas	Imlach	Sewell	Dowsett	Millington	Smith	Woods	Payne	Burnside	Horobin	Cutler	Fuller	Petchey	
1	2	3		6		9	4	8	10			5				11		7										2
		6		5		8	10	11	9		1	3			4		2	7										3
	3	4	2	5		9	6	11			1					7						10			8			4
	3	6	8	5		9	4	11	10							7	2		1									R
1	3	4	2	4		4	4	4	3		2	2			1	3	2	2	1			1			1			
						1			4																			

1965-66

Manager: Dick Graham until 3 January 1966; Arthur Rowe caretaker until April 1966, then Bert Head from 14 April 1966.

1	Aug	21	(a)	Birmingham C	L 1-2	Lawson	19,205
2		25	(h)	Bolton W	D 1-1	Lawson	20,843
3		28	(h)	Leyton O	W 2-1	Whitehouse, Woods	16,543
4	Sep	1	(a)	Bolton W	L 0-3		15,431
5		4	(a)	Middlesbrough	D 2-2	Lawson, Stephenson	10,160
6		8	(h)	Portsmouth	W 4-1	Kevan, Lawson, Burridge, Kellard	15,744
7		11	(h)	Huddersfield T	W 2-1	Kevan, Lawson	16,684
8		15	(a)	Portsmouth	D 1-1	Woods	18,926
9		18	(a)	Coventry C	W 1-0	Smith	25,203
10		25	(a)	Preston NE	L 0-2		12,661
11	Oct	2	(h)	Charlton A	W 2-0	Woods, Whitehouse	23,144
12		9	(h)	Bristol C	W 2-1	Kevan, Lawson	16,356
13		16	(a)	Manchester C	L 1-3	Oakes (og)	24,765
14		23	(h)	Rotherham U	D 2-2	Madden (og), Smith	15,833
15		30	(a)	Wolves	L 0-1		21,623
16	Nov	6	(h)	Norwich C	D 0-0		15,906
17		13	(a)	Bury	D 2-2	Burnside, Yard	7,689
18		20	(h)	Southampton	W 1-0	Kevan	12,697
19		27	(a)	Derby C	L 0-4		13,865
20	Dec	4	(h)	Cardiff C	D 0-0		11,527
21		11	(a)	Carlisle U	L 1-3	Kevan	9,577
22		18	(h)	Manchester C	L 0-2		12,847
23		27	(h)	Ipswich T	W 3-1	Stephenson 2, Smith	16,064
24	Jan	1	(a)	Bristol C	D 1-1	Long	16,456
25		8	(h)	Bury	W 1-0	Kember	13,699
26		15	(a)	Rotherham U	L 0-3		8,410
27		29	(h)	Birmingham C	W 1-0	Whitehouse	14,190
28	Feb	5	(a)	Leyton O	W 2-0	Whitehouse, Smith	7,508
29		11	(a)	Ipswich T	D 2-2	Whitehouse 2	9,151
30		19	(h)	Middlesbrough	D 1-1	Smith	13,902
31		26	(a)	Huddersfield T	D 1-1	Whitehouse	17,250
32	Mar	12	(h)	Coventry C	L 0-1		15,717
33		19	(h)	Preston NE	D 1-1	Stephenson	11,786
34		26	(a)	Charlton A	L 0-1		12,856
35	Apr	2	(a)	Norwich C	L 1-2	Sewell	11,215
36		8	(h)	Plymouth A	W 3-1	Burnside, Bannister, Kember	12,026
37		9	(h)	Wolves	L 0-1		14,403
38		11	(a)	Plymouth A	W 2-1	Yard, Bannister	11,289
39		16	(a)	Southampton	L 0-1		15,780
40		23	(h)	Derby C	D 1-1	Burnside	11,923
41		30	(a)	Cardiff C	L 0-1		9,577
42	May	7	(h)	Carlisle U	W 2-0	Bannister, Yard	9,413

FINAL LEAGUE POSITION: 11th in Division Two

Appearances
Sub Appearances
Goals

FA Cup

3	Jan	22	(a)	Carlisle U	L 0-3		13,740

Appearances
Goals

League Cup

2	Sep	22	(h)	Grimsby T	L 0-1		13,285

Appearances
Goals

Jackson	Howe	Whitehouse	Woods	Stephenson	Long	Smith	Burnside	Lawson	Kevan	Yard	Sewell	Payne	Kellard	Burridge	Stack	Wood	Millington	Bannister	Smout	Cutler	Kember	Imlach	
1	2	3	4	5	6	7	8	9	10	11													1
1	2	3	4	5				9	10	11	6	8	7										2
1	3	8	7	5		12		9*	10	4		6		2	11								3
1	3	2*	7	5		8		12	10	9		6			11	4							4
1	2		7	5	3		12	9	10	8		6	11			4*							5
1	2		7	5	3		8	9	10			6	11	4									6
	2		7	5	3		8	9	10	4			11	6			1						7
1			7	5	3		8	9	10		2	6	11	4									8
1		2	7	5	3	8	10			4			11			9		6					9
1		2	7	5	3		12	9	10*			4	11	8				6					10
1	3	4	7	5	2	10			9			8	11					6					11
1	3	8	7	5	2*			9	10	12		4	11					6					12
1	3	6	7	5	2		8	9	10			4	11										13
	3		7	5		10	8	9		4	2	6	11				1						14
1	3	7		5	2		10	8	9	11		4						6					15
1	3			5	4	7	9			8	2	6	11	10									16
1	3			5	4	7	8		10	9		6	11					2					17
1	2	6	11	5	4		9		10	8	3			7									18
1		6	11	5	3	8	9		10	7		2						4					19
		4	7	5	3	12	10	8	9	11	2							6	1*				20
1	3	4	7*		5	10	8	12	9	11	2							6					21
	3	7	8	5	6		9		10	11	2						1	4					22
1		6	7	5		8		9	10	11	2	4								3			23
1		6	3	5	4	8	12			11*	2	10								9	7		24
1	3	6	7	5	4	10	9				2									11	8		25
1	3	6	11	5	4	10	8		9		2										7		26
1	3	9		5	4	8	10			7*	2	6								11	12		27
1	3	9		5	4	8	10			7	2							6		11			28
1	3	9		5	4	8	10			7	2							6		11			29
1	3	9		5	4	10	8			7	2	6										11	30
1	3	9		5	4	8	12			7*	2	10						6				11	31
1	3				4	10	9			7	2	5						6			8	11	32
1	3			5	4	10	8	9		7	2							6				11	33
1	3		7	5	4	8*	10			9	2							6			12	11	34
1	3		7	5	4	9	10				2	6									8	11	35
1	3		7	5			10			9	2	4						6			8	11	36
1	3		7	5	6	12	10			9	2	4									8	11*	37
1	3		7	5	4	10	8			11	2	12						6		9*			38
1	3		7	5			9			10	2	6						4			8	11	39
1	3		7	5			10			9	2	6						4			8	11	40
1	3		7	5			10			9	2	12				4		6*			8	11	41
1	3		7	5						9	2	10				4		6			8	11	42
38	35	24	32	40	32	23	31	15	21	33	28	27	13	7	2	5	3	22	1	7	11	12	
						3	4	2		1		2									2		
		7	3	4	1	5	3	6	5	3	1		1	1				3			2		

2 own-goals

	3	6	7	5	4	10	8			9	2						1				11		3
	1	1	1	1	1	1	1			1	1						1				1		

1			7	5	3	9	8		10	4			11			2		6					2
1			1	1	1	1	1		1	1			1			1		1					

1966-67

Manager: Bert Head

1	Aug	20	(h)	Carlisle U	W 4-2	White 2, Woodruff 2	11,374
2		23	(a)	Bristol C	W 1-0	Burnside	13,365
3		27	(a)	Blackburn R	L 1-2	Woodruff	15,015
4		31	(h)	Bristol C	W 2-1	Woodruff, Kember	16,478
5	Sep	3	(h)	Bolton W	W 3-2	Woodruff, Kember, Imlach	16,578
6		7	(a)	Wolves	D 1-1	Kember	18,000
7		10	(a)	Charlton A	D 1-1	Woodruff	16,986
8		17	(h)	Derby C	W 2-1	Woodruff, Kember	17,617
9		24	(a)	Plymouth A	L 0-1		12,865
10	Oct	1	(a)	Huddersfield T	W 2-0	Kember, Stephenson	12,609
11		8	(h)	Northampton T	W 5-1	Dyson 3, Woodruff 2	18,507
12		15	(a)	Millwall	D 1-1	Dyson	28,664
13		22	(h)	Rotherham U	D 1-1	Payne	19,486
14		29	(a)	Preston NE	L 0-1		13,471
15	Nov	5	(h)	Bury	W 3-1	Dyson, O'Connell, Kember	12,810
16		12	(a)	Coventry C	W 2-1	C.Jackson, Kember	23,035
17		19	(h)	Norwich C	D 0-0		17,114
18		26	(a)	Birmingham C	L 1-3	C.Jackson	16,820
19	Dec	3	(h)	Portsmouth	L 0-2		15,700
20		10	(a)	Hull C	L 1-6	White	21,818
21		17	(a)	Carlisle U	L 0-3		10,324
22		26	(a)	Cardiff C	W 2-1	White, Long	17,158
23		27	(h)	Cardiff C	W 3-1	Dyson 2, Woodruff	13,553
24		31	(h)	Blackburn R	W 2-1	C.Jackson, Kember	17,703
25	Jan	14	(h)	Charlton A	W 1-0	White	24,399
26		21	(a)	Derby C	L 0-2		15,996
27	Feb	4	(h)	Plymouth A	W 2-1	Woodruff, Bannister	17,695
28		11	(h)	Huddersfield T	D 1-1	Woodruff	18,927
29		25	(a)	Northampton T	L 0-1		13,081
30	Mar	7	(h)	Preston NE	W 1-0	O'Connell	19,719
31		11	(a)	Bolton W	D 0-0		9,617
32		18	(a)	Rotherham U	W 1-0	White	7,916
33		25	(h)	Millwall	L 1-2	Byrne	30,845
34		27	(h)	Ipswich T	L 0-2		16,029
35		28	(a)	Ipswich T	L 0-2		17,176
36	Apr	1	(a)	Bury	D 1-1	Kember	7,106
37		8	(h)	Coventry C	D 1-1	Kember	23,247
38		15	(a)	Norwich C	L 3-4	Payne, Bannister, Woodruff	13,714
39		22	(h)	Birmingham C	W 2-1	Woodruff, Dyson	13,064
40		29	(a)	Portsmouth	D 1-1	Woodruff	13,392
41	May	6	(h)	Hull C	W 4-1	Woodruff 2, Light 2	11,329
42		13	(h)	Wolves	W 4-1	Woodruff, Bannister, Dyson, Light	26,930

FINAL LEAGUE POSITION: 7th in Division Two

Appearances
Sub Appearances
Goals

FA Cup

3	Jan	28	(a)	Leeds U	L 0-3	37,768

Appearances
Sub Appearances
Goals

League Cup

2	Sep	13	(a)	Fulham	L 0-2	9,906

Appearances
Sub Appearances
Goals

Jackson J	Sewell	Howe	Payne	Stephenson	Bannister	Kember	Burnside	White	Woodruff	O'Connell	McCormick	Yard	Imlach	Long	Dyson	Jackson C	Wood	Robertson	Presland	Byrne	Parsons	Light	Brophy	Shaw	Smith	
1	2	3	4	5	6	7	8	9	10	11																1
1	2	3	4	5	6	7	8	9	10	11																2
1	2	3	4	5	6	7	8	9	10		11*	12														3
1	2	3	4	5	6	7	8	9	10				11													4
1	2	3	4	5	6	7	8	9	10				11													5
1	2	3	4	5	6	8		9	10			7	11													6
1	2	3	4	5	6	8		9	10			7	11													7
1		2	4	5	3	8			10	7				6	9	11										8
1		2	4	5	3	8			10	7				6	9	11										9
1			4	5	3	8			10	7				2	9	11	6									10
1		12	4	5	6	8*			10	7				2	9	11	3									11
1		2		5	6	8			10	7				3	9	11	4									12
1		2	4	5	6	8			10	7					9	11	3									13
1		2	9	5	6	8			11					4	10	7	3									14
1		2	4	5	3	8			10	7				6	9	11										15
1		2	4	5	6	8			10						9	11	3	7								16
1		2	4	5	6	8			10					12	9	11	3*	7								17
1		2	4	5	3	8			10		6				9	11		7								18
1		2	4	5	3	7		8	10						9	11	6									19
1			4	5	6	7		8	10					2	9		3	11								20
1	2		4	5	6	8		9	10*					3		11	12	7								21
1	2		4	5	6	8		9	10					3	7	11										22
1	2		4	5	6	8		9	10					3	7	11										23
1	2		4	5	6	8		9	10					3	7	11										24
1	2		4	5	6	8		9	10					3	7	11										25
1	2		4	5	6	8		9	10					3	7	11										26
1	2		8	5	6	10			9					3	7	11			4							27
1			4	5	6	8			10	7				3	9	11			2							28
1	2			5	6	8			10	11				3	7				4	9						29
1			4	5	6	7		9	10	11				3					2	8						30
1			4	5	6	7		9	10	11				3					2	8						31
1	3		4	5	6	7		9	10	11									2	8						32
1	3		4	5	6	7		9	10	11									2	8						33
1	3		4	5	6	8*			10					12	7	11			2	9						34
1	2		10	5	6				7	11				4	9				3	8						35
1	2		4	5	6	8*			7	11				12	9				3	10						36
1	2		4	5	6	8			7	11				12	9*				3	10						37
1	2		4	5	6	8			7	11					9				3	10						38
	2		4	5	6	8*			7	11				12	9				3	10	1					39
	2		4	5	6	8			7						9	11			3	10	1					40
	2		4	5	6				8	12					9	11			3	10	1	7*				41
	2		4	5	6				10						9	11			3	8*	1	7	12			42
38	26	17	40	42	42	39	5	19	42	20	2	2	4	20	30	24	9	5	16	14	4	2				
		1								1		1		5			1						1			
			2	1	3	10	1	6	18	2			1	1	9	3				1		3				

Jackson J	Sewell	Howe	Payne	Stephenson	Bannister	Kember	Burnside	White	Woodruff	O'Connell	McCormick	Yard	Imlach	Long	Dyson	Jackson C	Wood	Robertson	Presland	Byrne	Parsons	Light	Brophy	Shaw	Smith	
1	2*		8	5	6	10			9					3	7	11			4					12		3
1	1		1	1	1	1			1					1	1	1			1							
																								1		

Jackson J	Sewell	Howe	Payne	Stephenson	Bannister	Kember	Burnside	White	Woodruff	O'Connell	McCormick	Yard	Imlach	Long	Dyson	Jackson C	Wood	Robertson	Presland	Byrne	Parsons	Light	Brophy	Shaw	Smith	
1	2	3	4	5	6	8			10	11	9														7	2
1	1	1	1	1	1	1			1	1	1														1	

1967-68

Manager: Bert Head

1	Aug	19	(a)	Rotherham U	W 3-0	Woodruff, Payne, White	7,661
2		26	(h)	Derby C	W 1-0	Woodruff	17,875
3		30	(a)	Cardiff C	L 2-4	Byrne (pen), C.Jackson	14,780
4	Sep	2	(a)	Preston NE	D 0-0		13,313
5		6	(h)	Plymouth A	W 5-0	Woodruff 2, Payne, Byrne, Kember	16,372
6		9	(h)	Charlton A	W 3-0	Byrne, Woodruff 2	23,181
7		16	(a)	Hull C	D 1-1	Light	15,993
8		23	(a)	Aston Villa	W 1-0	Woodruff (pen)	12,484
9		27	(h)	Cardiff C	W 2-1	Kember, Woodruff	20,424
10		30	(h)	Queen's Park R	W 1-0	Long	38,006
11	Oct	7	(h)	Bristol C	W 2-0	Kember, Woodruff	19,938
12		14	(a)	Blackpool	L 0-2		20,905
13		23	(h)	Blackburn R	W 1-0	Byrne (pen)	23,771
14		28	(a)	Carlisle U	L 0-3		11,399
15	Nov	11	(a)	Huddersfield T	D 1-1	White	11,055
16		18	(h)	Millwall	D 2-2	White 2	30,304
17		25	(a)	Birmingham C	L 0-1		27,538
18	Dec	2	(h)	Bolton W	L 0-3		15,780
19		9	(a)	Middlesbrough	L 0-3		16,651
20		16	(h)	Rotherham U	W 1-0	White	13,541
21		23	(a)	Derby C	D 1-1	White	20,224
22		26	(h)	Portsmouth	D 2-2	Kember, Woodruff	23,122
23		30	(a)	Portsmouth	D 2-2	Stephenson, Tomkins	28,379
24	Jan	20	(h)	Hull C	L 0-1		15,431
25	Feb	3	(h)	Aston Villa	L 0-1		10,214
26		10	(a)	Queen's Park R	L 1-2	Tomkins	18,954
27		24	(a)	Bristol C	L 1-2	Woodruff	13,082
28	Mar	2	(h)	Blackpool	W 3-1	White, Kember, Lazarus	11,860
29		5	(a)	Charlton A	W 1-0	McCormick	20,201
30		16	(a)	Blackburn R	L 1-2	C.Jackson	10,204
31		23	(h)	Carlisle U	D 1-1	Lazarus	9,149
32		30	(a)	Ispwich T	D 2-2	Kember, C.Jackson	24,889
33	Apr	6	(h)	Huddersfield T	L 0-1		10,929
34		13	(a)	Millwall	L 1-5	Woodruff	14,782
35		15	(a)	Norwich C	L 1-2	Woodruff	16,343
36		16	(h)	Norwich C	W 6-0	Woodruff 2, Light, Lazarus, Vansittart 2	7,745
37		20	(h)	Birmingham C	D 0-0		14,949
38		27	(a)	Bolton W	D 2-2	Woodruff 2	6,600
39	May	1	(h)	Ipswich T	L 1-3	Woodruff	19,999
40		4	(h)	Middlesbrough	L 1-3	Lazarus	9,669
41		11	(a)	Plymouth A	L 1-2	Lazarus	4,768
42		15	(h)	Preston NE	W 2-0	Kember, C.Jackson	7,357

FINAL LEAGUE POSITION: 11th in Division Two

Appearances
Sub Appearances
Goals

FA Cup

3	Jan	27	(a)	Walsall	D 1-1	White	15,333
R		31	(h)	Walsall	L 1-2	Byrne	27,144

Appearances
Sub Appearances
Goals

League Cup

2	Sep	13	(a)	Barrow	L 0-1		7,908

Appearances
Sub Appearances
Goals

Jackson J	Sewell	Presland	Payne	Stephenson	Bannister	Kember	Byrne	White	Woodruff	Jackson C	Long	Light	McCormick	Dyson	Lazarus	Tomkins	Dawkins J	Vansittart	Hoadley	Oliver	Cook	
1	2*	3	4	5	6	7	8	9	10	11	12											1
1	2	3	4	5	6	7	9	10	8	11												2
1	2	3	4	5	6	7	8	9	10	11												3
1	2	3	4	5	6	7	9		10	11	8											4
1	2	3	4	5*	6	8	9		10	11	12	7										5
1	2	3	4		6	8	9		10	11		7	5									6
1		3	4		6	8	9		10	11	2	7	5									7
1		3	4		6	8		12	10	11	2	7*	5	9								8
1		3	4		6	8		12	10	11	2	7	5	9*								9
1	2	3	4		6	8		9	10		11	7	5									10
1	2	3	4		6	8		9	10	11*	12	7	5									11
1	2	3	4		6	8	9		10	11	12	7*	5									12
1	2	3	4		6	8	9		10	11		7	5									13
1	2*	3	7	4	6	8	9		10	12	11		5									14
1		3	4	5	6	8	9	7	10	11	2											15
1		3	4	5	6	8	9	7	10	11	2											16
1		3	4	5	6	8		7	10	11	2			9								17
1		3	4	5	6	8	9	7	10	11*	2			12								18
1		3	4	5	6	8	9	7	10	11	2											19
1	2	3	4	5	6	8	10	9	11						7							20
1		2	4	5	6	8	10	9	11				3		7							21
1		2	4	5	6	10	8	9	11	12			3*		7							22
1		3	4	5	6	10		9	8		2				7	11						23
1	2	3		5	6	8	10	9	11						7*	12	4					24
1	2	3		4	6	8	9		10	7			5			11						25
1	2	3		4	6	8	9		10		12		5		7*	11						26
1	2		4	5	3	8		9	10				6		7	11						27
1	2	3	4	5	12	8		9	10				6*		7	11						28
1	2	3	4		6	8	11	9	10				5		7							29
1	2	3	4		6	8	9		10	7		12	5*			11						30
1	2	3	4		6	8			9	11					7	10		5				31
1	2	3	4		6	8			9	12	11				7	10*		5				32
1	2	3	4		6	8			9	12			5		7	10*		11				33
1	2	3	4		6	8			9		11		5		7	10						34
1	2	3	4		6	8			9				5		7	11		10				35
1	2	3	4		6*	8			9	12		11	5		7			10				36
1	2	3	4		6	8			9			11	5		7	12		10*				37
1	2		4		6	8			9			11	5		7	10*			12	3		38
1	2	3	4		6	8			9			11	5		7			10*	12			39
1	2	6	4			8			9			11	5		7					3	10	40
1	2	3	4		6				9		11	8	5		7	10						41
1	2	3	4		6	8			9	10		11	5		7							42
42	31	40	39	20	40	41	22	18	42	22	14	16	27	3	21	13	1	7		2	1	
					1			2		5	5	1		1		2			2			
			2	1		7	4	7	18	4	1	2	1		5	2		2				

Jackson J	Sewell	Presland	Payne	Stephenson	Bannister	Kember	Byrne	White	Woodruff	Jackson C	Long	Light	McCormick	Dyson	Lazarus	Tomkins	Dawkins J	Vansittart	Hoadley	Oliver	Cook	
1		3	4	5	6	8	10	9	11*		2	7					12					3
1		3	4*	5	6	8	9				2	10			7	11	12					R
2		2	2	2	2	2	2	1	1		2	2			1	1						
																	2					
							1	1														

Jackson J	Sewell	Presland	Payne	Stephenson	Bannister	Kember	Byrne	White	Woodruff	Jackson C	Long	Light	McCormick	Dyson	Lazarus	Tomkins	Dawkins J	Vansittart	Hoadley	Oliver	Cook	
1	2	3	4		6	8	9		10	11	7*	12	5									2
1	1	1	1		1	1	1		1	1	1		1									
												1										

1968-69

Manager: Bert Head

1	Aug	10	(a)	Cardiff C	W 4-0	Payne, C.Jackson 2, Blyth	16,359
2		14	(h)	Huddersfield T	W 2-1	Lazarus 2	16,620
3		17	(h)	Birmingham C	W 3-2	C.Jackson 2, Payne	17,679
4		20	(a)	Middlesbrough	L 0-4		21,622
5		24	(a)	Bury	L 1-2	Blyth	7,811
6		28	(h)	Norwich C	W 2-0	C.Taylor, Woodruff	12,857
7		31	(h)	Charlton A	D 3-3	C.Taylor, Blyth, C.Jackson	22,991
8	Sep	7	(h)	Carlisle U	W 5-0	C.Taylor 2, Kember 2, Lazarus	15,170
9		13	(a)	Fulham	L 0-1		23,132
10		21	(h)	Preston NE	L 1-2	C.Jackson	13,577
11		28	(a)	Portsmouth	D 3-3	C.Jackson, Kember, Woodruff	18,998
12	Oct	5	(h)	Sheffield U	D 1-1	Woodruff	16,978
13		9	(a)	Norwich C	W 1-0	Lazarus	18,993
14		12	(a)	Aston Villa	D 1-1	Bannister	15,887
15		19	(h)	Bristol C	W 2-1	Lazarus, Woodruff	15,033
16		26	(a)	Blackpool	L 0-3		15,224
17	Nov	2	(h)	Bolton W	W 2-1	C.Jackson, Payne	13,027
18		9	(a)	Oxford U	W 2-0	Kember, Woodruff	10,444
19		16	(h)	Blackburn R	W 1-0	C.Jackson	13,505
20		23	(a)	Millwall	W 2-0	Woodruff, Lazarus	27,913
21		30	(h)	Derby C	L 1-2	McCormick	20,751
22	Dec	7	(a)	Hull C	L 0-2		13,785
23		14	(h)	Aston Villa	W 4-2	C.Taylor 2, Hoy, A.Taylor	11,071
24		26	(a)	Sheffield U	D 1-1	C.Jackson	21,682
25	Jan	11	(a)	Bolton W	D 2-2	Lazarus, Dawkins	9,082
26		25	(h)	Blackpool	L 1-2	Kember	17,003
27	Feb	22	(h)	Hull C	W 2-0	Lazarus, McCormick	14,172
28		25	(a)	Bristol C	D 1-1	Woodruff	14,695
29	Mar	1	(h)	Cardiff C	W 3-1	A.Taylor, Hoy, C.Taylor	19,663
30		5	(a)	Derby C	W 1-0	Woodruff	31,748
31		8	(a)	Birmingham C	W 1-0	Kember	25,298
32		15	(h)	Bury	W 1-0	Woodruff	19,439
33		19	(h)	Millwall	W 4-2	Woodruff 2, C.Taylor, McCormick	32,516
34		22	(a)	Charlton A	D 1-1	Hoy	32,768
35		26	(h)	Oxford U	D 1-1	C.Jackson	20,158
36		29	(a)	Carlisle U	W 2-1	Lazarus, Marsland (og)	8,172
37	Apr	4	(h)	Middlesbrough	D 0-0		43,381
38		5	(h)	Portsmouth	W 3-1	Sewell (pen), Kember, C.Jackson	24,830
39		8	(a)	Huddersfield T	D 0-0		12,113
40		12	(a)	Preston NE	D 0-0		10,245
41		19	(h)	Fulham	W 3-2	Lazarus, C.Jackson, Kember	36,126
42		28	(a)	Blackburn R	W 2-1	C.Jackson, Lazarus	4,777

FINAL LEAGUE POSITION: 2nd in Division Two

Appearances
Sub Appearances
Goals

FA Cup

3	Jan	4	(a)	Charlton A	D 0-0		32,334
R		8	(h)	Charlton A	L 0-2		39,404

Appearances
Sub Appearances
Goals

League Cup

2	Sep	4	(h)	Preston NE	W 3-1	C.Jackson 2, Payne	12,574
3		24	(a)	Orient	W 1-0	C.Taylor	13,617
4	Oct	16	(h)	Leeds U	W 2-1	C.Jackson, C.Taylor	26,217
5		30	(a)	Burnley	L 0-2		17,895

Appearances
Sub Appearances
Goals

Jackson	Sewell	Presland	Payne	McCormick	Bannister	Lazarus	Kember	Jackson C	Blyth	Taylor C	Woodruff	Hoadley	Long	Dawkins	Hoy	Loughlan	Taylor T	Snowdon	
1	2	3	4	5	6	7	8	9	10	11									1
1	2	3	4	5	6	7	8	9	10	11									2
1	2	3	4	5	6	7	8	9	10	11									3
1	2	3	4	5	6	7	8	9	10	11									4
1	2	3	4	5	6	7	8	9	10		11								5
1	2		4	5	3	7	8	9	6	11	10								6
1	2		4	5	3	7	8	9	6	11	10								7
1	2		4	5	3	7	8	9	6	11	10								8
1	2		4	5	3	7	8	9	6		10	11							9
1	2		4	5	3	7	8	9	10	11			6						10
1			4	5	3		8	9	6	11	10		2	7					11
1			4	5	12		8*	9	6	11	10			7	2	3			12
1			4*	5	12	7	8	9	6	11	10				2	3			13
1				5	4	7	8	9	6	11	10				2	3			14
1	12			5	4	7	8	9	6*	11	10				2	3			15
1			4	5		7	8	9	6	11	10				2	3			16
1	2		4	5		7	8	9		11	10				6	3			17
1	2		4	5		7	8	9			10				6	3	11		18
1	2		4	5		7	8	9			10				6	3	11		19
1	2		4*	5		7	8	9	12		10				6	3	11		20
1	2			5		7	8	9	6		10				4	3	11		21
1	2			5		7*	8	9	6	12	10				4	3	11		22
1	2			5			8	9	6	11	10				4	3	7		23
1			2	5		7	8	9	6	11	10					3	4		24
1	2		4	5		7	8	9	6					10		3	11		25
1	2		4	5		7	8	9			10				6	3	11		26
1	2		4	5		7	8	9		11					6	3	10		27
1	2			5		7	8		6	12	9			10*	4	3	11		28
1	2			5		7	8		6	11	9				4	3	10		29
1	2			5		7	8		6	11	9				4	3	10		30
1	2			5		7	8		6	11	9				4	3	10		31
1	2			5		7	8		6	11	9				4	3	10		32
1	2			5		7	8		6	11	9				4	3	10		33
1	2			5		7	8		6	11	9				4*	3	10	12	34
1	2		3	5		7	8	4	6	11	9*						10	12	35
1	2		4	5		7	8	9	6	11							10	3	36
1	2		4	5		7	8	9		11					6	3	10		37
1	2		4	5		7	8	9		11					6	3	10*	12	38
1	2		4	5		7	8	9		11					6	3	10		39
1	2		4	5		7	8	9		11					6	3	10		40
1	2		4	5		7	8	9		11					6	3	10		41
1	2		4	5		7	8	9	6	11*						3	10	12	42
42	35	5	30	42	13	38	42	34	31	32	30	1	2	4	26	29	25	1	
	1				2				1	2								4	
	1		3	3	1	11	8	14	3	8	11			1	3		2		

1 own-goal

Jackson	Sewell	Presland	Payne	McCormick	Bannister	Lazarus	Kember	Jackson C	Blyth	Taylor C	Woodruff	Hoadley	Long	Dawkins	Hoy	Loughlan	Taylor T	Snowdon	
1	2		4	5		7	8	9		11	10				6	3			3
1	2		4	5		7*	8	9	6	11	10					3	12		R
2	2		2	2		2	2	2	1	2	2				1	2			
																	1		

Jackson	Sewell	Presland	Payne	McCormick	Bannister	Lazarus	Kember	Jackson C	Blyth	Taylor C	Woodruff	Hoadley	Long	Dawkins	Hoy	Loughlan	Taylor T	Snowdon	
1	2		4	5	3	7	8	9	6	11	10								2
1	2		4	5	3		8	9	6	11	10			7					3
1				5	4	7	8	9	6	11	10				2	3			4
1	2		4	5		7	8	9*	6	11	12				10	3			5
4	3		3	4	3	3	4	4	4	4	3			1	2	2			
											1								
			1					3		2									

1969-70

Manager: Bert Head

1	Aug	9	(h)	Manchester U	D 2-2	Blyth, Queen	‡ 48,610
2		13	(h)	Sunderland	W 2-0	Taylor, Queen	28,897
3		16	(a)	Everton	L 1-2	Blyth	50,700
4		20	(a)	Sunderland	D 0-0		16,192
5		23	(h)	Tottenham H	L 0-2		39,494
6		27	(h)	Liverpool	L 1-3	Sewell	36,639
7		30	(a)	Chelsea	D 1-1	Hoy	41,908
8	Sep	6	(h)	Stoke C	W 3-1	Bartram, Lazarus, Woodruff	26,745
9		13	(a)	Coventry C	D 2-2	Queen 2	29,314
10		20	(h)	West Brom A	L 1-3	C.Jackson	27,682
11		27	(a)	Nottingham F	D 0-0		23,250
12	Oct	4	(h)	Newcastle U	L 0-3		28,407
13		8	(h)	Everton	D 0-0		33,967
14		11	(a)	Burnley	L 2-4	Kember, Queen	12,640
15		18	(h)	Leeds U	D 1-1	Queen	31,910
16		25	(a)	Sheffield W	D 0-0		19,162
17	Nov	1	(h)	Arsenal	L 1-5	Bartram	34,903
18		8	(a)	West Ham U	L 1-2	Bonds (og)	31,515
19		15	(a)	Ipswich T	L 0-2		18,041
20		22	(h)	Wolves	W 2-1	Dawkins 2	23,585
21		29	(a)	Southampton	D 1-1	Kember	19,876
22	Dec	6	(h)	Derby C	L 0-1		20,833
23		13	(h)	Coventry C	L 0-3		16,763
24		20	(a)	Stoke C	L 0-1		12,426
25		26	(a)	Tottenham H	L 0-2		32,845
26		27	(h)	Chelsea	L 1-5	Queen	‡ 49,498
27	Jan	10	(a)	West Brom A	L 2-3	Queen, C.Jackson	20,907
28		17	(h)	Nottingham F	D 1-1	Payne	22,531
29		31	(a)	Newcastle U	D 0-0		35,440
30	Feb	11	(h)	Burnley	L 1-2	Queen	20,857
31		14	(a)	Manchester U	D 1-1	Sewell (pen)	55,262
32		21	(h)	Sheffield W	L 0-2		25,723
33		28	(a)	Leeds U	L 0-2		37,138
34	Mar	11	(a)	Manchester C	W 1-0	Queen	25,381
35		14	(h)	Southampton	W 2-0	C.Jackson, Hoy	20,867
36		18	(a)	Wolves	D 1-1	Kember	20,594
37		21	(a)	Derby C	L 1-3	C.Jackson	30,192
38		24	(h)	West Ham U	D 0-0		34,801
39		28	(h)	Ipswich T	D 1-1	McCormick	27,499
40		30	(a)	Arsenal	L 0-2		34,244
41	Apr	3	(a)	Liverpool	L 0-3		30,999
42		6	(h)	Manchester C	W 1-0	Hoy	27,704

FINAL LEAGUE POSITION: 20th in Division One

‡ Ground attendance record (broken twice).

Appearances
Sub Appearances
Goals

FA Cup

3	Jan	3	(h)	Walsall	W 2-0	Gregg (og), Blyth	17,015
4		24	(a)	Tottenham H	D 0-0		43,949
R		28	(h)	Tottenham H	W 1-0	Queen	45,980
5	Feb	7	(h)	Chelsea	L 1-4	Hoy	48,479

Appearances
Sub Appearances
Goals

League Cup

2	Sep	3	(h)	Cardiff C	W 3-1	Sewell 2 (2 pens), Bartram	18,616
3		24	(h)	Blackpool	D 2-2	James (og), Queen	17,990
R		30	(a)	Blackpool	W 1-0	Hoadley	13,973
4	Oct	14	(h)	Derby C	D 1-1	C.Jackson	30,539
R		29	(a)	Derby C	L 0-3		33,059

Appearances
Sub Appearances
Goals

Jackson J	Sewell	Loughlan	Hoy	McCormick	Hynd	Lazarus	Kember	Jackson C	Queen	Blyth	Taylor T	Woodruff	Bartram	Hoadley	Payne	Oliver	Dawkins	Tomkins	Vansittart	Pinkney	Thorup	Tambling	Scott	
1	2	3	4	5	6	7*	8	9	10	11	12													1
1	2	3	4	5	6		8	9	10*	11	7	12												2
1	2	3	4	5	6		8	9	10*	11	7	12												3
1	2	3	4	5	6		8	9*		11	7	10	12											4
1	2	3	4	5	6		8			11	7	10*	9	12										5
1	2	3	4	5	6		8			11	7	10	9											6
1	2	3*	4	5	6		8			11	7	10	9	12										7
1	2		4	5		7	8		12	6	11	10*	9	3										8
1	2	3	4	5	6	7*	8	9	10		11			12										9
1	2	3		5	6	7	8	9	10	4*	11			12										10
1	2	3	4	5			7	9	10	6	12		8*	11										11
1	2	3	4	5	6		8	9	10	11				7										12
1	2*	3	4	5	6		7	9	10	12	11		8											13
1		3		5	6		7	9	10		11	8		2	4									14
1		3		5	6		7	9*	10		11	8	12	4	2									15
1		2	10	5	6		7		9		11				4	3	8							16
1		2		5	6		7		10		8	9	11	3	4									17
1		2	9	5	6		7		10	3	8				4		11							18
1	2			5	3		7	10	9	6		8			4		11							19
1	2		8	5	6		7		9					3	4		10	11						20
1	2		8	5	6		7		9					3	4		10	11						21
1	2	3		5	6		7		9					8	4		10	11						22
1	2			5	6		8		10	11			9*	3	4		7		12					23
1	2		10*	5	6		7		8	12				3	4			11	9					24
1	2			5	6		8		10	4				3			7	9*	11	12				25
1	2	3		5	6				10	8				4*			7		11	9	12			26
1	2	3		5	6			9	10	11	7				4							8		27
1	2	3	8	5	6			9	10		11				4							7		28
1	2	3	8		9*			12	10	6	7			5	4							11		29
1	2	3	8	5	9				10	6	11				4								7	30
1	2	3		5	12			9	10	6	11			8	4								7*	31
1	2	3		5			8*	9	10	6	11			12	4								7	32
1	2	3		5	6			9	10	8	11				4								7	33
1	2		8	5			7		10	6	11			3	4								9	34
1	2		7	5			8	9	10	6	11			3	4									35
1	2		9	5			8		10	6	11			3	4								7	36
1	2		9	5			8	11	10	6				3	4								7	37
1	2		9	5			8		10	6	11			3	4								7	38
1	2		10	5			8		9	6	11			3	4								7	39
1	2		9	5			8		10	6	11			3	4								7	40
1	2			5			8		9	6	11			3	4		10						7	41
1	2		9	5			8	11	10	6	7			3	4									42
42	37	26	28	41	29	4	35	20	37	31	30	9	8	24	27	1	10	5	3	1		3	11	
					1			1	1	2	2	2	2	5					1	1	1			
	2		3	1		1	3	5	9	2	1	1	2		1		2							

1 own-goal

Jackson J	Sewell	Loughlan	Hoy	McCormick	Hynd	Lazarus	Kember	Jackson C	Queen	Blyth	Taylor T	Woodruff	Bartram	Hoadley	Payne	Oliver	Dawkins	Tomkins	Vansittart	Pinkney	Thorup	Tambling	Scott	
1	2	3		5	6				10	12				8	4		9*		11	7				3
1	2	3	8*	5	9			11	10	6	7			12	4									4
1	2	3	8	5*	9			11	10	6	7			12	4									R
1	2	3	11	5	9				10	6	7			8	4									5
4	4	4	3	4	4			2	4	3	3			2	4		1		1	1				
										1				2										
			1						1	1														

1 own-goal

Jackson J	Sewell	Loughlan	Hoy	McCormick	Hynd	Lazarus	Kember	Jackson C	Queen	Blyth	Taylor T	Woodruff	Bartram	Hoadley	Payne	Oliver	Dawkins	Tomkins	Vansittart	Pinkney	Thorup	Tambling	Scott	
1	2		4	5	6		8			11	7	10	9	3										2
1	2	3		5		11	7	9*	10	6		8	12	4										3
1	2	3	4	5	6		7	9	10	11	12			8*										R
1		3		5	6		7	9	10		11	8		4	2									4
1		2		5	6		7	12	10		8	9*		3	4		11							R
5	3	4	2	5	4	1	5	3	4	3	3	4	1	5	2		1							
								1			1		1											
	2							1	1				1	1										

1 own-goal

1970-71

Manager: Bert Head

No	Month	Day	Venue	Opponent	Result	Scorers	Attendance
1	Aug	15	(a)	West Brom A	D 0-0		24,766
2		19	(h)	Manchester C	L 0-1		35,118
3		22	(h)	Newcastle U	W 1-0	Birchenall	27,287
4		25	(a)	Liverpool	D 1-1	Queen	47,612
5		29	(a)	Stoke C	D 0-0		13,469
6	Sep	2	(h)	Blackpool	W 1-0	Queen	26,296
7		5	(h)	Nottingham F	W 2-0	Scott, Queen	26,510
8		12	(a)	Huddersfield T	W 2-0	Kember, Queen	18,820
9		19	(h)	Tottenham H	L 0-3		41,308
10		26	(a)	Everton	L 1-3	Scott	43,463
11	Oct	3	(h)	Southampton	W 3-1	Queen 2, Birchenall	26,663
12		10	(a)	Manchester U	W 1-0	Tambling	42,979
13		17	(h)	West Brom A	W 3-0	Tambling 2, Birchenall	28,330
14		24	(h)	West Ham U	D 1-1	Taylor	41,486
15		31	(a)	Burnley	L 1-2	Taylor	12,848
16	Nov	7	(h)	Leeds U	D 1-1	Sewell	37,963
17		14	(a)	Arsenal	D 1-1	Birchenall	34,503
18		21	(a)	Coventry C	L 1-2	Kember	23,054
19		29	(h)	Wolves	D 1-1	Scott	22,605
20	Dec	5	(a)	Ipswich T	W 2-1	Sewell (pen), Kember	19,344
21		12	(h)	Derby C	D 0-0		24,418
22		19	(a)	Newcastle U	L 0-2		21,740
23	Jan	9	(a)	Manchester C	L 0-1		27,240
24		13	(h)	Chelsea	D 0-0		40,489
25		16	(h)	Liverpool	W 1-0	Queen	28,253
26		30	(a)	Wolves	L 1-2	Birchenall	20,233
27	Feb	6	(h)	Ipswich T	W 1-0	Wall	23,482
28		17	(a)	Derby C	L 0-1		25,521
29		20	(h)	Coventry C	L 1-2	Birchenall	24,114
30		27	(h)	Burnley	L 0-2		20,436
31	Mar	6	(a)	West Ham U	D 0-0		26,157
32		13	(h)	Arsenal	L 0-2		35,022
33		20	(a)	Leeds U	L 1-2	Birchenall	31,871
34		24	(h)	Huddersfield T	L 0-3		16,646
35		27	(a)	Nottingham F	L 1-3	Birchenall	16,507
36	Apr	3	(h)	Stoke C	W 3-2	Kember, Birchenall, Wharton	16,963
37		10	(a)	Chelsea	D 1-1	Scott	38,953
38		17	(h)	Manchester U	L 3-5	Birchenall, Tambling, Queen	39,145
39		24	(a)	Tottenham H	L 0-2		28,619
40		26	(a)	Blackpool	L 1-3	Queen	8,905
41	May	1	(h)	Everton	W 2-0	Hoadley, Kember	21,590
42		4	(a)	Southampton	L 0-6		15,980

FINAL LEAGUE POSITION: 18th in Division One

Appearances
Sub Appearances
Goals

FA Cup

Round	Month	Day	Venue	Opponent	Result	Scorers	Attendance
3	Jan	2	(h)	Chelsea	D 2-2	McCormick, Birchenall	42,123
R		6	(a)	Chelsea	L 0-2		55,074

Appearances
Sub Appearances
Goals

League Cup

Round	Month	Day	Venue	Opponent	Result	Scorers	Attendance
2	Sep	9	(h)	Rochdale	D 3-3	Birchenall, Jenkins (og), Payne	16,265
R		14	(a)	Rochdale	W 3-1	Queen, Scott, Taylor	8,911
3	Oct	7	(h)	Lincoln C	W 4-0	Blyth 2, Tambling, Birchenall	16,988
4		28	(h)	Arsenal	D 0-0		40,451
R	Nov	9	(a)	Arsenal	W 2-0	Queen, Tambling (pen)	45,026
5		18	(a)	Manchester U	L 2-4	Queen, Taylor	43,241

Appearances
Sub Appearances
Goals

Jackson	Sewell	Wall	Payne	McCormick	Blyth	Scott	Kember	Queen	Birchenall	Tambling	Taylor A	Hoadley	Humphries	Proven	Dawkins	Loughlan	Wharton	Pinkney	
1	2	3	4	5	6	7	8	9	10	11									1
1	2	3	4	5	6	7	8	9	10	11									2
1	2	3	4	5	6		8	9	10	11	7								3
1	2	3		5	6		8	9	10	11	7*	4	12						4
1	2	3		5	6		8*	9	10	11	7	4	12						5
1	2	3	8	5	6	11*		9	10		7	4	12						6
1	2	3	4	5	6	11	8	9*	10		7		12						7
1	2	3	4	5	6	11	8*	9			7			10	12				8
1	2	3	4	5	6	11	8	9		7	12	10*							9
1	2	3	4	5	6	11	8	9		10	7								10
1	2	3	4	5	6		8	9	10	11	7								11
1	2	3	4	5	6		8	9	10	11	7								12
1	2	3	4	5	6		8		10	11	7	9							13
1	2	3	4	5	6		8	9*	10	11	7	12							14
1	2	3	4	5	6		8		10	11	7	9							15
1	2	3	4	5	6	8		9	10	11	7								16
1		3	4	5	6	11	8	9	10		7	2							17
1		3	4	5		11	8			9*	7	10	12		6	2			18
1		3	4	5	6	11	8	9			7	10				2			19
1	2	3	4	5	6	11	8	9	10		7								20
1	2	3	4*	5	6	11	8		10		7	9	12						21
1	2			5	6	11	8		10		7	3	9		4				22
1	2	3			6		8	9	10		7	5	11		4				23
1	2	3			6		8	9	10		7	5	11		4				24
1	2	3			6		8	9	10		7	5	11		4				25
1	2	3			6		8	9	10		7	5			4		11		26
1	2	3	8		6		10		9		11	5			4		7		27
1	2	3	11		6		8	9	10			5			4		7		28
1	2	3	11		6	12	8	9*	10			5			4		7		29
1	2	3	4		6		8	9	10		11	5					7		30
1	2		4	3	6	12		9*	10	8	11	5					7		31
1	2	3	11	5	6	7*	8		9	10		4	12						32
1		3	2	5	6	12	8		9	10	11	4					7*		33
1		3	2	5	6		8		9	10	11	4					7		34
1		3	2	5	6	7	8		9	10	11	4							35
1	12	3	2*	5		11	8		10	9	6	4					7		36
1	2	3		5*		8	6	12	9	10	11	4					7		37
1		3	2	5		11	8	12	10	9	6	4					7*		38
1		3	2*	5	6	12	8	10	9	7	11	4							39
1	2	3			5	7	6	10	9	8*	11	4					12		40
1		3		5	6	12	4	10	9*	8	11	2					7		41
1	12	3			6	9	4	10		8	11	5*				2	7		42
42	31	40	31	32	38	21	39	29	36	26	36	31	4	1	9	3	13		
	2					5		2			1	1	7		1		1		
	2	1				4	5	9	10	4	2	1					1		

Jackson	Sewell	Wall	Payne	McCormick	Blyth	Scott	Kember	Queen	Birchenall	Tambling	Taylor A	Hoadley	Humphries	Proven	Dawkins	Loughlan	Wharton	Pinkney	
1	2	3	4*	5	6	11	8	9	10		7	12							3
1	2	3		5	6	11	8	9	10		7	12			4*				R
2	2	2	1	2	2	2	2	2	2		2				1				
												2							
				1					1										

Jackson	Sewell	Wall	Payne	McCormick	Blyth	Scott	Kember	Queen	Birchenall	Tambling	Taylor A	Hoadley	Humphries	Proven	Dawkins	Loughlan	Wharton	Pinkney	
1	2	3	4	5	6	11		9	10*		7		8					12	2
1	2	3	4	5	6	11		9			7			10	8				R
1	2	3	4	5	6		8	9	10	11	7								3
1	2	3	4	5	6		8		10	11	7	9							4
1	2*	3	4	5		8		9	10	11	7	6				12			R
1		3	4	5	6	11	8	9	10*		7	2				12			5
6	5	6	6	6	5	4	3	5	5	3	6	3	1	1	1				
																2		1	
			1		2	1		3	2	2	2								

1 own-goal

1971-72

Manager: Bert Head

1	Aug	14	(h)	Newcastle U	W 2-0	Tambling, Taylor	25,281
2		18	(a)	Manchester C	L 0-4		27,103
3		20	(a)	Stoke C	L 1-3	Tambling	18,958
4		24	(h)	Liverpool	L 0-1		28,488
5		28	(h)	Nottingham F	D 1-1	Birchenall	17,699
6		31	(a)	Wolves	L 0-1		24,774
7	Sep	4	(a†)	Leeds U	L 0-2		18,715
8		11	(h)	Manchester U	L 1-3	Blyth	44,020
9		18	(a)	Tottenham H	L 0-3		37,239
10		25	(h)	Everton	W 2-1	Jenkins, Scott	25,594
11	Oct	2	(a)	Leicester C	D 0-0		28,493
12		9	(h)	West Brom A	L 0-2		22,399
13		16	(a)	Newcastle U	W 2-1	Tambling 2	20,510
14		22	(a)	Coventry C	D 1-1	Tambling	20,801
15		30	(h)	West Ham U	L 0-3		41,540
16	Nov	6	(a)	Derby C	L 0-3		30,380
17		13	(h)	Ipswich T	D 1-1	Wallace	18,462
18		20	(h)	Chelsea	L 2-3	Hughes, Queen	34,657
19		27	(a)	Arsenal	L 1-2	Craven	32,461
20	Dec	4	(h)	Sheffield U	W 5-1	Taylor, Hughes 2, Queen, McCormick	20,176
21		11	(a)	Huddersfield T	W 1-0	Tambling	11,692
22		18	(h)	Leeds U	D 1-1	Craven	31,456
23		27	(a)	Southampton	L 0-1		28,310
24	Jan	1	(h)	Tottenham H	D 1-1	Queen	35,841
25		8	(a)	Nottingham F	W 1-0	Wallace	19,033
26		22	(h)	Manchester C	L 1-2	Tambling	31,480
27		29	(a)	Liverpool	L 1-4	Wall	39,538
28	Feb	12	(h)	Coventry C	D 2-2	Craven, Queen	19,339
29		19	(a)	West Ham U	D 1-1	Payne	28,209
30	Mar	4	(a)	Ipswich T	W 2-0	Wallace, Tambling	17,222
31		11	(a)	West Brom A	D 1-1	Craven	17,217
32		18	(h)	Wolves	L 0-2		24,823
33		21	(a)	Everton	D 0-0		27,929
34		25	(a)	Manchester U	L 0-4		41,550
35		28	(h)	Derby C	L 0-1		21,158
36	Apr	1	(h)	Southampton	L 2-3	Craven, Kellard (pen)	23,776
37		3	(h)	Leicester C	D 1-1	Craven	23,736
38		8	(a)	Chelsea	L 1-2	Blyth	34,105
39		11	(h)	Arsenal	D 2-2	Kellard (pen), Craven	34,384
40		22	(a)	Sheffield U	L 0-1		23,250
41		26	(h)	Stoke C	W 2-0	Kellard (pen), Queen	24,550
42		29	(h)	Huddersfield T	D 0-0		18,120

FINAL LEAGUE POSITION: 20th in Division One

†Played at Leeds Road, Huddersfield. Leeds forced to play their first four home games on neutral grounds because of crowd trouble during 1970-71.

Appearances
Sub Appearances
Goals

FA Cup

3	Jan	15	(h)	Everton	D 2-2	Wallace 2	32,331
R		18	(a)	Everton	L 2-3	Tambling 2	45,408

Appearances
Sub Appearances
Goals

League Cup

2	Sep	7	(h)	Luton T	W 2-0	Queen, Taylor	13,838
3	Oct	5	(h)	Aston Villa	D 2-2	Craven, Tambling (pen)	21,179
R		13	(a)	Aston Villa	L 0-2		24,978

Appearances
Sub Appearances
Goals

Jackson	Payne	Wall	Kember	McCormick	Blyth	Wharton	Tambling	Birchenall	Queen	Taylor T	Hoadley	Scott	Loughlan	Jenkins	Bell	Kellard	Craven	Goodwin	Pinkney	Hughes	Wallace	Goldthorpe	
1	2	3	4	5	6	7	8	9*	10	11	12												1
1	2	3	4	5	6	7*	8		10	11	12	9											2
1	2	3	4	5	6	7	8*		10	11	12	9											3
1	2	3	4		6		8	9	10	11	5	7											4
1	2	3	8	5	6	7	10	9		11	4												5
1	2	3	4	5	6	10	8	9*	12	11	7												6
1	2	3	10	4	6	7*	8		9	11	5	12											7
1	4	3	8	5*	6		10			11	2	7	12	9									8
1	4	3	8	5	6		10*	11	7		2		12	9									9
1	4	3		5	6				10	11		12		9*	2	7	8						10
1	2	3		5	8				9	11					6	10	7	4					11
1	2	3		5	8				9	11					6	10	4	7					12
1	2	3			5		8*			11				9	6	7	4	10	12				13
1	2			5	4		7			3						10	9	8	6	11*	12		14
1	2	3		5	6		7			11						10	8	4		9*	12		15
1	2	5			4		7			11					3		8	6		9	10		16
1	2				6		7		8	3					5	10	4			9	11		17
1	2	3		5	6				8	10						4*	7	12		11	9		18
1	2	3		5	6				8	10						4	7			11	9		19
1	2	3		5	6				8	10						4	7			11	9		20
1	2	3		5	6		11*		8	10						4	7	12			9		21
1	2			5	6		11		8	10						4	7	3			9		22
1	2	3		5	6				8	10						4	7	12		11*	9		23
1		3		5	6		11		8	10						4	7	2			9		24
1	2	3		5	6		11		8	10						4	7				9		25
1	2	3		5	6		8			10						4	7*	12		11	9		26
1	2	3		5	6		10		8	11						4	7				9		27
1	2	3		5*	6		11		8	10						4	7	12			9		28
1	2			5	6		11		8	10						4	7	3			9		29
1	2			5	6		11		8	10						4	7	3			9		30
1	2	12		5*	6		11		8	10						4	7	3			9		31
1	2				6		11		8	10						4	7	3			9	5	32
1	2	12			6		11		8	10					5	4	7*	3			9		33
1	2	12			6*		11		8	10					5	4	7	3			9		34
1	2	12		5			11*		8	10					6	4	7	3			9		35
1	2	11		5	6				8	10					3	4	7				9		36
1	2	3		5	6				8	10						4	7	12		11*	9		37
1	2	3		5	6		11			10						4	7	8			9		38
1	2	3		5	6		11			10						8	7	4			9		39
1	2	3		5	6		11		12	10						4	7	8*			9		40
1	2	3		5	6		11		8	10						4	7				9		41
1	2	3		5	6		11		8	10						4*	7	12			9		42
42	41	32	9	35	41	6	33	5	31	41	6	4		4	10	32	33	18	1	10	27	1	
		4							2		3	2	2					7	1		2		
	1	1		1	2		8	1	5	2		1		1		3	7			3	3		

Jackson	Payne	Wall	Kember	McCormick	Blyth	Wharton	Tambling	Birchenall	Queen	Taylor T	Hoadley	Scott	Loughlan	Jenkins	Bell	Kellard	Craven	Goodwin	Pinkney	Hughes	Wallace	Goldthorpe	
1	2	3		5	6				8	10						4	7			11	9		3
1	2	3		5	6		11			10						4	7			8	9		R
2	2	2		2	2		1		1	2						2	2			2	2		
							2														2		

Jackson	Payne	Wall	Kember	McCormick	Blyth	Wharton	Tambling	Birchenall	Queen	Taylor T	Hoadley	Scott	Loughlan	Jenkins	Bell	Kellard	Craven	Goodwin	Pinkney	Hughes	Wallace	Goldthorpe	
1	4	3	8	5	6		10		9	11	2	7											2
1	2	3		5	6		9		10	11							8	4	7				3
1	2	3		5	6		9			11				10			8	4	7				R
3	3	3	1	3	3		3		2	3	1	1		1			2	2	2				
							1		1	1							1						

1972-73

Manager: Bert Head until 30 March 1973, then Malcolm Allison.

1	Aug	12	(a)	Stoke C	L 0-2		22,564
2		15	(h)	Derby C	D 0-0		25,105
3		19	(h)	Liverpool	D 1-1	Taylor	30,054
4		22	(a)	Everton	D 1-1	Jenkins	38,429
5		26	(a)	Birmingham C	D 1-1	Queen	31,066
6		29	(h)	Manchester C	W 1-0	Barrett (og)	24,731
7	Sep	2	(h)	Newcastle U	W 2-1	Kellard (pen), Wallace	21,749
8		9	(a)	Tottenham H	L 1-2	Knowles (og)	28,545
9		16	(h)	West Brom A	L 0-2		17,858
10		23	(a)	Southampton	L 0-2		15,469
11		30	(h)	Norwich C	L 0-2		21,255
12	Oct	7	(h)	Coventry C	L 0-1		22,229
13		14	(a)	Wolves	D 1-1	Hinshelwood	20,630
14		21	(h)	Arsenal	L 2-3	Craven 2	35,865
15		28	(a)	West Ham U	L 0-4		28,894
16	Nov	4	(h)	Everton	W 1-0	Rogers	28,614
17		11	(a)	Derby C	D 2-2	Rogers, Craven (pen)	26,716
18		18	(h)	Leeds U	D 2-2	Craven 2	38,167
19		25	(a)	Chelsea	D 0-0		36,608
20	Dec	9	(a)	Ipswich T	L 1-2	Hughes	18,077
21		16	(h)	Manchester U	W 5-0	Mulligan 2, Rogers 2, Whittle	39,484
22		23	(a)	Leicester C	L 1-2	Rogers	16,962
23		26	(h)	Southampton	W 3-0	Craven, Rogers 2	30,935
24		30	(a)	Liverpool	L 0-1		50,862
25	Jan	20	(a)	Newcastle U	L 0-2		24,660
26		27	(h)	Tottenham H	D 0-0		44,531
27	Feb	10	(a)	West Brom A	W 4-0	Whittle 2, Possee 2	14,829
28		17	(h)	Stoke C	W 3-2	Possee, Whittle, Rogers	32,099
29	Mar	2	(a)	Coventry C	L 0-2		24,902
30		6	(h)	Birmingham C	D 0-0		26,014
31		10	(h)	Wolves	D 1-1	Rogers	30,967
32		13	(h)	Sheffield U	L 0-1		23,976
33		24	(h)	West Ham U	L 1-3	Possee	36,915
34		26	(a)	Arsenal	L 0-1		41,879
35		31	(h)	Chelsea	W 2-0	Phillip, Cannon	39,325
36	Apr	7	(a)	Sheffield U	L 0-2		21,398
37		11	(a)	Manchester U	L 0-2		46,895
38		14	(h)	Ipswich T	D 1-1	Rogers (pen) 2, Possee 2	14,829
39		20	(h)	Leicester C	L 0-1		36,817
40		21	(a)	Leeds U	L 0-4		31,173
41		24	(a)	Norwich C	L 1-2	Rogers (pen)	36,922
42		28	(a)	Manchester C	W 3-2	Rogers 2 (1 pen), Craven	34,784

FINAL LEAGUE POSITION: 21st in Division One

Appearances
Sub Appearances
Goals

FA Cup

3	Jan	13	(h)	Southampton	W 2-0	Rogers, Cooke	31,604
4	Feb	3	(a)	Sheffield W	D 1-1	Craven	35,156
R		6	(h)	Sheffield W	D 1-1*	Phillip	44,071
2R		19	(n†)	Sheffield W	L 2-3*	Payne, Rogers	19,150

*After extra-time. †Played at Villa Park, Birmingham.

Appearances
Sub Appearances
Goals

League Cup

1				Bye			
2	Sep	8	(h)	Stockport C	L 0-1		11,463

Appearances
Sub Appearances
Goals

Jackson	Payne	Wall	Pinkney	McCormick	Blyth	Craven	Wallace	Jenkins	Kellard	Taylor T	Queen	Roffey	Tambling	Hinshelwood M	Philip	Hughes	Mulligan	Cooke	Hammond	Bell	Rogers	Whittle	Possee	Cannon	
1	2	3	4	5	6	7	8	9	10	11															1
1	2	3	8	5	6	7	10	9	4	11															2
1	2	3*	8	5	6	7	10	9	4	11	12														3
1	2		7	5	6	8*	9	10	4	11	12	3													4
1	2		7	5	6		9	10	4	11	8	3													5
1	2		8	5	6		10	9	4	11	7	3													6
1	2		7	5	6	12	8	9	4	11	10*	3													7
1	2		7	5	6	12	9	10	4	11		3	8*												8
1	2		7	5	6		8	9	4	11	10	3													9
1	2		7	5		8	12	9*	10	6		3	11	4											10
1	2		7	6		8		9	4			3		10	5	11									11
1	8		12	5	6	9			10	11				3*	4		2	7							12
	8		7	5	6	9				3			12	10	4		2*	11	1						13
	2		7	5	6	9				3			8	10	4			11	1						14
	2		7	5	6	9				3			11	10	4			8	1						15
1	8				6	9				3					4	7	2	10		5	11				16
1	8				6	9			12	3					4*	7	2	10		5	11				17
1	8				6	9				3					4	7	2	10		5	11				18
1	8				6	9				3					4	7	2	10		5	11				19
1	8				6	9*			12	3					4	11	2	10		5	7				20
1	8				6					3					4	7	2	10		5	11	9			21
1	8				6	12				3					4	7	2*	10		5	11	9			22
1	2		12		6	8*				3					4	7		10		5	11	9			23
1	2		7		6					3		8			4			10		5	11	9			24
1	2				6	9				3					4	7		10		5	11	8*	12		25
1	2				6	9				3					4			10		5	11	8	7		26
1	6											3		7	4		2	10		5	11	8	9		27
1					6					3				8	4		2	10		5	11	9	7		28
	2				6	12				3				8	4			10	1	5	11*	9	7		29
1	2				6	12				3				8*	4			10		5	11	9	7		30
1	2				6	8				7		3			4			10		5	11	9			31
1	2				6	9*				10		3			4			8		5	11	7	12		32
1					6					3		2		8	4			10		5	11	9	7		33
1	5				6	12				3		2		10	4			8			11	7	9*		34
1	8				5					3				10	4		2				11	9	7	6	35
1	8				5					3				10	4		2				11	9	7	6	36
1	11				5	12				3				8*	4		2	10				9	7	6	37
1	8	6			5					3		4					2	10			11	9	7		38
1	8				5	6				3		4					2	10			11	9	7		39
1	12				5					2		3		6*	10		4	8			11	9	7		40
1	8				5	9				3		4			6		2	10			11		7		41
1	8				5	9				3		2			4		6	10			11		7		42
38	39	4	15	15	39	23	9	11	12	40	4	19	4	16	30	10	19	29	4	18	26	20	15	3	
	1		2			7	1		2		2		1										2		
						7	1	1	1	1	1			1	1	1	2				13	4	4	1	

2 own-goals

Jackson	Payne	Wall	Pinkney	McCormick	Blyth	Craven	Wallace	Jenkins	Kellard	Taylor T	Queen	Roffey	Tambling	Hinshelwood M	Philip	Hughes	Mulligan	Cooke	Hammond	Bell	Rogers	Whittle	Possee	Cannon	
1	2				6	9				3					4	7		10		5	11	8			3
1	7				6	9				3					4		2	10		5	11	8			4
1	7				6	9*				3					4		2	10		5	11	8		12	R
	7				6	12				3				10*	4		2		1	5	11	8		9	2R
3	4				4	3				4				1	4	1	3	3	1	4	4	4		1	
						1																		1	
	1					1									1			1			2				

Jackson	Payne	Wall	Pinkney	McCormick	Blyth	Craven	Wallace	Jenkins	Kellard	Taylor T	Queen	Roffey	Tambling	Hinshelwood M	Philip	Hughes	Mulligan	Cooke	Hammond	Bell	Rogers	Whittle	Possee	Cannon	
1	2		7	5	6	10*	9	8	4	11	12	3													2
1	1		1	1	1	1	1	1	1	1		1													
											1														

1973-74

Manager: Malcolm Allison

1	Aug	25	(h)	Notts C	L 1-4	Rogers	20,841
2	Sep	1	(a)	West Brom A	L 0-1		18,037
3		8	(h)	Middlesbrough	L 2-3	Blyth, Cannon	17,554
4		11	(h)	Aston Villa	D 0-0		20,858
5		15	(a)	Bolton W	L 0-2		18,392
6		17	(a)	Blackpool	L 0-1		9,323
7		22	(h)	Cardiff C	D 3-3	P.Hinshelwood, Rogers 2	17,789
8		29	(a)	Sheffield W	L 0-4		12,861
9	Oct	2	(h)	Blackpool	L 1-2	Rogers	18,080
10		6	(h)	Luton T	L 1-2	Rogers	19,790
11		13	(a)	Oxford U	D 1-1	Rogers	10,161
12		20	(h)	Carlisle U	L 0-1		19,678
13		23	(a)	Aston Villa	L 1-2	Jeffries	26,670
14		27	(a)	Sunderland	D 0-0		31,935
15	Nov	3	(h)	Nottingham F	L 0-1		21,881
16		10	(a)	Bristol C	W 1-0	Whittle	15,488
17		17	(h)	Millwall	D 1-1	Whalley	30,054
18		24	(a)	Portsmouth	D 2-2	Rogers 2 (1 pen)	14,211
19	Dec	1	(h)	Swindon T	W 4-2	Rogers, Possee, Anderson, P.Taylor	17,881
20		8	(a)	Hull C	L 0-3		7,996
21		15	(a)	Preston NE	D 1-1	Whittle	9,121
22		22	(h)	Sheffield W	D 0-0		16,240
23		26	(a)	Orient	L 0-3		20,611
24		29	(a)	Middlesbrough	L 0-2		26,115
25	Jan	1	(h)	West Brom A	W 1-0	Rogers	23,338
26		12	(h)	Bolton W	D 0-0		15,804
27		20	(a)	Notts C	W 3-1	Barry, Possee 2	14,478
28	Feb	3	(h)	Preston NE	W 2-0	Possee, P.Taylor	24,575
29		17	(h)	Oxford U	W 2-0	P.Taylor 2 (1 pen)	23,169
30		23	(a)	Luton T	L 1-2	Possee	14,287
31	Mar	3	(h)	Orient	D 0-0		29,056
32		9	(h)	Sunderland	W 3-0	Rogers 2, Belfitt (og)	16,529
33		16	(a)	Carlisle U	L 0-1		6,964
34		23	(h)	Bristol C	W 3-1	Possee 2, Rogers (pen)	16,690
35		30	(a)	Nottingham F	W 2-1	Possee, Rogers	16,340
36	Apr	6	(h)	Portsmouth	D 0-0		23,662
37		12	(a)	Fulham	W 3-1	Possee, Johnson 2	22,877
38		13	(a)	Millwall	L 2-3	P.Taylor, Rogers (pen)	19,770
39		16	(h)	Fulham	L 0-2		32,124
40		20	(h)	Hull C	L 0-2		21,408
41		27	(a)	Swindon T	W 1-0	P.Taylor	11,964
42		30	(a)	Cardiff C	D 1-1	Jump	26,781

FINAL LEAGUE POSITION: 20th in Division Two

Appearances
Sub Appearances
Goals

FA Cup

3	Jan	5	(h)	Wrexham	L 0-2		16,119

Appearances
Sub Appearances
Goals

League Cup

2	Oct	9	(a)	Stockport C	L 0-1		8,501

Appearances
Sub Appearances
Goals

Hammond	Roffey	Taylor T	Chatterton	Bell	Blyth	Possee	Cooke	Whittle	Swindlehurst	Rogers	Cannon	Jackson	Whalley	Philip	Hinshelwood M	Hinshelwood P	Pinkney	McBride	Mulligan	Jefferies	Barry	Wall	Tambling	Taylor P	Anderson	Lindsey	Johnson	Jump	Hill	
1	2	3	4	5	6	7	8	9	10*	11	12																			1
1	2	3	9	5	6	7	10	8		11	4																			2
	2	3	10	5	6	7		9		11	4	1	8																	3
	2	3	10		6	7	12	9		11	4	1		5	8*															4
	2*	3	10		5	7	12	9		11	4	1		6	8															5
		3			6	7	8			11		1		4	2	9	10	5												6
		3			6	7	8*	9		11		1		5	4	10	12		2											7
1		6*				7	9		12	11					8	10			4	2	5	3								8
1		3				7	8			11	4					9	10		2	6	5									9
1		3				7	8*	9	12	11	4								2	6	5		10							10
1		3				9	8			7	4			10					2	6	5			11						11
1		3			6	9	8			10	7									4	5	2		11						12
1		3			6	9	8			10	11								2	4	5			7						13
1		3			4*	9	8			10	11								2	6	5	12		7						14
1						9	8		10	11	6*		12						2	4	5	3		7						15
1						8	7	12	9	11			4						2	6*	5	3		10						16
1						7		12	9	11			8						2	4	5	3*		10	6					17
1		3				7		9		11	6		8						2	4				10	5					18
1		3				7		9		11			8							2	5			10	4	6				19
1		3				7		9	12	11	5		8							2*				10	4	6				20
1			2			8		9		11											5			10	6	4	7	3		21
1		3			6			10		11									2		5			7			8	4	9	22
1		3			6			10	12	9									2		5			7		11*	8	4		23
1										11									2	4	5			7	6	10	8	3	9	24
1										10									2	7	5			11	4	8	6	3	9	25
1		3			4					10										7	5			11		8	6	2	9	26
1					4	8				10										7	5	3		11	9		6	2		27
1					6	8				10										7	5	3		11			4	2	9	28
1					6	8		10												7	5	3		11			4	2	9	29
1					6	8				10										7		3		11	5		4	2	9	30
1					6				8	10										7		3		11	5		4	2	9	31
1					6	7				10									2	8	5			11			4	3	9	32
1					4	7				10									2	8	5			11			6	3	9	33
1					6	7		9		10									2	8	5			11			4	3		34
1					4	7		9		10										8	5	2		11			6	3		35
1					4	7		9		10									2	8	5			11			6	3		36
1					6	8		9		10									2	7	5			11			4	3		37
1			12		6	8		9		10*										7	5			11	2		4	3		38
1					6	8		9		10									2	7	5			11			4	3		39
1					6	8		12		10									2	7*	5			11			4	3	9	40
1					4	7		9		10									2		5			11			6	3	8	41
1					6	8		9		10									2	7	5			11			4	3		42
37	5	20	6	3	29	36	13	22	5	41	13	5	6	5	5	4	2	1	24	31	31	11	1	32	11	7	22	22	12	
			1				2	3	4		1		1				1		1			1								
					1	9		2		15	1		1			1				1	1			6	1		2	1		

1 own-goal

Hammond	Roffey	Taylor T	Chatterton	Bell	Blyth	Possee	Cooke	Whittle	Swindlehurst	Rogers	Cannon	Jackson	Whalley	Philip	Hinshelwood M	Hinshelwood P	Pinkney	McBride	Mulligan	Jefferies	Barry	Wall	Tambling	Taylor P	Anderson	Lindsey	Johnson	Jump	Hill	
1							12			10									2	7*	5			11	4	8	6	3	9	3
1										1									1	1	1			1	1	1	1	1	1	
							1																							

Hammond	Roffey	Taylor T	Chatterton	Bell	Blyth	Possee	Cooke	Whittle	Swindlehurst	Rogers	Cannon	Jackson	Whalley	Philip	Hinshelwood M	Hinshelwood P	Pinkney	McBride	Mulligan	Jefferies	Barry	Wall	Tambling	Taylor P	Anderson	Lindsey	Johnson	Jump	Hill	
1		3		5		7	12			11	4			10	2*					6			8			9				2
1		1		1		1				1	1			1	1					1			1			1				
							1																							

1974-75

Manager: Malcolm Allison

1	Aug	17	(a)	Brighton & HA	L 0-1		26,235
2		24	(h)	Tranmere R	W 2-1	Blyth, Swindlehurst	14,816
3		31	(a)	Halifax T	L 1-3	Whittle	3,295
4	Sep	7	(h)	Swindon T	W 6-2	Jump, Swindlehurst 2, Whittle 2 (1 pen), Chatterton	13,964
5		13	(a)	Southend U	W 1-0	Chatterton	17,394
6		18	(a)	Hereford U	L 0-2		8,488
7		21	(h)	Wrexham	W 2-0	Taylor, Chatterton	13,226
8		24	(h)	Preston NE	W 1-0	Hill	19,680
9		28	(a)	Huddersfield T	W 1-0	Chatterton	6,524
10	Oct	1	(h)	Grimsby T	W 3-0	Whittle, Evans, Taylor	19,105
11		5	(h)	Chesterfield	L 1-4	Taylor	19,310
12		12	(a)	Bournemouth	L 0-4		10,407
13		19	(h)	Walsall	W 1-0	Whittle	15,029
14		22	(h)	Blackburn R	W 1-0	Taylor	17,754
15		26	(a)	Port Vale	L 1-2	Taylor	5,148
16	Nov	2	(h)	Peterborough U	D 1-1	Taylor	18,226
17		6	(a)	Blackburn R	D 1-1	P.Hinshelwood	13,612
18		9	(a)	Bury	D 2-2	Whittle, Swindlehurst	6,727
19		16	(h)	Plymouth A	D 3-3	Whittle, Swindlehurst, P.Hinshelwood	19,308
20		30	(h)	Charlton A	W 2-1	Cannon, Chatterton	24,274
21	Dec	7	(a)	Watford	W 2-1	Whittle, Taylor	11,065
22		20	(a)	Colchester U	D 1-1	Evans	6,914
23		26	(h)	Southend U	D 1-1	Swindlehurst	21,652
24		28	(a)	Gillingham	L 1-3	Wiltshire (og)	14,555
25	Jan	4	(h)	Hereford U	D 2-2	Taylor, Chatterton	16,893
26		11	(h)	Watford	W 1-0	Hill	17,055
27		18	(a)	Charlton A	L 0-1		25,535
28		25	(a)	Aldershot	L 1-2	Hill	8,790
29	Feb	1	(h)	Bury	D 2-2	Swindlehurst 2	15,046
30		8	(a)	Peterborough U	D 1-1	Whittle	7,698
31		15	(h)	Aldershot	W 3-0	Swindlehurst, Taylor, Whittle	15,394
32		22	(a)	Plymouth A	W 1-0	Swindlehurst	21,022
33		28	(h)	Halifax T	D 1-1	Swindlehurst	18,024
34	Mar	8	(a)	Preston NE	D 1-1	Swindlehurst	12,119
35		15	(h)	Huddersfield T	D 1-1	Taylor	15,043
36		18	(h)	Brighton & HA	W 3-0	Taylor (pen), J.Johnson, Swindlehurst	18,799
37		22	(a)	Swindon T	D 1-1	Swindlehurst	11,545
38		25	(h)	Colchester U	W 2-1	Evans, Cannon	16,851
39		31	(a)	Wrexham	D 0-0		5,833
40	Apr	5	(h)	Port Vale	D 1-1	Taylor (pen)	14,930
41		8	(a)	Grimsby T	L 1-2	Wall	8,381
42		12	(a)	Chesterfield	L 1-2	Hill	6,020
43		19	(h)	Bournemouth	W 4-1	Hill 2, Cannon, M.Hinshelwood	12,591
44		25	(a)	Walsall	L 0-3		6,001
45		29	(h)	Gillingham	W 4-0	Whittle 2, Taylor 2	13,442
46	May	7	(a)	Tranmere R	L 0-2		2,025

FINAL LEAGUE POSITION: 5th in Division Three

Appearances
Sub Appearances
Goals

FA Cup

1	Nov	27	(a)	Tooting & Mitham	W 2-1	P.Hinshelwood, Whittle	10,000
2	Dec	14	(a)	Plymouth A	L 1-2	Swindlehurst	17,473

Appearances
Sub Appearances
Goals

League Cup

1	Aug	21	(a)	Watford	D 1-1	Lindsay	10,643
R		27	(h)	Watford	W 5-1	Taylor, Whittle 2, Chatterton, Butler (og)	12,801
2	Sep	10	(h)	Bristol C	L 1-4	Whittle (pen)	16,263

Appearances
Sub Appearances
Goals

Hammond	Mulligan	Jump	Jeffries	Blyth	Johnson J	Whittle	Lindsay	Hill	Rogers	Taylor	Swindlehurst	Barry	Davies	Chatterton	Burns	Cannon	Venables	Evans	Ayres	Hinshelwood P	Hinshelwood M	Johnson P	Love	Wall	Holder	Sansom	Kemp	
1	2	3	4	5	6	7	8	9*	10	11	12																	1
1		3	4	5	6	7	8		10*	11	12	2	9															2
1		3	4	5	6	7	8			11	12	2	9*	10														3
1		3	5	6	4	7	8		12	11	9	2*		10														4
		3	5		4	8	7			11		2	9	10	1	6												5
		3	5*		12	8	7			11	9	2		10	1		4	6										6
		2			3	7	8			11	9	5		10	1		4	6										7
		3			5	8*	7	9		11		2		10	1		4	6	12									8
		3			8	7	6	9*				2		10	1	12	4	5	11									9
		3			5	8	7			11	9	2*		10	1	12	4	6										10
		3			7	8*	6	9		11		2		10	1		4	5		12								11
		12	7		2	8	6	9*		11				10	1	3	4	5										12
		3	5		2	8	7			11	12				1	10	4*	6	9									13
		3	10		5	8	7			11	9				1	2		6		4								14
		2	5		4	10	8			11	9				1	3*		6	12	7								15
1		2	6*		4	8	7			11	9					3		5	12	10								16
1		2	10		5	8	7			11	9			12		3		6		4*								17
1		2	6		4	8	7			11	9					3		5		10								18
1		2	5		7	8	12			11*	9					3	4	6		10								19
		2	5			8				11	9			7	1	3	4	6		10								20
		2	5			8*	12			11	9			7	1	3	4	6		10								21
	2		5			8				11	9			7	1	3	4	6		10								22
	2		6			10		12		11	9			7	1	3	4	5		8*								23
	2		5			8	9	10		11				7	1	3	4	6										24
	2		5		4			10		11	9	12		8	1	3		6				7						25
	2		5		4			10		11	9			8	1	3		6				7						26
	2		5		12	10	4	9						7	1	3		6	11			8*						27
	2		5		4	8		9						7	1	3		6			10		11*	12				28
	7		5		4	8		9		11	10				1	3		6						2				29
	7		5		4	8		10		11	9				1	3		6						2				30
	2		5		4	7		9		11	10				1			6						3	8			31
	2		5		4	7		9		11	10				1			6						3	8			32
	2*		5		4	8		9		11	10			12	1	3		6							7			33
			5		4			9		11	10*			7	1	3		6				12		2	8			34
			5		4			9		11	10			7	1	3		6			12			2	8			35
			5		4			9		11	10			7	1	3		6			8			2				36
			5		4	7		9		11	10				1	3		6			8			2				37
			5		4	7		9		11	10				1	3		6			8			2				38
			5		4	7		9		11	10				1	3		6			8			2				39
	3*		5		4	7	12	9		11	10				1	6					8			2				40
			5		3	7		9*		11	10			12	1	6					8			2	4			41
			5			7		9		11	10				1	3		6			8			2	4			42
			5			7		9		11	10				1	3		6			8			2	4			43
			5			7		10		11	9				1	3		6			8			2	4			44
			5			7		9		11	10				1	3		6			8			2	4			45
			5			7*		12		11	9				1	6					8			2	4	3	10	46
8	14	20	41	4	34	41	20	27	2	43	34	10	3	22	38	34	14	38	3	10	12	3	1	17	11	1	1	
		1			2		3	2	1		4	1		3		2			3	1	2	1		1				
		1		1	1	12		6		14	14			6		3		3		2	1			1				

1 own-goal

Hammond	Mulligan	Jump	Jeffries	Blyth	Johnson J	Whittle	Lindsay	Hill	Rogers	Taylor	Swindlehurst	Barry	Davies	Chatterton	Burns	Cannon	Venables	Evans	Ayres	Hinshelwood P	Hinshelwood M	Johnson P	Love	Wall	Holder	Sansom	Kemp	
1		2	5			8				11	9			7		3	4	6		10								1
	2		5			8	12			11	9			7	1	3	4	6		10*								2
1	1	1	2			2				2	2			2	1	2	2	2		2								
							1																					
						1														2								

Hammond	Mulligan	Jump	Jeffries	Blyth	Johnson J	Whittle	Lindsay	Hill	Rogers	Taylor	Swindlehurst	Barry	Davies	Chatterton	Burns	Cannon	Venables	Evans	Ayres	Hinshelwood P	Hinshelwood M	Johnson P	Love	Wall	Holder	Sansom	Kemp	
1	2*	3	5	6	4	8	7		10	11	9					12												1
1		3	5	6	4	8	7			11	9	2		10														R
1		3	5	6	4	8	7		12	11	9*	2		10														2
3	1	3	3	3	3	3	3		1	3	3	2		2														
									1							1												
						3	1			1				1														

1 own-goal

1975-76

Manager: Malcolm Allison

1	Aug	16	(h)	Chester	W 2-0	Chatterton, Kemp	13,009
2		23	(a)	Chesterfield	W 2-1	Kemp, Holder	5,386
3		30	(h)	Colchester U	W 3-2	Evans 3	13,713
4	Sep	6	(a)	Cardiff C	W 1-0	Kemp	10,479
5		13	(h)	Rotherham U	W 2-0	Evans, Kemp	16,421
6		16	(a)	Walsall	D 1-1	Evans	5,496
7		20	(a)	Shrewsbury T	W 4-2	Swindlehurst, Kemp, Taylor, Durban (og)	7,480
8		23	(h)	Brighton & HA	L 0-1		25,606
9		27	(h)	Sheffield W	D 1-1	Kemp	14,840
10	Oct	4	(a)	Port Vale	D 0-0		6,121
11		11	(h)	Grimsby T	W 3-0	Evans, Kemp, Swindlehurst	15,552
12		18	(a)	Preston NE	D 0-0		10,971
13		21	(h)	Hereford U	D 2-2	Swindlehurst, Taylor (pen)	20,232
14		25	(h)	Southend U	D 1-1	Taylor	18,438
15	Nov	1	(a)	Halifax T	W 3-1	Cannon, Swindlehurst, Taylor	3,282
16		4	(a)	Swindon T	W 2-1	Swindlehurst 2	10,599
17		8	(h)	Peterborough U	D 1-1	Chatterton	19,000
18		15	(a)	Wrexham	W 3-1	Swindlehurst 2, Kemp	5,878
19		29	(h)	Mansfield T	W 4-1	Swindlehurst 2, M.Hinshelwood, Evans	15,701
20	Dec	6	(a)	Bury	W 1-0	Kemp	10,035
21		20	(a)	Millwall	L 1-2	Swindlehurst	9,841
22		27	(a)	Aldershot	L 0-1		13,997
23		30	(h)	Gillingham	L 0-1		20,919
24	Jan	6	(h)	Walsall	L 0-1		16,181
25		10	(a)	Colchester U	W 3-0	Taylor (pen), Swindlehurst, Whittle	6,240
26		17	(h)	Shrewsbury T	D 1-1	J.Johnson	16,531
27		31	(a)	Hereford U	D 1-1	Swindlehurst	12,970
28	Feb	3	(a)	Rotherham U	L 1-4	Swindlehurst	7,633
29		7	(h)	Swindon T	D 3-3	Taylor (pen), Chatterton 2	15,844
30		18	(a)	Peterborough U	L 0-2		13,308
31		21	(h)	Wrexham	D 1-1	Chatterton	16,944
32		24	(a)	Brighton & HA	L 0-2		33,300
33		27	(a)	Southend U	W 2-1	Wall, Taylor (pen)	13,500
34	Mar	9	(h)	Port Vale	D 2-2	Chatterton, Swindlehurst	23,014
35		13	(a)	Grimsby T	W 2-1	Taylor 2	8,412
36		16	(h)	Preston NE	W 2-0	Taylor, Swindlehurst	22,213
37		20	(a)	Mansfield T	D 1-1	Taylor	12,990
38		27	(h)	Bury	W 1-0	Chatterton	21,328
39		30	(h)	Millwall	D 0-0		34,893
40	Apr	7	(a)	Sheffield W	L 0-1		11,909
41		10	(h)	Cardiff C	L 0-1		25,603
42		13	(h)	Halifax T	D 1-1	Martin	19,175
43		17	(a)	Gillingham	W 2-1	Cannon, Ley (og)	12,880
44		20	(h)	Aldershot	D 0-0		25,549
45		28	(h)	Chesterfield	D 0-0		27,961
46	May	4	(a)	Chester	L 1-2	Taylor (pen)	6,702

FINAL LEAGUE POSITION: 5th in Division Three

Appearances
Sub Appearances
Goals

FA Cup

1	Nov	22	(h)	Walton & Hersham	W 1-0	Kemp	16,241
2	Dec	13	(a)	Millwall	D 1-1	Swindlehurst	14,920
R		16	(h)	Millwall	W 2-1	Kemp, Taylor (pen)	18,284
3	Jan	3	(a)	Scarborough	W 2-1	Taylor, Evans	8,001
4		24	(a)	Leeds U	W 1-0	Swindlhurst	43,116
5	Feb	14	(a)	Chelsea	W 3-2	Taylor 2, Chatterton	54,407
6	Mar	6	(a)	Sunderland	W 1-0	Whittle	50,850
SF	Apr	3	(n†)	Southampton	L 0-2		52,810

†Played at Stamford Bridge, London.

Appearances
Sub Appearances
Goals

League Cup

1	Aug	19	(h)	Colchester U	W 3-0	Swindlehurst, Kemp 2	10,006
		25	(a)	Colchester U	L 1-3	Chatterton	3,912
2	Sep	9	(a)	Doncaster R	L 1-2	J.Johnson	6,268

Appearances
Sub Appearances
Goals

Burns	Wall	Johnson J	Holder	Jeffries	Hinshelwood M	Hill	Chatterton	Kemp	Swindlehurst	Taylor	Evans	Cannon	Hammond	Hinshelwood P	Jump	Whittle	Johnson P	Sansom	Martin	
1	2	3	4	5	6	7	8	9	10	11										1
1	2	3	11	5	4	7	8	9	10		6									2
1	2		8	5	4	7		9	10	11	6	3								3
	2		4	5	8	7		10	9	11	6	3	1							4
	2		8	5	4		7	9	10	11	6	3	1							5
	2		8	5	4		7	9	10	11	6	3	1							6
	2		8	5	4		7	10	9	11	6	3	1							7
	2	12	8	5	4		7*	9	10	11	6	3	1							8
	2	8	7	5	4*			10	9	11	6	3	1	12						9
	2	10	7	5	4			9		11	6	3	1	8						10
	2	8	7	5	4			9	10*	11	6		1	12	3					11
		8	7	5	4			9	10	11	6	3	1		2					12
		4	8	5			12	9	10	11	6	3*	1		2	7				13
	2	8	4	5				9	10	11*	6		1	12	3	7				14
	2	8	4				7	9	10	11	6	5	1		3					15
	2	4	8	5			7	9	10	11	6	3	1							16
	2	8	4	5			7	9	10		6	3	1			11				17
	2	8	4	5			7	9	10	11	6	3	1							18
	2	4		5	8*		7	9	10	11	6	3	1			12				19
	2	8			4		7	9	10	11	6	3	1		5					20
	2	8		5	4		7	9	10	11	6	3	1							21
	2	4	12	5	8		7	9*	10	11	6	3	1							22
	2	12	4	5	8		7		10*	11	6	3	1	9						23
	2				8		7	9	10	11	6	3	1		5	4				24
	2	4			8		7		10	11	6	3	1		5	9				25
	2	4			8		7		10	11	6	3	1		5	9				26
	2			4	8		7		10	11	6	3	1		5	9				27
	2			4	8		7		10	11	6	3	1		5	9				28
	2			4	8		7		10	11	6	3	1		5	9				29
	2		11	4	8		7	9	10		6	3	1		5					30
	2		11	4*	8		7	9	10		6	3	1		5		12			31
	2		11	4	8		7		10	9	6	3	1		5					32
	2		5	4	8		7		10	11	6	3	1			9				33
	2		4	5	8*		7	12	10	11	6		1		3	9				34
		8	6	4			7		10	11	5		1		3	9		2		35
	2	8	4*				7		10	11	6	3	1		5	9			12	36
	2	8		4			7		10	11	6	3	1		5*	12			9	37
	2	12	4	5			7		10	11	6	3	1			9			8	38
		8	4	5			7		10	11	6	3	1		2	9				39
	2	8	4	5			7		10		6	3	1			9			11	40
	2	8	4	5			7		10	11	6	3	1			9				41
	2	7						12	10*	11	6	3	1		5	9		4	8	42
	2	7							10	11	6	3	1		5	9		4	8	43
	2						8	12	10*	11	6	3	1		5	9		4	7	44
	2						7	9		11	6	3	1		5		10	4	8	45
	2						7	9		11	6	3	1		5		10	4	8	46
3	42	26	30	35	28	4	36	27	43	41	45	40	43	2	25	20	2	6	8	
		3	1				1	3						3		2	1		1	
	1	1	1		1		7	9	16	12	7	2				1			1	

2 own-goals

Burns	Wall	Johnson J	Holder	Jeffries	Hinshelwood M	Hill	Chatterton	Kemp	Swindlehurst	Taylor	Evans	Cannon	Hammond	Hinshelwood P	Jump	Whittle	Johnson P	Sansom	Martin	
	2	4	8	5			7	9	10	11	6	3	1							1
	2	4			8		7	9	10	11	6	3	1		5					2
	2	4		5	8		7	9	10	11	6	3	1			12				R
	2		4*		8		7	9	10	11	6	3	1		5	9				3
	2			4	8		7		10	11	6	3	1		5	9				4
	2			4	8		7		10	11	6	3	1		5	9				5
	2		4	5	8		7		10	11	6	3	1			9				6
	2	8	4	5			7		10	11	6	3	1			9				SF
	8	4	4	6	6		8	4	8	8	8	8	8		4	4				
																1				
							1	2	2	4	1					1				

Burns	Wall	Johnson J	Holder	Jeffries	Hinshelwood M	Hill	Chatterton	Kemp	Swindlehurst	Taylor	Evans	Cannon	Hammond	Hinshelwood P	Jump	Whittle	Johnson P	Sansom	Martin	
1	2	3	12	5	4*	7	8	9	10	11	6									1
1	2	3	12		4	7	8*	9	10	11	6	5								
	2	12	8	5	4	7*		9	10	11	6	3	1							2
2	3	2	1	2	3	3	2	3	3	3	3	2	1							
		1	2																	
		1					1	2	1											

1976-77

Manager: Terry Venables

1	Aug	21	(h)	York C	W 1-0	Taylor	14,426
2		24	(a)	Grimsby T	W 1-0	Kemp	5,841
3		27	(a)	Tranmere R	L 0-1		4,940
4	Sep	4	(h)	Chester	L 1-2	Swindlehurst	12,746
5		11	(h)	Bury	W 2-1	Evans, Silkman	12,390
6		18	(a)	Peterborough U	D 0-0		8,489
7		25	(h)	Mansfield T	W 2-0	Perrin, Swindlehurst	14,268
8	Oct	2	(a)	Brighton & HA	D 1-1	Cannon	27,059
9		9	(h)	Oxford U	D 2-2	P.Hinshelwood, Swindlehurst	17,339
10		16	(a)	Preston NE	L 1-2	Chatterton	10,524
11		23	(h)	Rotherham U	W 2-1	Swindlehurst, Evans	13,819
12		26	(h)	Shrewsbury T	W 2-1	Chatterton, Perrin	15,809
13		30	(a)	Walsall	D 0-0		6,033
14	Nov	2	(a)	Swindon T	D 1-1	Perrin	11,317
15		6	(h)	Reading	D 1-1	Swindlehurst	15,322
16		9	(a)	Sheffield W	L 0-1		14,899
17		27	(h)	Chesterfield	D 0-0		13,618
18	Dec	18	(h)	Northampton T	D 1-1	Silkman	10,642
19		27	(a)	Gillingham	W 3-0	Swindlehurst, Silkman, Perrin	11,237
20	Jan	1	(a)	Reading	D 0-0		11,851
21		3	(h)	Walsall	W 3-0	Chatterton, Harkouk, Holder (pen)	17,614
22		15	(h)	Grimsby T	W 2-1	Chatterton, Silkman	13,638
23		22	(a)	York C	L 1-2	Harkouk	3,427
24	Feb	1	(h)	Port Vale	W 2-0	Chatterton, Perrin	10,691
25		5	(h)	Tranmere R	W 1-0	Holder (pen)	14,288
26		12	(a)	Chester	L 1-2	Harkouk	5,442
27		19	(a)	Bury	W 1-0	Perrin	5,120
28		22	(h)	Portsmouth	W 2-1	Cannon, Harkouk	16,483
29		26	(h)	Peterborough U	D 0-0		16,623
30	Mar	2	(a)	Lincoln C	L 2-3	Swindlehurst, Brennan	8,280
31		5	(a)	Mansfield T	L 0-1		10,944
32		12	(h)	Brighton & HA	W 3-1	Harkouk 2, Swindlehurst	28,677
33		15	(a)	Northampton T	L 0-3		6,253
34		19	(a)	Oxford U	W 1-0	Perrin	6,872
35		22	(h)	Preston NE	W 1-0	Bourne	14,993
36	Apr	2	(a)	Rotherham U	D 1-1	Harkouk	8,353
37		5	(h)	Gillingham	W 3-1	Bourne 2, Holder (pen)	17,477
38		9	(a)	Portsmouth	D 0-0		14,108
39		12	(h)	Swindon T	W 5-0	Bourne 2, Holder (pen), Graham, Harkouk	18,501
40		16	(a)	Shrewsbury T	D 1-1	Graham	4,240
41		23	(h)	Sheffield W	W 4-0	Evans, Bourne, Henson (og), Harkouk	20,018
42		26	(a)	Port Vale	L 1-4	Bourne	3,990
43		30	(a)	Chesterfield	W 2-0	Harkouk, Chatterton	5,122
44	May	3	(h)	Wrexham	W 2-1	P.Hinshelwood (pen), Swindlehurst	18,583
45		7	(h)	Lincoln C	W 4-1	P.Hinshelwood 2 (2 pens), Bourne, Perrin	18,305
46		11	(a)	Wrexham	W 4-2	Swindlehurst, Perrin, Harkouk, Bourne	18,451

FINAL LEAGUE POSITION: 3rd in Division Three

Appearances
Sub Appearances
Goals

FA Cup

1	Nov	20	(a)	Brighton & HA	D 2-2	Evans, Harkouk	29,510
R		23	(h)	Brighton & HA	D 1-1*	Harkouk	29,174
2R	Dec	6	(n†)	Brighton & HA	W 1-0	Holder	14,118
2		11	(h)	Enfield	W 4-0	Swindlehurst 2, Silkman, P.Hinshelwood	13,570
3	Jan	8	(a)	Liverpool	D 0-0		44,730
R		11	(h)	Liverpool	L 2-3	P.Hinshelwood, Graham	42,664

*After extra-time. †Played at Stamford Bridge, London.

Appearances
Sub Appearances
Goals

League Cup

1	Aug	14	(h)	Portsmouth	D 2-2	Kemp 2	12,936
		17	(a)	Portsmouth	W 1-0	Taylor	9,774
2		31	(h)	Watford	L 1-3	Swindlehurst	14,105

Appearances
Sub Appearances
Goals

Hammond	Wall	Sansom	Holder	Cannon	Evans	Chatterton	Hinshelwood M	Kemp	Swindlehurst	Taylor	Harkouk	Hinshelwood P	Walsh	Silkman	Burns	Jump	Perrin	Smillie	Heppolette	Graham	Brennan	Hilaire	Bourne	Murphy	Caswell	
1	2	3	4*	5	6	7	8	9	10	11	12															1
1	2	3	4	5	6	7	8	9		11	10															2
1	2	3	4	5	6	7	8*	9	10	11		12														3
1	2	3	4	5	6	7			9	11			8	10												4
	2	3		5	6	7		9	10*		12	8		11	1	4										5
1	2	3		5	6	7			9	11		8		10		4										6
1	2	3		5	6	7			9	11		8				4	10									7
1	2	3	12	4	6	7			9			8		11*		5	10									8
1	2	3		4	6	7			10			8				5	9	11								9
1	12	3	4	2	6	7			9*			8				5	10		11							10
1		3	4	2	6	7			9			8				5	10		11							11
1		3	11	2	6	7			10			8				5	9		4							12
1		3	11	2	6	7			10			8				5	9		4							13
1		3	11	2	6	7			10			8				5	9		4							14
1	12	3	11	2	6	7			10			8*				5	9		4							15
1		3	11	2	6	7			10			8				5	9		4							16
1		3	7	5	6				10		11	2					9		4	8						17
1		3	4*	5	6	12			10			2		11			9		7	8						18
1		3	4	5	6				10			2		11			9		7	8						19
1		3	4	5	6				10			2		11			9		7	8						20
1		3	4	5	6	8					10	2		11			9		7							21
1		3	4	5	6	7			12		10	2		11*			9			8						22
1		3	4	5	6	7					10	2		11			9			8						23
1		3	4	5	6	7			10*		8	2		11			9		12							24
1		3	4	5	6	7					8	2		12			9		11*	10						25
1		3	4	5	6	7*			10		8	2					9		12	11						26
	2	3	4	5	6	7			10		11	8			1		9									27
	2	3	4	5	6	7			10		11	8		9	1											28
		3	4	5	6	7			10		11	2		12	1		9			8*						29
	2	3		5	6				10		11	8		7*	1		9				4	12				30
	2	3	4	5	6				10		11*	7		12	1		9			8						31
	2	3	4	5	6				10		11	7			1					8		12	9*			32
	2	3		5	6				10		11	7			1		4			8			9			33
		3	4	6	5	12			10		11*	2			1		7			8			9			34
		3	4	5	6	12			10*		11	2			1		7			8			9			35
		3	4	5	6	7			12		11*	2			1		8			10			9			36
		3	4	5	6	10			12		11	2			1		7*			8			9			37
		3	4	5	6	7			10		11*	2		12	1					8			9			38
		3	4	5	6	10			7		11	2			1					8			9			39
		3	4	5	6	7			10		11	2			1					8			9			40
		3	4	5	6				10		11	2		7	1					8*			9	12		41
		3	4	5	6				7		11*	2		10	1					8		12	9			42
		3		5	6	4			10*		11	2		7	1		8				12		9			43
		3		5	6	4			10			2		8	1		7			11			9			44
		3	4	5	6	12			10			2		11	1*		7			8			9			45
		3	4	5	6	7			8		12	2		11*			10						9		1	46
25	15	46	37	46	46	33	3	4	39	6	25	42	1	19	20	12	33	1	13	23	1		15		1	
	2		1			4			3		3	1		4					2		1	3		1		
			4	2	3	6		1	10	1	11	4					9			2	1		9			

1 own-goal

Hammond	Wall	Sansom	Holder	Cannon	Evans	Chatterton	Hinshelwood M	Kemp	Swindlehurst	Taylor	Harkouk	Hinshelwood P	Walsh	Silkman	Burns	Jump	Perrin	Smillie	Heppolette	Graham	Brennan	Hilaire	Bourne	Murphy	Caswell	
1	5	3	11	2	6	7			10		12	8					9		4*							1
1	5	3	4	2	6	7			10		11*	8				12	9									R
1	2	3	4	5	6				10*		12	8		11			9		7							2R
1		3	4	5	6				10			2		11			9		7	8						2
1		3	4	5	6	7			10			2		11			9			8						3
1		3	4	5	6	7			10		12	2		11*			9			8						R
6	3	6	6	6	6	4			6		1	6		4			6		3	3						
											3					1										
			1		1				2		2	2		1						1						

Hammond	Wall	Sansom	Holder	Cannon	Evans	Chatterton	Hinshelwood M	Kemp	Swindlehurst	Taylor	Harkouk	Hinshelwood P	Walsh	Silkman	Burns	Jump	Perrin	Smillie	Heppolette	Graham	Brennan	Hilaire	Bourne	Murphy	Caswell	
1	2	3	4	5	6	7	8	9	10*	11	12															1
1	2	3	4	5	6	7	8	9	10	11																
1	2	3	4	5	6	7			10	11*			9	8							12					2
3	3	3	3	3	3	3	2	2	3	3			1	1												
											1										1					
								2	1	1																

1977-78

Manager: Terry Venables

No	Month	Day	Venue	Opponent	Result	Scorers	Attendance
1	Aug	20	(a)	Millwall	W 3-0	Evans, Hilaire, Chatterton	14,856
2		23	(h)	Mansfield T	W 3-1	Harkouk 2, M.Hinshelwood	19,001
3		27	(h)	Hull C	L 0-1		14,382
4	Sep	3	(a)	Burnley	D 1-1	Chatterton	10,441
5		10	(h)	Sunderland	D 2-2	Bourne, Swindlehurst	21,305
6		17	(a)	Sheffield U	W 2-0	Swindlehurst, Harkouk	14,451
7		24	(h)	Bolton W	W 2-1	Harkouk, Chatterton	23,604
8	Oct	1	(h)	Fulham	L 2-3	Harkouk 2	28,343
9		4	(a)	Blackpool	L 1-3	Chatterton	9,369
10		8	(a)	Stoke C	W 2-0	Chatterton, Perrin	17,749
11		15	(h)	Southampton	L 1-2	Perrin	22,652
12		22	(a)	Brighton & HA	D 1-1	P.Hinshelwood	28,208
13		29	(h)	Charlton A	D 1-1	Chatterton	25,994
14	Nov	5	(a)	Oldham A	D 1-1	Perrin	7,775
15		12	(h)	Tottenham H	L 1-2	Harkouk	40,277
16		19	(a)	Orient	D 0-0		10,037
17		26	(h)	Cardiff C	W 2-0	Chatterton (pen), Perrin	16,139
18	Dec	3	(a)	Blackburn R	L 0-3		12,119
19		10	(h)	Notts C	W 2-0	Cannon, Walsh	14,608
20		17	(a)	Tottenham H	D 2-2	Swindlehurst 2	33,211
21		26	(h)	Luton T	D 3-3	Silkman 2, Sansom	22,027
22		27	(a)	Bristol R	L 0-3		11,688
23		31	(a)	Mansfield T	W 3-1	Sansom, Swindlehurst 2	9,291
24	Jan	2	(h)	Millwall	W 1-0	P.Hinshelwood	27,010
25		14	(a)	Hull C	L 0-1		5,617
26		21	(h)	Burnley	D 1-1	Hilaire	15,159
27	Feb	11	(h)	Sheffield U	W 1-0	Swindlehurst	13,391
28		25	(a)	Fulham	D 1-1	Nicholas	14,160
29	Mar	4	(h)	Stoke C	L 0-1		14,702
30		11	(a)	Southampton	L 0-2		22,480
31		14	(a)	Sunderland	D 0-0		15,962
32		18	(h)	Brighton & HA	D 0-0		26,305
33		24	(a)	Charlton A	L 0-1		14,971
34		25	(h)	Bristol R	W 1-0	Cannon	13,428
35		27	(a)	Luton T	L 0-1		9,816
36	Apr	1	(h)	Oldham A	D 0-0		11,272
37		8	(a)	Cardiff C	D 2-2	Chatterton (pen), Harkouk	9,328
38		15	(h)	Orient	W 1-0	Swindlehurst	15,414
39		18	(a)	Bolton W	L 0-2		23,980
40		22	(a)	Notts C	L 0-2		7,710
41		25	(h)	Blackpool	D 2-2	Swindlehurst, Chatterton (pen)	11,115
42		29	(h)	Blackburn R	W 5-0	Harkouk, Walsh, Swindlehurst 3	12,664

FINAL LEAGUE POSITION: 9th in Division Two

Appearances
Sub Appearances
Goals

FA Cup

Round	Month	Day	Venue	Opponent	Result	Scorers	Attendance
3	Jan	2	(a)	Hartlepool U	L 1-2	Chatterton	9,502

Appearances
Sub Appearances
Goals

League Cup

Round	Month	Day	Venue	Opponent	Result	Scorers	Attendance
1	Aug	13	(a)	Brentford	L 1-2	Harkouk	8,930
		16	(h)	Brentford	W 5-1	Cannon, Graham, Salmon (og), Harkouk 2	10,684
2		30	(h)	Southampton	D 0-0		19,565
	Sep	13	(a)	Southampton	L 1-2*	Perrin	19,836

*After extra-time

Appearances
Sub Appearances
Goals

Caswell	Nicholas	Sansom	Cannon	Evans	Chatterton	Graham	Hilaire	Perrin	Bourne	Harkouk	Wall	Hinshelwood P	Hinshelwood M	Silkman	Burns	Swindlehurst	Brennan	Gilbert	Jump	Blyth	Holder	Walsh	Fenwick	Murphy	Smillie	Burridge	Boyle	Fry	
1	2	3	4	5	6	7	8	9	10	11*	12																		1
1		3	5	6	8		7	10	9	11		2	4*	12															2
		3	5	6	8	4	7*	9	10	11		2			1	12													3
	5	3		6	8	4		9	10	11*	12	2			1	7													4
		3	5	6	8	4		9	10	11		2			1	7													5
		3	5	6	8	4	9		10	11		2			1	7													6
		3	5	6	8	4	7		9	11		2			1	10													7
		3	5	6	7		8	12	9	10		2			1	11*	4												8
		3	4		8	5	9		10	11		2			1	7		6											9
		3	5		7	4	8	9	10		6	2			1	11													10
		3	5		4		8	9	10	11	6	2			1	7													11
		3	5		8	4	9	12	10	11	6	2			1	7*													12
		3	5		8	4	9	12	10	11	6	2			1	7													13
		3	5		8	4	9	10		11*	6	2			1	7			12										14
		3	5		8	4	9	10		11		2			1	7				6									15
		3	5		8	4	9	10		11		2			1	7				6									16
		3	5		8	4	9	10				2		11	1	7				6									17
		3	5		8	4	9	10				2		11	1	7				6									18
	6	3	5		8		9					2		11	1	7					4	10							19
	6*	5	4		8					10		2		11	1	7					3		9	12					20
	6	3	5		7					10		2		11	1	9					4	12	8						21
	2		5		8		7				3			11	1	9		6				10		4					22
	7	3	5		8				10			2	12	11*	1	9		6			4								23
	7	3	5		8				10			2		11	1	9		6			4								24
	7	3							10			2	8	11	1	9		6		5	4								25
	7	3					8		10*			2		11	1	9		6		5	4				12				26
	7	3	5				8			10		2		11*	1	9		6			4	12							27
	7	3	5			12	8			10		2		11	1	9*		6			4								28
	5	3	6			8	7			10*		2		11	1	9					4	12							29
	6	3	5			4	9					2*		11	1	7						10	8	12					30
	6	3	5			8						2		12	1	9					7	10	4	11*					31
	7	3	5			8						2				9		6				10	4	11		1			32
	7	3	5			8	12					2				9		6				10	4	11*		1			33
	10	3	5				12					2		11		8		6			4	9	7*			1			34
		3	5		4		7					2		11*		9					8	10		12		1	6		35
	7	3	5		8					11		2		12		10		6				9	4*			1			36
	7	3	5		8					11		2				9		6			4*	10		12		1			37
		3	5		8		12			11		2		7		9		6			4	10*				1			38
	11	3	5		8		10					2		7		9		6					4			1			39
		3	5		7		9			10		2		11		8		6					4			1			40
	4	3	5		8		12			11*		2		7		9		6				10				1			41
	4	3	5		8					11		2		7		9		6				10						1	42
2	23	41	39	8	32	20	26	12	17	26	6	40	2	21	29	39	1	18		6	15	13	10	4		10	1	1	
						1	4	3			2		1	3		1			1			3		4	1				
	1	2	2	1	9		2	4	1	9		2	1	2		12						2							

Caswell	Nicholas	Sansom	Cannon	Evans	Chatterton	Graham	Hilaire	Perrin	Bourne	Harkouk	Wall	Hinshelwood P	Hinshelwood M	Silkman	Burns	Swindlehurst	Brennan	Gilbert	Jump	Blyth	Holder	Walsh	Fenwick	Murphy	Smillie	Burridge	Boyle	Fry	
	7	3	5		8				10			2		11	1	9		6			4								3
	1	1	1		1				1			1		1	1	1		1			1								
					1																								

Caswell	Nicholas	Sansom	Cannon	Evans	Chatterton	Graham	Hilaire	Perrin	Bourne	Harkouk	Wall	Hinshelwood P	Hinshelwood M	Silkman	Burns	Swindlehurst	Brennan	Gilbert	Jump	Blyth	Holder	Walsh	Fenwick	Murphy	Smillie	Burridge	Boyle	Fry	
		3	5	6	8	4	7	10	9	11		2			1														1
		3	5	6	8	7	4	9	10	11		2			1														
		3	5	6	8	4		9	10	11		2			1	7													2
		3	5	6	8	4		9	10	11*	12	2			1	7													
		4	4	4	4	4	2	4	4	4		4			4	2													
											1																		
			1			1		1		3																			

1 own-goal

1978-79

Manager: Terry Venables

1	Aug	19	(a)	Blackburn R	D 1-1	Swindlehurst	9,463
2		22	(h)	Luton T	W 3-1	Swindlehurst, Hilaire, Murphy	17,639
3		26	(h)	West Ham U	D 1-1	Gilbert	32,611
4	Sep	2	(a)	Sheffield U	W 2-0	Hilaire, Elwiss	17,388
5		9	(h)	Sunderland	D 1-1	Chatterton (pen)	21,112
6		16	(a)	Millwall	W 3-0	Murphy, Chatterton, Nicholas	11,693
7		23	(h)	Oldham A	W 1-0	Swindlehurst	18,318
8		30	(a)	Stoke C	D 1-1	Murphy	19,070
9	Oct	7	(h)	Brighton & HA	W 3-1	Hilaire 2, Swindlehurst	33,685
10		14	(a)	Preston NE	W 3-2	Walsh 2, Elwiss	10,795
11		21	(a)	Wrexham	D 0-0		15,132
12		28	(h)	Fulham	L 0-1		28,733
13	Nov	4	(a)	Burnley	L 1-2	Chatterton (pen)	11,067
14		11	(h)	Blackburn R	W 3-0	Walsh, Swindlehurst 2 (1 pen)	17,006
15		18	(a)	West Ham U	D 1-1	Elwiss	31,245
16		21	(h)	Sheffield U	W 3-1	Elwiss, Nicholas, Swindlehurst	19,504
17		25	(a)	Cardiff C	D 2-2	Elwiss, Swindlehurst	8,739
18	Dec	2	(h)	Newcastle U	W 1-0	Elwiss	19,287
19		9	(a)	Notts C	D 0-0		11,011
20		16	(h)	Leicester C	W 3-1	Cannon, Swindlehurst, Elwiss	17,330
21		23	(a)	Cambridge U	D 0-0		8,081
22		26	(h)	Bristol R	L 0-1		21,605
23		30	(h)	Orient	D 1-1	Hilaire	20,100
24	Jan	20	(h)	Millwall	D 0-0		21,142
25	Feb	10	(h)	Stoke C	D 1-1	Walsh	23,313
26		17	(a)	Brighton & HA	D 0-0		23,795
27		24	(h)	Preston NE	D 0-0		17,592
28	Mar	3	(h)	Wrexham	W 1-0	Walsh	15,154
29		10	(a)	Fulham	D 0-0		16,654
30		14	(a)	Sunderland	W 2-1	Hilaire, Cannon	34,986
31		24	(a)	Luton T	W 1-0	Nicholas	11,008
32		27	(a)	Charlton A	D 1-1	Swindlehurst	15,065
33		31	(h)	Cardiff C	W 2-0	Smillie, Walsh	18,672
34	Apr	3	(a)	Oldham A	D 0-0		5,620
35		7	(a)	Newcastle U	L 0-1		18,860
36		10	(h)	Cambridge U	D 1-1	Swindlehurst	21,795
37		14	(a)	Bristol R	W 1-0	Walsh	10,986
38		17	(h)	Charlton A	W 1-0	Murphy	30,000
39		20	(a)	Leicester C	D 1-1	Hinshelwood	16,767
40		28	(h)	Notts C	W 2-0	Swindlehurst, Murphy	23,880
41	May	5	(a)	Orient	W 1-0	Swindlehurst	19,945
42		11	(h)	Burnley	W 2-0	Walsh, Swindlehurst	‡ 51,801

FINAL LEAGUE POSITION: 1st in Division Two. ‡Ground attendance record

Appearances
Sub Appearances
Goals

FA Cup

3	Jan	9	(a)	Middlesbrough	D 1-1	Walsh	21,441
R		15	(h)	Middlesbrough	W 1-0	Sansom	23,119
4		29	(h)	Bristol C	W 3-0	Nicholas, Fenwick, Kember	21,463
5	Feb	26	(h)	Wolves	L 0-1		26,790

Appearances
Sub Appearances
Goals

League Cup

2	Aug	29	(a)	Bristol C	W 2-1	Murphy, Swindlehurst	10,433
3	Oct	4	(a)	Aston Villa	D 1-1	Chatterton (pen)	30,690
R		10	(h)	Aston Villa	D 0-0*		33,155
2R		16	(n†)	Aston Villa	L 0-3		25,445

*After extra-time. †Played at Highfield Road, Coventry.

Appearances
Sub Appearances
Goals

Burridge	Hinshelwood	Sansom	Nicholas	Cannon	Gilbert	Chatterton	Murphy	Swindlehurst	Elwiss	Hilaire	Fenwick	Silkman	Walsh	Kember	Smillie	Hazell	Sealy	
1	2	3	4	5	6	7	8*	9	10	11	12							1
1	2	3	4	5	6	7	8	9	10	11								2
1	2	3	4	5	6	7	8	9	10	11								3
1	2	3	4	5	6	7	8	9	10	11								4
1	2	3	4	5	6	7	8*	9	10	11		12						5
1	2	3	4	5	6	7	8	9	10	11								6
1	2	3	4	5	6	7	8	9	10	11								7
1	2	3	4	5	6	7	8	9	10	11								8
1	2	3	4	5	6	7	8	9*	10	11			12					9
1	2	3	4	5	6	7	8		10	11			9					10
1	2*	3	7		6	4	8	9	10	11	5		12					11
1		3	7	5*	6	4	8	9	10	11	2		12					12
1		3	7	5	6	4	12	9	10*	11	2			8				13
1		3	7	5	6		8	9		11	2		10	4				14
1		3	7	5	6		8	9	12	11*	2		10	4				15
1		3	7	5	6		8	9	10*		2		11	4	12			16
1		3		5	6		8	9	11	12	4		10	7*		2		17
1		3		5	6		8	9	10		7		11	4		2		18
1		3		5	6		8	9	10		2		11	7		4		19
1		3	7	5	6		8	9	10		2		11	4				20
1	2	3	7	5	6			9	10*	12	8		11	4				21
1		3	7	5	6		8	9		12	2		11	4*	10			22
1		3	7	5	6		8*	9		10			11	4	12	2		23
1	2	3	7	5	6		8*	9		12	10		11	4				24
1	2	3	7	5	6		8	9			10		11	4				25
1	2	3	7	5	6		10	9			8		11	4				26
1	2	3	7	5	6		8	9			10*		11	4	12			27
1	2	3	7	5	6		8*	9		11			10	4	12			28
1	2	3	7	5	6		8	9		11			10	4				29
1	2*	3	7	5			8	9		10	12		11	4		6		30
1	2	3	7	5	6		8	9		11			10	4				31
1	2	3	7	5	6		8	9		10			11	4				32
1	2	3	7	5	6		8	9					11*	4	10		12	33
1	2	3	7	5	6		8				12		10	4	11*		9	34
1	2	3	7	5	6		8	9		12	10*		11	4				35
1	2	3	7*	5	6		8	9		10			11	4	12			36
1	2	3	7	5	6		8	9*			12		11	4			10	37
1	2	3		5	6		8	9			7		11	4			10	38
1	2	3		5	6		8	9		12	7		11	4*			10	39
1	2	3	7	5	6		8	9		11			10	4				40
1	2	3	7	5	6		8	9		11	4		10					41
1	2	3	7	5	6		8	9		11			10	4				42
42	31	42	37	41	41	13	40	40	19	25	20		30	29	3	5	4	
							1		1	6	4	1	3		5		1	
	1		3	2	1	3	5	14	7	6			8		1			

Burridge	Hinshelwood	Sansom	Nicholas	Cannon	Gilbert	Chatterton	Murphy	Swindlehurst	Elwiss	Hilaire	Fenwick	Silkman	Walsh	Kember	Smillie	Hazell	Sealy	
1	2	3	7	5	6		8	9			10		11	4				3
1	2	3	7	5	6		8			10	9		11	4				R
1	2	3	7	5	6		8	10			9		11	4				4
1	2*	3	7	5	6		8	9		12	10		11	4				5
4	4	4	4	4	4		4	3		1	4		4	4				
										1								
		1	1								1		1	1				

Burridge	Hinshelwood	Sansom	Nicholas	Cannon	Gilbert	Chatterton	Murphy	Swindlehurst	Elwiss	Hilaire	Fenwick	Silkman	Walsh	Kember	Smillie	Hazell	Sealy	
1	2	3	8	5	6	4	7	9	10	11								2
1	2	3	7	5	6	4	8	9	10	11								3
1	2	3	7	5	6	4	8	9*	10	11			12					R
1	2	3	7	5*	6	4	8		10	11	12		9					2R
4	4	4	4	4	4	4	4	3	4	4			1					
											1		1					
						1	1	1										

1979-80

Manager: Terry Venables

1	Aug	18	(a)	Manchester C	D 0-0		40,681
2		21	(h)	Southampton	D 0-0		31,756
3		25	(a)	Middlesbrough	D 1-1	Swindlehurst	24,521
4	Sep	1	(h)	Derby C	W 4-0	Flanagan 2, Nicholas, Swindlehurst	25,127
5		8	(a)	Wolves	D 1-1	Swindlehurst	24,580
6		15	(h)	Aston Villa	W 2-1	Murphy 2	28,156
7		22	(a)	Stoke C	W 2-1	Hilaire, Cannon	19,255
8		29	(h)	Ipswich T	W 4-1	Swindlehurst, Hinshelwood, Francis (pen), Cannon	29,885
9	Oct	6	(h)	Tottenham H	D 1-1	Walsh	45,296
10		9	(a)	Southampton	L 1-4	Hinshelwood	23,174
11		13	(a)	Everton	L 1-3	Flanagan	30,645
12		20	(h)	Bristol C	D 1-1	Cannon (pen)	27,333
13		27	(a)	Bolton W	D 1-1	Smillie	15,132
14	Nov	3	(h)	Manchester C	W 2-0	Walsh, Swindlehurst	29,443
15		10	(h)	Arsenal	W 1-0	Swindlehurst	42,887
16		17	(a)	Manchester U	D 1-1	Swindlehurst	52,800
17		24	(h)	Coventry C	D 0-0		26,209
18	Dec	1	(a)	Leeds U	L 0-1		21,330
19		8	(h)	Nottingham F	W 1-0	Walsh	34,782
20		15	(a)	Liverpool	L 0-3		42,898
21		26	(a)	Brighton & HA	L 0-3		28,358
22		29	(h)	Middlesbrough	L 1-2	Francis (pen)	24,880
23	Jan	1	(h)	Norwich C	D 0-0		30,254
24		12	(a)	Derby C	W 2-1	Walsh 2	16,872
25		19	(h)	Wolves	W 1-0	Flanagan	22,577
26		26	(h)	West Brom A	D 2-2	Hilaire, Kember	23,258
27	Feb	2	(a)	Aston Villa	L 0-2		29,469
28		9	(h)	Stoke C	L 0-1		21,181
29		19	(a)	Ipswich T	L 0-3		23,012
30		23	(h)	Everton	D 1-1	Walsh	22,857
31	Mar	1	(a)	Bristol C	W 2-0	Nicholas, Flanagan	15,947
32		8	(h)	Bolton W	W 3-1	Gilbert, Hilaire, Murphy	18,728
33		15	(a)	Tottenham H	D 0-0		28,419
34		22	(a)	Arsenal	D 1-1	Sansom	37,606
35		29	(h)	Manchester U	L 0-2		33,003
36	Apr	1	(a)	West Brom A	L 0-3		17,090
37		5	(h)	Brighton & HA	D 1-1	Cannon	31,466
38		7	(a)	Norwich C	L 1-2	Francis	17,562
39		12	(h)	Leeds U	W 1-0	Hilaire	25,318
40		19	(a)	Coventry C	L 1-2	Hilaire	14,401
41		26	(h)	Liverpool	D 0-0		45,583
42	May	3	(a)	Nottingham F	L 0-4		24,529

FINAL LEAGUE POSITION: 13th in Division One

Appearances
Sub Appearances
Goals

FA Cup

3	Jan	5	(a)	Swansea C	D 2-2	Kember, Walsh	17,970
R		8	(h)	Swansea C	D 3-3*	Hinshelwood, Fenwick, Hilaire	27,006
2R		14	(n†)	Swansea C	L 1-2	Boyle	20,012

*After extra-time. †Played at Ninian Park, Cardiff.

Appearances
Sub Appearances
Goals

League Cup

2	Aug	29	(a)	Stockport C	D 1-1	Flanagan	6,193
	Sep	4	(h)	Stockport C	W 7-0	Murphy, Francis, Flanagan 2, Walsh 2, Hilaire	18,465
3		25	(h)	Wolves	L 1-2	Flanagan	30,645

Appearances
Sub Appearances
Goals

Burridge	Hinshelwood	Sansom	Nicholas	Cannon	Gilbert	Murphy	Francis	Swindlehurst	Flanagan	Hilaire	Fenwick	Walsh	Kember	Smillie	Boyle	Goodchild	Fry	Brooks	
1	2	3	4	5	6	7	8	9	10	11									1
1	2	3	4	5	6	7	8	9	10	11									2
1	2	3	4	5	6	7	8	9	10	11*	12								3
1	2	3*	4	5	6	7		9	10	11		12	8						4
1	2	3	4	5	6	7	8	9	10	11									5
1	2	3	4	5	6	7*	8	9	10	11		12							6
1	2	3	4*	5	6	7	8	9	10	11			12						7
1	2	3	4	5	6	7	8	9	10	11									8
1	2	3	4	5	6	7	8	9*	10	11		12							9
1	2	3	4	5	6	7		9	10	11		12	8*						10
1	2	3	4	5	6	7*	8	12	10	11		9							11
1	2	3	4	5	6	7			10	11		9	8						12
1	2	3	4	5	6*	7			10	11		9	8	12					13
1	2	3	4	5	6	7		10		11*		9	8	12					14
1	2	3	4	5	6	7	8	10		11		9							15
1	2	3	4	5	6	7	8*	10	9	11		12							16
1	2	3	4	5	6	7	8	10	9	11*		12							17
1	2	3	4	5	6	7*	8	10		11		9	12						18
1	2	3	4	5	6	7*	8	10		11	12	9							19
1	2	3	4	5	6	7	8	10		11		9							20
1	2	3*	4	5	6	7	8	10	9	11	12								21
1	2		6	4	5	7	8	10*	9	11	3	12							22
1	2		4	5	6	7*	8		9	11	3	10	12						23
1	2			3	6			7		11	8	9	4	10*	5	12			24
1	2			3	6	7		12	10	11*	8	9	4		5				25
1	2	3		5	6	7	8*	12	10	11		9	4						26
1	2	3	7	5			8*	12	10	11	9		4		6				27
1	2	3	4	5	6	12		9	10	11	8*		7						28
1	2	3	4	5	6	7	8		10	11		9							29
1	2		4	5	6	7	8		10	11	3	9							30
	2	3	4	5	6	7	8		10	11		9					1		31
	2	3	4	5	6	7	8		10	11		9					1		32
	2	3	4	5	6	7	8		10	11		9					1		33
	2	3	4	5	6	7	8		10	11		9					1		34
	2	3	4	5	6		8		10	11	7	9					1		35
	2	3	4	5	6		8*		10	11	7	9		12			1		36
1	2	3	4	5	6	7	8		10	11				9					37
1	2	3	4	5	6	7*	8		10	11	12			9					38
1	2*	3	4	5	6		8		10	11	7			9				12	39
1	2	3	4	5		7	8		9	11				10	6				40
1	2		4	5	6	7*	8		9	11	3	10			12				41
1	2	3	4	5	6	7	8		10	11		9							42
36	42	36	39	42	40	36	34	21	36	42	11	22	10	5	4		6		
						1		4			4	7	3	3	1	1		1	
	2	1	2	4	1	3	3	7	5	5		6	1	1					

Burridge	Hinshelwood	Sansom	Nicholas	Cannon	Gilbert	Murphy	Francis	Swindlehurst	Flanagan	Hilaire	Fenwick	Walsh	Kember	Smillie	Boyle	Goodchild	Fry	Brooks	
1	2		4	5	6	12	8		10*	11	3	9	7						3
1	2			5	6	8*		9		11	3	10	4	7		12			R
1	2			3	6	7		9		11	8	10	4		5				2R
3	3		1	3	3	3	1	2	1	3	3	3	3	1	1				
						1										1			
	1									1	1	1	1		1				

Burridge	Hinshelwood	Sansom	Nicholas	Cannon	Gilbert	Murphy	Francis	Swindlehurst	Flanagan	Hilaire	Fenwick	Walsh	Kember	Smillie	Boyle	Goodchild	Fry	Brooks	
1	2	3	4	5	6	7		9	10	11			8						2
1	2	3	4	5	6	7	8*	9	10	11		12							
1	2	3	4	5	6	7	8	9	10	11									3
3	3	3	3	3	3	3	2	3	3	3			1						
												1							
						1	1		4	1		2							

1980-81

Manager: Terry Venables until 30 October 1980; Ernie Walley until 1 December 1980; Malcolm Allison until 26 January 1981, then Dario Gradi.

1	Aug	16	(a)	Liverpool	L 0-3		42,777
2		19	(h)	Tottenham H	L 3-4	Hilaire, Smillie, Cannon	27,102
3		23	(h)	Middlesbrough	W 5-2	Allen 3 (1 pen), Sealy, Francis	16,713
4		30	(a)	Wolves	L 0-2		20,601
5	Sep	6	(a)	Coventry C	L 1-3	Allen	13,091
6		13	(h)	Ipswich T	L 1-2	Lovell	24,282
7		20	(a)	Everton	L 0-5		26,950
8		27	(h)	Aston Villa	L 0-1		18,398
9	Oct	4	(h)	West Brom A	L 0-1		16,081
10		11	(a)	Sunderland	L 0-1		25,444
11		18	(h)	Leicester C	W 2-1	Hilaire, Allen (pen)	16,387
12		21	(h)	Southampton	W 3-2	Flanagan 3	20,630
13		25	(a)	Leeds U	L 0-1		19,208
14		29	(a)	Norwich C	D 1-1	Francis	15,782
15	Nov	1	(h)	Manchester U	W 1-0	Nicholas	31,181
16		8	(a)	Birmingham C	L 0-1		16,910
17		12	(a)	Tottenham H	L 2-4	Hilaire, Walsh	25,777
18		15	(h)	Liverpool	D 2-2	Francis (pen), Walsh	31,154
19		22	(a)	Stoke C	L 0-1		13,422
20		29	(h)	Manchester C	L 2-3	Walsh, Sealy	16,575
21	Dec	6	(a)	Nottingham F	L 0-3		20,223
22		13	(h)	Norwich C	W 4-1	Allen 2, Murphy, Francis	15,257
23		20	(a)	Southampton	L 2-4	Sealy, Allen	19,352
24		26	(h)	Arsenal	D 2-2	Sealy 2	29,850
25		27	(a)	Brighton & HA	L 2-3	Murphy, Gregory (og)	27,367
26	Jan	10	(h)	Stoke C	D 1-1	Boyle	14,154
27		17	(h)	Wolves	D 0-0		15,080
28		31	(a)	Middlesbrough	L 0-2		16,099
29	Feb	7	(a)	Ipswich T	L 2-3	Walsh, Mariner (og)	25,036
30		17	(h)	Coventry C	L 0-3		12,268
31		21	(a)	Aston Villa	L 1-2	Hinshelwood	27,203
32		28	(h)	Everton	L 2-3	Allen (pen), Hilaire	14,594
33	Mar	7	(a)	West Brom A	L 0-1		15,999
34		14	(h)	Sunderland	L 0-1		16,748
35		21	(a)	Leicester C	D 1-1	Price	15,176
36		28	(h)	Leeds U	L 0-1		15,053
37	Apr	4	(a)	Manchester U	L 0-1		37,974
38		11	(h)	Birmingham C	W 3-1	Langley 2, Lovell	9,820
39		18	(h)	Brighton & HA	L 0-3		18,792
40		20	(a)	Arsenal	L 2-3	Price, Langley	24,346
41		25	(h)	Nottingham F	L 1-3	Smillie	12,138
42	May	2	(a)	Manchester C	D 1-1	Walsh	31,017

FINAL LEAGUE POSITION: 22nd in Division One

Appearances
Sub Appearances
Goals

FA Cup

3	Jan	3	(a)	Manchester C	L 0-4		39,347

Appearances
Sub Appearances
Goals

League Cup

2	Aug	26	(a)	Bolton W	W 3-0	Murphy 2, Flanagan	9,931
	Sep	2	(h)	Bolton W	W 2-1	Francis, Allen	15,536
3		24	(a)	Tottenham H	D 0-0		29,654
R		30	(h)	Tottenham H	L 1-3*	Allen (pen)	26,885

*After extra-time

Appearances
Sub Appearances
Goals

Barron	Hinshelwood	Fenwick	Nicholas	Cannon	Gilbert	Smillie	Francis	Allen	Flanagan	Hilaire	Murphy	Sealy	Leahy	Lovell	Brooks	Walsh	Boyle	Fry	Gennoe	Carter L	Goodchild	Dare	Banfield	Price	Bason	Langley	Paul	
1	2*	3	4	5	6	7	8	9	10	11	12																	1
1		3	2	5	6	7*	8	9	10	11	4	12																2
1		3	2	5	6	7	8	9	10		4	12	11*															3
1		3		5	6		8	9	10	11	4	12	7*	2														4
1	2	3		5	6	7	8	9	10	11	4																	5
1	2	3		5	6	7	8	9	10	11		12		4														6
1	2	3		5	6	7	8	9	10		11			4	12													7
1	2	3	4	5	6	7		9	10		11	8																8
1	2	3	4	5	6	7*	8	9	10	11						12												9
1	2	3	4	5	6		8	9	7	11						10												10
1	2	3	4	5	6	12	8	9	7	11*						10												11
1	2	3	4	5	6		8	9	7	11						10												12
1	2	3	4	5	6		8*	9	7	11				12		10												13
1	2	3	4	5	6	11*	8		10			12		7		9												14
1	2	3	4	5	6	11	8		10					7		9												15
1	2	3	4	5	6	11			10*		8			7		9	12											16
1	2	3	4	5	6		8		10	11				7		9												17
1	2	3	4	5	6		8		10*	11		12		7		9												18
1		3	4	5	6		8		10	11				7		9	2											19
1	4	3		2	6		8*		10	11		12		7		9	5											20
1	2	3	4	5	6		8	10		11		7				9												21
1	2		4	5	6		8	9		11	7*	10				12	3											22
	2		4	5	6		8	9		11	7	10					3	1										23
	2		4	5	6	12	8	9		11*	7	10					3	1										24
	2		4	5		11	8	9			7	10		6*	12		3	1										25
	2		4	5	6	12	8			11*		9		7			3		1	10								26
	2		4	5	6	11	8	10			7	9					3		1									27
	2		4	5	6	11		10				9		7	8*		3		1		12							28
1	3		8		4	7		9			10			2	6	11	5											29
	2		4			8		9		10	7*				6	11	5	1				3	12					30
	2		4			7		9		11		10			8		5	1				3	6					31
1	2		4		6	7*		9		11		10		3	8		5			12								32
1	2		4		6					11		9		7	8	10	5						3					33
1	2			5*	7	6				11				3	8	9								4	12	10		34
1	2				6					11				3	8	9	5							4	7	10		35
1	3				6					11	12			2*	8	9	5							4	7	10		36
1	3				6					11				2	8	9	5							4	7	10		37
	3				6					11				2	8	9	5	1						4*	7	10	12	38
1	3			6	12					11				2	8	9*	5							4	7	10		39
1	3			5	6			9*		11	12			2	8									4	7	10		40
1	3			5	6	11					4			2	8	9									7	10		41
1	3			5	6	7				11*	12				8	9								4	2	10		42
33	38	21	28	33	38	21	25	25	20	31	15	12	2	24	15	23	19	6	3	1		2	2	8	8	9		
					1	3					4	7		1	2	2	1			1	1		1		1		1	
	1		1	1		2	4	9	3	4	2	5		2		5	1							2		3		

2 own-goals

Barron	Hinshelwood	Fenwick	Nicholas	Cannon	Gilbert	Smillie	Francis	Allen	Flanagan	Hilaire	Murphy	Sealy	Leahy	Lovell	Brooks	Walsh	Boyle	Fry	Gennoe	Carter L	Goodchild	Dare	Banfield	Price	Bason	Langley	Paul	
	2		4*	5	6	11					7	9		8		10	3	1			12							3
	1		1	1	1	1					1	1		1		1	1	1										
																					1							

Barron	Hinshelwood	Fenwick	Nicholas	Cannon	Gilbert	Smillie	Francis	Allen	Flanagan	Hilaire	Murphy	Sealy	Leahy	Lovell	Brooks	Walsh	Boyle	Fry	Gennoe	Carter L	Goodchild	Dare	Banfield	Price	Bason	Langley	Paul	
1		3	2	5	6		8	9	10	11	4*	12	7															2
1		3		5	6	7	8	9	10	11	4*			2	12													
1	2	3	4	5	6	7	8	9	10		11																	3
1	2	3	4	5	6	7*	8	9	10		11	12																R
4	2	4	3	4	4	3	4	4	4	2	4		1	1														
												2			1													
							1	2	1		2																	

1981-82

Manager: Dario Gradi until 10 November 1981, then Steve Kember.

1	Aug	29	(h)	Cambridge U	W	2-1	Hinshelwood 2 (2 pens)	11,201
2	Sep	2	(a)	Norwich C	L	0-1		14,434
3		5	(a)	Sheffield W	L	0-1		18,476
4		12	(h)	Charlton A	W	2-0	Walsh 2	14,227
5		19	(a)	Queen's Park R	L	0-1		17,039
6		22	(h)	Orient	W	1-0	Hilaire	11,061
7		26	(h)	Shrewsbury T	L	0-1		9,037
8	Oct	3	(a)	Leicester C	D	1-1	Hilaire	12,558
9		10	(h)	Rotherham U	W	3-1	Smillie, Brooks, Langley	8,021
10		17	(a)	Wrexham	W	1-0	Lovell	4,795
11		24	(h)	Derby C	L	0-1		11,127
12		31	(a)	Luton T	L	0-1		11,712
13	Nov	7	(h)	Blackburn R	L	1-2	Cannon (pen)	9,452
14		21	(a)	Oldham A	D	0-0		5,581
15		24	(h)	Norwich C	W	2-1	Mabbutt 2	9,010
16		28	(h)	Bolton W	W	1-0	Jones (og)	8,889
17	Dec	5	(a)	Barnsley	L	0-2		14,877
18	Jan	19	(h)	Sheffield W	L	1-2	Wicks	8,289
19		26	(a)	Cambridge U	D	0-0		3,505
20		30	(h)	Queen's Park R	D	0-0		15,267
21	Feb	6	(a)	Charlton A	L	1-2	Brooks	9,072
22		21	(a)	Orient	D	0-0		5,132
23		27	(a)	Rotherham U	L	0-2		10,007
24	Mar	9	(h)	Cardiff C	W	1-0	Langley	6,526
25		13	(a)	Derby C	L	1-4	McAlle (og)	10,248
26		17	(a)	Chelsea	W	2-1	Marbutt, Murphy	13,894
27		20	(h)	Luton T	D	3-3	Smillie 2, Marbutt	12,001
28		23	(h)	Leicester C	L	0-2		9,506
29		27	(a)	Blackburn R	L	0-1		8,362
30		31	(a)	Newcastle U	D	0-0		21,610
31	Apr	3	(h)	Grimsby T	L	0-3		7,541
32		9	(a)	Watford	D	1-1	Giles	18,224
33		12	(h)	Chelsea	L	0-1		17,189
34		17	(h)	Oldham A	W	4-0	Hilaire 2, Marbutt 2	6,720
35		20	(a)	Grimsby T	W	1-0	Hilaire	7,646
36		24	(a)	Bolton W	D	0-0		6,280
37		27	(h)	Watford	L	0-3		12,355
38	May	1	(h)	Barnsley	L	1-2	Marbutt	7,500
39		4	(a)	Shrewsbury T	L	0-1		3,159
40		8	(a)	Cardiff C	W	1-0	Marbutt	5,762
41		11	(h)	Wrexham	W	2-1	Wilkins 2	7,272
42		15	(h)	Newcastle U	L	1-2	Murphy (pen)	8,453

FINAL LEAGUE POSITION: 15th in Division Two

Appearances
Sub Appearances
Goals

FA Cup

3	Jan	2	(a)	Enfield	W	3-2	Price, Hilaire 2	3,467
4		23	(h)	Bolton W	W	1-0	Cannon (pen)	9,719
5	Feb	13	(h)	Orient	D	0-0		14,501
R		16	(a)	Orient	W	1-0	Smillie	10,067
6	Mar	6	(a)	Queen's Park R	L	0-1		24,653

Appearances
Sub Appearances
Goals

League Cup

2	Oct	6	(a)	Doncaster R	L	0-1		7,783
		27	(h)	Doncaster R	W	2-0	Cannon (pen), Murphy	7,819
3	Nov	11	(a)	Sunderland	W	1-0	Cannon	11,139
4	Dec	15	(h)	West Brom A	L	1-3	Langley	10,311

Appearances
Sub Appearances
Goals

Barron	Hinshelwood P	Dare	Price	Cannon	Gilbert	Smillie	Murphy	Walsh	Langley	Hilaire	Hughes	Bason	Brooks	Lovell	Wicks	Leahy	Galliers	Mabbutt	Boulter	Giles	Fry	Wilkins	Baxter	Nebbeling	
1	2	3	4	5	6*	7	8	9	10	11	12														1
1	2	3	4	5	6	7		9	10			8	11*	12											2
1	2	3	4	5	6	7		9	10		12	11		8*											3
1	2		4	3	6	8		9	10	11		7			5										4
1	2		6	3	5	8		9	10	11*	12	7			4										5
1			4	3	6	8		9	10	11		7		2	5										6
1			4	3	6	8		9	10	11		7		2*	5	12									7
1		3	4	5	6	8			10	11	9	2	7*	12											8
1				5	6	8	4	12	10		9	2	7	3		11*									9
1				5	6	8	4	9*	10	11	12	2	7	3											10
1				5	6	8	4		10	11	9*	2	7	3			12								11
1			12	5	6	8	4		10			2	11*	3			7	9							12
1			11	5	6	8	4*		10	12		2		3			7	9							13
1			7	5		8	4		10*	11		2		6			12	9	3						14
1			7*	5		8	4		9	11		2		6			12	10	3						15
1				5		8	4		9	11			7	6			2	10	3						16
1				5		8	4		9	11			7	6			2	10	3						17
1	2			6		8	4	9		11			12	7*	5			10	3						18
1	2			6		8	4	9*		11			7		5		12	10	3						19
1	2			6		8	4	9		11			7		5			10	3						20
1	2			6		8	4	9		11			12		5			10*	3	7					21
1	2		12	6		8			9	11			7		5			10	3	4*					22
1	2*			4	6	8			9	11			7		5			10	3	12					23
				9	6	8*	4		12	11				2	5			10	3	7	1				24
1	2			5	6	8	4			11			9	3				10		7					25
1	2			9	6	8	4		11						5			10	3	7					26
1	2			11	6	8	4		9*	12					5			10	3	7					27
1	2			11	6	8	4		9	7			12		5			10	3*						28
1	2		4	11					9	8		12	5	6*				10	3	7					29
1	3		4	5	6	8			9			2	11					10		7					30
1	3			5	6	8			9	12		2*	11	4				10		7					31
1	3		4	5	6	8				11			9	2				10		7					32
1	3		4	5	6	8				11			9	2				10		7					33
1	3			5	6	8				11			9	2			4	10		7					34
1	3			5	6	8				11			9	2			4	10		7					35
1	3			5	6	8				11			9	2			4	10		7					36
1	3			5	6	8	12			11			9	2			4*	10		7					37
1	3			5	6	8	4			11				9				10	2	7*		12			38
1	3		4	5	6	8	9			11*				2				10		7		12			39
1	2		9*	5	6	8	4			11				3				10		7		12			40
1				5	6*	8	4			11		2		3			12	10		7		9			41
				5		8	4			11				2				10		7	1	9	3	6	42
40	27	4	17	42	31	41	24	12	25	33	3	17	22	28	14	1	8	31	16	20	2	2	1	1	
			2				1	1	1	3	4	1	3	2		1	5			1		3			
	2			1		3	2	2	2	5			2	1	1			8		1		2			

2 own-goals

Barron	Hinshelwood P	Dare	Price	Cannon	Gilbert	Smillie	Murphy	Walsh	Langley	Hilaire	Hughes	Bason	Brooks	Lovell	Wicks	Leahy	Galliers	Mabbutt	Boulter	Giles	Fry	Wilkins	Baxter	Nebbeling	
1	2		7	6		8	4	9*		11				12	5			10	3						3
1	2			6		8	4	9		11			7		5			10	3						4
1	2			6		8	4	9	12	10*			7		5			11	3						5
1	2		12	6		8	4*		9	11			7		5			10	3						R
1	2			9	6	8	4			11					5			10	3	7					6
5	5		1	5	1	5	5	3	1	5			3		5			5	5	1					
			1						1																
			1	1		1				2															

Barron	Hinshelwood P	Dare	Price	Cannon	Gilbert	Smillie	Murphy	Walsh	Langley	Hilaire	Hughes	Bason	Brooks	Lovell	Wicks	Leahy	Galliers	Mabbutt	Boulter	Giles	Fry	Wilkins	Baxter	Nebbeling	
1		3*	4	5	6	8			10		9	2	7	12		11									2
1			7	5	6	8	4		10	11		2	12	3		9*									
1			7	5	6	8	4		10	11	9	2		3											3
1			10*	5		8	4	12	9	11		2	7	6					3						4
4		1	4	4	3	4	3		4	3	2	4	2	3		2			1						
								1					1	1											
				2			1		1																

1982-83

Manager: Alan Mullery MBE

1	Aug	28	(h)	Barnsley	D 1-1	Hilaire	7,549
2	Sep	4	(a)	Rotherham U	D 2-2	Hinshelwood, Mabbutt	6,989
3		7	(h)	Shrewsbury T	W 2-1	Mabbutt, Hilaire	6,578
4		11	(h)	Blackburn R	W 2-0	Mabbutt, Hilaire	7,529
5		18	(a)	Carlisle U	L 1-4	Hinshelwood	4,390
6		25	(h)	Middlesbrough	W 3-0	Mabbutt 2, Edwards	7,689
7		28	(a)	Queen's Park R	D 0-0		12,194
8	Oct	2	(a)	Bolton W	L 0-1		5,804
9		9	(a)	Burnley	L 1-2	Hinshelwood	6,429
10		16	(h)	Oldham A	W 1-0	Mabbutt	6,843
11		23	(a)	Newcastle U	L 0-1		22,554
12		30	(h)	Fulham	D 1-1	Hilaire	14,912
13	Nov	6	(a)	Chelsea	D 0-0		15,169
14		13	(h)	Leeds U	D 1-1	Mabbutt	11,673
15		20	(a)	Leicester C	W 1-0	Mabbutt	8,616
16		27	(h)	Wolves	L 3-4	Cannon, Jones, Hinshelwood	10,225
17	Dec	4	(a)	Grimsby T	L 1-4	Cooper (og)	5,295
18		11	(h)	Sheffield W	W 2-0	Hinshelwood, Langley	8,498
19		18	(a)	Derby C	D 1-1	Langley	13,207
20		27	(h)	Charlton A	D 1-1	Jones	17,996
21		28	(a)	Cambridge U	L 0-1		4,822
22	Jan	1	(h)	Leicester C	W 1-0	Langley	8,801
23		3	(h)	Rotherham U	D 1-1	Hinshelwood (pen)	7,704
24		15	(a)	Barnsley	L 1-3	Jones	10,120
25		22	(h)	Queen's Park R	L 0-3		14,621
26	Feb	5	(a)	Shrewsbury T	D 1-1	Hinshelwood (pen)	3,716
27		22	(h)	Bolton W	W 3-0	Edwards 2, Brooks	4,456
28		26	(a)	Oldham A	L 0-2		9,780
29	Mar	5	(h)	Newcastle U	L 0-2		10,239
30		12	(a)	Fulham	L 0-1		11,234
31		19	(h)	Chelsea	D 0-0		13,437
32		26	(a)	Leeds U	L 1-2	Murphy (pen)	13,973
33	Apr	2	(h)	Cambridge U	D 0-0		5,495
34		4	(a)	Charlton A	L 1-2	Brown	7,836
35		9	(h)	Carlisle U	W 2-1	Rushbury (og), Brown	5,696
36		16	(a)	Blackburn R	L 0-3		4,635
37		23	(h)	Grimsby T	W 2-0	Hilaire, Brooks	5,909
38		30	(a)	Wolves	L 0-1		12,523
39	May	7	(h)	Derby C	W 4-1	Nebbeling, Mabbutt 2, Hughton	8,464
40		10	(a)	Middlesbrough	L 0-2		10,014
41		14	(a)	Sheffield W	L 1-2	Murphy	11,154
42		17	(h)	Burnley	W 1-0	Edwards	22,714

FINAL LEAGUE POSITION: 15th in Division Two

Appearances
Sub Appearances
Goals

FA Cup

3	Jan	8	(h)	York C	W 2-1	Lovell, Langley	7,831
4		29	(h)	Birmingham C	W 1-0	Edwards	12,327
5	Feb	19	(h)	Burnley	D 0-0		14,949
R		28	(a)	Burnley	L 0-1		16,150

Appearances
Sub Appearances
Goals

League Cup

1	Aug	31	(h)	Portsmouth	W 2-0	Hinshelwood 2	6,631
	Sep	14	(a)	Portsmouth	D 1-1	Lovell	10,698
2	Oct	6	(a)	Peterborough U	W 2-0	Edwards 2	3,798
		26	(h)	Peterborough U	W 2-1	Mabbutt, Hilaire	4,502
3	Nov	9	(h)	Sheffield W	L 1-2	Mabbutt	8,146

Appearances
Sub Appearances
Goals

Barron	Hinshelwood	Williams	Hughton	Cannon	Gilbert	Giles	Murphy	Langley	Mabbutt	Hilaire	Lovell	Edwards	Nebbeling	Brooks	Jones	Fry	Locke	Brown	Wilkins	Price	
1	2	3	4	5	6	7	8*	9	10	11	12										1
1	2	3	4	5	6	7*	8		10	11	12	9									2
1	2	3	4	5	6	7	8		10	11		9									3
1	2	3	4	5	6	7			10	11	8	9									4
1	2	3	4	5	6	7			10	11	8	9									5
1	2	3	4	5	6	7			10	11	8	9									6
1	2	3	4	5	6	7		9	10	11	8										7
1	2	3	4	5	6	7			10	11	8	9									8
1	2	3		5	6	7	4*	9	10	11	8		12								9
1	2	3	4	5	6	7			10	11	8	9									10
1			8	5	6	7			10	11	4	9	2	3							11
1			8	5	6	7	3		10	11	4	9	2								12
1	6		8	5		7	3		10	11	4	9	2								13
1	6		8	5		7	3	12	10	11	4	9*	2								14
1	6		8	5*	2	7	3	9	10	11	4		12								15
1	6		8	5	2	7	3		10	11	4				9						16
1	6		8	5	2	7	3	10		11	4				9						17
	6		8	5	2	7	3	10		11			4		9	1					18
	6		8	5	2	7	3	10		11			4		9	1					19
	6		8	5	2	7	3	10		11			4		9	1					20
	6		8	5	2	7	3	10		11			4		9	1					21
	6		8	5	2	7*	3	10		11	12		4		9	1					22
	6		8	5	2	7		10		11	3		4		9	1					23
	6		8	5		7		10*		11	3	12	4		9	1	2				24
	6		8	5		7		10		11		12	4	3*	9	1	2				25
	6		8	5	2		3	10		11		7			9	1	4				26
	6			5	2		3	10		11		7		8	9	1	4				27
	6		4		2	12	3	10		11		7*	5	8	9	1					28
			6	5		7	3	10		11			4	8	9	1	2				29
	6		8	5			3	10		11			4		9	1	2	7			30
	6		8	5		10	3			11			4		9	1	2	7			31
			8	5	6	10	3			11			4		9	1	2	7			32
			8	5	6	10	3	12		11			4*		9	1	2	7			33
			8	5	6	10	3	9*	12	11			4			1	2	7			34
	2		4	5	6	7	10		8	11						1	3	9			35
	3		8	5	6	10			9	11			4*			1	2	7	12		36
	2		8	5	6	10			9	11			4	3		1		7			37
	2		8	5		10	6		9	11			4	3		1		7			38
	2		4	5	6	7	10		8	11			3			1		9			39
	2		4	5	6		10	7	8	11			3			1		9			40
	2*		4	5	6	7	10	12	8	11		9	3			1					41
			4	5	6	7	10*	12	8	11		9	3			1	2				42
17	35	10	40	41	34	37	30	20	24	42	16	16	26	7	18	25	13	11			
						1		4	1		3	2	2						1		
	7		1	1			2	3	10	5		4	1	2	3			2			

2 own-goals

Barron	Hinshelwood	Williams	Hughton	Cannon	Gilbert	Giles	Murphy	Langley	Mabbutt	Hilaire	Lovell	Edwards	Nebbeling	Brooks	Jones	Fry	Locke	Brown	Wilkins	Price	
	6		8	5	2	7		10		11	3		4		9	1					3
	6		8	5	2		3	10		11		7			9	1	4				4
	6			5	2	12	3	10		11		7		8	9*	1	4				5
	6			5	2		3	10		11		7		8	9	1	4				R
	4		2	4	4	1	3	4		4	1	3	1	2	4	4	3				
						1															
								1			1	1									

Barron	Hinshelwood	Williams	Hughton	Cannon	Gilbert	Giles	Murphy	Langley	Mabbutt	Hilaire	Lovell	Edwards	Nebbeling	Brooks	Jones	Fry	Locke	Brown	Wilkins	Price	
1	2	3	4	5		7		9	10*	11	8		6							12	1
1	2	3	4	5	6		8		10	11	7	9									
1	2	3		5	6	7	4		10	11	8	9									2
1			4	5	2	7			10	11	3	9	6	8							
1	2		4	5		7	8	12	10	11	3*	9	6								3
5	4	3	4	5	3	4	3	1	5	5	5	4	3	1							
								1												1	
	2								2	1	1	2									

1983-84

Manager: Alan Mullery MBE

1	Aug	27	(h)	Manchester C	L 0-2		13,362
2	Sep	3	(a)	Shrewsbury T	D 1-1	Cummins	3,849
3		6	(a)	Huddersfield T	L 1-2	Cummings	7,814
4		11	(h)	Fulham	D 1-1	Wilson (og)	11,327
5		17	(a)	Newcastle U	L 1-3	Evans	22,774
6		27	(h)	Portsmouth	W 2-1	Wilkins, Hateley (og)	8,486
7	Oct	1	(a)	Middlesbrough	W 3-1	Hilaire, Evans 2	8,927
8		8	(a)	Cambridge U	W 3-1	Hilaire, Giles, Evans	4,323
9		15	(h)	Derby C	L 0-1		7,081
10		22	(a)	Grimsby T	L 0-2		6,500
11		29	(h)	Barnsley	L 0-1		6,377
12	Nov	5	(a)	Leeds U	D 1-1	Giles	14,847
13		8	(h)	Cardiff C	W 1-0	Murphy	5,299
14		12	(h)	Oldham A	W 2-1	McCulloch, Murphy	5,481
15		19	(a)	Chelsea	D 2-2	Locke, Evans	19,060
16		26	(h)	Sheffield W	W 1-0	Giles	11,263
17	Dec	3	(a)	Swansea C	L 0-1		7,000
18		11	(h)	Carlisle U	L 1-2	Stebbing	6,460
19		17	(a)	Blackburn R	L 1-2	Evans	4,,794
20		26	(h)	Brighton & HA	L 0-2		13,781
21		27	(a)	Charlton A	L 0-1		10,224
22		31	(h)	Shrewsbury T	D 1-1	Stebbing	5,275
23	Jan	14	(a)	Manchester C	L 1-3	Giles	20,144
24		21	(h)	Newcastle U	W 3-1	McCulloch, Mabbutt, Gilbert	9,464
25	Feb	4	(h)	Middlesbrough	W 1-0	Nicholas (pen)	4,819
26		11	(a)	Fulham	D 1-1	McCulloch	9,119
27		18	(a)	Barnsley	D 1-1	Nicholas	6,233
28		25	(h)	Grimsby T	L 0-1		5,956
29	Mar	3	(h)	Leeds U	D 0-0		8,077
30		10	(a)	Oldham A	L 2-3	Barber, Cummins	4,138
31		17	(h)	Huddersfield T	D 0-0		5,003
32		24	(a)	Portsmouth	W 1-0	Evans	10,237
33	Apr	1	(h)	Cambridge U	D 1-1	Murphy	5,276
34		7	(a)	Derby C	L 0-3		10,903
35		14	(h)	Chelsea	D 0-0		20,540
36		17	(a)	Cardiff C	W 2-0	Smith (og), Cummins	4,091
37		21	(a)	Brighton & HA	L 1-3	Nicholas	15,214
38		23	(h)	Charlton A	W 2-0	Cannon, Mabbutt	7,818
39		28	(a)	Sheffield W	L 0-1		27,287
40	May	5	(h)	Swansea C	W 2-0	Cannon, Mabbutt	5,318
41		7	(a)	Carlisle U	D 2-2	Giles, Barber	3,013
42		12	(h)	Blackburn R	L 0-2		5,078

FINAL LEAGUE POSITION: 18th in Division Two

Appearances
Sub Appearances
Goals

FA Cup

3	Jan	7	(h)	Leicester C	W 1-0	Gilbert	11,497
4		28	(h)	West Ham U	D 1-1	McCulloch	27,590
R		31	(a)	West Ham U	L 0-2		27,127

Appearances
Sub Appearances
Goals

League Cup

1	Aug	30	(h)	Peterborough U	W 3-0	Hilaire 2, Brooks (pen)	3,975
	Sep	14	(a)	Peterborough U	L 0-3*		3,504

*Aggregate 3-3, Peterborough United won 4-2 on penalties.

Appearances
Sub Appearances
Goals

Wood	Locke	Gilbert	Hughton	Lacy	Cannon	Evans	Murphy	Cummins	McCulloch	Hilaire	Brooks	Giles	Nebbeling	Stebbing	Fashanu	Strong	Wilkins	Nicholas	Lindsay	Martin	Mabbutt	Barber	
1	2	3	4	5	6	7	8*	9	10	11	12												1
1	2	3	4	5	6			9	10	11	8	7											2
1	2	3	4	5	6			9	10	11	8	7											3
1	2*	3			5		10	8		11	7	12	4	6	9								4
1		2	4	5		11	8	10	9			7	6			3							5
1		2	4	5		8	10			11		7	6			3	9						6
1			4	5		8		10		11		7	6	2		3	9						7
1	10		4	5		8				11		7	6	2		3	9						8
1	2*	12	4	5	9	10	8			11		7	6			3							9
1		2	3	5	6	8	4			11		7					9	10					10
1			3	12	6	8				11		7	5	2		4*	9	10					11
1	4	5	3		6	8				11		7		2			9	10					12
1	2	6	3		5	8	12		9	11		7		4*				10					13
1	2	6	3		5*	8	4		9	11		7		12				10					14
1	2	6	3	10	5	8	7		9	11				4									15
1	2	6	3	8	5		4		9	11		7		10									16
1	2	6	3	12	5*	8	4		10	11		7		9									17
1	2	6	3	5			4		9*	11			12	10					7	8			18
1	2	6	3	5		10	8		9	11			12	4		7*							19
1	2	6	3	5		8	7		10	11			12	4*				9					20
1	2	6	3	5			4		9	11*		7	8	10							12		21
1	2	6	3	5			4					7	9	8				11			10		22
1	2		3				6		9	11		7	5	4				10			8		23
1	2	6	3		5		12		9*	11		7		4				10			8		24
1	2	6	3		5				9	11		7		4				10			8		25
1	2*	6			5	12	3		9	11		7		4				10			8		26
1	2				5	8	3		9	11		7	6	4				10					27
1	2			12	5*		3	8		11		7	6	4				10				9	28
1	2	6			5	12	3	8	9*	11		7		4				10					29
1	2	6		9	5		3	8		11				4				10				7	30
1	2	6		10	5		3	8		11				4			9					7	31
1	2	6	9		5	8	3			11				4				10				7	32
1	2	6	9		5	8	3	12		11				4*				10				7	33
1	2	6	9		5	8*	3	4	7	11								10				12	34
1	2	6	3	7	5				9	11				4				10				8	35
1	2	6	3	10	5			7	9	11				8				4					36
1	2	6	3	8	5			7	9	11		12		4*				10					37
1	2	6	3		5		4	8	9	11		7*						10			12		38
1	2	6	3		5		4	8	9	11								10			7		39
1			3	6	5		4	7*		11		12		2				10			8	9	40
1	2	6	3	5			4			11		8						10			7	9	41
1	2		3	5			10	9		11		7	6	4							8		42
42	36	33	35	24	30	19	30	17	25	40	3	26	13	30	1	7	7	25	1	1	9	8	
		1		3		2	2	1			1	3	3	1							2	1	
	1	1			2	7	3	4	3	2		5		2			1	3			3	2	

3 own-goals

Wood	Locke	Gilbert	Hughton	Lacy	Cannon	Evans	Murphy	Cummins	McCulloch	Hilaire	Brooks	Giles	Nebbeling	Stebbing	Fashanu	Strong	Wilkins	Nicholas	Lindsay	Martin	Mabbutt	Barber	
1	2	6	3	5					9	11		7		4				10			8		3
1	2	6	3		5				9	11		7		4				10			8		4
1	2	6	3*		5	12			9	11		7		4				10			8		R
3	3	3	3	1	2				3	3		3		3				3			3		
						1																	
		1							1														

Wood	Locke	Gilbert	Hughton	Lacy	Cannon	Evans	Murphy	Cummins	McCulloch	Hilaire	Brooks	Giles	Nebbeling	Stebbing	Fashanu	Strong	Wilkins	Nicholas	Lindsay	Martin	Mabbutt	Barber	
1	2	3	4	5	6	7*		9	10	11	8	12											1
1	2	3		6	5*		10	8		11	4	7	12		9								
2	2	2	1	2	2	1	1	2	1	2	2	1			1								
												1	1										
										2	1												

1984-85

Manager: Steve Coppell

1	Aug	25	(h)	Blackburn R	D 1-1	Cummins	6,764
2	Sep	1	(a)	Shrewsbury T	L 1-4	Sparrow	3,414
3		8	(h)	Birmingham C	L 0-2		6,519
4		15	(a)	Brighton & HA	L 0-1		15,044
5		18	(a)	Sheffield U	W 2-1	Mahoney, Murphy	12,701
6		22	(h)	Leeds U	W 3-1	Cummins (pen), Irvine, Murphy	9,460
7		29	(a)	Manchester C	L 1-2	Irvine	20,252
8	Oct	7	(h)	Barnsley	L 0-1		6,252
9		13	(a)	Carlisle U	L 0-1		3,156
10		20	(a)	Wolves	L 1-2	Cummins (pen)	6,665
11		27	(h)	Fulham	D 2-2	Irvine, Nicholas (pen)	8,035
12	Nov	4	(a)	Wimbledon	L 2-3	Nicholas (pen), Mahoney	7,674
13		6	(h)	Shrewsbury T	D 2-2	Mahoney, Murphy	4,002
14		10	(h)	Huddersfield T	D 1-1	Aylott	4,906
15		17	(a)	Portsmouth	D 1-1	Barber	12,656
16		25	(h)	Oldham A	W 3-0	Aylott, Mahoney, Sparrow	4,502
17	Dec	1	(a)	Middlesbrough	D 1-1	Aylott	4,688
18		9	(h)	Cardiff C	D 1-1	Aylott	6,004
19		15	(a)	Grimsby T	W 3-1	Barber, Gray, Nicholas	5,814
20		26	(h)	Charlton A	W 2-1	Mabbutt, Nicholas	9,540
21		29	(a)	Oxford U	L 0-5		11,522
22	Jan	1	(a)	Notts C	D 0-0		5,715
23	Feb	2	(h)	Manchester C	L 1-2	Gray	7,668
24		5	(h)	Oxford U	W 1-0	Aylott	6,489
25		16	(a)	Huddersfield T	L 0-2		5,678
26		24	(h)	Wimbledon	L 0-5		8,005
27	Mar	2	(a)	Fulham	D 2-2	Gray, Stebbing	7,654
28		9	(h)	Wolves	D 0-0		5,413
29		17	(h)	Carlisle U	W 2-1	Barber 2	4,330
30		23	(a)	Barnsley	L 1-3	Gray (pen)	4,174
31		30	(h)	Sheffield U	L 1-3	Droy	4,552
32	Apr	2	(h)	Brighton & HA	D 1-1	Aylott	8,025
33		6	(a)	Charlton A	D 1-1	Aylott	6,131
34		8	(h)	Notts C	W 1-0	Cannon	4,744
35		13	(a)	Leeds U	L 1-4	Finnigan	12,286
36		16	(a)	Birmingham C	L 0-3		10,271
37		20	(h)	Portsmouth	W 2-1	Droy, Gray	10,215
38		23	(a)	Blackburn R	W 1-0	Irvine	9,725
39		27	(a)	Oldham A	L 0-1		2,628
40	May	4	(h)	Middlesbrough	W 1-0	Cannon	4,900
41		6	(a)	Cardiff C	W 3-0	Aylott, Galloway, Irvine	5,207
42		11	(h)	Grimsby T	L 0-2		4,923

FINAL LEAGUE POSITION: 15th in Division Two

Appearances
Sub Appearances
Goals

FA Cup

3	Jan	5	(a)	Millwall	D 1-1	Mahoney	11,015
R		23	(h)	Millwall	L 1-2	Aylott	10,735

Appearances
Sub Appearances
Goals

League Cup

1	Aug	27	(h)	Northampton T	W 1-0	Nicholas	3,752
	Sep	4	(a)	Northampton T	D 0-0		2,979
2		25	(a)	Sunderland	L 1-2	Cummins	11,696
	Oct	13	(h)	Sunderland	D 0-0		6,871

Appearances
Sub Appearances
Goals

Wood	Locke	Sparrow	Stebbing	Whyte	Hughton	Irvine	Murphy	Aylott	Nicholas	Cummins	Cannon	Mahoney	Barber	Lindsay	Nebbeling	Mabbutt	Galloway	Gray	Finnigan	Taylor	Droy	
1	2	3	4	5	6	7	8	9	10	11												1
1	2	3	4	5	6	7*	8	9	10	11		12										2
1	2	3		5	12	7	8	9	10	11	6	4*										3
1	2	3	4	5		7	8		10	11	6	9*	12									4
1	2	3	4	5		7	8		10	11	6	9										5
1	2	3	4	5		7	8		10	11	6	9										6
1	2	3	4	5		7	8		10	11	6	9										7
1	2	3	4	5		7	8	9	10	11	6											8
1	2	3	4*	5	12	7	8	9	10	11	6											9
1	2	3	4*	5	12	7	8	9	10	11	6											10
1		3	12	5	2	7	8	9*	10		6	11	4									11
1			12	5	2	7*	8	9	10		6	11	4	3								12
1*			7	5	2		8	9	10		6	11	4	3			12					13
1		3			2	7	8	9	10		6	11	4		5							14
1		3			2	7	8	9	10		6	11	4		5							15
1		3			2	7	8	9	10		6	11	4		5							16
1		3			2	7	8	9	10		6	11	4		5							17
1		3			2	7	8	9	10		6	11*	4		5			12				18
1		3			2	7		9	10		5	11	4		6			8				19
1		3			2*	7		9	10		6	11	4		5	12		8				20
1	2	3				7		9	10		6	11*	4		5	12		8				21
1	2	3				7		9	10*		6	11	4		5	12		8				22
1	2*	3			11	7	8	9			6		4		5	12		10				23
1	2	3			11	7	8	9			6		4		5			10				24
1	2*	3			11	7	8	9			6		4		5			10	12			25
1	2	3			11	7*	8	9			6		4		5	12		10				26
1	2	3	5		11	7	8				6		4					10	9			27
1	2	3	5		11	7	8				6		4					10	9	12		28
1	2	3	5		11		8				6		4			7		10	9			29
1	2		5		3		8	12			6		4		11	7		10*	9			30
1	2		11		3		8	9			6					7		10	4*	12	5	31
1		3	8		2			9			6			11				10	4	7	5	32
1		3	8*		2		12	9			6			11				10	4	7	5	33
1		3			2		8	9			6			11				10	4	7	5	34
1		3			2	12	8	9			6			11				10*	4	7	5	35
1	2	3				7	8	9			6			11*				12	4	10	5	36
1	2	3	11			7	8	9			6							10		4	5	37
1	2	3	11*			7	8	9			6			12				10		4	5	38
1	2	3			12	7	8	9			6		10	11*	5					4		39
1		3	11		2	7	8*	9			6		10		5		12			4		40
1		3	11		2	7		9			6			8			10			4	5	41
1		3	11*		2	7	8	9			6			12			10			4	5	42
42	25	38	22	13	28	34	35	34	22	10	40	17	22	9	16	3	2	19	10	11	10	
			2		4	1	1	1				1	1	2		5	2	2	1	2		
		2	1			5	3	8	4	3	2	4	4			1	1	5	1		2	

Wood	Locke	Sparrow	Stebbing	Whyte	Hughton	Irvine	Murphy	Aylott	Nicholas	Cummins	Cannon	Mahoney	Barber	Lindsay	Nebbeling	Mabbutt	Galloway	Gray	Finnigan	Taylor	Droy	
1	2	3				7	8	9			6	11	4	10	5							3
1	2	3				7	8	9	10		6	11	4		5							R
2	2	2				2	2	2	1		2	2	2	1	2							
								1				1										

Wood	Locke	Sparrow	Stebbing	Whyte	Hughton	Irvine	Murphy	Aylott	Nicholas	Cummins	Cannon	Mahoney	Barber	Lindsay	Nebbeling	Mabbutt	Galloway	Gray	Finnigan	Taylor	Droy	
1	2	3	4*	5	6	7	8	9	10	11		12										1
1	2	3		5	6	7	8	9	10	11		4										
1	2	3	4	5	12	7	8*		10	11	6	9										2
1		3	4*	5	2	7	8	9	10	11	6	12										
4	3	4	3	4	3	4	4	3	4	4	2	2										
					1							2										
									1	1												

1985-86

Manager: Steve Coppell

1	Aug	18	(a)	Shrewsbury T	W 2-0	Barber, Gray	4,293
2		24	(h)	Sunderland	W 1-0	Droy	7,040
3		27	(a)	Carlisle U	D 2-2	Aylott, Barber	3,080
4		31	(h)	Huddersfield T	L 2-3	Barber 2	6,026
5	Sep	7	(a)	Charlton A	L 1-3	Gray (pen)	6,637
6		14	(h)	Fulham	D 0-0		6,381
7		18	(a)	Norwich C	L 3-4	Gray 2 (1 pen), Droy	13,475
8		21	(h)	Millwall	W 2-1	Barber, Gray	8,713
9		28	(a)	Stoke C	D 0-0		7,130
10	Oct	1	(h)	Hull C	L 0-2		5,003
11		5	(a)	Middlesbrough	W 2-0	Barber, Ketteridge	4,991
12		12	(h)	Oldham A	W 3-2	Irvine, Taylor, Wright	5,243
13		19	(a)	Portsmouth	L 0-1		16,538
14		26	(h)	Blackburn R	W 2-0	Barber, Wright	5,408
15	Nov	2	(a)	Bradford C	L 0-1		5,604
16		9	(h)	Grimsby T	W 2-1	Droy, Taylor	4,620
17		16	(a)	Leeds U	W 3-1	Cannon, Finnigan 2	10,378
18		23	(h)	Barnsley	W 1-0	Taylor	5,625
19		30	(a)	Sheffield U	D 0-0		13,765
20	Dec	7	(a)	Hull C	W 2-1	Aylott 2	6,058
21		15	(h)	Shrewsbury T	L 0-1		8,253
22		22	(a)	Sunderland	D 1-1	Barber	16,710
23		26	(h)	Wimbledon	L 1-3	Droy	7,929
24	Jan	1	(a)	Brighton & HA	L 0-2		15,469
25		11	(h)	Charlton A	W 2-1	Finnigan, Taylor	11,523
26		18	(a)	Huddersfield T	D 0-0		5,729
27		25	(h)	Norwich C	L 1-2	Barber	8,369
28	Feb	1	(h)	Carlisle U	D 1-1	Gray	3,744
29		15	(a)	Blackburn R	W 2-1	Gray, Wright	4,825
30	Mar	8	(h)	Middlesbrough	W 2-1	Taylor, Wright	4,863
31		15	(a)	Oldham A	L 0-2		3,726
32		18	(h)	Stoke C	L 0-1		4,501
33		22	(a)	Fulham	W 3-2	Taylor (pen), Ketteridge, Wright	4,951
34		29	(h)	Brighton & HA	W 1-0	Brush	9,124
35	Apr	1	(a)	Wimbledon	D 1-1	Wright	8,429
36		5	(h)	Bradford C	W 2-1	Gray, Brush	5,079
37		8	(h)	Portsmouth	W 2-1	Gray 2	11,731
38		12	(a)	Grimsby T	L 0-3		4,222
39		19	(h)	Leeds U	W 3-0	Wright, Irvine 2	6,285
40		22	(a)	Millwall	L 2-3	Higginbottom, Ketteridge	5,618
41		26	(a)	Barnsley	W 4-2	Wright 2, Aylott, Ketteridge	3,862
42	May	3	(h)	Sheffield U	D 1-1	Higginbottom	6,375

FINAL LEAGUE POSITION: 5th in Division Two

Appearances
Sub Appearances
Goals

FA Cup

3	Jan	6	(h)	Luton T	L 1-2	Taylor	9,886

Appearances
Sub Appearances
Goals

League Cup

1	Aug	20	(a)	Charlton A	W 2-1	Barber 2	4,930
	Sep	3	(h)	Charlton A	D 1-1	Gray	6,051
2		24	(h)	Manchester U	L 0-1		21,506
	Oct	9	(a)	Manchester U	L 0-1		26,118

Appearances
Sub Appearances
Goals

Wood	Hughton	Lindsay	Ketteridge	Droy	Cannon	Irvine	Stebbing	Barber	Gray	Sparrow	Finnigan	Aylott	Wright	Higginbottom	Galloway	Locke	Taylor	Brush	Nebbeling	O'Doherty	Howard	Hardwick	
1	2	3	4	5	6	7	8	9	10	11													1
1	2	3	8	5	6	7		11	10		4	9											2
1	2	3	8	5	6	7		11	10		4	9											3
1	2	3*	8	5	6	7		11	10		4	9	12										4
1	2	3	8	5	6	7*		11	10		4			12	9								5
1		3*	8	5	6	7		9	10		4		12	11		2							6
1			8	5	6	7		9	10	3	4		12	11*		2							7
1			8	5	6	7		9	10	3	4					2	11						8
1			8	5	6	7	11	9	10	3	4		12			2*							9
1			8	5	6	7	11	9	10	4*	12					2		3					10
1			8		6	7		9	10	11*	12					2	4	3	5				11
1				5	6	7		9			8	10*	12	11		2	4	3					12
1				5	6	7		11			8	10	9			2	4	3					13
1		3			6	7		9			8	10	12	11		5*	4			2			14
1		3		5	6	7		10			8	9	12	11*			4			2			15
1			11	5	6	7		10	12		8	9*					4	3		2			16
1			11	5	6	7		10			8	9					4	3		2			17
1			11	5	6	7		10*			8	9	12				4	3		2			18
1			11	5	6	7		10			8	9					4	3		2			19
1			11	5	6	7		10*			8	9	12				4	3		2			20
1			11	5	6	7		10			8*	9	12				4	3		2			21
1			11	5	6	7		10				9	8				4	3		2			22
1	12		11	5	6	7		10				9	8				4	3*		2			23
1	3		11	5	6	7		10			8*	9	12			2	4						24
1	3			5	6	7		10	9		11		8				4				2		25
1	3			5	6	7*		10	9		11		8	12			4				2		26
1	3				6			10	9	11	7		8				4		5		2		27
1					6	7		10	9	3	8		12	11*			4		5		2		28
1				5	6	7		10	9	11	8*		12				4	3		2			29
			8	5	6	7		10	9	11*			12				4	3		2		1	30
			8	5	6	7		10	9	11			12				4	3		2*		1	31
	2*		8		6	7		10	9	11			12				4	3	5			1	32
1			8		6	7		10	9		2		11				4	3	5				33
1			8		6	7		10*	9		2		11	12			4	3	5				34
1			8		6	7		10	9		2		11				4	3	5				35
1			8		6	7		10*	9		2		11	12			4	3	5				36
1			8		6	7			9		2		11	10			4	3	5				37
1		12	8		6	7			9		2		11	10			4	3	5				38
1			8		6	7			9		2		11	10			4	3	5				39
1			8		6	7*		12	9		2		11	10			4	3	5				40
1			8		6	7		4	9*		2	12	11	10				3	5				41
1			8		6	7		4	9		2*	12	11	10				3	5				42
39	10	8	33	27	42	41	3	38	29	12	34	16	16	12	1	10	31	26	14	13	4	3	
	1	1						1	1		2	2	16	4									
			4	4	1	3		9	10		3	4	9	2			6	2					

Wood	Hughton	Lindsay	Ketteridge	Droy	Cannon	Irvine	Stebbing	Barber	Gray	Sparrow	Finnigan	Aylott	Wright	Higginbottom	Galloway	Locke	Taylor	Brush	Nebbeling	O'Doherty	Howard	Hardwick	
1	3		11	5	6	7		10*	9				8	12		2	4						3
1	1		1	1	1	1		1	1				1			1	1						
														1									
																	1						

Wood	Hughton	Lindsay	Ketteridge	Droy	Cannon	Irvine	Stebbing	Barber	Gray	Sparrow	Finnigan	Aylott	Wright	Higginbottom	Galloway	Locke	Taylor	Brush	Nebbeling	O'Doherty	Howard	Hardwick	
1	2	3	8	5	6	7		9	10	11	4												1
1	2	3	4	5	6	7		11	10		8		9*		12								
1			8	5	6	7	11	9	10	3	4					2							2
1	3		8		6	7		9	10*		11	12				2	4		5				
4	3	2	4	3	4	4	1	4	4	2	4		1			2	1		1				
												1			1								
								2	1														

1986-87

Manager: Steve Coppell

1	Aug	23	(a)	Barnsley	W 3-2	Barber, Brush, Wright	4,629
2		30	(h)	Stoke C	W 1-0	Barber	6,864
3	Sep	3	(a)	Bradford C	W 2-1	Irvine, Ketteridge	3,856
4		6	(a)	Derby C	L 0-1		12,058
5		9	(h)	Huddersfield T	W 1-0	Droy	6,601
6		13	(h)	Sheffield U	L 1-2	Irvine	7,003
7		20	(a)	Blackburn R	W 2-0	Taylor, Gray	5,921
8		27	(h)	Reading	L 1-3	Taylor (pen)	7,926
9	Oct	4	(h)	Millwall	W 2-1	Otulakowski, Finnigan	8,150
10		11	(a)	Leeds U	L 0-3		14,316
11		18	(a)	Birmingham C	L 1-4	Taylor	5,987
12		25	(h)	Shrewsbury T	L 2-3	Wright, Finnigan	4,865
13	Nov	1	(a)	Plymouth A	L 1-3	Taylor	11,708
14		8	(h)	Grimsby T	L 0-3		5,052
15		15	(h)	Ipswich T	D 3-3	Bright, Taylor, Wright	7,138
16		22	(a)	Oldham A	L 0-1		6,708
17		29	(h)	Sunderland	W 2-0	Finnigan, Bright	6,930
18	Dec	6	(a)	Portsmouth	L 0-2		10,907
19		13	(h)	Hull C	W 5-1	Taylor (pen), Barber, Gray, Finnigan 2	4,839
20		20	(a)	Huddersfield T	W 2-1	Bright 2	4,181
21		26	(h)	Brighton & HA	W 2-0	Irvine, Barber	10,365
22		27	(a)	Ipswich T	L 0-3		15,007
23	Jan	1	(a)	West Brom A	W 2-1	Barber, Bright	8,420
24		3	(h)	Derby C	W 1-0	Gray	9,526
25		24	(h)	Barnsley	L 0-1		6,011
26	Feb	7	(a)	Stoke C	L 1-3	Ketteridge	13,156
27		14	(h)	Bradford C	D 1-1	Gray	5,129
28		21	(a)	Reading	L 0-1		7,209
29		28	(h)	Blackburn R	W 2-0	Wright, Irvine	5,891
30	Mar	14	(h)	Birmingham C	W 6-0	Wright 2, Gray, Taylor, Cannon, Finnigan	6,201
31		17	(a)	Sheffield U	L 0-1		6,647
32		21	(h)	Leeds U	W 1-0	Gray (pen)	8,781
33		24	(a)	Shrewsbury T	D 0-0		2,555
34		28	(a)	Millwall	W 1-0	Bright	6,285
35	Apr	4	(a)	Grimsby T	W 1-0	Bright	3,071
36		11	(h)	Plymouth A	D 0-0		10,589
37		18	(h)	West Brom A	D 1-1	Taylor	7,127
38		20	(a)	Brighton & HA	L 0-2		10,062
39		25	(h)	Oldham A	W 2-1	Wright, Bright	6,097
40	May	2	(a)	Sunderland	L 0-1		11,461
41		4	(h)	Portsmouth	W 1-0	Wright	18,029
42		9	(a)	Hull C	L 0-3		7,656

FINAL LEAGUE POSITION: 6th in Division Two

Appearances
Sub Appearances
Goals

FA Cup

3	Jan	11	(h)	Nottingham F	W 1-0	Irvine	11,618
4		31	(a)	Tottenham H	L 0-4		29,603

Appearances
Sub Appearances
Goals

League Cup

2	Sep	24	(h)	Bury	D 0-0		4,017
	Oct	7	(a)	Bury	W 1-0	Wright	3,347
3		29	(h)	Nottingham F	D 2-2	Irvine, Gray	12,020
	Nov	5	(a)	Nottingham F	L 0-1		13,029

Appearances
Sub Appearances
Goals

Wood	Finnigan	Stebbing	Taylor	Brush	Cannon	Irvine	Ketteridge	Barber	Wright	Otulakowski	Droy	Gray	Higginbottom	Sparrow	O'Doherty	Nebbeling	Bright	O'Reilly	Salako	
1	2	3	4	5	6	7	8	9	10	11										1
1	2		4	3	6	7	8	9	10	11	5									2
1	2		4	3	6	7	8	9	10	11	5									3
1	2		4	3	6	7*	8	9	10	11	5	12								4
1	2		4	3	6		8	9	10	11	5	7								5
1	2		4	3	6	7	8	9	10		5	12	11*							6
1	2*		4	3	6	7	8	9	10		5	12	11							7
1	2		4	3	6	7	8	12	10		5	9	11*							8
1	2	7	4	3	6		8		10	11*	5	9	12							9
1	11	2	4	3	6	7*	8	9	10		5		12							10
1	7	2	4	3*	6		8	9	10	11	5		12							11
1	12	2	4		6	7	8		10	11	5	9*		3						12
1	12	2	4		6	7			10	11	5	9*	8	3						13
1	9	2	4		6	7	8		10	11*		12			3	5				14
1	3	2	4		6	7*	8		10	11				12		5	9			15
1	12	2	4		6	7*	8		10	11				3		5	9			16
1	11	2	4		6		8		10			7		3		5	9			17
1	11	2	4		6		8	10				7		3		5	9			18
1	11	2	4		6		8	10				7		3		5	9			19
1	8	2	4		6	7		11				10		3		5	9			20
1	8	2	4		6	7		11	12			10		3*		5	9			21
1	3	2	4		6	7	12	11*	8			10				5	9			22
1	3	2	4		6	7	8	11	10							5	9			23
1	3	2			6	7	8	11	10			4				5	9			24
1	7	2	4	3	6		8	11*				10					9	5	12	25
1	12	2	4*	3	6		8	11	10			7					9	5		26
1	12	2	4	3	6	7	8		10			11				5	9*			27
1			4	3	6	7	8	11	10						2	5	9			28
1	2		4		6	7	8	11	10					3		5	9			29
1	2	12	4		6	7		11	10*			8		3		5	9			30
1	2		4		6	7		11	10			8		3		5	9			31
1	2		4		6	7		11	10			8		3*		5	9	12		32
1	2		4		6	7		11	10			8			3		9	5		33
1	2	7	4		6			11	10*			8			3		9	5	12	34
1	2	12	4		6	7		11	10*			8			3		9	5		35
1	2		4		6	7		11	10			8			3		9	5		36
1	8		4		6	7		11	10						3	2	9	5		37
1	8		4		6	7		11	10						3	2	9	5		38
1	11		4		6	7			10			8			3	2	9	5		39
1	11*		4		6	7		12	10			8			3	2	9	5		40
1	11*		4		6	7			10			8			3	2	9	5	12	41
1	11		4		6	7			10			8			3*	2	9	5	12	42
42	36	21	41	15	42	33	25	29	37	12	12	26	4	12	12	23	28	12		
	5	2					1	2	1			4	3	1				1	4	
	6		8	1	1	4	2	5	8	1	1	6					8			

Wood	Finnigan	Stebbing	Taylor	Brush	Cannon	Irvine	Ketteridge	Barber	Wright	Otulakowski	Droy	Gray	Higginbottom	Sparrow	O'Doherty	Nebbeling	Bright	O'Reilly	Salako	
1	3	2			6	7	8	11	10			4					9	5		3
1	7	2	4	3*	6		8	11				10	12				9	5		4
2	2	2	1	1	2	1	2	2	1			2					2	2		
													1							
						1														

Wood	Finnigan	Stebbing	Taylor	Brush	Cannon	Irvine	Ketteridge	Barber	Wright	Otulakowski	Droy	Gray	Higginbottom	Sparrow	O'Doherty	Nebbeling	Bright	O'Reilly	Salako	
1	2*		4	3	6	7	8	9	10		5	14	11†		12					2
1	11	2	4	3	6	7	8	12	10		5	9*								
1	12	2	4		6	7	8*		10	11	5	9		3						3
1	9	2	4		6	7	12	14	10	11†			8*		3	5				
4	3	3	4	2	4	4	3	1	4	2	3	2	2	1	1	1				
	1						1	2				1			1					
						1			1			1								

1987-88

Manager: Steve Coppell

1	Aug	15	(a)	Huddersfield T	D	2-2	Bright 2	6,132
2		22	(h)	Hull C	D	2-2	Gray 2 (2 pens)	6,688
3		29	(a)	Barnsley	L	1-2	Bright	4,853
4	Sep	1	(h)	Middlesbrough	W	3-1	Thomas, Bright 2	6,866
5		5	(a)	Birmingham C	W	6-0	Bright, Redfearn, Thomas, Gray 2 (1 pen), Cannon	7,011
6		8	(h)	West Brom A	W	4-1	Bright 2, Redfearn, Wright	8,554
7		12	(h)	Leicester C	W	2-1	Thomas, Wright	8,925
8		15	(a)	Sheffield U	D	1-1	Wright	7,767
9		19	(a)	Reading	W	3-2	Wright, Nebbeling, Bright	6,819
10		26	(h)	Ipswich T	L	1-2	Nebbeling	10,828
11	Oct	3	(a)	Shrewsbury T	L	0-2		3,999
12		10	(h)	Millwall	W	1-0	Bright	10,678
13		21	(a)	Aston Villa	L	1-4	Wright	12,755
14		24	(h)	Swindon T	W	2-1	Bright, Gray, (pen)	9,077
15		31	(a)	Bradford C	L	0-2		13,012
16	Nov	3	(h)	Plymouth A	W	5-1	Wright 3, Gray, Nebbeling	7,424
17		7	(a)	Bournemouth	W	3-2	Thomas, Bright 2	9,083
18		14	(h)	Stoke C	W	2-0	Bright, Wright	8,309
19		21	(a)	Blackburn R	L	0-2		6,372
20		28	(h)	Leeds U	W	3-0	Bright, Ashurst (og), Wright	8,749
21	Dec	5	(a)	Manchester C	W	3-1	Redfearn (pen), Bright 2	23,161
22		13	(h)	Sheffield U	W	2-1	Redfearn (pen), Barber	8,174
23		19	(a)	Hull C	L	1-2	Barber	6,780
24		26	(a)	Ipswich T	W	3-2	Redfearn (pen), Wright 2	17,200
25		28	(h)	Reading	L	2-3	Wright, Cannon	12,449
26	Jan	1	(h)	Barnsley	W	3-2	McGugan (og), Wright, Bailey	8,563
27		2	(a)	Leicester C	D	4-4	Barber, Pennyfather, Wright 2	10,104
28		16	(h)	Huddersfield T	W	2-1	Barber, Cannon	9,013
29		23	(a)	Middlesbrough	L	1-2	Wright	12,597
30		29	(a)	Oldham A	L	0-1		6,169
31	Feb	6	(h)	Birmingham C	W	3-0	Bright, Barber, Salako	8,809
32		13	(a)	West Brom A	L	0-1		8,944
33		27	(h)	Shrewsbury T	L	1-2	Redfearn (pen)	8,210
34	Mar	5	(h)	Oldham A	W	3-1	Wright, Nebbeling 2	7,032
35		12	(a)	Millwall	D	1-1	Cannon	12,815
36		19	(h)	Bradford C	D	1-1	Barber	9,801
37		27	(a)	Swindon T	D	2-2	Bright, Wright	12,915
38	Apr	2	(h)	Bournemouth	W	3-0	Redfearn 2 (2 pens), Bright	9,557
39		4	(a)	Stoke C	D	1-1	Bright	9,613
40		9	(h)	Aston Villa	D	1-1	Wright (pen)	16,476
41		23	(a)	Plymouth A	W	3-1	Barber, Bright 2	8,370
42		30	(h)	Blackburn R	W	2-0	Bright, Thomas	13,059
43	May	2	(a)	Leeds U	L	0-1		13,217
44		7	(h)	Manchester C	W	2-0	Nebbeling, Thomas	17,555

FINAL LEAGUE POSITION: 6th in Division Two

Appearances
Sub Appearances
Goals

FA Cup

3	Jan	9	(a)	Newcastle U	L	0-1		20,203

Appearances
Sub Appearances
Goals

League Cup

2	Sep	22	(h)	Newport C	W	4-0	Wright 2, Salako, Barber	6,085
	Oct	6	(a)	Newport C	W	2-0	Wright, Bright	1,303
3		28	(a)	Manchester U	L	1-2	O'Doherty	27,285

Appearances
Sub Appearances
Goals

Wood	Stebbing	Brush	Gray	Nebbeling	Cannon	Redfearn	Thomas	Bright	Wright	Salako	Barber	Finnigan	O'Reilly	O'Doherty	Shaw	Taylor	Burke	Howe	Pardew	Pennyfather	Bailey	Suckling	Pemberton	Powell	
1	2	3	4	5	6	7	8	9	10	11*	12														1
1	2	3	4	5	6	7	8	9	10	11															2
1	2	3	4	5	6	7	8	9	10	11*		12													3
1	2	3	4	5	6	7	8	9	10	11															4
1	2†	3	4	5	6	7	8	9*	10	11	12		14												5
1	2*	3	4	5	6	7	8	9	10	11			12												6
1		3	4	5	6	7	8	9	10	11*	12		2												7
1		3	4	5	6	7	8	9	10	11			2*	12											8
1		3†	4	5	6*	7	8	9	10	11	12			2	14										9
1			4	5		7	8	9	10	11				2	3	6									10
1			4	5		7	3	9	10	11	12			6	2*	8									11
1			4		6	7	8	9	10*	11	12			2			3	5							12
1			4	5	6	7	8	9	10	11				2				3							13
1			4	5	6	7	8	9	10	11*	12			2				3							14
1			4	5	6	7	8	9	10	11*	12			2			3								15
1	14		4	5	6	7	8	9	10	11*	12			2†			3								16
1	12		4	5	6	7	8	9	10		11			2*			3								17
1	2			5		7	8	9	10		11			6			3		4						18
1	2			5		7	8	9	10	12	11*			6			3		4						19
1	2			5	6	7	8	9	10		11						3		4						20
1	2			5	6	7	8*	9	10		11						3		4	12					21
1	2			5	6	7	8		10	11*	9	12					3		4						22
1	2			5	6	7	8		10		9						3		4*	11	12				23
1	2			5	6	7*	8		10	11	9						3		12	4					24
1	2			5	6	7	8		10	11	9*						3			4	12				25
1	2			5	6	7	8		10	11*	9						3			4	12				26
1	2			5	6	11	8		10		9*						3		7	4	12				27
	2			5	6	7		9	10		11						3		4	8		1			28
	2				6	7		9	10		11			5			3		4	8		1			29
	2†				6	7		9	10		11*	14		5			3		4	8	12	1			30
					6	11	8	9		12	10	5		2			3		7*	4		1			31
					6	11	8	9		7	10	5		2			3		12	4*		1			32
				12	6	7†	8	9	10	14	11*	5		2			3		4			1			33
				5	6	7	8	9	10		11	2					3		4			1			34
				5	6	7	8	9	10	12	11*	2					3		4			1			35
				5	6	7	8	9*	10	12	11	2					3		4			1			36
				5	6		8	9	10		11	2					3		4	7		1			37
				5	6	7	8	9	10		11	2					3			4		1			38
				5	6	7*	8†	9	10	12	11	2					3		14	4		1			39
				5	6		8	9	10	7*	11	2					3		14	4†		1	12		40
				5	6	7*	8	9		11	10	2					3			4		1	12		41
				5	6	7*	8	9	10	12	11	2					3			4		1			42
				5	6	7*	8	9	10	12	11	2					3			4		1			43
				5	6	7	8	9	10		11	2					3			4		1			44
27	19	9	17	38	40	42	41	38	41	23	28	14	2	16	2	2	31	3	16	18		17			
	2			1						8	9	3	2	1	1				4	1	5		2		
			6	6	4	8	6	24	20	1	7									1	1				

2 own-goals

Wood	Stebbing	Brush	Gray	Nebbeling	Cannon	Redfearn	Thomas	Bright	Wright	Salako	Barber	Finnigan	O'Reilly	O'Doherty	Shaw	Taylor	Burke	Howe	Pardew	Pennyfather	Bailey	Suckling	Pemberton	Powell	
1	2			5	6	11	8	12	10		9†	14		7*			3		4						3
1	1			1	1	1	1		1		1			1			1		1						
								1				1													

Wood	Stebbing	Brush	Gray	Nebbeling	Cannon	Redfearn	Thomas	Bright	Wright	Salako	Barber	Finnigan	O'Reilly	O'Doherty	Shaw	Taylor	Burke	Howe	Pardew	Pennyfather	Bailey	Suckling	Pemberton	Powell	
1			4*	5		7	8		10	11†	9			2	3	6			12					14	2
1			4	5		7	6	9	10†	11	3			2		8*		14	12						
1	14		4	5†	6	7	8	9	10	11*	12			2				3							3
3			3	3	1	3	3	2	3	3	2			3	1	2		1							
	1										1							1	2					1	
								1	3	1	1			1											

1988-89

Manager: Steve Coppell

1	Aug	30	(h)	Chelsea	D 1-1	Redfearn	17,490
2	Sep	3	(h)	Watford	L 0-2		10,474
3		10	(a)	Walsall	D 0-0		6,525
4		17	(h)	Shrewsbury T	D 1-1	Wright	7,006
5		20	(a)	Sunderland	D 1-1	O'Reilly	13,150
6		24	(a)	Portsmouth	D 1-1	Wright	11,249
7	Oct	1	(h)	Plymouth A	W 4-1	Wright, Thomas, Bright, Pardew	8,047
8		4	(h)	Ipswich T	W 2-0	Bright, Wright	10,325
9		8	(a)	Blackburn R	L 4-5	Thomas, Wright, Bright, O'Reilly	8,022
10		15	(a)	Bradford C	W 1-0	Wright	11,098
11		22	(h)	Hull C	W 3-1	Wright, Barber 2	8,464
12		25	(h)	Oxford U	W 1-0	Redfearn (pen)	10,114
13		29	(a)	Stoke C	L 1-2	Bright	9,118
14	Nov	5	(h)	Barnsley	D 1-1	Bright	7,768
15		12	(a)	Bournemouth	L 0-2		7,500
16		19	(h)	Leicester C	W 4-2	Thomas, Barber 2, Bright	8,843
17		26	(a)	West Brom A	L 3-5	Dyer, Nebbeling, Thomas	11,099
18	Dec	3	(h)	Manchester C	D 0-0		12,444
19		10	(a)	Birmingham C	W 1-0	Dyer	6,523
20		17	(h)	Leeds U	D 0-0		9,847
21		26	(a)	Brighton & HA	L 1-3	Wright	13,515
22		30	(a)	Oldham A	W 3-2	Thomas, Wright 2 (1 pen)	6,562
23	Jan	2	(h)	Walsall	W 4-0	Wright, Bright 3	9,352
24		14	(a)	Chelsea	L 0-1		24,184
25		21	(h)	Swindon T	W 2-1	Bright 2	8,109
26	Feb	4	(a)	Ipswich T	W 2-1	Wright 2 (1 pen)	14,569
27		11	(h)	Blackburn R	D 2-2	Wright, Bright	11,270
28		25	(h)	Bradford C	W 2-0	Bright 2	7,455
29	Mar	1	(a)	Oxford U	L 0-1		6,020
30		4	(h)	Bournemouth	L 2-3	Pemberton, Wright	10,022
31		11	(a)	Barnsley	D 1-1	Futcher (og)	7,055
32		18	(h)	Sunderland	W 1-0	Bright (pen)	9,108
33		24	(a)	Watford	W 1-0	Barber	15,095
34		27	(h)	Brighton & HA	W 2-1	Wright, Bright (pen)	14,384
35	Apr	1	(a)	Shrewsbury T	L 1-2	Madden	4,160
36		5	(a)	Leeds U	W 2-1	Wright, Madden (pen)	25,604
37		8	(h)	Oldham A	W 2-0	Barber, Bright	9,089
38		11	(a)	Hull C	W 1-0	Wright	5,050
39		15	(h)	Portsmouth	W 2-0	Wright, Bright	12,358
40		22	(a)	Plymouth A	W 2-0	Bright 2	8,492
41		25	(a)	Swindon T	L 0-1		11,045
42		29	(h)	West Brom A	W 1-0	Wright	13,728
43	May	1	(a)	Manchester C	D 1-1	Wright	33,456
44		6	(a)	Leicester C	D 2-2	Madden 2 (2 pens)	9,917
45		9	(h)	Stoke C	W 1-0	Madden (pen)	12,159
46		13	(h)	Birmingham C	W 4-1	Wright 3 Clarkson (og)	17,581

FINAL LEAGUE POSITION: 3rd in Division Two

Appearances
Sub Appearances
Goals

Play-offs

SF	May	21	(a)	Swindon T	L 0-1		16,656
		24	(h)	Swindon T	W 2-0	Bright, Wright	23,677
F		31	(a)	Blackburn R	L 1-3	McGoldrick	16,421
	June	3	(h)	Blackburn R	W 3-0*	Wright 2, Madden (pen)	30,000

*After extra-time

Appearances
Sub Appearances
Goals

FA Cup

3	Jan	7	(a)	Stoke C	L 0-1		12,294

Appearances
Sub Appearances
Goals

League Cup

2	Sep	27	(a)	Swindon T	W 2-1	Bright, Wright	7,084
	Oct	12	(h)	Swindon T	W 2-0	Henry (og), Thomas	6,015
3	Nov	1	(a)	Bristol C	L 1-4	Pardew	12,167

Appearances
Sub Appearances
Goals

Suckling	Pemberton	Burke	Pennyfather	Nebbeling	O'Reilly	Redfearn	Thomas	Bright	Wright	Salako	Pardew	Barber	Madden	Parkin	Hopkins	Hone	Shaw	Powell	Dyer	Hedman	McGoldrick	Harris	
1	2	3	4*	5†	6	7	8	9	10	11	12	14											1
1	2	3	4		6	7†	8	9	10	11	5*	14	12										2
	2	3			6	7	8	9	10		4	11		1	5								3
	2	3			6	7*	8	9	10	12	4	11		1	5								4
	2	3			6	7*	8	9	10	12	4	11		1	5								5
	2	3			6	7	8	9	10		4	11		1	5								6
	2	3			6	7	8	9	10		4	11		1	5								7
		3			6	7	8	9	10*	12	4	11		1	5	2							8
	2	3			6	7	8	9	10	12	4	11*		1	5								9
	2*	3			6	7	8	9	10		4	11		1	5		12						10
	2	3			6	7	8	9	10*	12	4	11		1	5								11
	2	3			6	7	8	9		10	4	11		1	5								12
	2	3*			6	7	8	9		10	4	11		1	5		12						13
	2				6	7	8	9	12	10	4	11		1	5			3					14
	2				6	7*	8	9	10		4	11		1	5			3	12				15
			3	6			8	9†	10*	12	4	11		1	5		2	14	7				16
	2		3*	6			8	9	10	12	4	11†		1	5		14		7				17
	2	3		6			8	9	10	12	4	11*		1	5				7				18
	2	3		6			8	9	10		4	11		1	5				7				19
	2	3		6			8	9	10		4	11		1	5				7				20
	2	3	12	6			8	9	10		4†	11*		1	5				7	14			21
1	2	3	4	6			8*	9	10	7	12	11			5								22
1	2	3	4	6				9	10*	7	8	11			5					12			23
1	2	3	4	6				9	10	12	8	11*			5						7		24
1	2	3	4	6				9	10		8	11			5						7		25
1	2	3	4		6			9	10		8	11			5						7		26
1	2	3	4		6			9	10	12	8*	11			5						7		27
1	2	3	4		6			9		10	8	11					5				7		28
1	2	3	4*		6			9		10	8	11	12		5						7		29
1	2	3			6			9	10		8	11	4		5						7		30
1	3*		12		6			9	10		8	11	4		5		2				7		31
1	2				6			9	10		8	11	4		5		3				7		32
1	2				6			9	10	12	8	11	4		5		3				7*		33
1	2	12			6			9	10		8	11	4		5		3*				7		34
1	2	3			6			9	10	12	8	11	4*		5						7		35
1	2	3			6			9	10		8	11	4		5						7		36
1	2	3			6			9	10		8*	11	4		5		12				7		37
1	2	3			6			9	10	12	8	11	4		5						7*		38
1	2	3			6			9	10	12	8	11	4		5						7*		39
1	2	3			6			9	10*	7	8	11	4		5		12						40
1	2	3			6			9	10	7	8	11	4		5							12	41
1	2	3			6†			9	10	7*	8	11	4		5		14				12		42
1	2	3						9	10		8	11	4*		5		6				7	12	43
1		3		6				9	10	12	8	11	4		5		2*			14	7*		44
1		3		6				9	10		8	11	4		5					2	7		45
1	2	3	8*	6				9	10	12		11	4		5†					14	7		46
27	42	38	13	14	32	15	22	46	41	12	43	44	17	19	43	1	8	2	6	1	20		
		1	2						1	16	2	2	2				6	1	1	4	1	2	
	1			1	2	2	5	20	24		1	6	5						2				

2 own-goals

Suckling	Pemberton	Burke	Pennyfather	Nebbeling	O'Reilly	Redfearn	Thomas	Bright	Wright	Salako	Pardew	Barber	Madden	Parkin	Hopkins	Hone	Shaw	Powell	Dyer	Hedman	McGoldrick	Harris	
1	2	3	12					9	10		8	11*	4		5					6	7		SF
1	2	3						9	10		8	11	4		5					6	7		
1	2	3	12					9	10		8	11	4*		5					6	7		F
1	2	3			6			9	10		8	11	4		5						7		
4	4	4			1			4	4		4	4	4		4					3	4		
			2																				
								1	3				1								1		

Suckling	Pemberton	Burke	Pennyfather	Nebbeling	O'Reilly	Redfearn	Thomas	Bright	Wright	Salako	Pardew	Barber	Madden	Parkin	Hopkins	Hone	Shaw	Powell	Dyer	Hedman	McGoldrick	Harris	
1	2	3	4	6			8	9	10	7		11			5								3
1	1	1	1	1			1	1	1	1		1			1								

Suckling	Pemberton	Burke	Pennyfather	Nebbeling	O'Reilly	Redfearn	Thomas	Bright	Wright	Salako	Pardew	Barber	Madden	Parkin	Hopkins	Hone	Shaw	Powell	Dyer	Hedman	McGoldrick	Harris	
	2	3				7	8	9	10		4	11		1	6	5							2
	2	3			6	7	8	9	10	12	4†	11*		1	5		14						
	2				6	7	8	9		10	4	11		1	5	3							3
	3	2			2	3	3	3	2	1	3	3		3	3	2							
										1							1						
							1	1	1		1												

1 own-goal

Palace Against Other League Clubs

Crystal Palace have played 99 clubs in the Football League since 1920. Below is the Palace record against each club. Some clubs changed their names (eg Small Heath became Birmingham then Birmingham City) and some clubs modified their titles (eg Leicester Fosse became Leicester City). In all cases the current name used by each club cover all games under previous names.

		HOME					AWAY				
	P	W	D	L	F	A	W	D	L	F	A
Aberdare Athletic	4	0	1	1	0	1	1	0	1	3	4
Accrington Stanley	2	1	0	0	9	2	1	0	0	3	2
AFC Bournemouth	64	19	7	6	60	29	3	8	21	31	75
Aldershot	48	16	6	2	44	16	6	4	14	25	40
Arsenal	12	1	2	3	8	14	0	2	4	5	10
Aston Villa	12	2	2	2	7	5	1	1	4	5	11
Barnsley	30	4	2	9	15	19	5	2	8	24	30
Barrow	6	2	1	0	15	4	2	0	1	4	1
Birmingham City	20	7	2	1	22	7	3	1	6	12	15
Blackburn Rovers	28	10	2	2	25	8	4	2	8	16	24
Blackpool	18	4	2	3	14	11	2	0	7	6	19
Bolton Wanderers	20	7	2	1	17	9	0	5	5	5	16
Bradford	12	4	2	0	14	2	0	1	5	3	15
Bradford City	14	5	2	0	15	4	3	2	2	5	5
Brentford	30	10	2	3	27	18	3	2	10	21	36
Brighton & Hove Albion	80	22	9	9	68	39	6	10	24	40	72
Bristol City	58	18	6	5	60	32	5	10	14	24	49
Bristol Rovers	52	19	2	5	52	23	7	5	14	30	50
Burnley	10	2	1	2	5	5	0	1	4	6	11
Bury	20	7	2	1	16	8	3	4	3	13	14
Cambridge United	8	1	3	0	4	3	1	2	1	3	2
Cardiff City	42	14	5	2	45	18	8	8	5	29	25
Carlisle United	26	7	3	3	24	13	1	5	7	15	29
Charlton Athletic	38	14	3	2	38	15	5	6	8	24	25
Chelsea	18	2	3	4	7	11	1	6	2	9	10
Chester City	10	2	1	2	14	10	1	0	4	5	10
Chesterfield	6	0	2	1	1	4	2	0	1	5	3
Colchester United	24	3	5	4	15	17	4	4	4	18	20
Coventry City	66	11	14	8	44	41	7	10	16	45	75
Crewe Alexandra	8	3	1	0	11	2	2	1	1	6	6
Darlington	6	3	0	0	9	3	2	1	0	6	2
Derby County	36	7	4	7	23	16	2	4	12	12	45
Doncaster Rovers	4	2	0	0	9	1	2	0	0	7	2
Everton	12	3	2	1	8	5	0	2	4	4	14
Exeter City	60	15	11	4	54	26	9	6	15	44	65
Fulham	32	6	6	4	26	21	3	6	7	17	25
Gateshead	12	2	3	1	8	6	2	2	2	7	7
Gillingham	56	15	6	7	63	33	8	8	12	37	45
Grimsby Town	22	7	0	4	18	12	5	1	5	10	14
Halifax Town	8	1	3	0	6	5	1	2	1	7	7
Hartlepool United	6	1	1	1	8	6	2	0	1	6	6
Hereford United	4	0	2	0	4	4	0	1	1	1	3
Huddersfield Town	26	5	5	3	15	13	5	5	3	13	11
Hull City	32	5	5	6	22	19	3	5	8	14	31
Ipswich Town	48	9	9	6	37	30	4	7	13	33	52
Leeds United	32	6	8	2	20	11	2	2	12	10	32
Leicester City	24	7	1	4	18	15	1	6	5	12	20

		HOME					AWAY				
	P	W	D	L	F	A	W	D	L	F	A
Leyton Orient	60	18	9	3	48	26	7	8	15	25	48
Lincoln City	4	1	0	1	5	4	0	0	2	4	6
Liverpool	12	1	3	2	5	7	0	1	5	2	15
Luton Town	36	10	6	2	45	25	3	4	11	24	43
Manchester City	24	4	2	6	11	13	4	3	5	14	18
Manchester United	18	3	2	4	17	17	1	2	6	5	17
Mansfield Town	18	8	1	0	29	8	2	4	3	9	11
Merthyr Town	12	5	1	0	17	2	1	2	3	9	16
Middlesbrough	26	7	3	3	25	16	2	5	6	10	20
Millwall	66	12	12	9	47	42	8	8	17	37	55
Nelson	2	0	1	0	1	1	0	0	1	2	4
Newcastle United	18	5	1	3	11	10	1	2	6	3	12
Newport County	52	18	7	1	65	18	11	6	9	41	37
Northampton Town	70	14	10	11	64	49	3	11	21	30	81
Norwich City	64	21	5	6	60	26	6	2	24	36	69
Nottingham Forest	18	3	3	3	12	14	2	1	6	5	16
Notts County	38	9	5	5	30	22	7	6	6	21	25
Oldham Athletic	32	12	1	3	33	15	2	3	11	12	25
Oxford United	10	3	2	0	7	3	2	1	2	4	7
Peterborough United	14	2	3	2	8	8	0	4	3	4	12
Plymouth Argyle	36	9	5	4	39	23	6	2	10	19	44
Portsmouth	30	10	2	3	29	16	1	11	3	14	17
Port Vale	38	8	7	4	22	14	4	3	12	18	44
Preston North End	20	7	2	1	12	3	1	5	4	6	10
Queen's Park Rangers	58	11	9	9	37	33	7	6	16	36	54
Reading	56	11	9	8	44	37	6	7	15	28	63
Rochdale	4	2	0	0	8	1	0	1	1	2	6
Rotherham United	20	7	3	0	20	7	2	3	5	10	18
Sheffield United	18	4	2	3	15	11	3	3	3	8	7
Sheffield Wednesday	22	5	3	3	16	8	1	1	9	3	20
Shrewsbury Town	42	7	7	7	33	29	3	10	8	24	29
Southampton	36	8	3	7	27	25	2	3	13	13	38
Southend United	64	18	8	6	65	41	9	6	17	47	70
Southport	6	2	1	0	8	2	1	1	1	6	6
Stockport County	10	4	1	0	12	3	1	2	2	7	10
Stoke City	30	8	2	5	22	14	2	6	7	12	22
Sunderland	16	5	2	1	12	4	1	5	2	4	5
Swansea City	10	2	2	1	10	5	0	1	4	1	8
Swindon Town	72	23	10	3	85	30	6	12	18	43	70
Thames	4	2	0	0	4	2	2	0	0	5	1
Torquay United	54	16	8	3	70	30	6	7	14	35	52
Tottenham Hotspur	14	0	3	4	6	13	0	2	5	5	15
Tranmere Rovers	4	2	0	0	3	1	0	0	2	0	3
Walsall	52	19	2	5	64	25	4	11	11	27	42
Watford	70	19	8	8	67	34	10	6	19	48	66
West Bromwich Albion	20	4	2	4	13	12	2	2	6	12	16
West Ham United	14	0	3	4	5	15	0	4	3	4	11
Wimbledon	4	0	0	2	1	8	0	1	1	3	4
Wolverh'ton Wanderers	26	5	5	3	20	13	1	4	8	8	17
Workington	6	1	1	1	5	4	1	1	1	5	2
Wrexham	16	7	1	0	18	6	5	3	0	16	9
York City	6	2	1	0	2	0	1	1	1	4	3
Total	2678	695	350	294	2378	1411	288	363	688	1450	2406

Anglo-Italian Cup

1971
May 26 v Cagliari (h) W 1-0
Tambling
Att: 19,326
May 29 v Inter Milan (h) D 1-1
Birchenall
Att: 25,752
Jun 1 v Cagliari (a) L 0-2
Att: 30,000
Jun 4 v Inter Milan (a) W 2-1
Tambling 2

1973
Feb 14 v Verona (h) W 4-1
Whittle 2, Bell, M.Hinshelwood
Att:7,436
Mar 21 v Bari (a) W 1-0
Possee
Att: 10,000

Apr 4 v Lazio (h) W 3-1
Craven 3
Att: 6,023
May 2 v Fiorentina (a) D 2-2
Possee 2
Semi-final (1st leg)
May 11 v Newcastle United (h) D 0-0
Att: 12,001
Semi-final (2nd leg)
May 21 v Newcastle United (a) L 1-5
Cannon
Att: 12,510

Three Palace stars in action. Bobby Tambling (above), Alan Birchenall (top, opposite) challenging Leeds' Jack Charlton, and Jim Cannon (bottom, opposite).

Texaco Cup

1971-72
Round 1 (1st leg)
Sep 13 v Hearts (a) L 0-1
Att: 9,500
Round 1 (2nd leg)
Sep 26 v Hearts (h) L 0-1
Att: 9,855

Football League Trophy

1982-3
Aug 14 v Brentford (a) D 2-2
Edwards, Brooks
Barron; P.Hinshelwood, Hughton, Cannon, Nebbeling, Gilbert, Langley(Brooks), Wilkins, Edwards, Murphy, Giles.
Att: 3,397

Shaun Brooks

Aug 17 v Wimbledon (h) W 1-0
Edwards
Fry; P.Hinshelwood, Hughton, Cannon, Nebbeling, Lovell, Langley(Annon), Wilkins, Edwards, Brooks, Giles.
Att: 2,852
Aug 21 v Millwall (h) L 0-3
Barron; P.Hinshelwood, Hughton, Cannon, Nebbeling, Gilbert, Langley, Brooks(Annon), Edwards, Wilkins (Lovell), Giles
Att: 4,844

Full Members Cup

1985-6
Round 1
Oct 16 v Brighton & HA (h) L 1-3
Aylott

K.Hughes; Locke, Brush, K.Taylor, Droy, Nebbeling, Irvine, Hughton(Stebbing), Barber, Aylott, Higginbottom(Wright).
Att: 2,207

Trevor Aylott

Round 2
Oct 23 v West Bromwich A (a) L 1-2
Cannon
Wood; O'Doherty, Brush(Lindsay), K.Taylor, Droy, Cannon, Irvine, Finnigan, Aylott, Barber (Wright), Higginbottom.
Att: 3,764

1986-7
Round 1
Sep 16 v Portsmouth (a) L 0-4
Wood; O'Doherty, Brush, K.Taylor, Nebbeling, Cannon, Finnigan(Gray), Ketteridge(Sparrow), Barber, Wright, Higginbottom
Att: 2,515

Simod Cup

1987-8
Round 1
Nov 11 v Oxford United (a) L 0-1
Wood; Stebbing, Burke, Pardew, Nebbeling, Cannon(O'Doherty), Redfearn, Thomas, Bright, Wright, Barber.
Att: 1,478

1988-9
Round 1
Nov 22 v Walsall (h) W 4-2
Barber, Dyer 2, Wright
Parkin; Shaw, Pennyfather, Pardew(Powell), Hopkins, Nebbeling, Dyer, Thomas, Bright, Salako(Wright), Barber.
Att: 2,893
Round 2
Feb 13 v Southampton (a) W 2-1
Wright, Dyer
Parkin; Pemberton, Burke, Pardew, Hopkins, Nebbeling, Dyer, Thomas, Bright, Wright, Barber.
Att: 4,914
Round 3
Jan 10 v Luton Town (h) W 4-1
Bright 3, Wright
Suckling; Pemberton, Burke, Pennyfather, Hopkins, Nebbeling, Salako(McGoldrick), Pardew, Bright, Wright, Barber.
Att: 5,842

Phil Barber

Round 4
Jan 28 v Middlesbrough (a) W 3-2
Pardew, Barber, Wright
Suckling; Pemberton, Burke, Pennyfather, Hopkins, Nebbeling, McGoldrick, Pardew, Bright, Wright, Barber.
Att: 16,314
Semi-final
Feb 22 v Nottingham Forest (a) L 1-3
Wright
Suckling; Pemberton, Burke, Pennyfather, Nebbeling(Shaw), O'Reilly, McGoldrick (Salako), Pardew, Bright, Wright, Barber.
Att: 20,374

Four players involved in the semi-final game against Nottingham Forest. Above: Richard Shaw. Above, opposite: Gary O'Reilly. Below: Ian Wright. Below, opposite: Gavin Nebbeling.

Football League Division Three South Cup

1933-4
Round 1
Jan 24 v Exeter City (a) L 6-11
Fyfe 2, Dawes 2, Thompson 2

1934-5
Round 2
Oct 17 v Cardiff City (h) W 3-1
Dawes 2, Rooke
Round 3
Feb 7 v Coventry City (a) L 1-5
Bigg

1935-6
Round 1
Sep 30 v Cardiff City (h) W 2-1
Manders, Waldron
Round 2
Oct 28 v Exeter City (h) W 4-2
Dawes 2, Birtley, Biggs
Round 3
Nov 11 v Southend United (h) W 3-2
Rooke 2, Hanson
Semi-final
Jan 11 v Coventry City (h) L 1-2
Birtley

1936-7
Round 1
Sep 30 v Brighton & HA (h) W 3-2
Waldron 2, Levene
Round 2
Oct 21 v Torquay United (a) L 0-1

1937-8
Round 1
Sep 27 v Mansfield Town (a) W 1-0
Robson
Round 2
Nov 17 v Bristol Rovers (a) L 0-5

1938-9
Round 2
Dec 10 v Brighton & HA (a) W 3-2
Robson 2, Steele
Round 3
Mar 8 v Reading (a) D 0-0
Replay
Mar 22 v Reading (h) W 6-4
Waldron 2, Steele, Robson 3
Semi-final
Mar 29 v Torquay United (a) L 2-4
Waldron, Opp own-goal

Crystal Palace at the start of 1937-8. Back row (left to right): Greener, Booth, Fielding, Jordan, Robson, Pritchard, F.Dawes, Owens, Blackman, Irwin. Second row: Quayle, Leivesley, Daniels, Walker, Bore, Chesters, Wilde, Shanks, Bigg, Turton. Seated: G.Stanbury, T.G.Bromilow (manager), F.E.Burrell, Dr T.E.M.Wardill, C.E.Truett, C.H.Temple, E.T.Truett, R.Cornell, R.H.E.Blaxill. On ground: Waldron, Davis, Beresford, Birtley, Collins, Horton.

Football League

1938-9
Aug 20 v Brighton & HA (h) W 5-0
A.Dawes 2, Horton 3
Att: 5,898

1939-40
Aug 19 v Brighton & HA (a) D 3-3
Robson, Waldron 2
Att: 4,500

Southern Professional Floodlight Cup

1955-6
Round 2
Oct 10 v West Ham United (a) L 0-3

1956-7
Round 1
Oct 2 v Arsenal (a) L 0-4

1957-8
Round 1
Oct 22 v Watford (a) L 1-4

1958-9
Round 1
Oct 13 v Reading (h) W 4-2
Round 2
Jan 19 v Millwall (a) D 1-1
Replay
Jan 28 v Millwall (h) W 3-2
Semi-final
Apr 1 v Luton Town (h) W 1-0
Barnett
Final
Apr 27 v Arsenal (h) L 1-2
Byrne
Att: 32,384

1959-60
Round 1
Oct 21 v Brentford (h) W 5-2
Easton 4, Sexton
Round 2
Dec 14 v Southampton (h) D 2-2
Barnett, Byrne
Replay
Jan 18 v Southampton (a) L 1-2
Roche

Full-back John Edwards, who joined Palace from non-League football in 1949 and made 223 League appearances for the club before being transferred to Rochdale ten years later.

Reserve Competitions

London Mid-week League

	P	W	D	L	F	A	Pts	Pos
1949-50	26	16	1	9	66	42	33	3rd
1950-51	30	9	4	17	56	79	22	12th
1951-52	20	5	3	8	21	37	13	*
1952-53	18	3	4	11	23	56	10	9th
1953-54	22	4	5	13	24	59	13	12th
1954-55	20	13	4	3	52	28	30	2nd
1955-56	14	5	1	8	21	35	11	6th
1956-57	12	1	3	8	13	31	5	7th
1957-58	14	7	3	4	39	26	17	3rd
1958-59	12	3	3	6	*	*	9	6th
1959-60	14	3	2	9	24	42	8	7th

* Final figures not known

South Eastern Counties

	P	W	D	L	F	A	Pts	Pos
1954-55	20	6	4	9	32	35	16	*
1955-56	20	5	4	11	36	57	14	8th
1956-57	24	12	4	8	64	71	28	6th
1957-58	28	7	2	19	62	135	16	13th
1958-59	30	3	4	23	42	97	10	16th
1959-60	26	12	5	9	59	51	29	5th
1960-61	28	11	4	13	64	87	26	9th
1961-62	26	11	4	11	51	57	26	9th
1962-63	30	8	6	16	60	83	22	13th
1963-64	30	8	8	14	57	99	24	11th
1964-65	30	10	3	17	59	81	23	12th
1965-66	30	10	8	12	63	65	28	11th
1966-67	30	12	8	10	68	58	32	7th
1967-68	30	15	3	12	76	75	33	9th
1968-69	32	17	3	12	77	68	37	6th
1969-70	30	8	7	15	44	55	23	12th
1970-71	30	12	8	10	55	47	32	7th
1971-72	30	17	4	9	73	44	38	5th
1972-73	32	14	5	13	73	62	33	6th
1973-74	32	13	7	12	56	45	33	9th
1974-75	30	13	4	13	45	57	30	8th
1975-76	30	9	4	17	46	57	22	12th
1976-77	30	9	9	12	44	56	27	10th
1977-78	30	7	8	15	34	44	22	15th
1978-79	30	14	5	11	58	54	33	7th
1979-80	30	12	6	12	45	62	30	9th
1980-81	30	7	7	16	30	52	21	14th
1981-82	30	10	6	14	40	54	26	10th
1982-83	8	1	2	5	7	24	4	†
1983-84	did not compete							
1984-85	22	11	2	9	41	47	24	4th
1985-86	26	8	4	14	58	71	20	11th
1986-87	28	28	5	5	77	39	41	2nd
1987-88	28	13	4	11	55	49	30	7th
1988-89	28	13	5	10	59	37	31	7th

† Withdrew in October

United League

	P	W	D	L	F	A	Pts	Pos
1905-06	18	13	1	4	51	21	27	2nd
1906-07	14	8	5	1	39	20	21	1st
1907-08	16	4	4	8	20	33	12	7th

London League

	P	W	D	L	F	A	Pts	Pos
1906-07	18	5	3	10	27	33	13	6th
1913-14	16	8	1	7	43	28	17	4th
1914-15	16	5	1	10	17	43	11	7th

London 'B' League

	P	W	D	L	F	A	Pts	Pos
1912-13	10	6	2	2	26	15	14	2nd

Western League

	P	W	D	L	F	A	Pts	Pos
1907-08	12	3	4	5	16	17	10	6th
1909-10	12	5	2	5	23	22	12	4th

South Eastern League

	P	W	D	L	F	A	Pts	Pos
1908-09	38	13	4	21	54	75	30	13th
1909-10	38	8	10	16	43	67	26	16th

Kent League

	P	W	D	L	F	A	Pts	Pos
1912-13	28	19	4	5	91	35	42	2nd

London Football Combination

	P	W	D	L	F	A	Pts	Pos
1919-20	36	13	6	17	56	70	32	8th
1920-21	36	12	7	17	41	80	31	8th
1921-22	40	20	4	16	63	80	44	4th
1922-23	40	18	9	13	68	63	45	5th
1923-24	44	20	6	18	81	85	46	5th
1924-25	44	12	17	15	62	76	41	8th
1925-26	44	15	9	20	57	71	39	8th
1926-27	42	16	8	18	81	94	40	13th
1927-28	42	7	11	24	63	123	25	22nd
1928-29	42	16	6	20	67	86	38	15th
1929-30	42	17	6	19	88	101	40	13th
1930-31	42	20	3	19	78	73	43	10th
1931-32	42	22	8	12	90	49	52	3rd
1932-33	46	22	8	16	104	84	52	7th
1933-34	46	20	5	21	110	104	45	13th
1934-35	46	22	6	18	101	91	50	6th
1935-36	46	21	10	15	102	98	52	7th
1936-37	46	17	12	17	74	82	46	12th
1937-38	46	18	8	20	89	101	44	14th
1938-39	46	19	7	20	92	89	45	13th

London Professional Mid-week League

	P	W	D	L	F	A	Pts	Pos
1932-33	14	4	2	8	33	38	10	7th

Football Combination

League

	P	W	D	L	F	A	Pts	Pos
1946-47	30	8	6	16	38	73	22	15th
1947-48	30	5	10	15	25	57	20	15th

Cup

	P	W	D	L	F	A	Pts	Pos
1947-48	14	4	2	8	18	28	10	6th

League

	P	W	D	L	F	A	Pts	Pos
1948-49	30	10	8	12	38	53	28	10th

Cup

	P	W	D	L	F	A	Pts	Pos
1948-49	14	4	3	7	9	20	11	7th

League

	P	W	D	L	F	A	Pts	Pos
1949-50	30	14	6	10	41	38	34	4th

Cup

	P	W	D	L	F	A	Pts	Pos
1949-50	14	3	4	7	19	25	10	6th

League

	P	W	D	L	F	A	Pts	Pos
1950-51	30	8	9	13	29	43	25	15th

Cup

	P	W	D	L	F	A	Pts	Pos
1950-51	14	3	3	8	12	27	9	8th

League

	P	W	D	L	F	A	Pts	Pos
1951-52	30	7	5	18	29	56	19	15th

Cup

	P	W	D	L	F	A	Pts	Pos
1951-52	14	4	2	8	26	35	10	4th

League

	P	W	D	L	F	A	Pts	Pos
1952-53	30	10	7	13	38	50	27	11th

Cup

	P	W	D	L	F	A	Pts	Pos
1952-53	14	4	0	10	10	29	8	8th

League

	P	W	D	L	F	A	Pts	Pos
1953-54	30	7	3	20	30	76	17	16th

Cup

	P	W	D	L	F	A	Pts	Pos
1953-54	14	2	2	10	12	35	6	8th

League

	P	W	D	L	F	A	Pts	Pos
1954-55	30	9	4	17	46	65	22	13th

Cup

	P	W	D	L	F	A	Pts	Pos
1954-55	14	2	3	9	16	32	7	8th

League

	P	W	D	L	F	A	Pts	Pos
1955-56	42	18	5	19	78	74	41	16th
1956-57	42	17	10	15	72	84	44	14th
1957-58	42	15	7	20	71	103	37	19th
1958-59	32	11	5	16	37	52	27	14th
1959-60	38	15	5	18	73	76	35	12th
1960-61	38	12	7	19	71	79	31	17th
1961-62	34	15	4	15	67	68	34	8th
1962-63	34	19	6	9	72	48	44	3rd
1963-64	34	11	12	11	59	54	34	9th
1964-65	34	14	3	17	57	57	31	10th
1965-66	34	11	4	19	48	80	26	14th
1966-67	32	11	4	17	51	71	26	15th
1967-68	40	16	8	16	67	71	40	6th
1968-69	25	16	3	6	47	31	35	5th
1969-70	25	11	7	7	43	30	29	9th
1970-71	42	11	14	17	54	58	36	14th
1971-72	40	19	10	11	65	52	48	3rd
1972-73	40	15	10	15	50	52	40	9th
1973-74	42	12	11	19	51	70	35	18th
1974-75	40	18	5	17	64	62	41	9th
1975-76	42	12	12	18	49	64	36	18th
1976-77	42	9	12	21	48	70	30	21st
1977-78	42	16	10	16	50	53	42	12th
1978-79	42	11	16	15	60	59	38	12th
1979-80	42	12	13	17	63	71	27	15th
1980-81	42	18	9	15	74	64	45	11th
1981-82	38	12	2	24	46	78	26	17th
1982-83	42	10	11	21	55	86	31	21st
1983-84	42	5	12	25	32	101	22	20th
1984-85	42	12	6	24	57	86	30	17th
1985-86	42	13	10	19	67	104	36	14th
1986-87	38	8	11	19	52	73	27	16th
1987-88	38	8	7	23	38	78	23	19th
1988-89	38	16	9	13	55	44	41	10th

Goalkeeper Bob Anderson, who joined Palace from Middlesbrough in October 1951 and left for Bristol Rovers in March 1953 after 38 League appearances. He ended his career with Bristol City.

Palace in the Southern League: Top: Harry Hanger in action against Swindon. Middle: Bob Spottiswood (left) and Jim Hughes (right). Bottom: Edwin Smith scores against Reading.

Southern League Summary 1905-1920

		Home					Away				
	P	*W*	*D*	*L*	*F*	*A*	*W*	*D*	*L*	*F*	*A*
Bradford	2	0	1	0	1	1	1	0	0	1	0
Brentford	16	5	2	1	13	8	1	2	5	6	10
Brighton & HA	20	3	6	1	15	8	4	1	5	10	16
Bristol R	20	8	2	0	30	11	1	7	2	12	13
Cardiff C	6	1	1	1	5	3	1	0	2	3	8
Coventry C	12	4	0	2	12	4	2	2	2	8	8
Croydon Common	4	1	0	1	3	5	1	1	0	2	1
Exeter C	16	4	3	1	10	1	1	5	2	10	12
Fulham *	4	1	0	1	5	3	0	1	1	3	4
Grays A	2	1	0	0	9	1	1	0	0	3	0
Leyton	14	4	2	1	16	8	5	1	1	11	4
Luton T	16	5	0	3	19	12	4	1	3	14	15
Merthyr	6	2	1	0	6	3	2	1	0	3	1
Millwall	20	9	0	1	21	3	3	3	4	7	8
New Brompton	20	5	2	3	21	15	2	3	5	14	21
Newport C	2	1	0	0	3	0	0	0	1	0	1
Northampton T	20	3	4	3	15	12	1	3	6	7	16
Norwich C	20	8	0	2	25	7	2	3	5	8	14
Plymouth A	20	5	1	4	15	12	1	6	3	7	12
Portsmouth *	20	8	1	1	19	9	1	5	4	4	14
Queen's Park R	20	6	1	3	21	11	3	2	5	12	17
Reading *	20	7	3	0	26	8	1	4	5	7	15
Southampton *	22	5	3	3	26	13	6	3	2	26	19
Southend U	12	1	4	1	8	4	1	3	2	7	10
Southern U	2	1	0	0	4	0	1	0	0	1	0
St Leonards	2	1	0	0	3	1	1	0	0	3	0
Stoke	4	1	0	1	2	2	0	1	1	1	2
Swansea T	2	1	0	0	2	1	1	0	0	1	0
Swindon T *	22	6	2	3	22	15	2	3	6	11	19
Tottenham H	4	0	0	2	0	3	1	0	1	2	4
Watford *	22	8	1	2	22	9	1	3	7	9	25
West Ham U*	20	4	3	3	18	16	4	4	2	15	10
Wycombe W	2	1	0	0	4	0	1	0	0	4	1
	414	120	43	44	421	209	57	68	82	232	300

*Reserves 1905-06

FA Youth Cup Record

1952-3
Round 1
v Gillingham (h) W 4-1
Round 2
v Brighton & HA (a) L 0-1

1953-4
Round 1
v Bexleyheath/Welling (a) L 3-5

1954-5
Round 1
Bye
Round 2
v Southampton (a) W 5-2
Round 3
v Chelsea (h) L 0-8

1955-6
Round 1
v Halling (Kent) (a) W
Round 2
Oct 29 v Gillingham (h) D 1-1
Replay
Nov v Gillingham (a) W 2-1
Round 3
Nov 28 v Bexleyheath (h) D 1-1
Replay
Dec 12 v Bexleyheath (a) L 3-5

1956-7
Round 1
Oct 3 v Lion Works (h) W 9-1
Round 2
Oct 22 v Bexleyheath (h) W 3-0
Round 3
Feb v West Ham United (a) L 2-6

1957-8
Round 1
Bye
Round 2
Oct 21 v Eastbourne (h) W 1-0
Round 3
v Bexleyheath (a) L 0-4

1958-9
Round 1
Bye
Round 2
Nov 10 v Eastbourne (h) L 1-4

1959-60
Round 1
Bye
Round 2
Nov 16 v Gillingham (h) W 11-0
Round 3
Jan 6 v West Ham United (h) L 0-5

1960-61
Round 1
Bye
Round 2
v Worthing (h) W 6-1
Round 3
v Charlton Athletic (a) L 0-3

1961-2
Round 1
Bye
Round 2
Nov 11 v Southampton (a) D 3-3
Replay
Nov 24 v Southampton (h) W 3-0
Round 3
Jan 15 v Brighton & HA (h) L 0-1

1962-3
Round 1
Bye
Round 2
Dec 10 v Bexleyheath (h) L 2-3

1963-4
Round 1
Nov 20 v Charlton Athletic (a) L 0-2

1964-5
Round 1
Dec 20 v Charlton Athletic (a) L

1965-6
Round 1
Nov 10 v Tooting & Mitcham (h) W 7-1
Round 2
Dec 8 v Chelsea (a) L 0-4

1966-7
Round 1
Nov 9 v Millwall (h) L 1-2

1967-8
Round 1
Nov 8 v Hayes (a) W 8-1
Round 2
Dec 5 v West Ham United (h) W 2-0
Round 3
Jan 18 v Watford (a) W 1-0
Round 4
Feb 13 v Charlton Athletic (h) W 2-1
Round 5
Feb 26 v Chelsea (a) W 5-3
Semi-final
Apr 3 v Coventry City (h) D 1-1
Replay
Apr 9 v Coventry City (a) L 0-2

1968-9
Round 1
Bye
Round 2
Nov 27 v Queen's Park Rangers (h) L 1-3

1969-70
Round 1
Bye
Round 2
Dec 1 v Millwall (a) L 1-2

1970-71
Round 1
Nov 7 v Brentford (a) W 5-2
Round 2
Dec 14 Luton Town (h) W 4-0
Round 3
Jan 11 v Fulham (a) L 1-2

1971-2
Round 1
Oct 26 v Brentford (a) W 4-2
Round 2
Nov 29 v Fulham (a) W 1-0
Round 3
Dec 15 v Tottenham Hotspur (h) W 1-0
Round 4
Jan 26 v Chelsea (a) L 0-3

1972-3
Round 1
Bye
Round 2
Nov 29 v Cambridge United (h) W 3-0
Round 3
Dec 20 v West Ham United (h) D 2-2
Replay
Jan 10 v West Ham United (a) L 2-4

1973-4
Round 1
Bye
Round 2
Nov 27 v Arsenal (a) L 0-3

1974-5
Round 1
Bye
Round 2
v Southampton (a) W 1-0
Round 3
Dec 19 v Fulham (a) L 0-3

1975-6
Round 1
Bye
Round 2
v Croydon (h) W 6-1
Round 3
Dec 22 v Aston Villa (h) W 1-0
Round 4
Jan 1 v Arsenal (a) W 2-0
Round 5
Feb 28 v Oldham Athletic (h) W 2-1
Semi-final
Mar 29 v West Bromwich A (a) L 2-3
Semi-final (2nd leg)
Apr 6 v West Bromwich A (h) L 0-2

1976-7
Round 1
Bye
Round 2
Dec 20 v Fulham (h) D 0-0
Replay
Jan 6 v Fulham (a) W 4-1
Round 3
Feb 1 v Arsenal (h) D 2-2
Replay
Feb 12 v Arsenal (a) D 0-0
2nd Replay
Feb 15 v Arsenal (at Tooting & Mitcham) W 4-0
Round 4
Mar 4 v Chelsea (a) W 3-2
Round 5
Mar 26 v West Bromwich A (h) W 3-0
Semi-final
Apr 6 v Tottenham Hotspur (h) W 2-0
Semi-final (2nd leg)
Apr 13 v Tottenham Hotspur (a) W 6-0
Final
May 5 v Everton (a) D 0-0
Final (2nd leg)
May 13 v Everton (h) W 1-0

1977-8
Round 1
Bye
Round 2
Dec 6 v Fulham (h) W 1-0
Round 3
Jan v Chelsea (a) W 3-0
Round 4
Feb 21 v Leeds United (h) D 0-0
Replay
Mar 7 v Leeds United (a) W 1-0
Round 5
Mar 22 v Port Vale (h) W 3-0
Semi-final (1st leg)
Apr 3 v West Bromwich A (h) D 1-1
Semi-final (2nd leg)
Apr 10 v West Bromwich A (a) D 0-0
Replay
Apr 13 v West Bromwich A (a) D 2-2
2nd Replay
Apr v West Bromwich A (h) W 3-0
Final
v Aston Villa (at Highbury) W 1-0

1978-9
Round 1
Bye
Round 2
Dec 21 v Fulham (a) W 2-0
Round 3
Jan 22 v Tottenham Hotspur(a) W 2-0
Round 4
Feb 20 v Manchester City (h) L 1-2

1979-80
Round 1
Bye
Round 2
Nov 27 v Orient (h) W 2-1
Round 3
Jan 8 v Southampton (a) L 1-2

1980-81
Round 1
Bye
Round 2
Nov 24 v Watford (a) L 0-3

1981-2
Round 1
Bye
Round 2
Dec 2 v Chelsea (h) L 0-1

1982-3
Round 1
Nov v Brentford (h) W 2-1
Round 2
Nov v Maidstone (h) W 4-2
Round 3
Dec 13 v West Ham United (a) L 1-7

1983-4
Round 1
Nov 14 v Faversham (a) W 2-1
Round 2
Dec 8 v AP Leamington (a) L 0-2

1984-5
Round 1
Nov 5 v Brentford (a) L 1-4

1985-6
Round 1
Nov 5 v Brentford (h) W 4-2
Round 2
Dec 3 v Southampton (h) L 3-7

1986-7
Round 1
Nov v Enfield (a) W 8-2
Round 2
Dec 8 v Croydon (a) W 2-0
Round 3
Feb 2 v Fulham (h) W 2-0
Round 4
Feb 17 v Charlton Athletic (h) L 0-1

1987-8
Round 2
Nov 30 v Wimbledon (a) L 0-1

1988-9
Round 2
Dec 6 v Southampton (h) W 2-1
Round 3
Jan 18 v Brentford (a) L 0-1

Millwall's Dave Bumstead saves on the line from Palace's Johnny Gavin at Selhurst Park on Good Friday 1961. The Lions won this Fourth Division match 2-0.

PALACE INTERNATIONALS

Appearances given here refer to caps won when with Crystal Palace. The Republic of Ireland first played as a separate nation in 1924. The first set of figures in the 'Total' indicate appearances and goals while with Palace and the second (in brackets) are international career totals.

ENGLAND

ALDERSON J.T. Total 1-0 (1-0)

10. 5.23	v France	W 4-1	Paris

BYRNE J.J. Total 1-0 (11-8)

22.11.61	v Northern Ireland	D 1-1	Wembley (Division Three player)

COLCLOUGH H. Total 1-0 (1-0)

16. 3.14	v Wales	W 2-0	Cardiff (Southern League player)

SANSOM K.G. Total 9-0 (86-1)

23. 5.79	v Wales	D 0-0	Wembley
22.11.79	v Bulgaria	W 2-0	Wembley
6. 2.80	v Republic of Ireland	W 2-0	Wembley
13. 5.80	v Argentina	W 3-1	Wembley
17. 5.80	v Wales	L 1-4	Wrexham (sub)
20. 5.80	v Northern Ireland	D 1-1	Wembley
24. 5.80	v Scotland	W 2-0	Glasgow
12. 6.80	v Belgium	D 1-1	Turin
15. 6.80	v Italy	L 0-1	Turin

TAYLOR P. Total 4-2 (4-2)

24. 3.76	v Wales	W 2-1	Wrexham (sub) (1 goal) (Division Three player)
8. 5.76	v Wales	W 1-0	Cardiff (1 goal)
11. 5.76	v Northern Ireland	W 4-0	Wembley
15. 5.76	v Scotland	L 1-2	Glasgow

WALES

BOYLE T. Total 2-1 (2-1)

24. 2.81	v Republic of Ireland	W 3-1	Dublin (1 goal)
16. 5.81	v Scotland	W 2-0	Swansea (sub)

DAVIES W.C. Total 2-0 (4-0)

7. 3.08	v Scotland	L 1-2	Dundee (Southern League player)
16. 3.14	v England	L 0-2	Cardiff (Southern League player)

EVANS I.P. Total 13-1 (13-1)

19.11.75	v Austria	W 1-0	Wrexham
24. 3.76	v England	L 1-2	Wrexham
24. 4.76	v Yugoslavia	L 0-2	Zagreb
8. 5.76	v England	L 0-1	Cardiff

Johnny Byrne, Third Division Palace's England Star.

14. 5.76	v Northern Ireland	W 1-0	Swansea
22. 5.76	v Yugoslavia	D 1-1	Cardiff (1 goal)
6.10.76	v West Germany	L 0-2	Cardiff
17.11.76	v Scotland	L 0-1	Glasgow
30. 3.77	v Czechoslovakia	W 3-0	Wrexham
28. 5.77	v Scotland	D 0-0	Wrexham
31. 5.77	v England	W 1-0	Wembley
3. 6.77	v Northern Ireland	D 1-1	Belfast
20. 9.77	v Kuwait	D 0-0	Kuwait

GILES D. Total 3-0 (12-2)

24. 3.82	v Spain	D 1-1	Valencia (sub)
31. 5.83	v Northern Ireland	W 1-0	Belfast (sub)
12. 6.83	v Brazil	D 1-1	Cardiff

JONES J.T. Total 5-0 (15-0)

12. 2.21	v Scotland	L 1-2	Aberdeen
4. 2.22	v Scotland	W 2-1	Wrexham
13. 3.22	v England	L 0-1	Liverpool
16. 3.21	v England	D 0-0	Cardiff
1. 4.22	v Ireland	D 1-1	Belfast

LOVELL S. Total 1-0 (6-0)

18.11.81	v USSR	L 0-3	Tbilisi (sub)

MILLINGTON A. Total 2-0 (21-0)

18.11.64	v England	L 1-2	Wembley
30. 5.65	v USSR	L 1-2	Moscow

NICHOLAS P. Total 17-1 (54-2)

19. 5.79	v Scotland	W 3-0	Cardiff (sub)
25. 5.79	v Northern Ireland	D 1-1	Belfast (sub)
2. 6.79	v Malta	W 2-0	Valletta (1 goal)
11. 9.79	v Republic of Ireland	W 2-1	Swansea
17.10.79	v West Germany	L 1-5	Cologne
21.11.79	v Turkey	L 0-1	Izmir
17. 5.80	v England	W 4-1	Wrexham
21. 5.80	v Scotland	L 0-1	Glasgow
23. 5.80	v Northern Ireland	L 0-1	Cardiff
2. 6.80	v Iceland	W 4-0	Reykjavik
15.10.80	v Turkey	W 4-0	Cardiff
19.11.80	v Czechoslovakia	W 1-0	Cardiff
24. 2.81	v Republic of Ireland	W 3-1	Dublin
16.11.83	v Bulgaria	L 0-1	Sofia *
6. 6.84	v Norway	L 0-1	Trondheim *
10. 6.84	v Israel	D 0-0	Tel Aviv *
17.10.84	v Spain	L 0-3	Saville

* While on loan from Arsenal

ROUSE R.V. Total 1-0 (1-0)

22. 4.59	v Northern Ireland	L 1-4	Belfast (First Division Four cap)

WALSH I. Total 14-7 (18-7)

11. 9.79	v Republic of Ireland	W 2-1	Swansea (1 goal)
21.11.79	v Turkey	L 0-1	Izmir
17. 5.80	v England	W 4-1	Wrexham (1 goal)
21. 5.80	v Scotland	L 0-1	Glasgow
2. 6.80	v Iceland	W 4-0	Reykjavik (2 goals)
15.10.80	v Turkey	W 4-0	Cardiff (1 goal)
19.11.80	v Czechoslovakia	W 1-0	Cardiff
24. 2.81	v Republic of Ireland	W 3-1	Dublin
25. 3.81	v Turkey	W 1-0	Ankara
16. 5.81	v Scotland	W 2-0	Swansea (2 goals)
20. 5.81	v England	D 0-0	Wembley
30. 5.81	v USSR	D 0-0	Wrexham
9. 9.81	v Czechoslovakia	L 0-2	Prague (sub)
14.10.81	v Iceland	D 2-2	Swansea

WILLIAMS J.W. Total 2-0 (2-0)

2. 3.12	v Scotland	L 0-1	Tynecastle (Southern League player)
13. 4.12	v Ireland	L 2-3	Cardiff (Southern League player)

NORTHERN IRELAND (and Ireland before 1924)

McCRACKEN R. Total 4-0 (4-0)

23.10.20	v England	L 0-2	Sunderland
22.10.21	v England	D 1-1	Belfast
4. 3.22	v Scotland	L 1-2	Glasgow
1. 4.22	v Wales	D 1-1	Belfast

REPUBLIC OF IRELAND

MULLIGAN P. Total 14-0 (50-0)

15.11.72	v France	L 1-2	Dublin
13. 5.73	v USSR	L 0-1	Moscow
16. 5.73	v Poland	L 0-2	Katowice
19. 5.73	v France	D 1-1	Paris
6. 6.73	v Norway	D 1-1	Oslo
21.10.73	v Poland	W 1-0	Dublin
5. 5.74	v Brazil	L 1-2	Rio de Janerio
8. 5.74	v Uruguay	L 0-2	Montivideo
12. 5.74	v Chile	W 2-1	Santiago
30.10.74	v USSR	W 3-0	Dublin
20.11.74	v Turkey	D 1-1	Izmir
11. 5.75	v Switzerland	W 2-1	Dublin
18. 5.75	v USSR	L 1-2	Kiev
21. 5.75	v Switzerland	L 0-1	Berne

MURPHY J.M. Total 3-0 (3-0)

11. 9.79	v Wales	L 1-2	Swansea
29.10.79	v USA	W 3-2	Dublin
26. 3.80	v Cyprus	W 3-2	Nicosia

'COMMONWEALTH' INTERNATIONALS

BULCOCK J. Total 2-0 (2-0)

23. 7.10 v South Africa	W 6-2	Johannesburg
30. 7.10 v South Africa	W 6-3	Cape Town

HAMILTON J. Total 4-0 (4-0)

27. 6.25 v Australia	W 5-1	Brisbane
4. 7.25 v Australia	W 2-1	Sydney
11. 7.25 v Australia	W 8-2	Maitland
18. 7.25 v Australia	W 5-0	Svdnev

HILAIRE V. Total 1-1 (1-1)

15.10.79 v New Zealand	W 4-1	Leyton (Brisbane Road) (1 goal)

SANSOM K.G. Total 2-0 (2-0)

28.11.78 v Czechoslovakia 'B'	W 1-0	Prague
12. 6.79 v Austria 'B'	W 1-0	Klagenfurt

FLANAGAN M. Total 1-1 (1-1)

15.10.79 v New Zealand	W 4-1	Leyton (Brisbane Road) (1 goal)

UNDER-21 & UNDER-23 INTERNATIONALS

ENGLAND

ALLEN C. Total 2-0 (3-0)

9. 9.80 v Norway	W 3-0	Southampton
14.10.80 v Romania	L 0-4	Ploieşti

BYRNE J.J. Total 6-4 (7-6)

8. 2.61 v Wales	W 2-0	Everton (Goodison Park)
1. 3.61 v Scotland	L 0-1	Middlesbrough
15. 3.61 v West Germany	W 4-1	Tottenham (1 goal)
9.11.61 v Israel	W 7-1	Leeds (2 goals)
29.11.61 v Holland	W 5-2	Rotterdam (1 goal)
28. 2.62 v Scotland	W 4-2	Aberdeen

FENWICK T. Total 3-0 (11-0)

9. 9.80 v Norway	W 3-0	Southampton
14.10.80 v Romania	L 0-4	Ploieşti
18.11.80 v Switzerland	W 5-0	Ipswich

GILBERT W.A. Total 11-0 (11-0)

6. 2.79 v Wales	W 1-0	Swansea
5. 6.79 v Bulgaria	W 3-1	Pernik
20.11.79 v Bulgaria	W 5-0	Leicester
9. 9.80 v Norway	W 3-0	Southampton
14.10.80 v Romania	L 0-4	Ploieşti
18.11.80 v Switzerland	W 5-0	Ipswich
28. 4.81 v Romania	W 3-0	Swindon
31. 5.81 v Switzerland	D 0-0	Neuchâtel
5. 6.81 v Hungary	W 2-1	Kezthely
8. 9.81 v Norway	D 0-0	Drammen (sub)
17.11.81 v Hungary	W 2-0	Nottingham

Opposite: Kenny Sansom began his England career as a Crystal Palace player. ➧

HILAIRE V. Total 9-1 (9-1)

20.11.79	v Bulgaria	W 5-0	Leicester (1 goal)
12. 2.80	v Scotland	W 2-1	Coventry
4. 3.80	v Scotland	D 0-0	Aberdeen (sub)
16. 4.80	v East Germany	L 1-2	Sheffield (Bramall Lane)
23. 4.80	v East Germany	L 0-1	Jena
9. 9.80	v Norway	W 3-0	Southampton
14.10.80	v Romania	L 0-4	Ploieşti
18.11.80	v Switzerland	W 5-0	Ipswich (sub)
7. 4.82	v Poland	D 2-2	West Ham (Boleyn Ground) (sub)

HINSHELWOOD P.A. Total 2-0 (2-0)

6. 9.77	v Norway	W 6-0	Brighton
23. 4.80	v East Germany	L 0-1	Jena

KEMBER S.D. Total 1-0 (1-0)

14.10.70	v West Germany	W 3-1	Leicester

PAYNE D. Total 1-0 (1-0)

1.11.67	v Wales	W 2-1	Swansea (sub)

SANSOM K.G. Total 8-0 (8-0)

19. 9.78	v Denmark	W 2-1	Hvidovre
6. 2.79	v Wales	W 2-0	Swansea
5. 6.79	v Bulgaria	W 3-1	Pernik
10. 6.79	v Sweden	W 2-1	Västerås
12. 2.80	v Scotland	W 2-1	Coventry
4. 3.80	v Scotland	D 0-0	Aberdeen
16. 4.80	v East Germany	L 1-2	Sheffield (Bramall Lane)
23 .4.80	v East Germany	L 0-1	Jena

STEPHENSON A. Total 3-0 (7-0)

12.10.66	v Wales	W 8-0	Wolverhampton
20.12.67	v Italy	W 1-0	Nottingham (City Ground)
7. 2.68	v Scotland	W 2-1	Glasgow

SUCKLING P. Total 5-0 (10-0)

16. 2.88	v Scotland	W 1-0	Aberdeen
22. 3.88	v Scotland	W 1-0	Nottingham (City Ground)
13. 4.88	v France	L 2-4	Besançon
27. 4.88	v France	D 2-2	London (Highbury)
28. 5.88	v Switzerland	D 1-1	Lausanne

SWINDLEHURST D. Total 1-0 (1-0)

15.12.76	v Wales	D 0-0	Wolverhampton

TAYLOR P. Total 4-4 (4-4)

29.10.74	v Czechoslovakia	W 3-1	London (Selhurst Park)(1 goal)
19.11.74	v Portugal	W 3-2	Estoril (1 goal)
28.10.75	v Czechoslovakia	D 1-1	Trnava (1 goal)
18.11.75	v Poland	W 2-0	London (Selhurst Park)(1 goal)

WALES

BOYLE T. Total 1-0 (1-0)

13.10.81 v France — W 2-0 Newport

EVANS I. Total 1-0 (3-0)

21. 1.75 v England — L 0-2 Wrexham (sub)

GILES D. Total 1-0 (4-0)

14.11.82 v Yugoslavia — L 0-2 Nikšić

JOHNSON J. Total 2-0 (2-0)

27. 2.74 v Scotland — L 0-3 Aberdeen
4. 2.76 v Scotland — L 2-3 Wrexham

NICHOLAS P. Total 2-0 (3-0)

8. 2.78 v Scotland — W 1-0 Chester
6. 2.79 v England — L 0-1 Swansea

ROUSE R.V. Total 1-0 (1-0)

10.12.58 v Scotland — W 1-0 Edinburgh (First Division Four player)

WALSH I.P. Total 1-0 (4-0)

6. 2.79 v England — L 0-1 Swansea

SCOTLAND

PHILIP I. Total 1-0 (1-0)

13. 2.73 v England — L 1-2 Kilmarnock

REPUBLIC OF IRELAND

O'DOHERTY K. Total 1-0 (1-0)

25. 3.85 v England — L 2-3 Portsmouth

FOOTBALL LEAGUE REPRESENTATIVES

JACKSON J.

17. 3.71. v Scottish League — W 1-0 Glasgow (Hampden Park)

ENGLAND TRIALISTS (Probables)

DAWES A.G.

25. 3.36 v Possibles — W 3-1 Manchester (Old Trafford)

OTHER REPRESENTATIVE MATCHES

LONDON (Inter-Cities Fairs Cup)

BERRY P.

16. 9.57 v Lausanne — L 1-2 Lausanne

TRUETT G.

16. 9.57 v Lausanne	L 1-2	Lausanne

DIVISION THREE SOUTH
BELCHER J.

8.10.56 v Division Three North	W 2-1	Coventry

HARRISON B.

30.10.57 v Division Three North	D 2-2	London (Selhurst Park)

SOUTHERN LEAGUE
BULCOCK J.

11. 4.10 v Football League	D 2-2	London (Stamford Bridge)

COLCLOUGH H.

9. 2.14 v Football League	L 1-3	New Cross
26.10.14 v Football League	L 1-2	Highbury
12.10.14 v Scottish League	D 1-1	New Cross

COLLYER H.

30. 9.12 v Football League	L 1-2	Manchester (Old Trafford)
14.10.12 v Scottish League	W 1-0	New Cross
15. 3.13 v League of Ireland	D 1-1	New Cross
11.10.13 v League of Ireland	L 1-4	Dublin
13.10.13 v Scottish League	L 0-5	Glasgow (Parkhead)

HANGER H.

14.10.12 v Scottish League	W 1-0	New Cross

JOHNSON J.

11. 4.10 v Football League	D 2-2	Stamford Bridge
30. 9.11 v League of Ireland	W 2-0	Belfast (Windsor Park)
2.10.11 v Scottish League	L 2-3	Glasgow (Shawfield)

SPOTTISWOOD R.

30. 9.12 v Football League	L 1-2	Manchester (Old Trafford)

ENGLAND AMATEUR INTERNATIONALS

BATEMAN B.J.

8.11.13 v Ireland	W 2-0	Belfast
15.11.13 v Holland	W 2-1	Hull
5. 6.14 v Denmark	L 0-3	Copenhagen
12. 6.14 v Sweden	W 5-1	Stockholm

ENGLAND YOUTH INTERNATIONALS

1961-62	Hames B.	G	5 v Scotland, Wales, Yugoslavia, Bulgaria, Northern Ireland
1963-64	Holsgrove J.	LH	2 v Northern Ireland, Scotland
1966-67	Hamilton I.	LB	3 v Scotland, Northern Ireland, Wales
1966-67	Tomkins L.	IL	3 v Scotland, Northern Ireland, Wales

Gary Stebbing

1966-67	Kember S.	IR	7	v West Germany, Scotland, Italy, Spain, Yugoslavia, France, USSR
1967-68	Broad W.	LB	1	v Scotland
1968-69	Gonzalez R.	LB	1	v Scotland
1969-70	Hoadley P.	RH	3	v Republic of Ireland, Republic of Ireland, Wales
1973-74	Swindlehurst D.	IR	3	v Wales, Holland (sub), Wales
1976-77	Sansom K.G.	LB	5	v Wales, Wales, Belgium, Iceland, Greece
1976-77	Hilaire V.M.	IL	3	v Belgium (sub), Iceland, Greece
1977-78	Hilaire V.M.	IL	5	v France, France, Turkey, Spain, Poland
1977-78	Fenwick T.W.	RH	7	v Uruguay, Hungary, France, France, Turkey, Spain, Poland
1977-78	Dare K.J.	LB	1	v Hungary
1977-78	Gilbert WA	LH	4	v France, Turkey, Spain, Poland
1978-79	MacKenzie S.	OR	8	v Belgium, Italy, Italy, Czechoslovakia, Malta, West Germany, Bulgaria, France
1978-79	Carter L.	IL	3	v Belgium, Italy, Italy
1978-79	Paul A.G.	OR	2	v Italy, Czechoslovakia
1978-79	Banfield N.A.	LH	3	v Malta (sub), Bulgaria, France
1979-80	Banfield N.A.	LH	7	v West Germany, Poland, Hungary, Czechoslovakia, Denmark, Northern Ireland, Portugal
1979-80	Banfield N.A.	LH	3	v Poland, Holland, Yugoslavia
1980-81	Banfield N.A.	LH	5	v Cameroon, Argentina, Australia, Egypt, Romania
1979-80	Brooks S.	LH	3	v West Germany, Poland, Hungary
1980-81	Brooks S.	LH	4	v Northern Ireland, Northern Ireland, Scotland, Austria
1979-80	Horn R.	G	1	v Denmark (sub)
1983-84	Stebbing G.	RB	2	v France, Qatar
1985-86	Stebbing G.	RB	7	v Switzerland, Hungary, West Germany, Yugoslavia, Iceland, East Germany, Russia
1986-87	Stebbing G.	RB	4	v Cameroon, USSR, Mexico, France
1987-88	Stebbing G.	RB	3	v Paraquay, China, Mexico

SCOTLAND YOUTH INTERNATIONALS

1971-72	Cannon J.A.	CH	4	v England, Hungary, West Germany, Russia

WALES YOUTH INTERNATIONALS

1975-76	Nicholas P.	LB	1	v Yugoslavia
1975-76	Walsh I.	CF	1	v Yugoslavia (2 goals)

Action from the England-Wales game at Selhurst Park in 1926.

Other Matches at Selhurst Park

Full International

1 Mar 1926	England 1	Wales 3	29,000

Under-23 International

29 Oct 1974	England 3	Czechoslovakia 1	22,799
18 Nov 1975	England 2	Portugal 0	19,472

Amateur Internationals

10 Nov 1923	England 3	Ireland 0	
16 Nov 1929	England 7	Ireland 2	
19 Sep 1953	England 0	South Africa 4	
18 Sep 1954	England 5	Ireland 0	
16 Mar 1962	England 3	Scotland 4	
20 Mar 1964	England 1	Scotland 0	5,000

League Match

3 Dec 1947	Millwall 2	Newcastle United 1	30,000

Division Three South v Division Three North Match

30 Oct 1957	South 2	North 2	12,690

Division Three Play-off Match

29 May 1987	Gillingham 0 Swindon Town 2	18,491

FA Cup Matches

29 Jan 1927	Corinthians 1 Newcastle United 3	(Radio broadcast)
21 Dec 1953	Brighton & HA 1 Wrexham 3	

Third Place Play-off Matches

7 May 1971	Stoke City 3 Everton 2	5,031
5 Feb 1974	Orient 0 Portsmouth 2	19,595
10 Feb 1975	Wimbledon 0 Leeds United 1	45,701
15 Dec 1979	Croydon 1 Millwall 1	9,815

Amateur Cup Final

18 April 1936	Casuals 1 Ilford 1	25,064

Amateur Cup Semi-finals

Mar 1932	Dulwich Hamlet 1 Kingstonian 0	
Mar 1938	Erith & Belvedere 4 Romford 2	
Mar 1951	Hendon 2 Pegasus 3	Replay
Mar 1967	Enfield 1 Walthamstow Avenue 0	
Mar 68	Sutton 0 Leytonstone 0	

Crystal Palace in 1933-4. Back row (left to right): Collier (trainer), Norris, Parker, Hayward, Goddard, Earle, Clarke, Edwards, Sparke, Turnbull (assistant trainer). Second row: Rossiter, Brown, Finn, Ward, Tyler, Dunn, Beby, Nicholas, Parry, Barrie, Wilde, Roberts. Seated: Simpson, Rooke, F.E.Burrell, M.Derisley, R.S.Flew, L.T.Bellatti, F.Gates, H.Watson-Humphries, J.Tresadern (manager), Thompson, Manders. On ground: Howe, Harry, Turner, Fyfe.

Attendance Records

Crystal Palace

FA Cup
35,000 14 Jan 1911 v Everton

The Nest

League
22,000 27 Dec 1920 v Brighton & HA *(£1,105)*

FA Cup
22,000 29 Jan 1921 v Hull C *(£1,430)*
25,000 28 Jan 1922 v Millwall *(£1,778)*

Selhurst Park

League
25,000 26 Dec 1924 v Portsmouth *(£1,585)*
48,610 9 Aug 1969 v Manchester U *(£16,250)*
49,498 27 Dec 1969 v Chelsea
51,482 11 May 1979 v Burnley

FA Cup
40,000 30 Jan 1926 v Chelsea *(£2,554)*
41,667 20 Feb 1965 v Nottingham F
45,384 10 Mar 1965 v Leeds U

Record Receipts

£103,173 v West Ham U FA Cup (Round 4) 28 Jan 1984

Crystal Palace in 1938-9. Back row (left to right): Birtley, Horton, Blackman, A.Dawes, Collins, F.Dawes, Owens, Hudgell, Jordan, Robson. Second row: Gregory, Leivesley, Daniels, Walker, Chesters, Tierney, Shanks, Brooks, Uren, Lewis. Seated: R.Greener, G.Stanbury, Dr T.E.M.Wardill, C.H.Temple, E.T.Truett, R.H.Blaxill, F.E.Burrell, T.G.Bromilow (manager), G.Irwin. On ground: Davis, Waldron, Trevor Smith, Bryson, Gillespie, Bigg, McLean.

Highest Scores

Home

Win	17-2	West Beckenham	24 April 4 1906	Friendly
	11-1	Caribbean XI	14 September 1959	Friendly
	10-1	Reading	4 March 1916	War
	10-1	Brighton & HA	3 January 1942	War
	10-1	Swindon T	10 November 1945	War
	9-0	Barrow	10 September 1959	Division Four
	9-1	Grays A	4 November 1905	Southern
	9-2	Accrington S	20 August 1960	Division Four
	8-0	Southampton	16 November 1912	Southern
	8-0	Exeter C	6 February 1937	Division Three South
	8-1	Watford	23 September 1959	Division Four
Draw	5-5	Plymouth A	28 November 1925	Division Three South
Defeat	1-6	Millwall	7 May 1927	Division Three South
	1-6	Nottingham F	27 January 1951	Division Three South

Away

Win	8-1	Brighton & HA	26 September 1942	War
	6-0	Everton	7 January 1922	FA Cup
	6-0	Exeter C	26 January 1935	Division Three South
	6-0	Birmingham C	5 September 1987	Division Two
	6-3	Swindon T	1 November 1952	Division Three South
Draw	4-4	Swindon T	6 April 1931	Division Three South
	4-4	Exeter C	12 November 1938	Division Three South
	4-4	Ipswich T	24 December 1949	Division Three South
	4-4	Gillingham	10 February 1952	Division Three South
	4-4	Doncaster R	2 January 1988	Division Two
Defeat	4-13	Manchester C	20 February 1926	FA Cup
	0-11	West Ham U	6 April 1918	War
	6-11	Exeter C	24 January 1934	Division Three South Cup
	2-10	Reading	4 September 1946	Division Three South
	0-9	Arsenal	6 February 1943	War
	1-9	Portsmouth	26 December 1944	War
	0-8	Spurs	16 February 1918	War
	0-8	Coventry C	6 February 1932	Division Three South
	0-8	Leyton Orient	12 November 1955	Division Three South
	1-8	Northampton T	27 October 1928	Division Three South
	1-8	Coventry C	9 November 1935	Division Three South
	2-8	Brentford	25 December 1930	Division Three South
	2-8	Chelsea	16 September 1944	War

Action at Selhurst during the 1946-7 season when the League programme was extended into June after a bad winter. Above: Dick Graham punches clear from a Watford attack. Opposite top: Palace outside-right Albert Mycock on the attack against Norwich City. Opposite bottom: Bill Bassett in action during the visit of Cardiff City.

Alfie Noakes, another Palace stalwart to make over 200 appearances.

Ted Ward

Phil Bates

Bill Hand

Joe Cartwright

Palace Career Records
Southern League 1905-1920

*Also played in the Football League

Player	Date signed	From	Date tranfd	To	S League App	S League Gls	FA Cup App	FA Cup Gls	TOTAL App	TOTAL Gls
*ALDERSON John Thomas	Jan 1919	Newcastle	1920	Div 3	42	0	1	0	43	0*
ASTLEY Horace	1905	Middlesbrough	1907	Bury	*19	1	13	4	32	5

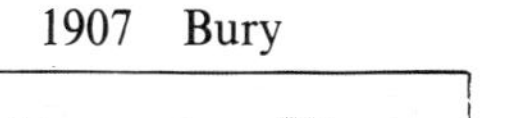

Ben Bateman

John Bowler

J.Bright

James Collins

Player	Date signed	From	Date tranfd	To	S League App	S League Gls	FA Cup App	FA Cup Gls	TOTAL App	TOTAL Gls
BAKER Robert W	1907	Redhill	1908		4	0	0	0	4	0
BALDING H A	1907	Bromley	1909		9	0	0	0	9	0
BARBER Thomas	1919	Aston Villa	1920	Merthyr	19	7	1	0	20	7
BARKER H	1908	Wimbledon	1909		6	1	0	0	6	1
*BATEMAN Benjamin	1913		1920	Div 3	75	4	3	0	78	4
*BATES Phillip	Mar 1919	Beckenham W	1921	Scunthorpe	25	1	1	0	26	1
BAUCHOP James Rae	Mar 1908	Norwich C	May 1909	Derby County	42	22	4	3	46	25
BEECH Daniel	1911	Mexborough	1913		4	0	0	0	4	0
BIRNIE Edward Lawson	May 1905	Newcastle	May 1906	Chelsea	*	2	7	1	7	3
BOURNE W J	1911	Sittingbourne	1913		9	4	0	0	9	4
BOWLER J	1914		1920		1	0	1	0	2	0
BOYD A	1911		1912		1	0	0	0	1	0
BRADLEY C E	1909	Leytonstone (amat)	1915	Barking	4	0	0	0	4	0
BRADSHAW	1905	Reserve	1906		0	0	0	0	0	0
BREARLEY John	7 May 1907	Spurs	1909	Millwall	71	3	7	1	78	4
BRIGHT John	1913	Sittingbourne	1914		18	9	2	0	20	9
BROWN William G	1907	Plymouth A	1908		0	0	0	0	0	0
BRYDEN	1905	Reserve	1906		0	0	0	0	0	0
BULCOCK Joseph	1909	Exeter C	Mar 1914	Swansea	131	2	8	0	139	2
CLARK Charles	1909	Plymouth A	1910		31	0	1	0	32	0
COLECLOUGH Horace	1912	Crewe A	1915	WWI	82	0	5	0	87	0
COLLINS Edward	1908	Carlisle	1910	Fulham	25	0	3	0	28	0
COLLINS James	1910		1915	WWI	50	2	1	0	51	2
COLLYER Harold W	1906	Catford Southend	1915	WWI	259	0	18	0	277	0

Player	Date signed	From	Date tranfd	To	S League App	S League Gls	FA Cup App	FA Cup Gls	TOTAL App	TOTAL Gls
*CONNER John	1919	Belfast Distillery	1920	Div 3	37	18	1	0	38	18
CRACKWELL Richard	1919		1920	Maidstone	33	1	1	0	34	1
DAVIES William C	Oct 1907	Stoke C	Aug 1908	WBA						
	May 1910	WBA	1915	WWI	192	21	14	3	206	24
EDWARDS Matthew	1905	Barnsley	1908		*44	5	14	0	58	5
FEEBURY Albert	1914	Coventry C	1920	Div 3	66	2	3	0	69	2

Harold Collyer

Albert Feebury

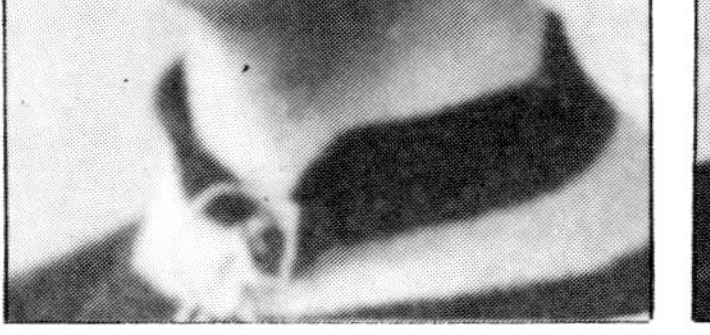

Harry Hanger

Charles Hewitt

Player	Date signed	From	Date tranfd	To	S League App	S League Gls	FA Cup App	FA Cup Gls	TOTAL App	TOTAL Gls
FORGAN Thomas H	1909	Gainsborough	1910		1	0	0	0	1	0
FORSTER William E	1906	Sheffield U	May 1908	Grimsby T	49	0	11	0	60	0
GARRATT George	May 1908	WBA	Oct 1913	Millwall	173	7	12	1	185	8
GIBSON Roberts J	Aug 1909	Bury	1910	Middlesbrough	2	1	0	0	2	1
GLOVER F	1910	Army (amat)	1911	Army	1	0	0	0	1	0
GOODHEAD	1910	Dartford (amat)	1911		1	0	0	0	1	0
GRAINGER John	1919		1920		1	0	0	0	1	0
GRANT	1905		1906		0	0	2	0	2	0
GRIFFIN Michael R	1909	Liverpool	1910		34	2	1	0	35	2
GREEN Albert	1919	Watford	1920	Sheppey U	9	2	0	0	9	2
GROVES F	1919		1920		1	0	0	0	1	0
HALL William	1907	Manchester City	1908		10	0	0	0	10	0
HANGER Harry	May 1909	Bradford City	1915	WWI	168	7	10	1	178	8
HARKER Richard	1905	Newcastle	1907	Hibernians	*					
	1911	Hearts	1912	Darlington	50	20	18	10	68	30
HATTON Albert	1910	Grimsby T	1912	Aberdare	43	0	2	0	45	0
HAYWOOD Adam	1908	Blackpool	1909	Coach	9	1	0	0	9	1
HEWITSON Robert	May 1905	Barnsley	14 Aug 1907	Oldham A	*36	0	15	0	51	0
HEWITT Charles	May 1910	WBA	1919	Hartlepools	144	39	11	3	155	42
HIGGINS H W	1907	Watford	1909	Watford	2	0	0	0	2	0
HODGKINSON Albert Victor	1906	Bury	May 1907	Southampton	5	1	0	0	5	1
HOOPER A	1914	Manchester United	1915	WWI	18	2	0	0	18	2
HUGHES James	1909	Liverpool	1920	Chatham	200	15	9	0	209	15
HULLOCK James	1908		1910	Third Lanark	8	0	0	0	8	0

A.Hooper K.R.G.Hunt James Hughes P.T.Keene

HUMPHRIES C	1910		1911		1	0	0	0	1	0
HUNT Kenneth R G (Rev)	1912	Wolves (amat)	1920	Wolves	16	0	0	0	16	0
HUNTER H	1906	Middlesbrough	1907		2	0	0	0	2	0
INNERD Wilfred	1905	Newcastle	1909	Shilden A	*95	4	22	3	117	7
ISLEY Arthur S	1919		1920	Div 3	8	0	0	0	8	0
JACKSON J B	Mar 1907	Portsmouth	Aug 1907		7	0	0	0	7	0

Player	Date signed	From	Date tranfd	To	S League App	S League Gls	FA Cup App	FA Cup Gls	TOTAL App	TOTAL Gls
JOHNSON Joshua	Nov 1907	Plymouth A	Jun 1919	Nottingham F	274	0	19	0	293	0
KEENE P T	1912		1915		15	3	2	0	17	3
KYLE J	1908	Woking	1909		3	0	0	0	3	0
LANE Harry William	1914	Manchester United	1915	WWI	16	4	0	0	16	4
LAWRENCE William H	Nov 1906	Summerstown (amat)	1913	Merthyr T	24	6	5	1	29	7
LEDGER William	1906	Royal Rovers	1907	Sunderland Close	11	0	2	0	13	0
LEE F R	1908	Rotherham Co	1909		6	2	0	0	6	2
LEWIS F E	1907		1909		17	0	1	0	18	0
*LITTLE Joseph	1919	Croydon Common	1920	Div 3	42	0	1	0	43	0
LITTLEWORT Henry Charles	1906	West Norwood	1907	West Norwood	1	0	0	0	1	0
LLOYD Herbert	1912	Rotherham	1913	Wolves	3	0	0	0	3	0
McGIBBON Charles Edward	1908	Gillingham	May 1909	Southampton	17	13	0	0	17	13
*MENLOVE Bert	1919	Southern Railway	1920	Div 3	12	6	0	0	12	6
MENZIES A	1906	Arthurlie	1907		4	0	0	0	4	0
MICHAEL A	1914	Worcester C	1915	WWI	1	0	0	0	1	0
MIDDLETON William G	1913	Birmingham (amat)	1920	Folkestone	32	7	2	1	34	8
MITCHELL H C	1910		1911		1	0	0	0	1	0
MOODY	1905	Reserve	1906		*0	1	0	0	0	1
MORTIMORE E	1912		1913	Mansfield	1	0	0	0	1	0
MOULT J	1909	Coventry C	1910		1	0	1	0	2	0
MYERS Ernest Colin	1909	Northfleet	1912	Hickleton Main	22	0	1	0	23	0
NEEDHAM Archibald	1905	Sheffield U	1909	Glossop	*84	25	20	2	104	27
OLIVER W	1905	Reserve	1906		*0	0	0	0	0	0

Player	Date signed	From	Date tranfd	To	S League App	S League Gls	FA Cup App	FA Cup Gls	TOTAL App	TOTAL Gls
O'CONNER Eric	1911	Catford Southend	1913		10	0	0	0	10	0
OWENS Issac	May 1907	Bristol Rovers	May 1908	Grimsby	22	7	0	0	22	7
PAGE David T	1911	Local	1912		1	0	0	0	1	0
PAYNE George Clark	1909	Spurs	Apr 1911	Sunderland	45	30	1	1	46	31
RANSOME	1906		1907		1	0	0	0	1	0
*RHODES Ernest	Oct 1913	Gravesend	1923	Sheppey	47	0	1	0	48	0
ROBERTS Richard James	1905	Middlesbrough	1909	Retired injury	*57	19	17	6	74	25
ROSS R	1905		1906		*0	3	0	0	0	3

Harry Lane

A.Michael

Bill Middleton

Ernest Rhodes

RYAN Charles W	1906	Nunhead	1909	Croydon Com	81	0	12	0	93	0
SANS Arthur	1906		1907		2	0	0	0	2	0
SANDERS Sidney C	1914	Nunhead	1919		1	0	0	0	1	0
SHAW H	1914	Metrogas	1915		6	0	0	0	6	0
SMITH Cyril	1919	Croydon Common	1920	Charlton Ath	7	0	0	0	7	0
SMITH Edwin Arthur	Dec 1911	Hull C	1920	Div 3	155	110	12	4	167	114
SMITH George	1907		1908		9	2	2	0	11	2
SPOTTISWOOD Robert	1909	Crewe A	Oct 1919	Clapton Orient	177	2	11	0	188	2
SWANN Hubert	1907	Plymouth A	1909	Queen's Park R	63	16	3	2	66	18
THOMPSON Frederick	4 May 1905	Portsmouth	Nov 1905	Fulham	0	0	0	0	0	0
THOMPSON George	1905	Newcastle	1906		*0	3	1	0	1	3
THOMPSON Henry	1910	Newcastle £25	1911		4	0	0	0	4	0
THORPE James	1908	Leeds City	1909		17	0	0	0	17	0
WALKER George	1905	Wolves	1909		*41	2	10	0	51	2
WALLACE Charles William	Jul 1905	Southwick	1 May 1907	Aston Villa	*37	8	14	1	51	9
WATKINS Walter Martin	1905	Sunderland	May 1906	Northampton	*0	8	6	6	6	14
WESTON W	1906	Sunderland	1907	Blackpool	6	1	1	0	7	1
WHIBLEY John	1911	Sittingbourne	1923	Sittingbourne	55	12	2	0	57	12
WHITE	1905		1906		0	0	0	0	0	0
WIGGINS R	1920		1921		1	0	0	0	1	0
WILLIAMS James William	1909	Birmingham	Feb 1914	Millwall	142	56	6	0	148	56
WILLIAMSON P	1911	Catford Southend	1913		2	0	0	0	2	0
WILLS Thomas	May 1906	Newcastle	1907	Carlisle	17	0	1	0	18	0
WILSON Albert J	1905	Streatham	1909		*4	0	0	0	4	0
*WOOD A	1919	Talbot Stead	1920	Div 3	13	1	0	0	13	1

Player	Date signed	From	Date tranfd	To	S League App	S League Gls	FA Cup App	FA Cup Gls	TOTAL App	TOTAL Gls
WOOD Frederick W Raymond	1913	Clapton	1914	Millwall (exch)	3	0	0	0	3	0
WOOD N A	1909		1910	Plymouth A	1	0	0	0	1	0
WOODGER George	1905	T.Heath Wednesday	30 Sep 1910	Oldham A£750	150	36	16	3	166	39
WOODHOUSE Charles	Sep 1910	Halesowen	7 Dec 1911	Died after illness	44	21	1	0	45	21
YORK W Ernest	1912	Kettering	1915	WWI	54	6	3	0	57	6
YOUNG John	Oct 1909	Hulford	1910		15	8	0	0	15	8

H.Shaw

Edwin Smith

Bob Spottiswood

John Whibley

Ernie York

Johnny McNichol, who made over 200 League and Cup appearances for Palace.

Crystal Palace Career Records 1920-1989

The following lists all players to have appeared in Football League, FA Cup and League Cup games for Palace. * Also Southern League † Still on staff *cs* close season ‡ not including war appearances § on loan # return from loan.

PLAYER	BIRTHPLACE	DATE	DATE SIGNED	FROM	DATE TRANSFERRED	TO	League App	League Gls	FA Cup App	FA Cup Gls	FL Cup App	FL Cup Gls	Total App	Total Gls
ADDINALL Albert W	Paddington	30 Jan 1921	Jul 1954	Brighton & HA	Jan 1955	Snowdon C	12	2	0	0	0	0	12	2
ALDERSON Jack*	Crook	28 Nov 1891	Jan 1919	Newcastle U	1924	Pontypridd	151	0	12	0	0	0	163	0
ALLEN Clive Darren	Stepney	20 May 1961	Aug 1980	Arsenal	Jun 1981	Queen's Park R	25	9	0	0	4	2	29	11
ALLEN James	Newcastle		Jan 1921	Walker Celtic	Jun 1924	Hartlepools U	16	0	0	0	0	0	16	0
ALLEN Ronnie	Fenton	15 Jan 1929	May 1961	West Bromwich A	16 Mar 1965	Wolves	100	34	7	3	2	0	109	37
ANDERSON Ben C	Aberdeen	18 Feb 1946	Nov 1973	Cape Town (SA)	1974		11	1	1	0	0	0	12	1
ANDERSON (Bob) John R	Newcastle	9 Nov 1924	Oct 1951	Blackhall Coll	Mar 53	Bristol Rovers	38	0	0	0	0	0	38	0
ANDREWS Cecil J	Alton	1 Nov 1930	Jun 1952	Portsmouth	Jun 1956	Queen's Park R	104	11	1	0	0	0	105	11
AYLOTT Trevor K C	Bermondsey	26 Nov 1957	18 Jul 1984	Luton T	22 Aug 1986	Bournemouth	50/3	12	2	1	3/1	0	55/4	13
AYRES Keith E	Oxford	15 May 1956	3 Nov 1973	Manchester U	Apr 1976	Contract cancelled	3/3	0	0	0	0	0	3/3	0
BAILEY Dennis	Lambeth	13 Nov 1965	Feb 1988	Farnborough	Feb 1989 † §	Bristol Rovers	0/5	1	0	0	0	0	0/5	1
BAILEY Roy N	Epsom	26 May 1932	Jun 1949	Juniors	15 Mar 1956	Ipswich T	118	0	1	0	0	0	119	0
BANFIELD Neil A	Poplar	20 Jan 1962	Aug 1979	Juniors	Dec 1983	Orient	2/1	0	0	0	0	0	2/1	0
BANNISTER Jack	Chesterfield	26 Jan 1942	1 Jul 1965	Scunthorpe U	23 Oct 1968	Luton T	117/3	7	3	0	6	0	126/3	7
BARBER Phil A	Tring	10 Jun 1965	Feb 1984	Aylesbury	†		168/28	20	7	0	10/3	3	185/31	23
BARKE Billy	(see Naylor)													
BARNES Howard	Wandsworth	Jan 1910	Oct 1931	Wimbledon	*cs* 1935		1	0	0	0	0	0	1	0
BARNES Victor	Twickenham	Aug 1903	3 Jun 1926	Kingstonians	*cs* 1928		4	1	2	0	0	0	6	1
BARNETT Tom	Muswell Hill	12 Oct 1936	1 Dec 1958	Chatham	Jun 1961		14	2	0	0	1	0	15	2
BARRIE George	Markinch		Jun 1929	Kettering T	15 Mar 1934	Gillingham	79	0	4	0	0	0	83	0
BARRON Paul G	Woolwich	16 Sep 1953	Aug 1980	Arsenal	Dec 1982	West Bromwich A	90	0	5	0	13	0	108	0
BARRY Roy A	Edinburgh	19 Sep 1942	26 Sep 1973	Coventry C	1 Feb 1975	Hibernians	41/1	1	1	0	2	0	44/1	1
BARTRAM Per	Denmark	8 Jan 1944	14 Aug 1969	Morton	Dec 1970	Morton	8/2	2	0	0	1	1	9/2	3
BASON Brian	Epsom	3 Sep 1955	Mar 1981	Plymouth A	Aug 1982	Reading	25/2	0	0	0	4	0	29/2	0
BASSETT Bill‡	Brithdir	8 Jun 1912	1942	Cardiff C	Jun 1949	Portmadoc coach	70	0	1	0	0	0	71	0
BATEMAN Ben*	Chelsea	20 Nov 1892	1913		Aug 1924	Dartford	98	6	5	1	0	0	103	7
BATES Phil*	Beckenham		Mar 1919	Beckenham W	May 1921	Scunthorpe U	40	2	2	0	0	0	42	2
BAXTER Paul A	Hackney	22 Apr 1964	Sep 1981	Tottenham H	Jun 1983	Leytonstone	1	0	0	0	0	0	1	0
BELCHER Jim A	Stepney	31 Oct 1932	Jun 1954	West Ham U	12 May 1958	Ipswich T	128	20	10	0	0	0	138	20
BELL Bobby	Cambridge	26 Oct 1950	23 Sep 1971	Blackburn R	1973	South Africa	31	0	4	0	1	0	36	0
BENNETT Ken E	Wood Green	2 Oct 1921	Jul 1953	Brighton & HA	Jul 1954	Tonbridge	17	2	0	0	0	0	17	2

Clive Allen

Phil Barber

PLAYER	BIRTHPLACE	DATE	DATE SIGNED	FROM	DATE TRANSFERRED	TO	League App	League Gls	FA Cup App	FA Cup Gls	FL Cup App	FL Cup Gls	Total App	Total Gls
BENNETT Ron	Hinckley	8 May 1927	Jan 1952	Portsmouth	Jul 1953	Brighton & HA	27	5	0	0	0	0	27	5
BERESFORD Frank E	Chesterfield	8 Oct 1910	22 Dec 1936	Luton T	9 Nov 1937	Carlisle U	3	0	0	0	0	0	3	0
BERESFORD Reg H	Walsall	3 Jun 1921	Aug 1948	Birmingham C	May 1949		7	1	0	0	0	0	7	1
BERRY Peter	Aldershot	20 Sep 1933	Aug 1951	Juniors	9 May 1958	Ipswich T	151	24	10	1	0	0	161	25
BERRY William G	Hackney	18 Aug 1904	Nov 1932	Brentford	Jun 1933	Bournemouth	17	4	0	0	0	0	17	4
BESAGNI Romo	Italy	22 Apr 1935	21 Oct 1952	Juniors	1953		2	0	0	0	0	0	2	0
BETTERIDGE Walter	Oakthorpe	Oct 1886	Jun 1928	Peterborough U	Aug 1929	Loughborough C	1	0	0	0	0	0	1	0
BIGG Bob‡	Croydon		Mar 1934	Redhill	*cs* 1939	Aldershot	109	41	5	0	0	0	114	41
BIRCH Billy	Southport	20 Oct 1944	Jun 1963	West Bromwich A	May 1964		6	0	0	0	1	0	7	0
BIRCHENALL Alan	East Ham	22 Aug 1945	3 Jun 1970	Chelsea	21 Sep 1971	Leicester C	41	11	2	1	5	2	48	14
BIRTLEY Bob	Easington	1908	26 Oct 1935	Coventry C	*cs* 1939	Gateshead	65	15	4	1	0	0	69	16
BLACKMAN Jack‡	Bermondsey	Jan 1911	28 Oct 1935	Queen's Park R	May 1946	Guildford	100	52	7	3	0	0	107	55
BLACKSHAW Bill	Ashton	6 Sep 1920	9 Jul 1949	Oldham A	17 Feb 1951	Rochdale	32	5	0	0	0	0	32	5
BLAKE William H	Worcester		Mar 1924	Kidderminster	*cs* 1926	Kidderminster	35	0	0	0	0	0	35	0
BLAKEMORE Cecil	Stourbridge	8 Dec 1897	Dec 1922	Redditch	May 1927	Bristol City	133	54	8	2	0	0	141	56
BLORE Vincent F	Uttoxeter		29 Oct 1936	West Ham U	Oct 1938	Exeter C	33	0	2	0	0	0	35	0
BLYTH Mel ☆	Norwich	28 Jul 1944	1 Jul 1968	Scunthorpe U	Sep 1974	Southampton	219/3	9	12/1	1	19	2	250/4	12
BOOTH Samuel	Northwich	30 Jan 1911	May 1935	Margate	Jun 1938	Southport	25	0	4	0	0	0	29	0
BOSTOCK Benjamin	Mansfield	19 Apr 1929	May 1946	Juniors	May 1951		3	0	0	0	0	0	3	0
BOULTER Dave	Stepney	5 Oct 1962	Jul 1980	Juniors	Jun 1981		16	0	5	0	1	0	22	0
BOURNE Jeffrey	Linton	19 Jun 1948	10 Mar 1977	Derby C	1 Mar 1978	Dallas Tornado	32	10	1	0	4	0	37	10
BOYLE Terry	Ammanford	29 Oct 1958	Jan 1978	Tottenham H	Oct 1981	Bristol City	24/2	1	2	1	0	0	26/2	2
BRAITHWAITE Ronnie S	Ash Vale	9 Apr 1931	Aug 1949	Army	*cs* 1953		3	0	0	0	0	0	3	0
BRENNAN Steve A	Mile End	3 Sep 1958	Feb 1976	Juniors	1 Aug 1978	Plymouth A	2/1	1	0	0	0/1	0	2/2	1
BRENNAN T	Calderbank		24 Dec 1930	Gillingham	*cs* 1931		2	0	0	0	0	0	2	0
BRETT Ron	Stanford-le-Hope	4 Sep 1937	Sep 1954	Juniors	Jun 1959	West Ham U								
			Mar 1962	West Ham U	30 Aug 1962	Deceased	44	13	6	0	0	0	50	13
BRIGGS George H	Shotten	27 Feb 1923	Nov 1947	Shotten Colliery	1955		146	4	7	0	0	0	153	4
BRIGHT Mark	Stoke	6 Jun 1962	26 Jan 1987	Leicester C	†		112	52	3/1	0	5	2	120/1	54
BROOKS John	Reading	23 Dec 1931	Jan 1964	Brentford	*cs* 1964	Stevenage	7	0	0	0	0	0	7	0
BROOKS Shaun	London	9 Oct 1962	Oct 1979	Juniors	Oct 1983	Orient	47/7	4	5	0	5/2	1	57/9	5
BROPHY Hugh	Dublin	2 Sep 1948	Jul 1966	Shamrock Rovers	1967		0/1	0	0	0	0	0	0/1	0
BROUGHTON Ted	Bradford	9 Feb 1925	Aug 1948	New Brighton	1954	Retired injury	96	6	4	0	0	0	100	6
BROWN Bert	Bristol	4 Mar 1934	Aug 1956	Exeter U	Jul 1959	Queen's Park R	3	0	0	0	0	0	3	0
BROWN Alister	Musselburgh	12 Apr 1951	Mar 1983	West Bromwich A	Aug 1983	Walsall	11	2	0	0	0	0	11	2
BROWN Charles G	Wandsworth	7 Dec 1909	Jun 1932	Hayes	Aug 1934	Watford	29	0	0	0	0	0	29	0
BROWN John	Belfast	1 Sep	11 Jun 1927	Merthyr T	*cs* 1928	Aberdare	8	3	0	0	0	0	8	3
BROWN Thomas B	Troed-y-rhiw	Jul 1912	*cs* 1933	Folkestone	*cs* 1934		5	0	0	0	0	0	5	0
BRUSH Paul	Plaistow	22 Feb 1958	Sep 1985	West Ham U	Jan 1988	Southend U	50/2	1	1	0	2	0	53/2	1
BUCKLEY Frank L	Lichfield	11 May 1922	Nov 1946	Notts C	*cs* 1952	Guildford C	69	0	4	0	0	0	73	0
BUNSTEAD Charles H	Croydon	8 Jan 1922	Aug 1948	Millwall	Nov 1951	Dover	53	0	2	0	0	0	55	0

☆ *includes 6 League appearances when on loan from Southampton in 1977-8.*

Shaun Brooks

Paul Brush

PLAYER	BIRTHPLACE	DATE	DATE SIGNED	FROM	DATE TRANSFERRED	TO	League App	League Gls	FA Cup App	FA Cup Gls	FL Cup App	FL Cup Gls	Total App	Total Gls
BURGESS 'Cam' A C	Birkenhead	21 Sep 1919	Sep 1951	Chester	Jul 1953	York C	47	40	3	0	0	0	50	40
BURKE David I	Liverpool	6 Aug 1960	Oct 1987	Huddersfield T	†		69/1	0	2	0	2	0	73/1	0
BURNS Tony	Edenbridge	27 Mar 1934	16 Oct 1973	Durban (S Africa)	15 Aug 1978	Plymouth	90	0	2	0	6	0	98	0
BURNSIDE Dave	Bristol	10 Dec 1939	24 Dec 1964	Southampton	7 Sep 1966	Wolves	52/4	8	5	2	1	0	58/4	10
BURRELL Lester F‡	Brighton	8 Aug 1917	1945	Margate	May 1948	Ipswich T	19	4	0	0	0	0	19	0
BURRIDGE John	Workington	3 Dec 1951	Mar 1978	Aston Villa	24 Dec 1980	Queen's Park R	88	0	7	0	7	0	102	0
BURRIDGE Peter J	Harlow	30 Dec 1933	28 Jun 1962	Millwall	25 Nov 1965	Charlton A	114	43	6	3	4	4	124	50
BUTLER Hubert	Atherton	11 Jul 1906	2 Jun 1928	Chorley	Jun 1932	Chester	108	31	16	8	0	0	124	39
BYRNE John	West Horsley	13 May 1939	14 May 1956	Juniors	Mar 1962	West Ham U								
			15 Feb 1967	West Ham U	16 Mar 1968	Fulham	238	90	18	11	2	0	258	101
CALLENDER Billy	Prudhoe	1903			26 Jul 1932	Deceased	202	0	22	0	0	0	224	0
CANNON James Anthony	Glasgow	2 Oct 1953	Oct 1970	Juniors	*cs* 1988	Croydon	568/3	30	42	1	43/1	3	653/4	34
CARSON Jim	Clydebank		1934	Bradford	*cs* 1936	Burnley	52	17	2	0	0	0	54	17
CARTER Leslie A	Farnborough	24 Oct 1960	Nov 1977	Juniors	Feb 1982	Bristol C	1/1	0	0	0	0	0	1/1	0
CARTWRIGHT Joe‡	Warrington	11 Dec ?	29 Jun 1921	Manchester C			19	4	2	0	0	0	21	4
CARTWRIGHT John	Northampton	5 Nov 1940	May 1961	West Ham U	1963	Wimbledon	11	1	1	0	0	0	12	1
CASWELL Peter D	Leatherhead	16 Jan 1957	5 Aug 1975	Juniors	Aug 1978	Crewe A	3	0	0	0	0	0	3	0
CHARLESWORTH George	Bristol	29 Nov	Mar 1929	Kettering T			21	9	0	0	0	0	21	9
CHARLTON Stan	Little Hulton	16 Nov 1900	15 May 1928	Exeter C	8 Oct 1932	Newport C	122	7	14	2	0	0	136	7
CHASE Charlie T	Steyning	31 Jan 1924	Jul 1948	Watford	1950	Retired	55	2	2	0	0	0	57	2
CHATTERTON Nicky	Norwood	18 May 1954	13 Mar 1972	Juniors	Nov 1978	Millwall	142/9	31	15	2	15	3	172/9	36
CHERRETT Percy	Bournemouth	12 Sep 1899	14 Sep 1975	Plymouth A	Sep 1927	Bristol C	75	58	6	7	0	0	81	65
CHESTERS Arthur	Salford	1912	20 May 1937	Exeter C	Feb 1941	Leicester C	78	0	7	0	0	0	85	0
CHILVERS Geoff T‡	Sutton	31 Jan 1925	1942	Sutton U	1954		118	1	5	0	0	0	123	1
CHOULES Len G	Orpington	29 Jan 1932	6 May 1951	Sutton U	1962	Romford	259	2	20	1	1	0	280	3
CLARKE George B	Bolsover	24 Jul 1900	May 1925	Aston Villa	*cs* 1933	Queen's Park R	274	98	25	7	0	0	299	105
CLARKE Wally H L	Anerley		*cs* 1933	Blackheath	1934	Folkestone	16	0	4	0	0	0	20	0
CLELLAND David	Netherburn	18 Mar 1924	Sep 1949	Brighton & HA	1950	Weymouth	2	0	0	0	0	0	2	0
CLIFFORD John C	Newport	24 Sep 1906	20 Feb 1932	Newport C	*cs* 1933	Newport C	12	0	0	0	0	0	12	0
CLOUGH Jimmy	Newcastle	30 Aug 1918	Sep 1947	Southport	May 1949	Southend U	68	12	4	1	0	0	72	13
COATES John	Limehouse	13 May 1920	1946	Local amateur	1947	Local	4	0	0	0	0	0	4	0
COLFAR Ray	Liverpool	4 Dec 1935	3 Nov 1958	Sutton U	1961	Cambridge U	41	6	3	0	0	0	44	6
COLLIER J			*cs* 1920	Blyth Spartans	1922	Retired	1	0	0	0	0	0	1	0
COLLINS Tony	Kensington	19 Mar 1926	Nov 1957	Watford	Jun 1959	Rochdale	57	14	6	2	0	0	63	16
COLLINS Nicholas‡	Chopwell		1934	Canterbury W	1946	Yeovil	142	7	9	0	0	0	151	7
COMRIE Malcolm	Dundee		15 Jun 1935	Burnley	*cs* 1936	York C	2	0	0	0	0	0	2	0
CONATY Thomas	North Shields		*cs* 1928	South Shields	*cs* 1929	Barrow	3	0	0	0	0	0	3	0
CONNER John*	Renfrew		*cs* 1919	Belfast Distillery	23 Nov 1922	Newport C	61	36	5	2	0	0	66	38
COOK Michael J	Belmont	25 Jan 1950	Feb 1968	Juniors	2 Aug 1969	Brentford	1	0	0	0	0	0	1	0
COOKE Charlie	St Monace	14 Oct 1942	Sep 1972	Chelsea	17 Jan 1974	Chelsea	42/2	0	3/1	1	0/1	0	45/4	1
COOPER George	Kingswinford	1 Oct 1932	Jan 1955	Brierley Hill All	Jan 1959	Rochdale	70	27	5	1	0	0	75	28

Johnny Byrne

Nick Chatterton

PLAYER	BIRTHPLACE	DATE	DATE SIGNED	FROM	DATE TRANSFERRED	TO	League App	League Gls	FA Cup App	FA Cup Gls	FL Cup App	FL Cup Gls	Total App	Total Gls
CORBETT John T	Bow	9 Jan 1920	Sep 1946	Swansea T	May 1947		1	1	0	0	0	0	1	1
CORRIGAN John	Addiewell	1947	1 May 1968	Stirling Albion	1970		0	0	0	0	0	0	0	0
COTTON Frederick	Halesowen	12 Mar 1932	Aug 1956		Jun 1957		4	1	0	0	0	0	4	1
COULSTON Walter	Warwell		*cs* 1936	Manchester C	*cs* 1937	Exeter C	12	1	0	0	0	0	12	1
COYLE Terrance	Broxbourne		12 Dec 1925	East Fife	1927		30	2	4	0	0	0	34	2
CRACKNELL Dick*	Newcastle		Jun 1923	Maidstone	*cs* 1926	Dartford	47	0	7	0	0	0	54	0
CRAVEN John R	St Annes	15 May 1947	Sep 1971	Blackpool	May 1973	Coventry C	56/7	14	5/1	1	3	1	64/8	16
CRILLY Tom	Stockton-on-Tees	20 Jul 1895	May 1928	Derby C	Jun 1933	Northampton T	116	1	10	0	0	0	126	1
CROMPTON Arthur W	Birmingham	9 Jan 1903	1 Feb 1934	Brentford	20 Sep 1935	Tranmere R	27	6	1	0	0	0	28	6
CROPPER Reginald W	Staveley	Jan 1902	3 Oct 1931	Norwich C	*cs* 1932	Mansfield T	3	1	0	0	0	0	3	1
CROSS Charles A	Coventry	15 May	1922	Coventry C	1928	Wolves	221	0	16	0	0	0	237	0
CUMMINS Stan	Sedgefield	6 Dec 1958	Aug 1983	Sunderland	30 Oct 1984	Sunderland	27/1	7	0	0	6	1	33/1	8
CUSHLOW Dick	Shotton	15 Jun 1920	Feb 1951	Derby C	*cs* 1952		28	0	0	0	0	0	28	0
CUTLER Paul	Welwyn G C	18 Jun 1946	6 Apr 1964	Juniors	Jul 1966	Nuneaton	10	1	0	0	1	0	11	1
DANIELS George	Winsford	1913	18 May 1937	Torquay U	*cs* 1939	Hartlepools U	7	0	0	0	0	0	7	0
DARE Kevin J	Finchley	15 Nov 1959	Feb 1977	Juniors	1982	Enfield	6	0	0	0	1	0	7	0
DAVIDSON Alex M	Longholm	6 Jun 1920	Aug 1948	Chelsea	1949		10	2	0	0	0	0	10	2
DAVIES Wyn R	Caernarfon	20 Mar 1942	19 Aug 1974	Blackpool §	18 Sep 1974	Blackpool	3	0	0	0	0	0	3	0
DAVIS Arthur G			*cs* 1928	Notts C	1929		5	1	0	0	0	0	5	1
DAVIS Hubert	Bradford	11 Aug 1906	28 Jun 1937	Leicester C	Jun 1940	Bradford	26	4	3	1	0	0	29	5
DAWES Albert G‡	Frimley Green	23 Apr 1907	22 Dec 1933	Northampton T	22 Dec 1936	Luton T								
			18 Feb 1938	Luton T	*cs* 1939	Aldershot	148	91	7	1	0	0	155	92
DAWES Frederick W‡	Frimley Green	2 May 1911	24 Feb 1936	Northampton T	1950	Assistant Manager	223	1	12	0	0	0	235	1
DAWKINS Trevor A	Rochford	7 Oct 1945	3 Oct 1967	West Ham U	Sep 1971	Brentford §	24/1	3	2/2	0	3	0	29/3	3
DEAKIN Frederick A	Birmingham	5 Feb 1920	Sep 1946	Birmingham C	1948		6	0	0	0	0	0	6	0
DEAKIN Mike R F	Birmingham	25 Oct 1933	12 Nov 1954	Bromsgrove	Oct 1959	Northampton T	143	56	8	7	0	0	151	63
DELANEY Louis P	Bothwell	28 Feb 1921	Nov 1949	Arsenal	1950		3	0	0	0	0	0	3	0
DEVONSHIRE Les	Acton	13 Jun 1926	Aug 1951	Chester	1955		82	12	4	0	0	0	86	12
DODGE Bill	Hackney	10 Mar 1937	Jul 1962	Tottenham H	1963	Kettering T	3	0	0	0	0	0	3	0
DONCASTER Dick	Barry	13 May 1908	1932	Exeter C	*cs* 1933	Reading	15	4	0	0	0	0	15	4
DOUGLAS Edward AC	Hebbern	26 Mar	Nov 1922	Crook T	*cs* 1923	Crook T/Brentford	2	1	0	0	0	0	2	1
DOWNS Ronnie	Southwark	27 Aug 1932	Dec 1952	Grove U	1954	Retired injury	23	2	0	0	0	0	23	2
DOWSETT GJ (Dickie)	Chelmsford	3 Jul 1931	Nov 1962	Bournemouth	*cs* 1965	Weymouth	54	22	0	0	2	0	56	22
DREYER Henry	Sunderland	9 Mar 1892	Jun 1921	South Shields	Oct 1923	Southend U	55	2	3	0	0	0	58	2
DROY Micky	Highbury	7 May 1951	Mar 1985	Chelsea	Nov 1986	Brentford	49	7	1	0	6	0	56	7
DUNN Ronald V	Southall	24 Nov 1908	1931	Army (Hounslow)	1937		167	0	8	0	0	0	175	0
DUNSIRE Andrew	Merthyr (Fife)		20 Mar 1929	Kettering T	12 Jul 1930	Dartford	5	1	0	0	0	0	5	1
DUTHIE John F	Fraserburgh	7 Jan 1903	1929	York C	1930	York C	13	3	0	0	0	0	13	3
DYER Alex	West Ham	14 Nov 1965	9 Nov 1988	Hull C	†		6/1	2	0	0	0	0	6/1	2
DYSON Barry J	Oldham	6 Sep 1942	12 Sep 1966	Tranmere R	19 Jan 1968	Watford	33/1	9	1	0	0	0	34/1	9
EARLE E James	Newbiggin	17 Jun	5 Aug 1933	Boston	1934		9	3	1	0	0	0	10	3

Stan Cummins

Micky Droy

PLAYER	BIRTHPLACE	DATE	DATE SIGNED	FROM	DATE TRANSFERRED	TO	League App	League Gls	FA Cup App	FA Cup Gls	FL Cup App	FL Cup Gls	Total App	Total Gls
EASTMAN Donald J	Eastry, Dover	9 Aug 1923	1940	Local (amateur)	1947		1	0	0	0	0	0	1	0
EASTON Harry	Shoreham	12 Sep 1938	30 Oct 1956	Juniors	1962	Gravesend	8	1	1	0	0	0	9	1
EDWARDS Ian R	Wrexham	30 Jan 1955	Jul 1982	Wrexham	1983		16/2	4	3	1	4	2	23/2	7
EDWARDS 'Jack' JW	Risca	6 Jul 1929	Sep 1949	Lovells A	Jun 1959	Rochdale	223	0	16	0	0	0	239	0
EDWARDS Leslie	Nuneaton	1912	*cs* 1933	Folkestone	*cs* 1936	Newport C	24	2	1	0	0	0	25	2
ELWISS Mike	Doncaster	2 May 1954	Jul 1978	Preston NE	Mar 1980	Preston NE §	19/1	7	0	0	4	0	23/1	7
EVANS A (Tony)	Liverpool	11 Jan 1954	Aug 1983	Birmingham C	Apr 1984	Wolves	19/2	7	0/1	0	1	0	20/3	7
EVANS Fred	Petersfield	20 May 1923	Mar 1951	Notts C	Jun 1953	Rochdale	52	11	1	0	0	0	53	11
EVANS Gwyn	Treorchy	24 Feb 1935	28 Mar 1955	Cumpare	1963	New Zealand	80	0	9	0	1	0	90	0
EVANS Ian P	Egham	30 Jan 1952	13 Sep 1974	Queen's Park R	Dec 1979	Barnsley	137	14	16	2	10	0	163	16
FARRELL Ray	Cardiff	31 May 1933	May 1957	Treharris	1959		5	0	0	0	0	0	5	0
FARRINGTON Roy	Tonbridge	6 Jun 1925	Nov 1947	Juniors	1949		3	0	1	1	0	0	4	1
FASHANU John	Kensington	18 Sep 1962	14 Aug 1983	Norwich C §	Sep 1983	Norwich C#	1	0	0	0	1	0	2	0
FEEBURY Albert	Hucknall	1891	*cs* 1914	Coventry C	1925	Folkestone	92	7	3	0	0	0	95	7
FELL Les	West Ham	16 Dec 1920	Oct 1952	Charlton A	1954	Margate	65	6	4	2	0	0	69	8
FELTON Robert F	Gateshead	12 Aug 1918	Sep 1946	Port Vale	1946		1	0	0	0	0	0	1	0
FELTON Vivien E	Southgate	13 Aug 1929	Aug 1954	Barnet	1956		2	0	0	0	0	0	2	0
FENWICK Terry	Seaham	17 Nov 1959	Dec 1976	Juniors	17 Dec 1980	Queen's Park R	62/8	0	7	2	4/1	0	73/9	2
FIELDING Horace	Heywood	14 Oct 1906	11 Mar 1937	Reading	1938	Mansfield T	22	1	0	0	0	0	22	1
FINN Arthur C	Folkestone	1913	20 May 1933	Folkestone	1934		9	0	0	0	0	0	9	0
FINNIGAN Tony	Wimbledon	17 Oct 1962	19 Mar 1985	Finland	29 Jul 1988	Blackburn R	94/11	10	2/1	0	7/1	0	103/13	10
FISHLOCK Lawrie	Battersea	2 Jan 1907	*cs* 1929	Dulwich H	*cs* 1932	Aldershot	18	2	1	0	0	0	19	2
FLANAGAN Mike	Ilford	9 Nov 1952	Aug 1979	Charlton A	Dec 1980	Queen's Park R	56	8	1	0	7	5	64	13
FLETCHER Charlie A	Hommerton	28 Oct 1905	*cs* 1928	Clapton Orient	*cs* 1929	Merthyr T	7	0	0	0	0	0	7	0
FLOOD Joe	Dublin		May 1926	Shamrock Rovers	1928		34	5	5	0	0	0	39	5
FORSTER Stanley	Aylesham	1 Nov 1943	Nov 1961	Margate	1963		2	1	0	0	1	0	3	1
FORWARD Fred	Croydon	8 Sep 1899	1921	Southern Railway	1924	Newport C	6	0	0	0	0	0	6	0
FOULDS Albert	Salford	8 Aug 1919	Jul 1953	Rochdale	Jan 1954	Crewe A	17	4	1	0	0	0	18	4
FRANCIS Gerry	Chiswick	6 Dec 1951	Jul 1979	Queen's Park R	Feb 1981	Queen's Park R	59	7	1	0	6	2	66	9
FREEMAN Alf	Bethnal Green	2 Feb 1920	Aug 1948	Southampton	1949		1	0	0	0	0	0	1	0
FROST Jack	Oakenshaw		24 May 1930	Arsenal	1931	Retired injury	4	2	0	0	0	0	4	2
FRY David	Bournemouth	5 Jan 1960	Jan 1977	Weymouth (amateur)	Jul 1983	Gillingham	40	0	5	0	0	0	45	0
FRY Bob	Pontypridd	29 Jun 1935	Apr 1956		1956	Bath C/to QPR	6	0	0	0	0	0	6	0
FULLER Bill	Brixton	6 Apr 1944	Jan 1963	Juniors	1965	Wellington	3	0	0	0	1	0	4	0
GAILLARD Marcel	Belgium	15 Jan 1927	Feb 1948	Tonbridge	Feb 1951	Portsmouth	22	3	0	0	0	0	22	3
GALLAGHER Hugh			*cs* 1926	Clyde			36	0	2	0	0	0	38	0
GALLIERS Steve	Fulwood	21 Aug 1957	Oct 1981	Wimbledon	Aug 1982	Wimbledon	8/5	0	0	0	0	0	8/5	0
GALLOWAY Steve	Hanover	13 Feb 1963	Oct 1984	Sutton U	Apr 1986	Cambridge U §	2/2	1	0	0	0/1	0	2/3	1
GAVIN Johnny	Limerick	20 Apr 1928	9 May 1959	Watford	1961	Cambridge C	66	15	2	2	0	0	68	17
GENNOE Terry	Shrewsbury	16 Mar 1953	Jan 1981	Southampton §	Feb 1981	Southampton#	3	0	0	0	0	0	3	0
GEORGE Ronald A	Bristol	14 Aug 1922	Feb 1947	Bristol Acto	Jul 1954	Colchester U	122	2	3	0	0	0	125	2

Tony Finnigan

Stephen Galloway

PLAYER	BIRTHPLACE	DATE	DATE SIGNED	FROM	DATE TRANSFERRED	TO	League App	League Gls	FA Cup App	FA Cup Gls	FL Cup App	FL Cup Gls	Total App	Total Gls
GILBERT Billy	Lewisham	10 Nov 1959	Dec 1976	Juniors	May 1984	Portsmouth	235/2	3	17	1	19	0	271/2	4
GILES David	Cardiff	21 Sep 1956	Mar 1982	Swansea C	Aug 1984	Birmingham C	83/5	6	5/1	0	5/1	0	93/7	6
GILL James J	Sheffield	9 Nov 1894	May 1928	Derby C	1929		10	3	0	0	0	0	10	3
GILLESPIE Ian‡	Plymouth	6 May 1913	Feb 1937	Harwich & Parkeston	13 Apr 1946	Ipswich T	21	4	5	1	0	0	26	5
GIRLING Howard‡	Birmingham	24 May 1922	1942		Feb 1947	Brentford £3,000	26	6	1	0	0	0	27	6
GLAZIER Bill	Nottingham	2 Aug 1943	Oct 1961	Torquay U (amateur)	16 Oct 1964	Coventry C £35,000	106	0	5	0	2	0	113	0
GODDARD Charles P	Ranceby	6 Apr 1910	1932	Northfleet	Oct 1935	Fulham	24	7	0	0	0	0	24	7
GOLDTHORPE Bobby	Osterley	6 Dec 1950	15 Jul 1968	Fulham	Dec 1972	Charlton A	1	0	0	0	0	0	1	0
GOODCHILD Gary	Chelmsford	27 Jan 1958	Dec 1979	Sweden	Mar 1981	Norway	0/2	0	0/2	0	0	0	0/4	0
GOODCLIFFE William G	London		1932	Dulwich H (amateur)	1936	Dulwich H	2	1	0	0	0	0	2	1
GOODWIN Sammy	Tarbolton	14 Mar 1943	Oct 1971	Airdrie	Oct 1972	Motherwell	18/7	0	0	0	2	0	20/7	0
GRAHAM George	Bargeddie	30 Nov 1944	13 Nov 1976	Portsmouth	1980	QPR Coach	43/1	2	3	1	4	1	50/1	4
GRAHAM Richard D (Dick)‡	Corby	6 May 1922	Dec 1945	Leicester C	1951	Retired injury	155	0	6	0	0	0	161	0
GRANT Walter A			1926	Raith Rovers	1928		21	5	0	0	0	0	21	5
GRAY Andy	Lambeth	22 Feb 1964	8 Nov 1984	Dulwich H	25 Nov 1987	Aston Villa	92/6	27	3	0	9/1	2	104/7	29
GREENER Bob	Birtley		Sep 1921	Birtley Colliery	4 Oct 1932	York C	290	5	24	1	0	0	314	6
GREENWOOD Alex	Fulham	17 Jun 1933	May 1954	Chelsea	Jun 1955	Scarborough	2	0	0	0	0	0	2	0
GREENWOOD Roy	Croydon	22 May 1931	Nov 1954	Beckenham	1959	Bedford T	111	0	5	0	0	0	116	0
GREGORY Charlie F‡	Doncaster	24 Oct 1911	15 Dec 1937	Reading	Jun 1946	Hartlepools U	43	9	0	0	0	0	43	9
GRIFFITHS Lewis	Pennycraig		May 1928	Torquay U	1930	Fulham	36	21	6	3	0	0	42	24
GRIMSHAW Colin	Betchworth	16 Sep 1925	Oct 1952	Arsenal	Jun 1954	Guildford	32	3	3	0	0	0	35	3
GROVES Fred	Lincoln		Aug 1924	Stoke	1926	Rhyl	14	2	1	1	0	0	15	3
GUNNING Harry	Leigh	8 Feb 1932	Jun 1954	West Ham U	6 May 1957	Reading	64	4	2	0	0	0	66	4
GUTHRIE James	Luncarty	6 Jun 1912	Oct 1946	Portsmouth	1947	PFA Chairman	5	0	0	0	0	0	5	0
HALLAM Charles	Longton	Apr 1899	Jun 1927	Stoke C	1928	Sandbach	2	2	0	0	0	0	2	2
HAMILTON James	Hetton-le-Hole		Dec 1922	Army	1931	Hartlepools U	180	5	16	1	0	0	196	6
HAMMOND Paul A	Nottingham	26 Jul 1953	Sep 1971	Thoneywood	Feb 1977	Tampa Bay	117	0	17	0	8	0	142	0
HAMPTON Colin M	Brechin	1 Sep	16 Dec 1925	Brechin			3	0	0	0	0	0	3	0
HANCOX Ray	Mansfield	1 May 1929	Aug 1950	Sutton U	Jun 1953	Southend U	20	2	0	0	0	0	20	2
HAND William R	Codnor	5 Jul 1898	Oct 1920	Sutton T	31 Oct 1925	Contract Cancelled	100	15	9	1	0	0	109	16
HANDLEY George H	Wednesbury		19 May 1934	West Bromwich A	1935		5	0	0	0	0	0	5	0
HANLON Wally	Glasgow	23 Sep 1919	Jul 1949	Bournemouth	Jun 1955	Sudbury T	125	8	4	1	0	0	129	9
HANN Ralph	Whitburn	4 Jul 1911	Apr 1947	Derby C Trainer	1947	Luton T Trainer	1	0	0	0	0	0	1	0
HANSON Fred	Sheffield	23 May 1915	4 May 1935	Wolves	1936	Rotherham U	1	0	0	0	0	0	1	0
HARDING Ted	Croydon	5 Apr 1925	1942	Coalville	22 May 1953	Whitstable	151	0	5	0	0	0	156	0
HARDWICK Steve	Mansfield	6 Sep 1956	Feb 1986	Oxford U §	Mar 1986	Oxford U#	3	0	0	0	0	0	3	0
HARKOUK Rachid P	Chelsea	19 May 1956	23 Jun 1976	Feltham	Jun 1978	Queen's Park R	51/3	21	1/3	2	4/1	3	56/4	26
HARPER Bill G	Wishaw	15 Nov 1900	23 May 1924	Manchester C	Oct 1926	Luton T	57	0	2	0	0	0	59	0
HARRIS Mark	Reading	15 July 1943	Jun 1988	Wokingham	†		0/2	0	0	0	0	0	0/2	0
HARRISON Bernie	Worcester	28 Sep 1934	Oct 1955	Portsmouth (amateur)	Aug 1959	Southampton	92	13	8	0	0	0	100	13
HARRY Albert	Kingston	8 Mar 1897	Jun 1921	Kingstonians	Aug 1934	Dartford	411	53	30	2	0	0	441	55

David Giles

Andy Gray

PLAYER	BIRTHPLACE	DATE	DATE SIGNED	FROM	DATE TRANSFERRED	TO	League App	League Gls	FA Cup App	FA Cup Gls	FL Cup App	FL Cup Gls	Total App	Total Gls
HAVELOCK Harry	Hull	20 Jan 1901	3 Nov 1927	Portsmouth	May 1931	Hull C	67	40	9	4	0	0	76	44
HAWKINS Alfred T	Malden	Oct 1904	7 Nov 1925	Southall	Jun 1927		20	8	2	1	0	0	22	9
HAYNES Alfred E	Suffolk	1910	17 Nov 1933	Arsenal	Jun 1936		48	1	3	0	0	0	51	1
HAYWOOD Jack	Warsop Vale	Oct 1903	10 Jun 1933	Bournemouth	Jun 1934		19	1	1	0	0	0	20	1
HAZELL Tony	High Wycombe	19 Sep 1947	17 Nov 1978	Millwall	20 Sep 1979	Charlton A	5	0	0	0	0	0	5	0
HEARN Frank	St Pancras	5 Nov 1929	Jun 1954	Northampton T	Jun 1955		8	1	0	0	0	0	8	1
HECKMAN Ron	Peckham	23 Nov 1929	Jul 1960	Millwall	1963	Bedford T	84	25	6	4	3	0	93	29
HEDMAN Rudi	Lambeth	16 Nov 1964	29 Dec 1988	Colchester U	†		1/4	0	0	0	0	0	1/4	0
HEDLEY Ralph	Byker	1897	6 Dec 1924	Hull C	Aug 1926	Durham C	4	0	0	0	0	0	4	0
HEINEMAN George H	Stafford	17 Dec 1905	18 Aug 1934	Coventry C	Aug 1935	Clapton Orient	25	0	1	0	0	0	26	0
HEPPOLETTE Ricky	India	8 Apr 1949	14 Oct 1976	Orient	24 Feb 1977	Chesterfield	13/2	0	3	0	0	0	16/2	0
HERBERT Trevor	Reading	3 Jun 1929	Jul 1950	Leyton Orient	Jun 1951		8	2	0	0	0	0	8	2
HEGGINBOTTOM Andy	Chesterfield	22 Oct 1964	1985	Cambridge U	Mar 1987	Maidstone U	16/7	2	0/2	0	2	0	18/9	2
HIGGINS Fred	Hackney	21 Jan 1930	Mar 1952	Wood Green	Apr 1954	Retired	11	0	0	0	0	0	11	0
HILAIRE Vince	Forest Gate	10 Oct 1959	26 Oct 1976	Juniors	18 Jul 1984	Luton T	239/16	29	16/1	3	21	4	276/17	36
HILL Michael R	Hereford	3 Dec 1947	Dec 1973	Ipswich T	Feb 1976	South Africa	43/2	6	1	0	3	0	47/2	6
HILLEY Cornelius	Glasgow		*cs* 1926	Third Lanark	Aug 1928	Thames	43	4	2	0	0	0	45	4
HINSHELWOOD Martin	Reading	16 Jun 1953	12 Aug 1970	Juniors	1978	Retired injury	66/3	4	7	0	6	0	79/3	4
HINSHELWOOD Paul	Bristol	14 Aug 1956	14 Aug 1973	Juniors	Aug 1983	Oxford U	271/5	23	26	4	17	2	314/5	29
HOADLEY Phil	Battersea	6 Jan 1952	15 Jan 1969	Juniors	Sep 1971	Orient	62/11	1	2/4	0	9	1	73/15	2
HODDINOTT Tom	Brecon	29 Nov 1894	*cs* 1923	Chelsea	Jun 1926	Rhyl	78	20	10	2	0	0	88	22
HOLDER Phil	Kilburn	19 Jan 1952	Feb 1975	Tottenham H	8 Mar 1979	Bournemouth	93/2	5	11	1	4/2	0	108/4	6
HOLMES Eddie	Manchester	15 Nov 1900	Sep 1926	Altrincham	Jun 1928	Reading	17	0	3	0	0	0	20	0
HOLSGROVE John	Southwark	27 Sep 1945	Feb 1964	Juniors	1 May 1965	Wolves	18	2	4	0	0	0	22	2
HOLTON Cliff	Oxford	29 Apr 1929	Dec 1962	Northampton T	6 May 1965	Watford	101	40	6	8	5	1	112	49
HONE Mark	Croydon	31 Mar 1968	Jan 1985	Juniors	†		4	0	0	0	3/1	0	7/1	0
HOPGOOD Ron	Battersea	24 Nov 1934	2 May 1957	Spicers A	Jun 1959	Folkestone	14	0	2	0	0	0	16	0
HOPKINS H	Pontypridd		1926	Barry T	1928		40	14	3	3	0	0	43	17
HOPKINS Idris	Merthyr	11 Oct 1907	Jun 1932	Dartford	Nov.1932	Brentford	4	0	0	0	0	0	4	0
HOPKINS Jeff	Swansea	14 Apr 1964	Aug 1988	Fulham	†		43	0	1	0	3	0	47	0
HOROBIN Roy	Brownhills	10 Mar 1935	2 Jul 1964	Peterborough U	1965	Weymouth	4	0	3	0	0	0	7	0
HORTON Jack	Castleford	14 Jul 1905	Jun 1937	Chelsea	May 1939		38	7	3	0	0	0	41	7
HOWARD Terry	Hornchurch	26 Feb 1966	Jan 1986	Chelsea §	Feb 1986	Chelsea#	4	0	0	0	0	0	4	0
HOWE Albert R H	Charlton	16 Nov 1938	Dec 1958	Faversham	Jan 1967	Orient	192/1	0	12	1	7	0	211/1	1
HOWE H	Hemel Hempstead		May 1933	Queen's Park R	Jun 1934	Rochdale	2	0	0	0	0	0	2	0
HOWELLS Ray G	Rhondda	27 Jun 1926	Jun 1947	Mid-Rhondda	6 Jul 1951	Exeter C	26	5	1	0	0	0	27	5
HOY Roger E	Poplar	6 Dec 1946	26 Sep 1968	Tottenham H	Jun 1970	Luton T	54	6	4	1	4	0	62	7
HUDGELL Arthur J	Hackney	28 Dec 1920	Dec 1937	Eton Manor	26 Jan 1947	Sunderland	25	1	1	0	0	0	26	1
HUGHES John (Yogi)	Coatbridge	3 Apr 1943	Oct 1971	Celtic	Jan 1973	Sunderland	20	4	3	0	0	0	23	4
HUGHES Stephen (Billy)	Folkestone	29 Jul 1960	Jul 1981	Gillingham	Mar 1982	Wimbledon	3/4	0	0	0	2	0	5/4	0
HUGHES William A	Colwyn Bay	2 Feb 1919	Feb 1951	Rochdale	Jun 1952		18	0	0	0	0	0	18	0

Mark Hone

Phil Hoadley

PLAYER	BIRTHPLACE	DATE	DATE SIGNED	FROM	DATE TRANSFERRED	TO	League App	League Gls	FA Cup App	FA Cup Gls	FL Cup App	FL Cup Gls	Total App	Total Gls
HUGHTON Henry T	Stratford	18 Nov 1959	Jul 1982	Orient	Sep 1986	Brentford	113/5	1	6	0	11/1	0	130/6	1
HUMPHREYS Gerald	Llandudno	14 Jan 1946	8 Jun 1970	Everton	Jan 1971	Crewe A	4/7	0	0	0	1	0	5/7	0
HUNT Michael H	Croydon		Dec 1924	Local professionals	Jun 1928		3	0	1	0	0	0	4	0
HYND J Roger S	Falkirk	2 Feb 1942	21 Jun 1969	Rangers	Jul 1970	Birmingham C	29/1	0	4	0	4	0	37/1	0
HYNON John C	Bath	19 Jan 1934	Aug 1954	Army	Jun 1955		1	0	0	0	0	0	1	0
IMLACH J J Stuart	Lossiemouth	6 Jan 1932	1962	Coventry C	Jan 1965	Dover								
			14 Feb 1966	Chelmsford	Mar 1967	Notts C Coach	51	3	0	0	3	0	54	3
IMRIE James	Markinch, Fife		Mar 1929	Kettering T	Aug 1931	Luton T	36	0	1	0	0	0	37	0
IRVINE Alan J	Glasgow	12 Jul 1958	Aug 1984	Everton	9 Jun 1987	Dundee U	108/1	12	4	1	12	1	124/1	14
IRWIN George W	Smethwick	7 Jan	*cs* 1921	West Bromwich A	*cs* 1923	Reading	16	0	0	0	0	0	16	0
IVEY Lawrence A	Abingdon	Oct 1900	1927	Amateur	Jun 1928		1	0	0	0	0	0	1	0
JACKSON Cliff	Swindon	3 Sep 1941	16 Sep 1966	Plymouth A	Aug 1970	Torquay U	100/6	26	5	0	8/1	4	113/7	30
JACKSON John Keith	Hammersmith	5 Sep 1942	Mar 1962	St Clement Danes Sch'l	16 Oct 1973	Orient	346	0	18	0	24	0	388	0
JAMES Wilfred H	Cross Keys	Apr 1904	1927	Newport C	Mar 1929	Notts C	4	1	0	0	0	0	4	1
JAMIESON Harold John	Wallsend	9 Dec 1908	Dec 1929	Crawcrook	24 Dec 1930	Gillingham	4	0	0	0	0	0	4	0
JEFFRIES Derek	Manchester	22 Mar 1951	Sep 1973	Manchester C	Jul 1977	Chester	107	1	9	0	6	0	122	1
JENKINS Ross A	Kensington	4 Nov 1951	5 Nov 1969	Juniors	3 Nov 1972	Watford	15	2	0	0	2	0	17	2
JEWETT George	Southampton	Apr 1906	May 1931	Southampton	1932		1	0	0	0	0	0	1	0
JOHNSON Jeff D	Cardiff	26 Nov 1953	Dec 1973	Swansea C	Jul 1976	Sheffield W	82/5	4	5	0	5/1	1	92/6	5
JOHNSON W Joseph	Wednesbury	23 Jun	1922	Cannock T	Jun 1925	Barnsley	29	6	2	0	0	0	31	6
JOHNSON Peter J	Hackney	18 Feb 1954	Jan 1975	Orient	Jun 1976	Bournemouth	5/2	0	0	0	0	0	5/2	0
JONES Chris H	Jersey	18 Apr 1956	Nov 1982	Manchester C	Sep 1983	Charlton A	18	3	4	0	0	0	22	3
JONES Edwin	Tyldesley		1924	Brighton & HA	1925		4	0	0	0	0	0	4	0
JONES Ivor J	Rhondda	1 Apr 1925	Jun 1946	Amateur	Jun 1947	Arsenal amateur	1	1	0	0	0	0	1	1
JONES J Tom	Rhosymedre	1887	Jun 1920	Stoke	Jul 1922	Coventry C	61	6	5	0	0	0	66	6
JONES Ken B	Wrexham	11 May 1937	1 Jun 1960	Wrexham	Mar 1961		4	0	1	0	0	0	5	0
JONES William Maurice	Liverpool	30 Nov 1919	May 1950	Swindon T	Mar 1951	Watford	17	3	1	0	0	0	18	3
JORDAN David	Belfast		14 May 1937	Wolves	Oct 1939	Ireland	7	0	0	0	0	0	7	0
JUMP Stewart Paul	Crumpsall	27 Jan 1952	Dec 1973	Stoke C	20 Mar 1978	USA	79/2	2	6/1	0	3	0	88/3	2
KEENAN Arnold	Ireland		29 Jul 1925	Glentoran	1926		4	0	0	0	0	0	4	0
KELLARD Robert Sidney W	Edmonton	1 Mar 1943	4 Sep 1963	Southend U	25 Nov 1965	Ipswich T								
			Sep 1971	Leicester C	29 Dec 1972	Portsmouth	120/2	10	7	0	7	0	134/2	10
KELLY John	Wishaw		14 May 1927	Gillingham	21 Jul 1928	Thames	22	0	1	0	0	0	23	0
KELLY Noel	Dublin	28 Dec 1921	Mar 1950	Arsenal	Aug 1951	Nottingham F	42	6	1	1	0	0	43	7
KEMBER Stephen David	Croydon	8 Dec 1948	8 Dec 1965	Juniors	22 Sep 1971	Chelsea								
			27 Oct 1968	Leicester C	1980	Vancouver Whitecaps	255/5	35	15	2	16	0	286/5	37
KEMP David Michael	Harrow	20 Feb 1953	Apr 1975	Slough T	10 Nov 1976	Portsmouth	32/3	10	4	2	5	4	41/3	16
KENNEDY Andrew Lynd	Belfast	1 Sep 1885	8 Sep 1920	Belfast Celtic	May 1922	Arsenal	4	0	1	0	0	0	5	0
KERRINS Patrick Michael	Fulham	13 Sep 1936	Jun 1960	Queen's Park R	Jul 1961	Southend U	5	0	0	0	1	0	6	0
KETTERIDGE Stephen J	Stevenage	7 Nov 1959	7 Aug 1985	Wimbledon	Jun 1987	Orient	58/1	6	3	0	7/1	0	68/2	6
KEVAN Derek Tennyson	Ripon	6 Mar 1935	29 Jul 1965	Manchester C	2 Mar 1966	Peterborough U	21	5	0	0	1	0	22	5

Steve Kember tangles with Chelsea's Alan Hudson.

PLAYER	BIRTHPLACE	DATE	DATE SIGNED	FROM	DATE TRANSFERRED	TO	League App	League Gls	FA Cup App	FA Cup Gls	FL Cup App	FL Cup Gls	Total App	Total Gls
KNOX Thomas	Wishaw Moor		May 1936	Notts C	9 Dec 1936	Norwich C	3	0	0	0	0	0	3	0
KURZ Frederick J ‡	Grimsby	3 Sep 1918	26 Dec 1945	Grimsby T	Aug 1951	Boston	148	50	3	0	0	0	151	50
LACY John	Liverpool	14 Aug 1951	Aug 1983	Tottenham H	Nov 1984	Norway	24/3	0	1	0	2	0	27/3	0
LANE John William	Birmingham	29 May 1902	29 Jan 1931	Brentford	Sep 1932	Aldershot	34	10	0	0	0	0	34	10
LANGLEY Thomas W	Lambeth	8 Feb 1958	Mar 1981	Queen's Park R	*cs* 1983	AEK Athens	54/5	9	5/1	1	5/1	1	64/7	11
LAWSON Frederick Ian A	Onslow	24 Mar 1939	6 May 1965	Leeds U	Aug 1966	Port Vale	15/2	6	0	0	0	0	15/2	6
LAZARUS Mark	Stepney	5 Dec 1938	15 Dec 1967	Queen's Park R	15 Oct 1969	Orient	63	17	3	0	4	0	70	17
LEAHY Stephen D	Battersea	23 Sep 1959	Oct 1976	Juniors	Apr 1982	Dartford	3/1	0	0	0	3	0	6/1	0
LEGG Henry G W	Swindon	Jul 1910	1930	Swindon T	1931		1	0	0	0	0	0	1	0
LEVENE David Jack	Bethnal Green	25 Feb 1908	6 Dec 1935	Tottenham H	1937		22	0	1	0	0	0	23	0
LEWIS Brian	Woking	26 Jan 1943	Apr 1960	Juniors	Jul 1963	Portsmouth	32	4	0	0	1	0	33	4
LEWIS Glynn ‡	Abertillery	3 Jul 1921	1941	RAF	Jul 1948	Bristol C	60	4	3	0	0	0	63	4
LEWIS Jack ‡	Walsall	26 Aug 1919	1938	West Bromwich A	Nov 1949	Bournemouth	123	6	3	0	0	0	126	6
LIDDLE James Sigsworth	Felling	Jul 1912	6 Jun 1936	Reading	1937		13	1	1	0	0	0	14	1
LIEVESLEY Leslie ‡	Staveley	Jul 1911	24 Apr 1937	Torquay U	1945	Italy (Coach)	75	3	7	0	0	0	82	3
LIGHT Daniel	Chiswick	10 Jul 1948	6 Dec 1965	Juniors	Aug 1968	Colchester U	18/1	5	2	0	0/1	0	20/2	5
LINDSAY Mark E	Lambeth	6 Mar 1955	Aug 1973	Juniors	1977	Tampa Bay Rowdies	27/3	0	1/1	0	4	1	32/4	1
LINDSEY David James	Havering	17 May 1966	May 1984	Juniors	Mar 1987	Welling U	18/3	0	1	0	2	0	21/3	0
LITTLE Joe*	Seaton Delaval		Jun 1919	Croydon Common	1926	Sittingbourne	199	0	18	0	0	0	217	0
LITTLE Roy	Manchester	1 Jun 1931	May 1961	Brighton & HA	May 1963	Dover	38	1	3	0	2	0	43	1
LLOYD James Clifford	Bristol		1930	Southend U	1932		14	0	2	0	0	0	16	0
LOCKE Gary Robert	Kingsbury	12 Jul 1954	Jan 1983	Chelsea	Mar 1986	Sweden	84	1	9	0	7	0	100	1
LONG Terry Alexandra	Tylers Green	17 Nov 1934	12 May 1955	Wycombe W	1970	Coach	432/10	15	30	1	8	1	470/10	18
LOUGHLAN John	Coatbridge	12 Jun 1943	26 Sep 1968	Morton	Mar 1972	Wrexham §	58/2	0	6	0	6/2	0	70/4	0
LOVE John E	Hillingdon	22 Apr 1951	Jan 1975	Staines	Jun 1976		1	0	0	0	0	0	1	0
LOVELL Stephen John	Swansea	16 Jul 1960	Aug 1977	Juniors	Mar 1983	Millwall	68/6	3	2/1	1	9/1	1	79/8	5
LUCAS Frederick Charles	Slade Green	29 Sep 1933	25 Oct 1963	Charlton A	Dec 1964		16	0	2	0	1	0	19	0
LUCAS Robert W	Bethnal Green	6 Jan 1925	Jun 1946	Hendon	Jun 1948		4	0	0	0	0	0	4	0
LUNNISS Roy E	Islington	4 Nov 1939	27 Apr 1960	Carshalton	May 1963	Portsmouth	25	1	0	0	2	0	27	1
MABBUTT Kevin Richard	Bristol	5 Dec 1958	Oct 1981	Bristol C	1985	USA	67/8	22	8	0	5	2	80/8	24
McBRIDE Andrew D	Kenya	15 Mar 1954	Oct 1971	Juniors	1974		1	0	0	0	0	0	1	0
McCORMICK James	Rotherham	26 Sep 1912	Feb 1949	Lincoln C	1949	Malta	13	2	0	0	0	0	13	2
McCORMICK John	Glasgow	18 Jul 1936	30 May 1966	Aberdeen	1973	Wealdstone	194	6	10	1	21	0	225	7
McCRACKEN Robert	Dromore	25 Jun 1900	Jun 1920	Belfast Distillery	Aug 1926	Portadown	175	1	15	1	0	0	190	2
McCULLOCH Andrew	Northampton	3 Jan 1950	Aug 1983	Sheffield W	Nov 1984	Aldershot	25	3	3	1	1	0	29	4
MacDONALD David Anderson	Dundee	9 May 1931	Mar 1951	Dundee Violet	1955		32	0	5	0	0	0	37	0
McDONALD Gordon	Hampstead	7 Feb 1932	Dec 1954	Eastbourne	Jul 1957	Swindon T	13	0	4	0	0	0	17	0
McDONALD Harry	Salford	11 Sep 1926	Sep 1950	Ashton U	Jul 1955	Kettering T	140	1	6	0	0	0	146	1
McGEACHIE George	Calder	26 Oct 1916	Jun 1951	Rochdale	Aug 1952	Wigan A	46	5	1	0	0	0	47	5
McGOLDRICK Edward J	London	30 Apr 1965	9 Jan 1989	Northampton T	†		20/1	0	0	0	0	0	20/1	0
McGREGOR John	Darlington		May 1932	Gillingham	Jun 1933		4	0	0	0	0	0	4	0

John McCormick and Liverpool's John Toshack.

PLAYER	BIRTHPLACE	DATE	DATE SIGNED	FROM	DATE TRANSFERRED	TO	League App	League Gls	FA Cup App	FA Cup Gls	FL Cup App	FL Cup Gls	Total App	Total Gls
McKENNA John Guthrie	Newcastle	Oct 1901	1923		Jun 1926	Walker Celtic	3	0	0	0	0	0	3	0
McMENEMY Frank	Rutherglen	1910	1936	Northampton T	1937	Guildford C	25	3	2	0	0	0	27	3
McNICHOL John	Kilmarnock	20 Aug 1925	13 Mar 1958	Chelsea	Jun 1963	Tunbridge Wells R	189	15	15	0	1	0	205	15
MADDEN David J	Stepney	6 Jan 1963	Aug 1988	Reading	†		17/2	5	0	0	0	0	17/2	5
MAHONEY Anthony J	Barking	26 Sep 1959	1984	Brentford	1985	Grays A	17/1	4	2	1	2/2	0	21/3	5
MANDERS Frank	Camberley	13 Jun 1914	Jul 1931	Aldershot	26 Oct 1935	Norwich C	98	31	5	2	0	0	103	33
MARSDEN Eric	Bolsover	3 Jan 1930	Apr 1950	Winchester	Oct 1952	Southend U	34	12	0	0	0	0	34	12
MARTIN Neil	Alloa	20 Oct 1940	Mar 1976	Brighton & HA	1976	St Patricks	8/1	1	0	0	0	0	8/1	1
MARTIN Wayne L	Basildon	16 Dec 1965	Jul 1982	Juniors	1984		1	0	0	0	0	0	1	0
MAY Harold C			Oct 1931	Woking	May 1934		31	10	1	0	0	0	32	10
MENLOVE Bert *	Croydon		1919	Southern Railway	Mar 1922	Sheffield U	48	13	5	3	0	0	53	16
MIDDLEMISS James	Benwell	Oct 1904	1924	Scotswood	Jun 1925		1	0	0	0	0	0	1	0
MILLARD Bert	West Bromwich	1 Oct 1898	23 Jul 1922	Coventry C	23 Oct 1924	Charlton A	34	4	1	0	0	0	35	4
MILLBANK Joseph H ‡	Edmonton	30 Sep 1919	Aug 1939	Wolves	Jul 1948	Queen's Park R	38	1	3	0	0	0	41	1
MILLIGAN A G			1920	Clyde	1921		2	1	0	0	0	0	2	1
MILLINGTON Anthony H	Hawarden	5 Jun 1943	16 Oct 1964	West Bromwich A	Mar 1966	Peterborough U	16	0	3	0	1	0	20	0
MOORE John			12 Dec 1925	Aberdeen	1926	Hamilton A	1	0	0	0	0	0	1	0
MORGAN Kenneth S	Swansea	28 Jul 1932	Oct 1955	Brentford	Jun 1956		2	0	0	0	0	0	2	0
MORGAN R L			1926	Amateur	Jun 1927		1	0	0	0	0	0	1	0
MORGAN William Albert	Old Hill	3 Nov 1900	Jul 1922	Coventry C	Jun 1925	Cradley Heath	76	14	8	2	0	0	84	16
MORRIS Frank	Penge	28 Mar 1932	Mar 1956		1957		8	0	0	0	0	0	8	0
MORTON Keith	Ferryhill	11 Aug 1934	Mar 1954	Army (Nat Serv)	Jul 1954	Sunderland	5	3	0	0	0	0	5	3
MOSS Donald Richard	Tamworth	27 Jun 1925	May 1953	Cardiff C	Mar 1957	Retired injury	56	2	2	0	0	0	58	2
MOYLE Walter	New Tredgar	Oct 1902	1928	Manchester U	1929	Merthyr T	5	1	0	0	0	0	5	1
MOYSE Alec R	Mitcham	5 Aug 1935	Feb 1956	Chatham	Aug 1958	Swindon T	4	1	0	0	0	0	4	1
MULCAHY Patrick Paul			Feb 1928	Annfield Plain	1929		23	5	0	0	0	0	23	5
MULHERON Peter	Glasgow	21 Jun 1921	Oct 1948	Tonbridge	1950	Tonbridge	38	2	2	0	0	0	40	2
MULLEN James W	Larne	10 Jan 1921	Jul 1948	Barrow	Feb 1949	Bristol C	10	0	1	0	0	0	11	0
MULLIGAN Patrick M	Dublin	17 Mar 1945	28 Sep 1972	Chelsea	Sep 1975	West Bromwich A	57	2	5	0	1	0	63	2
MURPHY Jerry Michael	Stepney	23 Sep 1959	Oct 1976	Juniors	Aug 1985	Chelsea	214/14	20	17/1	0	22	5	253/15	25
MURPHY John	Dowlais		30 Oct 1931	Fulham	1932		7	2	2	0	0	0	9	2
MURPHY Joseph Patrick	Waterford	30 Mar 1924	Feb 1949	Sherborne	Jul 1952	Bedford T	38	0	0	0	0	0	38	0
MURRAY James William	Lambeth	16 Mar 1935	Jul 1955	Juniors	Jun 1958	Walsall	37	13	1	1	0	0	38	14
MUXWORTHY Graham J	Bristol	17 Oct 1938	Sep 1957	Exeter U	1959	Chippenham	2	0	0	0	0	0	2	0
MYCOCK Albert	Manchester	31 Jan 1923	22 Jun 1946	Manchester U	Jul 1948	Barrow	58	9	3	0	0	0	61	9
NASH Edward Montague	Swindon	12 Apr 1902	Aug 1932	Brentford	1933		1	0	0	0	0	0	1	0
NASTRI Carlo L F	Finchley	22 Oct 1935	18 Jul 1958	Kingstonians	1960		2	0	0	0	0	0	2	0
NAYLOR William Henry ‡	Sheffield	23 Nov 1919	25 Jan 1939	Hampton Sports	11 Feb 1947	Brentford	18	8	1	2	0	0	19	10
NEBBELING Gavin Mark	Johannesburg	15 May 1963	Aug 1981	Arcadia Shepherds	July 1989	Fulham	146/5	8	5	0	8/1	0	159/6	8
NELSON David	Douglas Water	3 Feb 1918	Mar 1952	Queen's Park R	1953	Ashford T	12	0	0	0	0	0	12	0
NEWMAN Ronald Vernon	Portsmouth	19 Jan 1934	Oct 1962	Leyton Orient	Sep 1963	Gillingham	6	0	1	0	0	0	7	0

Tony Mahoney

Wayne Martin

PLAYER	BIRTHPLACE	DATE	DATE SIGNED	FROM	DATE TRANSFERRED	TO	League App	League Gls	FA Cup App	FA Cup Gls	FL Cup App	FL Cup Gls	Total App	Total Gls
NICHOLAS George A	Barnsley	26 Feb 1908	3 Dec 1930	Treharris	Aug 1935	Dartford	39	0	0	0	0	0	39	0
NICHOLAS Peter	Newport	10 Nov 1959	Dec 1976	Juniors	10 Mar 1981	Arsenal								
			Oct 1983	Arsenal	30 Jan 1985	Luton T	174	14	11	1	14	1	199	16
NICHOLSON George H			29 Sep 1923	West Stanley	1924	Dundee U	2	0	0	0	0	0	2	0
NIXON Joseph	Prudhoe		Dec 1920		May 1927		29	1	2	0	0	0	31	1
NOAKES Alfred George	Stratford	14 Aug 1933	16 Jun 1955	Sittingbourne	Jul 1962	Portsmouth	195	14	14	0	0	0	209	14
NORRIS Frank H	Birmingham	14 Aug 1907	20 May 1933	West Ham U	Dec 1934	France	11	4	1	0	0	0	12	4
O'CONNELL Brian E (Pat)	Fulham	13 Sep 1937	1 Jul 1966	Fulham	1967		20/1	2	0	0	1	0	21/1	2
O'DOHERTY Kenneth	Dublin	30 Mar 1963	1984	University (Dublin)	17 Jun 1988	Huddersfield T	41/1	0	1	0	4/1	1	46/2	1
OLIVER James	Uxbridge	28 Aug 1949	Mar 1967	Juniors	1970		3	0	0	0	0	0	3	0
O'REILLY Gary Mills	Isleworth	21 Mar 1961	5 Jan 1987	Brighton £40,000	†		46/3	2	2	0	2	0	50/3	2
ORR Robert	Hardgate		1926	Morton	1928	Retired	70	2	1	0	0	0	71	2
OSBORNE Ernest	Wolverhampton		26 May 1923	Evesham	1926	Lincoln C	30	3	0	0	0	0	30	3
OTULAKOWSKI Anton	Dewsbury	29 Jan 1956	May 1986	Millwall	1987	Hastings	12	1	0	0	2	0	14	1
OWENS Edward	Trimden Grange	1913	Jun 1934	Preston NE	Nov 1945	Bath C	164	0	8	1	0	0	172	1
PALETHORPE John T	Leicester	23 Nov 1909	1929	Maidenhead (amateur)	1930	Reading (amateur)								
			16 Oct 1936	Aston Villa		Chelmsford	38	11	5	0	0	0	43	11
PARDEW Alan A	Wimbledon	18 Jul 1961	17 Mar 1987	Yeovil	†		59/6	1	1	0	3/2	1	63/8	2
PARKER Edward BH	Anerley		1933	Local	1934	Mansfield T	2	0	0	0	0	0	2	0
PARKIN Brian	Birkenhead	12 Oct 1965	1 Jul 1988	Crewe A	†		19	0	0	0	3	0	22	0
PARRY Oswald	Dowlais	16 Aug 1908	May 1931	Wimbledon	15 Jun 1936	Ipswich T	142	0	8	0	0	0	150	0
PARSONS Frank R	Amersham	29 Oct 1947	26 Jul 1965	Juniors	Aug 1970	Cardiff C	4	0	0	0	0	0	4	0
PAUL Tony G	Isleworth	6 Apr 1961	Apr 1978	Juniors	Apr 1981	Croydon	0/1	0	0	0	0	0	0/1	0
PAYNE David R	Thornton Heath	25 Apr 1947	26 Oct 1964	Juniors	Aug 1973	Orient	281/3	9	16	1	18	2	315/3	12
PEMBERTON John	Oldham	18 Nov 1964	24 Mar 1988	Crewe A	†		42/2	1	1	0	3	0	46/2	1
PENN Frank R	Edmonton	15 Apr 1927	1949	Fulham (amateur)	1950		1	0	0	0	0	0	1	0
PENNYFATHER Glenn	Billericay	11 Feb 1963	3 Dec 1987	Southend U	†		31/3	1	1	0	0	0	32/3	1
PERRIN Stephen C	Paddington	13 Feb 1952	Mar 1976	Wycombe W	Mar 1978	Plymouth A	45/3	11	6	0	4	1	55/3	12
PETTITT Harold	Sydenham		Jul 1924	Kingstonians	1926		2	0	0	0	0	0	2	0
PETCHEY George W	Whitechapel	24 Jun 1931	24 May 1960	Queen's Park R		Retired to coach	143	12	7	0	3	0	153	12
PHILIP Iain F	Dundee	14 Feb 1951	Sep 1972	Dundee	17 Oct 1973	Dundee	35	1	4	1	1	0	40	2
PIERCE Barry John	Liverpool	13 Aug 1934	Aug 1955	Truro C	May 1959	Millwall	85	23	8	4	0	0	93	27
PINKNEY Alan J	Battersea	1 Jan 1947	Jul 1969	Exeter C	1974		19/5	0	1	0	3/1	0	23/6	0
POSSEE Derek James	Southwark	14 Feb 1946	Jan 1973	Millwall	Jul 1974	Orient	51/2	12	1/1	0	1	0	53/3	12
POTTER Raymond John	Beckenham	7 May 1936	May 1953	Juniors	Jun 1958	West Bromwich A	44	0	5	0	0	0	49	0
POWELL Chris	Lambeth	8 Sep 1969	24 Dec 1987	Juniors	†		2/1	0	0	0	0/1	0	2/2	0
PRESLAND Edward Robert	Waltham Cross	27 Mar 1943	Jan 1967	West Ham U	Oct 1969	Colchester U	61	0	3	0	1	0	65	0
PRICE David J	Caterham	23 Jun 1955	Mar 1981	Arsenal	Mar 1983	Orient	25/2	2	1/1	1	4/1	0	30/4	3
PRICE Ernest	Easington	12 May 1926	Jul 1951	Darlington	Jul 1953	Weymouth	34	5	1	0	0	0	35	5
PRIESTLY Gerald	Halifax	2 Mar 1931	Nov 1958	Grimsby T	Jul 1960	Halifax T	28	2	7	0	0	0	35	2
PRITCHARD Harvey John	Meridan	30 Jan 1918	9 Jun 1937	Coventry C	9 Mar 1938	Manchester C	30	6	5	2	0	0	35	8

Ken O'Doherty

Peter Nicholas

PLAYER	BIRTHPLACE	DATE	DATE SIGNED	FROM	DATE TRANSFERRED	TO	League App	League Gls	FA Cup App	FA Cup Gls	FL Cup App	FL Cup Gls	Total App	Total Gls
PROUDLER Arthur	Kingswinford	3 Oct 1929	Jun 1956	Aston Villa	1959	Dorchester	26	2	0	0	0	0	26	2
PROVEN David	Falkirk	11 Mar 1941	Jun 1970	Rangers	Mar 1971	Plymouth A	1	0	0	0	1	0	2	0
PURDON James Small	Glasgow	14 Mar 1906	10 Jun 1934	Bradford	Jul 1936	Southport	14	2	0	0	0	0	14	2
PYKE Malcolm	Eltham	6 Mar 1938	9 Jun 1959	West Ham U	Jun 1960	Dartford	2	0	0	0	0	0	2	0
QUAYLE Charles J	Ireland		1936	Drumcondra	1938	Bradford C	10	3	0	0	0	0	10	3
QUEEN Gerald	Glasgow	15 Jan 1945	Jul 1969	Kilmarnock	Sep 1972	Orient	101/7	24	7	1	11/1	5	19/8	30
RAINFORD John William	Camden Town	11 Dec 1930	Mar 1949	Juniors	May 1953	Cardiff C	64	8	3	2	0	0	67	10
RANDELL Ernest Albert W	Bognor Regis	13 Jan 1926	Jun 1953	Chelsea	1955	Bognor Regis	22	12	2	1	0	0	24	13
READ Thomas Albert	West Bromwich	2 Apr 1900	Jun 1935	Grimsby T	1936		16	0	0	0	0	0	16	0
REDFEARN Neil	Dewsbury	20 Jun 1965	31 Jul 1987	Doncaster R	18 Nov 1988	Watford	57	10	1	0	6	0	64	10
REDMOND Harold	Manchester	24 Mar 1933	Apr 1957	Tavistock	May 1958	Millwall	2	0	1	0	0	0	3	0
REECE Thomas Samuel ‡	Wolverhampton	17 May 1919	14 Sep 1938	Wolves	1948	Kidderminster H	76	5	4	0	0	0	80	5
REED George	Altofts	7 Feb 1904	1934	Plymouth A	1935	Clapton Orient	2	0	0	0	0	0	2	0
REES William	Swansea	30 Sep 1937	20 May 1959	Peterborough U	Jul 1960	Hastings	17	1	1	0	0	0	18	1
REEVE Frederick W	Clapton	1 May 1918	1935	Ashford	1937	Tottenham H	1	0	0	0	0	0	1	0
RHODES Ernest *	South Bank		Oct 1913	Gravesend	1923	Sheppey U	89	1	5	0	0	0	94	1
RIVERS Walter	Throckley	8 Jan	1 Jun 1929	Gillingham	1933	Queen's Park R	80	2	8	0	0	0	88	2
ROBERTS Charles Leslie	Halesowen	28 Feb 1901	Jul 1932	Exeter C	18 Jan 1934	Chester	45	18	3	2	0	0	48	20
ROBERTSON Peter	Dundee	1911	1933	Charlton A	1934	Dundee U	4	0	0	0	0	0	4	0
ROBERTSON Thomas	Coventry	28 Sep 1944	Nov 1966	St Mirren	1967		5	0	0	0	0	0	5	0
ROBSON Albert Proud ‡	Crook	14 Nov 1916	Dec 1934	Godalming	1948	Tunbridge Wells	85	22	3	1	0	0	88	23
ROCHE John A	Poplar	18 May 1932	15 May 1959	Millwall	1960	Margate	36	11	4	2	0	0	40	13
ROFFEY William R	Stepney	6 Feb 1954	May 1971	Juniors	Oct 1973	Orient	24	0	0	0	1	0	25	0
ROGERS Donald E	Paulton	25 Oct 1945	30 Oct 1972	Swindon T	Sep 1974	Queen's Park R	69/1	28	5	2	2/1	0	76/2	30
ROOKE Ronald Leslie	Guildford	7 Dec 1911	Mar 1933	Guildford C	22 Oct 1936	Fulham								
			Jun 1949	Arsenal	Nov 1950	Bedford T	63	32	1	0	0	0	64	32
ROSS Alex Malcolm	Glasgow	17 Dec 1923	Aug 1948	West Bromwich A	Aug 1951	Tonbridge	33	0	0	0	0	0	33	0
ROSSITER Abbott (Bud)	Ashford		1933	Folkestone	1935	Gillingham	24	0	3	0	0	0	27	0
ROUSE Raymond Victor	Swansea	16 Mar 1936	Aug 1956	Millwall	Aug 1963	Oxford U	238	0	17	0	2	0	257	0
RUMBOLD George A	Alton	10 Jul 1911	20 Oct 1934	Farringdon	Jun 1937	Clapton Orient	5	0	0	0	0	0	5	0
RUNDLE Charles Rodney	Fowey	17 Jan 1923	Jun 1950	Tottenham H	Aug 1952	Tonbridge	38	2	2	0	0	0	40	2
RUSSELL James Walker	Edinburgh	14 Sep 1916	Dec 1946	Norwich C	Jul 1948	New Brighton	44	6	0	0	0	0	44	6
RUTTER D Brian	Poplar	11 May 1933	1954	Cardiff (amateur)	1955		3	1	0	0	0	0	3	1
SALAKO John	Nigeria	11 Feb 1969	3 Nov 1986	Juniors	†		35/28	1	1	0	4/1	1	40/29	2
SALT Harold	Sheffield		Jan 1928	Grays Thurrock	May 1929	Brentford	42	1	2	0	0	0	44	1
SANDERS James Charles F	Marlborough	15 Oct 1932	17 Mar 1955	Bristol C	Oct 1960	Rochdale	46	0	4	0	0	0	50	0
SANSOM Kenneth Graham	Camberwell	26 Sep 1958	Dec 1975	Juniors	14 Aug 1980	Arsenal	172	3	11	1	14	0	197	4
SAUNDERS John Francis	Middlesbrough	24 Aug 1924	Aug 1954	Chelsea	May 1957	Chester	60	0	2	0	0	0	62	0
SAWARD Leonard R	Aldershot	6 Jul 1927	Mar 1949	Beddington	1952	Cambridge U	9	1	0	0	0	0	9	1
SCOTT James	Falkirk	21 Aug 1940	Feb 1970	Newcastle U	Jan 1972	Falkirk	36/7	5	2	0	5	1	43/7	6
SCOTT Lawrence	Sheffield	23 Apr 1917	18 Oct 1951	Arsenal Player-Man	Aug 1953	Retired (player)	28	0	2	0	0	0	30	0

John Salako

David Provan

PLAYER	BIRTHPLACE	DATE	DATE SIGNED	FROM	DATE TRANSFERRED	TO	League App	League Gls	FA Cup App	FA Cup Gls	FL Cup App	FL Cup Gls	Total App	Total Gls
SEALY Anthony John	Hackney	7 May 1959	29 Mar 1979	Southampton	Mar 1981	Queen's Park R	16/8	5	1	0	0/2	0	17/10	5
SEWELL John David	Brockley	7 Jul 1938	25 Oct 1963	Charlton A	5 Aug 1971	Orient	228/3	6	12	1	15	2	255/3	9
SEXTON David James	Islington	6 Apr 1930	May 1959	Brighton & HA	1960	Retired injury	27	11	1	1	0	0	28	12
SHANKS Robert ‡	Sunnyside	14 Dec 1912	15 May 1937	Swindon T	1946	Swindon T	18	0	0	0	0	0	18	0
SHAW Richard Edward	Park Royal	11 Sep 1968	4 Sep 1987	Juniors	†		10/7	0	0	0	1/1	0	11/8	0
SHAW Stuart	Liverpool	9 Oct 1944	Dec 1966	Everton	Mar 1967	Southport	0	0	0/1	0	0	0	0/1	0
SHERWOOD Jack Henry W	Reading	3 Sep 1913	1949	Aldershot	1950		2	0	0	0	0	0	2	0
SILKMAN Barry	Stepney	29 Jun 1952	4 Aug 1976	Hereford U	Oct 1978	Plymouth A	40/8	7	5	1	1	0	46/8	8
SILLE Leslie T	Liverpool	12 Apr 1928	Sep 1948	Ipswich T	Feb 1949	Tranmere R	3	0	0	0	0	0	3	0
SIMPSON Peter	Leith	13 Nov 1904	Jun 1929	Kettering T	15 Jun 1935	West Ham U	180	154	15	12	0	0	195	166
SIMPSON William George	Glasgow	22 May 1928	Jul 1952	Aston Villa	1955		38	13	0	0	0	0	38	13
SKINGLEY Brian G	Romford	28 Aug 1937	Sep 1958	Bristol R	Jul 1959	Queen's Park R	11	0	1	0	0	0	12	0
SMILLIE Andrew Thomas	Minster Sheppey	15 Mar 1941	Jun 1961	West Ham U	Jul 1963	Scunthorpe U	53	23	5	1	1	2	59	26
SMILLIE Neil	Barnsley	19 Jul 1958	Oct 1975	Juniors	Aug 1982	Brighton & HA	71/12	7	7	1	7	0	85/12	8
SMITH Edwin Arthur *	Birmingham	1884	Dec 1911	Hull C	1922		25	11	0	0	0	0	25	11
SMITH George Charles	Portsmouth	24 Mar 1919	Jul 1950	Southampton	1951		7	0	0	0	0	0	7	0
SMITH John Trevor ‡	West Stanley	8 Sep 1910	4 Feb 1938	Fulham £2,500	1945	Yeovil T	57	14	2	0	0	0	59	14
SMITH Keith Wilson	Woodville	15 Sep 1940	3 Nov 1964	Peterborough U	Nov 1966	Darlington	47/3	13	4	1	2	0	53/3	14
SMITH Lewis F	Bilsworth		Mar 1925	Hampstead	1929		45	1	3	1	0	0	48	2
SMITH Thomas		6 Oct ?	Jun 1932	Sunderland	1933		9	1	0	0	0	0	9	1
SMITH Wilfred	Sheffield	28 Mar 1910	Jul 1935	Burnley	1936		2	0	0	0	0	0	2	0
SMITH William Shiel	South Shields	22 Oct 1903	27 Oct 1933	Brentford	May 1936	Burnley	38	1	3	0	0	0	41	1
SMOUT John R	Newtown	30 Oct 1914	Aug 1965	Juniors	Jun 1966	Exeter C	1	0	0	0	0	0	1	0
SNOWDEN Brian V S	Bishop Auckland	1 Jan 1935	Feb 1969	USA	1969		1/4	0	0	0	0	0	1/4	0
SOMERFIELD Alfred G	South Kirby	22 Mar 1918	Sep 1947	Wrexham	1948		10	3	2	0	0	0	12	3
SPARROW Brian E	Bethnall Green	24 Jun 1962	Jul 1984	Arsenal	1987	Enfield	62/1	2	2	0	7	0	71/1	2
STACK William J	Liverpool	19 Jan 1948	18 Jan 1965	Juniors	May 1967	Chelmsford	2	0	0	0	0	0	2	0
STANBURY George Horace	Plymouth	24 Oct 1905	1934	Gillingham Coach	1935	Assistant Trainer	1	0	0	0	0	0	1	0
STEBBING Gary S	Croydon	11 Aug 1965	Aug 1983	Juniors	1988	Belgium	95/7	3	6	0	7/1	0	108/8	3
STEELE Ernest	Middleton	18 Jun 1908	29 Sep 1938	Millwall	Sep 1939	Rochdale	30	8	2	0	0	0	32	8
STEPHENSON Alan C	Cheshunt	26 Sep 1944	15 Feb 1962	Juniors	12 Mar 1968	West Ham U	170	13	8	0	7	0	185	13
STEVENS Leslie William G	Croydon	15 Aug 1920	Aug 1950	Bradford	Jun 1951	Tonbridge	20	2	1	0	0	0	21	2
STONE Edward L	Aberdeen	5 Jan 1942	May 1961	Charlton A	Jun 1963		1	0	0	0	0	0	1	0
STOREY Thomas	Colne	23 Nov	Jul 1920	Middlesbrough	Jul 1922	Coventry C	52	4	0	0	0	0	52	4
STRANG Richard	Rutherglen		23 May 1924	Birmingham	31 Oct 1925	Poole T (dismissed)	24	0	0	0	0	0	24	0
STRONG Leslie	Streatham	3 Jul 1953	Aug 1983	Fulham	Oct 1984	Rochdale N/C	7	0	0	0	0	0	7	0
STUBBS Alfred T	West Ham	18 Apr 1922	Dec 1946	Juniors	1947		3	0	0	0	0	0	3	0
SUCKLING Perry	Leyton	12 Oct 1965	14 Jan 1988	Manchester C	†		44	0	1	0	0	0	45	0
SUMMERSBY Roy D	Lambeth	19 Mar 1935	8 Dec 1958	Millwall	May 1963	Portsmouth	176	59	13	1	1	0	190	60
SURTEES Hubert	Durham	16 Jul 1921	Aug 1949	Watford	1951	Snowdon Colliery	5	0	0	0	0	0	5	0
SWAN Christopher Samuel	Byker	4 Dec 1900	18 May 1929	Hull C	1932	Scarborough	6	0	0	0	0	0	6	0

Dave Sexton

Brian Sparrow

PLAYER	BIRTHPLACE	DATE	DATE SIGNED	FROM	DATE TRANSFERRED	TO	League App	League Gls	FA Cup App	FA Cup Gls	FL Cup App	FL Cup Gls	Total App	Total Gls
SWANNELL John			Oct 1960	Hendon (amateur)	Oct 1960	Hendon	0	0	0	0	1	0	1	0
SWIFT Arthur	Hartlepool	1892	1920	West Bromwich A	1921	Coach	1	0	0	0	0	0	1	0
SWINDLEHURST David	Edgware	6 Jan 1956	22 Jan 1973	Juniors	Dec 1980	Derby C	221/16	73	22	5	17	3	260/16	81
TAMBLING Robert Victor	Storrington	18 Sep 1941	Jan 1970	Chelsea	Oct 1973	Cork Hibs	67/1	12	1	2	7	3	75/1	17
TAYLOR Anthony	Glasgow	6 Sep 1946	31 Oct 1968	Morton	Aug 1974	Southend U	192/3	8	11/1	0	14/1	3	217/5	11
TAYLOR Colin	Stourbridge	24 Aug 1940	May 1968	Walsall	14 Sep 1969	Walsall	32/2	8	2	0	4	2	38/2	10
TAYLOR John William	Durham	10 Jul 1926	1948	Bishop Auckland (am)	1949	Dartford (amateur)	2	0	0	0	0	0	2	0
TAYLOR Kevin	Wakefield	22 Jan 1961	27 Jul 1984	Derby C	Oct 1987	Scunthorpe U	85/2	14	2	1	7	0	94/2	15
TAYLOR Peter John	Rochford	3 Jan 1953	11 Oct 1973	Southend U	30 Sep 1976	Tottenham H	122	33	11	4	9	2	142	39
TAYLOR Robert John	Croydon	16 Mar 1936	1954	Fulham (amateur)	Sep 1956	Gillingham	2	0	0	0	0	0	2	0
TELLING Hubert	Swindon	1913	1936	Reading	1937	Hartlepools U	3	0	0	0	0	0	3	0
THOMAS Geoffrey	Manchester	5 Aug 1964	1987	Crewe A	†		63	11	2	0	6	1	71	12
THOMAS John E	Walsall	15 Jul 1922	Oct 1948	West Bromwich A	1952	Cambridge T	52	17	1	0	0	0	53	17
THOMAS Robert Albert	Stepney	2 Aug 1919	Sep 1952	Fulham	1955	Tunbridge Wells	96	31	6	2	0	0	102	33
THOMPSON Leonard	Sheffield	18 Feb 1901	10 Jun 1933	Arsenal	1934		2	0	0	0	0	0	2	0
THOMS Harold	Stockton	19 Nov	May 1928	Derby C	1929		6	1	1	0	0	0	7	1
THORPE Albert Edward	Pilsley	14 Jul 1910	25 Oct 1935	Norwich C	1936		4	0	0	0	0	0	4	0
THORUP Borge	Denmark	4 Oct 1943	Mar 1969	Morton	1969	Morton	0/1	0	0	0	0	0	0/1	0
TILSTON Thomas Arthur	Chester	19 Feb 1926	Feb 1954	Wrexham	Jul 1956	Chelmsford	58	14	1	0	0	0	59	14
TIZARD Charles Walter			1934	Winchester	1935	Northampton T	4	0	0	0	0	0	4	0
TOMKINS Leonard A	Isleworth	16 Jan 1949	Apr 1967	Juniors	1970	Canada	18/2	2	1	0	0	0	19/2	2
TONNER John (Jack)	Holytown	20 Feb 1898	May 1927	Fulham	1928	Thames	24	7	0	0	0	0	24	7
TONNER Samuel	Dunfermline	10 Aug	Aug 1926	Bristol C	1927	Armadale	2	0	1	0	0	0	3	0
TOOTILL Alfred‡	Ramsbottom	12 Nov 1908	26 Nov 1938	Fulham	1945	Retired	1	0	0	0	0	0	1	0
TOWNSEND Donald Edward	Swindon	17 Sep 1930	Jul 1962	Charlton A	1965	Retired	77	0	2	0	3	0	82	0
TRUETT Geoffrey	West Ham	23 May 1935	4 Jun 1957	Wycombe W	Jul 1962	Tonbridge	38	5	1	0	0	0	39	5
TURNBULL Robert Hamilton	Dumbarton	22 Jun 1894	11 Jul 1931	Southend U	May 1933	Trainer	2	0	0	0	0	0	2	0
TURNER William	Tipton	16 Nov 1901	4 May 1925	Bromsgrove	Jun 1936	Worcester C	285	36	21	1	0	0	306	37
TURTON Geoffrey F	Sheffield	1914	Mar 1936	Gillingham	Jun 1938		12	0	2	0	0	0	14	0
UPHILL Dennis Edward	Bath	11 Aug 1931	Oct 1960	Watford	1963	Rugby T	63	17	9	3	2	0	74	20
VANSITTART Thomas	Merton	23 Jan 1950	Apr 1967	Juniors	Feb 1970	Wrexham	10/1	2	1	0	0	0	11/1	2
VENABLES Terrence F	Dagenham	6 Jan 1943	Sep 1974	Queen's Park R	1975	Coach	14	0	2	0	0	0	16	0
WAITE Norman			*cs* 1921	Preston Colliery	Jun 1923		16	3	0	0	0	0	16	3
WALDRON Ernest	Birmingham	3 Jun 1913	1934	Bromsgrove	Nov 1946	Aberdeen	80	29	6	2	0	0	86	31
WALKER George	Musselburgh	24 May 1909	Jun 1936	Notts C	Jul 1939	Watford	102	1	9	0	0	0	111	1
WALL Peter Thomas	Shrewsbury	13 Sep 1944	3 Jun 1970	Liverpool	1978	USA	167/10	3	15	0	15/1	0	197/11	3
WALLACE William B S	Kirkintilloch	23 Jun 1941	Oct 1971	Celtic	Oct 1972	Dumbarton	36/3	4	2	2	1	0	39/3	6
WALLEY Keith J	Weymouth	19 Oct 1954	Aug 1973	Juniors	1974		6/1	1	0	0	0	0	6/1	1
WALSH Ian Paul	St Davids	4 Sep 1958	Oct 1975	Juniors	Feb 1982	Swansea T	101/16	23	11	2	2/3	2	114/19	27
WALSH Thomas	Bolton		1 May 1928	Bristol C	Jun 1929		8	1	1	0	0	0	9	1
WALTERS Thomas C			14 May 1932	Bolton W	May 1933	Exeter C	14	4	0	0	0	0	14	4

Kevin Taylor

Dave Swindlehurst

PLAYER	BIRTHPLACE	DATE	DATE SIGNED	FROM	DATE TRANSFERRED	TO	League App	League Gls	FA Cup App	FA Cup Gls	FL Cup App	FL Cup Gls	Total App	Total Gls
WARD Edward	Cowpan	16 Jun 1896	24 Jun 1922	Newcastle U	Jun 1923	Nelson	4	0	0	0	0	0	4	0
WARD Thomas Edward G	Chatham	27 Apr 1914	5 Aug 1933	Chatham	Jun 1934	Grimsby T	7	0	2	0	0	0	9	0
WATERFIELD George S	Swinton	2 Jun 1901	15 Jun 1935	Burnley	Jun 1936		2	0	0	0	0	0	2	0
WATSON George Sutton	Milton Regis	10 Apr 1907	13 Sep 1930	Maidstone	12 Dec 1931	Clapton Orient	2	0	0	0	0	0	2	0
WATSON John F	Hamilton	31 Dec 1917	Jul 1949	Real Madrid	Aug 1951	Canterbury C	61	1	2	0	0	0	63	1
WATSON John Gordon	Cambois	1912	30 May 1936	Coventry C	May 1937		12	3	0	0	0	0	12	3
WEBB Ronald Charles T	Brentford	13 Mar 1925	Sep 1946	Queen's Park R	1948		3	0	0	0	0	0	3	0
WELLS Albert F	Watford		1921	Ramsgate	Jun 1923		5	0	0	0	0	0	5	0
WERGE Edward	Sidcup	9 Sep 1936	May 1961	Charlton A	Dec 1966	Orient (after S Africa)	83	6	6	1	2	0	91	7
WETHERBY Thomas	Worcester		Jun 1928	Newport C	Jun 1931		65	0	6	0	0	0	71	0
WHARTON Terrence J	Bolton	1 Jul 1942	27 Jan 1971	Bolton W	Dec 1971	South Africa	19/1	1	0	0	0	0	19/1	1
WHIBLEY John *	Sittingbourne		1911	Sittingbourne	May 1923	Sittingbourne	91	15	2	1	0	0	93	16
WHITAKER William Paul	Charlton	20 Dec 1922	Jun 1950	Huddersfield T	Jul 1951	Cambridge U	35	1	1	0	0	0	36	1
WHITE Thomas	Musselburgh	12 Aug 1939	May 1966	Aberdeen	Feb 1968	Blackpool	37/2	13	1	1	9	9	38/2	14
WHITEAR John Michael	Isleworth	31 May 1935	May 1956	Aston Villa	May 1957		5	1	0	0	0	0	5	1
WHITEHOUSE Brian	West Bromwich	8 Sep 1935	19 Nov 1963	Wrexham	Mar 1966	Charlton A	82	17	6	0	4	0	92	17
WHITTLE Alan	Liverpool	10 Mar 1950	9 Dec 1972	Everton	Sep 1976	Orient	103/5	19	10/1	2	3	3	116/6	24
WHITWORTH George H *	Northampton	14 Jul 1896	Mar 1922	Northampton T	May 1925	Sheffield W	111	48	7	2	0	0	118	50
WHYTE Chris Anderson	Hornsey	2 Sep 1961	23 Aug 1984	Arsenal §	8 Nov 1984	Arsenal#	13	0	0	0	4	0	17	0
WICKS Stephen John	Reading	3 Oct 1956	Jun 1981	Queen's Park R	Mar 1982	Queen's Park R	14	1	5	0	0	0	19	1
WILCOCKSON Ernest S	Poplar	11 May 1905	Jun 1930	Crittals	Jun 1932	Dartford	5	1	1	0	0	0	6	1
WILDE Jimmy William C	Lyndhurst	24 Sep 1904	17 Nov 1928	Army	1938	Retired	270	5	22	1	0	0	292	6
WILKINS Paul	Hackney	20 Mar 1964	Jan 1982	Tottenham H	Jun 1984	Preston NE	9/4	3	0	0	0	0	9/4	3
WILLARD Jessie C T F	Chichester	16 Jan 1924	Jul 1953	Brighton & HA	1955	Retired injury	46	5	1	0	0	0	47	5
WILLIAMS Gary S Peter	Liverpool	8 Mar 1954	Jul 1982	Brighton & HA	1984	Retired injury	10	0	0	0	3	0	13	0
WILLIAMSON William T	Cowdenbeath		Jun 1927	Dunfermline A	Nov 1927	Dunfermline A	6	1	0	0	0	0	6	1
WILSON Albert ‡	Rotherham	28 Jan 1915	2 Jan 1939	Mansfield T	Jun 1946	Rotherham U	20	6	0	0	0	0	20	6
WOAN Alan Esplin	Liverpool	8 Feb 1931	Oct 1959	Northampton T	Feb 1961	Aldershot	41	21	4	2	1	0	46	23
WOOD A H *	Walsall		1919	Talbot Stead	1922	Coventry C	34	9	4	1	0	0	38	10
WOOD Brian T	Hamworthy	8 Dec 1940	8 May 1961	West Bromwich A	Dec 1966	Orient	142/1	1	5	3	4	0	151/1	4
WOOD George	Douglas	26 Sep 1952	Aug 1983	Arsenal	Jan 1988	Cardiff C	192	0	9	0	17	0	218	0
WOOD James	Royston		15 Jun 1935	West Ham U	1936		10	4	0	0	0	0	10	4
WOODRUFF Robert W	Highworth	9 Nov 1940	Jun 1966	Wolves	20 Nov 1969	Cardiff C	123/2	48	4	0	9/1	0	136/3	48
WOODS Charles Morgan P	Whitehaven	18 Mar 1941	26 Nov 1964	Bournemouth	8 Jul 1966	Ipswich T	49	6	1	0	1	0	51	6
WOODS Raymond	Peterborough	27 Apr 1930	Jun 1953	Southend U	Jan 1955	Folkestone	18	0	0	0	0	0	18	0
WRIGHT Ian Edward	Woolwich	3 Nov 1963	1985	Greenwich B	†		135/18	61	4	0	10	5	149/18	66
WYATT George Albert	Whitechapel	28 Mar 1924	Nov 1947	Juniors	1949		7	0	0	0	0	0	7	0
YARD Ernest J	Stranraer	3 May 1941	1 May 1961	Bury	11 Nov 1966	Reading	35/2	3	1	0	1	0	37/2	3

Ian Wright gets the better of Chelsea's Graham Roberts.

Tommy Reece

Fred Dawes

Fred Kurz

Ron George

Alf Stubbs

Ray Howells

Bill Bassett

Frank Buckley

SUBSCRIBERS

Presentation Copies
1 Crystal Palace Football Club
2 The Football League • 3 The Football Association
4 R G Noades

5 Mike Purkiss
6 Rev Nigel Sands MA
7 Mike Ryan
8 Duncan Watt
9 D T Bryant
10 J A Harris
11 John Treleven
12 William Dee
13 J S Pyke
14 Gerald Hill
15 J M Moore
16 A P J M Otten
17 Christopher Minchin
18 Esa Kautonen
19 Greg Wall
20 Geir Juva
21 Lars-Olof Wendler
22 P W Stevenson
23 Simons Martin
24 Harald Lohr
25 Surapot Saengchote
26 Kåre M Torgrimsen
27 David J Godfrey
28 M Swart
29 A Young
30 Keith Lowe
31 R G Woolman
32 Richard Stocken
33 Gordon Small
34 John Motson
35 S P Tomlin
36 P H Whitehead
37 Phil Soar
38 G D Painter
39 Harvey Paterson
40 P (Phil) A L Huffer
41 B Kitcherside
42 Robert Rouse
43 A Larcombe
44 Richard Paton
45 Neil Harris
46 Ian Weller
47 Chris Richards
48 Richard Dulwich
49 Fred Einar Tappenden
50 Fin Barr Francis Hilton
51 David Burchell
52 M J Bashford
53 Michael Gould
54 David Simpson
55 Paul King
56 Alan Palmer
57 David Brown
58 P Scoble
59 Russell McGuinness
60 M E Parsons
61 Keith Booles
62 Steve Johnson
63 Leslie Lightfoot
64 Kevin Barthrop
65 John Moule
66 Charles Bake
67 Howard Baker
68 Peter Wallington
69 D R Green
70 D J Gadd
71 Miss G Vary
72 Dawn Leggett
73 S A Embleton
74 Stuart Davidson
75 Andrew Clark
76 Ian R King
77 Ian R King
78 E Mayer
79 Mervyn Powell
80 Ian Harraden
81 R P Lisney
82 Dave Mathews
83 Steve South
84 L F Stevens
85 D P Allchurch
86 V Pearce
87 D M G Kendrick
88 Simon Pearson
89 Terry Willard
90 Neil Stevenson
91 'Steve' Stevenson
92 Harry Kay
93 Derek Hyde
94 Geoff Allman
95 R J Gamble
96 B H Standish
97 David Keats
98 Moira & Frederick Furness
99 Fred Lee
100 Donald Noble
101 Kevin C Wyatt
102 Peter Lunn
103 D A R H Webster
104 R D N Wells
105 David Robert Earnshaw
106 Dave Hillam
107 Michael Royle
108 Peter Kendall
109 Colin Cameron
110 Cliff Atkins
111 Gary Wynne
112 John Qvarnberg
113 R A Kelly
114 Robert Stevens
115 David Sarah
116 David London
117 Peter Skinner
118 Stephen J Curl
119 Richard J Green
120 Sarah Clarke
121 Tony Peisley
122 Tony Peisley
123 Stuart Williams
124 Colin Paul Howlett
125 Andrew D Wickens
126 Brian Stacey
127 Neil Cooper
128 A E Feasey
129 Lou & Audrey Hurley
130 J Crawley
131 Graham Axtell
132 K J Lineker
133 Joe Grech
134 Muriel Arrow
135 Michael Green
136 David Sammut
137 David Boakes
138 S L Hutson
139 D C Allen
140 G J Richardson
141 John Stephens
142 Steve Burrows
143 Harry Fortey
144 Paul A Grant
145 Edward H Grant
146 Keith Mintrim
147 J V McGhie
148 David McCarthy
149 Tim Barnes
150 Paul Jackson
151 Thomas Maslona
152 Graham Paris
153 Annette Legg
154 Matthew Leatt
155 Peter E Gee
156 Dominic Harper
157 David Fraser
158 G W Greenwood
159 Philip Clucas

160 M J Moran
161 K A Sinclair
162 Stephen Carleton
163 John Macdonald
164 P J Jieve
165 Alan H White
166 Matthew Chandler
167 Ian Griffin
168 Robert Bance
169 R Peters
170 J D Cobb
171 Garry Harwood
172 Andrew Corras
173 Sandra Alder
174 Neil Chatterjee
175 Eric H Tarrant
176 Philip Longster
177 Colin Hollingsworth
178 M N Winter
179 John Kain
180 Graham Hoy
181 Morgan Michie
182 C Winter
183 M Elrick
184 M Druce
185 R J Roberts
186 Paul Everett
187 Mr Shorter
188 Brian Thorne
189 Martin D'Rozario
190 Michael D'Rozario
191 Brian Coulter
192 Martin Clark
193 Richard Tilly
194 Stephen Ratcliff
195 John Hambrook
196 C Ellwood
197 Barry Couldrick
198 J B Rickard
199 Tony Evans
200 J A Kallend
201 F R Holyoake
202 Stephen Sherriff
203 Keith Orr
204 Roy Bridewell
205 Nigel K A Green
206 Derek Howlett
207 W W Boakes
208 Darrell S M Bourne
209 C R Killick
210 S Killick
211 Michael D Bushell
212 Cameron D H McCrea
213 Peter Dunkley
214 T M Brown
215 M P Hand
216 John Gunn
217 John E Corps
218 Peter Pickup
219 Ian Willott
220 D E Harries
221 Ian M Goldsmith
222 Nicholas Burrell
223 Adrian J Waddington
224 Christopher Stone
225 Eric Fowler
226 Mrs C V Shirley
227 Geoffrey W Smith
228 S H Dexter
229 Kevin Webb
230 David Ballam
231 Mark Gardiner
232 Gary Frost
233 Neil Philip Smith
234 Neil Tester
235 Dean J D Vokes
236 Kevin Powell
237 Christopher Hazelton
238 John G Axtell
239 Graham Turner
240 G W Harris
241 John Roberts
242 David Frampton
243 Colin Ferguson Duncan
244 Colin Ferguson Duncan
245 L K C Brooks
246 Ron & Bob Reeves
247 James Barrett
248 Paul Smith
249 Stephen Warwick
250 Trevor Stotten
251 Michael John Horgan
252 K B Priestley
253 Martin Stanford
254 Janet Lloyd
255 D B Stannard
256 Andrew Failes
257 Andrew Failes
258 Tom Littlewood
259 Andrew Drysdale
260 Peter G Figgess
261 John E Craker
262 P Friend
263 Mrs M Mahon
264 Gary Keith Palmer
265 John Churchill
266 David Churchill
267 Alexander Newman
268 M W J Chilver
269 J D Welsh
270 T Richards-Jones
271 P J Targett
272 John McBride
273 Justin Mandry
274 Neil Witherow
275 R L Mayers
276 Ian Spires
277 P S Newman
278 H C Telling
279 Graham John Complin
280 Colin Hambleton
281 Miss S Wright
282 Matthew Vile
283 J K Sisley
284 George Dunk
286 Paul Heaney
287 Paul Firmage
288 Roy White
289 K F Atkins
290 Richard L Gribble
291 Andrew Kelly
292 E Wheeler
293 Tim Harrison
294 Martin Winters
295 Ian Bessick
296 Graham Harris
297 Sarah Oldfield
298 J K Miller
299 John Swain
300 R J Garrett MA
301 Peter Oliver
302 Derek John Belbin
303 David Warwick
304 Miss S E Wiseman
305 George Zeleny
306 J W Cleary
307 Clive Jones
308 Neil Gunn
309 M Raynsford
310 J F Cotton
311 Keith Townsend
312 John David Smith
313 Harry Gibson
314 Sebastian Vance
315 Alan George
316 James Piddock
317 Clive Rowland
318 James Waters
319 Deano Standing
320 Cllr A J Pelling
321 P Jarrett
322 A Sewell
323 J Williams
324 R H Minchin
325 Arthur Henshall
326 Robert Plows
327 A M Regelous
328 Paul Newcomb
329 A J Hindley
330 Eric Heesom
331 Anders Johansson
332 J Gardiner
333 Ian Griffiths
334 Ake Axelsson
335 W D Phillips
336 Derek Jones
337 Harry Thompson
338 Dave Helliwell
339 Adrian Figgess
340 Tony Ward

341 Michael J Heffernan
342 Peter J Loaring
343 Peter Rollitt
344 A Bailey
345 Peter J G Lynch
346 Patrick Maw
347 Adrian Alan Walton
348 Maurice P West
349 Michael King
350 Paul K H Baker
351 Clive Southby
352 Gavin Dunn
353 Jason Moore
354 M J Meech
355 Autoplan Limited
356 Alfred E Willson
357 G C Potter
358 Vince Holub
359 Peter O'Kill
360 Mrs Jan Rich
361 Gary Hartnell
362 David Daniels
363 Gordon Wright
364 P S Garlinge
365 Malcolm Larkins
366 D L Lawn
367 F J Lavender
368 S M Musgrove
369 Michael McCauley
370 Barry Richardson
371 Mark Evetts
372 R F Elliott
373 Ian Seres
374 Ricky Ballantine
375 R Bevan
376 David Johnson
377 Ian Eagle
378 A Fells
379 Michael A Nash
380 Paul Paternoster
381 Richard Greatorex
382 Roy Nassé
383 Barry Gibbs
384 W E Austin
385 J A Austin OBE
386 Angus W Rodger
387 K Evans
388 Richard Melik
389 J A Claassen
390 C Creech
391 Martin Goble
392 Colin Medcalf
393 Neil Baker
394 G R Clarke
395 Peter J Bourne
396 Andrew Anderson
397 Michael Kennett
398 P J Donohue
399 Ian Way
400 Roger F Wallis
401 Bruce Paton
402 Nick Crivich
403 John Stephen Clark
404 G Cook
405 Jamie Wimble
406 Rob Marsden
407 Michael Van-Boolen
408 Dave Storrier
409 Brian Read
410 John Kooyman
411 John Turner
412 Alf Ford
413 Andy Southern
414 Dave Erny
415 Harry Arnold
416 Warren Bullock
417 Jason Wells
418 Peter Anthony Giles
419 David Tompsett
420 Geoff Haywood
421 D W Bateman
422 Stephen Moss
423 J D George
424 David A Evans
425 Robert Ainger
426 John Ainger
427 D Maurice
428 Chris Errington
429 David Wimble
430 T A Godwin
431 J F Holroyd
432 Philip Odell
433 Raymond Shaw
434 Graham Arnold
435 Colin Ricketts
436 Paul Andrew Younger
437 Dan Tier
438 R G Strudwick
439 Roger Browne
440 J & M Hoath
441 M D Rickard
442 D A Rickard
443 J R Ramage
444 Paul Clark
445 Philip Anthony Adams
446 Roger Cochrane
447 Les Gold
448 Hugh O Garland
449 M D Redmill
450 R Redmill
451 J Maytom
452 Graham Thorn
453 Andrew Day
454 Richard Gallard
455 A S Winch
456 James S Boardman
457 M F Draper
458 S M Woollacott
459 Leslie Newman
460 Bernard Roberts
461 Ken Pringle
462 J Ringrose
463 Barry Rowbotham
464 Terry Austin
465 Des Beamish
466 C A Warner
467 C A Warner
468 Stewart Fell
469 Douglas Lamming
470 Mike Vickers
471 Simon Paul Robert Tidy
472 Mike A Thorn
473 Mark Picksley
474 Nigel & Rita Broadway
475 Steven Endacott
476 Peter Davis
477 John Campion
478 Karen Hughes
479 Keith Sussemilch
480 Matthew James Pyett
481 Tony & Pam Thornburn
482 Trond Isaksen
483 Robert Riviere
484 Philip Gerrish
485 Richard A Baker
486 P F Cuthbert
487 R G Lee
488 Ian Monk
489 Bill French
490 Paul Spiller
491 C Reynolds
492 M J Denney
493 Lisa Wright
494 J True
495 Michael Beauchamp
496 Andrew Pudney
497 Mark Fox
498 Phil Thomas
499 A P Dean
500 David John Smith
501 James Ward-Davis
502 D A Marshall
503 Andy Russell
504 Peter Edwards
505 T R C Dunford
506 Ian Andrew Lyons
507 Miss S J Eaves
508 Nathan Burr
509 C Arch
510 Roger Dickson
511 P M Baars
512 Michael Vagg
513 Diana Cowell
514 J M Lockton
515 Mrs O B Smith
516 David Edwards
517 Anthony Baughen
518 Graham Sanders
519 Steve Mobbs
520 K Jeffery

521 D W Ridgwell
522 John P Davidge
523 Gary Martyn
524 Sports Marketing (South Australia)
525 Geoffrey Wright
526 Tony Bond
527 Stephen Page
528 B J Harris
529 Steven Read
530 Keith McLoughlin
531 Mark Keegan
532 Trevor Clark
533 Nigel Collison
534 Ian D Barnes
535 Thomas McCann
536 G T Stevens
537 Ted Oddy
538 Jonathan S Barker
539 Simon J Barker
540 Gary Morris
541 Clive Ward
542 Miss D P Bendall
543 L A Zammit
544 P Furmanski
545 Steve Mosham
546 Steve Mosham
547 M T Grosse
548 Neil Spires
549 Ian Spires
550 Adrian Rowbotham
551 Peter Surry
552 Andy Dunican
553 Peter N Goodbody
554 Robert Smith
555 Keith David Oakley
556 Roger Wash
557 Derek Miles
558 Matthew Pemble
559 Edward Lonsdale
560 Ian T Richardson
561 Roger Drayton
562 Paul Nightingale
563 David John Kemp
564 Andrew Brenner
565 F Waters
566 Robert Oakes
567 John Oakes
568 Colin M Darnell
569 P C Bonthrone
570 Paul Stringer
571 Martin Newman
572 G Greenfield
573 A F Brooker
574 Brian Mason
575 Kevin Mason
576 David Gregg
577 Tony R Woollaston
578 Michael P Freyone
579 Raymond F Way
580 Paul Owen
581 L F Hedges
582 T Terry
583 Dr C J Morton
584 Peter Baxter
585 Stanley A Robinson
586 F Beale
587 Robert Salter
588 Jason Boyce
589 O Malyan
590 G M Bastin
591 Robbie Carpenter
592 Paul Tant
593 Kim J Duke
594 Charlie Chainsaw
595 P R Wardley
596 Terry Goose
597 Paul R Wright
598 Michael J Edwards
599 Richard Gee
600 G C Penfold
601 F E Penfold
602 C Morley
603 K E Purkiss
604 K E Purkiss
605 K E Purkiss
606 David Downs
607 Norman Green
608 J C C M Rose
609 Graham Brown
610 Colin Readman
611 Nicos Christodoulou
612 Ian Chapman
613 Kevin Day
614 James McDaid
615 Tracey Dyer
616 Barbara White
617 I R McRae
618 Anthony Philip Harvey
619 R M Leonard
620 Philip C B Smith
621 Paul Mathews
622 John Collins
623 David Collyer
624 Ian Duggan
625 Paul Twitchett
626 Antony Paul Auger
627 Mrs J A Hillarby
628 Ian Mathews
629 Wayne Smith
630 Mike Mannion
631 P M Wallis
632 Mike Harragin
633 J de Sayrah
634 Paul A Attwater
635 Gary Bowman
636 Richard Fordham
637 Mrs G M Holbourn
638 P J Holbourn
639 William Shindler
640 Richard Goldring
641 Simon Lane
642 Terry Morley
643 Mark T Green
644 Steve Gillham
645 Ron Steele
646 Antony Bennett
647 John Anthony Gillis
648 L E Wayman
649 David Gettins
650 N L Higerty
651 Brett Kemp
652 John Wales
653 Paul Jerome
654 David John Eley
655 John R Challis
656 Paul Cleal
657 Martin Bayntun
658 Roy Tedman
659 J M Littlechild
660 Keith Tickner
661 G R Tessier
662 Tony Humphreys
663 A Denholm
664 Luke & Keith Remnant
665 Richard Woodhead
666 Andrew Noble
667 Stephen M Fetherston
668 A & M Shepherd
669 Richard Mortimer
670 John A R Gillgrass
671 Martin Roberts
672 Jim Evans
673 Matthew Browne
674 Malcolm J Henderson
675 Chris Whetherly
676 Phil Nicholson
677 Richard J Goward
678 Peter S D Carpenter
679 Nigel Chaffer
680 Keith Chaffer
681 Alan Bissenden
682 J L Lockton
683 C R Attewell
684 D P Ames
685 Paul J Smith
686 J R Rishworth
687 Gary Sutton
688 Ian Lingham
689 Jack Burgess
690 Rita Carter
691 Toby Kinder
692 I R Hamilton
693 Christopher Sandy
694 R Clausen-Thue
695 K P Shore
696 B V Beswick
697 Nick Crowe
698 M Kaczmarczyk
699 Shani Carson

700 John Gill
701 N Crimp
702 John Vince
703 Stephen Berridge
704 Barbara Neal
705 M C Baker
706 C A Duneclift
707 Bryan N Bisland
708 Philip Hall
709 Steve Francis
710 John Andrew Reed
711 Dr S J Harrison
712 J R Green
713 Miss Hazel Young
714 Philip I Northwood
715 Antony Massarella
716 Ian Reynolds
717 C W Forbes
718 S Lochinger
719 N Deards
720 Miss D Weston
721 Anthony Pettet
722 Trevor Brand
723 J D Townsley
724 David Agates
725 M Kelly
726 Andrew J Phillips
727 Stephen A S Curtis
728 Martyn Charles Vallas
729 Keith Burgess
730 Ted Gates
731 David Slawson
732 Paul Bradshaw
733 J W H Gilbert
734 Shaun Bullock
735 Miss Allison Duffy
736 Sanderstead Fruit & Deli
737 D W Jones
738 Phil Johnson
739 M J Youngman
740 Antony Dilley
741 Jon Weaver
742 Mike Clark
743 Garry Belcher
744 Ian Pressman
745 David Murphy
746 Darren Maeers
747 Tony Matthews
748 Keith Edwards
749 Domenico Polimeno
750 Ian Wilkins
751 Gary Casey
752 David Green
753 Martin Putt
754 Stuart Gibbon
755 Roger Hall
756 David Marritt
757 Colin Wilson
758 J Roy Nash
759 Lee English
760 T E O'Neill
761 Ben Evans
762 Richard J Chace
763 David Barker
764 Antony Walters
765 A R Marritt
766 R T Milsted
767 S D Blackwell
768 R Blenman
769 Bryan Rootes
770 Bob Ashby
771 Grahame Church
772 Barry Hyne
773 M J Murphy
774 S C Burchett
775 Paul Jackson
776 Derrick Rushworth
777 J Taylor
778 C J Chapman
779 James Purr
780 Peter Moody
781 B J Naldrett
782 Philip Ramsey
783 Paul Jenner
784 Philip Petrou
785 Gary Parsons
786 Tasos D Botsis
787 D Gold
788 Ian Mattocks
789 B G Masters
790 Terry Brigden
791 Andrew Fraser
792 Richard Bushell
793 Jerry Hedges
794 S A Williamson
795 Michael Angell
796 Graham Angell
797 R J Horsford
798 B V White
799 Richard Woodland
800 Keith Hathaway
801 Brian Newell
802 David Peter Iverson
803 Richard Wilson
804 Ashley Royston
805 Graham Attaway
806 Nicholas Lindsey
807 Derek Bardwell
808 Andrew D McVicar
809 David Brian Sparrow
810 Brian J Sparrow
811 T J Cole
812 Barry Carter
813 C S Gormley
814 Gary Prior
815 A D Powe
816 P Appleton
817 Mark Booth
818 Daniel Miller
819 Patrick Kenyon
820 Robert Brooks
821 Peter Saunders
822 I D G Hamilton
823 Allan Weale
824 A McCulloch
825 A McCulloch
826 Keith Miles
827 David Durell
828 F T Stevens
829 Ian Wood
830 R W Griffin
831 Martin E E Fletcher
832 Graham Hinks
833 Tony Lewis
834 Mark C Towersey
835 Ray Blaquiere
836 J Ramsey
837 C M Mills
838 James Boots
839 David Kentish
840 Philip Walter
841 Kevin Buckland
842 Martin Frelford
843 T J Anderson
844 Iain Gordon
845 Clifford R Gavercole
846 David Corbett
847 J M Getgood
848 Mrs M Getgood
849 David Simmons
850 Paul A Sawyers
851 Anton Rippon
852 John Grainger
853 Ray Yeomans
854 Graham Hales
855 J P Cheadle